# The Mamluk Sultanate

The Mamluk Sultanate ruled Egypt, Syria, and the Arabian hinterland along the Red Sea. Lasting from the deposition of the Ayyubid dynasty (c. 1250) to the Ottoman conquest of Egypt in 1517, this regime of slave-soldiers incorporated many of the political structures and cultural traditions of its Fatimid and Ayyubid predecessors. Yet, its system of governance and centralization of authority represented radical departures from the hierarchies of power that predated it. Providing a rich and comprehensive survey of events from the Sultanate's founding to the Ottoman occupation, this interdisciplinary book explores the Sultanate's identity and heritage after the Mongol conquests, the expedience of conspiratorial politics, and the close symbiosis of the military elite and civil bureaucracy. Carl F. Petry also considers the statecraft, foreign policy, economy, and cultural legacy of the Sultanate, and its interaction with polities throughout the central Islamic world and beyond. In doing so, Petry reveals how the Mamluk Sultanate can be regarded as a significant experiment in the history of state-building within the premodern Islamic world.

CARL F. PETRY is the Hamad Ibn Khalifa Al Thani Professor of Middle East Studies and Professor of History at Northwestern University. He is the author of *The Civilian Elite of Cairo in the Later Middle Ages* (1982), *Twilight of Majesty: The Reigns of al-Ashraf Qaytbay and Qansuh al-Ghawri in Egypt* (1993), *Protectors or Praetorians? The Last Mamluk Sultans and Egypt's Waning as a Great Power* (1994), and *The Criminal Underworld in a Medieval Islamic Society: Narratives from Cairo and Damascus under the Mamluks* (2012), and is the editor of *The Cambridge History of Egypt: Islamic Egypt, 640–1517* (1998). His research has been supported by the J. S. Guggenheim Foundation, the Institute for Advanced Study, the American Research Center in Egypt, and the American Council of Learned Societies.

T0382276

# The Mamluk Sultanate

## *A History*

Carl F. Petry

*Northwestern University*

CAMBRIDGE
UNIVERSITY PRESS

**CAMBRIDGE**
**UNIVERSITY PRESS**

University Printing House, Cambridge CB2 8BS, United Kingdom

One Liberty Plaza, 20th Floor, New York, NY 10006, USA

477 Williamstown Road, Port Melbourne, VIC 3207, Australia

314–321, 3rd Floor, Plot 3, Splendor Forum, Jasola District Centre,
New Delhi – 110025, India

103 Penang Road, #05-06/07, Visioncrest Commercial, Singapore 238467

Cambridge University Press is part of the University of Cambridge.

It furthers the University's mission by disseminating knowledge in the pursuit of education, learning, and research at the highest international levels of excellence.

www.cambridge.org
Information on this title: www.cambridge.org/9781108471046
DOI: 10.1017/9781108557382

© Carl F. Petry 2022

This publication is in copyright. Subject to statutory exception and to the provisions of relevant collective licensing agreements, no reproduction of any part may take place without the written permission of Cambridge University Press.

First published 2022

*A catalogue record for this publication is available from the British Library.*

*Library of Congress Cataloging-in-Publication Data*
Names: Petry, Carl F., 1943- author.
Title: The Mamluk Sultanate : a history / Carl F. Petry, Northwestern University, Illinois.
Description: Cambridge, United Kingdom ; New York, NY : Cambridge University Press, 2022. | Includes bibliographical references and index.
Identifiers: LCCN 2021050093 (print) | LCCN 2021050094 (ebook) | ISBN 9781108471046 (hardback) | ISBN 9781108456999 (paperback) | ISBN 9781108557382 (epub)
Subjects: LCSH: Mamelukes–History. | Egypt–History–1250-1517. | Islamic Empire.
Classification: LCC DT96 .P48 2022 (print) | LCC DT96 (ebook) | DDC 962/.02–dc23/eng/20220107
LC record available at https://lccn.loc.gov/2021050093
LC ebook record available at https://lccn.loc.gov/2021050094

ISBN 978-1-108-47104-6 Hardback
ISBN 978-1-108-45699-9 Paperback

Cambridge University Press has no responsibility for the persistence or accuracy of URLs for external or third-party internet websites referred to in this publication and does not guarantee that any content on such websites is, or will remain, accurate or appropriate.

To Bruce D. Craig
Steadfast Khushdash and
Advocate for Mamluk Studies

# Contents

# Figures

# Maps

# Maps

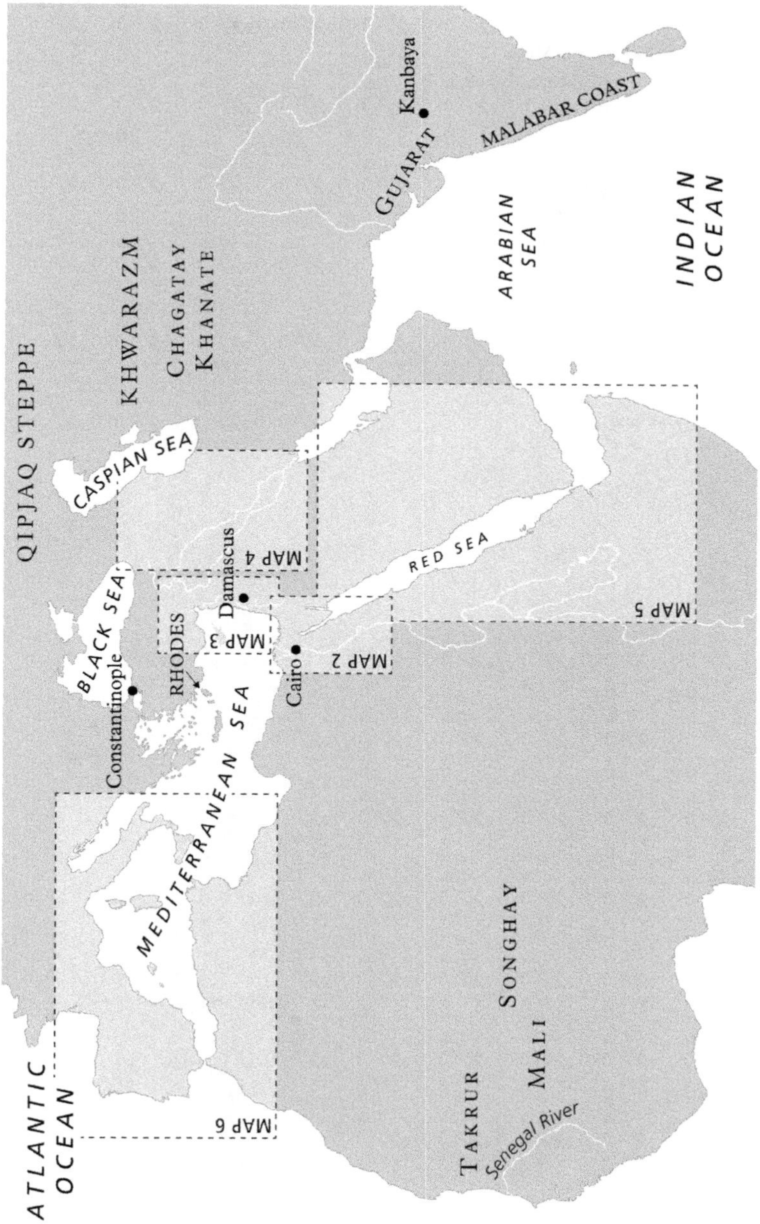


1 Africa, Eurasia

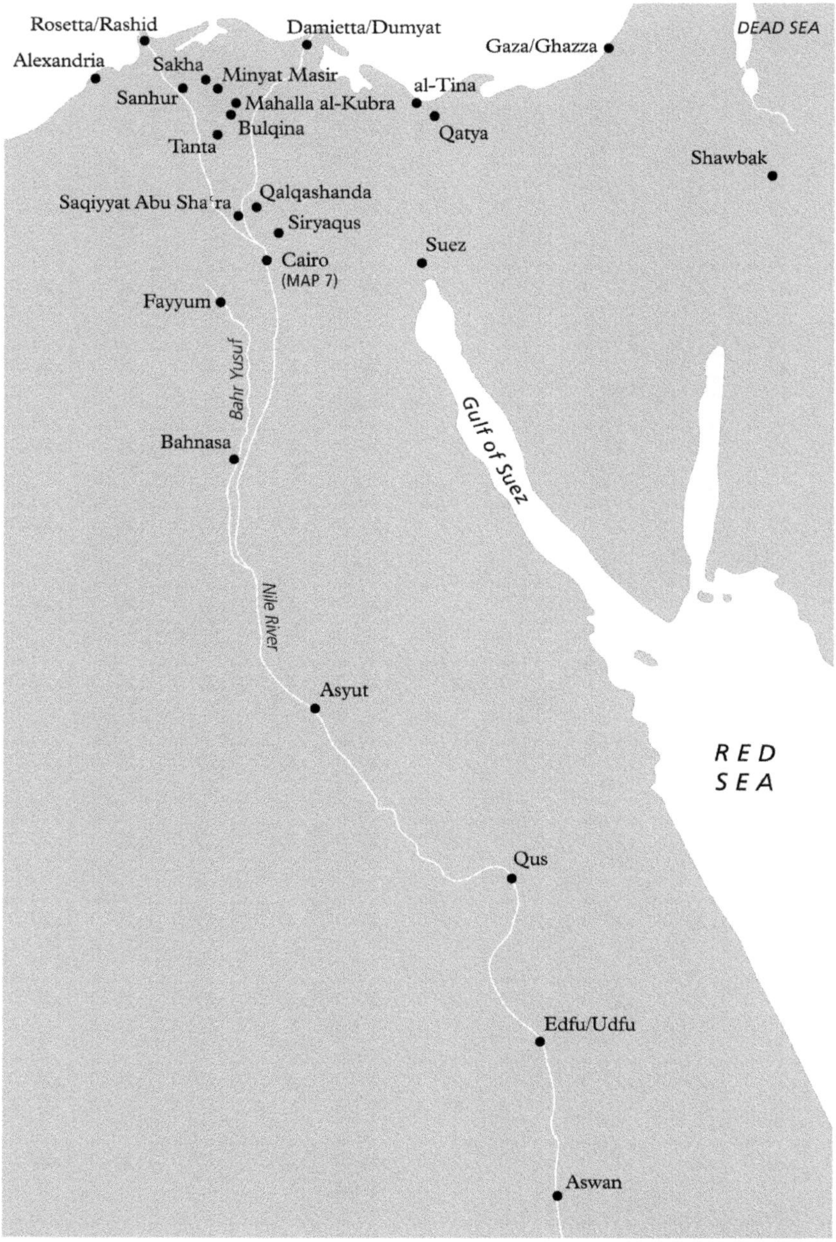


2 Egypt, Nile Valley

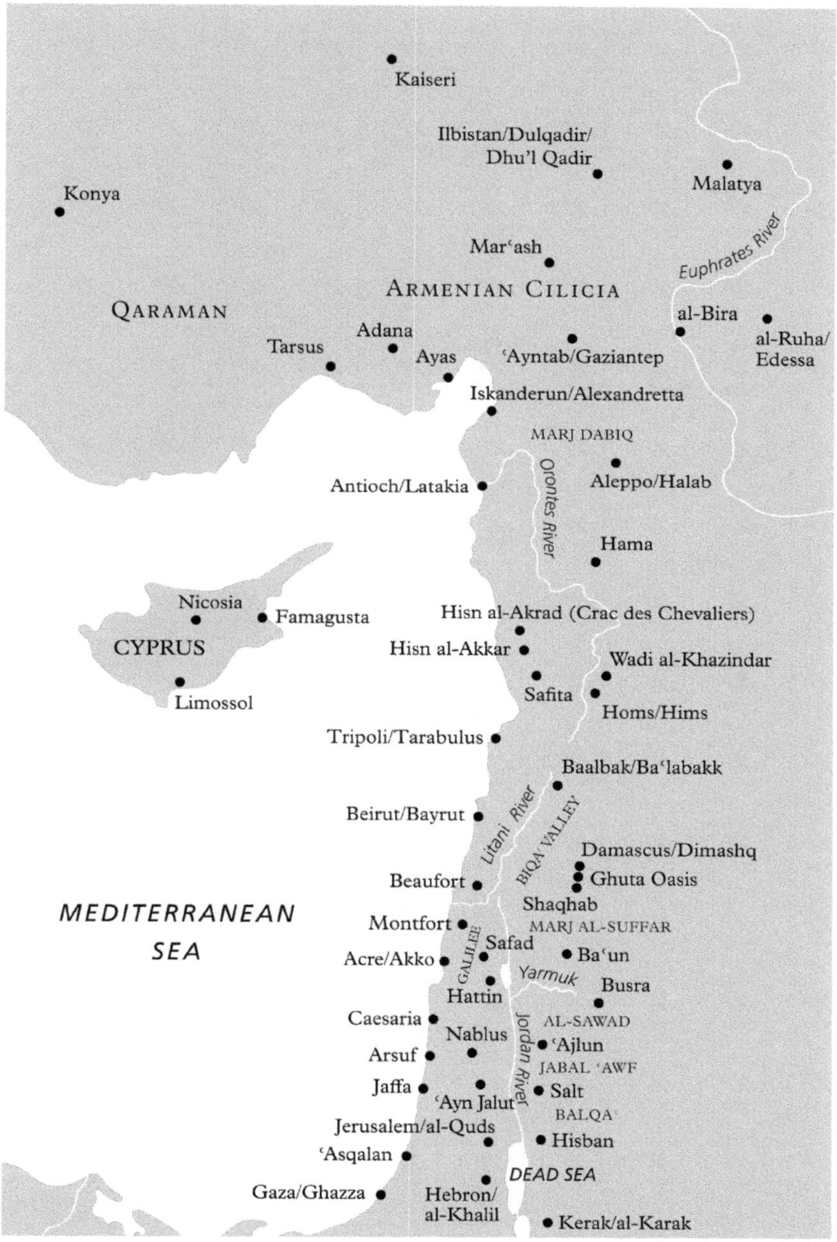
Kaiseri
Ilbistan/Dulqadir/
Dhu'l Qadir
Malatya
Konya
Euphrates River
Mar'ash
ARMENIAN CILICIA
QARAMAN
al-Bira
Adana
Tarsus
Ayas
'Ayntab/Gaziantep
al-Ruha/
Edessa
Iskanderun/Alexandretta
MARJ DABIQ
Antioch/Latakia
Orontes River
Aleppo/Halab
Hama
Nicosia
Famagusta
CYPRUS
Limossol
Hisn al-Akrad (Crac des Chevaliers)
Hisn al-Akkar
Wadi al-Khazindar
Safita
Homs/Hims
Tripoli/Tarabulus
Baalbak/Ba'labakk
Beirut/Bayrut
Litani River
BIQA' VALLEY
Damascus/Dimashq
Ghuta Oasis
Beaufort
Shaqhab
MEDITERRANEAN
SEA
Montfort
MARJ AL-SUFFAR
GALILEE
Safad
Acre/Akko
Ba'un
Yarmuk
Hattin
Busra
Caesaria
Jordan River
AL-SAWAD
Nablus
'Ajlun
Arsuf
JABAL 'AWF
Jaffa
Salt
'Ayn Jalut
BALQA'
Jerusalem/al-Quds
Hisban
'Asqalan
DEAD SEA
Gaza/Ghazza
Hebron/
al-Khalil
Kerak/al-Karak

3 Syria, Eastern Anatolia, Cyprus

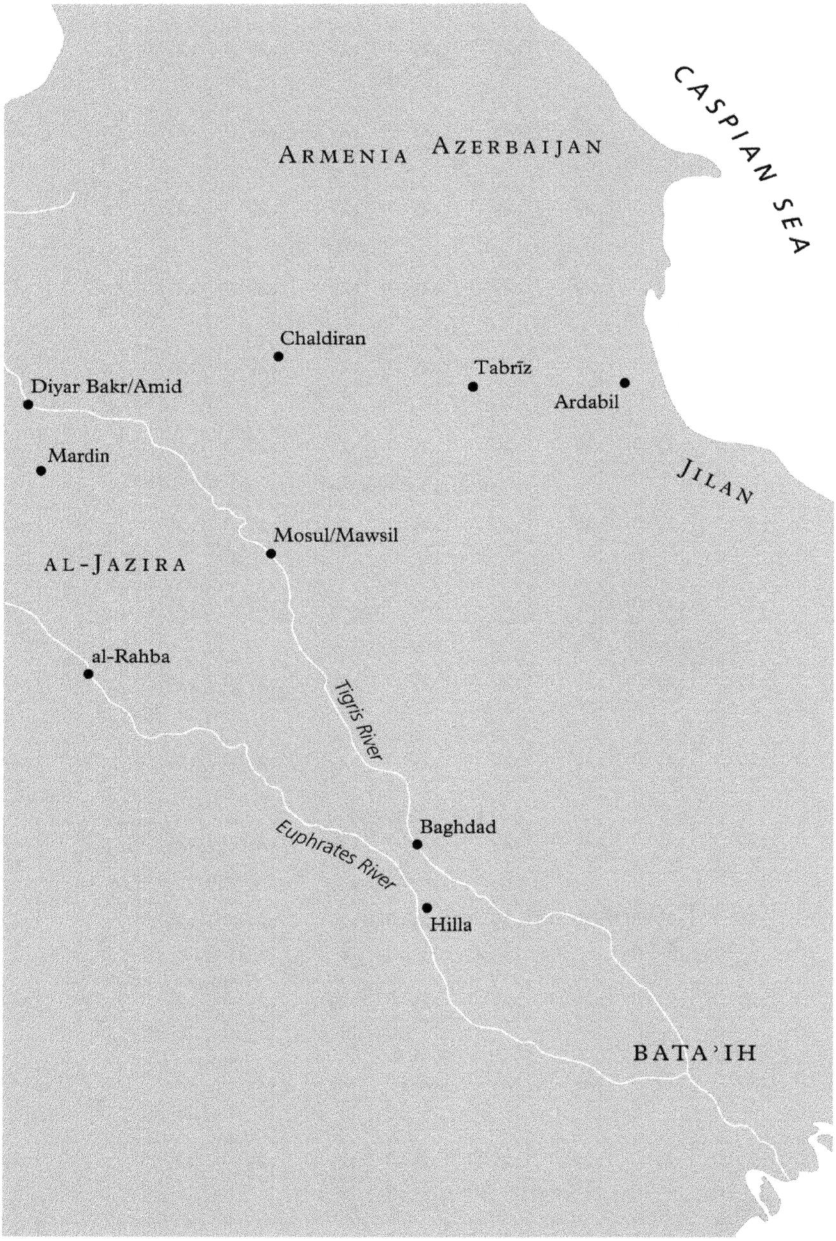


4 Iraq, Western Iran

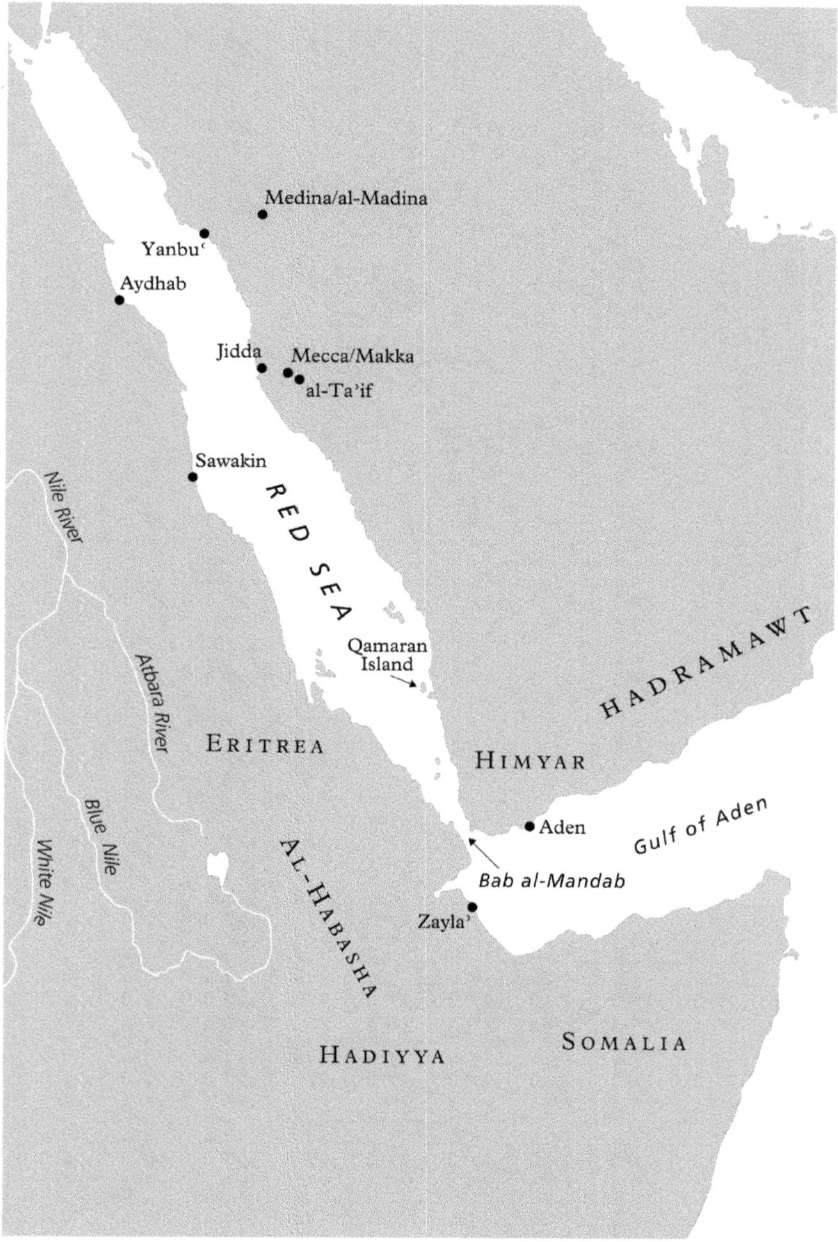


5 Arabian Peninsula, Northeast Africa

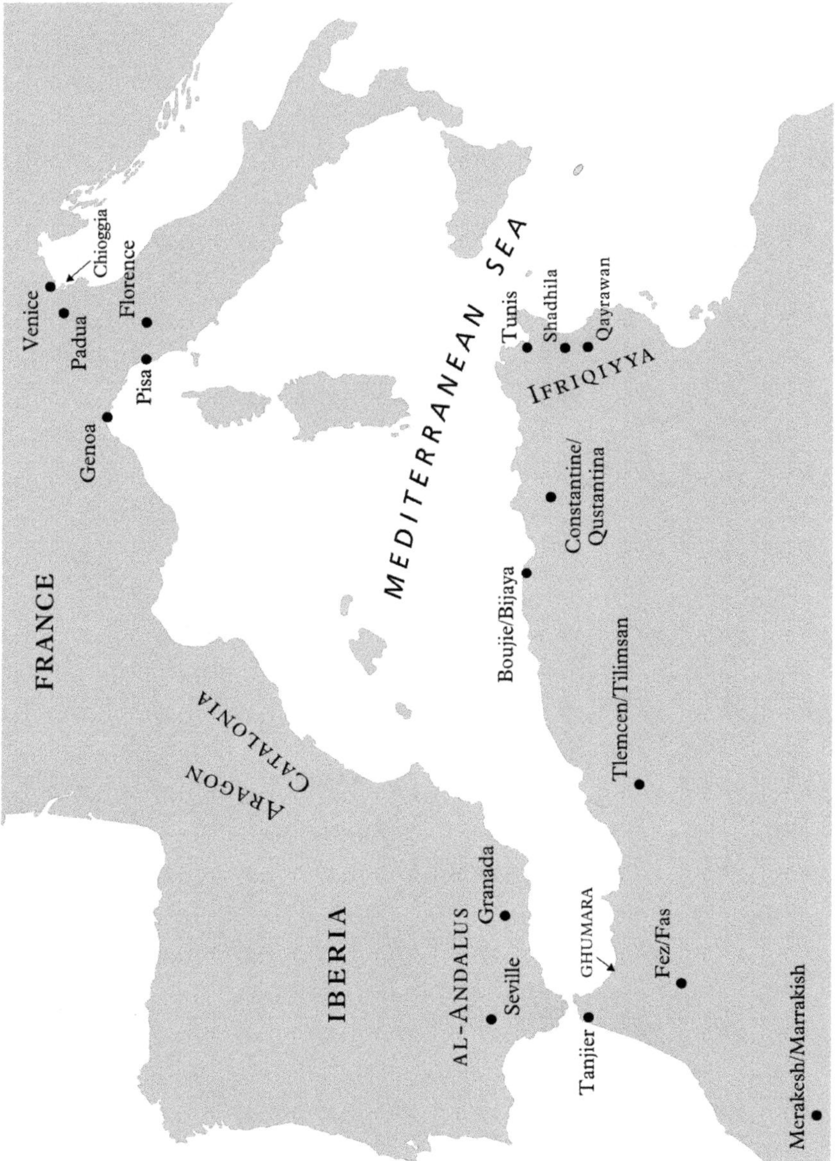


6 North Africa (Maghrib), Mediterranean Europe

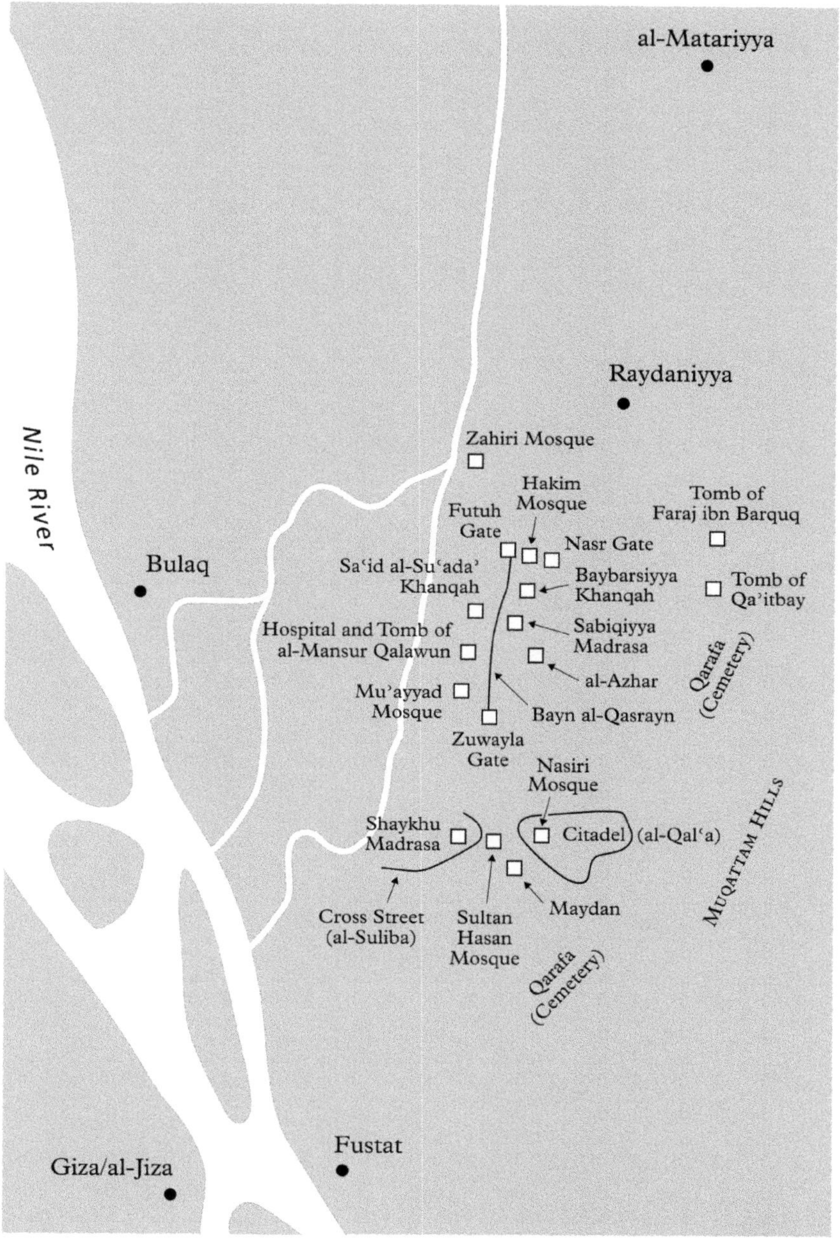
al-Matariyya
Raydaniyya
Nile River
Bulaq
Zahiri Mosque
Hakim Mosque
Futuh Gate
Tomb of Faraj ibn Barquq
Nasr Gate
Sa'id al-Su'ada' Khanqah
Baybarsiyya Khanqah
Tomb of Qa'itbay
Hospital and Tomb of al-Mansur Qalawun
Sabiqiyya Madrasa
al-Azhar
Qarafa (Cemetery)
Mu'ayyad Mosque
Bayn al-Qasrayn
Zuwayla Gate
Nasiri Mosque
Shaykhu Madrasa
Citadel (al-Qal'a)
Muqattam Hills
Cross Street (al-Suliba)
Sultan Hasan Mosque
Maydan
Qarafa (Cemetery)
Fustat
Giza/al-Jiza

7 Cairo and environs

# Introduction

In 784H/1382CE, North African historian and political philosopher Ibn Khaldun (d. 808/1406) arrived in Alexandria, Egypt's Mediterranean port, ostensibly on his way to pilgrimage in Mecca but in fact as a refugee from political controversy in the Maghrib. Ibn Khaldun's fame had preceded him, and the reigning Sultan, al-Zahir Barquq, appointed him senior judge of the Maliki school of Islamic law in Cairo, the first of several prestigious offices he would hold as a jurist and scholar. Ibn Khaldun spent the rest of his life in the city revising his monumental history of North Africa and the central Islamic lands, *Kitāb al-ʿibar*. Ibn Khaldun is known to the modern world primarily for his analysis of social structures in a volume titled *al-Muqaddima fi'l-ta'rīkh* (Introduction to History), which he wrote as an explanatory preamble to his larger work (cf. Chapter 6). While the *Muqaddima* overshadows the *Kitāb al-ʿibar* in contemporary scholarship, Ibn Khaldun expressed in the latter his esteem for the regime that, ironically, would grant him sanctuary years later:

When the [ʿAbbasid] state was drowned in decadence and luxury and donned the garments of calamity and impotence and was overthrown by the heathen Tatars [the Mongols], who abolished the seat of the Caliphate and obliterated the splendor of the lands, and made unbelief prevail in place of belief, because the people of the faith, sunk in self-indulgence, preoccupied with pleasure and abandoned to luxury, had become deficient in energy and reluctant to rally in their defense, and had stripped off the skin of courage and the emblem of manhood – then it was God's benevolence that He rescued the faith by reviving its dying breath and restoring the unity of the Muslims in the Egyptian realms (*al-diyār al-Miṣriyya*), preserving the order and defending the walls of Islam. He did this by sending to the Muslims, from this Turkish nation (*al-ṭā'ifat al-turkiyya*) and from among its great and numerous tribes, rulers to defend them and totally loyal helpers. They were brought from the House of War to the House of Islam under the rule of slavery (*riqq*), which hides in itself a divine blessing. By means of bondage they learn glory and blessing and are exposed to divine providence; cured by slavery, they enter the Muslim religion with the firm resolve of true believers and yet with nomadic virtues (*akhlāq badawiyya*) unsullied by debased nature, unadulterated with the filth of pleasure, undefiled by the ways of civilized living, and with their ardor unbroken by the profusion of luxury. The slave merchants bring them to Egypt in batches, like sand-grouse to the watering places (*al-qaṭan naḥwa al-mawārid*), and government buyers have them displayed for inspection and bid for them, raising the price above their value. They do this in order not to subjugate them, but to intensify loyalty, increase power, and strengthen zeal. They choose from each group, according to what they observe of the characteristics of the race and the tribes. Then they place them in a government barracks where they give them good and fair treatment, educate them, have them taught the Qur'an and kept at their religious studies until they have a firm grasp of this. Then they train them in archery and fencing, in horsemanship, in hippodromes, and in thrusting with the lance and striking with the sword until their arms grow strong and skills become firmly rooted. When the masters know that they have reached the stage of readiness to defend them, even to die for them, they double their pay and increase their grants (*iqṭāʾ*), and impose on them the duty to improve themselves in the use of weapons and horsemanship, and so also to increase the number of men of their own races (*ajnāsihim*) in the realm for that purpose. Often, they place them in service to the state and appoint them to high offices. Some of them are chosen to sit on the throne of the Sultans and direct the affairs of the Muslims, in accordance with divine providence and with the mercy of God to His creatures. Thus, one intake succeeds another and generation follows generation, and Islam rejoices in the benefit which it gains through them, and the branches of the kingdom flourish with the freshness of youth.[1]

Ibn Khaldun's praise for this cadre of slave-soldiers was not meant as effusive acclaim of utopian guardians or gratitude for sanctuary offered to a refugee. He credited these individuals for providing security to the Islamic heartland from conquest by unbelievers and salvation from moral decay on the part of indigenous Muslims themselves. The characteristics Ibn Khaldun attributed to these slave-soldiers encompass the qualities he found requisite to the revitalization of Islam as a religion and the endurance of the polity necessary for its fluorescence in his own day.

The survey that follows examines these qualities in the context of the regime in which they achieved their fullest development: the Sultanate that ruled Egypt, Syria, and the Arabian hinterland along the Red Sea from 648/1250 to 922/1517. The institution of Mamluk military slavery had its origins centuries earlier in the centralized Caliphate during the formative era of Islamic history in regions known today as the Middle East (Northeast Africa, Southwest Asia). The traits Ibn Khaldun emphasized have received attention in many contexts of scholarly inquiry for more than a century. In the past several decades, they have been subjected to revisionist approaches reflective of analytical currents prevalent in disciplines of the humanities and social sciences at the present time. The survey also takes stock of these shifting currents to indicate how they are reshaping the field of medieval Islamic history itself.

Several overviews of the Mamluk institution and its manifestation as an autonomous state centered in Cairo have appeared since the emergence of this field as a distinctive branch of premodern Islamic historiography. Notable among these in English are by Robert Irwin,[2] Linda Northrup,[3] Jean-Claude

Garcin,[4] and Amalia Levanoni.[5] Similar outlines have appeared in Arabic, French, German, Hebrew, Japanese, and Turkish. So, what justifies the publication of this survey? To date, no endeavor to depict the evolution of the Mamluk State beyond a summation of its political trajectory has appeared in a single volume. Given this regime's complexities and the range of studies devoted to its development, no analysis of this scope can credibly claim to be comprehensive. The current bibliography is vast, its subjects varied. What this work attempts to do is revisit the qualities Ibn Khaldun attributed to this cadre from the perspective of recent scholarship in the humanities and social sciences. Ibn Khaldun's own opinions about the Mamluks constitute a special aspect of historiographical inquiry into his broader worldview. As the reader will observe upon perusal of the following work, these qualities have prompted a wide range of reactions that embrace diverse approaches in several fields. Beyond historiography, the disciplines of anthropology, archaeology, art and architecture, gender and literary studies, education and pedagogy, politics, political economy, and religious studies are evident in the scholarship cited. While the author's own views are apparent, the survey's overriding objective has been to suggest how this scholarship has reshaped contemporary understanding of Egyptian and Syrian History during the late medieval and early modern period – and continues to do so.

The survey is presented in seven chapters. Chapter 1 provides a synopsis of events from the Sultanate's founding to the Ottoman occupation in 922/1517. Chapter 2 considers the regime's identity and sense of heritage in the era following the Mongol conquests throughout the region. It outlines procedures of training for Mamluk cadets in the Islamic religion and military arts, the hierarchy of positions held by senior officers, and the competitive ethos that pervaded the military elite's ranks. Chapter 3 addresses the Sultanate's interaction with other polities in the central Islamic world, East and South Asia, Mediterranean Europe, and Africa beyond its borders (Takrur, Abyssinia, and the Maghrib). Chapter 4 examines the Sultanate's administration, the bureaucracy that managed it, the civil judiciary and scholastic classes that presided over litigation and education, and the agents of religious service who upheld a stance of distinction from their learned counterparts. Chapter 5 appraises issues of political economy: agriculture and land use, taxation, interregional and local commerce, commodity prices, salaries and wages, and procedures of revenue extraction (formal and clandestine) imposed by the regime to address cash shortfalls. Chapter 6 considers the Sultanate's cultural legacy, its sponsorship by the military elite, the evolution of literary production (poetry and prose), and the dramatic growth of historiography. Chapter 7 examines the rural setting, issues surrounding its lack of visibility in sources, gender relations, the status of religious minorities (Christians and Jews), and diversity in religious practice, especially as measured by popular identity with Sufism.

Matters of chronology, events, persons, locales, and institutions are cited initially according to their listing in the *Encyclopaedia of Islam*, second and third editions (*EI2*/*EI3*), as first lines of reference to a source with internationally recognized standards for accuracy and scope. Arabic diacritics conform to the Romanization Tables for Arabic of the American Library Association/ Library of Congress. They are limited to terms or phrases in italics, when precise transliteration is indicated. Dates are listed as Hijri (H) and Common Era (CE).

Several individuals who are authorities on the history of medieval Egypt and Syria read chapters of this work during the drafting process: Li Guo, John Meloy, Adam Sabra, Warren Schultz, and Terry Wilfong. Their insights and criticisms were invaluable and are deeply appreciated; any errors of fact or interpretation are the author's responsibility. I also owe a debt of gratitude to Olaf Nelson of Chinook Design for drawing the maps that locate sites noted in the text.

# 1 Synopsis of Events

### The Mamluk Institution

The regime that ruled over Egypt, Syria, and the Red Sea between the mid-seventh and early tenth Hijra / thirteenth and sixteenth CE centuries incorporated many of the political structures and cultural traditions of its Fatimid and Ayyubid predecessors. Yet, its system of governance and centralization of authority represented departures from hierarchies of power and collective rule characterizing the regimes that antedated it. The Mamluk Sultanate can therefore be regarded as an experiment in the history of state-building within the premodern Islamic world. Since the Sultanate proved durable, controlling Egypt, Syria, and the Levant for two and a half centuries – the final episode of the region's status as an independent power in premodern times – it left an indelible imprint on its Ottoman successors and the cultural legacy of the central Arab lands.

The Mamluk institution preceded the Sultanate's establishment by several centuries. Its origins can be traced to the caliphal empire created in provinces of the former Byzantine and Sassanid realms (Northeast Africa, Southwest Asia) conquered by Bedouin tribal armies in the seventh and eighth centuries CE. The Caliphate formally legitimated its authority to rule on the principle of successorship (ar. *Khilāfa*) to the Prophet Muhammad. Following the assumption of this office by the Umayyad governor of Damascus, Muʿawiya ibn Abi Sufyan, in 41/661, the Caliphate in practice functioned as a dynastic monarchy that relied on loyalty from Arab Bedouin cadres stationed in garrisons strategically located throughout these territories. When opposition to Umayyad privileging of Arab ethnic hegemony coalesced around the insurrectionary movement of the ʿAbbasids in Iraq between 96/715 and 132/750, the Umayyad Dynasty faced hostility on the part of converts to Islam from non-Arab origins (the emerging majority) that proved insurmountable. The ʿAbbasid Dynasty that succeeded to the Caliphate in 132/750 lasted for half a millennium before its own demise at the hands of Mongols invading from Central Asia in the mid-thirteenth century. It owed its longevity (if not its territorial integrity) in part to the formation of military institutions that adapted to post-Umayyad ethnic diversity in the now-global Muslim community.

The term *Mamlūk* itself is a passive participle of the Arabic root *mīm-lām-kāf* (to own/possess) and literally means "one owned." In a military context, it referred to a slave trained specifically for martial duties. While often distinguished from chattel slaves (*ʿabd*/*ʿabīd*) according to ethnicity or "race," mamluks derived in fact from a disparate range of backgrounds and should not be envisioned on a simplistic basis of "color" (i.e., "white"). Yet, following the extension of caliphal suzerainty over western Central Asia, Turkic tribal groups assumed a pronounced place among the mamluk cadres in this institution during its formative phase. Although several Umayyad Caliphs made sporadic use of mamluk slave-soldiers, the ʿAbbasids utilized them as a prominent element of their military apparatus, in particular after the reign of Caliph al-Muʿtasim bi'llah Muhammad (218/833–227/842), of partial Turkish origin himself.[1] Because descendants of the original Bedouin conquerors had largely assimilated among indigenous populations, the ʿAbbasids could not count on support from a favored regional element, as had the Umayyads. They therefore adopted a policy of reliance on cadres without ties to the original conquerors. Slaves imported from non-Muslim populations, as property of the ruling authorities were an important component of the new military order. Since in principle, these slaves owed their status and power to the ruler or oligarchy who acquired them (either by purchase or as war prisoners), their loyalty could be trusted. Such was the expected outcome in theory.

The training procedures devised for mamluk slave-soldiers were designed to emphasize their elite status in society. Their patrons sought to separate them from the indigenous population to impede their assimilation, which was presumed to stir up divided loyalties and provoke a deterioration of group solidarity. The initial rationale behind these policies of isolation from civilian society stemmed from efforts by the early Caliphs to preserve the martial spirit of their Bedouin forces by stationing them in military camps away from the conquered populace. Since the Bedouin Arabs were eventually free to settle as they wished, this objective was unsustainable. But the ideal of their pristine valor, unsullied by contact with civilian masses, remained to inspire subsequent rulers and their advisors. Distinction from the local society was more effectively achieved with corps of imported slaves.

The consequences of separation for these slaves did not promote the unequivocal dependence and reliability initially envisioned, however. The competitiveness drilled into mamluk cadets combined with their sense of isolation to encourage simultaneous feelings of disdain for civilians and vulnerability as a minority to animosity from the majority. Discouraged from identifying with local masses, mamluks often came to consider themselves a privileged caste who could lay claim to an outsized share of a state's fiscal assets in return for the security they provided. Once entrenched in a political system, their behavior soon confirmed that the implementation of a military monopoly led to political manipulation at high levels, and even to outright control. Few regimes succeeded in restricting their slave-soldiers solely to military functions that served their patrons' interests. The histories of several regimes witnessed the effective supplanting of the ruler's independent political authority. In some instances, he became a figurehead exploited by his own slaves to mask their actual supremacy.

## Ayyubid Origins (521/1127–647/1249)

The institution of mamluk slave-soldiers did not supplant alternate systems of military recruitment, especially following the political disintegration of the ʿAbbasid Caliphate into an array of autonomous principalities emerging across Northeast Africa and Southwest Asia. In particular the rise of the Saljuk Sultanate throughout the Iranian regions during the tenth and eleventh centuries CE promoted the salience of free-born soldiers, again frequently of Turkic origin. These either served princes as officers or struck out on their own to found self-governing polities. When the so-called Great Saljuk empire in Iran (431/1040–590/1194) devolved into a network of polities formally subordinate but autonomous in practice, they were often controlled by individuals formally installed as *atābaks* or governors ruling in the name of the distant Sultan. Among these polities, the regime established in the northern Iraqi city of Mosul in the twelfth century CE was destined to attain hegemony over greater Syria and the Nile Valley, and to set in motion forces that would lead to formation of the Mamluk Sultanate in Egypt and Syria.

The principality in question was founded by an officer *(amīr)*: ʿImad al-Din Zangi, Atabak of Mosul (r. 521/1127–541/1146).[2] Zangi carved out an autonomous dominion inclusive of northern Iraq *(al-Jazīra)* and Syria as an offshoot of the Great Saljuk empire. He appointed a son, Nur al-Din Mahmud (r. 541/1147–569/1174), as governor of Damascus. Nur al-Din was concerned over the vulnerability of the Fatimid Shiʿi Caliphate in Egypt (297/909–567/1171) during its final decades due to internal restiveness, manipulation of the ruling dynasty by aggressive viziers, and the threat of invasion by European knights in the aftermath of the First Crusade (491–92/1098–99). He therefore sent several adjutants, of Kurdish origin, ostensibly to aid the current vizier and create a unified front against subsequent Crusades but in reality to explore the feasibility of occupying Egypt. The officer in charge was Asad al-Din Shirkuh ibn Shadhi. His nephew, Salah al-Din Yusuf ibn Ayyub (the Crusaders' Saladin), assumed command of the Syrian army in Egypt upon Shirkuh's death in 564/1169.[3] Salah al-Din deposed the last Fatimid Caliph in 567/1171 and proclaimed the restoration of Sunnism as the official practice of Islam in Egypt. The Azhar Mosque, formerly center of worship for the Ismaʿili Shiʿi Mission (*Daʿwa*), was converted to Sunni orthodox service.

Salah al-Din founded a dynasty, named for his own father Najm al-Din Ayyub (Shirkuh's brother), that linked Egypt to several principalities in Syria and the Jazira as an imperial federation ruled by his descendants. During his reign (564/1169–589/1193), Salah al-Din exploited this empire to confront the Crusader Kingdom of Jerusalem. He granted strategic garrison towns to members of his family as appanages while retaining the office of Sultan in Cairo for himself. The Ayyubid Dynasty projected an aura of unity over Egypt and Syria that lasted to the mid-seventh/thirteenth century. Salah al-Din scored several victories over the Crusaders (in particular at *Ḥaṭṭīn*, 583/1187), after which Muslim rule was restored to Jerusalem. But Salah al-Din failed to dislodge the Crusaders from Syria, and his successors in Cairo eventually adopted a policy of détente with remaining Crusader strongholds on the coast and interior. Salah al-Din presided over an ambitious building program in Cairo that included construction of the Citadel (*al-Qalʿa*) as the seat of government on the Muqattam Heights overlooking the city, and its surrounding walls. Cairo's medieval architectural profile dates from his reign.

Under the last Ayyubid Sultan, al-Malik al-Salih Ayyub (r. 637/1240–647/1249) ibn al-Malik al-Kamil Muhammad (r. 615/1218–635/1238), internal quarrels between branches of the Ayyubid Dynasty throughout Syria and ethnic tensions among factions of the army stationed in Cairo induced al-Salih to import upward of 1000 mamluk slave-soldiers from the Qipjaq Turkish Steppes in western Central Asia as his personal bodyguard. Housed in a garrison on the Nile, several units of these mamluks were subsequently known as Bahri or "Riverine." In the aftermath of al-Salih's death, a power struggle led to a coup, and foundation of a new regime, destined to preside over Egypt's final epoch as a regional power before modern times.

## From Junta to Sultanate: A Tumultuous Decade (647/1249–658/1260)

Sultan al-Salih Ayyub had named the regiment of mamluks purchased and trained as his personal guard the *Ṣāliḥiyya* after himself. Al-Salih's final year (647/1249) was marked by an invasion of the Nile Delta by King Louis IX of France. The French Crusaders initially occupied the city of Damietta (*Dumyāṭ*) but were subsequently defeated by competing mamluk units, who exploited the crisis to advance their own interests. The French monarch was captured and held for ransom. Following al-Salih's death, his son and heir, al-Muʿazzam Turan Shah, departed his own base in al-Jazira to claim the Sultanate in Cairo. Turan Shah manifested his intent to supplant with his own trusted adjutants the Mamluk officers who had risen to prominence in the oligarchy surrounding his father. Alarmed over the prospect of demotion following their successful repulsion of the French, these officers assassinated Turan Shah (28

Muharram 648/May 2, 1250). Effectively presiding over a junta, the officers initially weighed offering the Sultanate to reigning Ayyubid amirs in Syria – in particular al-Nasir Yusuf ibn al-ʿAziz Muhammad of Aleppo and Damascus. But their ultimate choice devolved upon a unique claimant – al-Salih's widow, a former concubine of Armenian descent named Tree of Pearls (ar. *Shajar al-Durr*).[4]

The officers' decision was motivated by Shajar al-Durr's support for several subunits within the Salihi regiment, in particular the band known as "Riverine" (*Baḥriyya*), noted above. Having received lucrative land allotments (*iqṭāʿ*s) granted by her, the Bahriyya were prepared to acknowledge Shajar al-Durr's leadership. But rival units contended that a valid succession was limited to a legitimate member of the Ayyubid Dynasty. Thus, when a senior officer named al-Muʿizz Aybak, head (*atābak*) of the Salihiyya regiment, was finally acclaimed as Sultan, he was compelled formally to share the office conjointly with a grandson of the former Ayyubid ruler al-Kamil, al-Ashraf Musa, along with al-Salih's widow, whom Aybak married. Aybak's reign (648/1250–655/1257) was plagued by factional insurgencies, intensified by the arrival in Cairo of mamluk squadrons defecting from their Ayyubid masters in Syria to seek their fortunes in Cairo. His assassination in 655/1257 was rumored to have occurred at Shajar al-Durr's instigation, when she became alarmed over the prospect of abandonment for a spouse more suited to Aybak's ambitions: a daughter of Badr al-Din Lu'lu', Atabak of Mosul (the principality that had sponsored the Ayyubid Dynasty). Within the following week, Shajar al-Durr was herself murdered, allegedly by members of Aybak's faction. Aybak's adolescent son, al-Mansur ʿAli (r. 655–57/1257–59), was installed as nominal Sultan, while one of Aybak's colleagues in the Salihiyya regiment, Sayf al-Din Qutuz, exercised actual authority.[5]

The turbulence of these events depicts the fragility of a junta devoid of stable leadership and wracked by internecine strife. A threat of invasion on the part of the Mongol occupiers of Iraq exacerbated these tensions. The Mongol Ilkhan Hulegu had sacked Baghdad, fabled seat of the ʿAbbasid Caliphate, in 656/1258. In the aftermath of his victory, which shook the Sunni Islamic world, Hulegu manifested his intention to invade the Levant and subsequently Egypt. Qutuz deposed ʿAli on grounds of juvenile incompetence in the face of a foreign menace, claimed the Sultanate, and proceeded to apprehend members of rival mamluk factions he suspected of undermining his rule. Among these members were several amirs of the Bahri unit, who had absconded to Gaza on the Sinai–Palestine border to avoid arrest as rebels. It was under these circumstances that one of the officers emerged to prominence in the historical narratives: the future Sultan, al-Zahir Baybars.

After Hulegu's forces occupied Aleppo and Damascus early in 659/1260, Sultan Qutuz defiantly anticipated their campaign against Egypt. Upon receipt of the Khan's emissaries, who presented an ultimatum to submit, with emphasis on the Sultan's status as a former slave (despite belonging to the Khwarazmian Dynasty), Qutuz met their insult with his own and ordered their execution. Aware that his act would be interpreted as a declaration of war, Qutuz reconciled with Ayyubid princes who had not yielded to the Mongols, along with the rebel Bahri officers in Gaza, and assembled an army composed of seasoned mamluk cavalry, Egyptian conscripts, and Ayyubid horsemen to confront Hulegu's host. But the massive invasion did not occur. Upon learning of the Great Khan Mongke's death back in China (657/1259), Hulegu called off the invasion and returned to Azerbaijan to await the outcome of Mongke's succession. Qutuz exploited the opportunity to assert his authority over Syria. Joined by the previously disaffected Bahri amirs, Qutuz led his coalition forces into Palestine. The remaining Mongol detachments, commanded by Hulegu's adjutant Kitbugha, confronted his army on 26 Ramadan 658/September 3, 1260, at a site known as ʿAyn Jalut (Spring of Goliath).

Despite their depleted numbers, the Mongols fought vigorously. Their defeat was in large measure due to the adroit tactics adopted by several officers on the Mamluk side, in particular Baybars. The victory achieved at ʿAyn Jalut by Qutuz's forces did not terminate Mongol intervention in Syria. But its successful blockage of the seemingly invincible Mongol advance on a global scale conveyed a powerful message that enhanced the stature of those officers who pulled it off. In anticipation of rewards that included governorships and land grants in Syria, several of them were disappointed by Qutuz's apparent favoritism of individuals in his personal retinue. When Qutuz failed to award Baybars rule over Aleppo, he joined other disaffected amirs in a plot to assassinate Qutuz on his way back to Egypt via Gaza. Since Baybars allegedly inflicted the fatal wound (disputed in some sources), his coconspirators ultimately acclaimed him as Qutuz's natural successor according to Turkic customary law. Upon their acknowledgment, Baybars demanded their oaths (*buyūʿ*) of loyalty, which were sworn only after Baybars acknowledged their own prerogatives as peers in the future ruling oligarchy. Baybars then assumed the Sultanic office on 17 Dhu'l-Qaʿda 658/October 24, 1260, in Cairo with the honorific title (*laqab*) "Mastering" (in God: *al-Ẓāhir [bi'llāh]*).

## The Reign of al-Zahir Baybars al-Bunduqdari (658/1260–676/1277)

Baybars is regarded as the architect of the imperial state that would unite Egypt and Syria over the decades following his enthronement.[6] He spent his early years enlarging the Mamluk military institution, subjecting it to rigorous training, consolidating the bureaucratic apparatus that funded its expenses via iqtaʿ property allotments (of land and urban real estate), and aggrandizing his personal household. During his seventeen-year reign, Mamluk contingents in the army would, conservatively measured, double or possibly triple from the 10,000 cavalry troops who had served Qutuz. Although Baybars attempted to promote a dynastic succession by installing his young son Berke as co-sultan, the senior amirs in his coalition dismissed the boy as a figurehead and upheld the tradition of peer acclamation by right of proven merit and division of power by negotiation. Baybars's signal achievement in politics resulted from his success at working with a contentious oligarchy of senior officers who regarded themselves as coequals with rights to share control over the state's assets. By stabilizing the ruling oligarchy, Baybars was able to avoid the destructive insurrections that had marred the preceding decade.

With regard to foreign policy, Baybars did not immediately exploit his victory at ʿAyn Jalut by prolonging hostilities with the Mongols whose outcome was dubious for either side. Instead, he set out to arrange an expedient coexistence with the Ilkhanate in Iran, in part to impede possible collusion between the Mongols and European powers that remained committed to the Crusader enterprise. Yet, Baybars also pragmatically admitted to his service bands of Mongols who had turned renegade against the Ilkhanid regime because of internal disputes or rivalries within their own ranks. Referred to as al-Wafidiyya (in this context: "defectors," cf. Chapter 2), these bands, whose members derived from diverse tribes within the Mongol military consortium, sought asylum under the Sultanate and would figure prominently in factional politics and military operations during future reigns.

Keenly aware of his predecessors' reputation as usurpers who had supplanted a legitimate royal dynasty, Baybars capitalized on the arrival in Cairo of one Abu'l-Qasim Ahmad, who claimed to be an uncle of the last ʿAbbasid Caliph in Baghdad, al-Mustaʿsim, whom the Mongols had executed in 656/1258. Bedouin tribesmen in Syria had apprehended this individual in the Iraqi–Syrian desert and sent him to Damascus during Qutuz's reign. Baybars now summoned the refugee and installed him as Caliph with the title of al-Mustansir II. He then proclaimed the ʿAbbasid Caliphate renewed in the Mamluk capital, secure from threats by unbelievers.[7] When al-Mustansir was killed during an abortive expedition to reconquer Baghdad, Baybars raised another claimant to the ʿAbbasid house to the Caliphate with the title of al-Hakim. While subsequent incumbents who occupied the caliphal office exercised little political power, their presence lent the new regime prestige throughout the Sunni Islamic world. Their function as legitimators of the officers who gained the Sultanate countered the perceived stain of their status as military slaves and betrayers of legitimate dynasties.

Baybars remained meteorically active throughout his reign. His seventeen years of rule can be regarded as an extended campaign, interrupted by pauses primarily to reinvigorate his troops and take stock of strategic shifts in the power balance between regional competitors. While Baybars presided over a significant consolidation of domestic administration in Egypt, he focused on realizing territorial objectives achieved by military successes abroad. Having demonstrated conspicuous military prowess and tactical skills before his arrival in Cairo and induction into al-Salih's Bahri corps, Baybars had already earned a reputation for effective leadership of troops (the nisba title *Bunduqdārī* refers to "crossbowman," although it was actually associated with Baybars's purchaser).

As Sultan, Baybars's primary goal was termination of the residual Crusader presence in greater Syria. Over a decade and a half of field battles and skirmishes, he largely realized it. Between 659/1261, when Baybars initiated his sieges of Crusader strongholds, and his death in Damascus on 29 Muharram 676/July 1, 1277, the Sultan had raided, occupied, or compelled to recognize him as suzerain the sites of: Jaffa, Acre, al-Karak, Caesaria, Arsuf, Safad, Beaufort, Tripoli, Hama, Hims, Antioch, Hisn al-Akrad (Crac des Chevaliers), Safita, Hisn al-ʿAkkar, Montfort, al-Bira on the Euphrates, and Cilician Armenia (**Fig. 1.1**). He solidified his control over Gaza, Damascus, and Aleppo during repeated visits and replenishing of garrisons there with troops of proven loyalty. In the final years of his reign, Baybars invaded southeastern Anatolia and challenged the legitimacy of regional Saljuk rulers on grounds of their vassalage to the Ilkhans in Iran. In the early 670s/1270s, expeditions under his adjutant officers confronted the Christian kingdom in Nubia and established the Sultanate's presence in ports on the Red Sea. Thus, when Baybars succumbed to a draft of (possibly poisoned) Qumiz (fermented mare's milk) in the Syrian capital, he had set the stage for a union between Egypt and Syria far more cohesive than his Fatimid or Ayyubid predecessors had achieved. His successors would finalize it.

## The Qalawunid Succession and Quasi-Dynasty (676/1277–709/1310)

Baybars was succeeded by his son Berke (after his mother's Khwarazmian ancestor who had assisted al-Salih; his name is frequently given as Baraka in Arabic sources). Despite Baybars's elaborate measures to ensure his son's accession, Berke unsettled the senior amirs, who had effectively shared authority with the deceased sultan. They therefore compelled him to abdicate in Rabiʿ I 678/August 1279 and accept exile with control over the former Crusader stronghold of al-Karak east of the Jordan River. The amirs then raised his seven-year-old brother Salamish to the Sultanate with the title al-ʿAdil, his installation a stopgap measure while the ruling oligarchy determined who merited their acclamation. Their choice ultimately went to al-Mansur Qalawun al-Alfi (the *nisba*-title denoting his purchase price of 1000 dinars, the high sum due to his good looks).[8] Qalawun (r. 678/1279–689/1290) had

Fig. 1.1 Bridge with lion blazons built by Sultan Baybars
Known as the Bridge of Jindas (ar. *Jisr Jindas*), a village near modern Lod, Israel. The inscription dates from 672/1273 and glorifies Sultan Baybars for building the bridge. The inscription is flanked by two lions (or leopards), Baybars's heraldic symbols.
(Credit: by IAISI/Getty Images)

risen to prominence during Baybars's reign as one of his most influential and powerful adjutants. His accession was soon challenged by another senior amir, Sunqur al-Ashqar (on 12 Dhu'l-Hijja 678/April 26, 1280), who had received the governorship of Damascus during negotiations preceding Qalawun's enthronement. Qalawun and Sunqur belonged to the aging coterie of Salihi officers who surrounded Baybars; neither regarded the other as superior in rank. Their contestation for power might have extended indefinitely had not the Mongols intervened.

The Ilkhanids sent an expeditionary force into northern Syria in Jumada I 679/September 1280. Qalawun and Sunqur reached a rapprochement in which the former recognized the latter as overlord of several sites in northern Syria while the latter acknowledged Qalawun as Sultan in Cairo. Their agreement stemmed from necessity; the Ilkhanids planned a major campaign to restore their hegemony over the region. The battle occurred near Hims on 14 Rajab 680/October 29, 1281. Despite their inferior numbers, Qalawun and Sunqur defeated the Ilkhanids, their success due in part to the adept maneuvers of Bedouin auxiliaries. The ruling Ilkhan Abaqa planned another expedition but died the next year. His passing relieved the immediate Mongol threat.

Qalawun's military record sustained the Cairo Sultanate's hegemony in central Syria and Nubia but did not equal Baybars's exceptional accomplishments. Although relations with the Mongols stabilized during his reign, regions north of Aleppo became effectively a buffer between Damascus Province and the Ilkhanate. Residual Crusader elements and local tribal bands roamed them under semi-autonomous conditions. Qalawun's domestic administration proved more effective. The Sultan adopted policies attractive to Cairo's mercantile elite. Taxes and tariffs regarded as extortionist under Shariʿa law were rescinded. Qalawun styled himself a defender of judicial equity and religious propriety. He generously supported renovations of revered holy sites such as the Aqsa Mosque in Jerusalem, the Prophet's Mosque in Medina, and the Shrine of the Biblical Patriarch Ibrahim in Hebron (*al-Khalīl*). In Cairo, Qalawun built and endowed a hospital regarded as a marvel of healing, the project calculated to garner popular support (**Fig. 1.2**). With regard to the military elite, Qalawun swelled its ranks, purchasing many junior recruits from non-Turkish regions. Circassians appeared among their ranks as a significant component and formed a regiment titled "Burji" after a tower in the Citadel where they were garrisoned.

Qalawun died on 7 Dhu'l-Qaʿda 689/November 11, 1290. Upon his death, his younger son al-Ashraf Khalil (r. 689/1290–693/1293) succeeded. Qalawun had relied on his eldest son al-Salih ʿAli's assistance as effective co-ruler in Egypt during his absences in Syria. But ʿAli died in 687/1288, leaving his less admired brother unopposed despite his lack of popularity. Khalil nonetheless proved himself a forceful militarist. His agenda of rigorous training produced

Fig. 1.2 Sultan Qalawun hospital site
A massive complex in Cairo, constructed by Sultan al-Mansur Qalawun in 682–83/1284–85. Located on the Bayn al-Qasrayn street at the center of the former Fatimid district in Cairo, the site includes a hospital *(bīmāristān)*, a madrasa, and his mausoleum *(qubba/ḍarīḥ)*.
(Photo by Michel Setboun/Corbis via Getty Images)

impressive results. On 17 Jumada I 690/May 18, 1291, Khalil's army occupied the heavily fortified Crusader port and stronghold of Akko/Acre, thereby securing the Sultanate's control over central and southern Syria. Khalil laid plans for an expedition against the Ilkhanate that included the re-conquest of Baghdad. Had he survived, this project might have altered the regional balance of power. But Khalil had made enemies among several of his senior adjutants and provincial governors who considered their interests slighted, notwithstanding their service during the campaigns. During a hunting trip on 13 Muharram 693/December 14, 1293, several of these fatally ambushed him. The conspirators included his once-trusted deputy Baydara al-Mansuri, one of the most respected senior officers of the realm.

Khalil's assassination set off turmoil that was not resolved for seventeen years. Of the conspirators who had sought to seize the Sultanate, Baydara was murdered after less than a week. Ultimately, in Muharram 693/December 1293, a coterie of contending amirs enthroned Khalil's eight-year-old brother, al-Nasir Muhammad, once again exploiting the status of Qalawun's line to bide for time as they maneuvered to gain ultimate power. An officer who had not belonged to Khalil's circle, Zayn al-Din Kitbugha (of Mongol origin, but no relation to the Ilkhanid commander), eventually won out. Kitbugha defeated his preeminent rival, the vizier ʿAlam al-Din Sanjar al-Shujaʿi, purged the army of Khalil's Ashrafi mamluks, and exiled the boy-sultan to al-Karak in Muharram 694/December 1294. Kitbugha assumed the Sultanate with the title of al-ʿAdil, but held it himself for only two years before voluntarily leaving the office to his deputy (*nāʾib al-sulṭān*), Husam al-Din Lajin.[9] An officer of Greek origin, Lajin had plotted to assassinate his superior, who resolved the dispute by abdicating and acceptance of retirement to a post in Syria. Lajin assumed the Sultanate with the title of al-Mansur in 696/1296. His own tenure was brief. When rival factions impugned Lajin's distribution of iqtaʿ allotments to his supporters, they murdered him and raised al-Nasir Muhammad to the Sultanate a second time on 11 Rabiʿ II 698/January 16, 1299.

Al-Nasir Muhammad returned to Cairo from al-Karak. Having reached the age when he could credibly assume command of the army, al-Nasir confronted the Ilkhan Ghazan at the site of Wadi al-Khazindar near Hims (28 Rabiʿ I 699/ December 23, 1299). Ghazan had renewed the long-standing Mongol project of conquering the Levant and invaded Syria with a large host. Due in part to their numerical inferiority, the forces led by al-Nasir were defeated and withdrew in disarray (**Fig. 1.3**). Although Ghazan occupied Hims and Damascus, his hold over Syria remained tenuous due to foraging issues and widespread ambivalence by the local populace. In Cairo, al-Nasir Muhammad reequipped his army for a campaign to restore Mamluk rule over Syria, funded by forced expropriations from the Egyptian populace. Before the expedition set out, al-Nasir received news that Ghazan had withdrawn, leaving diminished garrisons in Damascus and Hims. Al-Nasir ultimately negotiated the submission of their commanders. Realizing that the Ilkhan remained intent on invading the Levant at a future date, al-Nasir invited the former Sultan Kitbugha back to service as governor in Hama and elevated his major-domo (*Ustādār*), Baybars al-Jashankir, to lead the Mamluk army in Syria. Further skirmishes culminated in a decisive clash at the site of Marj al-Suffar in which the Mamluks routed the Ilkhanids (2 Ramadan 702/April 20, 1303). The battle effectively terminated Ilkhanid prospects for authority in Syria. Al-Nasir Muhammad could legitimately claim sovereignty over the province.

Notwithstanding his augmented stature, al-Nasir continued to find himself buffeted by competition between several rivals, among whom his major-domo, Rukn al-Din Baybars al-Jashankir (Court Taster), and deputy-sultan, Sayf al-Din Salar (a Mongol officer of the Oirat Wafidiyya faction who rose to prominence during Qalawun's reign), stood out. Al-Nasir retreated back to al-Karak in 708/1309, while Baybars prevailed in his contest with Salar and claimed the Sultanate as al-Malik al-Muzaffar (r. 708/1309–709/1310). By this time, al-Nasir Muhammad had acquired skill in the game of factional politics.

Fig. 1.3 Battle in Wadi al-Khazindar
Depiction of fourteenth-century ms. of battle at site of Wadi al-Khazindar near Hims between the Mongols led by Ilkhan Ghazan and the Mamluks headed by Sultan al-Nasir Muhammad ibn Qalawun near Hims (28 Rabiʿ I 699/December 23, 1299).
(Photo by: Universal History Archive/Universal Images Group via Getty Images)

Over the following year, al-Nasir profited from his refuge in al-Karak to build his own following of mamluks (some of whom had served his father [*Manṣūrīs*], others recruited personally from his own resources [*Nāṣirīs*]), and Bedouin loyalists in the Karak vicinity who stood to gain from his successful consolidation of power. Al-Nasir Muhammad returned to Cairo in Shawwal 709/March 1310, deposed and terminated Baybars, and set about securing himself in the Sultanic office. His strategy proved successful. Al-Nasir would reign independently for three decades and preside over a period widely regarded as the Sultanate's halcyon era.

## The Third Reign of al-Nasir Muhammad ibn Qalawun (709/1310–741/1341)

Al-Nasir Muhammad confronted the legacy of conspiracy and turbulence engendered from the preceding decades of strife with policies that deviated from his eminent predecessors', Baybars al-Bunduqdari and al-Mansur Qalawun.[10] While his immediate goal was to entrench himself at the apex of authority, al-Nasir's alterations in recruitment, promotion, and training of military personnel were to have consequences long after his reign. Primary among al-Nasir's concerns was the endemic threat of competition for the Sultanic office, which had affected his own fear of deposition deeply. Al-Nasir therefore systematically eliminated those officers who had manipulated him in his previous reigns as a figurehead. Their removal by imprisonment, exile, or execution cleared the way for al-Nasir's own, theoretically loyal, cadres. But their expulsion also resulted in the disappearance of senior staff skilled in warfare and factional infighting by long-term experience. Al-Nasir's own identity within the military elite, more precisely its lack, is significant.

As a *walad al-nās* or son of a mamluk recruited by purchase as a slave, al-Nasir did not regard himself as a soldier who owed allegiance to a patron. He rather saw himself as heir to a dynasty and thereby a supreme patron by royal right. Traditions of martial expertise or barracks camaraderie (*khushdāshiyya*) meant little to al-Nasir personally, in particular since he had observed at close range how tenuous these proved to be during the infighting that marked his first two reigns. By contrast, al-Nasir realized that in matters of survival, loyalty topped military expertise and martial ethos with regard to his security in office. Al-Nasir also understood that his personal status as a walad al-nas remained a matter of scorn among soldiers recruited as indentured guardians of their patron and honed as effective praetorians. He accordingly began to advance individuals from backgrounds diverse in many ways except for their common ambivalence toward the exclusive cadres of first-generation mamluk slave-soldiers.

From al-Nasir Muhammad's reign, the cohesion that had its origin in the Qipjaq cadres acquired and trained by al-Salih Ayyub began to dissipate, as individuals who entered military service from contrasting milieus advanced to prominence. While ethnic solidarity, allegedly prized among the Mamluk corps, remained more significant as an ideal rather than a reality even in its formative stage under the regime's founders, from al-Nasir's reign it was diluted by individuals whose origins spanned the eastern Mediterranean, Caucasus, and Southwest Asia more generally. Although cadet trainees in elite units were still acquired via purchase, the merchants who collected them interacted with diverse ethnicities across these regions who were ready to offer their offspring (male and female) for cash or career opportunities. Dialects of Turkish and later Circassian remained media of discourse among Mamluk cadres by ingrained tradition rather than by ethnic descent. And facility in Arabic or Persian increasingly marked cultural attainment and formal learning among all military ranks (cf. Chapter 6). Al-Nasir, who himself had not experienced the rigors of intense military training, was prepared to value loyalty over martial skill and to regard the former as primary in the process of recruitment, promotion, and pay. Thus, during al-Nasir Muhammad's three decades of independent rule, the Mamluk institution diverged from its profiles of the formative period.

Al-Nasir also faced a fiduciary issue with profound implications for the future trajectory of the economy. Acting on the precedent set by the forced expropriations that had funded his earlier campaigns against the Mongols, al-Nasir Muhammad experimented with a variety of measures to raise the funds necessary to satisfy the demands of cadres progressively motivated by fiscal reward rather than pride over loyalty and quality of service. During al-Nasir's reign, the *rawk* or cadaster, systematic taxation of rents from agrarian properties held as *iqta*ʿ allotments throughout the realm and based on surveys of yields according to district, became a foundation of fiduciary support for the military establishment. But since the sums acquired from these excises rarely satisfied the demands of troops when summoned to campaigns, the regime progressively exploited tactics of confiscation imposed on elements in society presumed to hold substantial assets in cash, commodities, or real estate. These tactics will be discussed subsequently (cf. Chapter 5). While their origins predated the Mamluk regime, they became vital components of the Sultanate's fiduciary system during al-Nasir Muhammad's third reign.

These measures, however onerous to those on whom they were imposed, did not degrade the performance of martial forces at al-Nasir's disposal. The Sultan recognized that the corps of Royal (*Sulṭānī*) Mamluks remained crucial to his power base and did not diminish their stipends. In 711/1312, they led his army to defeat the last noteworthy invasion of Syria by the Ilkhanids. Ten years later, the two regimes concluded a peace treaty that formally terminated the era of warfare between them. The Ilkhanate itself would soon fragment into a series of local regimes in Southwest Asia, each with distinctive political aspirations. With the end of this rivalry on a global scale, the Sultanate would enter a period of economic growth and cultural florescence that was sustained for several decades despite the pernicious fiduciary policies imposed to shore up the military. The Sultan declared himself a guardian of productive sectors in society and promoted policies to enhance commerce foreign and domestic. He abolished a network of abusive taxes deemed inconsistent with Shariʿa law and initiated reforms of currency aimed at curbing debasement of coinage. The program of infrastructural development and ceremonial building that marked al-Nasir's era became legendary throughout the region, the object of admiration and praise by foreign observers.

Yet, al-Nasir Muhammad's recruitment policies did not eliminate the potential for factional strife within the military institution. Upon his death on 21 Dhu'l-Hijja 741/June 7, 1341 at the age of fifty-four, competition for the Sultanate reemerged under the aegis of al-Nasir's numerous progeny. The quasi-dynasty over which they presided maintained a degree of stability that mitigated inter-factional tensions until the emergence of a new style of governance with the accession of al-Zahir Barquq in 784/1382.

## The Qalawunid Lineage: Figureheads and Power Brokers (741/1341–784/1382)

The four decades that intervened between al-Nasir Muhammad's passing and Barquq's accession are frequently depicted as a period of prolonged competition between a coterie of senior officers who had served the deceased sultan as his adjutants. They expediently installed his descendants in the Sultanic office while they conspired among themselves as arbiters of genuine power. This impression, promoted by chroniclers, is valid in some measure but misses the rationale behind such an extended process of succession within the Qalawunid lineage. The amirs who enthroned these figureheads were not motivated exclusively by expedience. They owed their own careers to the Qalawunid Dynasty and did not envisage abandoning it to appropriate Sultanic authority on their own. Their mind-set qualifies another widely held impression of antipathy toward dynastic succession fundamental to an idealized ethos of first-generation primacy among the Mamluk elite. Several of the sons and grandsons of al-Nasir Muhammad who occupied the Sultanate were in fact pawns of manipulative amirs. But they embodied a legacy these amirs regarded as essential to their own hegemony. Its preservation served to legitimate their jockeying for influence and sharing of prerogatives at the realm's summit. When the Qalawunid succession finally ended, its termination resulted from political circumstances that can be discerned in hindsight but were not apparent to contemporary political actors.

Al-Nasir Muhammad himself had groomed his oldest son, Anuk, for the succession. When Anuk predeceased the sultan in 739/1339, al-Nasir's choice went to the third, Abu Bakr, who formally succeeded. Al-Nasir's passing over the second son, Ahmad, opened the door to intrigue among two senior amirs, Bashtak and Qawsun, who mutually conspired to assume final authority behind their control of the new incumbent. When Abu Bakr sought to free himself from the officer who won out, Qawsun, the latter exiled him to Upper Egypt in less than a year. Qawsun then turned to al-Nasir's adolescent son Kuchuk, whom he regarded as more malleable. Yet, Qawsun's envisioned ploy failed due to opposition from viceroys (*nuwwāb al-salṭāna*) in Damascus and Aleppo and counter-conspiracy by the officers sent to arrest the second son, Ahmad, who was based in the fortress of al-Karak. By Rajab-Shaʿban 742/January 1342, both Kuchuk and Qawsun had been eliminated and Ahmad enthroned as al-Malik al-Nasir. Ahmad felt insecure about departing his stronghold for Cairo and its threat of betrayal by his alleged benefactors. He therefore announced the Sultanate's transfer to al-Karak. Resistance by senior amirs in Egypt was predictable, and five months later Ahmad was replaced by his half-sibling Isma'il, who was enthroned as al-Malik al-Salih on 12 Muharram 743/June 17, 1342. Isma'il occupied the Sultanate for three years until his own death due to illness on 22 Rabi' 746/July 23, 1345. The contrast between his professed piety and fondness for concubines did not alarm the senior amirs, whose rivalries Isma'il tolerated, in part to secure their support for expeditions to occupy al-Karak, eliminate Ahmad, and secure his treasure.

Upon Isma'il's death another sibling, Sha'ban, was elevated as al-Malik al-Kamil.[11] Sha'ban's tenure aroused widespread antipathy among the senior amirs and hosts of Nasiri Mamluks who resided in the capital with no licit patron. When sales of lucrative offices became rampant to stave off fiscal deficits, insurrection erupted in the person of Yalbugha al-Yahyawi, na'ib of Damascus, in 747/1346. Following Yalbugha's declaration of revolt, several amirs in Cairo deposed Sha'ban and enthroned his half-brother Hajji as al-Malik al-Muzaffar on 3 Jumada II 747/September 21, 1346. The new sultan sought to secure his position by lavishly stipending units of former Nasiri mamluks whose finances had been precarious since their patron's death in 741/1341. On 12 Ramadan 748/December 16, 1347, he followed his predecessors in deposition and execution.

The preceding sequence of successions occurred under unsettled circumstances affecting the larger society. During the mid-seventh/fourteenth century, waves of plague epidemic altered the demography of Egypt and Syria, adversely impacting the economy and arousing resentment among competing Mamluk units angered over reductions in pay and rations. Hajji was followed by another of al-Nasir Muhammad's progeny, al-Nasir Hasan, who faced a now-familiar milieu of conspiracy and unrest. Hasan's efforts to build a coalition of loyal amirs through a variety of fiscal stratagems led to his own deposition on 17 Jumada II 752/August 11, 1351, followed by the enthronement of yet another sibling, al-Salih Salih. Four years later, Salih was removed and Hasan restored. Hasan emerged from house confinement in the harem to occupy the Sultanate a second time. He accelerated his agenda of buying praetorian favor by advancing second-generation descendants of Mamluks (*awlād al-nās*) to ranks formerly the prerogative of first-generation recruits. The resulting resentment led to Hasan's removal on 12 Jumada I 762/March 20, 1361. Despite the similarity of his termination to his predecessors' fate, Hasan was not a cipher. His alleged fiduciary corruption seems to have succeeded to the extent that al-Nasir Hasan financed construction of lavish buildings, in particular his vast tomb-mosque that stands today opposite the Citadel on the Maydan (**Fig. 1.4**).

The amir who led the revolt against Hasan, Yalbugha al-'Umari al-Khassaki, presided over the elevation of al-Mansur Muhammad, a son of the former

Fig. 1.4 Mosque of Sultan al-Nasir Hasan ibn Qalawun
Mosque/madrasa constructed on the Maydan facing the Citadel between 757 and 64/1356 and 1363; among the most prominent medieval Islamic structures in Cairo. Lithography by David Roberts, ca. 1845.
(Photo by adoc-photos/Corbis via Getty Images)

sultan Hajji. Muhammad lasted in the Sultanate until 5 Shaʿban 764/May 20, 1363, when Yalbugha replaced him with a son of Sultan Hasan, the second Shaʿban, who took the title al-Malik al-Ashraf. Yalbugha now wielded supreme power while holding the office of atabak al-ʿasakir. His attempts to counter what he perceived as a decline in discipline in the Mamluk corps by imposing training regimens practiced in Baybars's and Qalawun's time provoked the new cadres who had emerged from among the awlad al-nas and other newcomers. His tenure was also undermined by shifts in commercial activity throughout the eastern Mediterranean. Following the occupation of Acre/Akko in Qalawun's reign, ports in Cilician Armenia had emerged as entrepôts of European trade. The Sultanate organized expeditions to occupy this territory, efforts that were blocked by an invasion of Alexandria headed by the Lusignan ruler of Cyprus, Peter I (24 Muharram 767/October 11, 1365).[12] The immediate consequence of these events was a shift in the balance of trade that, at least temporarily, weakened the local economy. These events combined to undermine Yalbugha's position, and he suffered execution after a revolt on the part of disaffected troops in 767/1365. For his part, Sultan Shaʿban II continued in office until 6 Dhu'l-Qaʿda 778/March 17, 1377. He proved himself an effective ruler credited with rectifying excesses of his predecessors and bettering the conditions of the Mamluk units who supported him. Yet, the second Shaʿban was to share his predecessors' fate. When the Sultan prepared to make the Hajj to Mecca, disaffected officers who had moved up the ranks as mamluks formerly held by Yalbugha occupied the Citadel in Cairo. They executed Shaʿban by strangulation (an honorable death according to military tradition). Prominent among them was the individual who would preside over the formation of a new regime and political order, the Amir Barquq.

## Al-Zahir Barquq and Establishment of the "Circassian" Regime (784/1382–801/1399)

Following Shaʿban's termination, Barquq and the other conspirators installed his adolescent son, ʿAli, as al-Malik al-Mansur. Barquq belonged to the Yalbughawi faction of the Burji Circassian regiment of Mamluks whose origin dated from al-Mansur Qalawun's time.[13] He had advanced to prominence in the service of the Atabak Yalbugha al-Khassaki during the 760s/1360s. Upon Yalbugha's death in 767/1365, Barquq became embroiled in several insurrectionary movements until he attached himself to al-Ashraf Shaʿban's retinue, received further promotions, and was awarded the post of arms bearer (*Silāḥdār*). After Shaʿban's death, Barquq was promoted to the rank of amir of forty, along with another mamluk, Baraka (Berke), by supporters of al-Mansur ʿAli in return for their part in terminating one of the leading plotters against Shaʿban, the Amir Qaratay. By 783/1381, Barquq had ousted his former comrade Baraka and become the commander of armed forces in Cairo (*atābak al-ʿasākir*). He had married a daughter of the Viceroy of Damascus, Tashtimur al-ʿAlaʾi (another senior Yalbughawi officer), as a means of allying with a potential successor to Shaʿban and competitor for command of the army in Cairo. But, attuned to the shifting currents of conspiracy, Barquq plotted to eliminate Tashtimur and emerged himself as effective ruler in Cairo. When al-Mansur ʿAli succumbed to the plague on 23 Safar 784/May 8, 1382, Atabak Barquq initially acquiesced to his colleagues' demand for the accession of Shaʿban's younger son Hajji as al-Malik al-Salih. But within the year, Barquq removed Hajji (the second of this name) and assumed the Sultanate on grounds of impending disorder in Syria. He took the title al-Malik al-Zahir as a declaration of his succession paralleling his great predecessor's, the Sultanate's founder, al-Zahir Baybars.

Upon his enthronement, Barquq (r. 784/1382–801/1399, with interregnum), whose personal name was "Plum" in Arabic (given by his original purchaser because of his bulging eyes), planned to bolster his position by promoting mamluks from rival factions to gain their support. While this attempt at coalition building would produce positive results in the long term, its immediate consequence was exposure to plots by his rivals. Two of these seized the opportunity: Yalbugha al-Nasiri, governor (*nāʾib*) of Aleppo, and Timurtash (known as Mintash), na'ib of Tripoli after dismissal from Barquq's service in disgrace. Their conspiracy erupted in open rebellion, to which other Syrian governors joined. Barquq swore oaths of renewed loyalty from his officers in Cairo and then sent an expeditionary force to confront Yalbugha al-Nasiri outside of Damascus. The battle occurred on 11 Rabiʿ I 791/March 10, 1389 and resulted in a rout of Barquq's troops. Yalbugha proclaimed himself master of Syria while Barquq hastily organized a new army to confront a probable invasion of Egypt. Yalbugha and Mintash reached Matariyya, north of Cairo, and on 15 Jumada I/May 12 again met Barquq, whose own adjutants were poised to transfer their allegiance to the rebels. Since the encounter ended indecisively, Barquq retreated to the Citadel in Cairo. After a second engagement beneath Cairo's walls, Barquq went into hiding. Yalbugha and Mintash entered the city and ultimately occupied the Citadel. Barquq was apprehended and jailed while the conspirators convened with the assembled amirs and the Caliph to decide their course of action. After heated discussions, they decided to dethrone Barquq, exile him to al-Karak, and re-install Hajji, who would serve as a front for the new junta. Hajji, now fourteen, took the title al-Mansur (25 Jumada II 791/May 22, 1389).

The rebels proved incapable of duplicating Barquq's coalition. Their occupation deteriorated into street fighting between Yalbugha, ensconced in the Citadel, and Mintash, who raised a force from troops discontented with their reward for abandoning Barquq. Mintash laid siege to the Citadel – bombarding it with projectiles hurled from his base in the massive mosque of Sultan Hasan across the square. Yalbugha now found himself facing the desertion of followers that Barquq had suffered. He succumbed to Mintash, who imprisoned him in Alexandria. For his part, Barquq had not remained idle. Aware of the strife in Cairo, he garnered support from Bedouin tribes in the vicinity of al-Karak and led them back toward the Egyptian frontier. After defeating the governor of Gaza, he proceeded toward Damascus and vanquished a contingent of troops stationed there at the site of Shaqhab, where a century earlier the Ilkhanid army had been routed. Realizing the menace emerging in Syria, Mintash departed Cairo at the head of a large host, accompanied by his sultan-ward Hajji, the Caliph, and senior magistrates (17 Dhu'l-Hijja 791/December 7, 1389). Upon his arrival at Gaza, he found the garrison had largely deserted to join Barquq. When Mintash finally confronted Barquq, again at Shaqhab (3 Safar 792/January 21, 1390), the former sultan lost the initial encounter but rallied a band of intrepid supporters (less than forty) and raided Mintash's camp. Seizing its baggage, Barquq regrouped his troops and inflicted a defeat against Mintash, who retreated to occupy Damascus. Al-Mansur Hajji and the Caliph swore oaths of loyalty to Barquq, who returned to

Cairo to receive his reconfirmation in the Sultanate by acclamation of officers and troops who had awaited the contest's outcome (15 Safar 792/February 2, 1390). Hajji formally abdicated and lived in honorable retirement for two decades.

The rebel Mintash was unwilling to reconcile, however. Over the next four years, this redoubtable individual sought sanctuary and won support to challenge Barquq's suzerainty from amirs in Aleppo (twice), Tripoli, Hims, Hama, Damascus (twice), and Baʿlabakk before he was finally betrayed by a Bedouin chieftain in northern Syria. Turned over to the governor of Aleppo, Mintash was tortured to force his revelation of money caches he had hidden. When he refused, Mintash was decapitated and his head displayed in public squares as it made its way to Cairo. Barquq ordered celebrations for a week upon its arrival.

Barquq renewed his agenda of replacing soldiers and officers who had served his predecessors (veteran Mamluks) with troops he purchased himself. To fund their substantial cost, Barquq founded a "Special Bureau" (*al-dīwān al-mufrad*), which initially paid their stipends from iqtaʿ allotments formerly held by deposed Qalawunids. He established a policy that would be maintained through the Sultanate's subsequent history (cf. Chapter 5). While personnel originating in Circassian territories figured prominently in Barquq's regiments, recruits (*julbān*) appeared in their ranks from diverse regions throughout Southwest Asia, the Balkans, and farther afield. Many accepted indentured status of their own volition to join the Sultanate's prestigious military elite. By contrast, the presence of Turkic recruits diminished significantly, their former homelands no longer disposed to export manpower to foreign rulers. Barquq's enlistment program had long-lasting consequences: soldiers and officers who bore the Zahiri nisba would assume notable roles in the regime's ruling hierarchy over the following decades. During Barquq's reign, many senior members of the military elite maintained close ties with relatives in their places of origin. Barquq himself invited his father, Anas, to join him in Cairo as an honored guest.

Barquq also established ties with diverse elements of Cairo's civilian populace (*al-ʿāmma*), in particular their plebeian constituents. In this, Barquq displayed an astute grasp of mass politics and its impact on potential insurgencies. Barquq was aware of their presence in riots that had unsettled, and frequently controlled, Cairo's streets during former reigns. He realized that mobs often dismissed as rabble or riff-raff (*zuʿar*) by "respectable" classes of society (*al-nās*) fought vigorously alongside low-ranked recruits who were inclined to rebel for higher stipends and preference over their competing brigades. Their distinction from common criminals was inconspicuous. Barquq therefore reached out to some of the least reputable groups among the masses, so-called *harafīsh* or members of the more informal Sufi orders and day laborers often impressed into forced labor on public works projects such as canal digging or street clearing. In return for sporadic distribution of food and money, and appointment as de facto police in their urban wards, these harafish were prepared to back the sultan in the advent of insurrection from potential rivals. Barquq was thus acknowledged by chroniclers for his pragmatic liberality with regard to the common people. Their support, however inchoate, was to constitute a significant aspect of his reign's organization, a fact on which the chroniclers dwelled at length. Barquq's munificence to the more eminent Sufi orders was no less visible. The sultan contributed generously to the endowments of Cairo's Sufi hospices (*khānqāhs*), whose residents dependably lauded his rule and, if not endorsed, at least countenanced his policies (cf. Chapter 7). Barquq's eulogizers noted his personal identity with Sufi spirituality, depicting it as a signal – and admirable – aspect of his character.

Barquq's second reign continued with few foreign hazards. The Central Asian conqueror Timur Lenk (Tamerlane) had subdued the Iraqi regions by 789/1387. In 795/1393, Barquq's Ottoman contemporary in Anatolia, Sultan Bayazid I (r. 791/1389–804/1402), sent emissaries inviting the Egyptian Sultanate to join with him in an alliance against Timur's advance further west. The deposed Jalayirid ruler of Baghdad, Ahmad ibn Uways, arrived in Cairo on 7 Rabiʿ I 796/January 10, 1394, seeking asylum from Timur's invasion. Barquq welcomed him with honors. When he subsequently received a demand from Timur for submission, Barquq had its courier executed and laid preparations for an expedition to confront him. To counteract his troops' minimal enthusiasm for the venture, Barquq demanded a requisition of 200,000 dinars from Cairo's spice merchants to fund their bonuses as special compensation. Accompanied by Ahmad ibn Uways and the Caliph, Barquq thus proceeded to al-Bira on the Euphrates. But Timur had altered his own campaign plans to quell restiveness in the Iranian regions he had already occupied. He put off his advance through Syria and departed Mesopotamia for Iran, leaving a contingent of troops behind. After clashing with Barquq's forces, the contingent retreated in defeat, freeing Barquq to return to Cairo in stages, with a sojourn in Damascus to assign commanders to regional fortresses. Ahmad ibn Uways reclaimed his rule in Baghdad.

Barquq spent his remaining years in the capital. His health declined, marked by seizures that may have signaled epilepsy. He died on 15 Shawwal 801/June 20, 1399, after convening his senior adjutants to endorse the succession of his first-born son, Faraj. Effective founder of the so-called Circassian regime, Barquq had held power, either as Atabak formally subordinate to the last Qalawunid figureheads or as Sultan independently, for two decades. The unrelieved list of conspiracies and rivalries on which contemporary historians laid stress as markers of his reign should not mask either Barquq's success at surmounting them or the underlying stability that they superficially obscured.

Barquq's signal achievement in fact emerged from the durability of the system he engendered. The ruling institution during the subsequent Circassian period would continue to endure myriad conspiracies and insurrections. But each episode of unrest was followed by a durable reign that increasingly penalized plotting and rebellion with exile (often to al-Karak or Jerusalem) or forced retirement through house arrest (frequently in Alexandria) rather than with torture or execution. Barquq set the precedent for this shift and his successors ultimately upheld it.

## The Reigns of Faraj and Shaykh: Rivalry, Invasion, Reconsolidation (801/1399–825/1422)

Barquq's son, Faraj, was acknowledged as Sultan on the day of his father's death with the laqab al-Nasir. Initially regarded as a figurehead in the precedent already fixed by numerous adolescent successors exploited by senior amirs, Faraj was formally enthroned as ruler several months later (Rabiʿ I 802/November 1399), due to their failure to settle the accession on one of their own. Historians of the period castigated Faraj's reign (801/1399–815/1412, with interregnum) as among the least worthy in the Sultanate's history.[14] Faraj's deportment, described by them in lurid detail, does reveal unsavory characteristics. But the circumstances surrounding his accession, at the age of eleven, and repeated attempts at his deposition by ruthless adjutants provide a mitigating context. And the intensity of this youth's desire to survive formidable odds cannot be ignored. Faraj managed to dispense with the guardians appointed by his father – Taghri Birdi al-Bashbughawi (parent of the eminent historian, cf. Chapter 6) and Aytmish al-Bajasi – after several months. He faced more determined threats from officers holding positions of authority over troops in Cairo or stationed as governors in Syria. Prominent among the latter was Tanam, viceroy of Damascus. When a group of officers who identified with the Turkish faction, and were aggrieved over Barquq's Circassian appointments, attacked the Citadel, Faraj's own coterie of junior officers and pages successfully fought them off. Several of the assaulters fled to Damascus, where they were granted asylum by Tanam, who prepared to invade Egypt and besiege the capital. But Faraj, despite his novice age, managed to assemble a host composed of his own backers who stood to lose everything if he were removed. They were determined to bring the war to Tanam in Damascus. Faraj defeated Tanam during his initial expedition (3 Shaʿban 802/March 30, 1300), but subsequent insurrections erupted throughout his reign.

Six years later, Faraj endured deposition in favor of his own brother ʿAbd al-ʿAziz (al-Malik al-Mansur, installed on 25 Rabiʿ I 808/September 20, 1405) at the instigation of the amirs Yashbak al-Shaʿbani, Baybars the Atabak al-ʿAsakir, and the aforementioned Taghri Birdi, who were countering claims to the Sultanate by rebellious officers in Syria. Although Faraj was restored only seventy days later, challenges to his position continued. Faraj was compelled to organize six expeditions in total to play competing officers off against each other. Faraj's ability to outflank these intimidating rivals is indicative of political acumen remarkable for a youth of his age. Yet, this sagacity did not compensate for traits denounced by historians as greed or openness to sycophantism. The historian al-Maqrizi castigated Faraj for presiding over a deteriorating fisc and appointing counselors chosen for praise rather than for offering feasible means of avoiding insolvency. Ultimately, Faraj failed to sustain his efforts at balancing contending adversaries. He was deposed a second time in Damascus (25 Muharram 815/May 7, 1412). Faraj was imprisoned until summoned before a panel of Syrian officers and jurists, prominent among whom were Shaykh al-Mahmudi and Nawruz al-Hafizi, who declared him unfit to rule. His execution followed on 16 Safar/May 28. The incumbent ʿAbbasid Caliph al-Mustaʿin succeeded him until the Amir Shaykh, who had confronted Faraj with the death warrant, was installed as Sultan.

The prominent foreign event of Faraj's turbulent reigns occurred in 803/1400–01, when Timur Lenk again invaded the Syro-Palestinian corridor with the presumed intention of ravaging Egypt. After Timur besieged and sacked the fortress city of Aleppo, Faraj was reluctantly placed at the head of an expedition to block his advance, commanded by several senior officers. After the expedition reached Damascus, rumors of atrocities inflicted on the inhabitants of Aleppo unsettled both Faraj and his subordinates. Versions as to whether the sultan or these officers made the decision to abandon the city vary, but they departed before Timur's army arrived. Damascus was left to negotiate its own surrender. Among Faraj's retinue that had accompanied the expedition was the distinguished historian Ibn Khaldun, who remained in Damascus and personally interviewed the conqueror (cf. Chapter 6). Timur himself was reported to have appreciated the martial qualities of the Mamluk troops and the bargaining skills of the civilian population. He allegedly attributed the army's weaknesses to its leader's incompetence and officers' discord. Whatever Timur's estimation of the Sultanate's military effectiveness, his decision to depart Syria was motivated by strategic issues originating elsewhere. Reacting to the Ottoman Sultan Bayazid's aggressive expansion into eastern Anatolia and supplanting fellow Muslims, Timur elected to challenge him. Southern Syria and Egypt were thus spared an invasion due to external factors.

Despite Faraj's unflattering reputation, contemporary historians acknowledged his contribution to Cairo's architectural heritage. In fulfillment of his father's wish to be interred in the vast cemetery east of the city, among the tombs of saints and savants, Faraj commissioned the construction of a funerary hospice (*khānqāh*) for Sufi mystics to shelter his father's remains (and his own,

Fig. 1.5 Funerary hospice and mausoleum built for Sultan al-Zahir Barquq by his son, al-Nasir Faraj
Constructed between 803–14 and 1400–11 in the Desert Cemetery east of medieval Cairo.
(Photo by Boyer/Roger Viollet, January 1, 1912 via Getty Images)

although his demise and burial in Damascus forestalled this objective). Faraj did not live to witness completion of the complex, which required eleven years (**Fig. 1.5**). Although its dedication presumably occurred during the reign of Faraj's eventual successor, al-Mu'ayyad Shaykh, no trust (*waqf*) document survives to confirm either the precise date or services the foundation was to provide (such as the scholastic curriculum of a madrasa). The monument itself has been admired by local commentators and modern architectural historians as one of the exceptional structures of the Mamluk Sultanate in Cairo.[15] Its rectangular design around a courtyard, anchored at its east end by two masonry domes (largest of their kind constructed in the Mamluk period, with diameters of 14.3 meters) and on the west side by two imposing minarets, remains among the distinctive features of Cairo's medieval mortuary zone (**Fig. 1.6**). Faraj intended to surround the foundation with markets and commercial institutions. While these plans did not materialize at the time of Faraj's death, they qualify the historians' dismissal of this individual as a ruler devoid of vision with regard to practical matters.

Fig. 1.6 Interior of south dome in funerary hospice/mausoleum built for Sultan al-Zahir Barquq
(Photo by Michel Setboun/Corbis via Getty Images)

Preceding Faraj's deposition, the Amirs Shaykh and Nawruz had informally divided the realm into Egyptian and Syrian spheres, with Shaykh presiding over the former (as *Atābak al-ʿAsākir*) and Nawruz the latter (as *Nāʾib* or Viceroy). Shaykh allowed the Caliph al-Mustaʿin to occupy the Sultanate for seven months before assuming it himself, with the title al-Malik al-Muʾayyad (1 Shaʿban 815/November 6, 1412). Shaykh had initially arrived in Cairo the same year as Barquq's father, Anas (783/1383), around the age of twelve.[16] He was presented to Barquq, who held the post of Atabak al-ʿAsakir. Barquq admired the boy for his skill in horsemanship (*furūsiyya*) and such martial arts as lance casting, archery, swordsmanship, and wrestling (*ṣirāʿ*). Barquq elevated Shaykh to the status of "intimate" (*khaṣṣakī*), i.e., member of the Sultan's personal guard, despite the cadet's brashness, because he found his company agreeable. Barquq promoted Shaykh to the rank of amir of ten soon before the insurrection of Yalbugha and Mintash. He participated in the battle at Shaqhab (12 Safar 794/January 9, 1392), following which he was jailed at the Khizanat al-Shamaʾil prison in Cairo, reserved for treasonous prisoners. Barquq released Shaykh upon his own restoration. Shaykh served as commander of the Pilgrimage (*Amīr al-Ḥajj*; year 801/1398–99) after Barquq's death and then as governor of Tripoli (*Ṭarābulus*) following Faraj's accession, before participating in the expedition against Timur Lenk. Shaykh was captured but made an escape fit for adventures in the *Arabian Nights*. During Timur's departure from Damascus, Shaykh managed to seize a "baggage animal" (*dābba*, probably a donkey) and rode to a village in Safad province. From there he returned to Tripoli (in disguise since the town was controlled by Timur's troops), took ship to al-Tina, and proceeded over land to Qatya, where he sought sanctuary from its prefect (*wālī*). The latter initially found Shaykh's tale bogus but was sweet-talked into giving him a horse, on which Shaykh made it back to Cairo, where he described his escape to the incredulous court (**Fig. 1.7**). Shaykh resumed his governorship in Tarabulus and was then promoted Na'ib of Damascus, the senior post in Syria, where he was stationed when the final fitnas against Faraj broke out.

Two years after his accession, insurrection simmering between Shaykh and Nawruz erupted into open revolt (817/1414). Nawruz had rejected the Caliph's deposition from the Sultanate and declared his autonomy in Damascus. Shaykh led an expedition, defeated Nawruz on the field, and besieged him in the Damascus Citadel, from which he lured the rebel viceroy with the promise of safe-conduct and negotiation of their differences. These proceeded cordially but were sealed with Nawruz's arrest and execution the evening of their signing. The jurists who drew up the safe-conduct had deliberately inserted grammatical errors to invalidate the document.

Nawruz's execution failed to resolve the insurrection. Several governors appointed by Shaykh rebelled, their disloyalty prompting a second expedition the next year (818/1415). Following a third campaign to finalize his control over Syria (820/1417), Shaykh proceeded north into Asia Minor. His goal was re-imposition of the Sultanate's suzerainty over Southeastern Anatolia, disrupted by Timur's invasion. The Conqueror had restored the autonomy of several principalities (*beyliks*) annexed by the Ottomans over recent decades. In the aftermath of his return to Central Asia, his Turcoman clients, the Aq-Qoyunlu (White Sheep) and Qara-Qoyunlu (Black Sheep) tribal federations, had occupied the Diyar Bakr (*Amid*) region and northern Mesopotamia respectively. Situated between these rivals, rulers of two beyliks attempted to assert their own plans for influence: the Dhu'l-Qadrids of Ilbistan and the Qaramanids centered at Konya. Sultan al-Mu'ayyad initially focused on the Cilician town of Tarsus, which the Qaraman ruler, Mehmed Bey, had taken from Shaykh's client during Timur's invasion. Two years after Shaykh's successful recapture of Tarsus, his son al-Sarimi Ibrahim invaded Qaraman territories (822/1419) and restored Mamluk suzerainty over Kaiseri. He proceeded on toward Konya, the Qaraman capital and seat of earlier Saljuk traditions of regional hegemony in Asia Minor. Ibrahim elected to stop short of Konya, due to concern among his adjutants (and likely his father) over exceeding the strategic limits of a feasible occupation (and provoking a hostile

Fig. 1.7 Soldier in pursuit
Scene from an eighth/fourteenth c. Mamluk manual on horsemanship, military arts, and technology: *Nihāyat al-su'l wa'l-umniyya fī ta'allum a'māl al-furūsiyya* (An End of Questioning and Desiring [Further Knowledge] concerning Learning of the Different Exercises of Horsemanship), from the British Library's collection of Arabic manuscripts (Add. MS 18866).
(Photo by Werner Forman/Universal Images Group/Getty Images)

reaction from the Ottomans). The Sultanate's northern frontier of influence was thus effectively drawn between the two towns. The Qaraman beylik would continue to pursue its own goals of regional dominion in future decades, with open conflict erupting during Qayitbay's reign during the latter ninth/fifteenth century. Shaykh and his heir thus succeeded in returning the political status of southeastern Anatolia to the condition that had prevailed prior to Timur's invasion.

Shaykh pursued no further campaigns during his reign. Funds to support further expeditions were lacking. Plague epidemics revisited major cities in 818–19/1415–16 and 824/1420. Much of Upper Egypt had passed under Bedouin (*ʿurbān*) control, which remained resistant to efforts by the central authority to diffuse it. The diwan al-mufrad founded by Barquq continued as the prime source of fiduciary support for the military institution. Amirs assigned its management resorted to forced purchases imposed on the civil populace of crop staples yielded from iqtaʿ estates at inflated prices, booty extracted from defeated Bedouin tribes, and confiscation of assets held by the mercantile establishment in Cairo to shore it up. Shaykh had intended to reform the army along models pursued by Barquq, but fiscal shortfalls aborted his plan of importing Turks to balance off Circassians. Identities that had shifted during Faraj's conflicts resulted in a new status quo, marked by Zahiri veterans, largely Turkish, occupying the amiral ranks while new recruits (*Julbān*, now largely Circassian, but interspersed with other ethnicities) remained non-commissioned with limited chances for promotion. From al-Muʾayyad's time, the term of active service for Julban recruits imported by the ruler was confined to his reign. At his death, they were discharged to be replaced by his successor's own troops. Effectively disenfranchised, these soldiers sought employment in households of amirs who could afford them or in less formal circumstances. They evolved into a disruptive element, aggrieved over their status and exploiting their military training to provoke riots incessantly and demand ad-hoc payments from asset holders in return for their protection. They would also infiltrate the Shariʿa judicial system, effectively intimidating magistrates to decide cases on the basis of the highest bidder for their "insurance" services.

Al-Muʾayyad Shaykh adapted his personal situation to these prevailing trends. With some success, since when he expired, his personal treasury was rumored to include 1,500,000 dinars. Contemporary chroniclers gave his reign mixed reviews. At once depicted as munificent with regard to his support of the judiciary, literati, and custodians of formal religion, Shaykh was simultaneously castigated for profiting from the pernicious economic policies noted above. Personally devout, several biographers acknowledged the depths of Shaykh's admiration for traditions of the Prophet (*Ḥadīth*), to the extent that eminent transmitters assumed a prominent place in his court ceremonials and

Fig. 1.8 Mosque of Sultan al-Mu'ayyad Shaykh
Constructed between 817/1414 and 824/1421; the Sultan established a mosque, madrasa, and hospice (*khānqāh*) for Sufis.
(Photo by Michel Setboun/Corbis via Getty Images)

campaigns abroad (**Fig. 1.8**). They also appreciated al-Mu'ayyad's skill in dealing with adjutants and senior civil officials, masking shrewd assessments of character behind a jocular façade of easygoing banter that aimed at manipulating opposition into agreement without overt pressure or humiliation. Yet, despite this genial aura, al-Mu'ayyad seems not to have secured long-term camaraderie in the khushdash tradition (cf. Chapter 2). The sultan's convivial façade did not offset the frequent imprisonments or exiles that stalled or terminated many aspiring careers. However substantive the rumored hoard of his treasury, it dissipated among senior amirs after his death (9 Muharram 824/ January 14, 1421), leaving whoever followed short of funds. The biographer al-Sakhawi claimed that not a single senior amir bothered to attend al-Mu'ayyad's funeral. At his corpse washing, no towels to dry the body were found among the deceased's possessions. To cover his genitals, a Saʿidi (Upper Egyptian) scarf from a slave girl had to suffice.

Al-Mu'ayyad Shaykh had groomed his son, al-Sarimi Ibrahim, to succeed him. Ibrahim had participated in Shaykh's third expedition into Cilicia and the Qaramanid territories, virtually as his father's second in command. But Ibrahim died the following year (15 Jumada I 823/June 27, 1420) in his twenties, leaving his ailing father with a second son, a toddler under two years old: Ahmad. The child was nonetheless removed from the harem nursery and formally installed as sultan with the laqab al-Muzaffar. Distraught by the ceremony and acclamation by the assembled courtiers, he cried continuously. Given his age, al-Mu'ayyad had appointed Tatar, one of his closest adjutants and fellow Zahiri amir, as one of three trusted regents. Tatar, who had risen to the rank of Presider over Council (*Amīr Majlis*) under Shaykh, assumed full authority over his charge but was immediately challenged by the viceroy of Damascus, Qanibay. Tatar led an expedition, as his ward's guardian, to Damascus, defeated the viceroy, proceeded on to Aleppo to accept its submission, and then returned to Damascus.

After arresting his predecessor's veteran Mamluks, Tatar deposed al-Muzaffar Ahmad and claimed the Sultanate with the laqab al-Malik al-Zahir (29 Shaʿban 824/August 29, 1421). Tatar immediately declared his own son, al-Salih Muhammad, a boy of ten, as his heir, but several months later expired from an undisclosed illness (4 Dhu'l-Hijja 824/November 30, 1421). Similar to Shaykh, Tatar had designated a confidant as regent for his son, a comrade who had accompanied him to Damascus as his second in command: Barsbay al-Duqmaqi, who had already attained prominence among the coterie of amirs originally promoted by al-Zahir Barquq. His regency did not go uncontested, however. A fellow Zahiri, Janibak al-Sufi, disputed his claim and attempted to organize an assault on the Citadel but lost out and retired to Giza across the river, accompanied by a group of disaffected officers. A second endeavor to supplant Barsbay failed, and the rebels were imprisoned. The oligarchy of senior officers then deposed al-Salih and acclaimed Barsbay as Sultan, who chose the laqab al-Ashraf (8 Rabiʿ II 825/March 31, 1422).

## The Reign of al-Ashraf Barsbay (825/1422–841/1438)

Barsbay stands large among the rulers of the later Sultanate.[17] Yet, he remains an enigma whose accomplishments on the territorial front were qualified by policies that contemporary observers regarded as detrimental to the domestic economy. Barsbay's early career paralleled the pattern now typical of individuals who had reached the regime's summit. Purchased as a recruit by Barquq, he advanced up the ranks during service to several senior amirs and both Barquq's successors, Faraj and Shaykh. He participated in the coalition that had deposed Faraj and became one of Shaykh's confidants. Shaykh appointed Barsbay to his first governorship, of Tarabulus, from which he was dismissed by the Viceroy of Damascus, Qanibay. Since this individual had subsequently contested Tatar's succession, the new sultan appointed Barsbay his senior executive adjutant (*dawādār al-kabīr*, literally: inkstand holder), making him second in command. Barsbay's attainment of the ultimate office thus conformed with past precedent.

Events from abroad soon prompted Barsbay to initiate the long-term campaign against Cyprus that became the hallmark of his reign. During the ninth/fifteenth century, piracy by European corsairs in the Mediterranean (notably Catalan and Genoese, labeled as "Frankish" or *Ifranjī* in Arabic texts) had progressed from a sporadic nuisance to a serious threat to commerce conducted through the Sultanate. From Shaykh's reign, they had raided ships departing the Sultanate's ports of Alexandria and Damietta. When Barsbay learned of these assaults, and of corsair activity along the Levantine coast that originated from the Lusignan Kingdom of Cyprus, he impounded goods held legitimately by Frankish merchants in the affected sites as collateral for restitution. Since this reprisal targeted parties innocent of the actual depredations, the sultan's response compromised extant, and mutually profitable, trade agreements with commercial powers in Europe, as emphasized by the sultan's fiscal staff. Barsbay therefore laid plans for more far-reaching reprisals that addressed protection of foreign commerce more broadly.

These initially focused on monetary reforms. In Safar 829/December 1425, Barsbay promulgated an edict restricting the use of European currency in the realm. He envisioned replacing it with coins imitating European issues (primarily Italian ducats). Specie called "*Ifrantī*," i.e., Frankish dinars, were minted and placed in circulation to replace European currency, which was widely preferred by merchants throughout the eastern Mediterranean and the Levant. Since agents of commerce both local and foreign reacted adversely, the initiative actually repressed profits from trading activity among all parties concerned. Undeterred by these negative consequences, Barsbay ultimately ordered the issuance of dinars that were to substitute for existing indigenous currency throughout the realm. Since these bore the sultan's laqab, they became known as "Ashrafis." Minted with a standard of gold content equal to that of the ducat, their circulation would affect commerce throughout the region for decades (cf. Chapter 5, Addendum).

Barsbay's primary concern addressed piracy, and his attention thus turned to corsairs operating out of Cypriot ports. In Ramadan 825/August 1424, the sultan sent several ships to Cyprus for reconnaissance about political tensions on the island. They landed at the town of Famagusta, then controlled by the Genoese, where they were positively received and encouraged to raid the Lusignan port of Limassol. Upon accomplishing this goal, the ships returned to Egypt with booty and a recommendation to invade. Barsbay subsequently ordered construction of warships at Bulaq, Cairo's Nile port, for a second expedition, which departed in the summer of 828/1425. At Tripoli on the north Syrian coast, several more were mustered. These landed again at Famagusta on 20 Ramadan/August 5. The Sultanate's forces conducted raids, engaged the Cypriot fleet, and confronted a Lusignan detachment before departing when word spread that the King Janus was personally mobilizing a host capable of a genuine threat. Upon their return to Cairo, their commander led a triumphal procession toward the citadel comprised of several hundred prisoners, camels bearing loads of booty, and captured armaments. The following year, John VIII Palaiologos, the Byzantine Emperor, sent an emissary to Cairo warning that if the Sultanate pursued further assaults on its Lusignan ally, reprisals would follow. Barsbay dismissed the emperor's admonition as void of enforcement and dispatched his third expedition on a larger scale than its predecessors.

The Egyptian fleet landed at the port of Limossol and razed its fortress on 26 Shaʿban 829/July 3, 1426. The Sultanate's host proceeded toward Nicosia, seat of the Lusignan regime, and met its army led by King Janus (24 Shaʿban 829/ July 1, 1426). The initial contingent, composed of Royal Mamluks who were leading their mounts on foot due to the heat, had progressed ahead of the main Egyptian force with the expectation that the Cypriots would await them outside the city walls. Janus had anticipated their vulnerability and surprised them with his host massed to attack. But the Royal Mamluks retrieved a near loss by hastily mounting a charge that observers considered a near-suicide. The Mamluks, allegedly numbering no more than seventy, drove through the ranks of Cypriot knights and infantry, breaking their formation until the main force caught up. The Egyptians thus scored a stunning success. Janus was taken prisoner and the Lusignan palace in Nicosia was looted. The victorious army returned to Cairo and staged another triumphal procession in which the captive king was prominently humbled before the Sultan (8 Shawwal 829/August 13, 1426). Janus was held until European missions in Cairo raised his ransom. He then returned to Cyprus as the sultan's vassal on condition of paying an annual tribute. After Janus's death six years later, Barsbay confirmed the rule of his infant son John, who was compelled to reaffirm his vassalage to the Sultan and yield up the tribute, which had fallen in arrears. The Sultanate maintained its claim of suzerainty over Cyprus in coming decades, although the overarching goal of curtailing piracy was less effectively realized. Internal struggles within the Lusignan Dynasty would also involve Barsbay's successors, as will be noted.

Following his defeat of the Lusignan monarch, Barsbay was preoccupied by challenges from regimes in the East that had their origins in large part from developments in the western Arabian Peninsula (*Ḥijāz*) and Red Sea. From Baybars's time, the Sultanate had assumed the prerogative of supplying the mantle (*Kiswa*) draped ceremoniously over the Kaʿba Shrine after it arrived in Mecca at the end of the annual Mahmal caravan. Timur Lenk's son and successor, Shah Rukh (r. in Iran 811/1407–850/1447), now arrogated this prerogative several times, thereby asserting his precedence over the Sultanate as senior ruler of the Islamic Commonwealth. In 838/1434, Sultan Barsbay formally confronted Shah Rukh's challenge by convening the four senior qadis to debate the legitimacy of his claim. Although only the Hanafi judge disavowed the Timurid's assertion, Barsbay acted on the silence of the other three to reassert the primacy of the Sultanate's prerogative. He recommended that Shah Rukh sell the mantle he offered and feed the indigent of Mecca with its proceeds. During Barsbay's reign, the Sultanate would bolster its influence over the Hijaz by binding the Sharifs of Mecca more closely to its authority and reining in the regional tribes, with more ambivalent results (cf. Chapters 3, 5).

Barsbay's action with regard to Shah Rukh's challenge emerged from a broader context of regional influence and global commerce. The Red Sea remained a crucial link in trade connecting South and East Asia with the central Islamic lands and, more importantly, with Mediterranean Europe. The latter zone had become accustomed to a wide array of commodities, of which spices uniquely cultivated in the Indian sub-continent or the Indonesian archipelago were only the most prominent examples. Since pepper ranked among the most lucrative of these, its traffic had assumed a significant place in the global commerce that transited the Red Sea from the Indian Ocean. The Sultanate accordingly aimed at preserving its monopoly over this crucial trade route. During the early decades of the ninth/fifteenth century, the nautical focus of ships arriving from the Indian Ocean shifted from Aden in the Yemen to Jidda in the Hijaz, due to extractions imposed on local spice traders by the Rasulid ruler of Yemen. The spice trade itself in Egypt had been conducted since Fatimid times by a network of merchants referred to in Arabic sources as Karimis. Their stature had become symptomatic of the proverbial affluence associated with the alleged heyday of the regional economy that extended from the High Caliphate through the Fatimid period (358/969–567/1171).

The Timurid invasions affected, at least temporarily, the movement of these commodities across the land route between China and Iran, diverting them through the Indian Ocean and the Red Sea. Placement of their commerce under state control had been entertained by regimes in Egypt from the imposition of militarist rule under Salah al-Din in the sixth/twelfth century. These inclinations became more pronounced after the Sultanate's foundation, when need for income to meet the military's inflating demands inexorably outgrew revenues provided by existing sources from iqta‘ yields and domestic taxes. Whether Barsbay actually merits the opprobrium cast on him by contemporary historians for imposing a state monopoly over pepper can be debated, but they concurred in attributing the responsibility for it to him (832/1428). Barsbay's edict compelled European merchants to purchase spices from regime agents at prices fixed to generate maximum revenues rather than by competitive market forces. The results were cumulative and detrimental to Egypt's spice trade. The Karimi merchants progressively diminished as managers of the spice trade. The monopoly itself served to prompt the European mercantile establishment to seek alternative routes, a motive that eventually led to discovery of nautical routes around the horn of Africa and across the Atlantic. These transitions, with global consequences, emerged from multiple causes that were developing independently from conditions in the central Islamic lands. But since Barsbay and his successors imposed state monopolies over other, more staple commodities such as sugar and textiles, the precedent was set for more interventions in the future.

Barsbay's challenges from eastern regimes were not resolved by repudiating Shah Rukh's bid to provide the Kiswa mantle. The Timurid had previously issued diplomas of investiture to several princes who disputed the Egyptian sultan's claims of suzerainty. Among the more aggressive of these was Qara Yuluk ʿUthman Bey, chieftain of the Aq-Qoyunlu federation (r. 805/1403–839/1435). Following his defeat of the Lusignan monarch, the sultan engaged Qara Yuluk, who was asserting his own expansionist ambitions to the west of his stronghold in Diyar Bakr/Amid. Barsbay led an expedition that occupied al-Ruha/Edessa but failed to conquer Amid. Qara Yuluk launched his own campaign, fought Barsbay to a draw (8 Shawwal 836/May 28, 1433), and negotiated the Sultan's recognition of his sovereign rights over Diyar Bakr in return for his vague pledge to acknowledge the latter's suzerainty as preeminent ruler. The sultan's worries over unrest to the north were further exacerbated by the reappearance of a former rival, the regent preferred by al-Zahir Tatar to guard Shaykh's heir, Janibak al-Sufi. Supplanted by Barsbay, Janibak had escaped from prison in Alexandria and made his way to the northern marches, where he successively allied himself with several of the individuals contesting the Sultan's suzerainty. Barsbay's forces defeated Janibak at ʿAyntab (25 Dhu'l-Hijja 839/July 10, 1436), but he managed to escape and sought sanctuary with Qara Yuluk's sons. They ultimately found his presence a liability and turned him over to the governor of Aleppo, who imprisoned him until his death (26 Rabiʿ II 841/October 27, 1437). Thus was Barsbay finally relieved of threats from the North.

Notwithstanding his aggrandizement of the Sultanate's regional stature, Barsbay's personal image among period commentators remained ambivalent. Their consistent attribution of corrupt methods for extracting revenues extended even to funding of his imposing monuments. The biographer al-Sakhawi quoted such authorities as al-Maqrizi, who claimed that Barsbay defrayed the steep costs of constructing his grand madrasa by charging pilgrims returning from the Hajj a fine for overstaying their sojourn in Mecca more than a month after performing the required rituals. When Barsbay elected to repeal or reduce some of the measures he had imposed, he was allegedly motivated by a fear of his own mortality. He nonetheless succumbed to the plague on 13 Dhu'l-Hijja 841/June 7, 1438 after lingering several months.

Barsbay had formally confirmed his fourteen-year-old son Yusuf as his successor, who was installed with the laqab al-ʿAziz that day. Barsbay had appointed one of his senior adjutants, the amir Jaqmaq al-Jarkasi al-ʿAlaʾi al-Zahiri, as regent. Predictable quarrels erupted between officers who had served all the rulers since Barquq's time, but after three months, Jaqmaq neutralized their opposition, exiled Yusuf to Alexandria, and assumed the Sultanate with the laqab al-Zahir (19 Rabiʿ I 842/September 9, 1438).

## From Jaqmaq to Qayitbay: Upholding the Status Quo (842/1438–872/1468)

Jaqmaq (r. 842/1438–857/1453) was advanced in age upon his usurpation.[18] Like his predecessors, he had initiated his career as a recruit in Barquq's service. After al-Muʾayyad Shaykh supplanted Faraj, he invalidated Jaqmaq's arrest, restored him to his Khassaki status and returned his amirship of ten. From that time, Jaqmaq advanced through a series of offices, adroitly avoiding conflicts between restive groups of veteran Mamluks. Jaqmaq cultivated characteristics of the ideal khushdash throughout these years and made few enemies. He became one of Barsbay's trusted confidants throughout the latter's reign and, after his death, assumed power with little resentment. The governors in Syria had initially proclaimed their support for Yusuf, as a means of declaring their own autonomy. Their rivalry did not last, and by 843/1439, Jaqmaq's position was secure.

Jaqmaq's signal venture in foreign policy was his three expeditions against the island of Rhodes in the Aegean, held by the Hospitaler Knights of St. John. These occurred between 844/1440 and 848/1444, without success. The Knights of St. John remained entrenched on Rhodes, succumbing to a Muslim ruler decades later during the Ottoman Suleiman Qanuni's reign. Jaqmaq managed to uphold the vestiges of the Sultanate's suzerainty in Cyprus, despite disputes within the Lusignan house. With regard to relations with Shah Rukh, Jaqmaq rescinded Barsbay's disclaimer of his Kiswa bid. Following the repulsion of his second expedition against Rhodes, Jaqmaq willingly received an embassy from Shah Rukh and agreed to allow him to dispatch the Mahmal caravan to Mecca (15 Ramadan 848 /November 27, 1444). Jaqmaq aimed at quieting unrest in eastern Anatolia and sustained positive relations with the Ottomans.

Jaqmaq's domestic policies broadly upheld the monopolies imposed by Barsbay, despite formal rescinding of several tariffs, pledges to reform arbitrary price setting for staple commodities, and promises to curb corruption in the fiscal bureaucracy. In fact, Jaqmaq was to show himself astute at masking confiscations and extortion of assets with elaborate ploys justified by Islamic Law. To abet this stratagem, Jaqmaq assembled a host of jurists skilled in manipulating property law and in particular questions of precedence with regard to Christian places of worship. Jaqmaq personally regarded his actions as fully compliant with Shariʿa. He became renowned for his piety and admiration for Islamic learning. While miserly to his military colleagues, he gave lavishly to custodians of formal belief. In contrast to the public's antipathy toward several of his predecessors, when Jaqmaq expired, at the age of 80 (3 Safar 857/February 13, 1453), the masses genuinely mourned his passing.

Jaqmaq's son ʿUthman acceded to the Sultanate with the laqab al-Mansur. A young adult of 18 years, ʿUthman attempted to buy the support of rival veteran mamluks with dinars so debased that they cast them away in contempt. The Atabak al-ʿAsakir appointed by his father, Jaqmaq – Inal al-ʿAlaʾi al-Zahiri al-Nasiri – moved to occupy the Citadel, aided by a trusted group of fellow Zahiri amirs familiar with the fortress. Inal's status as the most senior officer in the realm upon Jaqmaq's death rendered his own installation inevitable, although not without protest. Inal understood the risk of assuming power with a depleted treasury (despite Jaqmaq's tactics) and unruly Julban recruits and had resisted an initial offer on grounds of penury. He ultimately negotiated terms that involved stipendiary reductions reluctantly acceptable to the oligarchy of grand amirs who controlled the veteran soldiers at the core of the army and was acclaimed to the Sultanate by the Caliph and four senior judges two months after Jaqmaq's death.

Inal (r. 857/1453–856/1461, known as *al-Ajrūd*; beardless) was the last sultan to have begun his career as a purchased recruit in service to Barquq.[19] Manumitted and promoted to Khassaki status by al-Nasir Faraj, he received his amirship of ten under al-Muzaffar Ahmad ibn Shaykh in 824/1421. He rose through the ranks during Barsbay's reign, attaining the office of second guard captain (*raʾs nawba al-thānī*). Barsbay appointed him naʾib of Gaza in 831/1439, his first governorship. He accompanied Barsbay's expedition against Qara Yuluk ʿUthman, in which he distinguished himself despite its failure to occupy Diyar Bakr/Amid. Barsbay promoted him to the ultimate rank of officer of 100 and commander of 1000 (*amir miʾa wa-muqaddam alf*) and awarded him the governorship of al-Ruha (Edessa). Inal occupied several regional posts in Syria until his former khushdash Jaqmaq summoned him back to Cairo as Senior Executive Secretary (*Dawādār Kabīr*). He participated in Jaqmaq's abortive assaults on Rhodes and attained the penultimate office of Atabak al-ʿAsakir in 850/1446, all without ever having been arrested.

Inal was seventy-three at his enthronement. He was fated to rule during one of the most dramatic events in Islamic History: the conquest of Constantinople by the Ottoman Sultan Mehmed II Fatih. An embassy arrived in Cairo with the news on 23 Shawwal 857/October 27, 1453. Inal duly ordered celebrations to commemorate the accomplishment. Whether he and his colleagues appreciated its global implications is less clear. The fall of Constantinople to the Ottomans marked their rise to the zenith of great power status, while the Cairo regime remained territorially static and subject to irremediable fiscal shortfalls – and the attendant unrest within the military class they provoked (cf. Chapter 2). Ottoman aggression was moving inexorably east, with pressure on the principalities that occupied the marcher regions on the Mamluk Sultanate's northern frontier. The wars over their control that broke out during Inal's reign would become the central focus of the Mamluks' foreign policy in its final decades.

The succession issue in Cyprus also reignited when the Lusignan monarch, John II, died on 16 Ramadan 862/July 28, 1458. John had remained an obedient vassal of the Mamluk Sultan but upon his death his office was disputed by his legitimate daughter, Charlotte, and his illegitimate son, James (ar. *Jākum*), known as "the Bastard." James arrived at the Citadel (28 Ramadan 863/May 29, 1459) to request Inal's support, which the Sultan initially pledged. Inal bestowed a robe of honor on James and prepared an expedition to invade the island and enforce his claim. But Charlotte's advocates devised a counter-strategy. The following year, the Mamluk emissary to Cyprus returned to Cairo (1 Jumada II 864/March 24, 1460), escorting a contingent of Cypriot notables who endorsed Charlotte's claims. They secretly offered Inal a bribe that exceeded what James had promised to shift the sultan's support to the Princess. Inal, and more significantly his senior officers who were similarly induced, covertly agreed. They announced their affirmation of Charlotte's claim during the reception originally scheduled to honor James. Stunned by his abandonment, James called upon his patron's honor, seemingly to no avail. But in the evening, partisans of James offered the amirs a larger bribe and regained their backing of him. When confronted by them the next day as an ignominious betrayer, Inal reversed his position again and confirmed James as the genuine heir, his illegitimacy having no bearing under Shariʿa since the father's identity was not at issue. An expedition subsequently departed, defeated Charlotte's faction, and installed James as king. He would reign until 1473, to be followed by his Venetian wife. The Venetians would annex the island outright in 1489.

The regime's depleted fisc, which had precipitated this incident, remained straitened. Inal was compelled to disenfranchise his predecessor's Julban recruits to make room for those he had purchased himself. Their cost, combined with short-term pay-offs to stymie incessant revolts by the Julban, brought the government to insolvency. Inal and the ruling oligarchy responded by increasing sales of lucrative offices and judgeships, placing individuals who settled suits for bribes rather than legal equity. The offering of iqtaʿ allotments for money hastened the alienation of properties previously belonging to the state and granted out as usufruct in return for military service. The kharaj land tax they formerly owed was lost. The regime's attempted withdrawal of debased silver and gold coinage dating to Barsbay's time remained ineffective since they were largely replaced with copper issues (*fals*). Precious metal virtually disappeared from circulation among the masses. Inal himself presided over a lax oligarchy that ceased to witness the conspiracy of earlier decades but allowed discipline to slacken among the ranks. The Julban indulged in endemic disorder that the sultan left unchecked. Contemporary biographers depicted him as unsteadfast and pliable, referring to the Cypriot affair as typical of his amorality.

Inal expired on 15 Jumada I 865/February 26, 1461. His son Ahmad succeeded with the laqab al-Mu'ayyad. His position was challenged by two contestants: the governor of Damascus, Janam al-Ashrafi, and Janibak al-Zahiri, former governor of Jidda. Janibak ultimately persuaded veteran mamluks of former sultans to back a compromise candidate: Ahmad's Atabak, Khushqadam al-Mu'ayyadi. Their coalition occupied the Citadel with minimal resistance, sent Ahmad off to exile in Alexandria, and acclaimed Khushqadam (17 Ramadan 865/June 26, 1461), who chose the laqab al-Zahir. Khushqadam's background was termed "*Rūmī*" or Anatolian, with possible Greek ethnicity.[20] Because he was not Circassian, his accession was initially accepted as temporary. But Khushqadam managed to placate his rival from Damascus, Janam, whom he persuaded to disband an invasion of Egypt with a confirmation of his autonomy in Damascus, bolstered with a substantial bribe (Shawwal 865/July 1461). Several months later, Khushqadam undermined Janam's governorship in Damascus. Janam sought sanctuary with the Aq-Qoyunlu ruler Uzun Hasan, who granted the deposed governor troops to launch an expedition back into Syria. The expedition proved abortive and Janam ended up killed during a subsequent campaign in al-Ruha/Edessa the next year. Khushqadam also managed to outmaneuver his coalition partner, Janibak. Although he had made Janibak his second in command as Dawadar kabir, Khushqadam persuaded veteran mamluks opposed to the Zahiri faction that Janibak's presence was inimical to their own security. They therefore plotted to assassinate Janibak, which they accomplished (Dhu'l-Hijja 867/August 1463).

Khushqadam's reign (865/1461–872/1467) witnessed foreign events that evolved from previous developments. The Sultanate's suzerainty over Cyprus continued, although when Khushaqadam's resident insulted King James over the legitimacy of his position, James killed him in battle and took control over Famagusta. A succession dispute within the Turkoman Dhu'l-Qadrid ruling family of Ilbistan resulted in the contestants whom the sultan backed suffering defeat at the hands of an opponent supported by the Ottomans, who would loom large in wars during Qayitbay's reign: Shah Suwar (cf. Chapter 3). On the domestic front, Bedouin Arab tribes aggressively contested the Sultanate's authority. Khushqadam sent expeditions against the Labid tribe in the Delta province of Buhayra between 866–69/1462–65 and against the Hawwara tribe that dominated Upper Egypt (872/1467), with no appreciable results.

Khushqadam died on 10 Rabiʿ I 872/October 9, 1467. The oligarchy of senior amirs immediately settled on his Atabak Yalbay al-Mu'ayyadi, who lasted two months before being replaced by an amir who had advanced during Jaqmaq's reign, Timurbugha al-Zahiri. Ongoing unrest brought on his deposition on 6 Rajab 872/January 31, 1468. Timurbugha willingly gave way to the accession of a close comrade, Qayitbay al-Mahmudi al-Zahiri Jaqmaq, who was destined to rule twenty-eight years.

### The Reigns of al-Ashraf Qayitbay and Successors (872/1468–906/1501)

Qayitbay was purchased in 839/1435–36 by the slave merchant Mahmud ibn Rustam, who recruited adolescents from the Circassian districts of the Caucasus.[21] Past twenty when he arrived in Cairo, he caught the notice of Sultan Barsbay's staff because of his skill in horsemanship and lance-casting. Upon Barsbay's death, the trainee entered the service of Sultan Jaqmaq, who manumitted him, granted the status of Khassaki, and assigned him to the Dawadar's staff as an assistant. Under Sultans Inal and Khushqadam, he attained the ranks of amir tabalkhanah (possessor of a drum band and ownership of forty mamluks) and finally muqaddam alf (commander of 1000), the highest grade. He had previously served as superintendent of provisions (*shādd al-Sharābkhānah*). During his brief tenure as sultan, Yalbay appointed Qayitbay captain of the mamluk guard (*ra's nawba al-nuwwāb*) and Timurbugha his second in command as Atabak. Superficially, Qayitbay's trajectory paralleled those who made it to the regime's apex. Yet, Qayitbay emerges from the narrative sources as something of a dark horse, without enemies but also void of distinction. Qayitbay's lack of notoriety may reflect aspects of character that set him apart from other figures prominent in the Sultanate's politics. Qayitbay displayed a disinclination, even repugnance, for the conspiratorial ambitions that defined the Mamluk institution throughout so much of its history. Qayitbay's reputation for equanimity in his dealings with colleagues, widely praised in the sources, stemmed from this aversion to conspiracy. Qayitbay demonstrated this predisposition in his treatment of Timurbugha upon his accession. The new sultan agreed to Timurbugha's request for an honorable retirement to Damietta. Qayitbay would show similar magnanimity toward other deposed rulers and their progeny.

Qayitbay's humane stance combined with the depths of his respect for the Shariʿa and personal piety to inspire admiration and respect. The signal aspects of his reign emerged in foreign affairs and the sultan's even-handed relations with military subordinates, Julban recruits, bureaucratic and judicial officials, and custodians of religion. With regard to foreign affairs, the central issue focused on the frontier principalities in Asia Minor and tensions between the rivals for their influence. The prominent figure was Shah Suwar (r. 871/1466–877/1472), who had secured his rule over the Dhu'l-Qadrid

Principality of Ilbistan during Khushqadam's reign (cf. Chapter 3). While claiming to uphold neutrality between the Ottomans and Mamluks, Shah Suwar covertly sought Ottoman support. For his part, Qayitbay openly backed the Qaramanid ruler Ahmad, who aimed at stalling Ottoman encroachment. In his first three regnal years, Qayitbay sent two expeditions against Shah Suwar, which ended in defeat, due in part to Shah Suwar's strategic skill but also to internal rifts between contingents within the Mamluk forces. When Shah Suwar lost aid from the Ottomans after Qayitbay ceased backing Ahmad, he was finally defeated after a series of battles in 876/1471, led by Qayitbay's field commander, the Dawadar Yashbak min Mahdi. Shah Suwar was compelled to retreat to his fort, having abandoned his wife and family in haste. He held out until offered surrender with retention of his rulership as a vassal but was betrayed, conducted to Cairo, and executed along with notables of his retinue.

Other prominent adversaries included Uzun Hasan, prince of the Aq-Qoyunlu federation (r. 861/1467–882/1478), who aggressively extended his influence from Diyar Bakr/Amid east against the Qara-Qoyunlu federation and Samarqand in Central Asia and west against the Ottomans. The Ottoman Sultan Mehmet II (2nd r. 855/1451–886/1481) defeated Uzun Hasan 876/1471, but after Uzun died in 880/1475, his second son, Yaʿqub, revived his father's expansionist ambitions, with less success. Yaʿqub extended an invitation to another of Qayitbay's senior commanders, Yashbak min Mahdi, to participate in Yaʿqub's campaign against al-Ruha/Edessa, in return for autonomous authority over the province. Yashbak, whose positive ties to Qayitbay precluded any insurgency at home, readily accepted and scored quick victories but was killed during his siege of the town (cf. Chapter 2). This demise of Qayitbay's senior general was followed by an intensification of hostilities with the Ottomans after the accession of Mehmet's successor, Bayazid II (r. 886/1481–918/1512). Qayitbay had accepted a request for sanctuary from Bayazid's rival and exiled brother, Jem, which Bayazid interpreted as endorsement of Jem's claim. Qayitbay also supported Ala' al-Dawla, Dhu'l-Qadrid ruler of Ilbistan (r. 884/1479–921/1515), in the latter's resistance to the Ottomans. Confrontations continued through the 880s and early 890s over the cities of Tarsus, Adana, Malatya, and Iskanderun, culminating in Atabak Azbak's defeat of the Ottomans at Qaysariyya/Kaiseri in central Anatolia (895/1490). Since both sides now faced exhaustion, a settlement was concluded the following year. The remainder of Qayitbay's reign was free of foreign conflicts.

Qayitbay's relations with both his subordinate officers and line troops were stable in comparison with those of his peers throughout the Circassian period. The Julban recruits persisted in fomenting riots for back pay, but not to the extent of their restiveness during Qansawh al-Ghawri's reign. Qayitbay's stance of equity impressed his subordinates sufficiently to diffuse their conspiratorial leanings until the end of his reign. Qayitbay's relationship with his fiscal bureaucracy exhibited refinement of the symbiosis between militarist authorities and civil managers of assets that matured during the ninth/fifteenth century. Techniques of extraction, bribery, and confiscation were applied systematically rather than reformed. Qayitbay's relations with the civil judiciary and custodians of religion reflected the sincerity of his commitment to rule as a defender of Shariʿa and Sunni orthodox belief. The expenses of Qayitbay's military campaigns, plus the costs to purchase his host of recruits (ca. 8,000), may have exceeded seven million dinars and clearly posed a drain on the economy (cf. Chapter 5). Yet, Qayitbay's consistency with regard to the extractive techniques noted above enabled asset holders and revenue producers to function within predictable parameters. Contemporary historians noted the extensive building programs and enhancement of rural infrastructure during Qayitbay's reign that extended beyond the capital Cairo to the provinces in Egypt and Syria (**Fig. 1.9**). Overall, they depicted an impression of prosperity not seen in the realm since al-Nasir Muhammad's time more than a century earlier.

Fig. 1.9 Fountain (*Sabīl*) endowed by Sultan al-Ashraf Qayitbay in Jerusalem Constructed in 892/1487 as part of the Sultan's charitable donations to the precinct of the Haram al-Sharif (Temple Mount), Israel (UNESCO World Heritage List, 1981).
(Photo by DeAgostini/Getty Images)

Nonetheless, these costs were borne in an environment of plague epidemics that sapped both the rural and urban populations. Agriculture, especially in Upper Egypt, declined with many tracts reverting to Bedouin pastoralism. In the coming half century, the commercial revolution that spurred drastic shifts in nautical trade routes would profoundly alter the Sultanate's centrality to global commerce.

Thus, when Qayitbay expired on 27 Dhu'l-Qaʿda 901/August 8, 1496, the Sultanate's economy was depressed, the population in decline, and the political milieu tense after the inevitable weakening of a ruler who had held power so long. That the Sultanic office would stabilize once again is more remarkable than the infighting that did erupt. Qayitbay's son Muhammad, born during the sultan's old age, was fourteen when he succeeded to the Sultanate with the laqab al-Nasir. Prior to that event, contemporary sources described him minimally, and when they did their comments were derogatory and emphasized the boy's predilection for association with groups outside the ruling class.[22] Qayitbay himself suspected that his son was plotting with potential contestants for his office and forced Muhammad to live as an ordinary trainee in the barracks with duties that included sweeping stable waste. When al-Nasir did take power, his intention to set up a new military contingent recruited from black slaves trained in firearms conformed with his previous consortiums. The extant ruling oligarchy were predictably repelled, however, and they acted on their repugnance by assassinating al-Nasir (5 Rabiʿ I 904/October 31, 1498). He was followed by a maternal uncle, al-Zahir Qansawh, whose accession resulted from machinations of several potential candidates, prominent among whom was the amir al-ʿAdil Tuman Bay. Tuman Bay had designs on the Sultanate himself but settled on Qansawh while he laid plans for his own accession. Tuman Bay eventually succeeded in driving Qansawh from the Citadel (Dhu'l-Qaʿda 905/June 1500) but reluctantly yielded to primacy of place and accepted installation of the Atabak Janbalat. Tuman Bay subsequently declared himself sultan during an expedition to quell a revolt in Damascus against Janbalat, returned to force him out, and assumed the office (Jumada II 906/January 1501). Three months later, al-ʿAdil faced deposition himself. His successor was a senior amir and former khushdash whose previous career had been spent largely in Syria and the frontier provinces. His selection stemmed in part from his status as an outsider who had not actively involved himself in court politics during the reigns of Qayitbay or his son.

## The Reigns of Qansawh al-Ghawri, al-Ashraf Tuman Bay, and the Ottoman Conquest (906/1501–923/1517)

This successor was Qansawh al-Ghawri, whom al-ʿAdil Tuman Bay had appointed Dawadar Kabir upon his enthronement. When al-ʿAdil was deposed, al-Ghawri protested the rump oligarchy's devolution on him of an office that had become high-risk. Under these circumstances, his demurral may have been genuine. According to contemporary sources, Qansawh al-Ghawri had emerged to prominence from obscurity. Details on his youth or early adulthood in Circassia, his importation to Cairo, martial training, factional alliances, or initial promotions are lacking in comparison with detailed biographies of his peers.[23] Al-Ghawri arrived in Cairo to commence his training during Qayitbay's first years. He was stationed in the Ghawr barracks of the Citadel, from which he took his only nisba. He was appointed inspector (*kāshif*) of iqtaʿ estates in Upper Egypt (Dhu'l-Qaʿda 886/December 1481–January 1482). Since he was sixty at his accession (1 Shawwal 906/April 20, 1501), Qansawh al-Ghawri had already turned forty when he received his first formal posting. And he was therefore well past twenty when he entered Qayitbay's service as a cadet. The beginning of al-Ghawri's career as a mature adult qualifies the widely held impression of youthful cadets starting out as *ingénue* adolescents. Al-Ghawri had likely shaped his values long before. Al-Ghawri was promoted amir of ten in Rabiʿ II 889/April–May 1484, possibly in preparation for service during the forthcoming Ottoman expedition. He began an extended tour of duty in the northern marches after assignment to the governorship of Tarsus. In Rabiʿ II 894/March 1489, al-Ghawri was transferred to the chamberlainship (*ḥajaba*) of Aleppo. He rose in Qayitbay's estimation when he successfully suppressed a rebellion against the city's governor that threatened to wipe out its entire garrison. Sultan al-Nasir Muhammad II granted him the rank of commander of 1000 and appointed him governor of Malatya in Asia Minor. Al-Nasir's ephemeral successor, al-Zahir Qansawh, advanced him to the guard captaincy (*ra's nawba*: 3 Dhu'l-Qaʿda 905/May 31, 1500). As al-ʿAdil Tuman Bay's khushdash, he joined him in the expedition to Damascus to quell the revolt against Janbalat, after which Tuman Bay declared against his patron. Tuman Bay made al-Ghawri his executive adjutant (*dawādār kabīr*), thus his second in command. When his comrade was removed, al-Ghawri found himself enmeshed in the fractious oligarchy of contenders.

After al-ʿAdil's deposition, the oligarchy considered his Atabak, Tanibak, for the office. But Tanibak adjudged the position too dangerous to proceed when he learned of the widespread hostility toward him. The amirs Qayt al-Rajabi and Misirbay al-Muqaddam then proposed Qansawh al-Ghawri. Al-Ghawri's protestation was so vehement that they secured his agreement only when the deposed al-Zahir Qansawh swore allegiance in return for amnesty, and al-ʿAdil was apprehended and executed. Qansawh al-Ghawri's hold on power remained tenuous for several months, in which even the supporters above conspired against him. When al-Ghawri finally managed to consolidate his position, new personalities formed the core of his inner circle. Prominent among these was the son of a Bedouin groom in the Citadel stables: Zayn al-Din Barakat ibn Musa, who became al-Ghawri's financial counselor and strategist for revenue extraction. Another was his brother's son, Tuman Bay, whom al-Ghawri installed as Dawadar (4 Jumada II 913/October 11, 1507). Zayni Barakat would serve al-Ghawri as his agent of revenue procurement (cf. Chapter 5), while Tuman Bay became his second in command.

Qansawh al-Ghawri confronted fiscal shortfalls throughout his reign (906/1501–922/1516). He inherited their causes, the primary of which were the transformations within the military elite that generated large numbers of disenfranchised soldiers who demanded ad-hoc stipends to desist from rioting. The long-term consequences of plague, Bedouin resurgence, fallowing of formerly productive agrarian land, imposition of monopolies over commodity production, and European piracy also strained the economy. Al-Ghawri was castigated for measures his critics, in particular the historian Ibn Iyas, condemned as extortionist.[24] But this simplistic impression of al-Ghawri as a fiscal predator is misleading. Al-Ghawri was prepared to reward entrepreneurship when he encountered it. And he also contemplated a substantive reform of the military institution. Al-Ghawri recognized the threat, and opportunities, posed by the development of gunpowder technology that had emerged in Europe and was adopted by the Ottomans. He set up a foundry to produce cannons in 913/1507 and organized a new unit that was trained in firearms. They were referred to as the Fifth Corps (*al-Ṭabaqa al-Khāmisa*) because they were conscripted outside the traditional system of recruitment and training for mamluks and did not advance through the several grades of promotion. Their ranks were filled with Turkman, Persians, progeny of mamluks (*awlād al-nās*), and artisans. Intense resistance to them from the Mamluk ranks prohibited al-Ghawri from deploying them widely before his fatal encounter with the Ottomans, but he did not allow their drilling to elapse.

The figure of prominence in Syria during al-Ghawri's reign was the amir Sibay, who had opposed him in 910/1504–05 but subsequently settled into mutual recognition after his appointment as governor of Damascus (17 Shawwal 911/March 13, 1506). Sibay acknowledged al-Ghawri's suzerainty thereafter and organized several campaigns to curb resistance from local Bedouin tribes that threatened regional security and access to routes into the Hijaz.

More ominous portents emerged from European expansion into the Indian Ocean. At the end of the ninth/fifteenth century, the Portuguese rounded the horn of Africa and established missions on the Indian subcontinent and in the Persian Gulf. Regimes in Egypt had heretofore assumed no European presence there. The Portuguese aimed at blocking Muslim commerce from the Red Sea, a stance that motivated the Sultanate to send an expedition to support the ruler of Gujarat, Mahmud Shah, against their presence (Jumada II 911/November 1505).

The expedition confronted the Portuguese several times until it was defeated (Shawwal 914/February 1509), after which the Sultanate ceased to maintain a presence in the Indian Ocean. Al-Ghawri enlisted Ottoman aid in naval stores to build war ships in the Gulf of Suez. When the Portuguese attacked Aden (Muharram 919/March–April 1513), the Fifth Corps was sent to guard the new fleet in Suez. Two years later, a joint expedition with Mamluk and Ottoman contingents set sail for the Yemen. Although Aden was not recovered, the expedition founded a base there that the Ottomans would subsequently exploit.

Concurrent with developments in the Red Sea was the emergence of a new political order in Persia. From 906/1501, Shah Ismaʿil Safawi had emerged from Ardabil in Azerbaijan to create an aggressive imperial state in Iran, Mesopotamia, and the Jazira. Ismaʿil styled himself the charismatic leader of Twelver Shiʿism and openly challenged the Sunnism upheld by the Ottomans (cf. Chapter 3). The Ottoman and Safavid armies met at the site of Chaldiran (2 Rajab 920/August 23, 1514) in a battle won decisively by the Ottomans. When the Ottoman Sultan Selim I (r. 918/1512–926/1520) defeated the Dhu'l-Qadrid ruler ʿAlaʾ al-Dawla for refusing aid during the Safavid campaign, the governors of Damascus (*Sībāy*) and Aleppo (*Khāʾir Bak*) became alarmed over Selim's intentions. They pressured Qansawh al-Ghawri to organize an expedition in defense of Syria. Al-Ghawri departed Cairo (15 Rabiʿ II 922/May 18, 1516) accompanied by the Caliph and four senior qadis. Despite its lavish trappings the host numbered only 529 royal Mamluks and 5,000 troops. Al-Ghawri had left his nephew Tuman Bay as his deputy in Cairo, but emptied the Citadel of treasures accumulating there since Salah al-Din's time, possibly as revenue for bonuses if his army defeated the Ottomans but also as a cache he could fall back on if revolts occurred in his absence. The army proceeded through Gaza to Damascus, where al-Ghawri found Sibay initially hesitant to commit his own forces to the campaign. After al-Ghawri's persuasion, the combined army advanced to Aleppo, where the sultan and two governors awaited Selim's decision to follow up his defeat of Ismaʿil with a campaign further into Iran. When they learned that Selim reacted to their muster in Aleppo by marching toward Syria, the die was cast.

The battle occurred at the site of Marj Dabiq north of Aleppo on 25 Rajab 922/August 24, 1516. Notwithstanding the Ottomans' numerical advantage, the royal Mamluk contingent mounted a charge that paralleled the maneuver that had vanquished King Janus in Cyprus. Their audacity surprised Selim and scattered his forces. But when al-Ghawri delayed his recruits, the royal Mamluks suspected betrayal and held back. It was then that the governor of Aleppo Khaʾir Bak broke ranks and departed with his troops for Hama. Khaʾir Bak had secretly negotiated with Selim to abandon the sultan in return for a high post after an Ottoman victory. When discipline broke down, al-Ghawri

Fig. 1.10 Bab Zuwayla on south wall of medieval Cairo
Gate constructed in 485/1092 during the Fatimid period and named for the Zuwayla army unit recruited from the town of that name in Fazzan district (modern Libya); the two minarets were added by Sultan al-Mu'ayyad Shaykh to serve his adjacent mosque.
(Credit: Luis Dafos/Getty Images)

was reported to have fainted and fallen from his horse. His body was not recovered. After the battle, survivors found themselves denied access to Aleppo and had to make their way back to Damascus, harassed by the local populace. Selim tarried in Aleppo and inventoried the treasure al-Ghawri had deposited in its Citadel. The historian Ibn Iyas claimed that the value of coin, bullion, and fine armaments collectively amounted to 100 million dinars (*mi'at alf alf*).[25] However exaggerated this figure, Selim discovered a windfall that would finance subsequent campaigns.

When news of the defeat reached Cairo, the remaining oligarchy of amirs proclaimed Tuman Bay sultan (13 Ramadan 922/October 10, 1516).[26] He intended to confront Selim in the Gaza region, but the oligarchy objected. Tuman Bay then prepared a line of defense at al-Raydaniyya north of Cairo, bolstered by the artillery al-Ghawri had cast. The Ottomans overwhelmed this barricade and attacked Cairo (29 Dhu'l-Hijja 922/January 22, 1517). Tuman Bay escaped to al-Bahnasa in Middle Egypt with a remnant of his army. He was defeated and captured at al-Jiza (10 Rabiʿ I 923/April 2, 1517), brought back to Cairo, and hanged at the Zuwayla Gate twelve days later (**Fig. 1.10**). Before his execution, he asked the assembled populace to recite the opening sura of the Qur'an three times. The governor of Aleppo, Kha'ir Bak, was rewarded for his betrayal with the viceroyship of Cairo. Egypt and Syria became provinces of the Ottoman Empire. As an independent state, the Mamluk Sultanate had ceased to exist.

# 2 Ethos of the "Slave-Soldiers" Regime

The polity that established itself in Cairo, and subsequently over Egypt, Syria, Southeastern Asia Minor, and Western Arabia, did not define itself with the Arabic word for a slave-soldier. The phrase "Mamluk Sultanate" is a creation of modern scholarship, which drew upon the term to depict the system of governance these slave-soldiers devised over time. Indigenous chroniclers referred to this regime most frequently as *dawlat al-atrāk*, or "state of the Turks." Mention of the term "mamluk" in fact unduly highlighted the origins of the new ruling elite as slaves of the former Ayyubid ruler whose office they had usurped. In practice, during the 267 years of the independent Sultanate, the majority of individuals who were enthroned as sultans did not initiate their careers as slaves purchased for military service. Of forty-four individuals who attained the position, fewer than half personally shared this background as mamluks of the first generation. The others were installed through dynastic inheritance or other circumstances.[1] They wished to emphasize neither the founders' inceptive status as a free ruler's property nor their legacy as usurpers who had deposed a legitimate patron. These markers were regarded as stigmatizing, the object of scorn and denigration by contemporary sovereigns elsewhere who claimed their offices by descent from dynasts. Allusion to Turkish ethnicity more accurately depicted the background of dominant elements within this cadre during the Sultanate's formation and evolved into a potent symbol of esteemed stature that persisted after the cadre's ethnic diversification.[2] Notwithstanding its exogenous fabrication, the phrase "Mamluk Sultanate" is now widely applied to the military elite as a whole, inclusive of both first-generation troopers and their descendants. With the qualifications noted above, it will designate the state under consideration in the discussion that follows.

The term "Turk" itself evoked long-standing impressions of military competence and aggressive leadership that the Sultanate's ruling hierarchy sought to emulate. These impressions emerged from a rich legacy of values, real or imagined, that the military elite tapped to formulate its own stance of governance and leadership. Preeminent among these values were attitudes about the Sultanate's principal rival during its formative years: the Mongol imperium (specifically, the Ilkhanate in Iran and Iraq) and the behavioral norms of the cavalry warriors who built it. Idealization of martial ethics attributed by ruling elites to nomadic tribes long predated the eruption of the Mongols on the Islamic world in the seventh/thirteenth century and indeed the emergence of Islam much earlier. Specific to the Islamic context, recruitment of cadres from western Central Asia who were regarded as proficient in warfare to staff military institutions dated from the formation of the ʿAbbasid Caliphate between the second/eighth and fourth/tenth centuries.

The Turkish-speaking contingents who rose to prominence in caliphal armies brought with them more than combat techniques or tactical skills that had proved effective during centuries of intertribal strife. They also implanted concepts of personal valor, initiative, and pragmatic agility on the mentalities of ruling classes that were vivid and durable.[3] Valor and agility implied a capacity to adapt one's personal position to rapidly changing circumstances and flexible alliances. Loyalties were conditional rather than absolute and shifted according to coalitions that themselves altered continuously according to circumstances of the moment. Fortunes of clans and tribes remained pragmatically volatile; their leaders measured success by their capacity to exploit this intrinsic instability to score military victories, recruit aggressive followings, and profit from strategic weaknesses among their rivals. In such a milieu, commitment to a mindset that prized adroitness outranked loyalty rigidly fixed on an individual or group. The mentality that embraced this style of behavior persisted over such a broad swath of (largely tribal) territories because all those who participated understood its code of ethics and accepted the expediency inherent to it as requisite to success and stature. Bonds of personal attachment were therefore not ineluctably violated when political circumstances warranted betrayal of a proven comrade to achieve an effective outcome or gain of power.

These behavioral norms were recognized for their effectiveness by the caliphal government. Lacking the institutional identity among its subject populations requisite to enlistment of a "citizen army," the Caliphate relied on troop cadres recruited from Central Asian tribes for two purposes: a) to preserve its own hegemony over these (increasingly disparate) subject populations and b) to defend its frontiers from invasion by marauders (often Central Asians themselves) who embodied the norms noted above and recurrently menaced the Caliphate's territorial integrity. As noted in Chapter 1, the cadres who were recruited initially from Turkic regions to realize these goals did not uniformly serve as mamluk slave-soldiers. Service was performed under a variety of statuses that ranged from purchased mamluk slaves, to free soldiers of fortune who offered their service for pay or promotion, to entire tribal federations who acknowledged caliphal suzerainty in exchange for provincial governorships and autonomous authority over subject populations. But the norms of personal agility, transient loyalties, and strategic pragmatism infused the value systems of these cadres regardless of their personal status. And overall, their military service was effective. In fact, the political cohesion of the High Caliphate, and its successor states, owed its durability in large measure to the security from internal insurrection and protection from external invasion they provided over long periods of time.

The Mongols' incursions of the sixth/thirteenth century enhanced the trends considered above but did not supplant a sense of autonomy from them among their opponents. The unprecedented scope of the Mongols' territorial conquests combined with the effectiveness of their draconian tactics of combat to promote an impression of exceptional dexterity and power.[4] Yet, contemporary regimes were more inclined to exploit Mongol military prowess for the purpose of resisting further expansion into their own territories by welcoming renegades from Mongol armies rather than for acknowledging Mongol suzerainty. Initial incursions of the Mongols into Islamic lands occurred during the final decades of Ayyubid rule in Egypt and Syria. The last Ayyubid Sultan in Cairo, al-Malik al-Salih, took advantage of the Mongols' defeat of the Khwarazmian Principality in western Central Asia to embrace large numbers of refugees fleeing from the conquerors. The tradition of *Wāfidiyya*, or "defectors"/"immigrants," began with al-Salih's enlistment of several thousand Khwarazmian troops in his wars against rival Ayyubid amirs in Syria.[5] Although the Khwarazmian contingents failed to secure a permanent foothold in Syria, despite their effectiveness in battle, the precedent was set for the recruitment of either refugees fleeing from Mongol pillaging or rebels from among the Mongols' own ranks seeking asylum in rival regimes. Successive bands of Wafidiyya troops were valued for their martial prowess but denied parity in the upper ranks of the emerging military elite.

The individual most impressed with Mongol martial proficiency, Sultan al-Zahir Baybars, was also adept in exploiting their skills to prevent their former regime in Iran from encroaching on his territories (**Fig. 2.1**). Baybars's ambivalent admiration for Mongol militarism was dramatically shown by a ceremonial act that ironically ended his life. Having returned to Damascus from a successful campaign against the Mongol Ilkhan Abaqa in Ilbistan (located in eastern Anatolia), in which he thwarted his opponent's plan to occupy northern Syria, Baybars drank multiple draughts of *Qumiz* (fermented mare's milk), which proved fatal. He died the following day (29 Muharram 676/July 1, 1277), whether by poison or excess consumption (the sources differ on this issue).[6] The *Qumiz* quaffing ceremony was regarded throughout the central Islamic lands as a potent ritual of acclamation for accomplishment in battle and confirmation of royal authority. Some historians of the period explained Baybars's act as evidence for his deep-rooted esteem for Mongol martial traditions, an interpretation revived in certain scholarly circles more recently. These chroniclers went on to infer that Baybars effectively

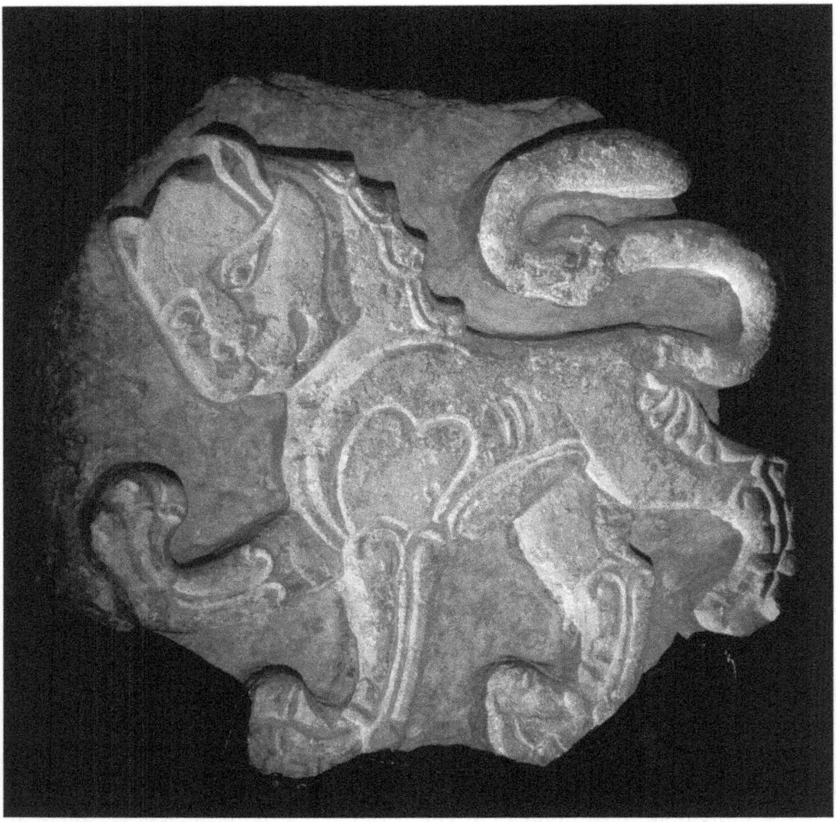

Fig. 2.1 Heraldic lion blazon of Sultan al-Zahir Baybars
(Photo by Werner Forman/Universal Images Group/Getty Images)

proclaimed his own acknowledgment of Mongol suzerainty over the Mamluk realm in Cairo and Damascus. They asserted that Baybars was positively disposed to granting precedence to the Mongol legal code or Yasa over the Shariʿa as the basis at least for juridical praxis among the military class. They further claimed that Baybars had named his son Berke after a grandson of Jenghis Khan via his eldest son Juchi, ruler of the Golden Horde, as an act of formal submission to him. These interpretations have been refuted. Baybars' namesake for his heir was in fact Husam al-Din Berke Khan, grandfather of the son's mother and the officer who had led the Khwarazmian Wafidiyya contingent that assisted al-Malik al-Salih against his Ayyubid rivals. The Mongol Yasa never gained serious credence as a replacement for either the Shariʿa or customary Turkic law in the Mamluk court.

The Wafidiyya themselves, their contribution to the Sultanate's consolidation notwithstanding, rarely infiltrated its elite ranks. As free men, they could not acquire the status of Royal Mamluks (the ruling caste's crucial element), who were recruited during the regime's formative stages exclusively from military slaves. Their influence would manifest itself in training procedures for cadets, in which Mongol tactics of horse riding, archery, and lance casting were readily adopted, and in strategic formations for combat in the field. But they were denied entry into the highest circles of power. As noted above, Mamluk sultans valued the Wafidiyya as instruments to thwart the incursion of invaders from whose regimes they had defected.

## Cadets in Training: Inculcating a Ruling Class

Critics of the military elite among the literary classes opined about the mediocre level of formal learning among the cadres of Mamluk cadets. They emphasized ubiquitous mispronunciation or faulty grammar among those who studied Arabic and claimed that ignorance of the language remained widespread throughout their ranks. Yet, the survival of texts copied by cadets, from training manuals, Qur'anic and Hadith transcriptions, and poetic anthologies – or original commentaries on them authored by senior officers – suggests a more receptive environment for erudition within their barracks culture (cf. Chapter 6). Since the Mamluk Institution had evolved over centuries preceding the Sultanate's founding in Cairo, its formal goal – defense of Sunni Islam – entailed an agenda of inculcation with regard to the religion's textual and legal foundations that had matured into a substantive curriculum. While the depth of its comprehension varied significantly according to age, origins, and political turmoil affecting barracks life for cadets, all experienced some degree of exposure to the tenets of Islam along with their military training.[7]

Cadets arrived in Cairo at dissimilar stages – from childhood through adolescence to adult maturity – and occasionally at advanced ages. Territories amalgamated by geographers as the "Qipjaq Steppe" encompassed a wide region populated by disparate tribal groups. After the Sultanate's formative period, slaves could be traced to many lands between the Balkans and India; they exhibited global diversity. The circumstances under which slaves were acquired – seized as war booty, kidnapped during intertribal raiding, requisitioned by tax levies, or purchased from clans willing to sell them – mitigated against common upbringings or uniform passages from site of origin to the barracks in Cairo. Contemporary sources reveal slaves traversing routes that crossed the Black Sea on ships from the Crimea to the Dardanelles or proceeding overland in caravans west through Bulgaria or east through the Caucasus and Armenia.[8] During periods of Mongol regional hegemony under the Golden Horde, slave merchants (ar. *khawājāt*, from a

Farsi root for "master") tended to exhibit Persianate backgrounds. Later on, when Ottomans controlled the straits, Genoese merchants held a near monopoly over their trade due to treaties (capitulations) signed with sultans in Constantinople (cf. Chapter 5). A static image of "green" impressionable youths naively landing in the big city is thus misleading. They also represented a mix of ethnic backgrounds and political heritages that a generalized designation as "Turkic" could not efface. Among such a multifarious cohort, aptitudes for literary instruction varied widely, although whether their inherent facility in martial arts was more pronounced may also be questioned. According to cursory references in contemporary sources, the younger a cadet was upon entry of service, the more readily he gained proficiency in Arabic. Or in Qipjaq Turkish – the language of military instruction – for that matter, since cadets spoke a variety of dialects when they arrived in Cairo, not all of them Turkish. Whatever their disparity in ages and languages, cadets were expected to attain some proficiency in both literary and spoken Arabic.

Upon arriving in Cairo, cadets divided into cohorts of 20–25 pupils and were assigned to a preceptor (*muʿallim*) whose task was instruction of Arabic and tenets of Islam. At least, this was the ideal. On the ground, political circumstances and fiscal stringencies affected class sizes and quality of instructors. Preceptors differed considerably in their credentials, but the sources indicate that Sultans and their confidants took the matter of qualifications seriously with regard to their wards' instruction and appointed preceptors whose resumés were credible. Many had received formal madrasa educations. The Qur'an served as the basis for both linguistic study and religious inculcation. Commentators on education in the barracks outlined several cycles of schooling, up to four of one to three years each, before a cadet reached the age of readiness for military drilling, not earlier than fifteen, at which time a youth was deemed prepared for the physical rigor of martial arts. Even in prosperous times, barracks life was intentionally severe and aimed at equating endurance with spiritual dedication.

Methods of instruction adhered to the traditional pedagogical focus on memorization, recitation, and copying of verses from the Qur'an and other texts, reinforced by drills. With regard to mastery of script, contemporary commentators mentioned exercises in calligraphy in tandem with copying. The Qur'an served as the foundation of religious instruction and likely remained the principal text of study for a majority of cadets who did not exhibit an aptitude for more advanced learning. The commentators nonetheless discussed training in Islamic Law (*Sharīʿa*) and Jurisprudence (*fiqh*) as the twin disciplines that paralleled religion in ranked importance and followed logically from assimilating the Qur'an. Learning how Islam functioned to regulate society was regarded as essential for the class that would determine its politics and defend its frontiers. After these foundational fields, texts attributed to Mamluk authors or copyists included grammars of literary Arabic (*fuṣḥá*) and Qipjaq Turkish, lives of the Prophet Muhammad, recensions of Prophetic Traditions (*Ḥadīth*), prayer books, handbooks of instruction for governance (frequently titled "mirrors for princes"), manuals of warfare, and poetic anthologies (among the genres diffused most broadly among cadets of all ranks and abilities; cf. Chapter 6). Formats of poetic verses evoking piety and spiritual consciousness appearing in these compilations suggest their arrangement for oral chanting in genres performed by Sufi mystic orders that had permeated the larger Muslim society in the later medieval period. Preceptors often belonged to these orders and infused their mystic beliefs about Divine awareness and affinity among their impressionable charges.

Commentators on barracks life and cultural inclinations of the Mamluk elite often remarked about the receptiveness of this cadre to mystic communion with God. Arguments about a predisposition to embrace Sufi visions of Divine omnipresence embedded among tribal populations from which cadets were recruited continue to provoke debates that remain robust. That Sufism contributed significantly to the collective and individual identities of the Mamluk corps is widely recognized, whether stemming from religious legacies that predated a cadet's arrival from Central Asia or from the socialization he experienced in the barracks. Sufi orders figured large in the politics of the Mamluk Sultanate because of the empathy toward them widespread among all ranks of the military class. The influence of Sufi orders and their prominent members on political currents throughout Egyptian society was appreciated by the oligarchy that ruled the state. Sultans were alert to their opinions about faith, justice, and Divine retribution for corruption and overbearing conceit that awaited those who transgressed their privileges to oppress fellow believers. The place of Sufism in Mamluk society more broadly will be considered subsequently (cf. Chapter 7).

Competence in translation of Arabic texts into Turkish was a skill entailed by the prevalence of the latter language as the lingua franca of barracks parlance and training. The identity of those who authored these texts points to the elite among the mass of cadets who rose to its senior ranks and provides evidence that their stature rested on more than proficiency in martial arts or agility in political rivalry.

Upon completion of their literary and religious instruction, usually by their middle teens, the cadets commenced upon their formal military training. It focused on horsemanship and mastery of cavalry tactics of warfare. When the Sultanate was founded, horsemanship (ar. *furūsiyya*) had evolved into a sophisticated system of mounted combat, hearkening back to a legacy attributed to the era of the initial Arab Conquests (first/seventh century).[9] Illustrated manuals of practice date from the ʿAbbasid Caliphate and richly elucidate equipage of mounts and riders, specialized weapons, and strategic maneuvers.

In Cairo, training exercises were conducted at several fields (ar. *maydān/ mayādīn*) laid out below the Muqattam Citadel and other locations in the capital's vicinity (allegedly eight during the Sultanate's height: seventh/thirteenth centuries; half as many by its later period: ninth/fifteenth c. when the city had fallen into partial ruin; only the penultimate Sultan, Qansawh al-Ghawri, built a new one). Cadets initially learned skills of mounting and handling a horse on wooden models that bucked and lunged to throw their rider. They transitioned to live horses only after proving their capacity to stay astride without a saddle (**Fig. 2.2**). Combat training included archery, lance casting, and sword play, conducted while a horse ran at top speed. Aerial photography around the ʿAbbasid capitals of Baghdad and Samarra has revealed racecourses laid out in diverse forms during the second/eighth–third/ninth centuries, around which opposing squadrons of trainees confronted each other at full gallop to place several arrows in their adversaries' target shields. Tracks of these forms have not been discerned in Egypt or Syria, but similar exercises of archery or lance casting for cadets while mounted on a dashing horse are described in manuals from the Mamluk period (**Fig. 2.3**).

Horse herds were pastured in fields located within the Giza and Fayyum Provinces on allotments (*iqṭāʿ*s) held by the Sultan and senior officers and stabled near the barracks and maydans. Contemporary sources attribute the maturation of cadets' training procedures to the years between the reigns of al-Zahir Baybars and al-Nasir Muhammad ibn Qalawun (658/1260–741/1341). Chroniclers noted the diligence of several sultans who personally oversaw the drilling of cadets they had purchased for promotion to the ranks of Royal Mamluks. These individuals, whose own proficiency at horsemanship and tactics was acknowledged, included Baybars himself (the Sultanate's archetypal figure), al-Mansur Qalawun. al-Zahir Barquq, al-Mu'ayyad Shaykh, and al-Ashraf Qayitbay. By contrast, the sovereign regarded as presiding over the Sultanate at its zenith, al-Nasir Muhammad ibn Qalawun, had not risen from the ranks of imported cadets and lacked exposure to the training rigors they had endured. While adept at leading troops from backgrounds outside the formal Mamluk cadres, he did not share the dedication to these tactics of peers who had survived them (cf. Chapter 1).

The military institution of the Mamluk Sultanate morphed along divergent lines as it evolved over two and a half centuries. Whether Royal Mamluks recruited via purchase from Qipjaq tribes in western Central Asia ever formed the exclusive core of the army even during the so-called ascendant era noted above is qualified by frequent reference to rulers readily conscripting troops from outside their ranks who fought effectively when exigency demanded ad-hoc strategies. But the training procedures for the cavalry units described above persisted to the Sultanate's final decades, when rulers began seriously to contemplate alternative approaches to armament and training. The storied

Fig. 2.2 Rider unseated from galloping horse
Scene from *Nihāyat al-Su'l*, eighth/fourteenth c. manual of horsemanship.
(Photo by Werner Forman/Universal Images Group/Getty Images)

resistance to adoption of firearms by the Mamluk military institution continues to stimulate discussion. While reasons behind their opposition have focused on alleged atrophy and ingrained disdain for innovation, a more practical cause may derive from the weight of heavy fire pieces and loading procedures

Fig. 2.3 Riders in a team game cantering around the Maydan Pool
Scene from *Nihāyat al-Su'l*, eighth/fourteenth c. manual of horsemanship.
(Photo by Werner Forman/Universal Images Group/Getty Images)

cumbersome on a horse running at full speed rather than from inflexible disdain for innovation.

An important dimension of a cadet's tutelage in the barracks involved the special quality of his guardians. These individuals were primarily eunuchs (*ṭawāshī/ṭawāshiyya*; *khādim/khuddām*) assigned to oversee their charges' upbringing before manumission, under circumstances unique to their impressionability as adolescents and the regime's goal of forging abiding bonds of camaraderie among them.[10] The eunuchs themselves were enlisted from a category of slaves originating largely in Sudanic Africa or Abyssinia (*al-Ḥabasha*; cf. Chapter 3). Castration was performed on these slaves while adolescents before their own arrival in Cairo. Period sources also insinuated that the protection the eunuchs provided involved isolation from the cadets' adult peers until they had reached sexual maturity. Few alluded in detail to the cadets' personal lives and intimate contacts in the barracks, but many remarked on the pivotal role played by their eunuch guardians in forming their character and group solidarity. Since sexual identities and mores vary by culture and time, a precise sense of what guardianship actually involved in the training schools remains elusive without relevant commentary by contemporary observers. Simplistic banning of same-gender intimacy is unlikely since the sources do not dwell on prohibitions against such contact among cadets of a similar age. What does emerge is the proscription of such intimacy between minors and adults, as defined by customary and religious law. Inferences in the sources imply undermining of cohort bonds rather than warping of personal character as the potential threat to a cadet's character; denunciations of sinful debauchery are confined to sporadic alcohol or drug use.

The eunuchs' influence was not confined to sheltering their charges from vice. Eunuchs had risen to prominence in court and military circles long before the advent of Islam. Their role as guardians of harems loomed large from the eastern Mediterranean to China since ancient times. In the Mamluk training barracks, they served as role models for the cadets, likely due to bonds fortified through trust and constancy uncompromised by intimate desire. To what extent the eunuch guardians participated in the cadets' military exercises is unclear since eunuchs rarely attained formal status as soldiers within the Mamluks' ranks. Nor do the sources link their ethnic origins as Africans to qualities unique to their services in the barracks. But they uniformly depict them as powerfully influencing the development of their wards' character. Eunuchs and cadets shared a severed tie to immediate kin groups, a sense of uprootedness, that may have intensified the special camaraderie so central to the barracks identity the Sultanate sought to nurture – and thereby promote loyalty to regime rather than family.

Upon completion of their military training, cadets were formally manumitted by conversion to Islam and appointment to the base ranks of adult soldiers. While their induction to the Community of Believers technically terminated any stigma associated with chattel slavery, they proudly retained their identity as Mamluks: those owned (by the ruler) and sworn to his protection, defense of his realm, and security of its order and religion. They set out on their formal careers with this ceremony.

## Organization, Ranks, and Titles

Units of the Mamluk army were organized according to antecedents of rank that appeared during the Ayyubid Dynasty but assumed their mature categories during the formative years between the reigns of al-Zahir Baybars and al-Nasir Muhammad ibn Qalawun. The most prominent of these categories were the Royal Mamluks, so designated because they were the ruling Sultan's own property (*al-Mamālīk al-Sulṭāniyya*). Referred to in period sources as "purchased" (ar. *mushtarawāt*) or "imported" (*ajlāb, julbān*), these individuals enjoyed primacy in the Sultanic regime and, theoretically, owed their loyalty exclusively to their royal patron who had bought them. Their preeminence was dependent upon their stature as first-generation slave-soldiers, their prerogatives and proximity to the Sultan denied to other categories.[11]

The elite among the Sultan's mamluks were his personal guard, referred to as "intimate" (*khaṣṣakī*). They had attracted the attention of their preceptors and trainers as talented quick starters and were brought to the Sultan's notice upon their manumission. In addition to the protection they offered the ruler, the Khassakiyya initially performed as cup bearers, pen-box holders, armor bearers, and other duties suited to his proximity. They were the most likely to receive early promotion to the several stages of command as officers (*amīr/umarā'*). But they were also subject to abrupt demotion upon the Sultan's death, since his successor suspected their loyalty and sought to supplant them with his own trusted mushtarawat. Mamluks of a former ruler were downgraded immediately at his death to the status of "slaves of previous sultans" (*mamālīk al-ṣalāṭīn al-mutaqaddima*) or "veterans" (*qarāniṣa*). Stripped of their special privileges, these faced dismissal, physical ejection from the barracks, and unemployment unless hired by a senior officer (and potential rival of the incumbent ruler). Some Sultans took draconian measures to secure their ascendance: arrest, exile, and even execution of their predecessors' troops. The majority of mamluks from former regimes did adjust to their disenfranchisement but continued to identify – vehemently – with their previous patron and claimed his nisba as their agnomen (i.e., a mamluk purchased by al-Zahir Baybars, al-Mansur Qalawun, or al-Ashraf Barsbay referred to himself as a Zahiri, a Mansuri, or an Ashrafi). Due to their martial competence and previous hegemony, these contingents of former rulers formed the most aggressive factions within the military establishment, contending incessantly with each other but united in unstable coalitions by their antipathy toward mushtarawat of the current ruler.

Command over mamluks purchased by the Sultan (other than his own *khaṣṣakī*s) was distributed among several ranks of officers (*umarā'*), the most senior (and highly stipended) of whom also acquired contingents of their own. Individuals advanced through several stages of promotion: officers of ten (*umarāʾ ʿashara*) received an allotment (*iqṭāʿ*) sufficient to arm, pay, and supply horses to ten mamluks; officers of forty (*umarāʾ arbaʿīn*) received an allotment supporting forty and the right to maintain a marching band (*ṭabalkhāna*) with four drummers; officers of one hundred (*umarāʾ miʾa*) were granted iqtaʿs substantive enough to maintain a hundred soldiers and authority of command (*taqaddima*) over 1000. The band accompanying their maneuvers could number eight drummers.[12]

During the Sultanate's formative years, to the third reign of al-Nasir Muhammad ibn Qalawun (709/1310), this cursus of advancement was rigorously determined by quality of leadership and military performance. Line troopers whose service during campaigns was exemplary or who aided the Sultan or a senior officer in distinctive ways were advanced to the initial rank of ten, with an iqtaʿ stipend of 9,000–12,000 dinars per annum. For the next promotion, recognizing further achievement, an amir of forty received an iqtaʿ yielding 20,000–30,000/annum. At the highest level, an amir of 100 and commander of a thousand might be granted iqtaʿs yielding between 100 and 200 thousand dinars yearly, often supplemented by revenues from fiscal offices or ad-hoc sources to support their contingent of mamluks and household of extended family and civil staff. Individuals who reached the most senior rank had frequently belonged to the circle of barracks comrades in training (*khushdāshiyya*), among whom the reigning Sultan had begun his career. They had risen with him through the ranks, outmaneuvered their rivals, and attained positions of authority at the apex of the military hierarchy. Their maturity and records of distinction, combined with their proximity to the Sultan, qualified them for membership in the oligarchy that ruled the state and balanced off the myriad factions competing for access below them. These most senior officers possessed assets sufficient to import their own mamluks from abroad or to employ veteran soldiers of former rulers (who were designated "*sayfī*" mamluks due to their patrons' right to wear swords).

The preceding outline most accurately conformed to actual practice during the Sultanate's formation. After his final ascension, Sultan al-Nasir Muhammad initiated alterations to it that would continue to the Sultanate's end and transform the process significantly (or dilute it, according to critics).[13] As noted previously, al-Nasir Muhammad acquired the ultimate office by right of inheritance, albeit after two abortive terms that decisively influenced his outlook on authority and determination to endure. Al-Nasir had experienced neither the martial training through which cadets advanced (or failed) in the barracks nor the powerful bonds of camaraderie forged between them as they competed with their peers for promotion and rewards upon manumission. He interpreted his legitimacy as a dynastic right and evinced little respect for a *corsus honorum* through which he had never passed but from which he had suffered derision and insurrection. While al-Nasir continued to indulge his

Fig. 2.4 Mamluk and Bedouin lithograph
From *Galleria universale di tutti i popoli del mondo, ossia storia dei costumi, religioni, riti, governi d'ogni parte del globo* (Gallery and history of all peoples, customs, religions, rituals, governments from all over the globe), Volume II, Plate III, published by Giuseppe Antonelli, 1838, Venice.
(Photo by DEA/Icas94 / De Agostini Picture Library via Getty Images)

corps of purchased Mamluks, he was prepared to seek loyalty among cadres of personnel who diverged from the upper ranks of the military elite: former Royal Mamluks demoted after their patron's demise but adept at factional infighting, free soldiers who offered their service for hire, Bedouin cavalry whose knowledge of combat tactics in the desert had proved valuable during campaigns, and a host of civil bureaucrats skilled in unorthodox means of raising revenue (**Fig. 2.4**). Historians who observed Al-Nasir Muhammad's tactics alternated between castigation for deviating from the "classic" model of exclusive reliance on Mamluks formally trained and appreciation for the military edifice that kept him in office through three turbulent decades and made his regime the region's preeminent power.

Subsequent rulers who introduced reforms of their own included al-Zahir Barquq (784/1382–801/1399), al-Mu'ayyad Shaykh (815/1412–824/1421), al-Ashraf Barsbay (825/1422–841/1438), al-Ashraf Inal (857/1453–865/1461), al-Ashraf Qayitbay (872/1468–901/1496), and Qansawh al-Ghawri (906/1501–922/1516). These rulers adopted measures that shared only the goals of strengthening their forces and securing their positions. Otherwise, their tactics contrasted: recruiting elite personnel from dissimilar ethnicities (Barquq), reliance on combat performance rather than ascribed reputation of units (Shaykh), advancement of cadres descended from former Mamluks (Barsbay), fomenting discord and indiscipline between rival factions (Inal), enlargement of the corps of Royal Mamluks (Qayitbay), and enlisting personnel from outside the established military cadres for training in firearms (Qansawh al-Ghawri). These rulers pursued their policies under conditions of fiscal stringency.

Costs of importation, training, and maintenance were compounded by reduction of personnel due to several plague epidemics that decimated populations in Southwest Asia and the Mediterranean between the thirteenth and sixteenth centuries.[14] Personnel recently imported to replenish the Mamluk ranks from regions outside zones of infection lacked the immunity of residents in areas exposed to previous epidemics and died in greater numbers. Rulers goaded to replace their losses faced expenses exceeding the capacity of licit revenue sources (taxes on agrarian land and tariffs on domestic/foreign commerce). They resorted to ad-hoc measures that ranged from: forced purchases of staple commodities placed under government monopolies (such as sugar) at prices above market value, appropriations negotiated with holders of agrarian land and urban real estate, manipulation of charitable trusts (*awqāf*) for seizure of yields, and confiscation of assets hoarded by officials arrested on charges of corruption that verged on extortion. The consequences of these tactics for the regime's economy will be considered subsequently (cf. Chapter 5). Relevant to this discussion, several rulers spent lavishly on their efforts to shore up their military contingents; Sultan Qayitbay himself is alleged to have exceeded seven million dinars during his reign of twenty-eight years. Qansawh al-Ghawri's efforts to found artillery pieces were derided as much for their exorbitant cost as for their humiliating failures.

Figures for the cadres of the military institution overall differ according to numbers listed in encyclopedias of bureaucratic practice and diplomacy, manuals of warfare, or narrative chronicles of specific events. For the formative period between 1260 and 1341 noted above, these converge around a group of twenty-four senior amirs of 100/commanders of 1000, with overall numbers of mamluk troops between 24,000 and 30,000. After al-Nasir Muhammad's reign, these figures fluctuated but generally decreased over time, despite agendas of replenishment pursued by rulers like Inal or Qayitbay. When Qansawh al-Ghawri led his army out of Cairo to confront the massive host assembled by the Ottoman Sultan Selim Yavuz in 922/1516, it was alleged to exceed 5000 only slightly overall, inclusive of non-Mamluk auxiliaries.

These auxiliaries had themselves acquired distinctive characteristics throughout the Sultanate's development. During its formative phase, the ruling oligarchy attempted to confine the elite military ranks to mamluks purchased from the Qipjaq Steppes. Membership, with attendant duties and prerogatives, was closed to their descendants. These offspring of first-generation slave-soldiers were designated "sons of the people" (s. *walad*, pl. *awlād al-nās*), the term "people" (*nās*) referring to the military elite specifically and the upper classes generally, in contrast to the masses (*al-ʿāmma*).[15] They frequently bore Arabic names and did not undergo the rigors of training experienced by their fathers. Their position in the military hierarchy evolved over time: from assignation to duties subordinate to the formal mamluk cadres and receipt of lesser iqtaʿs during the early years, to a gradual diminution of their official functions and reduction of their fiscal allotments. In the decades following the reign of al-Nasir Muhammad, during which the military establishment was opened to outsiders from diverse backgrounds, references to awlad al-nas who could not trace their origins to the military elite increased noticeably. By the so-called Circassian period, following the reign of al-Zahir Barquq, persons claiming to be awlad al-nas represented a wide range of civilian backgrounds but little training in traditional martial arts. The prerogative they sought, according to observers who criticized their presence as corrupt and even parasitical, involved access to a secure, if modest, pension – for which the recipient had bribed official members of the Mamluk elite. Yet, when Qansawh al-Ghawri founded his so-called Fifth Corps (*al-ṭāʾifat al-khāmisa*) of soldiers trained in the use of firearms (arquebuses), the chroniclers derisively noted that awlad al-nas were prominent among them. Al-Ghawri apparently regarded them as less resistant to experiments with untraditional weapons than were his Royal Mamluks who spurned them.

Similar conditions applied to a broader auxiliary group: the "circle" or *ḥalqa*. The term referred originally to an entourage surrounding sultans of the early junta days who had pledged themselves to his security in an environment of endemic assault and assassination. From these Praetorian beginnings, the Halqa assumed the status of free troops who, as infantry, had not entered the military elite via the cursus of mamluk slave-soldiers. They looked back to the founder of the Ayyubid regime: Salah al-Din Yusuf, whose armies were composed primarily of free cavalrymen.[16]

As the Mamluk Sultanate evolved, Halqa troops served both the Sultan and his senior officers. Their numbers seem to have peaked around 20,000, when they formed discrete squadrons of some forty foot soldiers, each under the command of captains who did not answer to Mamluk superiors. Nor did they owe their stipends to the fiscal bureaus that salaried Mamluk troops. But, over time, the Halqa itself morphed into a less cohesive entity, subjected to diminished status, sporadic pay, and wider representation of social groups. By the Circassian period, the Halqa had become largely synonymous with the ranks of awlad al-nas. Both groups had been effectively marginalized by the Royal Mamluks of reigning sultans or the contentious factions of their demoted predecessors, who together made up the core of the formal military institution.

Neither unit had access to horses. Yet, when chroniclers remarked on the composition of personnel departing Cairo on campaigns, they routinely mentioned the awlad al-nas and Halqa as components of these forces. For what purposes they were to serve remains unclear, but they seem to have more readily coordinated their efforts with other auxiliary units, such as Bedouin or Turkmen, despite their status as infantry. When the historian Ibn Iyas reflected over reasons behind Qansawh al-Ghawri's defeat by the Ottomans at the Battle of Marj Dabiq (922/1516), he noted that tensions had already heightened between mamluk cavalrymen and awlad al-nas foot soldiers.[17] At the battle's critical juncture, the awlad al-nas joined Turkmen squadrons when the latter abandoned the field to follow al-Ghawri's traitorous colleague, Kha'ir Bak. Members of the Halqa were among the elements most readily disposed to adapt their positions to new realities of rule under the Ottoman occupiers and would merge themselves into the hybrid military order that evolved after the Occupation.

## Offices and Conditions of Service

Chroniclers and encyclopedists of the Mamluk Sultanate referred frequently to offices held by the officers who formed the ruling oligarchy. Titles of these offices depicted formal duties, actual performance of which varied according to the personnel appointed to them and the circumstances under which they fulfilled their charges.[18] Foremost among these were "deputy" sultans (s. *Nā'ib*, pl. *Nuwwāb al-Salṭana*), effectively viceroys, who were formally positioned to assume command in the advent of the sovereign's demise. They frequently stood in for him as the final magistrate in the biweekly appellate audiences in the Citadel or Stables that received petitions from plaintiffs disputing decisions imposed by judges in the Shariʿa civil courts. After al-Zahir Baybars's time, deputy sultans ruled over the Empire's provinces in Syria: Damascus, Aleppo, Hims, Hama, and Tripoli. In theory subordinate to the Sultan in Cairo, in practice they governed their territories autonomously except in times of war, when they were expected to obey their sovereign's call for muster.[19] These viceroys were distinguished from the supreme commander of the Sultan's armies (*Atābak al-ʿAsākir*), appointed from among his closest senior amirs and based in Cairo. The Atabak served the monarch as his chief strategist and marshal, the individual who actually led campaigns in the field.

Their names loom large in the roster of battles fought during the Sultanate's history, and several predictably plotted to succeed their former khushdash to the royal office.

Ranked officially after the Atabak al-ʿAsakir was the captain of the guard (*Ra'.s Nawba*). Initially intended to regiment the unruly ranks of amirs, guard captains ultimately held responsibility for disciplining the entire host of mamluks in Cairo. Under al-Zahir Barquq, himself a radical reformer of the military institution who weeded out elements loyal to the Qalawunid quasi-dynasty, the office was titled *Ra's Nawbat al-Nuwwāb*. Its incumbent was now empowered to put down disputes between factions of Qaranis, Sultani, and Sayfi Mamluks; and revolts on the part of Julban line troops rioting for pay increases and despoiling Cairo's markets. Only slightly lower in rank to the Raʾs Nawba was the master of arms (*Amīr Silāḥ, Silāḥdār*), with authority over the royal arsenal (*Zardkhāna*) and manufacture of weapons. This official, also among the Sultan's close confidants, paralleled the guard captain's position because of his control over the regime's crucial instruments of enforcement. In practice, the Sultan himself frequently took over allotment of royal armaments himself, relegating the Amir Silah to an honorary post of leading the royal arms bearers during ceremonials. The Amir Silah technically oversaw the arsenal warden (*Zardkāsh*), who supervised its employees. Chroniclers who described criminal activity regarded arsenal staff as among the most susceptible to bribery and espionage due to illicit arms trafficking by plotters of insurgencies against the regime, foreign and domestic (**Fig. 2.5**). Parallel in status to the Amir Silah was the senior master of horse (*Amīr Ākhūr*), who managed the Citadel stables, where he was officially stationed, and the royal horse herds pastured in Giza and the Fayyum. The host of minor officials who answered to him (upwards of forty), each with a specific task that ranged from details of foddering to polishing saddles and bridles, was commensurate with the primacy of cavalry in the military institution.

The Sultan's advisory council, in effect the regime's ruling oligarchy, convened in a chamber presided over by its superintendent (*Amīr Majlis*), who guarded its proceedings and arranged appointments of the royal household with court physicians and oculists. Among the Sultanate's most influential officials of administration who assembled there were: the senior chamberlain (*Ḥājib al-Ḥujjāb*), grand secretary (*Dawādār*: "holder of the ink stand"), treasurer (*Khāzindār*), and "master of the house" (*Ustādār*: majordomo). Individuals appointed to these positions numbered among the Sultan's closest comrades from their barracks days, rose to the oligarchy's uppermost ranks alongside him, and sometimes conspired against him to gain the sovereign office. The chamberlain ordered the sultan's audiences, arranged sequences of petitioners appealing lower court rulings and bureaucrats presenting their reports or accounts, presented ambassadors and foreign delegations,

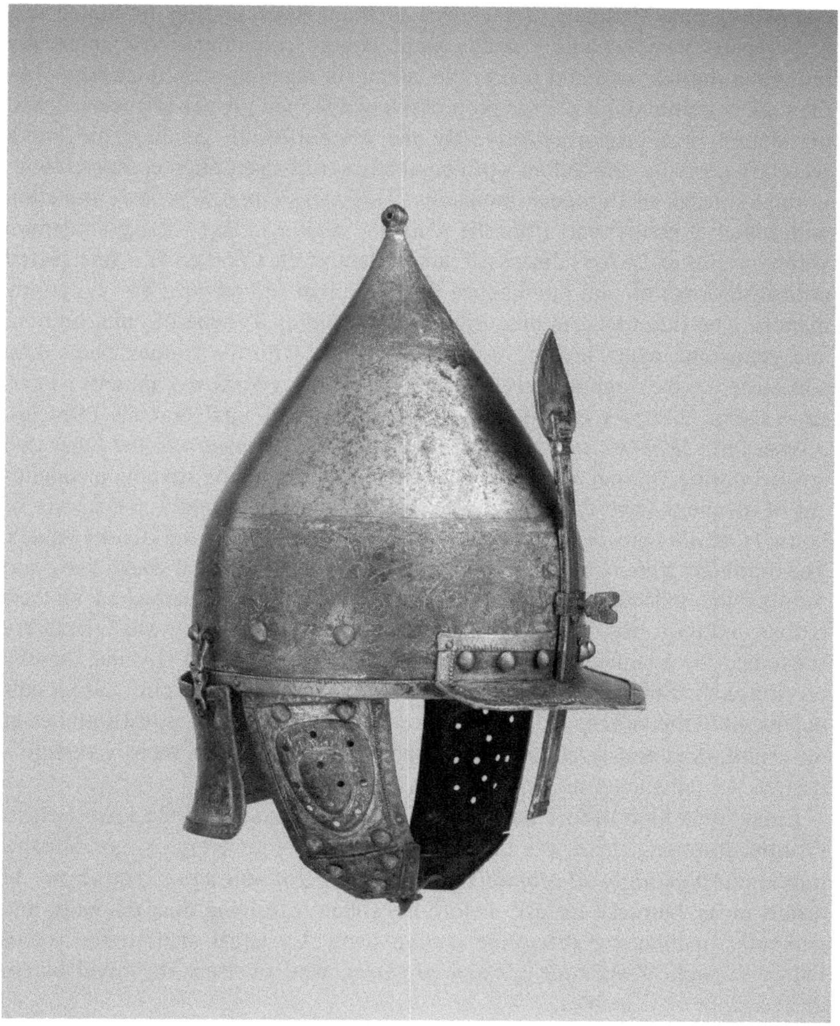

Fig. 2.5 Helmet, ca. 1500–25
Possibly Turkish, Istanbul, in the style of Turkman armor, steel, iron, gold, copper alloy; one of the few conical helmets of the period to retain its original brim, nasal, cheeks, and nape defense. The brass trim, engraved with a zigzag motif, is typical of Mamluk and Ottoman helmets about 1500.
(Photo by: Sepia Times/Universal Images Group via Getty Images)

and oversaw the hierarchy of attendees at ceremonials. During the Sultanate's early years, the Dawadar's duties were largely ceremonial. He physically presented the ink well and pen to the sultan for signatures on documents. As the regime matured, his charge progressively assumed greater importance, and his stature rose proportionately. By the ninth/fifteenth century, the grand secretary served as the Sultan's principal advisor of state, often compared with prime ministers of European monarchs. This *Dawādār Kabīr*, in conjunction with his civil counterpart from the learned (*ʿulamāʾ*) class – the confidential secretary (*Kātib al-Sirr*, discussed subsequently; cf. Chapter 4) – interpreted critical information and intelligence for the Sultan and advised him on policy matters. The treasurer had authority over the Sultan's cache of coin, bullion, and gems and, again ideally, worked in tandem with his civilian peers who administered the regime's fiscal bureaus: viziers (*Wuzarāʾ*) initially; later: supervisors (*Nuẓẓār*) of the army (*Jaysh*), tax and iqtaʿ bureaus (*Dawla*), private fund (*Khāṣṣ*), and "special" bureau (*Dīwān al-Mufrad*), the latter two created during Barquq's reign to provide him with income streams independent of revenues from the state treasury (cf. Chapter 5). Finally, the master of house (*Ustādār*) presided over the sovereign's household in the Citadel Palace. The *Ustādār Kabīr* supervised those who staffed the royal magazines and supplied the ranks of attendants and mamluks in the Citadel barracks with their rations and uniforms. From Barquq's reign, after the vizierate was effectively subsumed, he assumed authority over the Khass and Mufrad Diwans, thereby serving as the Sultan's effective minister of finance for the Empire. Individuals appointed to this office, and who survived in it, amassed the largest fortunes of the realm, dexterously aligning their enormous wealth with their sovereign's designs for enhancing his power.

Eunuchs in high offices held the rank of amir, usually of the lowest class. Prominent among them was the commander of the sovereign's mamluks-in-training (*Muqaddam al-Mamālīk*), responsible for mustering squadrons of cadets in the barracks for drill before the sultan, resolving their disputes, and generally maintaining discipline among them. Of equal station: the senior Palace eunuch (*Zimāmdār, Zimām al-Qaṣr*), who oversaw the royal harem and its store of valuables.

Security over the Citadel and Cairo at large was assigned respectively to amirs of forty: the deputy (*Nāʾib al-Qalʿa*), responsible for guarding the winding staircase entry gate to the Fortress; and the governor of Cairo (*Wālī al-Qāhira*), chief of police and upholder of order over the capital. Officers with parallel duties included: the senior armor bearer (*Amīr Jāndār*), who meted out punishments ordered by the sultan, and guarded the arsenal and royal encampment during campaigns in the field; and the adjutant of the army (*Naqīb al-Jaysh*), responsible for security over public processions and journeys outside the capital. These offices changed over time: the former was largely replaced by the Ra'ʾs Nawba, the latter combined with the chief of police. Each commanded a staff of armed bailiffs (*Bardadāriyya*) who acted as enforcers and inspectors (*Shādd, Mushidd*) who monitored revenue-generating agencies: markets, granaries, oil presses, sugar mills, the Nile port of Bulaq, canals, and pious trust properties (*a̲wqāf*). During the ninth/fifteenth century, the office of Naqib al-Jaysh in particular extended its ad-hoc (nefarious, according to contemporary commentators) influence over litigation in the civil Shariʿa courts. Filers of suits came to rely on intercessions on the part of bailiffs to gain a positive judgment, in return for which they paid bribes.

The evolution of the army adjutant's office was both symbolic of contrasts between formal duties and actual functions and symptomatic of the contexts behind them. All of the preceding appointments merged official charges with ad-hoc functions that amounted to lofty sinecures to some degree. Few of them were distinct or mutually exclusive. While the Atabak al-ʿAsakir or Dawadar Kabir clearly served as senior commander of armed forces or executive adviser to the monarch respectively, all acted in a wide range of other capacities as well. And all appointees exploited their positions to build fortunes. Following the pivotal reign of al-Nasir Muhammad ibn Qalawun, the official dimension of service for office holding in the ruling oligarchy steadily eroded in importance while the unofficial aspect gained proportionately. This transformation did not go unnoticed by chroniclers, who denounced it as corrupt and debilitating to the regime's effectiveness – not to mention its commitment to just governance. The unanimity of their censure must be considered in light of the milieu in which the ruling oligarchy operated.

## Legacy, "Conspiracy," or Both?

Politics within the Mamluk military institution initially come across as inherently faction-ridden and intrinsically violent. The detailed narratives by contemporary observers who chronicled the Sultanate's political history may leave their readers with contradictory impressions of exceptional volatility and persistent durability. From a superficial perspective, these impressions should have been mutually incompatible. But upon scrutiny of specific events, the record of Mamluk politics qualifies a judgment of endemic violence and clarifies the context behind its longevity. With regard to volatility, chroniclers targeted prominent actors in the game of politics – those whose stories made gripping reads. Their careers, loaded with conflicts, plots, and rivalries, depict the minority who contended for power. Trajectories for the less active majority remain less visible in the narratives. Impressions of hyper-charged conflict ubiquitously pursued throughout all levels of the Mamluk elite are misleading. While line troops certainly indulged in confrontational acts such as riots or work stoppages that subjected civil society to disorder, they adopted these measures as tactics to negotiate pay increases or terms of service, much as a modern union bargains to enhance its leverage. As demonstrations, their insurrections aimed at staging potential clout rather than inflicting serious damage of benefit to no one. Within the ranks of amirs, many officers remained fixed at lower levels of promotion, their inertia due either to mediocre service records or simple resignation to one's lot and a pragmatic desire to avoid risks of advancement. Prudence often trumped ambition in a middle-ranked officer's scale of options. Chroniclers tended to ignore their mundane careers to focus on turbulent biographies of major actors who took risks. Reasons behind the regime's endurance are more complex and emerge from the enduring appeal of a nostalgic dynastic ideal juxtaposed against concepts of comradeship acknowledged by all those who identified as members of the Mamluk institution, regardless of rank. These concepts emerged from circumstances of the Sultanate's formation.

Chroniclers of the Sultanate pointed to eschewal of dynastic rule by its founders, who allegedly chose to posit ultimate authority exclusively on autocrats rising from slave origins. Succession to genuine power was not hereditary. The actual process was more nuanced and revealed tensions between two contrasting perceptions of succession rather than mutual rejection of either. With regard to persistence of a dynastic legacy, the Sultanate's founders remained sensitive to the act of usurpation that had originally placed them at the head of a realm. They never disavowed succession by inheritance in principle, despite the relegation of many royal heirs to the status of fronts while senior officers of their fathers jockeyed among themselves over who would control the Sultanate. Dismissal of these heirs as uniformly ephemeral discounts the agility of several who succeeded in holding power for enough time to qualify as autonomous sovereigns who made effective policy decisions. The endurance of the Qalawunid quasi-dynasty for a century (678/1279–784/1382) is testimony to more than persistence by default.[20] The prestige linked to Qalawun's descendants lent the officers who gained the Sultanic office through conflict an aura of legitimacy they would lack if they seized power with no show of respect for the family of an esteemed progenitor they formally were sworn to protect. When al-Zahir Barquq finally did away with the Qalawunids, he acted to model his behavior after the precedent set by an even greater progenitor, the founder Baybars, whose agnomen Barquq appropriated for himself. Amirs who succeeded to the Sultanate for the half-century after Barquq initiated their own careers they had cherished as officers in his service. A similar process applied to amirs originally acquired by Shaykh, Barsbay, and Jaqmaq.[21] By Qayitbay's time, the practice of executing a previous sultan's offspring had been replaced by his honorary exile to Alexandria. A similar policy applied to many senior amirs, now permitted retirement to one of the holy cities: Jerusalem, Hebron, or Medina.

Yet, nostalgic renown accruing to this dynastic legacy did not invalidate the prerogative of accession through merit gained over a career of proven performance and leadership by individuals who started out as imported slaves for whom competition was engrained. Those who succeeded in consolidating their positions, and went on to productive reigns, belonged to the class of Royal Mamluks imported from abroad and drilled as cadets – with the exception of al-Nasir Muhammad ibn Qalawun, whose route to the Sultanate via inheritance made him unique. Membership in the cadre of first-generation slaves therefore became the idealized qualification for aspiring to the realm's highest office and holding on to it. Most of these prominent sultans reached the top after decades of military service. Along with their military distinction, they brought to it networking skills and political savvy, essential for the deal cutting requisite to enlisting their peers' acclamation and support – rather than insurrection – from those whose own ambitions had been thwarted. In short, when they were positioned to compete for the supreme office, they were prepared not only to win it but also to consolidate it and move on to conducting substantive policy rather than merely conspiring to survive. Experience learned through years of interacting with ruthless colleagues truly mattered.[22] No matter how close they were personally, their potential for rivalry could not be discounted. These individuals had frequently governed provinces in Egypt or Syria in virtual autonomy. They had purchased and trained squadrons of their own mamluks, built up households of personal retainers, and hired staffs of bureaucrats who managed revenues from their land allotments (*iqṭāʿāt*) and private estates. In short, those whom contemporary biographers named as the Sultanate's prominent rulers exhibited the requisite qualifications long before their enthronements. Yet, they all lived with the prospect of conspiracy, a condition seemingly endemic to the culture of the Mamluk institution at all levels.

Conspiracy is a term loaded with nefarious inferences. Betrayal and malfeasance are conjured up as affiliates. With regard to the Mamluk institution, its negative connotations belie a process of aggressive competition and adroit maneuvering instilled in mamluk cadets from the time of their arrival in the barracks. While their naiveté as "raw recruits" cannot be uniformly assumed, these adolescents were largely separated from their families and isolated from the indigenous population until their manumission. They matured in a barracks culture that emphasized their distinction from the masses, marked by military prowess and intense group loyalty (*khushdāshiyya*). Bonds formed during these barracks years became the underlying foundation of personal trust and mutual reliance among them. But trust and reliance did not rule out opportunism or duplicity. It is the incongruity implicit in this fusion of seemingly opposite traits that complicates discerning a rationale behind their behavior. However enigmatic these traits may have seemed, they were deeply ingrained and shaped a mamluk's outlook toward his colleagues for the rest of his life.

Cadets realized early on that to advance meant to outwit one's opponents: those recruits belonging to rival units bound to serve amir patrons who intrigued among themselves incessantly for preferment, the ultimate goal of which was the throne itself.

Factional rivalry was legitimized as the appropriate process through which power was distributed and authority decided. Considered essential to attaining military valor and political competence, the capacity to compete aggressively became the aptitude requisite to success as the mamluk elite defined it. Factional rivalry was therefore anticipated rather than disavowed by aspiring mamluk trainees. Their skill in practicing it was rewarded by promotion; their failure to outflank opponents led to stalled advancement. From a positive perspective, this process self-selected combative high achievers who learned how to inspire confidence among followers, strategize intuitively, and score victories against formidable odds. On the negative side, conspiratorial politics promoted a milieu of tension and paranoia over potential insurrection that permeated the military hierarchy and persisted throughout the Sultanate's history. Whether conspiracy contributed to alleged tendencies toward introversion and conservatism pervading the mamluk elite remains another question, about which debate continues.[23]

But the durability of the edifice cannot be ignored. The independent Mamluk state endured for two and a half centuries. It presided over the final era when a great power flourished indigenously in the Central Arab lands. It achieved a union between Egypt and Syria that has not been duplicated since. The Sultanate owed its longevity as much to the stability of its governance as to the prowess of its military cadres. How was stability possible in a system that epitomized competition, if not conspiracy? It was for two reasons. First, the military class confined competition largely to itself. Although the Mamluk institution ruled the Empire through close interaction with a host of civilian adjutants who oversaw the realm's administration, these adjutants were largely spared the factional infighting that so preoccupied the militarists. They became entangled only when their duties involved them in their patrons' own conspiracies or when they were suspected of withholding funds, the amassing of which had been the basis of their appointment. For most of the population, since they had no say in politics, they remained outside its intrigues. The masses did influence decisions taken by the ruling oligarchy in a variety of indirect ways, which are considered subsequently. But their exclusion as nonparticipants rendered them immune for the most part.

The second reason involved a deep-rooted awareness of the special context of competitiveness that was imbedded within the military institution at all levels. Each member, every subgroup within the Mamluk caste, embraced the milieu in which they plotted their political courses. Under such circumstances, rivalry or conspiracy between individuals was normative rather than exceptional and a powerful conditioner of comradeship. Friendships were pliable and constrained by circumstances that shifted according to the pragmatic requirements of coalition building and effectiveness in battle. In this light, "betrayal" itself became a malleable concept that mitigated against feelings of "wrongness" or "deceit" when former comrades turned on each other for political gain. This malleability could coexist with loyalties that ran deep among former cadets whose identities with their regiment and original patrons weathered passing skirmishes and lasted throughout their careers. A mamluk trooper or officer remained a Zahiri (Barquq) or Ashrafi (Barsbay), even if he eventually plotted against a fellow Zahiri or Ashrafi when advancement or ad-hoc coalition warranted such action. And those sultans who did build lasting regimes skillfully managed to reconcile seemingly intractable contenders who elected to work together for their common goal: shared hegemony.

This mindset can be seen in an example noted by a contemporary observer: the ambivalent relationship between Sultan Qayitbay and one of his closest colleagues, the Grand Amir Yashbak min Mahdi. Yashbak had shared apprenticeship as a junior officer with Qayitbay. Both had trained and were manumitted as Royal Mamluks of al-Zahir Jaqmaq (Qayitbay was acquired as a guardsman by Barsbay in the sultan's final years; there is no record of his status as a cadet). Later in Jaqmaq's reign, they were promoted to the lower and medial ranks of amirs; during the tenures of his successors, Inal and Khushqadam, both joined the elite oligarchy of senior officers who commanded 1000 mamluks. Despite their parallel trajectories to the summit of the military hierarchy, they were polar opposites. Qayitbay was a cautious calculator with a reputation for sober reasoning and moral integrity. He exuded an aura of piety and reverence for the religious Law that would serve him well during his long reign. Yashbak was an impetuous warrior whose courage and ruthlessness inspired fear and respect in equal measure among his military colleagues and the civil populace. When Qayitbay consolidated his hold on the Sultanate, he appointed Yashbak his Dawadar, with the intent of exploiting the amir's formidable style of leadership on the battlefield. Yashbak's draconian tactics had first shown their effectiveness when Jaqmaq dispatched him to Upper Egypt to quell revolts by the Hawwara Bedouin tribe, which had seized control of several districts and usurped rents from iqtaʿs reserved for the military class. Yashbak adopted measures of intimidation that included flaying his most obstinate opponents and stuffing their skins with straw to form manikins set up as warnings against repeated insurgencies. Yashbak would go on to further accomplishments that culminated in his successful campaign against the Dhu'l-Qadrid rebel Shah Suwar in southeastern Anatolia (cf. Chapter 1). Yashbak's aggressive personality was matched by abiding ambition; he thirsted for supreme power. Yet, he faced an untenable dilemma since his comradeship with Qayitbay prevented an act of betrayal so long as the sultan, his khushdash, reigned.

Qayitbay himself resolved Yashbak's quandary, and potential menace, by allowing his most redoubtable officer to depart for a venture of foreign conquest on his own. In 885/1480, Yashbak received emissaries from Yaʿqub, son of Uzun Hasan and thus heir to the Aq-Qoyunlu federation in Iraq and western Iran.[24] The emissaries privately informed Yashbak that the son's position was tenuous and that his subordinates would welcome restoration of order by so daunting a warrior as the Grand Dawadar. Yashbak found this prospect appealing and feasible, as did Qayitbay, who regarded the venture as a means to relieve himself of a challenge to his own tenure and, at the same time, to establish a trusted ally in a strategically important territory that compromised his suzerainty over Syria – all this while preserving his comrade's honor and cementing his friendship. Yashbak's expedition ended in disaster, due in large measure to his impetuosity. After pursuing a Bedouin chief, who was marauding throughout northern Syria, to the town of al-Ruha (Edessa) in Aq-Qoyunlu territory east of the Euphrates, Yashbak placed it under siege. Rashly underestimating the sagacity of its commander, Yashbak committed errors of judgment that resulted in his defeat and execution. While Qayitbay genuinely mourned Yashbak's loss, his grief was tempered by the pragmatic removal of a khushdash whose loyalty was compromised by ambition and potentially a threat.

The long-term effects of tensions arising from this milieu of endemic competition, if not conspiracy, were not uniformly construed as positive. Throughout the Sultanate's final decades, these tensions combined with perceptions of a stagnating economy and awareness of shifts in the regional order to alarm members of the military hierarchy about the Sultanate's future prospects in a turbulent world. During the reign of Qayitbay's eventual successor, Qansawh al-Ghawri, a growing number of officers considered hedging their future by seeking service in a rival's court. Their concerns mounted after the Ottoman Sultan Selim Yavuz defeated the Safavid Shah Ismaʿil at Chaldiran on 3 Rajab 920/August 23, 1514. In the aftermath of a battle widely interpreted as altering the balance of power to the Sultanate's detriment, an amir named Khushqadam (no relation to the former sultan) whom al-Ghawri had publicly disgraced secretly departed Cairo for Alexandria and then Istanbul. The historian Ibn Iyas gave the following account of his audience in the Ottoman capital:

> Khushqadam incited the Ottoman ruler against the sultan, informed him about the latter's tyrannical and oppressive acts, described his illegal monthly and weekly taxes imposed on commodity sellers, and dwelt on his forced exchanges of gold and silver currency at unfavorable rates. He told him many other stories in this vein about the sorry state of affairs in Egypt. He even reported on the unruly condition of the Egyptian

armies, and how this might be exploited. He deplored the immorality of Egyptian qadis, their habitual acceptance of bribes before pronouncing judgments. He urged the Ottoman ruler to march against the sultan's realm, stressing how simple its conquest would be. He explained to him how he should deploy his fleet against Alexandria and Damietta. Henceforth, the Ottoman's ambition was inspired to conquer Egypt. God remains the master of its future.[25]

As the renegade officer's list of liabilities indicated, al-Ghawri's regime faced difficulties on several fronts. But the Ottoman ruler paid heed to the weakness of paramount significance: the unruly condition of the Egyptian armies. This deficiency was crucial to chances for success of a future invasion by a foreign rival. Ibn Iyas made certain to highlight it as a means of underscoring the cumulative legacy of strain stemming from fissures within the Sultanate's military institution that had become irremediable within the larger web of difficulties impinging upon it. The historian regarded "unruliness" in the army's ranks as a root cause behind its defeat.

# 3 The Mamluk Sultanate from a Global Perspective

The Mamluk Sultanate inherited a centuries-old world view from its Fatimid and Ayyubid forebears, compounded by dedication to preservation of the status quo in foreign affairs. The founding generation of amirs occupied themselves with construction of a cohesive territorial union on the remnants of the Fatimid and Ayyubid empires. Their hegemonic vision was thus shaped by strategic imperatives for supremacy in the eastern Mediterranean and Southwest Asia prevalent three centuries earlier: dominion over the Palestinian corridor, the upper Euphrates marches, the Nile Valley, and the Red Sea.[1] Historically, foreign enemies had passed through Syria to menace Egypt. Accordingly, no alien power could be allowed dominance over the Syrian littoral. Southeastern Anatolia and the Jazira between the Iraqi rivers served as buffers shielding the Sultanate from regimes seen as inherently unstable. The Delta and Upper Valley of Egypt generated the agrarian produce on which the military establishment relied. Protected by surrounding deserts, they were accessible to armies from the south via Aswan, the east from Sinai, and the west along the Mediterranean coast. The Mamluk oligarchy prioritized barring these sites of entry to any hostile regime. Finally, the Red Sea linked the Mediterranean to the Indian subcontinent and East Asia, sources of lucrative foreign commodities passing on to Europe. Until the navigational revolution at the end of the ninth/fifteenth century, the Mamluk Empire straddled one of the most important commercial arteries of interregional trade during the Middle Ages. Its bureaus extracted revenues from the commerce in spices, textiles, and other luxury items transiting the Red Sea entrepôts on their way to consumers on both shores of the Mediterranean (cf. Chapter 5).

Of different but symbolic significance, the holiest cities of Islam were accessed from Red Sea ports. As destinations for thousands of pilgrims, Mecca and Medina lent an aura of legitimacy to the regime, ensuring their safety. From its inception, the Mamluk Sultanate acted as guardian of the holy cities. Since Jerusalem and Hebron also lay within its domain, this state enjoyed a status unique among Muslim empires. No other was so well placed for rendering equivalent service to the Islamic Commonwealth. Protecting the passage of pilgrims and promoting their fulfillment of religious obligations represented fundamental contributions by the Sultanate to the Commonwealth's integrity. Successive rulers emphasized their custodianship over the holy places in titles, inscriptions, and proclamations.

Sultan al-Zahir Baybars (r. 658/1260–676/1277) made a dramatic gesture toward realizing these objectives at the regime's outset when he succeeded in relocating the ʿAbbasid Caliphate to Cairo after its incumbent was executed by the Mongols besieging Baghdad in 656/1258.[2] While the transplanted Caliph exercised no substantive authority and was compelled to preside over the enthronement of whomever the senior amirs acclaimed as sultan, he remained the formal head of the Sunni Islamic community. His presence in Cairo lent respectability to a regime that sought to mitigate the stigma of its origins as a junta that had eliminated a legitimate dynastic ruler. The Sultanate's foreign rivals did not allow its rulers to forget that they had initiated their careers as slaves, imported from regions peopled by unbelievers. The Mamluk oligarchy thus nurtured the ʿAbbasid "Shadow Caliphs" until the regime's demise. Following his victory, the Ottoman Sultan Selim I abstained from assuming the title.

These strategic and symbolic principles pertained to the past, however. The early Mamluk sultans built their reputations as monarchs of international stature by defeating enemies whose agendas of conquest no longer resonated with a shifting global order. They had repelled Mongol invaders from Central Asia and expelled Crusader occupiers from Western Europe, both representatives of ideologies or incentives outmoded by the late ninth/fifteenth century. Changes in military technology and maritime practice were limiting the capacity of nomadic tribes from the Central Asian outback to overrun sedentary populations or monopolize trade routes. Intimidating as they were, the predations of Timur Lenk (Tamerlane, r. 771/1369–807/1405) marked the end of an epoch rather than presaging a future one. The peculiar combination of commercial pragmatism, religious fervor, and territorial ambition that had ignited the Crusader movement in the eleventh century could no longer be resurrected in the Europe of 1500. The crude mercantilism that had motivated Italian trading states to finance the Crusader enterprise had now been replaced by more sophisticated concepts of international markets, integrated currencies, and negotiated relations with governments irrespective of their religion (cf. Chapter 5). These republics viewed the Mamluk Empire as a partner with which one did business. Its cooperation mattered more than its confrontation.

Throughout its tenure, the Mamluk Sultanate sought to preserve hegemony over its disparate territories by upholding the status quo it had assumed from the Crusader and Mongol periods. For a century and a half, the regime succeeded. During the reigns of rulers who pursued military agendas outside Egypt such as Baybars, al-Mansur Qalawun (678/1279–689/1290), al-Nasir Muhammad I (third r. 709/1310–741/1341), al-Ashraf Barsbay (r. 825/1422–841/1437), or al-Ashraf Qayitbay (872/1476–901/1496), rival states acknowledged an effective equilibrium championed by the Mamluks that assured a balance of power, if not full peace, in this turbulent zone. But after 1450, shifts in the world order manifested themselves obtrusively. In Iran and Iraq, a new kind of overlord was forging aggressive confederacies from the patchwork of nomadic tribes and caravan towns that had emerged in the aftermath of the Mongols and Timurids. At the close of the fifteenth century, this region produced a charismatic leader in the person ofIsmaʿil Safawi, who exploited Twelver Shiʿi dogma and imperialist drive to create an ideologically cohesive kingdom in the Persian heartland for the first time since the Mongol invasions.

Further west, the frontier principality (*beylik*) of ʿUthman, on the threshold of the Byzantine remnant, had expanded into a formidable military power with dominion over territories in Europe and Asia. By the latter decades of the ninth/fifteenth century, the Ottomans' conquests had brought them disquietingly close to the Mamluk frontiers. They now posed as rivals with little respect for the status quo. Finally, the Europeans had emerged as shapers of commercial dealings in the international marketplace. Their societies were in the process of creating economic institutions that were aggressive, expansive, and dismissive of extant spheres of influence. Bureaucrats and merchants in Mamluk service minimally sensed their own growing dependence on European crafts and currency sources, but they found the European presence in both the Mediterranean and Red Seas a tangible threat. Therefore, by 1500 the Mamluk Sultanate was facing the emergence of a new global system. How did it respond?

Mamluk foreign policy aimed, as its primary objective, at preserving stasis. While such a goal may seem uninspiring to modern strategists, it was rooted in practical experience with interstate relations in the central Islamic lands. The superficial fragility of ties between sovereign states and their clients in this region masked a set of concepts all shared to varying degrees. While many competed for suzerainty, regional prominence, or control over trade routes, few envisioned realigning the profile of international politics they had inherited from the post-Mongol order. Principles of universal Islamic empire under the Prophet's Caliph-successors now found their expression primarily in cultural and religious patterns mutually embraced by most polities in the area. After the passing of Mongol hegemony, local rivalries posed few challenges to these patterns, since the temporary dominance of one regime over its neighbors rarely resulted in profound cultural or religious discontinuity. Following disruptions inflicted by the Mongol invasions, resurgent regimes laid considerable store on preservation of traditions from the earlier classical era. Since change was more likely to disturb or disorient than to invigorate or renew, the Mamluk Sultanate in particular looked back to achievements of an idealized golden age rather than forward to an uncertain future. Maintenance of stasis assured continuity of political systems that enabled these traditions to endure.

The Mamluk Sultanate, caretaker of the ʿAbbasid Caliphate as noted above, posed as regional champion of Sunni orthodoxy. The Caliph's presence gave Cairo primacy of diplomatic protocol over other Muslim capitals. Princes or chieftains recently ensconced by coups often requested formal confirmation of their positions from the Caliph in Cairo. His unique authority to grant such endorsements lent the sultan who protected him a prestige no other Muslim ruler could claim. During the fourteenth and fifteenth centuries, Cairo was recognized as the preeminent seat of authority among Sunni Muslims. Envoys ascended to the Citadel to pay their respects and present the sultan with entreaties for support, proposals for regulating trade, requests for safe transit, and pleas for sanctuary from rivals or hostile relatives. Mamluk sultans, several of whom owed their thrones to intrigue or had seized them by force, cherished the status they enjoyed in consequence of patronizing the Commander of Believers. His presence symbolized idealized traditions from the golden age they sought to emulate.

Since the Mamluk military hierarchy was composed of slave-soldiers imported from foreign lands (or descended from those who had) and trained for years before performing their allotted duties, their purchase and schooling were costly. The regime husbanded its investment by avoiding losses on the battlefront. Although the performance of Mamluk armies was impressive, the relative paucity of their campaigns after Qalawun's death in 689/1290 bespeaks the regime's reluctance to squander its reserve of seasoned troops. The Mamluk Sultanate routinely brandished its military apparatus before visiting dignitaries in elaborate displays. But it exhausted the diplomatic measures in its chancery's arsenal before resorting to armed conflict. Few doubted the Mamluks' combat ability if compelled to use it. But ritual shows of strength often sufficed to dissuade a rival from open confrontation.

## Statecraft

In light of these motives for caution and restraint, the axioms of Mamluk statecraft reveal their rationale. These may be summarized as follows: commitment to coexistence, reliance on negotiation to resolve disputes, recognition of mutually defined spheres of influence, and acknowledgment of strategic and commercial interests superseding political or sectarian differences between states. Officials in the Mamluk bureaucracy noted distinctions between coexistence and peace. The former implied resignation to the reality of a potentially hostile rival's presence, without according it formal recognition or confronting it in open warfare. This nuanced approach enabled the Mamluk chancery to deal with any state whose pragmatic objectives coincided with its own while expending little time soul-searching over that state's internal behavior or confession. A commitment to coexistence provided the Sultanate a convenient means of bypassing declaration of Jihad, or holy war, against an enemy of Islam. As self-proclaimed defenders of Sunni Orthodoxy, sultans paid lip service to this hallowed principle of communal defense. In practice, they devised excuses to avoid it. Implementation of Jihad would compromise the regime's fundamental imperative of upholding the status quo.

By the time of its late maturity, the Mamluk Sultanate had refined its diplomatic procedures. Receptions for emissaries were staged according to protocols initiated hundreds of years earlier and elaborated over the centuries. Honors shown a guest, the sultan's degree of intimacy toward him, terms employed in salutations, and the relative munificence of gifts exchanged established an ambassador's rank and the weight of his patron's missive before any negotiations began. These might be superficial if a policy decision had already been made or substantive if an emissary brought with him a detailed treaty agenda, outlining privileges of foreign merchants, delimiting borders, encompassing zones of free trade, or resolving longstanding disputes. A decision to organize a military expedition would be reached only after discussions failed.

The roster of treaties Mamluk rulers and their counselors negotiated with their contemporaries in both Christian and Muslim states discloses the Sultanate's conception of world order as a network of interlocking interests, each dependent on the others for efficient transfer of commodities, setting of tariffs, assurance of safe conduct and diplomatic immunity, and guarantee of access to holy places.[3] The Mamluk regime upheld the principle of shared interests as an overreaching goal outweighing parochial quarrels or religious differences. These axioms thus aimed at maintaining the prevalent balance of power. The extant rank and prerogatives of rulers would be defended, since the Mamluk sultan already claimed primacy in the hierarchy of monarchs and could only lose stature in the advent of change. Preservation of stasis thus became an ideal fundamental to the regime's stance. The Sultanate eschewed deviations from this objective. Unfamiliar ideologies of relations between states, expansive visions of imperialism, or experiments with untried styles of diplomacy found minimal receptivity. The inclination for their reception remained ambivalent if not hostile. So long as no rival regime initiated such experiments, the Sultanate managed to maintain its primacy. When radical changes altered the political map, the regime faced challenges.

## The Syrian Littoral: Suzerainty versus Autonomy

Attempts by Egyptian rulers to control the Syrian corridor date back to the Pharaonic era in Antiquity. Following the Arab Conquest, Egypt extended its hegemony over this heterogeneous region intermittently during the Tulunid and Fatimid periods (254/868–292/905, 297/909–567/1171 respectively).

Under the Ayyubids (from 564/1169), the sultan in Cairo formally presided over a federation of principalities extending to al-Jazira and ruled semi-autonomously by branches of the dynasty. Sporadically interrupted by insurgencies from within or foreign incursions, Egyptian authority under the Mamluks would be restored when an oligarchy capable of mustering a strong expeditionary force reasserted itself in Cairo.[4] The strategic necessity of securing the Syrian corridor from hostile powers had outranked all other contingencies from the perspective of sultans and their colleagues since the reign of al-Zahir Baybars. This architect of the Mamluk state invested his energies throughout his career to subduing Ayyubid claimants, Crusader remnants, or rebellious officers in the Syrian towns who profited from the new regime's consolidation to declare their dissociation (cf. Chapter 1). Once they had subdued residual opposition, Baybars and his eventual successor Qalawun established the distinctive model alternating between dominion and autonomy that would characterize Syro-Egyptian relations until the Sultanate's termination.

The region was divided into two main provinces. Damascus (*Dimashq, al-Shām*) exercised military jurisdiction over central and southern Syria (the term "Palestine" [ar. *Filasṭīn*] resonated in local parlance from Roman times but had no political designation during the Mamluk period).[5] It included: Jerusalem (*al-Quds*), Nablus, Safad, Hebron (*al-Khalīl*), and the fortress of al-Karak, district garrison for territories east of the Jordan River. Second was Aleppo (*Ḥalab*), with authority over Hims, Hama, Beirut, Tripoli (*Ṭarābulus*), and more distantly several march towns in southeastern Anatolia (prominently: *Adana*, *ʿAynṭāb* [Gaziantep], *al-Bīra*, *Diyār Bakr*, *Ilbistān*, *Malaṭya*, *Marʿash*, *al-Ruhā* [Edessa] and *Ṭarsūs*) (**Fig. 3.1**). For administrative centers of secondary rank, the sultan appointed governors (ar. *nuwwāb*) from medial echelons of his officers, most of whom had emerged to notability in his corps of favored troops (*al-khaṣṣakiyya*). Those he reserved for the two provincial capitals, effectively as viceroys, were chosen from the circle of his closest colleagues. These individuals, in Arabic "deputy sultans" (*nuwwāb al-salṭana*), had usually risen to the apex of the military hierarchy as grand amirs of one hundred and commanders of a thousand. They already presided over vast households and troop detachments of their own before they assumed their postings in Syria. Placing senior officers who had matured in Cairo and had attained distinction in statecraft was considered essential to inculcating the identity that bound these primary provincial centers to Cairo, seat of imperial power.

But their appointment carried risks. All of these officers, whether based in the two provincial capitals or the more peripheral centers, were steeped in the factional rivalries of the imperial metropolis. Despite their exercise of executive authority locally, many regarded their appointments as temporary – and involuntary – separations from participation in the politics that drove the

Fig. 3.1 Citadel at Aleppo
Constructed seventh/thirteenth to tenth/sixteenth centuries; detail of ramp connecting upper and lower entry gates.
(Credit: Luis Dafos/Getty Images)

regime and aimed at its supreme office. They longed to return and chafed in their provincial postings they considered virtual exile. Several plotted to rally contingents from their garrisons to aid them in their bids for attainment of a high position in the Cairo oligarchy or the Sultanate itself. Others were satisfied to remain entrenched at their stations with local authority and exploited their autonomy to build personal fiefdoms planned to last their careers. Still others were prepared to connive with rulers of regional powers who challenged the Cairo Sultanate's stance of imperial hegemony. All of them imitated the cultural and political milieus they had grown up with in the capital to varying degrees. The unity over which they presided created a special kind of interdependence between Egypt and Syria that could bolster its security cordon while weathering the episodes of sedition that periodically roiled it.

The control exercised by viceroys sent from Cairo was paralleled by the influence of a civil bureaucracy and judiciary also appointed by the central regime. Similar to the policy prevalent in the capital, four senior justices (ar. *qāḍī/quḍāh*), one per canonical school of law (*madhhab*), presided over a host of subordinates in Damascus and Aleppo, whose jurisdiction reached to outlying districts inhabited largely by villagers and Bedouin pastoralists.

The sultan allowed viceroys some leeway in choosing personnel to staff their administrative bureaucracies but retained his prerogative of selecting the senior magistrates. Upon the advice of their four counterparts in Cairo, he balanced prominent representatives of local ʿulamaʾ families against Cairenes whose reputations were established before they assumed their provincial judgeships. The senior levels of the Syrian judiciary therefore comprised a second component of an imperial system that bound the regional capitals to the ruling center. A fraternity of legist-scholars, many of whom had studied in lecture circles at the same madrasas in Cairo, served as penultimate appellate judges and interpreters of a uniform Sunni Shariʿ tradition throughout this politically fractious zone.

Appointees to governorships in the provincial capitals or district centers ran the gamut from potential insurgents whose ambitions looked either to supplanting the autocrat or carving out an autonomous principality, to officers with parochial visions, content with authority over a locale and loyal to the sovereign who had ensconced them in it. An outstanding example of the latter during the Sultanate's so-called ascendant phase may be seen in the career of the Amir Tankiz al-Husami al-Nasiri, confidant of Sultan al-Nasir Muhammad ibn Qalawun.[6] This individual was imported to Cairo for training as a cadet after Sultan Qalawun's death in 689/1290. Purchased by Qalawun's son and heir al-Ashraf Khalil, he was acquired by his eventual successor al-Mansur Lajin but was passed on to al-Nasir Muhammad following his second accession upon Lajin's murder in 698/1299. Tankiz was formally manumitted and advanced to the rank of Khassaki by al-Nasir Muhammad, to whom he owed his early career and cemented ties as a comrade (*khushdāsh*). Tankiz participated in the battle of Wadi al-Khazindar near Hims (699/1299), which resulted in Ghazan Khan's defeat of al-Nasir's forces but distinction for Tankiz who rendered his patron military service that was noticed and appreciated. When Sultan al-Nasir scored a decisive victory over the Ilkhanids at Marj al-Suffar near Damascus (702/1303), terminating the Mongol threat to Syria, Tankiz attained further renown.

Al-Nasir's defeat of the Ilkhanids did not resolve competition among aggressive amirs for his office in Cairo. When he withdrew to al-Karak a second time, his khushdash Tankiz accompanied him. During al-Nasir's campaign to regain his position (cf. Chapter 1), he sent Tankiz to the governor of Damascus, Jamal al-Din Aqush al-Afram, with a missive inviting his support against the reigning Sultan in Cairo, al-Muzaffar Baybars II. Since al-Afram remained loyal to Baybars, he dealt with Tankiz as a provocateur and reluctantly released him only after harsh treatment and a stay in prison. Upon his return to al-Karak, al-Nasir promised to replace al-Afram with Tankiz as Na'ib al-Sham, which he did two years after his ascension to the Sultanate the third time in Shawwal 709/March 1310.

Al-Nasir's installation of Tankiz in this highest provincial office broke precedent since he had not advanced to the penultimate rank of amir mi'a wa-muqaddam alf, after a proven record of service to the sovereign. His appointment was indicative of al-Nasir's own departure from the *cursus honorum* for advancement to senior posts established by the regime's founders. Al-Nasir looked for empathy and trust among his subordinates while holding officers who had attained their status by demonstrating a knack for aggression and conspiracy suspect, however exemplary their military performance. Tankiz fulfilled his patron's expectations and went on to a career as Na'ib al-Sham that lasted almost three decades.

Tankiz ruled the Damascus Province as a vice sultan, acting as principal intermediary between the ruler and governors of the other Syrian provinces and districts. Missives to and from the sovereign passed his inspection, enabling Tankiz, as al-Nasir's essential conduit, to at once rein in amirs who were potential insurgents and provide his patron with intelligence and advice about their own stratagems and those of foreign rivals. Tankiz's unswerving loyalty and service were the decisive qualities that bound him to al-Nasir as his prime khushdash. Familial ties cemented this exceptional camaraderie. Tankiz gave al-Nasir the slave Tughay, whom the sultan made his favored concubine and second wife. He bestowed one of his daughters on al-Nasir in marriage. Two of al-Nasir's daughters married Tankiz's sons.

Tankiz went on to parallel his sovereign's agenda for massive urban renewal in Cairo by initiating a building program in Damascus that had no antecedent. Tankiz's biographers listed a host of imposing structures constructed out of the viceroy's personal fortune: mosques, madrasas, libraries, Sufi hospices, caravansaries, bridges, gardens, and orchards, not only in the city but elsewhere in the province of al-Sham. The sums they recorded as paid out for their construction were similarly exceptional. Tankiz's effective reign as the "Malik al-Sham" impacted the cultural milieu in Damascus as well. The spurt of Damascene scholarly writing – in particular belles-lettres, history, and theology – prompted by his largesse would establish Syrian authors as a group distinct from their Egyptian counterparts in both theme and quality during the later medieval period (cf. Chapter 6).

Yet, the camaraderie that bound Tankiz to al-Nasir Muhammad for almost three decades did not counteract the fear of betrayal endemic to the Mamluk oligarchy. In 740/1340, Sultan al-Nasir Muhammad arrested Tankiz, confiscated his fortune, imprisoned him in Alexandria, and finally had him executed. Reasons circulating by rumor involved insinuations of latent treachery by amirs angling for power around the aging sultan. The extent of Tankiz's fortune and its potential for attracting insurgents also caused al-Nasir unease. Contemporary historians considered Tankiz's removal from office as the end of a "golden age" in Damascus during the late medieval period. The city's subsequent history was marked by an unsettled economy and political turbulence, paralleling the decades of tension in Cairo that intervened between al-Nasir Muhammad's death and the accession of al-Zahir Barquq (784/1382).

From the mid-eighth/fourteenth through the ninth/fifteenth centuries, Damascene politics broadly reflected conditions throughout the Syrian provinces that persisted into the Ottoman occupation. Feuds smoldering among garrison officers, often within the same town, periodically erupted into open conflict. Troop factions lined up behind their commanders to pillage the civilian populace. Compounding their vendettas was a trend toward extortion by fiscal officials sent from Cairo to collect taxes and monitor trade. As the central regime sought to counter insolvency through clandestine measures of acquiring revenue, it became more tolerant of similar procedures in the provinces. Inhabitants of Syrian towns reacted more violently against such oppression than did their counterparts in Cairo, where the largest troop contingents were stationed and police authorities were more brutally effective. A vivid example of popular resistance occurred in Damascus during Sultan Qayitbay's reign. In Safar 882/May–June 1477, the sultan's intendant of military fiefs (*nāẓir al-jaysh*), Shihab al-Din Ahmad al-Nabulusi, was attacked by a mob for hoarding wheat stores.[7] Al-Nabulusi had speculated in construction licenses, selling building rights to contractors who skirted structural codes for the highest fees. He aided acquisitive heirs to propertied estates in their plans to alienate religious trusts. He had profited from stockpiling grain reserved for troop rations, selling it when prices rose steeply and placating squadron leaders for the loss with bribes. Assigned by Qayitbay to supply his quota of tax revenues, few questions asked, he reliably met his patron's requests. The masses reached their limit when bread became scarce. They drove al-Nabulusi from his residence, set it ablaze, and pursued him to the Umayyad Mosque, where he sought sanctuary until a commission of inquiry arrived from Cairo several weeks later. When Qayitbay was apprised of al-Nabulusi's devices, he ordered his imprisonment and confiscated his fortune (estimated to exceed a million dinars). The commission addressed many claims from plaintiffs over sums al-Nabulusi had allegedly swindled from them. While litigation dragged on for years, the chroniclers dwelled on al-Nabulusi's case primarily because of its notoriety. Many officials similarly implicated managed to evade restitution and retired with their gains intact. And despite the undercurrent of corruption, rhythms of official business in the provinces continued unaffected. The narrative sources are replete with references to the Sultanate's agents traveling from Cairo to the Syrian towns bearing edicts requisitioning supplies, altering tariffs, or setting infantry quotas from local militias.

From the unstable years following Sultan al-Nasir Muhammad's death, the potential for sedition on the part of viceroys in Syria who contemplated supplanting their sovereign in Cairo perturbed every sultan who suspected his subordinates' ambitions. Their worries intensified during the last half-century before the Ottoman occupation in 922/1517. Sultan Qansawh al-Ghawri in particular had reason to be wary of his appointees. Syrian partisans of his Atabak, Qayt al-Rajabi, schemed to unseat him and acclaim the marshal as sultan.[8] The inciter of their plot, the governor of Tarabulus, Dawlatbay, had been a partisan of the former sultan al-ᶜAdil Tuman Bay, now incarcerated by al-Ghawri in Alexandria. Dawlatbay broke his allegiance to al-Ghawri in 910/1504. He convinced the viceroy of Aleppo, Sibay, to join his insurgency. Dawlatbay took control of northern Syria and proceeded south toward Damascus. He and Qayt al-Rajabi had secretly planned to partition the Empire. Once the Atabak joined his ally in Damascus, the two would combine forces, march on Cairo, rally disaffected officers, and dethrone al-Ghawri. Dawlatbay and Sibay would subsequently divide Syria between them while Qayt assumed power in Egypt. Al-Ghawri became aware of this conspiracy immediately before Qayt was scheduled to depart, ostensibly on an inspection tour of Syria. The sultan arrested al-Rajabi and designated a more reliable associate, Azdamur al-Dawadar, to lead the tour.

When news of al-Rajabi's arrest reached Syria, enthusiasm for the rebellion evaporated. The Aleppo viceroy, Sibay, concluded that he stood to gain more autonomy in his base by reconciling with al-Ghawri rather than risking an open break.[9] In Rabiᶜ I 911/August 1505, Sibay sent a mediator to profess his renewed loyalty if a pardon were extended to him. He was prepared to submit personally before the sultan at the Citadel in Cairo if protected by a writ of safe-conduct (*amāna*). Al-Ghawri granted his request and received him in the audience hall. Sibay arrived carrying his mantle of office with his personal emblems torn off as a sign of submission. Al-Ghawri forgave him and offered to appoint him viceroy of Damascus – which was a shrewd move on several counts. The current Na'ib al-Sham, Arikmas min Tarabay, had alienated all factions of civil notables in the city and was driven out by an angry mob. Al-Ghawri offered the most prestigious governorship in the Empire to a capable administrator in return for his oath of loyalty. Sibay swore his allegiance on an ᶜUthmani copy of the Qur'an, which the Caliph held out to him. Sibay then signed a written pledge of obedience witnessed by all four senior magistrates. Sibay upheld his vow. In return, he exercised unchallenged rule over Damascus for the next eleven years while acknowledging al-Ghawri's suzerainty.

Compounding the threat of sedition by Mamluk governors was the problem of Bedouin predation. The Syrian Sahel was inhabited largely by desert nomads. Some districts, such as Nablus and Hawran, lay under the control of semi-sedentary shaykhs whose succession Cairo symbolically confirmed. Other tribal confederations roved widely, raiding villagers and townspeople when they perceived weakness within provincial Mamluk garrisons.[10] During the Sultanate's later decades, the tribe of Al Fadl pillaged Hama and other north Syrian towns frequently. Qayitbay's ambitious adjutant, the Dawadar Yashbak min Mahdi, engaged in his unlucky bid for independent authority on the pretense of apprehending the tribe's aggressive chief, Sayf, who had taken shelter in the town of al-Ruha (Edessa). Yashbak's miscalculation of its commander's resistance led to his capture and execution (cf. Chapter 2). Among the boldest raiders were the Banu Lam, who plundered districts east of the Jordan. Stories circulated in Cairo of fantastical beings so formidable that the redoubtable tribe fled their territories.[11] In 896/1491, the governor of al-Karak reported their repeated encounters with a demon of human shape but monstrous size who feasted on raw flesh. Depleting the Banu Lam's herds, this creature was impervious to arrow or lance wounds and devoured his attackers alive if he caught them. The Banu Lam allegedly abandoned their grazing grounds and turned to raiding because of their intimidation. Whether such tales were fanciful or based on some kernel of fact, they underscored the looseness of Mamluk authority over the Bedouin of Syria. As the Sultanate's internal difficulties worsened, these tribes intensified their predation.

By the turn of the tenth/sixteenth century, the Syrian provinces were restive within the Mamluk orbit. Tied to the ruling institution in Cairo more than two centuries earlier as a barrier to invasion, these districts now exhibited antipathy over control from Egypt. Since their own military contingents had eroded the sultan's suzerainty, they responded ambivalently to his calls for muster when he planned expeditions against foreign regimes they were covertly prepared to acknowledge. After Qansawh al-Ghawri's army scattered in defeat before Selim I, survivors found no haven in the garrison towns of Syria. Both inhabitants and prescient commanders were ready to shift their allegiance to the more successful invader.

## Al-Hijaz: The Hasanid Sharifate between Mamluk Amirs and Clan Rivals

The Mamluk Sultanate claimed the Hijaz (Western Arabian Peninsula) as part of the legacy it inherited from the Ayyubids. The region's central political figures were Sharifs in Mecca descended from Hasan ibn Abi Talib (and thus the Prophet Muhammad's lineage via his first cousin). They established themselves in the Holy City during the fourth/tenth century.[12] The Sharifs extended their direct rule over Mecca's environs, the neighboring town of al-Ta'if, and the port of Jidda on the Red Sea. More than 200 miles northeast, the oasis town of Medina, seat of the Prophet's post-Hijra mission and burial, lay outside their jurisdiction and was governed by another (often rival) branch of the Hasanid line. Salah al-Din Yusuf (Saladin), founder of the Ayyubid

Sultanate in Cairo, authorized his brother, Turan Shah, to cross the Red Sea from Upper Egypt to invade the Hijaz and Yemen (569–70/1174–75). Although reassertion of Egyptian control and restoration of Sunni primacy over the holy cities remained the dynasty's formal reasons behind their occupation, reaping gains from taxes (*ᶜmaks/mukūs*) on the lucrative trade from South Asia through the Red Sea figured large among their motives.[13] Salah al-Din himself had abolished the tax previously authorized by the Fatimids on pilgrims who arrived for the Hajj or ᶜUmra (noncompulsory pilgrimage), in part to diminish the financial burden on making the voyage that had substantially reduced the numbers who elected to depart from Egypt. Salah al-Din aimed to make up revenues lost to the Sharifs by granting them a yearly subsidy in dinars and grain. His Ayyubid and Mamluk successors would periodically renew the policy, at least in principle, since in practice lapses occurred frequently and provided Sharifs with excuses to renew the impost on pilgrims.

Sharifs of Mecca during the late Ayyubid and Mamluk periods may be traced back to the reign of an amir who belonged to a branch of the Hasanid line based near the coastal town of Yanbuᶜ: Qatada ibn Idris (b. ca. 540/1145–46).[14] After rallying tribes in Yanbuᶜ's vicinity, Qatada drove the incumbent Sharifs from Mecca (597/1201) and engaged upon a campaign to assert its isolation from political control by the ᶜAyyubids in Cairo or religious authority by the ᶜAbbasid Caliph in Baghdad. Qatada never managed to dislodge the Hasanid amirs of Medina but died at his son Hasan's hand while planning an expedition against the oasis town (618/1221). Hasan's act was motivated by trepidation over his father's preference of a relative to succeed him. His own tenure was compromised since the Ayyubid amir in Yemen, al-Masᶜud Yusuf, reimposed the dynasty's direct control over Mecca two years later (619/1223). Since the Ayyubids' restoration in Mecca was itself brief due to their supplanting in Yemen by the Rasulids (629/1232), political authority over the town would alternate between the two dynasties until the ascension of the next significant Sharif, Abu Numayy Muhammad, whose rule would approach half a century (652/1254–700/1301). Sharif Abu Numayy proved himself adroit at navigating shifts in political currents throughout the region. Accurately forecasting the power of the Mamluk regime's architect, al-Zahir Baybars, as an empire builder, Abu Numayy pledged his allegiance and received Baybars's endorsement of his own position over his rival uncle, Idris. In return for acknowledging Mamluk suzerainty in Mecca, signaled by recitation of Baybars's titles during Friday prayer in its Great Mosque, Abu Numayy received an annual stipend of 20,000 dirhams from the Sultan, formally to eliminate the pilgrim tax.

Baybars made the Hajj to Mecca in 667/1269 and compelled the Sharif to swear an oath not to reimpose the tax on pilgrims who joined the caravan from

Egypt to reach the holy cities. Abu Numayy complied until Baybars's death in 676/1277, after which he reinstated it. Assessment of the pilgrim tax would fluctuate along with excises on commodities arriving from South Asia according to interventions on the part of sultans in Cairo and their adjutants assigned to Mecca and Jidda. Members of the Qatadid house who contested among themselves for the Amirate of Mecca (the Sultanate's title for the Sharifal office) would proclaim the abolition of these taxes as a means of garnering the regime's endorsement. While sultans continued to oppose the pilgrim tax, they were less immune to the allure of proceeds from excises on expensive wares from India. After the death of al-Nasir Muhammad ibn Qalawun (741/1341), rising revenues generated from these taxes paralleled increases in the volume of trade in South Asian commodities (prominently silk and spices) offloaded in Jidda for passage to the Mediterranean and Europe. Given the fiscal stringencies confronting the Sultanate that became chronic during the interval between al-Nasir's demise and al-Zahir Barquq's ascension (784/1382), the Cairo Sultanate intensified its control over Mecca and Jidda to secure a revenue source that steadily inflated. Jidda's centrality as a port was on the rise. Dissolution of the Ilkhanate in Iran and Iraq had lessened the viability of the overland route from South and East Asia while the Egyptian Red Sea port at Aydhab no longer served as a significant transit site.

Throughout the second half of the eighth/fourteenth century, tensions fluctuated between Mamluk agents, Meccan Sharifs, and Rasulid rulers in Yemen for overseeing regional politics and maximizing gains from commercial taxes. These tensions were complicated by contradictions between idealized principle and pragmatic gain. In 766/1365, Sultan al-Ashraf Shaᶜban issued a decree revoking excises of all kinds in the Holy City and its port. Since revenue losses to the Sharifs were considerable, Shaᶜban authorized an annual subsidy of 160,000 dirhams from the royal treasury, a policy certain to alarm fiscal officials in Cairo and a possible reason for the sultan's eventual removal. When Meccan politics stabilized again during the long reign of Sharif Hasan ibn ᶜAjlan, a descendant of Abu Numayy (798/1395–829/1426 with interregnum), the Sharif took measures to promote Jidda's monopoly over commerce from South Asia, which in turn prompted the Sultanate to intervene more directly in Sharifian politics. Hasan reconciled with the Rasulid regime in Yemen to end their embargo of Jidda against ships transiting Aden into the Red Sea. His policy reaped gains from customs duties substantial enough to motivate a complex response from Cairo that would be repeated under various guises until the Sultanate's termination. During the reigns of al-Muʾayyad Shaykh and his three ephemeral successors (815/1412–825/1422), regime amirs were sent to Mecca and Jidda leading troop squadrons ostensibly to abolish taxes on pilgrims and foodstuffs. Unofficially, they arrived to tighten their control over the two towns and enlarge the regime's share of their commercial taxes. The monopolies, imposed over a host of commodities processed domestically or transiting from abroad that became a signal prop of the Sultanate's fiscal policy under Barsbay, germinated as a concept during these interventions in Sharifian politics ordered by his predecessors.

Sultan Barsbay (r. 825/1422–941/1438) installed Hasan's son, Barakat, as Sharif of Mecca at a formal ceremony in Cairo upon his father's death (829/1426).[15] The son had assumed Hasan's duties several years earlier (821/1418) and was experienced at dealing with the Sultanate's officers. Barsbay extracted an oath from Barakat that he comply with the Sultanate's primacy as collector of customs duties. But Barsbay also recognized the advantage of working with a subordinate who stood to gain from the relationship and who faced potential resistance from parties denied a share they were accustomed to receive.[16] When members of Barakat's ʿAjlan clan protested being left out, the sultan agreed to restore to Barakat a third of the total yield from excises on cargoes arriving from South Asia. Barsbay also allowed the Sharif to retain yields from taxes on cargoes from Egypt, Yemen, and the Maghrib. Barakat managed to retain his office for several decades until his death (829/1426–859/1455), although he was unseated by his brothers, ʿAli and Abu'l-Qasim, between 845/1442 and 850/1446. Barsbay increased Barakat's allowance to 50 percent in 840/1436–37, but when al-Zahir Jaqmaq (r. 842/1438–857/1453) succeeded him, he reduced it to a quarter and claimed three-fourths of proceeds from all other excises. Jaqmaq demanded Barakat's presence in Cairo several times to inventory his receipts, and when the Sharif refused, the sultan replaced him with ʿAli (845/1441), then resident in Cairo. Jaqmaq sent ʿAli at the head of a substantial force before which Barakat departed to seek refuge in Yemen, where he raised a following sufficient for his recapture of Mecca and Jidda.

Barakat confronted merchants and vessel captains with exorbitant tax increases, proceeds from which he claimed exclusively.[17] His brother ʿAli then drove Barakat out a second time but was himself supplanted by Abu'l-Qasim, who arrived with the pilgrimage caravan from Egypt bearing the sultan's endorsement. Mecca and Jidda remained roiled between disputes among clan factions aligned with the contending brothers, who repeatedly violated interim agreements. Finally, an ʿalim resident in Mecca, ʿAbd al-Kabir ibn ʿAbd Allah al-Hadrami, negotiated a settlement they were prepared to accept (848/1445). Abu'l-Qasim agreed to remit Barakat a sum amounting to 2000 ducats in three allotments over several months and grant him a third of the Sharif's share of duties collected in Jidda. Whether the Sultanate's portion was reallocated the settlement did not specify, although a substantive decrease is unlikely. In any case, two years later Barakat regained the Sharifate, again with the Sultanate's manipulative backing. He held it until his death, upon which his son Muhammad succeeded. Abu'l-Qasim died in Cairo (853/1449) after a futile attempt to win back the Sultanate's support.

Sharif Muhammad was destined for a reign that was lengthy (859/1455–903/1497) and stable compared to his predecessors'. Three sultans – Inal, Khushqadam and Qayitbay – presided over the Empire during his tenure. Several senior officers oversaw the regime's monitoring of taxes, notable among whom was an amir initially installed as customs inspector (*shadd*) by Jaqmaq: Janibak al-Zahiri (849/1445).[18] Janibak succeeded in enhancing the regime's percentage of customs revenues to the extent that he was acknowledged as the virtual "viceroy" (*nāʾib*) of Jidda, despite the informal status of this title. He also amassed a fortune that enabled him to purchase several villages in Egypt and Syria, which he converted into trusts (*awqāf*) for his personal use. Janibak rose to the pinnacle of the ruling oligarchy in Cairo through Jaqmaq's remaining years and Inal's reign. When he was appointed grand secretary (*dawādār*) and majordomo (*ustādār*), he was compelled to resign his position in Jidda. Yet, he was reinstated three more times because of his consistent increase of tax proceeds. Janibak recognized that his performance as shadd was responsible for his ascent and preferred his residence in Jidda to the tension-ridden milieu of regime politics in Cairo. His apprehension was astute since, following Khushqadam's enthronement, the new sultan feared his influence over the faction of Zahiri amirs in Cairo, despite the support Janibak had proffered him against his competitors. Khushqadam plotted Janibak's assassination in 867/1463, a fate he might have avoided had he remained in Jidda.

Shifts in tax policies by amirs of Yemen adversely affected the numbers of vessels from South Asia offloading their cargos in Jidda during Qayitbay's reign. In the final decades of the ninth/fifteenth century, the Rasulids reduced their excises to render their port at Aden more competitive in comparison with Jidda, where rates were rising. Qayitbay had initially issued decrees equalizing shares received by the regime and the Sharif. But during the 890s/1490s, fiscal exigencies in Cairo compelled the sultan to increase the regime's take until by 899/1494 the state demanded them all, leaving the Sharifate officially with none. Whether these decrees were effectively enforced is unclear from spotty evidence. And when Qansawh al-Ghawri commenced upon the Sultanate's final phase, dramatic shifts in the international scene would alter the status of both Aden and Jidda.

The Portuguese rounded Africa and entered the Indian Ocean at the turn of the tenth/sixteenth century. They immediately sought to establish bases on the Malabar (Southwest) coast of India and aimed at harassing the Red Sea nautical route. In 911/1505, al-Ghawri sent an expedition commanded by the amir Husayn Mushrif al-Kurdi to aid Mahmud Shah, ruler of Gujarat, that included arquebusiers who had been training outside the formal Mamluk ranks. Amir Husayn fortified Jidda against a possible Portuguese invasion and established a rapport with Sharif Barakat II ibn Muhammad, recently reinstated over his brother Humayda. When the Ottoman Sultan Selim I defeated al-Ghawri in 922/1516 and his nephew Tuman Bay the following year, Sharif Barakat acknowledged his sovereignty; in return, the Ottoman reconfirmed Barakat's office, which he would hold to 931/1525.

## The East Anatolian Marches: Mamluk Suzerainty, Local Ferment

Mamluk influence over territories in southeastern Anatolia north of Aleppo alternated between direct rule and peripheral clientship. Situated between competing regional powers, these marches sporadically asserted claims for local authority in the guise of local dynasties that sought to attain independent sovereignty. Prominent among them was the line of Turkmen amirs (Turkish: beys) who took the title "Dhu'l-Qadr" (Arabic: Possessing Power, Turkish: Dulghadir, Dulqadir) for their principality (*beylik*).[19] Its founder was Qaraja ibn Dulghadir, who in 735/1335 exploited the succession crisis after the death of the Ilkhan Abu Saʿid in Iran to occupy Ilibistan, for which he received a diploma of investiture from Sultan al-Nasir Muhammad two years later. Qaraja lost out in a power struggle with a rival bey, who turned him over to the Sultanate for execution (754/1553). His son Khalil managed to regain some of the Dhu'l-Qadrid patrimony but convinced the Cairo regime that his ambitions challenged their hegemony over the "Euphrates Corridor" north of Aleppo when he advanced upon the Mamluk stronghold in Malatya. Sultan Barquq arranged for his assassination by another Turkmen chief in 788/1386. Khalil's brother Suli allied himself with the Amir Mintash, who had rebelled against Barquq and was assembling a force to overthrow him (cf. Ch. One). Following Mintash's defeat, Suli evaded capture and established contact with Timur Lenk, proposing to guide his invasion into Syria. While Barquq ultimately arranged Suli's murder (800/1398), the Ottoman Sultan Bayazid I decided the succession's eventual outcome by forcing Suli's son out of Ilbistan and establishing Khalil's heir, Nasir al-Din Muhammad, as bey (801/1399).

Muhammad survived Timur's temporary occupation of Anatolia and reigned to 846/1442. Whether he would have retained his autonomous position under Bayazid remains indeterminate, due to the expansionist Ottoman's own defeat and termination by Timur (804/1402). Muhammad skillfully managed to maintain positive relations with both Mamluks and Ottomans. He married one of his daughters to Bayazid's successor, Mehmet I, and another to Sultan Jaqmaq years later. Muhammad participated in Egyptian campaigns against the neighboring Qaraman Beylik, for which he received the central Anatolian town of Kayseri from Sultan al-Mu'ayyad Shaykh. When the Qaramanlis reoccupied Kayseri, the Ottoman Sultan Murad II restored it to Muhammad. The Dhu'l-Qadrid balance between the two Sultanates continued under

Muhammad's successor, Suleiman (r. 846/1442–858/1465), who agreed to a marital alliance between his daughter and Murad's son, the future Mehmet II. But when the Aq-Qoyunlu amir Uzun Hasan (r. 856/1452–882/1478) had designs for hegemony over the region, disputes erupted between Suleiman's sons following his death, backed by their respective sponsors. Suleiman's immediate successor, Malik Arslan, was caught up in tensions between Mamluks and Ottomans as they sought to bolster their positions before the Aq-Qoyunlu threat. In Cairo, Sultan Khushqadam suspected Malik Arslan of weakness after he abandoned Ilbistan to Uzun Hasan. Khushqadam had granted refuge to Malik Arslan's brother, Shah Budaq. After Khushqadam instigated Malik Arslan's assassination in Ilbistan, Dhu'l-Qadrid notables rejected Shah Budaq's claim and appealed to the Ottoman ruler Mehmet II for aid. Mehmet backed the succession of another brother, Shah Suwar, whom he had supported.[20] Mehmet invested Shah Suwar as wali (governor) of territories his father Suleiman had ruled but did not grant him title to the Dhu'l-Qadrid Beylik and omitted Kayseri from its jurisdiction. Yet, Shah Suwar would present the Mamluk Sultanate with one of its severest challenges before the Ottoman Conquest.

Shah Suwar's ultimate goal aimed at creation of an autonomous principality resistant to claims from both the Mamluk and Ottoman Sultanates. It was this threat by an ambitious insurgent prepared to battle his siblings and disrupt the established balance of power that alarmed the ruling oligarchy in Cairo. Shah Suwar's actions later dissuaded the Ottomans under Mehmet's more cautious successor, Bayazid II (r. 886/1481–918/1512), from risking a major confrontation with the Mamluks over dominance in southeastern Anatolia. Since Shah Suwar intended to augment his autonomy from Istanbul by nullifying Mamluk suzerainty on his own terms, the Ottomans were willing to accept elimination of an insubordinate client if he proved incapable of throwing off Cairo's suzerainty. Shah Suwar initiated his campaign by seizing several towns north of Aleppo late in Sultan Khushqadam's reign. He defeated a force sent by Khushqadam to recover them and reinstall Shah Budaq early in 872/1467. Shah Suwar then occupied ʿAyntab (*Gaziantep*), a move that prompted Khushqadam's successor, Qayitbay, to send a second expedition later that year (Dhu'l-Qaʿda 872/May 1468).

When Shah Suwar vanquished this detachment, its effect was traumatic in Cairo. The Mamluk Sultanate's stature as the regional great power had been compromised. The historian Ibn Taghri Birdi depicted the regime's state of depression as follows:

> The populace was agitated. The catastrophe weighed heavily on them all, even the religious minorities (*ahl al-dhimma*). ... The Sultan's despondency was magnified since, as a consequence of these disasters, his valor was diminished by Shah Suwar – the weakest, the least of Turkmen tribesmen. Shah Suwar did battle against the Egyptian army ... the effectiveness of which had been unparalleled. Yet they suffered

defeat at the hands of this lowly man, minimal of power, junior in age, distant from authority. But God's will prevailed.[21]

In the defeat's aftermath, the Sultanate could no longer assume with confidence its hold over Aleppo, northern bastion of Mamluk authority. When Shah Suwar sent adjutants of Qayitbay's Atabak, Janibak Qulaqsiz, commander of the expedition whom he held captive, to demand his ransom, Qayitbay refused compliance to save face. Qulaqsiz's own staff in Cairo had to raise the money. The Egyptian sultan's acceptance of such a demand from a provincial upstart was tantamount to attribution of peer status, a gesture Qayitbay disavowed. Once his regime perceived the gravity of Shah Suwar's threat, offers of adjudication from Shah Suwar were rebuffed. Acceptance of a mediator's credentials symbolized acknowledgment of his overlord's legitimacy, and Qayitbay now resolved to discredit Shah Suwar as a rebel who held stability in contempt. From the Sultanate's perspective, he behaved as an outlaw to be dealt with as a criminal. In subsequent proclamations, the regime referred to Shah Suwar as "the Forsaken" (*al-Makhdhūl*) or "the Dissident" (*al-Khārijī*).[22]

Yet, Shah Suwar's successes gave observers throughout the region pause for reflection over the sultan's apparent incapacity to rein in this rebel. They prompted the Mamluk oligarchy to intensify their efforts to subdue him – to ultimate effect. Shah Suwar's subsequent campaigns, frequently against his own brothers who appealed to Mamluk or Ottoman backing, resulted in less positive outcomes. Sultan Qayitbay finally achieved Shah Suwar's demise in Dhu'l-Hijja 876/June 1472 when his adjutant Yashbak min Mahdi lured Shah Suwar from the fortress to which he had retreated. Violating a promise of safe conduct, Yashbak took Shah Suwar prisoner and brought him to Cairo for trial before the four senior qadis. Condemned as a traitor, Shah Suwar was hanged at the Zuwayla Gate along with three siblings who had stood by him (Rabiᶜ I 877/August 1472).

Sultan Qayitbay and his oligarchy had achieved their immediate objective with Shah Suwar's termination, at a formidable cost in arms and money. But did they realize their larger goal: restoration of the status quo in the marcher zone? Other amirs and beys in the region had observed Qayitbay's handling of the rebellion. If he had failed to remove a rebel from a minor house, how profitable was their own fealty? Suzerain loyalty in these tumultuous times was tenuous. Client chieftains respected an overlord who projected power effectively. Allegiance to a sovereign whose authority was perceived as eroding diminished a client's stature at home. Their own security would require seeking out patronage elsewhere. A rebel's successful pursuit of autonomy encouraged others to consider the option. Shah Suwar's insurgency thus posed a larger danger than his occupation of provincial towns or humiliation of the Sultan's troops. Qayitbay and his colleagues recognized the uprising's broader implications. Unchecked, Shah Suwar might have initiated a domino effect culminating in the Empire's dismemberment. It is in this light that Qayitbay's perseverance and expenditures should be interpreted. His designation of Yashbak finally resuscitated a faltering enterprise and brought Shah Suwar to execution as a traitor. But Shah Suwar's legacy could not be undone. Even though Shah Suwar's rival brother, Shah Budaq, was reinstated as the Sultanate's client, he did not extinguish his sibling's record of insurgency. Nor was Shah Suwar's example lost on more powerful rulers who contemplated challenging the status quo for their own purposes.

Shah Budaq soon found his position contested by another brother who would figure prominently in subsequent events: ʿAlaʾ al-Dawla Bozkurt. ʿAlaʾ al-Dawla had allied himself with the Ottomans toward the end of Mehmet II's reign. He had married a daughter to Mehmet's son, the future Bayazid II. ʿAlaʾ al-Dawla enlisted Ottoman support to supplant Shah Budaq in Dhu'l-Hijja 885/February 1481. ʿAlaʾ al-Dawla proved himself an adroit navigator of the shifting political currents in the marcher zone. He therefore held his position for thirty-five years (885–921/1480–515). Vacillating between alliances with the Mamluk and Ottoman Sultanates, ʿAlaʾ al-Dawla managed to exploit their war, which continued through 896/1490, to occupy strategic fortresses, surrendering them to one side or the other in return for safeguarding his hold over the principality. When Bayazid II decided to depose ʿAlaʾ al-Dawla and restore his brother Shah Budaq a second time (894/1489), ʿAlaʾ al-Dawla successfully enlisted Mamluk support to regain his office. Shah Budaq was exiled to Egypt where he succumbed to the plague.

Over the following two decades ʿAlaʾ al-Dawla engaged in the turbulent events surrounding invasions by the Aq-Qoyunlu amir Uzun Hasan and the meteoric Safavid Shah Ismaʾil. When ʿAlaʾ al-Dawla sought to supplant Safavid control over such strategic towns as Diyar Bakr, he prompted Shah Ismaʾil's occupation of Ilbistan itself. ʿAlaʾ al-Dawla's machinations ultimately aroused the ire of the Ottoman Sultan Selim I Yavuz ("Grim"), who regarded his denial of support for Selim's campaign against Ismaʾil as treasonous. Selim received intelligence that ʿAlaʾ al-Dawla had harassed Ottoman supply lines at the instigation of Sultan Qansawh al-Ghawri. Following Selim's defeat of Ismaʿil at Chaldiran (Shaʿban 920/August 1514), he resolved to eliminate ʿAlaʾ al-Dawla and charged one of Shah Suwar's sons, ʿAli Bey, now a provincial governor (*sanjak bey*) in his service, with the task. ʿAli Bey defeated ʿAlaʾ al-Dawla (Rabiʿ II 921/June 1515) and delivered his head to Selim, who sent it on to Qansawh al-Ghawri in Cairo as a warning of future retribution.

ʿAli Bey succeeded to the Beylik of Dhu'l-Qadr. He participated actively in Selim's campaign in Egypt that terminated the Mamluk Sultanate, leading a squadron during the Battle at Marj Dabiq in which Qansawh al-Ghawri was killed and joining the initial occupiers of Cairo who executed his successor

Tuman Bay. He subsequently gained valor as a suppressor of the Jalali revolt in eastern Anatolia and the rebellion of Jan-Birdi al-Ghazali in Aleppo (late 926–early 927/1520–21). His eminence prompted the resentment of Ottoman Supreme Commander, Farhad Pasha, who induced Selim's successor, Suleiman, to have him executed. With ʿAli Bey's death, the Dhu'l-Qadrid Principality was formally extinguished in the Mamluk period. Beys of several other principalities in this marcher zone engaged in similar attempts, either to proclaim their autonomy or to gain leverage by playing off the larger powers. But the Dhu'l-Qadrids stand out as the most significant clients contending for influence and affecting the Mamluk Sultanate's foreign policy in the region.

## Challengers to Mamluk Suzerainty from Iran

During the Mamluk Sultanate's tenure, four regimes in Iran contested its claim to hegemony in Southwest Asia: the Mongol Ilkhans, the Timurids, the Aq-Qoyunlu Federation, and the Safavid Monarchy. The term "*Īlkhān*" (alternative meanings: "subordinate khan," "commander of domain") referred to rulers over the Mongol regime established through conquest in Iran and Iraq by Hulegu (r. 654/1256–663/1265), a grandson of Jenghis (*Chinggis*) Khan.[23] Sent by his brother, Great Khan Mongke, in 651/1253 to eliminate the Ismaʿili Assassin sect, Hulegu subsequently invaded central Mesopotamia and terminated the ʿAbbasid Caliphate in Baghdad (Safar 656/February 1258). The following year, Hulegu crossed the Euphrates, advanced into Syria, besieged and sacked Aleppo, and accepted the surrender of Damascus. Hulegu was motivated to encroach upon territories under Mamluk suzerainty by an overarching ideology of expansion on a global scale that was central to the concept of Universal Empire, in which Mongols had a heaven-sent mission to impose their hegemony over all peoples. The Ilkhanate Hulegu founded in Southwest Asia would adhere to this ideology, although its efforts at implementation were stymied by Mamluk resistance.

Hulegu did not remain to consolidate his position in Syria, withdrawing to Azerbaijan because of the contested succession in Mongolia after Mongke's death (657/1259). He left his field commander, Kitbugha, in charge of a troop contingent with orders to extend the occupation east across the Jordan and south toward Jerusalem. Kitbugha advanced as far as Gaza, from where he sent a threatening missive in Hulegu's name to Sultan Qutuz in Cairo, demanding his submission. Qutuz rejected this call to surrender (cf. Chapter 1), resolved a dispute with his rival Baybars al-Bunduqdari, organized an expedition under their joint command, and drove the Mongols from Gaza (Shaʿban 658/July 1260). Kitbugha reconvened his contingent in the Biqaʿ Valley (in modern Lebanon) and then positioned himself at the site of ʿAyn Jalut (ar. Spring of Goliath, in modern Israel) to await the Mamluks. The battle occurred on 25 Ramadan 658/September 3, 1260. Clashes continued through the day until a squadron of Ayyubid cavalry deserted the Mongols who had pressed them into service, and their commander Kitbugha was killed. Both Qutuz and Baybars held up their troops' resolve and distinguished themselves in the fighting (Qutuz survived his horse being shot from under him). Following their rout, the Mongols temporarily abandoned territories west of the Euphrates to the Mamluks.

Although the Battle of ʿAyn Jalut did not end the war between Ilkhanids and Mamluks, it provided the new Sultanate in Cairo with prestige that mitigated its origins by usurpation and bolstered its credibility as a military power.[24] Two decades would elapse before the Mongols attempted another invasion on a large scale. The intervening period was marked by forays on the part of Sultan Baybars across the Euphrates or north into the east Anatolian marches and incursions by Mongol commanders to counter them. The next invasion was ordered by Hulegu's successor, Ilkhan Abaqa (r. 663/1265–681/1282).[25] Having failed to persuade several European powers and the Papacy to participate in a joint campaign against the Mamluks, Abaqa in 679/1280 assembled a host that approached 40,000 cavalry, supported by auxiliaries of Armenians, Georgians, and Turkmen that may have numbered 30,000. Having elected not to cross the Euphrates, Abaqa placed his brother Mongke Temur in command of the army that advanced into Syria. The reigning Mamluk Sultan, Baybars's ultimate successor Qalawun, joined forces with his governor of Damascus, Sunqur al-Ashqar, and entered Syria with a smaller host composed of 800 Royal Mamluks and 4000 Halqa soldiers, augmented by contingents from Syrian garrisons and a company of Bedouin cavalry. The combatants met near Hims (14 Rajab 680/October 28, 1281) in a confrontation inflicting severe losses on both sides. Although the Mongol commander Mongke Temur was wounded, the Sultanate carried the day because of its aggressive Bedouin brigade.

Abaqa's death the following year initiated a second hiatus to the war that lasted until the fateful battle of Wadi al-Khazindar, again near Hims (28 Rabiʿ I 699/December 23, 1299). Desultory efforts by Abaqa's successor, his brother Ahmad Teguder (r. 681/1282–683/1284), to reconcile with the Mamluks had produced no substantive results. The battle itself, under the command of Ilkhan Ghazan (r. 694/1295–703/1304),[26] inflicted the sole serious defeat suffered by the Cairo Sultanate during the conflict. Yet, since Ghazan departed Syria soon after occupying Hims and Damascus, his adjutants were unable to sustain the Ilkhanate's presence in Syria. Sultan al-Nasir Muhammad replenished his army, which scored a decisive victory over the Mongols at Marj al-Suffar near Damascus (2 Ramadan 702/20 April 1303), their loss effectively bringing an end to further confrontations on Syrian territory. Ilkhan Uljaytu Khudabanda (r. 703/1304–716/1316) was persuaded by Qara Sunqur, an amir in revolt against al-Nasir, to attempt an invasion but was prevented from crossing the Euphrates at the river fortress al-Rahba, which held out against a brutal siege by the Mongols (711/1312). While al-Nasir Muhammad ordered several raids into Ilkhanid territory over the coming decade, neither side was eager for further incursions on a large scale. Uljaytu's son, Abu Saᶜid (r. 716/1316–736/1335), preoccupied by fiscal deficits and deteriorating control over provincial rivals at home, was reluctant to attempt his predecessors' aggressive actions.[27]

Late in 720/early 1321, Abu Saᶜid's senior adjutant, Chupan, dispatched a merchant of mamluk slaves, al-Majd al-Sallami, to Cairo with a proposal for a peace settlement (*ṣulḥ*).[28] The proposition mutually invalidated claims to extradite renegades from either side, banned Bedouin or Turkmen from raiding Ilkhanid territory with the Sultanate's inducement, opened both regimes to mutual trade, and sanctioned a Hajj caravan conveying a Kaᶜba Mantle (*kiswa*) to depart Iraq annually for the Hijaz. Its banners would bear the titles of the Egyptian sultan and Iranian Ilkhan. Sultan al-Nasir Muhammad agreed to the proposal, which effectively formalized the *status quo ante bellum*. He sent al-Sallami back to Tabriz with a positive response and 50,000 dinars. Over the next two years, subsequent envoys refined the agreement, which was ratified in 723/1323.[29] The sixty-year war between the Mamluk Sultanate and Mongol Ilkhanate had concluded. The treaty itself was testimony to how far the Mongol ideology of Universal Empire had waned. It also testified to the viability of the Sultanate's commitment to maintenance of the status quo.

The Sultanate's interaction with the campaigns of Timur Lenk and his son/successor Shah Rukh occurred during the reigns of Barquq, his son Faraj, Barsbay, and Jaqmaq. Timur's rationale for imperial expansion was an attempt to replicate Jenghis Khan's goal of Universal Empire, similar to the impetus behind formation of the Ilkhanate a century earlier. Timur (r. 771/1370–807/1405) contested with a host of rival chieftains, initially in the western Chagatay Khanate of Central Asia.[30] He combined tactical insight with exceptional force to defeat or outmaneuver his opponents. He also inspired the horsemen of the Chagatay tribal federation (*ulus*), who made up the core of his military cadre, to share his hegemonic vision and martial aggression, the consequence of which was an unbroken series of conquests east into the Indus Valley and west into Iran, the Turkic Steppes, the central Arab lands, and Anatolia during the final decades of the eighth/fourteenth century.

Sultan Barquq initiated a potential confrontation with Timur by offering sanctuary to Ahmad ibn Uways, the Jalayarid ruler of Iraq whom the Chagatayid Conqueror had deposed (796/1394). When Timur called upon Barquq to acknowledge his suzerainty, the sultan executed the courier who brought the summons and organized an expedition to block his invasion of Syria. Barquq led his detachment to al-Bira on the Euphrates to await the invader but learned that Timur had delayed his progression west to suppress insurgencies in Iran. Barquq's troops defeated the contingent Timur had left behind and therefore secured the Syrian corridor for the remainder of his reign. Timur took up his campaign against the Mamluks after the accession of Barquq's adolescent son, al-Nasir Faraj. Faraj's retreat to Cairo and abandonment of Damascus to negotiate its surrender to Timur seemingly left southern Syria and Egypt open to invasion, a threat avoided by opportune circumstance (cf. Chapter 1). Timur elected to put off his advance toward Egypt to counter the imperial agenda of a rival who matched his own aggressiveness, the Ottoman Bayazid I Yilderim. Following his defeat of Bayazid at Ankara (19 Dhu'l-Hijja 804/July 20, 1402) and temporary dismemberment of Ottoman domains in Anatolia, Timur turned his attention toward east Asia and an invasion of China that was aborted by his own death. The Mamluk Sultanate was thus spared.

Timur's son and ultimate successor, Shah Rukh (r. 811/1409–850/1447), entertained no plan of military engagement with the Sultanate but challenged its stance of primacy among Muslim powers.[31] His claim to priority over the Mamluk Sultanate with regard to authorizing a pilgrimage caravan bearing a mantle (*kiswa*, not the *mahmal*) to drape the Kaᶜba in Mecca drew on the precedent set by terms of the treaty that ended the Ilkhanid–Mamluk war more than a century earlier. While Sultan Barsbay dismissed it as the presumption of a secondary – and inferior – power, Jaqmaq more pragmatically acknowledged its authorizer as a sovereign of equal standing by permitting the Iraqi caravan to convey the Timurid mantle. Jaqmaq's gesture was typical of stances adopted by rulers during the Sultanate's latter decades when new actors were challenging the extant balance of power. They indicated the regime's readiness to accommodate claims to equivalency by rivals who confined their expressions to ceremony rather than resorting to military aggression. Maintaining a cordial relationship with Timur's successor minimized the prospect of provoking his style of belligerence and devastation.

The Aq-Qoyunlu ("White Sheep") Turkmen confederation emerged as a significant force in politics of Southwest Asia during the second half of the ninth/fifteenth century, following the Ilkhanate's decline.[32] Its Bayandur tribe produced a line of leaders, of whom Hasan (known as "Tall" [Turkish: *Uzun*, Arabic: *Ṭawīl*]; r. 861/1457–882/1478) ibn ᶜAli ibn Qara Yuluk ᶜUthman engaged the Mamluk Sultanate in a complex balancing act that fluctuated between aggression and submission.[33] During his first decade in power, Uzun Hasan won a series of battles against two of his opponents, Jahan Shah of the Qara-Qoyunlu Federation and the Timurid ruler of Bukhara, Abu Saᶜid, that established the Aq-Qoyunlu as the Ottomans' chief impediment to their drive east. It was under these circumstances that Uzun Hasan crafted his opportunistic relationship with the Mamluks, whom he predicted would regard the Ottoman advance with ambivalence. Egyptian chroniclers took note of Uzun Hasan late in 872/1468 after his defeat of Jahan Shah. Since the recently enthroned Qayitbay was preoccupied with consolidating his position, the event figured minimally in affairs at court. But the historian Ibn Taghri Birdi did appreciate its potential for destabilizing the Iranian zone. He stated that Hasan's victory set in motion "numerous battles and disputes in the eastern regions between a host of Turkmen and others that would require a month to relate. A vast number were killed."[34] Uzun Hasan initially avoided proclaiming his feat as a provocation and presented himself to the sultan as a deferential ally. He sent an emissary to congratulate Qayitbay for his accession. Others followed with reassuring pledges of their patron's allegiance: "Rejoicing over the sultan's acclamation, he regarded himself as his Mamluk and affirmed his service. The Sultan's wishes were his commands."[35]

Hasan kept up the dispatch of couriers conveying his promises of fidelity, while he eliminated residual opponents in Iran and the marcher territories. Sultan Qayitbay received conflicting reports about the outcome of a confrontation between Uzun Hasan and Jahan Shah's son, Hasan ᶜAli, who had rallied survivors of his father's army in a countermove against the Aq-Qoyunlu. When Uzun Hasan's success was confirmed, Qayitbay and his oligarchy recognized that a new regime had consolidated its authority over the Iranian zone. Events the following year substantiated their apprehension. In Dhu'l-Hijja 873/June–July 1469, a courier arrived in Cairo with the severed head of the Timurid Abu Saᶜid. Uzun Hasan was alleged to have attacked him in revenge for his support of Hasan ᶜAli. The emissary asked Qayitbay's permission to impale the head on a lance and parade it through Cairo's streets, preceded by heralds and torchbearers. The Sultan refused on grounds that such a display violated Abu Saᶜid's rights as a believer and had the head interred. More pragmatically, Qayitbay avoided augmenting Uzun Hasan's standing by celebrating his victory. Instead, he ordered a formal procession with his Royal Mamluks through the city to impress upon the emissary the Egyptian sultan's superior status.

Qayitbay learned of Uzun Hasan's first foray into Mamluk territory in Rabiᶜ II 875/September–October 1470, when the Viceroy of Aleppo sent a messenger bearing the news. Although encouraged by Shah Suwar's defeat of the Egyptian army, Hasan limited the expedition to raids in the vicinity of al-Bira and al-Ruha (Edessa) without overtly threatening either town. But in Dhu'l-Qaᶜda 876/April–May 1472, he sent another missive that reopened the issue of a Kaᶜba mantle. Claiming his prerogative as successor to the Timurids, Uzun Hasan demanded to send a Kiswa to Mecca on Shah Rukh's precedent, as sanctioned by Sultan Jaqmaq. He also vouched for Shah Suwar's good behavior, offering bond money in return for the Sultan's pardon. Qayitbay now regarded Hasan's actions as an affront, since by interceding for Shah Suwar's future conduct, he was acting as his true suzerain in the Sultan's place. And by claiming the mantle right, he was elevating his regime to the Sultanate's level.

After Yashbak min Mahdi captured Shah Suwar, Uzun Hasan took the part of a patron defending a wronged client and initiated open hostilities with the Sultanate. In Jumada II 877/November–December 1472, he sent a contingent under his son Ughurlu Muhammad to besiege al-Bira and al-Ruha. Qayitbay responded by sending his Atabak to reinforce Aleppo and Yashbak to confront the Aq-Qoyunlu. Hasan sent missives throughout the marcher territories that drew upon Qur'an verses to assert his stature as God's legitimate representative rather than the Sultan. Subsequent reports reached Cairo that the governor of al-Bira had driven off the Aq-Qoyunlu contingent. Word soon followed from Aleppo that the viceroy had apprehended forty spies who had covertly entered the city, fomented opposition to the Sultan's rule there, and sent back intelligence about discord among barracks factions. Given the deteriorating situation, Yashbak departed for the Euphrates frontier immediately upon his arrival in Aleppo (Shawwal 877/March 1473). Appreciating Yashbak's formidable renown, Hasan assumed command over his cavalry camped near al-Bira. The two met in battle (Dhu'l-Qaᶜda/March) in which the Aq-Qoyunlu were defeated and a son of Hasan was killed. Hasan retreated in such haste that he abandoned his archive. Upon its examination, Yashbak discovered correspondence Hasan had sent to European courts offering collusion with them against the sultans of both Cairo and Istanbul. Reading from these letters in Aleppo's Great Mosque, Yashbak condemned Uzun Hasan as a traitor to his coreligionists. Qayitbay himself had received confirmation of Hasan's strategy from the Ottoman ruler, who had arrested his ambassador crossing Anatolia toward Europe. Letters were intercepted that urged Frankish princes to attack Egypt and Asia Minor by sea while Hasan invaded by land.

After his failure at al-Bira, Uzun Hasan attempted no further military actions against the Mamluk State. But his diplomatic endeavors continued. At the end of 877/May 1473, the intendant (*mubāshir*) of the Pilgrimage returned to Cairo with news of an incident involving the Hajj caravan from Iraq. Two of Hasan's agents, an officer and magistrate, had intimidated imams in Medina. They had pressured them to preach the Friday Sermon (*khuṭba*) at the Prophet's Mosque with Uzun Hasan's titles: *al-Malik al-ᶜĀdil Ḥasan al-Ṭawīl, Khādim al-Ḥaramayn* ("The Just Monarch, Hasan the Tall, Servant of the Two Sanctuaries."[36] After they departed, the clerics had written to Sharif Muhammad ibn Barakat, informing him of their act. Muhammad apprehended the provocateurs outside of Mecca and sent them to Cairo for interrogation. When they were questioned, they disclosed Hasan's intent to pose himself as Guardian of the Holy Places once he supplanted the Egyptian sultan. Since the Iraqi caravan had departed for the Hijaz before Hasan's defeat at al-Bira, Qayitbay dismissed his agents' plot and released them as a sign of both disdain and good will, at Yashbak's inducement. Early in 879/May–June 1474, Uzun Hasan reconciled with Qayitbay, who pledged no further retribution. In his final years, Hasan faced insurrection from his own family. His son, Ughurlu Muhammad, who had led the first expedition against al-Bira, fell out with his father and requested aid from the Viceroy of Aleppo. Ughurlu's mother presented herself at the Citadel in Cairo as an intermediary between her son and husband. Although Qayitbay received her with honors and lodged her in the harem under his wife's care, he remained noncommittal on the matter of her son's claims. He later welcomed Ughurlu Muhammad's heir, whom he retained as his ward in Cairo.

In Shaᶜban 883/October–November 1478, news of Uzun Hasan's death reached Cairo. His oldest surviving son, Khalil, had been acclaimed as leader of the Aq-Qoyunlu but was soon deposed by rebellious subordinates. The son who followed him, Yaᶜqub, reconsolidated his father's base and reigned for more than a decade (883/1478–896/1490). It was during his tenure that Yashbak launched his abortive attempt at kingship in the frontier zone between the Mamluk and Aq-Qoyunlu Empires. From the long view, Uzun Hasan's imperial venture caused minimal difficulty for the Mamluk regime, compared with challenges elsewhere. Yet, Hasan's strategic balancing of rivalry and reconciliation set him apart from his contemporaries. Hasan's overtures to Christian rulers were not unique; their distinction emerged from his simultaneous stance as a more genuine defender of the faith than the Sultan in Cairo. For his part, Qayitbay took military action against Uzun Hasan only when he infringed on Mamluk territory and disrupted the status quo. The ruling oligarchy perceived the latent menace: Hasan's actions set a precedent for subsequent dynasts in Iran, who combined charisma with doctrine to inspire a different style of imperial competition.

Three decades intervened before such an incident occurred. In Safar 908/August–September 1502, reports of another incursion across the frontier of Aleppo province reached Cairo. Identity of its instigator was obscure at this date. In 908/1502, the historian Ibn Iyas limited his reference to him as "Shah Ismaᶜil al-Sufi" (the Mystic), without elaborating on his genealogy, ideological leanings, or motives for invasion.[37] His only descriptive term was revealing, however. Ibn Iyas labeled Ismaᶜil a "dissident" (*khārijī*); whether in the context of political disruption or doctrinal heterodoxy is indeterminate. Throughout their comments about Ismaᶜil's conquests, until his defeat at Chaldiran (2 Rajab 920/August 23, 1514) by the Ottoman Sultan Selim I, Egyptian chroniclers took little note of his Twelver Shiᶜi revivalism. Ismaᶜil was depicted essentially as an incarnation of Uzun Hasan and his predecessors who emerged from Iran to challenge the status quo. In fact, Ismaᶜil was more than an ambitious warlord who united tribes into an ephemeral imperial entity, disintegrating soon after its formation. Although Ismaᶜil's political mission, closely tied to his religious charisma, did not recover from Chaldiran, the regime he founded under the sectarian doctrine he shaped would outlast him.

These portents were not envisioned in Cairo when the first Safavid raid was reported in 908. Yet, in light of Uzun Hasan's precedent, Sultan Qansawh al-Ghawri mobilized troops to confront the incursion. When news arrived of the Safavids' departure, al-Ghawri called off the expedition. Isma<sup>c</sup>il's elite cadre, known as Kizilbash (literally, "Red Heads," from their distinctive head gear), did not replicate the menace posed by Shah Suwar or Uzun Hasan to the Mamluk Sultanate. Their tactics, with regard to territories west of Iran, seemed to aim more at fomenting unrest than their systematic absorption into an imperial domain. Until Chaldiran, the Safavids remained more inclined to inculcate their propaganda of invincibility rather than to consolidate their conquests.

After 918/1512, Sultan al-Ghawri's relations with Isma<sup>c</sup>il became more focused – but on their shared opponent, the newly enthroned Ottoman Sultan, Selim I. Several months before Chaldiran (Rabi<sup>c</sup> I 920/April–May 1514), al-Ghawri equivocated when Selim requested his aid against Isma<sup>c</sup>il. Although both the Ottomans and Mamluks defended Sunnism, al-Ghawri recognized that no variant of Shi<sup>c</sup>ism posed a realistic challenge to religious observance in his realm at either the formal or popular levels. By contrast, Selim was confronting a tangible threat from Safavid agents to his authority in eastern Anatolia. While Qansawh al-Ghawri could afford indifference to Isma<sup>c</sup>il's doctrinal "aberrations," he could not ignore the implications of continued Ottoman expansion east toward territories in the Mamluks' sphere of influence. As a pragmatist, al-Ghawri would continue to keep his options open until the Ottoman–Safavid encounter at Chaldiran, prepared to exploit the prospect of his rivals weakening each other and subsequently to deal with a diminished victor. Chaldiran's outcome upended this stratagem. The extent of Selim's victory effectively neutralized Safavid interventionism for the indefinite future and left the Mamluks to confront an emboldened rival who suspected al-Ghawri of opportunism, if not duplicity.

## The Ottomans: Contesting the Status Quo

Relations between the Mamluk and Ottoman Sultanates attracted attention in sources by Egyptian and Syrian authors following the Ottomans' recovery after their defeat by Timur Lenk at Ankara (804/1402). Having retained their hold over Europe below the Danube, the Ottomans restored their dominion throughout western and central Anatolia during the next half-century. By the time of Qayitbay's accession (872/1468), they had regained their status as a regional power, on a firmer institutional foundation than at the turn of the ninth/fifteenth century. The reign of Mehmet II Fatih ("Conqueror," 855/1451–886/1481), which witnessed the occupation of Constantinople, was lauded by these authors as an era of renewed Muslim hegemony of benefit to both powers. The ruling oligarchy in Cairo accorded Mehmet status as a peer of his Mamluk counterpart. In his obituary of Mehmet, the historian Ibn Iyas extolled him as:

> the glorious and omnipotent sultan, indomitable warrior, master of Anatolia, custodian of Constantinople; an illustrious and esteemed sovereign, superior to all his forbears in the House of ʿUthman. All the universe acknowledged his justice. He exhibited morality, wisdom, rectitude, generosity. He possessed a vast fortune, commanded invincible armies. He expanded his domain at the expense of infidel nations.[38]

Ibn Iyas did not acclaim figures like Shah Suwar, Uzun Hasan, or Ismaʿil Safawi in this fashion. The eulogy attributed to Mehmet essential ideals of monarchy according to Islamic Law. That he concluded with praise for Mehmet's aggression against "infidel" states rather than fellow Muslims was placed for effect. Ibn Iyas looked back on the Conqueror's reign as a positive time of mutual respect between two bastions of Sunnism, in contrast with the threat of impending invasion by Selim I during Qansawh al-Ghawri's tenure. In those propitious days, both empires allegedly shared common goals with minimal friction. Each respected the prevailing political order and cooperated to uphold it. Ibn Iyas's tribute omitted signals of Ottoman aggression toward Muslim states that antedated al-Ghawri's time. During Qayitbay's early years, the ruler of the Qaraman Beylik in southeastern Anatolia sent entreaties to Cairo for help against his aggressive neighbor.[39] Once this hold-out of resistance to Ottoman expansion was absorbed, the two empires shared a common frontier. Past precedent implied antagonism for those who contested adjacent fields of influence with the House of ʿUthman. The Ottomans found friendship for distant allies more plausible than for regimes nearby.

After Qayitbay's accession, Mamluk–Ottoman relations evolved from cordial coexistence to escalating rivalry, stand-off, and, ultimately, confrontation. These phases in the two states' interaction denote a contrast in imperialist ideologies. The Mamluk Sultanate rarely allowed fixed doctrines to constrain its priorities. From its perspective, imperialism represented the most effective means of ensuring order among potentially acrimonious populations. Although the Sultanate formally pledged itself to defense of Sunnism, in practice it was prepared to tolerate regimes upholding divergent views of Islam. Non-Muslim states with significant commercial ties to Egypt and Syria maintained positive diplomatic relations for profitable reasons. To the ruling oligarchy, a prime benefit of imperialism was sustenance of their elite lifestyle. While the military class drained assets from productive sectors of society for conspicuous consumption, it recognized the link between dependable territorial control and reliable extractions. Confrontations with foreign competitors over ideological matters could result in losses of subject territories, irate sectarian groups, and thus reduced extractions. Time-tested stratagems aimed at preserving equilibrium coincided more positively with the Sultanate's goal of upholding the ruling elite's preeminence.

The Ottoman Sultanate developed under different circumstances. Founded on the northwestern frontier of the Muslim world at the threshold of Europe, the Ottoman state began as a minor principality (*beylik*). Drawn at its inception to the principle of *ghazwa* (Arabic: raiding) against unbelievers, early Ottoman war leaders conceived of their goal, and defined their legitimacy, through conquest. Territorial acquisition became an overriding objective. The Ottoman ruling class fixated not on preservation of a static geographic patrimony but rather on indefinite enlargement of a territorial network. Visions of universal dominion, derivative in part from an idealized Mongol model, motivated the actions of Ottoman rulers, at least to the death of Suleiman Qanuni (974/1566). In this context, the Ottoman ruling elite regarded the Mamluk fixation on the status quo ambivalently. They would regard its defenders as an impediment to their mission, despite their shared Sunni allegiance. To the Mamluks, peace meant preservation of the prevailing order among states. To the Ottomans, peace was equated with unified authority over the Dar al-Islam and regions beyond it. In Istanbul's view, until the mid- sixteenth century, the ideal international system was a single imperial confederacy, with resources sufficient to suppress discord, subdue recalcitrant clients, and integrate agriculturalists, pastoralists, merchants, and artisans in a cohesive whole. The Ottoman concept of religious unity paralleled this view. Not content with protecting holy sites, the Ottomans sought to impose Sunnism over Muslims under their rule. Tolerant of other monotheists, they disavowed sectarian pluralism within the Islamic Commonwealth. These contrasting perspectives therefore promoted tension between the two military elites. Episodes of cordiality signaled mutual crises both recognized as common threats. When their interests no longer coincided, conflict resumed.

Qayitbay's oligarchy adjusted their tactics to deal with the Ottomans' expansion through eastern Anatolia. Their goal of restoring the status-quo was visible in all of them. While Mehmet II lived, relations remained positive. Ottoman resistance to Uzun Hasan's ambitions motivated Mehmet to form a tacit alliance with Cairo. In return, Cairo overlooked Ottoman overtures toward Qayitbay's Lusignan vassal in Cyprus, or the Ottoman siege of Rhodes, held by the Templar Knights. The Egyptian chancery discerned potential Ottoman aggression in these actions but abided them as minimally disruptive to the extant balance. When Mehmet's son, Bayazid II (r. 886/1481–918/1512), pressured Shah Suwar's successors in Southeastern Anatolia, however, Qayitbay responded in kind. The Ottomans supported Shah Suwar's displaced brother, Shah Budaq, in his bid for autonomy from Cairo. They subsequently offered similar inducements to Qayitbay's own client,

ʿAlaʾ al-Dawla. The expeditions Qayitbay sent against both of them in 889–96/1483–91 reminded the Ottomans that the Mamluks had not surrendered their suzerainty over this region. After his defeats, Bayazid desisted from further confrontations over the Dhu'l-Qadrid march. His preference for coexistence did not sit well with his successor, Selim I.

Qansawh al-Ghawri's attempts to counter Ottoman expansion drew upon tactics from the past that proved inadequate when applied to a hegemonist like Selim. Al-Ghawri's decision to take the field himself at Marj Dabiq was reluctant, driven by calls for defensive action from the viceroys of Damascus and Aleppo (cf. Chapter 1). Yet, al-Ghawri was motivated by the partial success of a retaliation by Ismaʿil that had defeated an Ottoman contingent at Amida (*Diyār Bakr*) earlier in 922/1516. Given the possibility of further Safavid resistance distracting Selim, al-Ghawri held on to the chance that renewed conflict between the two might offer opportunities to exploit for his own gain. Circumstances leading to conflict stemmed from renewed Ottoman pressure on Cairo's Dhu'l-Qadrid client, ʿAlaʾ al-Dawla. When Shah Suwar's son, ʿAli Bey, revolted against ʿAlaʾ al-Dawla, he acted on Selim's impetus. ʿAlaʾ al-Dawla called upon al-Ghawri to defend him, but the sultan was not positioned financially or politically to replicate Qayitbay's reprisals decades earlier. Selim's defeats of his opponents are often attributed to his advantage in firepower. Yet, with regard to his confrontation of al-Ghawri at Marj Dabiq, desertion by senior officers contributed significantly to al-Ghawri's loss. Nonetheless, the Ottomans' readiness to innovate with artillery and firearms contrasted with the Mamluks' opposition to them. Al-Ghawri's experiments with artillery units had not advanced enough for their effective use against the Ottomans by 922/1516. Whether al-Ghawri's tactics would have progressed to successful application if confrontation with the Ottomans had been delayed remains speculative.[40] Al-Ghawri presided over a regime ambivalent about change. By contrast, the Ottoman Sultanate embraced innovation in the expansive phase of its evolution. Its commitment to imperialism by conquest overwhelmed the containment policies of its Mamluk rival.

## The Europeans: Transit, Commerce, Profit, and Piracy

Sustained relations between the European Mediterranean and the Islamic world date to the establishment of the ʿAbbasid Caliphate, which presided over the extension of trade networks to South and East Asia by land and sea (mid-third/eighth–fourth/tenth centuries). Emerging maritime powers in the Italian and Iberian Peninsulas and southern France that sought access to commodities produced in Asia systematized their commercial ties with Egypt and Syria, which straddled routes connecting the Mediterranean to these networks via the Red Sea and Indian Ocean (cf. Chapter 5). They also aggressively competed with each other for preference as trading partners with local Muslim regimes that simultaneously contended among themselves for regional control over these routes. Mamluk rule over Egypt and Syria followed the formation of the Mongol Imperium, which extended its dominion over the land route ("Silk Road") between the Black Sea and East Asia. While the Mongols did not terminate caravan trade across the Silk Road, their policies encouraged the European maritime powers to augment their commerce with the Cairo Sultanate during the Bahri period, which represented its halcyon era of transit trade.

Numerous cities appear among the roster of states engaging in commerce with the Mamluk Sultanate, but two stand out: Genoa and Venice. Intense rivalry, verging on military conflict, was the consistent feature of their interaction: with each other and mutually with the Sultanate. Between the mid-seventh/thirteenth and late eighth/fourteenth centuries, Genoa capitalized on advantages it derived from close ties with the Byzantines and Ilkhanids to assume a dominant position with the Cairo Sultanate in terms of trade, particularly in slaves. Unable to compete with the Genoese gain from its near-monopoly over northern routes to Central Asia, the Venetians focused on access to the Indian Ocean and South/Southeast Asia via the Red Sea. When both the Byzantine and Ilkhanid states were eclipsed by regimes with differing visions of regional power and commercial strategies, the Venetians pulled ahead of Genoa and emerged as the Mamluks' primary European trading partner (mid eighth/fourteenth–early tenth/sixteenth centuries; cf. Chapter 5).[41] Recognizing that they could not duplicate the former Genoese procurement of slaves, the Venetians focused on shipment of spices and silk from India, cotton and linen from Egypt and Syria. During the ninth/fifteenth century, the Venetians effectively marginalized their Italian competitors, while the ruling oligarchy in Cairo attempted to monopolize the transit in luxury items from Asia by supplanting the Karimi spice merchants who had controlled it independently. Whether the Venetians succeeded in blocking the rising presence of the Aragonese, Catalonians, or French is open to question, since merchants from these powers figured prominently during the Circassian Mamluk period.

Commercial ties between Genoa, Venice, and the Sultanate were complicated by events that adversely affected conditions under which they operated. Notable among these were: a) a ban on trade declared by the Papacy in 723/1323 and b) warfare instigated by the Lusignan king of Cyprus. The ban prohibited Christian trafficking with Muslims, in response to its claim that the Sultanate was restricting free access by pilgrims to Christian shrines in territories under its jurisdiction. Sanctions were officially severe: fines of half the value of any merchandise proved to have been imported from Egypt or Syria. Actual enforcement was problematic. The effectiveness of penalties for violation remained dubious because the Genoese and Venetians devised elaborate schemes of subterfuge, relying on intermediaries and carriers rendezvousing in neutral ports or entrepôts that refused to acknowledge Papal authority. In 745/1345 the Holy See submitted to mounting pressure from the Venetian Senate and lifted the ban. Venetian arbitrators renegotiated exchange and tariff conditions in force before 1323 with the Sultanate's agents.

The Cypriot war was more serious because of damage inflicted on the primary port of call for European vessels in Egypt. The Cypriot King Peter I (r. 760/1359–770/1369) attacked and pillaged Alexandria in 766/1365, inducing the sultan to arrest Christian merchants based there on charges of espionage and collaboration (cf. Chapter 1).[42] Several maritime engagements occurred over the next five years, until the Genoese and Venetians were able to broker an end to hostilities. A formal peace treaty was signed by representatives of the two republics plus Cyprus, Egypt, and Catalonia in 771/1370. King Peter I emerges from sources documenting the conflict as an enigma, a throwback to ideals of an archaic chivalry and religious zeal that were relevant to neither European nor Levantine commercial interests. The eagerness of the Genoese and Venetians to reduce tensions, with only muted opposition from Rome, underscored how outdated the Crusader ideal had become in the milieu of interstate commerce by the later Middle Ages. Nonetheless, the Cypriot affair was not a closed case from the Egyptian perspective. Convinced that the treaty provided no guarantee against piracy originating from Cypriot coastal towns, the Sultanate resolved to deal more forcefully with this menace in the future. Fifty-five years later, al-Ashraf Barsbay launched the naval expedition that resulted in the Sultanate's occupation of Cyprus. The question of Cypriot sovereignty continued to impair European–Levantine relations throughout the remainder of the ninth/fifteenth century.

Procedures governing the interaction of European and Egyptian or Syrian merchants varied during the two and a half centuries of the Mamluk Sultanate's tenure. But they adhered to a regimen that aimed at separating carriers of Asian goods from their European counterparts, who shipped them on to destinations on the north side of the Mediterranean. Depictions of Venetian activity offer the most details.[43] Convoys of ships sent by the Venetian Commune arrived in the port of Alexandria, to await inspection of cargoes by customs officials. Officially, their merchants and crews were restricted to structures designated for their residence while they awaited the arrival of commodities either locally produced (such as textiles or foodstuffs) or shipped from Asia via the Red Sea and transfer stations to the Nile Valley. Fleets sent from India, Indonesia, Malaysia, or China conveying spices, dyes, silk, and porcelains that were prized in Europe unloaded their cargoes at Aden or Hijaz ports, to be conveyed in vessels controlled by the Sultanate (initially under supervision by Karimi merchants, later by the Sultanate's own agents).

The regime's objective behind this procedure was collection of transfer tolls and tariffs on commodities. How effective the policy of separation was in practice remains speculative, since contemporary narrative sources sporadically mentioned the presence of Venetians and other Europeans in Cairo, Syrian ports, and even the Hijaz. But the importance of tolls and tariffs to the regime as a source of revenue remained essential to its fiscal policy. From the European perspective, they represented a hefty business cost. To Venetians dependent on the Red Sea artery, they were unavoidable. To Europeans elsewhere, such as the Portuguese looking South and West across the Atlantic, they stimulated exploration for alternate routes that offered the prospect of direct access and avoidance of intermediaries.

And indeed, the century beginning in 1450 C.E. would witness a navigational revolution with profound implications for societies of the Mediterranean basin and Southwest Asia that had played a central role in global trade for hundreds of years. To the ruling oligarchy of the later Mamluk Sultanate, these implications were recognized as disruptive of the status quo in ways that undermined a foundation of the regional economy. Disruption occurred on two fronts: piracy in the Mediterranean and arrival of Portuguese in the Indian Ocean and Red Sea. With regard to piracy, sporadic harassment of Muslim shipping in Mediterranean waters dated from the revival of Italian seafaring during the central Middle Ages. But as commercial activity increased during the eighth/fourteenth and ninth/fifteenth centuries, so did attacks by corsairs. In 876/1472, Sultan Qayitbay responded to assaults on Egyptian vessels sailing to the Delta ports of Rashid (Rosetta) and al-Tina with a plan for fortifying the coast.[44] He ordered construction of guard towers at several sites, the most imposing of which was in Alexandria. Qayitbay chose the location of the ancient Pharos Lighthouse at the harbor entry. A massive structure that cost 100,000 dinars, the tower served as an effective deterrent to assaults on the port (**Fig. 3.2**). Yet, Qayitbay's thinking did not envision taking the offensive. He took no measures to counter piracy with Egyptian vessels or hire European renegades to do so. No plans were laid for a naval response.

Sultan Qansawh al-Ghawri was more assertive. When raiding intensified between 913/1508 and 916/1511, al-Ghawri outfitted one of the few Mediterranean expeditions by the late Sultanate to follow Barsbay's invasion of Cyprus decades earlier (cf. Chapter 1). In Dhu'l-Qaᶜda 913/March 1508, al-Ghawri placed a senior officer in command of a flotilla charged with collecting naval stores from Ayas (Alexandretta) on the northeast coast of the Mediterranean. If European corsairs showed signs of hostility, he should attack them. Al-Ghawri's offensive resulted in the capture of many European ships raiding the Delta and Syrian coasts over the next two years. But when it was defeated in 916/1510 with a loss of eighteen vessels, al-Ghawri decided against risking further naval ventures. He took aim at a prominent Christian

Fig. 3.2 Fortress of Sultan Qayitbay at entry to Alexandria Harbor Constructed 882/1477.
(Credit: DEA/C. SAPPA/Photo by DeAgostini/Getty Images)

shrine by ordering the arrest of monks (*ruhbān*) resident at the Resurrection (*Qiyāma*) Church in Jerusalem.[45] These were confined to the Citadel in Cairo along with merchants and consuls from Alexandria and Damietta (*Dumyāṭ*), where they were compelled to draft letters demanding release of the captured ships and pledges of safe passage from European regimes accused of sponsoring piracy. Al-Ghawri actually threatened to demolish the Resurrection Church and hang the monks, despite their status as clerics. Al-Ghawri's threat exceeded his intent, since he placed the hostages under his fiscal secretary's supervision pending the Europeans' reply. Two years elapsed before it arrived.

In Safar 918/April–May 1512, an ambassador from the Doge of Venice presented himself at the Citadel.[46] The historian Ibn Iyas described the emissary as "an elderly man with a white beard and imposing deportment – a commanding presence." Outfitted in Chinese silk with gold embroidery, the ambassador brought gifts so profuse they required 200 bearers to convey them up the staircases to the audience hall. He offered crystal vases, velvet garments embossed with dragons, a great variety of silk and satin cloth, and "other precious items." While the Venetian emissary, with this display of Chinese finery, made his point about the overriding need for both sides to ensure the oriental trade, which no incident of piracy or sequestration of a holy site should threaten, he brought no promise of restitution. How al-Ghawri received his proposal for a negotiated settlement is unclear. But Ibn Iyas reported no subsequent acts of execution or demolition. Sultan and emissary may have reached a mutually acceptable arrangement allowing both parties to save face without open capitulation. The Resurrection Church was closed for an indefinite period, but it remained intact. Previous commercial treaties were reactivated as well. Whether the Venetians actually curbed piracy in the Mediterranean cannot be ascertained from Arabic sources, but the latter report no further raids during al-Ghawri's final years. The threat of such acts continued nonetheless, since no active steps had been taken to prevent them. The Ottomans would therefore inherit this abiding problem unresolved by the Mamluk regime. The maritime balance of power in the Mediterranean was shifting. How the Ottomans dealt with the Portuguese challenge further south revealed a preemptive response that also proved ineffective.

The Portuguese penetration of the Indian Ocean presaged direct European access to markets of South and East Asia previously monopolized by merchants from central Muslim states. Precisely when Portuguese mariners first entered the Red Sea is unclear in Arabic sources, but Ibn Iyas noted their presence in Dhu'l-Hijja 912/April–May 1507. Mamluk authorities had become aware of their maneuvers off the Indian littoral several years earlier, presumably from their own agents or local merchants who sent reports of Portuguese aggression. Al-Ghawri prepared his first expedition to strengthen fortifications along the Red Sea and Yemen coasts in 911/1505 (cf. Chapter 1). When the court in Cairo learned of Portuguese raiding north of the Bab al-Mandab Strait, in waters previously regarded as secure, rumors spread depicting their audacious tactics.[47] The Portuguese had breached a dyke allegedly constructed by Alexander the Great (referred to by Ibn Iyas as *Iskandar ibn Filibus al-Rūmī*) connecting the "Chinese and Roman Seas." They had worked for years to rupture it so that whole fleets could pass through. Now, twenty of their ships had appeared in the Red Sea and were ambushing Indian commercial vessels bound for Jidda and Sawakin. Although the sudden Portuguese presence caused alarm in Cairo, the Sultanate responded in kind. In 914/1508, al-Ghawri's first retaliatory contingent, commanded by the Amir Husayn Mushrif al-Kurdi, defeated several Portuguese squadrons in the Indian Ocean. Inspired by this victory, the sultan proceeded with his plan for building a Red Sea fleet capable of staving off the invaders and restoring the Egyptian trade monopoly. Soon after celebrating Husayn's achievement, al-Ghawri reviewed a regatta of ships he had commissioned for service in the Red Sea, the first in seventy years.

Al-Ghawri's efforts did not succeed. The following year brought reports of Husayn's defeat in several clashes with the Portuguese. Rulers of Indian states that exported spices to Egypt sent messengers with tales of European encroachment and requests for aid al-Ghawri was not positioned to provide.[48] Al-Ghawri issued a reply profuse with pledges of solidarity but vague on concrete proposals, which he sent with a eunuch official. The emissary visited allied Indian princes and urged their cooperation against European invaders. Although the courier returned months later (Muharram 917/March–April 1511), he brought no word of tangible resistance. Twelve months elapsed before the Amir Husayn arrived at the Citadel after an absence of seven years. Despite his poor showing against the Portuguese, Husayn had made contact with several Indian princes. When the Amir ascended to his audience, he was accompanied by an emissary of Muzaffar Shah ibn Mahmud, ruler of Kanbaya. This ambassador may have discussed the Portuguese presence during his briefing but was not preoccupied with it since he had come ostensibly to request a certificate from the Caliph confirming his patron's succession. His focus on a formal recognition of his sovereign brings into question the perception by Indian potentates of the extent to which the Portuguese threatened their interests. Concerned primarily over their profits from the spice trade, they might endorse the principle of Egypt's continued trade monopoly but cared less as to who actually purchased from them.

But al-Ghawri did appreciate their threat. When the Portuguese again entered the Red Sea (Rabiᶜ II 919/June–July 1513), he planned a second naval expedition. The Portuguese had besieged Sawakin after occupying Qamaran Island off the Arabian coast. Al-Ghawri began enlarging a shipyard in Suez at the southern end of the isthmus between the Delta and Sinai. He chose this campaign to try out his new Fifth Corps of arquebusiers, recruited from outside the Mamluk ranks and not opposed to new weaponry. Its members received training in firearms that Mamluk regulars scorned. The latter showed little enthusiasm for this venture and pressured al-Ghawri for additional bonuses, a demand he deferred for several months. He also considered leading the contingent himself to Suez. Having received an offer of assistance from an officer in the Ottoman navy, Salman al-Ra'is, al-Ghawri wished to impress on him his army's competence. Because of prolonged disputes over stipends, the expedition did not set out until early in 920/March 1514. Although plagued by unseasonable heat and polluted water supplies (larvae in transport skins), both cavalry troops and Fifth Corps arquebusiers reached Suez to join Salman, who had begun outfitting vessels. The meeting between Mamluk sultan and Ottoman admiral was cordial despite mounting tensions between Cairo and Istanbul over diplomatic issues elsewhere. Both governments shared an interest in blocking further European gains in the Red Sea.

The two regimes mounted a final nautical campaign against the Portuguese the next year (921/1515). Amir Husayn, having regained al-Ghawri's favor, shared command with Salman al-Ra'is. By Shaᶜban 922/August–September 1516, they had dislodged the Portuguese from their recently occupied enclaves in the Yemen. They were preparing their pursuit through the Bab al-Mandab when the historian Ibn Iyas interrupted his narrative of events in the Red Sea to focus on al-Ghawri's encounter with Selim Yavuz at Marj Dabiq. But the expedition's scale and partial success underscored the mutual recognition by the leading powers of the central Islamic world that a new entity challenged their commercial dominance. More noteworthy was its timing and coordination during a decline in Mamluk–Ottoman relations. Since Selim won out, his descendants would face the task of confronting the Europeans. Whether the Ottomans' response in future centuries extended the reactive policy of the Mamluks remains an open question. For its part, the Cairo Sultanate limited its tactics to thwarting rather than outflanking its European rivals.

## Africa beyond the Sultanate: Takrur, Abyssinia, and the Maghrib

Three regions on the African continent beyond Egypt appeared in Arabic sources compiled during the Mamluk period: *al-Takrūr*, a term that referred to Muslim territories in Central West Africa encompassing modern Mali and its environs; Abyssinia (modern Ethiopia, ar. *al-Ḥabasha*), in the seventh/thirteenth–ninth/fifteenth centuries a Christian realm in the Ethiopian Highlands under the rule of the Solomonic Dynasty; and states in the Maghrib or west Mediterranean zone of the Islamic world (modern Tunisia, Algeria, Morocco). With regard to Takrur, its origins point to a region along the Senegal River (often designated as the "*Nīl*" by Arabic geographers) inhabited by disparate ethnic groups, among whom the Fulbe were prominent by the third/ninth century.[49] To Arabic writers of the fifth/eleventh century onwards, Takrur was known as a kingdom whose founder, one War Jabi ibn Rabis (d. 448/1056–57) had allegedly converted its population to Islam. Al-Idrisi, the sixth/twelfth-century geographer who wrote prolifically about Takrur, emphasized the kingdom's mineral wealth and integration into trade networks linking it north to the Maghrib and east to the Nile Valley. By the Mamluk period, from the mid-eighth/fourteenth century, Takrur had become a generic name for Muslim West Africa and diverse persons who traced their ethnic identity to the region. Authors of biographical dictionaries and necrologies of prominent persons inserted at the close of entries for years or decades in historical chronicles listed individuals with the nisba "Takruri" in numbers indicative of an ethnic presence that was not numerous in comparison with communities from other geographic regions but well established in the Sultanate's urban milieu. Those persons depicted as eminent in commerce or learned in jurisprudence and theology were uniformly identified with the Maliki School (*madhhab*) of Sunni Law (*Sharīʿa*), consistent with the broader trend of legal affiliation throughout the Muslim West. They also consistently appeared as free individuals, with few ties to either the domestic slave population or to the military class of Mamluk recruits; this in contrast with the Abyssinian (*Ḥabashī*) presence, which figured prominently among the Sultanate's slave cadres.

In medieval Arabic historiography, one event takes precedence as the most famous incident linked to Takrur during the Mamluk period: the pilgrimage visit to Cairo of its monarch, Mansa Musa (r. 712/1312–737/1337), grandson of Abu Bakr Keita, himself a descendant of the Malian Empire's founders. Mansa (Manding for "King") Musa arrived at the Pyramid district west of the Egyptian capital on 15 Jumada II 724/June 9, 1324, on his way to perform the Hajj in Mecca.[50] He was accompanied by his first wife and a host of relatives and retainers and invested with a trove of gold – a feature of his visit that prompted commentary by contemporary observers and enhanced his stature to the reigning sultan, al-Nasir Muhammad ibn Qalawun. The Syrian chancery official and historian, Ibn Fadl Allah al-ᶜUmari, provided a detailed record of Mansa Musa's visit, based on discussions with the Wali of the Qarafa Cemetery District in Cairo, Abu'l-Hasan ᶜAli ibn Amir Hajib, who arranged the King's stay there and developed a personal friendship with him.[51] Mansa Musa described to Ibn Amir Hajib his kingdom, its size, population, resources, rivals, and leading personages at length. He related a story of his predecessor Muhammad, from a different branch of the dynasty, who had ventured upon a voyage with a large fleet of ships to explore the limits of the Atlantic Ocean and inhabitants of its unknown shores. When he failed to return, Mansa Musa took up rule over the kingdom in his own right.

On 16 Rajab/July 9, Mansa Musa ascended to the Citadel in Cairo for an audience with Sultan al-Nasir Muhammad. When informed that visitors were expected to prostrate themselves before the sultan's throne, Mansa Musa declined, declaring that he was no supplicant and bowed to none but God Himself. Sultan al-Nasir accepted the King's rationale for his refusal, but would not permit him to sit in his presence (according to al-ᶜUmari, the Sultan's host of ceremonies [*mihmāndār*] told him that al-Nasir actually did stand to welcome Musa, after he declined the prostration and sat him at his side). The audience then proceeded cordially. Although the King had studied literary Arabic, he refrained from speaking it and communicated through an interpreter. The Sultan interrogated the King about his realm and expressed particular interest in sources of his gold supply. He granted the King's request to meet with scholars and theologians before his departure to the Hijaz. He also welcomed him to shop Cairo's markets and emporia, with the encouragement to provide lavishly for his retinue. Mansa Musa readily accepted and purchased apparel for his retinue, said to exceed 1000 persons. He also bought a large number of female slaves. The King was alleged to have spent so much gold that its infusion into Cairo's money supply dropped the price of a gold dinar by six silver dirhams.[52] Mansa Musa returned from the pilgrimage imbued with renewed piety. He was accompanied by four individuals descended from the Prophet's line of Quraysh (*Shurufā'*), who intended to accompany him back to Mali and reside there permanently. For his part, Mansa Musa maintained close contacts with the Sultan's court and corresponded with rulers of neighboring Muslim states in West Africa and the Maghrib. In his later years, he intended to abdicate his position to his son and spend what time remained to him in Mecca as a spiritual sojourner but died before realizing this goal.

In 902/1496–97, more than a century and a half later, Askiya Muhammad, ruler of the Songhay Empire in West Africa, stopped in Cairo on his way to perform the Pilgrimage in Mecca. He met the eminent scholar Jalal al-Din al-Suyuti (cf. Chapter 6), who may have arranged an audience with the ʿAbbasid Caliph. Whether the Caliph invested Askia Muhammad with a brevet confirming his authority over the Empire is not certain, since al-Suyuti dated a meeting with the "ruler of Takrur" a decade earlier.[53] But al-Suyuti subsequently corresponded with Askiya Muhammad on principles appropriate to Muslim governance.

The East African realm prominently in contact with the Sultanate, the Christian Solomonic Dynasty of Abyssinia (*al-Ḥabasha*), maintained diplomatic relations strained by religious rivalry.[54] Their contexts encompassed appointment or confirmation of the Abyssinian Metropolitan (*Maṭrān*) by the patriarchal Coptic See of Alexandria (based in Cairo), mutual requests for protection of Christian or Muslim minorities under the aegis of the respective ruler, and commerce. When commerce was noted in Egyptian sources, it frequently mentioned trading in contraband arms or precious metals fashioned into Christian icons, the first for potential use against the Sultan's army, the second to promote Christian rituals and proselytize Muslims.

Persons of Habashi heritage appeared in these sources as free-born Muslims or as slaves with animist backgrounds manumitted to Islam. The free Muslims exhibited nomenclature indicating personal origins or ancestry linking them to regions in the Horn of Africa (modern Eritrea, Ethiopia, and Somalia). Those who attained stature as learned (*ʿulamā'*) or notables (*aʿyān*) initiated their careers in Cairo's college mosques, in particular al-Azhar, where hospices (*riwāq/arwiqa*) had been founded to house students from the region (**Fig. 3.3**). These were known by sites linked to the Horn of Africa: the *Riwāq al-Jabart* (Eritrea and Somalia) and *Riwāq al-Ziyāliʿa* (after *Zaylāʿ*, a Somali coastal port). Upon completion of their educations at the Azhar and elsewhere, these individuals formed a distinct community within Cairo's learned and Sufi mystic communities.[55] Several attained renown as revered luminaries, for whom shrines founded around their tombs attracted devotees from throughout the Nile Valley and beyond.[56] The vocation of one ʿAli ibn Yusuf ibn Ṣabr

Fig. 3.3 The main courtyard in Al-Azhar Mosque
Constructed from the fourth/tenth century ongoing; engraving from *Arabic Art in the monuments of Cairo*, 1869–77, by Emile Prisse d'Avennes (1807–79).
(Credit: DeAgostini Picture Library/Photo by DeAgostini/Getty Images)

al-Din al-Jabarti al-Azhari al-Shafiʿi illustrates the esteem attained by such a luminary. Following his completion of studies at the Azhar in 850/1445–46, ʿAli al-Jabarti departed Cairo to take up a life of pious poverty in Damascus, Baghdad, and Aleppo. He returned to Cairo twenty years later to reside at the Azhar, having acquired influence among a diverse circle of revered figures, international merchants, and military officers during his sojourn abroad.[57] In Baghdad, he received a robe of honor from an eminent member of the Qadiri Sufi order. Al-Jabarti's pious calling posed no barriers to his immersion in practical affairs, although he brokered his contacts with worldly groups from his abode of ascetic solitude on the roof (*saṭḥ*) of al-Azhar.

Habashi slaves were depicted in two categories: domestic servants in households (with Christian or animist identity, when rarely disclosed) or as eunuchs (*ṭawāshi/ṭawāshiyya*), converted to Islam from animism upon their manumission and designated for several distinctive forms of service.[58] Eunuchs gained prominence as stewards of sultans' tombs in Cairo, wardens of cadets in Mamluk barracks (*muqaddamūn al-mamālīk al-sulṭāniyya*, cf. Chapter 2), intendants of women in harems of the Sultan and senior officers, guardians (*khādim/khuddām*) of the Prophet's tomb in Medina, and custodians of pious foundations supporting the two Holy Shrines (*Ḥaramayn*) in Mecca and Medina.[59] Adolescent males were initially taken from the Muslim principality of Hadiyya in southwestern Ethiopia (whether by force or purchase is unclear) until its conquest by the Solomonic rulers (732/1332); they may subsequently have been collected from the Dar Fur region to the north. Castrated in Upper Egypt by Coptic Christians (due to the ban on Muslims performing this act under Shariᶜa), the boys received military training in the Mamluk barracks as a special corps separated from the non-emasculated Julban recruits. Those who attained prominence in historiographic sources held the offices of: barracks warden or supervisor as above (*muqaddam*), wardrobe keeper (*jamdār*), cup-bearer (*sāqī*), tutor of sultans' sons (*lālā*), superintendent of the royal courtyard (*shādd al-ḥawsh*) with responsibility for organizing ceremonies, treasurer-paymaster (*khāzindār*), and fiscal officer of the sultan's household (*zimām*).

While promotion to an officer's formal rank (of ten: *amīr ᶜashara*) at a level on par with that of a Royal Mamluk, junior grade, was restricted to barracks wardens, the subordinate status of the other posts did not prevent their holders from amassing substantial wealth. Paymasters and managers of the royal household in particular made fortunes, as attested by the frequency of corruption and embezzlement charges brought against them. Their value as enhancers of their patrons' even larger fortunes is also evident in the consistency of their restoration to former offices after confiscation and a "cooling off" period of temporary exile, often in the Sanctuary cities of the Hijaz. Their presence combined with the tomb/mosque guardians and waqf/trust custodians to form a singular Habashi presence in these cities. During their "retirement," many immersed themselves in study of the Qur'an, Hadith, and mysticism (*ṭasawwuf*). Although their condition as eunuchs closed off access to positions designating membership among the formally learned (*ᶜulamā'*), authors of biographical compendia acknowledged the expertise many attained and applauded the depths of their piety. The names that appear in their biographies or obituaries marked them as Muslims of a special kind. Virtually none bore appellations commonly linked to native-born believers, often constructed from the root *Ḥ M D* (praise). Rather, such agnomens as ᶜAnbar ("Amber"), Bashīr ("Glad Tidings"), Faraj ("Joy"), Fātin ("Alluring"), Jawhar ("Jewel"), Khāliṣ ("Sincere"), Marjān ("Coral," "Pearl"), Marzūq ("Blessed"), Miftāḥ ("Key"), Mithqāl ("[Gold] Nugget"), Mufliḥ ("Lucky"), Mukhtaṣar ("Epitome"), Qātim ("Dark"), Rayḥān ("Aromatic"), Saᶜd ("Fortunate"), Surūr ("Joy") tied these individuals to ornamental qualities or precious objects and were likely given to them after their castration from a category of sobriquets traditionally associated with the station to which they were now confined. They formed a central element of their identity and do not seem to have been scorned as stigmatizing.

An aspect of the outlook unique to these eunuchs can be discerned in their fixation on legacy. Since bequeathal to biological heirs was denied them, those possessed of means sought to leave their mark as patrons of pious charities that would continue after their deaths, thus perpetuating their names. An example emerges in the college of law (*madrasa*) founded in 763/1361–62 by Sabiq al-Din Mithqal al-Anuki al-Habashi (d. 776/1364–65), amir of ten and muqaddam al-mamalik to Sultan al-Ashraf Shaᶜban.[60] Mithqal purchased a plot of land east of the Qasaba avenue that separated the former caliphal palaces (*Bayn al-Qaṣrayn*) at the center of the former Fatimid city. He paid a high price for the plot to ensure that his college would be close to the royal foundations that lined the avenue north to south from the Bab al-Nasr to the Bab Zuwayla and gave it a scholastic luster acknowledged throughout the Sunni Islamic world (**Fig. 3.4**). The college's architects chose the cruciform hall (*īwān*) style to

Fig. 3.4 View of Bab al-Nasr
Bab al-Nasr (Succor Gate) constructed in 480/1087 as a principal entry to the city on Cairo's north wall.
(Credit: de Agostini/Getty Images)

emulate madrasas offering instruction in all four legal schools. The Sabiqiyya was among the first colleges to adapt this style to a curriculum limited to only one school (the *Shāfiʿī*) but open to students from the other three. Mithqal imported marble and porphyry from Italy to pave the floor and panel the prayer niche (*miḥrāb*) and cedar from Lebanon for the gilded ceiling. He set up an endowment (*waqf*) to support one senior professor (*mudarris*) of Shafiʿi jurisprudence (*fiqh*) and appointed an eminent shaykh, Siraj al-Din ʿUmar ibn al-Mulaqqin, as first recipient of its chair (*kursī*). The mudarris was assisted by two deputy instructors (*nuwwāb*), and a repetitor (*muʿīd*) to supervise drill of required texts with pupils. The waqf also endowed a library (*khizānat al-kutub*). Although Mithqal's madrasa was modest in scale compared with the royal foundations nearby, it was described by the topographer of Cairo, al-Maqrizi, as an architectural masterpiece. And its legacy outlasted the patron. Mithqal clashed with a senior officer in Sultan Shaʿban's oligarchy, Yalbugha al-ʿUmari al-Khassaki, likely due to competition for their sovereign's favor.[61] Yalbugha had Mithqal lashed, allegedly 600 strokes, from which he survived but was condemned and exiled to Aswan, subsequently Qus in Upper Egypt. After Yalbugha's death, Shaʿban recalled Mithqal and restored him to his former rank. Disabled from the severity of his scourging, Mithqal died soon after. His biographers pointedly stressed the perpetuity of the foundation he established, in contrast with the transience of his career. Temporality was marked by injustice but generosity was rewarded by lasting esteem.

References in contemporary sources to relations between the Sultanate and the Solomonic Kingdom are sporadic and focus on incidents illustrative of endemic Muslim–Christian tensions. Noteworthy among these was an espionage trial in Cairo that occurred during the reign of Sultan al-Ashraf Barsbay (825–41/1422–38).[62] The accused was a merchant of Iranian origin: Nur al-Din ʿAli ibn Muhammad al-Tabrizi al-ʿAjami, who had departed his native land to take up temporary residence in Cairo before setting out for the Solomonic Kingdom. Several chroniclers wrote detailed accounts of al-Tabrizi's activities when he arrived there, alleging his inclinations toward apostasy and arms smuggling. Although the historians differed in their versions of al-Tabrizi's illicit behavior, they concurred that he had aspired to visit the Solomonic Kingdom from childhood, with the inference that he was drawn to its Christian rituals. Once settled at the court of the Ethiopian ruler (*Yeshaq*, known in Arabic as *al-Ḥāṭī*; r. 1414–29), al-Tabrizi cultivated the favor of notables among the Kingdom's Christian inhabitants, offering to fashion, on his own initiative, gold crosses for their adornment or church services and readily selling – for profit – weapons that he had either brought with him personally from Egypt or could acquire from contacts back in Cairo. The chroniclers claimed that al-Tabrizi's activities had attracted the Ethiopian ruler's notice, who summoned him to join his entourage and to craft even more precious, gem-studded crosses and other Christian regalia. The ruler encouraged him to continue his arms trafficking. One author asserted that Yeshaq requested al-Tabrizi, during his travels to Europe, to purchase a nail alleged to have been among the three that fastened the Messiah on the True Cross at his crucifixion.

Several historians claimed that the Ethiopian ruler sent al-Tabrizi on a spy mission to plot an anti-Muslim crusade against the Sultanate. Reacting to an invasion of the Principality of Cyprus under the Lusignan Dynasty, at Sultan Barsbay's orders (cf. Chapter 1), King Yeshaq al-Hati was reported to have unleashed a persecution of Muslims throughout his realm. He supposedly entrusted al-Tabrizi with missives to monarchs in Europe (likely Aragon and France but depicted generically as "Franks" [*Firanj*]), inciting them to join a counter-invasion of Egypt. While they launched an invasion across the Mediterranean, the Ethiopians would proceed north, crossing the Sudd swamp in southern Sudan to the Nubian territories south of Aswan, from where they could attack the Sultanate on its southern flank. Their depiction laid out effectively a pincer operation, compelling the Cairo regime to confront Christian forces on two fronts. How feasible actualizing such a venture would have been is questionable. Contemporary sources provide little evidence that the Ethiopian monarchy could realistically plan, let alone carry out, a major expedition over land against the Mamluk Sultanate. The logistics would be formidable. The distance between the Abyssinian Highlands and Aswan on the Egyptian–Nubian border exceeds 2000 kilometers. An invasion route would traverse either the Sahara Desert or Nile swamps, both inhospitable to an expedition capable of challenging Mamluk garrisons in league with local Bedouin. From the European perspective, although Frankish regimes had landed troops on the Egyptian and Syrian coasts since the fifth/eleventh century, the chroniclers' renditions do not suggest their enthusiasm for this operation. To what extent Roman Catholic governments in Western Europe were disposed to heed schemes concocted by the ruler of a distant state whose Monophysite church likely appeared more alien than the Sunni Islam of the Cairo Sultanate, with which they were familiar, is problematic. The chroniclers indicated the Europeans' misgivings about al-Tabrizi's personal loyalties, which presumably came to light during the inquest following his arrest in Alexandria. The Europeans had reason to doubt the wisdom of involving themselves in a venture with minimal strategic prospects for success, but genuine chances for threatening their profitable trade with the power that monopolized access to the Red Sea and Indian Ocean.

Yet, the Sultanate did not dismiss this incident as trivial. The Solomonic Dynasty had previously warned of shutting off flowage from the Blue Nile, source of four-fifths of the water reaching Egypt, in response to the Sultanate's periodic closing of Christian shrines. For its part, the Cairo regime initiated a campaign of forced conversion of Nubians from Christianity to Islam, from Aswan on south. Alarm over a potential Christian fifth column lurking among Nubians in the Sudan, who chafed under Mamluk suzerainty, unsettled the ruling oligarchy in Cairo, especially after European powers intensified their own piracy in the Mediterranean. These worries would be exacerbated decades later when the Portuguese appeared with their vessels in the Red Sea. To what extent the Sultanate credited the Ethiopian monarch with the capacity to pose a tangible military threat is debatable. But its ire over al-Tabrizi's alleged espionage and overtures to Christians in the Ethiopian court was symptomatic of deeper concerns.

Al-Tabrizi's conspiracy had come to light when he returned to Alexandria from Europe, accompanied by two Ethiopian monks. A Muslim deck hand who had been impressed to the ship's crew as a slave disclosed his mission to port authorities. They impounded the ship's cargo and discovered al-Tabrizi's hidden missives. These were translated into Arabic while he and the monks awaited trial in Cairo. Sultan Barsbay consigned the case to the Maliki senior Qadi, Shams al-Din Muhammad al-Bisati, on 10 Jumada I 831/February 26, 1428. Since, in addition to the espionage charges, claims that al-Tabrizi had secretly converted to Christianity and sought to proselytize Muslims resident in Ethiopia were disputed by his supporters, including a Habashi eunuch in his service, the Qadi was initially unable to obtain a unanimous verdict from the assembled legists who heard the conflicting versions. After nine days of arguments over absolution or conviction, al-Bisati cast the deciding guilty vote. Al-Tabrizi was decapitated for apostasy and espionage in the square in front of the Salihiyya madrasa, where the four senior magistrates heard appellate cases. Before his execution, he pronounced attestations of personal witness twice, recited verses from the Qur'an, and declared his innocence of any religion other than Islam. The Sultan allowed al-Tabrizi's family to inter his body as a Muslim.

Contemporary sources recorded no subsequent events of this notoriety. But references to diplomatic contact with Ethiopia continued.[63] A prominent example was an embassy from the Solomonic Kingdom that arrived in Muharram 886/March 1481 during Sultan Qayitbay's reign. Qayitbay received the emissaries courteously, although they were not allowed to sit in his presence. The historian Ibn Iyas made no mention of the Tabrizi affair but noted that the Ethiopian ambassador conveyed a "sumptuous gift" to the sultan. He wished to deliver a request of the Coptic Patriarch to nominate a legate for the Church in his sovereign's realm.[64] Several decades elapsed before Ibn Iyas noted the final contact between the two states before the Ottoman occupation. On 25 Muharram 922/February 29, 1516, a second ambassador arrived in Cairo at the head of a large delegation.[65] Ibn Iyas described their apparel in detail, which he found remarkable for its lavishness when worn but was frequently absent since many members were partially nude. He claimed that the ambassador wore a helmet (*khudha*) capped with a pearl (*durra*) "of priceless value." The embassy was accompanied by the Coptic Patriarch in Alexandria, who intended to join its subsequent trip to Jerusalem, per the Ethiopian King's request to allow the delegation to visit the Resurrection Church. Sultan Qansawh al-Ghawri received only the ambassador and six adjutants but accorded them full honors. Upon hearing the Ethiopian king's letter, al-Ghawri granted his appeal. Ibn Iyas noted that after the session concluded, the delegation departed the Citadel under guard by the audiencer (*mihmāndār*) and chief of police (*wālī*), due to concerns over hostility from bystanders who had threatened to stone the procession. Although the embassy's appearance was a novelty due to the rarity of any formal presence from Ethiopia, anti-Christian feelings endured. The embassy left Cairo for Jerusalem but after insinuations of penury on the sultan's part. Al-Ghawri found the ambassador's obligatory "gift," in reality a bribe for permitting the pilgrimage, paltry, valued at no more than 5000 dinars. The sultan produced a list of gifts from previous embassies during the reigns of al-Nasir Muhammad ibn Qalawun, Barsbay, Jaqmaq, and Qayitbay that substantially exceeded this figure. He claimed that the gift to al-Nasir Muhammad was worth 100,000 dinars. While Ibn Iyas did not report the ambassador's response, he observed that the Solomonic Dynasty's wealth had declined in proportion to its lessening influence throughout the Horn of Africa. Some "sixty principalities along the Nile course" were now contending for power, to the dynasty's weakness. Soon after the Ottoman defeat over the Mamluk Sultanate, local Muslim insurgents would carve several of the Kingdom's provinces away. The Ethiopian regime itself would find salvation from intervention by the Portuguese.

During the era of Mamluk authority in Egypt and Syria, several dynasties ruled over territories in Muslim North Africa (*Ifriqiyya*, or the "West" [*Maghrib*]).[66] The Marinids succeeded the Almohads, presiding over a realm based at Fez (614–869/1217–465). In Tilimsan (*Tlemcen*), the Zayyanids exercised partial control over central Algeria (633–962/1236–555). The most significant dynasty in Ifriqiyya, based at Tunis, took its name from an influential figure among the earlier Almohads: Abu'l-Hafs ʿUmar al-Hintati. One of his descendants, as governor of Tunis, founded an autonomous regime that controlled Tunisia and eastern Algeria (Hafsids: 627–982/1229–574). Finally, a collateral branch of the Marinid line, the Wattasids, succeeded them in Fez (831–946/1428–549). From the Mamluks' perspective in Cairo, this region participated minimally in their political arena.

Data on migration and residence recorded in Arabic biographical literature (nouns of relation, usually geographic [*nisba*s]; sites of birth/death; and reports of travel [*riḥla*]) relevant to medieval Egypt and Syria indicate the Maghrib as producing a small percentage of personnel overall who traveled to and/or settled in the Sultanate from abroad between the sixth/thirteenth and ninth/fifteenth centuries – no more than 3–4 percent.[67] These individuals nonetheless formed a distinctive community in the Sultanate's cities. The regions of North Africa where sites of origin appeared most frequently were Ifriqiyya and al-Maghrib al-Aqsa (modern Tunisia and Morocco) and more locally the districts surrounding Fas (Fez) and Marrakish; and to the east the towns of Tilimsan (*Tlemcen*), Bijaya (*Boujie*), and Qustantina (*Constantine*). References to these centers outside the two central zones suggest their status as way stations and transit entrepôts for travelers between the Maghrib, Tunisia, and the Nile Valley. They also marked the northern termini of trade routes across the Sahara to states of central and western Africa. Premodern biographical sources highlight the careers of eminent militarists, literati, jurists, scholars, theologians, and merchants. The Maghribis they listed distinguished themselves in these fields. Such figures as the medieval globetrotter Shams al-Din Muhammad ibn ʿAbd-Allah al-Lawati al-Tanji, known as Ibn Battuta (703–70/79/1303–68/77),[68] who departed Tangier for journeys that took him to South and East Asia; or the historian Abu Zayd ʿAbd al-Rahman ibn Muhammad al-Hadrami, known as Ibn Khaldun (732–808/1332–406), who wrote a seminal analysis of the past based on principles of proto-social science (cf. Chapter 6) had their origins in the Maghrib. They were joined by many other persons of eminence in the world of commerce or learning. Whether the modest numbers in biographical sources are indicative of a larger demographic presence of North Africans from more diverse backgrounds is indeterminate. The life trajectories they depict do imply something of a wanderlust among persons from the far western Islamic lands, for whom performance of acts obligatory under Shariʿa, like the Hajj, required a lengthy journey to Egypt before heading East to the holy cities. But with respect to a significant legacy of nomadic migration throughout the Maghrib in previous centuries, the lack of ties connecting Bedouin tribes in North Africa to their counterparts in the Nile Valley during the Mamluk period is noticeable. While reports of local Bedouin raids, insurgencies, and control over rural populations fill Egyptian and Syrian chronicles, they rarely mention connections to inciters of such activity in North Africa.

Remarks in Arabic narrative sources about political events occurring in the Maghrib during the Mamluk period do not suggest levels of interaction with the Sultanate that parallel such ties to regions previously discussed in this chapter. They appear infrequently and primarily in the contexts of internal dynastic shifts or, especially in the ninth/fifteenth century, mounting assaults by Europeans. This dearth of commentary implies a mutual sense of deferential neutrality: an attitude that neither side regarded the other as inclined to interfere in its internal affairs or to alter the status quo in the regional balance of power. Although a tradition of substantive trade between the Nile Valley and North Africa may be discerned in a general sense in narrative sources, references to specifics are few in comparison with the profusion of their allusions to commerce between South or East Asia, the Mediterranean via the Indian Ocean and Red Sea, or sub-Saharan West Africa.

## Retrospect

The impression emerging from the previous appraisals of relations between the Mamluk Sultanate, its provinces, and neighboring powers is an abiding commitment to preservation of the status quo, a stance that contributed to the regime's stability and longevity in a volatile setting. Debates over whether the Sultanate's ruling oligarchy would have countered aggressors bent on challenging this commitment to stasis more successfully by adopting proactive policies, rather than containing them, remain unresolved. Their rhetoric is frequently couched in terms that infer inferiority on the part of an "oriental" mentality juxtaposed against the creativity of "innovative" newcomers ready to play under new rules. By criteria cited by indigenous commentators assessing crises they observed in situ, the Mamluk institution did confront significant challenges in its dealings with foreign powers. New actors were disrupting time-tested procedures of interaction formed in an international milieu relevant to the Crusader and Mongol periods that was no longer resonant with commerce and politics of the global order centuries later. Yet, the impression of stasis merits interrogation. The preceding discussion revealed resilience and adaptation in measures equal to inertia and stasis. How the Sultanate would have evolved had it not succumbed to the Ottomans remains an open question. An assumption that defeat was a foregone conclusion due to "fixation" on the status quo must be weighed against the Sultanate's success at integrating regions with disparate politics coherently in a turbulent environment over two and a half centuries – a track record not replicated since. The Ottoman regime that supplanted the independent Mamluk state would owe much of its own longevity to precedents adopted from its precursor.

# 4 Vocational Classes

## Bureaucrats, Magistrates, Scholastics, Clerics

The individuals who administered the Mamluk Sultanate exhibited expertise, attained through formal instruction or ad-hoc apprenticeship, that implied proficiency in diverse callings. Holding of multiple offices, often simultaneously, characterized their service and enhanced incomes substantially larger than fees or salaries tied to specific posts. While the Sultanate's officialdom assumed multiple roles, career paths of individuals qualify impressions of generalized multicompetence. Distinctions between personnel who staffed the fiscal bureaucracy, civil (*Sharīʿa*) judiciary, scholastic institutions, and clerical establishment were consistently discernible in their biographies. Yet, as a whole, these cadres constituted a broad social category, labeled in contemporary sources as "notables" (*aʿyān*) or "learned" (*ʿulamāʾ*), that shared qualities of expertise, status, and authority. Although their debt to the legacy of learned personnel that extended back to the ʿAbbasid period is apparent in their roster of activities or scholastic endeavors, the notables who managed the Sultanate in its imperial center or provincial capitals revealed traits that tied them more narrowly to administration, litigation, pedagogy, religious service, or artisanship in Egypt and Syria during the later Middle Ages (seventh/thirteenth–ninth/fifteenth centuries). Profiles in their biographies indicated diminishing crossover from one category to another as individuals advanced through their career trajectories.

### The Bureaucracy

Principal figures who staffed the Sultanate's bureaus (*dīwān/dawāwīn*) were: viziers, secretaries, supervisors, and chancellors. The official who had crowned the bureaucracy in its formative (*Baḥrī*) period was the vizier (ar. *Wazīr*) or "Prime Minister."[1] Initially charged with overseeing functions of the fiscal bureaucracy as a whole (accounting, supervision, taxation), the vizier's authority eroded, particularly during the regime's second (Circassian) phase, after the ascension of al-Zahir Barquq in 784/1382. By the Sultanate's latter decades, the vizier had been effectively supplanted by officials who supervised the Sultan's personal fisc (*nāẓir al-mufrad*), chancery (*kātib al-sirr*), or household (*ustādār*), all of whom were either senior officers or jurists with close ties to the ruler. By contrast, viziers in the late Sultanate were frequently recruited from the medial ranks of fiscal officialdom and confined to duties that involved procurement of revenues via clandestine procedures. Several belonged to the class of Coptic converts to Islam and lived with its ambivalent status in the bureaucracy. Assignment to the position carried minimal prestige and often signaled demotion to performance of tasks that, despite lucrative returns, signaled stymied status tainted by corruption.

The office that defined bureaucracy under the Mamluks was the secretary (*kātib/kuttāb/kataba*).[2] Having evolved over several centuries from its ʿAbbasid origins, the post manifested characteristics central to the civilian elite but distinct from the formal ranks of ʿulamaʾ, or those trained in Shariʿ Jurisprudence, Scholasticism, or Theology. Secretaries dealt in processing records. Skill in accounting and documentation was required; expertise in the Islamic sciences less so. Secretaries who staffed the Sultanate's bureaucracies were also adept at information gathering, in particular from fiscal records or archives. Their knowledge of assets licitly accessed via taxation or covertly tapped from concealed repositories rendered secretaries a crucial component of the regime's administration. Yet, their value as processors – or manipulators – of fiscal records did not assure entry to hierarchies of the learned. Although secretaries exhibited the pattern of multiple offices shared by other bureaucrats, they were among the least represented in legal, scholastic, or religious fields of any profession. By contrast, they monopolized the tax bureaus, from which positions they moved up toward more influential posts in the army bureau that dispensed stipends to soldiers, or supervision of the several diwans established by Sultans in their progressive privatization of revenues from state control. Most individuals who ultimately landed in the vizierate started out as *kuttāb al-dīwān*. Similar to viziers, many exhibited Coptic ancestry, a mark of dependent clients whose influence stemmed from their symbiotic ties to more powerful groups in the military establishment. Their service to such patrons was procurement of information or revenues, access to which the militarists' formal duties as law enforcers or defenders of public security officially limited.

At the apex of the bureaucratic hierarchy were fiscal supervisors or comptrollers (*nāẓir/nuẓẓār*).[3] Their postings dealt with overseeing budgets and distributing revenues. Officials holding the title of nazir administered the gamut of governmental bureaus and scholastic or religious institutions throughout the Sultanate (cf. offices listed in Chapters 2 and 5). Those in charge of diwan bureaus served the regime's interests by meeting its fiduciary goals as a primary expectation of their placement. Individuals appointed to oversee budgets of mosques, madrasas, hospices, and shrines were in theory more free of regime control, their autonomy upheld by the charitable endowments (*awqāf*) that financed institutional operations. Decisions as to choice of personnel were a perennial source of contention between the military and civil elites. Staffs of scholastic or religious institutions sought to nominate candidates from within their own ranks, while sultans or senior officers wished to appoint reliable clients who furthered their fiscal and political interests. As the Sultanate's financial system evolved toward privatization, the regime's encroachment on charitable endowments prompted selection of its own agents as supervisors. Since these individuals were simultaneously chief administrative officers over an endowed institution, such appointments affected all subordinate staff. Whether appointees exhibited scholarly aptitudes and clerical interests, or focused their objectives on fiscal gain, adverse consequences for staff were likely mitigated by the guarantee of functions prescribed by original donors of endowed trusts. Surpluses from waqf yields that exceeded funds requisite to maintaining designated charities enabled donors, their descendants, or regime appropriators to siphon off revenues without detriment to fulfillment of this objective.

Unlike secretaries, whose careers were often relegated to positions subordinate to wielders of power, supervisors were appointed from personnel accustomed to authority. Mamluk officers were conspicuous among their ranks. Yet, the judicial, scholastic, and clerical cadres were prominently represented as well. The marked presence of judges, professors, and rectors among *nuẓẓār* implies their success at maintaining a measure of control over the financial status and operational policies of their institutions. Overt defiance of interference from superiors was precarious and unproductive. Rather than risking open confrontation with the regime over an appointment (with the possible exception of staffs in large Sufi hospices, who enjoyed some immunity from regime interference), they resorted to subtler means of influencing nominations, such as bribery or favors and services more likely to influence a decision to their liking. Prayer and public praise for a reigning sultan proved efficacious. Rulers themselves were not uniformly committed to placing one of their own in this office. Upholding the integrity and endorsement of the learned community ranked high in their values.

Supervisors were installed in either governmental or institutional posts. Those in charge of scholastic or religious institutions conducted their offices within the sphere of the learned elite. Those in bureaus of government dealt with payment of troops and officials; building programs; troop and staff provisioning; maintenance of routes, ports, and sanctuaries; the burgeoning array of Sultanic private funds; the regime's commercial ventures; and taxation. ʿUlamaʾ or other civil notables were prominently represented. Supervisors of the army bureau (*nuẓẓār al-jaysh*), for example, were often civilians rather than Mamluks. The rapid turnover of incumbents in this office, despite its opportunities for illicit gain, indicates that risks accompanied profits. Officials placed in these positions were routinely subjected to public humiliations, confiscations, incarcerations, and physical abuse. Their treatment, seemingly wanton from a superficial perspective, was in fact the consequence of deliberate policy. If civilians, with few military or defensive options, were installed in these offices, they could offer little resistance to confiscation and harassment. The sultan retained ready access to revenues under their supervision. And, by focusing opprobrium for alleged corruption on these vulnerable clients, induced by the illicit activities for which they had been ensconced, sultans and amirs were able to collect revenues while dodging accusations of violating the Shariʿa themselves. Guilt was imposed on the occupants of offices covertly designed to expedite such graft. The ruler could pose as the arm of Law and collect the monetary benefits. This cycle predated the Mamluk period but became pronounced during the Sultanate's latter decades (ninth/fifteenth century). The frequency of Copts who were appointed fiscal supervisors paralleled their presence among secretaries. Their vulnerability to hostility from the Muslim majority heightened their value to the regime as dependent extorters of illicit revenues to make up for the shortfalls that were increasing in these decades. Intimidation was not confined to this minority. Supervisors who derived from elite Muslim backgrounds were equally susceptible to pressure from their sponsors for funds. They figured prominently among bureaucrats who amassed fortunes from their posts, only to endure confiscation and dismissal. That many reappeared after an interval of seclusion, either by exile or imprisonment, reinforces an established trajectory of temporary removal followed by restoration to their previous functions. A proven track record of procurement was too valuable to waste.

The office of Chancellor (literally, "Secretary of Confidence": *Kātib al-Sirr*) contrasted markedly from the ranks of fiscal secretaries.[4] The Chancellor's duties implied a close advisory relationship with the Sultan, his senior military officers, and provincial governors. Its incumbent held the highest status among civil personnel in the imperial court. The Katib al-Sirr presided over the Bureau of Documents and Diplomacy (*Dīwān al-Inshāʾ*), an agency also traceable to origins under the ʿAbbasid Caliphs. Under the Mamluk Sultanate, the Bureau had accumulated a trove of procedures for drafting documents composed for correspondence with the wide range of potentates and states, from Europe to South and East Asia, with which the regime maintained contacts. The huge manual of diplomatic practice authored by the ninth/fifteenth-century Diwan secretary al-Qalaqashandi (*Ṣubḥ al-Aʿshá fī Ṣināʿat al-Inshāʾ*) provides voluminous testimony to the elaboration of formulaic address, titles, and textual styles in use during the period (cf. Chapter 6).

But diplomatic protocol was not the Diwan's signal function from the regime's perspective. For the ruling oligarchy, provision of reliable intelligence constituted the Katib al-Sirr's essential charge. No other official was equally positioned to acquire it. The importance attached to this official may be discerned in the personnel appointed to the post. Sultans tended to select their confidential secretaries not from the ranks of bureau secretaries but rather from a cadre of individuals who had gained distinction in the upper echelons of fiscal bureaus or Shariʿa courts: supervisors and magistrates. The status of such individuals among the learned classes was unquestioned, in contrast with rank-and-file bureaucrats. Having access to more classified information than other officials closely associated with the ruling oligarchy brought kuttab al-sirr both benefits and liabilities. Rulers and senior officers relied on their intelligence chiefs for vital information, yet mistrusted them because of this knowledge and its potential value to rivals, domestic or foreign. Confidential secretaries were frequently dismissed, even jailed, if they were suspected of nurturing covert ties to possible contenders for the Sultanic office. Rulers were inherently wary of individuals intimately acquainted with the tactics that had abetted their own rise to ultimate power. Mastery of the Chancellery and its myriad facets was a talent both prized and suspected by the senior officers, who were vigilant of potential challengers to their authority.

The simultaneous value and risk associated with this office contributed to its uniquely cosmopolitan quality. Individuals foreign to Egypt often appeared among its incumbents. A pronounced Syrian presence is discernible, a phenomenon attributable to provincial governors or other senior officers stationed in the Levant who, upon their return to Cairo, were accompanied by their Syrian staff. Several of the Syrians who became Confidential Secretaries in Cairo had held the position under a provincial governor or received the post when their former patron assumed the Sultanate. These individuals combined two qualities as masters of intelligence. First, because of their ties to ʿulamaʾ diversely distributed throughout the Sultanate's realm, they were intimately informed about their myriad activities in Cairo and other provincial capitals. Many had seen service in other branches of the bureaucracy, judiciary, and scholastic establishment. Several belonged to eminent Syrian families connected to relatives in Cairo. Their cosmopolitan backgrounds heightened their familiarity with diplomacy and statecraft, more than any other civilian group in the Sultanate.

Second, as Syrians, most of these individuals owed their positions in Cairo to the military patrons to whom they had attached themselves during the latter's tours of duty abroad. In a competitive milieu in which qualified persons exceeded the limited positions available, a proven client relationship was essential to advancement.[5] The military hierarchy controlled access to diwan posts and manipulated their clients, binding them closely to fulfillment of their own interests. Syrians who attained bureaucratic prominence in Egypt owed their status to their sponsors. To secure it, they were pressured (and disposed) to perform the clandestine tasks of espionage and finessing of covert diplomacy demanded by their patrons. Syrians were more suited to these duties than

Egyptians because of their foreign origin and dependence on Mamluk sponsors in the imperial capital. Their patrons were aware of this when they appointed their *kuttāb al-sirr*.

The careers of two individuals, father and son, illustrate the qualities exemplified by Syrians who held the office. Both were born in the provincial capital of Hama. Nasir al-Din Muhammad ibn ʿUthman al-Hamawi al-Shafiʿi (769/1368–823/1420), known as Ibn al-Barizi, became confidential secretary in Hama and supervisor of the army in Aleppo (809/1406) before attracting the notice of al-Mu'ayyad Shaykh, then governor of Damascus. Shaykh appointed Nasir al-Din Friday preacher (*khaṭīb*) of the Umayyad Mosque in that city. Sultan Barquq's successor, Faraj, had installed him as Shafiʿi chief justice (*qāḍī al-quḍāh*) of Aleppo. When Shaykh deposed Faraj and assumed the Sultanate, he transferred Nasir al-Din to Cairo and eventually appointed him Katib al-Sirr (815/1413), at which post he remained for seven years until his resignation.[6] He was succeeded by his ambitious son, Kamal al-Din Muhammad, in 823/1420.[7] Exceeding his father's aspirations, Kamal al-Din nurtured close ties with Sultans Shaykh, Barsbay, and Jaqmaq. Under these rulers, Kamal al-Din became one of the most influential civil officials in the Empire. He held the posts of army supervisor in Cairo, confidential secretary, and two Shafiʿi judgeships in Damascus, confidential secretary in Cairo three times, khatib of the Umayyad Mosque, and Shafiʿi qadi of Damietta (*Dumyāṭ*), from which he retired. The list of intrigues in his biography was exceptional for its disclosure of political acumen, indicating that Kamal al-Din ibn al-Barizi exploited his office as chancellery head to supply his patrons, Jaqmaq in particular, with secret details about amirs suspected of treason or bureaucrats who were accumulating fortunes, ripe for confiscation.

Two other Syrian families paralleled the Barizis' prominence as chancellors: the houses of Muzhir and Shihna. The former initiated its rise in Cairo with the career of one Badr al-Din Muhammad ibn Muzhir al-Ansari al-Hanafi.[8] Employed by the Diwan al-Insha' in Damascus when al-Mu'ayyad Shaykh governed the city, he accompanied his patron to the Egyptian capital. Ascending through several posts, Badr al-Din became Confidential Secretary under Sultan Barsbay in 828/1425 and held the office for four years. His son, Jalal al-Din, succeeded him at the age of fifteen. Since his appointment had been purchased by family money, he was sacked after a few months.[9] But another son gained exceptional renown decades later. Zayn al-Din Abu Bakr Muhammad, born 832/1429 (the year of his father's death), excelled in scholastic pursuits but chose to enter the bureaucracy in his twenties.[10] He held supervisory positions in the royal stables, the diwan of minority taxes in Egypt and Syria, the influential Sufi Hospice of Saʿid al-Suʿada' in Cairo, the state treasury, and the army department before Sultan Khushqadam appointed him Katib al-Sirr in 867/1453. Zayn al-Din continued in this post for 25 years.

He served under four rulers, the last of whom, Qayitbay, regarded him as his indispensable aide from the learned elite. Zayn al-Din was the only civil official whose advice the Sultan allowed to counter the will of his most senior military adjutants, the Dawadar Yashbak min Mahdi or the Atabak Azbak min Tutukh. When Qayitbay was thrown from his horse and suffered a near-fatal fracture of his femur (891/1486), it was Zayn al-Din who took steps to quell rumors of his demise that were spreading throughout the capital and provinces. The historian Ibn Iyas credited him with staving off a succession crisis and deposition of his patron.[11] Two of Zayn al-Din's sons succeeded him to the office,[12] without duplicating his distinction.

The Shihna family belonged to the Syrian Hanafi elite. Their story in Cairo began with Muhibb al-Din Abu'l-Fadl Muhammad ibn Abu'l-Walid Muhammad ibn al-Shihna.[13] Son of an eminent jurist and scholar in Aleppo, Damascus, and Cairo, Muhibb al-Din left the Hanafi qadiship in Aleppo to try his luck in Cairo.[14] Although offered the Hanafi qadiship in the capital on the basis of his father's reputation, he lobbied Sultan Inal to appoint him Katib al-Sirr in 857/1453, lasted one year before dismissal, and served two terms as Hanafi chief qadi until he regained the Chancellorship five years later. Muhibb al-Din became embroiled in controversies surrounding the poetry of the eminent (or infamous) mystic ʿUmar ibn al-Farid (d. 632/1235) and was removed by Sultan Khushqadam, following his accession in 867/1463. Muhibb al-Din ended his career as rector of the mystic hospice founded by the Grand Amir Shaykhu on the Cross (*Ṣulība*) Street in Cairo. In retirement, Muhibb al-Din revised his father's writings, amending his history of Aleppo (*al-Durr al-muntakhab li-taʾrīkh Ḥalab*). His son, Sari al-Din ʿAbd al-Barr, sought fame and fortune outside the Chancellorship. He focused his goal on the Hanafi judgeship, from which base he would gain notoriety during Qansawh al-Ghawri's reign.

## The Civil Judiciary

The personnel who presided over litigation in civil (*shārʿī*) or military (*ʿaskarī*) courts, the legal establishment, comprised the foundation of the learned elite in the Sultanate, as they did throughout pre-modern Islamic societies generally. Individuals appointed to the several categories of judge or magistrate (*qāḍī/quḍāh*) did not encompass the full range of occupations that touched on legal interpretation or service. Nor were all legal activities confined to formal litigation. Judges nonetheless were the essential component of the judiciary. Since their training in jurisprudence (*fiqh*) formed the curricular core in colleges of law (*madrasa/madāris*), their presence among the scholastic establishment was ubiquitous as well. Biographical sources and manuals of jurisprudence disclose a hierarchy of offices, ascending in rank, from the court notary or witness (*shāhid/shuhūd*), deputy judge (*nāʾib qāḍī*), full judge (*qāḍī/quḍāh*), to chief justice (*qāḍī al-quḍāh*). The latter represented the appellate authority for each of the four legal schools (*madhhab/madhāhib*) endorsed by the regime in a district or town. Other figures who performed legal services were custodial rectors of religio-academic institutions (*shaykh/shuyūkh*), inspectors/regulators of commerce in the market place (*muḥtasib/-āt*), and jurisconsults (*muftī/muftūn*) who issued opinions on the legality of issues debated in the courts. Among overseers of litigation, the court notary was the most junior but performed services essential to his superiors.

Shuhud evaluated the veracity of testimony of plaintiffs and defendants during hearings. They weighed the validity of statements made by each before a magistrate, submitted evaluations of plausibility, and provided assessments of character following a hearing's conclusion and departure of claimants from the chamber. In the absence of written evidence, certification of testimony heard by the judge was crucial. A shahid was chosen on the basis of discernment (*ʿaql*) and proven long-term residence in the district of a local court to ensure personal knowledge of litigants appearing before the magistrate. The office was, predictably, vulnerable to validation of dubious testimony in return for remuneration. Such temptation was augmented by the notaries' function as previewer of cases on a judge's roster. In practice, they largely determined the schedule of litigation a judge would hear and did much of the preliminary interrogation.[15]

Individuals appointed to judgeships rarely initiated their careers with independent authority to decide litigation. The majority started out as adjutants or "deputy" judges (*nāʾib qāḍī/nuwwāb al-quḍāh*), subordinate to a more senior magistrate. They frequently apprenticed to a father, grandfather, uncle, or in-law who presided over a court as a full judge. Circumstances affecting a novice's entry into the civil judiciary were not uniform in the diverse settings of Shariʿa courts throughout the Mamluk Sultanate. One cannot assume that individuals routinely advanced through the echelons of the judiciary through familial connections. Not all adjutants were able to secure full judgeships. Some spent their careers under the aegis of a higher magistrate. But the occupational trajectories of this category disclosed individuals who did rise to higher callings. Scholarly distinction and political connections consistently appeared as qualifications requisite to their appointment. Yet, the biographies of many luminaries on the bench began with reference to their service as adjutant judges. Regarding the senior judicial ranks as closed to them would be misleading. Across the Sultanate, profiles of membership within the most eminent ʿulamaʾ families revealed individuals who had begun their careers at the entry level of the judicial hierarchy.

Entitlement of a deputy judge to decide cases depended on the level of litigation. Hearing of a minor complaint or suit readily resolved to mutual satisfaction of all affected parties fell under an adjutant's jurisdiction. Cases involving more serious disputes or substantial assets were either appealed to a senior magistrate or bypassed the adjutant entirely to be placed on his superior's docket from the start. The annals of several chroniclers who served as deputy judges confirm their presence at hearings over notorious cases, in which their detailed depictions of acrimonious deliberations suggest their own lack of participation in reaching final decisions. Adjutant judges nonetheless initiated their service fully trained in jurisprudence and its allied disciplines. The vocational rosters of *nuwwāb al-quḍāh* disclose their integration within the ranks of scholars who staffed madrasas and other centers of learning throughout the Sultanate. Comparative studies with scholastic occupations reveal a high correlation between holders of madrasa professorships and adjutant judgeships. A symbiotic relationship may be discerned between the two groups, justifying their mutual designation as "jurist-scholars."[16]

Where did adjutant judges conduct their hearings? Unlike their superiors, for whom work settings were infrequently mentioned, it is at this base level of litigation where locales of district or ward courts may be discerned. Madrasas and markets appear as primary court sites, the former employing the professors of jurisprudence, who simultaneously presided over litigation as magistrates at the same venue. The latter convened adjutants and litigants at sites where the causes of disputes routinely occurred.

The divide between deputy and full judge was significant. Appointment to an autonomous judgeship marked entry to the penultimate rank of the judiciary and, more broadly, the cadre of civil notables (*aʿyān*) itself. While most individuals who attained autonomous judgeships had previously served as adjutants, the influence of family ties mattered in their advancement. Judgeships were frequently transferred between generations of established judicial families, from father to son, uncle to nephew, or between in-laws. Many deputies who did secure judgeships belonged to established lineages of magistrates and had apprenticed under the aegis of relatives. Adjutants who did not belong to judicial families were less successful in securing an autonomous judgeship. Yet, there were exceptions, and individuals without pedigree but offering erudite credentials, political connections, and fiscal resources often succeeded in gaining an appointment. Paralleling their simultaneous holding of madrasa professorships (primarily in jurisprudence and related fields), full judges were highly visible in the civil bureaucracy. Supervision of fiscal bureaus and endowed institutions provided a significant portion of a magistrate's income; the yield from a comptrollership (*naẓr*) likely exceeded his formal salary. Judges less frequently appeared among the ranks of executive offices monopolized by the military class. They derived principally from the civilian sector; few sought or were recruited for positions within Mamluk circles. But exceptions occurred in this elite category, as exemplified by the career of Mahmud ibn Muhammad al-Qaysari al-Rumi al-ʿAjami (d. 799/1397). An immigrant to Cairo from Anatolia, fluent in Arabic, Turkish, and possibly Persian, al-Qaysari occupied the army comptrollership (*naẓr al-jaysh*) during his tenure as qadi, from which position he dispensed the military payroll – and amassed a vast fortune.[17]

Magistrates often held (honorary) imamates (*imāmāt*) or Friday preacherships (*khaṭābāt*) in district mosques but rarely engaged in the more routine aspects of religious service, such as Qur'an reading, prayer calling, or time keeping. An indicator of mobility may be seen in the range of artisanal posts held by judges, presumably before their entry into the judicial class. Although numerically modest and usually limited to a single occurrence early in a future magistrate's career, references to perfume selling, comb fashioning, chickpea cooking, silk weaving, shoe cobbling, camel driving, bowl crafting, fire stoking in a bath, generalized merchandizing, and farming attest to the presence of individuals who started outside the learned classes and penetrated at least the lower or medial ranks of the judiciary.

Upward mobility was less evident in the roster of offices held by the ultimate figure of the civil judiciary: the *qāḍī al-quḍāh* or "judge of judges," chief justice of one of the four legal schools (*madhāhib: Shāfiʿī, Ḥanafī, Mālikī, Ḥanbalī*) endorsed by the Sultanate. Individuals who attained the supreme magisterial office revealed elite familial status, scholarly eminence, and personal ties to the highest military authorities or the autocrat himself. Many combined all three. Although appointment as qadi al-qudah marked the apex of a judicial vocation, it carried hazards of close association with the senior ranks of military officers who controlled the realm and drove its contentious politics. Chief justices served at the pleasure of the current sultan. They mediated between the ruling caste, disparate sectors of the civil elite, and, ideally, the broader masses of the population as a whole. The four senior qadis acted as the final adjudicators of the Shariʿa courts, hearing suits appealed by plaintiffs from lower tribunals. The regime exploited the office's vaulted status to pressure its incumbents, along with muftis, to formulate legal rulings on issues that advanced its own fiscal and political interests.[18] Senior qadis were expected to clothe the sultan's decisions, taken for political expedience, with legal justifications culled from the Sunna (*Qur'ān* and *Ḥadīth*) and written corpus of the four schools.

The complexities of this highest judicial office may be seen in the careers of its prominent – or notorious – incumbents. Numerous examples of individuals born into judicial "dynasties" may be discerned among the ranks of senior qadis. The roster of notable magistrates yielded by the Bulqini family exemplifies the significance of family ties. This lineage attained renown as jurist-scholars in the Delta town of Bulqina during the eighth/fourteenth century. Their eminence in Cairo may be traced to one Siraj al-Din ʿUmar al-Bulqini

(724/1324–805/1403), who set the precedent for the dynasty's distinction in the judiciary, politics, and scholasticism that lasted to the Sultanate's termination in 923/1517 and beyond.[19] Emigrating to Cairo at the age of fourteen to complete his studies, ʿUmar received his first teaching post at the Mosque of ʿAmr ibn al-Āṣ in old Cairo with the endorsement of his teacher and future father-in-law, Baha' al-Din ibn ʿAqil. He moved on to assume numerous professorships, held in tandem with appointments as jurisconsult in the Justice Palace (*muftī Dār al-ʿAdl*), senior magistrate of Old Cairo (*Fusṭāṭ*), and Shafiʿi chief justice in Damascus. Several of his sons and grandsons were appointed chief justices and jurisconsults of the Shafiʿi madhhab in Cairo. Their rosters of positions included professorships in jurisprudence (*fiqh*) and exegesis (*tafsīr*), military judgeships (*quḍāt al-ʿaskar*), comptrollerships of charitable trusts (*awqāf*) that endowed mosques and madrasas established by militarist luminaries, and rectorships (*mashāyikh*) of revered Sufi hospices. The career trajectories of many other senior magistrates paralleled the significance of judicial lineages, although few approached the Bulqinis' luster.

But scions of judicial dynasties did not monopolize the ranks of chief justices. Biographies of individuals who attained the office reveal a diverse range of backgrounds, scholastic attainment, and political circumstances. During the Mamluk period, several emerged as first-generation jurists from mercantile families. Some were rustics whose critics never ceased to deride them for their rhetorical infelicities, whatever their skill as litigators. Ties to the military elite leveraged so many successful appointments that this linkage, open or covert, may be regarded as essential, even for members of prominent lineages. Numerous career biographies mention notice of an aspiring magistrate by a powerful amir appreciative of valued service, a provincial governor sensing administrative talent, or the sultan himself seeking to add a shrewd litigator adept at the surreptitious aspects of procedures in court to his trusted circle of advisers. Especially during the Sultanate's latter decades, marked by endemic cash shortfalls that prompted unrest and insurgencies among the ranks of recruits and line troops, award of office often depended on large fees.[20] Appointments attained by several Bulqinis resulted from payments amounting to thousands of dinars. The Sultanate's penultimate autocrat, Qansawh al-Ghawri, was castigated by chroniclers for relying on sales of judicial postings to defray the demands of his increasingly obstreperous soldiers for stipends and ad-hoc "bonuses" in return for their service on expeditions. Such dealings the chroniclers denounced as corrupt did not emerge abruptly from the straitened circumstances of the late Sultanate, but may be discerned at its origins in the mid-seventh/thirteenth century. They preceded the regime's founding. Chroniclers also dwelled on individuals who exploited the power of their positions as ultimate appellate judges to amass copious fortunes. Bribery for false testimony, laundered trial records, or swayed verdicts were reported at every level of the judiciary – from sworn statements by shuhud witnesses to the senior magistrates themselves, pressured (and rewarded) for pronouncing judgments to the liking of powerful claimants and sponsors alike. The biographies of chief justices also reveal instances when an incumbent renowned for integrity refused to allow such graft to affect his decisions – often with precarious consequences, as noted in detail by chroniclers who described dismissal as the least dangerous result of verdicts angering the regime's political hierarchy. Mulcting, jail time, public humiliation, and physical abuse might threaten magistrates esteemed for their probity or status in a judicial dynasty.[21]

Circumstances affecting service at this highest judicial level may be seen in the careers of individuals who attained notoriety in the chroniclers' logs. In particular, the biography of Sari al-Din ʿAbd al-Barr ibn al-Shihna, chief Hanafi qadi under Sultan Qansawh al-Ghawri, reveals hazards and options navigated by a master of opportunism in the courts. Son of the former Katib al-Sirr and Hanafi Qadi Muhibb al-Din Muhammad, Sari al-Din ʿAbd al-Barr succeeded to his father's rectorship (*mashyakha*) of the Sufi Hospice in the Shaykhuniyya complex, a post with much prestige but modest income. His rise to prominence began with an appointment of convenience to the senior Hanafi qadiship, after the newly enthroned Qansawh al-Ghawri sought to remove his predecessor's client, Burhan al-Din Ibrahim ibn al-Karaki. Sari al-Din soon found an opportunity to prove his worth as an adjutant who could manipulate the law to alleviate his patron's fiscal exigencies. In Muharram 907/July 1501, al-Ghawri was short of money to meet his recruits' demand for increased bonuses.[22] He convened the Caliph and four senior qadis in special session to debate the legality of tapping trust (*waqf*) yields to make up the deficit. Sari al-Din elected not to join his colleagues at the session, where they denounced the ploy as misuse of sacrosanct assets and a violation of charity, third pillar of belief incumbent upon Muslims. Later in the day, he consulted with his patron alone to concoct licit justifications for al-Ghawri's proposal. The next day, al-Ghawri summoned all the judges and pressured the three recalcitrant hold-outs to acknowledge the validity of Sari al-Din's arguments. The sultan then charged his marshal (*atābak*), Qayt al-Rajabi, with confiscating yields of Cairo's waqfs for the year.

This was the first of many such tactics rigging legal statutes that Sari al-Din helped implement. Over the following years, he augmented his stature as the sultan's most favored jurist, an adjutant who "got things done." Sari al-Din would flourish in his special relationship with Qansawh al-Ghawri for more than a decade, until a spectacular case of spousal infidelity would bring him down. In Shawwal 919/December 1513, the wife of a Hanafi deputy judge was caught in a tryst that precipitated a clash of wills between the sultan and his senior jurists. Eager to show his defense of conjugal morality, al-Ghawri condemned the wife and her lover to death without consulting the four chief qadis, who formally reserved for themselves the ultimate authority to litigate morals crimes. When a deputy judge of the Shafiʿi rite disputed the sultan's verdict on grounds that the founder of his school, Imam al-Shafiʿi himself, had recommended clemency after "sincere repentance" even for proven fornicators, the chief justices – Sari al-Din included – rescinded their initial endorsement of the sultan's verdict. Outraged by their effrontery, al-Ghawri fired all four immediately, temporarily leaving the supreme judicial tribunal vacant.[23] Sari al-Din's storied career terminated abruptly, his demise proof that even a record of exceptional service could not palliate a perceived insult to a patron. To the sovereign, humiliation by a client was intolerable. Al-Ghawri could not forgive his adjutant who allowed legal principle to compromise loyalty. His condemnation of Sari al-Din, along with the other justices, also revealed how tenuous patron–client bonds were in the tumultuous milieu of the Sultanate's final decades, when rulers implicated in corruption themselves sought to diffuse criticism by elaborate shows of public morality.

An office central to legal authority from the perspective of regulating commercial practice was the market inspector (*muḥtasib*).[24] Although not formally viewed as a jurist involved with court litigation, the muhtasib's duties required knowledge of Shariʿa and customary law relative to standards of commodity production, access to markets, price setting, and penalties for corrupt dealings. Commentators often dwelled on the disparity between the muhtasib's formal role as guardian of licit commerce and his actual conduct, which was affected by the fiscal deficits that depressed the economy, especially during the Circassian period. The muhtasib became entangled in the web of price controls, forced purchasing of staple commodities by the regime, and tactics for maneuvering around them that had become normative ways of doing business. Without regime muscle, he was virtually powerless to confront the hordes of marauding recruits and out-of-service mamluks who terrorized markets in Cairo and other cities during the late Sultanate. The office's prestige as a reliable defender of commercial equity progressively diminished, although its significance as a fixer of clandestine arrangements grew proportionately as the economy worsened.

The muhtasib navigated complexities of the marketplace with dexterity because his rulings could be enforced by the state. His formal charges and covert dealings required experience gained more readily in the bureaucratic or executive realms than in the judiciary. The office most frequently held in tandem with the market inspectorship was the supervisor (*nāẓir*) of a fiduciary institution. For effective performance and advancement, connections to the financial bureaus ranked higher than formal training in Shariʿa. This weighting of practical expertise highlighted the contrast between the Shariʿa as a moral code and realities of actual praxis in the marketplace. The evolution of regime control over many applied aspects of the legal system, in which commerce loomed large, antedated the Mamluk period. To what extent the hisba office ever functioned with genuine autonomy is an open question. Certainly, under the Mamluks, the inspectorship fell increasingly within the regime's sphere of influence. The preponderance of revenue-related diwan positions in career trajectories of muhtasibs supports their principal service as extractors, an arm of the Sultanate's growing network of extortion. More Mamluk officers occupied this office than any other occupation of the legal category.

By contrast, muhtasibs were less visible in the scholastic or clerical components of the learned classes. Few derived from prominent ʿulamaʾ families. Individuals who styled themselves jurist-scholars seem to have rarely sought or attained the office. Yet, such eminent savants as the historian Taqi al-Din al-Maqrizi served as a muhtasib, and he was not alone among jurists who prefaced their judgeships with the post. The aforementioned Mahmud ibn Muhammad al-Qaysari did several stints as inspector between 778/1377 and 789/1387, from which he moved on to supervise the army bureau (*nāẓir dīwān al-jaysh*) before becoming Hanafi chief qadi.[25] Holding the post jointly with his judgeship was Sadr al-Din ʿAli ibn Muhammad ibn al-Adami decades later (816/1413–14), who advanced from similar offices in Damascus.[26] Contemporary to al-Maqrizi and his nemesis as historian was Badr al-Din Mahmud ibn Ahmad al-ʿAyni, whose knowledge of Turkish expedited his entry to circles of power within the Mamluk elite (cf. Chapter 6). He occupied the inspectorship before and after his two terms as Hanafi chief justice, his extended tenure indicative of his intimate knowledge of the regime's fiscal agenda.[27] The Maliki qadi Burhan al-Din Ibrahim ibn Muhammad al-Saʿdi al-Akhnaʾi served as muhtasib, supervisor of the royal magazines and hospital (*nāẓir al-khizāna, al-māristān*), before assuming the qadiship in 763/1359.[28] His career was unusual due to a shift in madhhab: from his father's Shafiʿi rite to the Maliki allegiance he shared with his brothers. The issue of madhhab is significant with regard to the market inspectorship. Al-Akhnaʾi was among the few non-Hanafis to occupy it. Alignment with this school favored among the ruling class was advantageous for aspirants to fiscal power over the commercial establishment and beyond.

The office of jurisconsult (*mufti/muftūn*), a legist qualified to issue opinions (*fatwā/fatāwa*) on questions submitted to them by litigants in court or from political authorities seeking justification for their rulings under law, routinely appeared in biographies of rising jurists.[29] But its occurrence was rarely linked to the inferences of power or efficacy associated by chroniclers with the preceding positions. In the Sultanate's judicial hierarchy, the most prominent jurisconsults either staffed the Palace of Justice (*Dār al-ʿAdl*), which convened in Cairo and the provincial capitals, or occupied the post autonomously in Jerusalem (*al-Quds*). Appointed by the ruler, these individuals responded to appellate cases judged to be in need of validation according to principles of Shariʿa that were unresolved in antecedent court proceedings. Although their opinions formally represented a legal question's conclusive interpretation, in practice muftis seem to have ranked below the status of senior judges. Mention of the office usually occurred in the middle of a jurist's *cursus honorum*, rather than as its ultimate attainment. Due to the formal training in fiqh requisite to a jurisconsult's duties, muftis routinely held instructorships in colleges of Law. The term mudarris appeared consistently in their job rosters.

Contrasts in status between a judgeship and jurisconsult may be seen in the career of one Shams al-Din Muhammad ibn ʿAbd Allah al-Absi al-Dayri al-Maqdisi. Son of a merchant from Nablus, al-Maqdisi distinguished himself as a scholar in Jerusalem, Damascus, and Cairo. When al-Muʾayyad Shaykh was governor of Damascus, he appointed al-Maqdisi Hanafi jurisconsult of Jerusalem. After he became sultan, Shaykh summoned al-Maqdisi to Cairo as chief Hanafi Qadi in 816/1413. Regarded by powerful amirs and influential civilians as excessively honest – and averse to profitable corruption – al-Maqdisi resigned from his post voluntarily after three years rather than face the prospect of dismissal. Having persuaded al-Muʾayyad Shaykh to install him as rector (*shaykh*) of his new hospice for Sufis, al-Maqdisi arranged a comfortable retirement for himself in this sinecure. The integrity that had prompted al-Muʾayyad Shaykh to grant al-Maqdisi his post as mufti in Jerusalem worked against him in the more potent office of Hanafi chief qadi in Cairo.[30]

## Scholastic Practice

Scholarship beyond the acquisition of basic literacy and religious precepts was conducted along procedures that had matured centuries before the Sultanate's founding. The formal institutions where it was pursued, in particular the college of law (*madrasa/madāris*), had spread throughout the central Islamic lands during the Ayyubid period (564/1169–650/1252). The madrasa did not monopolize scholastic pedagogy. Instruction occurred in mosques (district: *jāmiʿ/jawāmiʿ* or congregational: *masjid/masājid*), hospices for Sufis (*ribāṭ/-āṭ, khānqāh/-āt*), or privately in study circles endowed by wealthy patrons. The principal agent of higher learning in a college or mosque was the mudarris, frequently translated as "professor," albeit "instructor" more closely approaches its literal meaning.[31] A mudarris in a college occupied a post funded by a charitable trust (*waqf*) that stipulated this position among its roster of charitable functions. The post itself was frequently termed a "chair" (*kursī*), since the instructor sat or stood while lecturing to students seated on the floor. Professors expounded on a wide range of texts in the Sunni corpus, reciting them aloud (with the aid of repetitors: *muʿīdūn*, or drill instructors) to set examples of grammatical rules and instill paradigms of diction that students were to memorize – ideally verbatim. Madrasa personnel consociated with figures in the judiciary, as previously noted. Both vocational cadres shared a common demography, studied in similar venues, and had interiorized the same curriculum.

The subjects that formed the core of higher learning have been termed "Islamic Sciences," since they derived from the foundational sources of the Islamic religion: Revelation (*Qur'ān*) and Prophetic Tradition (*Ḥadīth*). Jurisprudence (*fiqh*), or legal study within tenets of one or more of the four Sunni schools Shariʿa endorsed by the Sultanate, is assumed to have comprised the essence of a jurist-scholar's training. Texts authored by founders of each school, followed by the myriad treatises of elucidation and interpretation that emanated from them over the centuries, had evolved into a prodigious corpus of scholarly discourse by the late medieval period in the central Islamic lands. Biographies of individual scholars indicate specialization within particular lines of thought or accumulated case rulings. The aggregate lists of treatises mastered by individual luminaries nonetheless reveal numerous lengthy works memorized and elaborated to refine particular topics. "Mastery" of a text or subject involved memorization of its contents, allegedly without error or deviation from the original, as certified by attestation of peer witnesses in a document (*ijāza*) that validated the recipient's authority to teach and transmit it. Disciplines ancillary to acquiring expertise in jurisprudence were Qurʾanic exegesis (*tafsīr*), Prophetic Traditions (*Ḥadīth*), Divine ordinances/precepts (*Farā'iḍ*), paradigms of recitation (*qirā'a*), grammar (*naḥw*), and diction/logic (*manṭiq*). References to specific works certified in individual biographies suggest that a majority of scholastic personnel focused on a limited body of works committed to memory for exposition to students. Their biographies also indicate that brief commentaries (*sharḥ/shurūḥ*) abridging lengthier texts figured prominently in lists certifying erudition for many scholars and often served as the basis for their receipt of ijazas. Composition and sale of such commentaries had become a standard feature of madrasa learning by the Mamluk period – and a source of income for their compilers.

Contemporary biographical sources sporadically mention erudition in disciplines apart from the Islamic Sciences. History (*Ta'rīkh*), literature (*Adab*), mathematics (primarily algebra [*al-Jibr*] and geometry [*Handasa*]), medicine (*Ṭibb*), and time/date keeping (*Mīqāt*) emerge among the most cited. The circumstances under which these were acquired remain elusive, since formal coursework was largely restricted to legal and religious subjects. Inferences to them in biographies signal individualized study on a scholar's personal initiative – separate from routine pedagogy. Learning by apprenticeship in situ that required practical training along with exposure to texts was the likely medium of instruction for medicine and timekeeping (hospitals, observatories). Yet, the production of extensive works, notably in historiography, suggests access to madrasa libraries stocked in these fields and consulted by practitioners. Citations of sources by authors indicate more than familiarity with extant bodies of scholarship in shared disciplines. Especially in Syria, evidence may be discerned of collegiality visible in "schools" of distinctive approaches to definition of topics, stylistic expression, and citation of previous or contemporary authors (cf. Chapter 6).[32] The issue of collegiality in madrasa networks of the Mamluk period is complicated by the lack of terms depicting faculties organized along lines of their counterparts in medieval European universities. All formal sites of higher learning remained institutions dedicated to religious service. While waqf deeds list teaching posts that spell out pedagogical duties and remuneration, they provide little in the way of hierarchical organization, such as "departments" or "seminars." None of these institutions operated according to charters, formally incorporated under law. Teaching methods seem to have been confined to one-on-one relationships between scholar and student. Studies of madrasa networks in the Sultanate's large cities do indicate varying degrees of institutional prominence, as measured by both numbers of students attending and their ranked placement, post-departure, in offices within the bureaucracy, judiciary, or religious institution. A student who attended a modest college that maintained a single mudarris expounding on texts in one madhhab tended not to rub shoulders with the future luminaries trained in such regionally prominent centers as the Azhar, or colleges surrounding the great tomb-mosque of Sultan Qalawun along the Bayn al-Qasrayn avenue in the center of Cairo (**Fig. 4.1**). These drew students from throughout the central Islamic lands. Studies of comparative placement give the edge of enhanced opportunities for appointment as supervisor of a lucrative bureaucracy or senior judge to persons receiving ijazas from staff at these elite madrasas. Yet, the environment in which either one studied shared the same basic relationship of single mentor to student.[33]

In what setting, then, did eminent scholars who worked outside the purview of madrasas and mosques produce their works? Little in the biographies of such figures as the historians Ibn Khaldun or al-Maqrizi indicates research or composition in a collegiate setting. One assumes much the same context for literary compositions, although sultans convened festive public readings by prominent poets (cf. Chapter 6). Although both Ibn Khaldun and al-Maqrizi held teaching positions in madrasas – in the Maghrib, Egypt, and Syria respectively – each produced his compendia largely solo, away from a collegiate milieu over bouts of unemployment. Some historians were commissioned by senior officials of the ruling class, including the sultan. They wrote with the expectation of preferment for choice offices close to the ruling oligarchy. Yet, others produced their works, apparently to suit personal motives without remuneration. Al-Maqrizi retired from service in the bureaucracies or courts

Fig. 4.1 Facade of the Mausoleum of Sultan Qalawun
Constructed in 682–83/1284–85 on the Bayn al-Qasrayn Street in the former Fatimid District of Cairo, the complex served as a madrasa, tomb, and hospital.
(Photo by Angelo Hornak/Corbis via Getty Images)

to devote himself to writing his topographical survey of Cairo and histories of Egyptian regimes from the Fatimids to his own day. Since al-Maqrizi was acerbically critical of officials high in the Sultanate, pointedly jabbing at several rulers, he did not aim to please potential patrons. But others did. The chronicler Ibn al-Sayrafi al-Jawhari, whose gossipy logs divulge a trove of intrigues and scandals among bureaucrats and jurists, dedicated his works to Sultan Qayitbay, although without evoking a positive response.[34] The issue of context for scholarship produced outside the formal Islamic Sciences thus remains an open question. Solitary pursuit of projects or study in private circles of thinkers with shared interests are possible venues hinted in biographical sources. Actual milieus are speculative.

The adjutant most frequently mentioned in biographies of professors was the repetitor (*muʿīd/-ūn*). He was charged with drill and stylized recitation of texts regarded as canons for proficiency in a discipline or competence in a special subject.[35] Memorization was central to the traditional educational process at all levels – from the Qur'an at its initial stage to complex treatises regarded as the core of a learned science at the culmination of a scholar's training. Accurate rendition and transmission were considered essential, gate markers of a scholar's prerogative to interrogate a treatise's premises or, more seriously, dispute it openly. Discursive inquiry beyond boundaries set by conventions among previous generations of savants who had determined valid interpretations by collective consensus could licitly proceed only after accuracy was certified. Fulfillment of this objective was the muʿid's task. Assuring transmission of a text without errors of grammar or elocution, according to established patterns of recitation, was the repetitor's formal mission. In practice, few may have met this standard. But it remained the ultimate definition of proficiency and the goal of students seeking formal certification via the ijaza and entry to the ranks of the learned elite. Repetitors therefore served as more than drill instructors. Ideally, they were guides (*murshidūn*), caretakers of their students' moral compass. The muʿid channeled them along the "straight paths" of inquiry endorsed as sound by the scholarly canons of the period and transmitted to subsequent generations without deviation from their tenets.

### Custodians of Religion

For the Sultanate's Muslim communities, principally Sunni during the Mamluk period, the personnel who presided over religious service represented their medium for devotion conveyed through worship and performance of pious acts. While manifestations of piety were extraordinarily diverse, their expression in rituals centered on institutions where the faithful congregated: mosques, shrines, tombs of saints, and mystic hospices. The individuals who staffed these institutions emerge as a group singular within the larger category of the formally learned (*ʿulamāʾ*) for their relative parochialism and distinction from judicial or scholastic professions. Nor did they exhibit the signs of social isolation discernible among several categories of bureaucrats. Muslims descended from Copts were conspicuously absent from their ranks. A majority of individuals engaged in religious service whose genealogies trace their geographic roots were closely linked to the regions where their postings were located. Lineage ties to the Nile Delta and vicinity of Cairo were pronounced for religious functionaries in the Sultanate's capital. Although magistrates and scholastics were visible among them, the mutuality of professional traits and shared offices so evident for jurist-scholars was less noticeable among staffers of religious institutions. By contrast, they figured prominently in elementary education, since for Muslims, literacy was often initiated with reading the Qurʾan. While summaries of civilian careers in biographical dictionaries focus on eminent jurist-scholars and their attainments, sporadic references to activities associated with elementary education indicate its inclusion within the roster of fields embraced by the ʿulamaʾ. But, viewed collectively, religious functionaries derived from broader status groups than jurist-scholars, who often were born into prominent literary families. Nonetheless, prayer leaders and sermon preachers did appear within these families, although their origins implied close ties to zones surrounding their institutional bases.

The offices linked to religious service notably listed in biographical sources were prayer leaders (*imām/aʾimma*), sermon preachers (*khaṭīb/khuṭabāʾ*), Qurʾān reciters (*muqriʾ/maqāriʾ*), and transmitters of Prophetic Traditions (*muḥaddith/-ūn*). Individuals for whom prayer leading appeared as a formal post (*manṣib*) in a mosque, madrasa, or khanqah were typically funded from a charitable trust (*waqf*) with prescribed duties and a set wage.[36] Many received the post as an honorarium, following a series of previous appointments as jurists or pedagogues from which they resigned, retired, or were dismissed. Reference to an imamate thus often signaled termination of a career, rarely in the bureaucracy, more frequently in the judiciary or academy. Imams were also engaged in elite households, effectively as chaplains tending to their members. The most noteworthy of such a posting was the Sultanic court itself, to which individuals renowned for both erudition and piety ministered to the highest status group in the realm.

Their calling brings into focus its special relationship with the Mamluk ruling elite. While imams minimally appeared in the roster of secular offices held by civilians closely associated with senior militarists, they exercised a profound influence over the mamluks' spiritual lives. The systemic violence often attributed to the military caste as the predestined outcome of their barracks upbringing, training in martial arts, and embrace of conspiracy as a path to promotion may seem paradoxical when compared to the depths of religious feeling they manifested. Fear over salvation denied after death meted out as retribution for sins committed in a turbulent life cannot fully explain this sentiment. The mamluks did take their charge as defenders of Sunni Islam to heart. They were also moved by tenets of Divine intimacy expressed in Sufi rituals that granted a seeker special rapport with God. It is no coincidence that the office most closely associated with the imamate was rectorship (*mashya-kha*) over a Sufi hospice. The military elite sought to cultivate favor with inmates in Sufi khanqahs, whose influence over the masses, the equivalence of "public opinion," they recognized as potent. Mamluk officers, with the sultan at their apex, lavishly endowed the mosques, hospices, and tombs in which imams joined Sufi shaykhs and Qurʾan readers (discussed below) in reading scripture over their graves.[37]

Biographical sources aimed at elite careers and slanted impressions toward individuals at prestigious institutions with connections to the ruling class. Imams who populated the myriad ranks of local mosques in cities, not to mention their counterparts in rural settings, likely did not exhibit the credentials of luminaries lauded in the dictionaries. Nor did they match their judgeships and academic posts. Whether their training extended appreciably beyond the Qurʾan and basic tenets of the faith remains unknown.

Preachers of the Friday sermon (*khuṭba*) performed a dual role: enjoining a congregation to fulfill its faith obligations and communicating temporal events during the obligatory weekly prayer at midday. Both called forth rhetorical virtuosity, pious erudition, and political acuity.[38] Appointment as a khatib in a prominent mosque acknowledged eminence accrued in the Islamic sciences and cognizance of events vitally affecting the state. Khatibs acquired special renown for skill in imparting the latter. The khutba began with invocation of the secular authority's titles. A congregation was thus informed as to the continuity or disruption of the regime under which they lived. Additionally, the khutba could reveal by inference and circumspect phrasing a wide range of political information concerning the regime's policies and agenda for future actions. Events affecting the public interest were proclaimed openly. The sermon thereby served as a semiofficial news medium. It was eagerly anticipated in major centers of worship, particularly in Cairo and the Syrian capitals at times of momentous political shifts, internal disruption, or events abroad. To forcefully merge political information with moral exhortation, a khatib needed political acumen along with erudition and piety. Of necessity, he would associate with senior officials who kept him abreast of the Sultanate's policies. For these reasons, individuals appointed to preacherships often appear to have been ensconced in the upper ranks of the ʿulamaʾ. Khatibs mutually held a range of offices appropriate to the significance of this post. Their occupational contour paralleled that of jurists and scholastics more closely than for other offices in this category. But, at the same time, the preachership retained the autonomy characteristic of religious functionaries generally. Although alert to the regime's designs, khatibs themselves rarely served as blatant instruments of their imposition. Yet, the khatibs' presence in the bureaucracy (in particular as fiscal supervisors) reinforces an impression of familiarity with these stratagems. Conversely, holders of preacherships tended to be less directly involved with mundane religious procedures (such as prayer calling) than were other religious functionaries. Qurʾan readers enacted perhaps the most performative rituals in religious service: Muqri's recited verses, or the entire scripture, during annual festivals of the Muslim calendar, prayer services, and familial events such as circumcisions, marriages, and funerals.[39] Recitation of the Qurʾan was considered essential for obsequies and wakes over the grave. Intoning scripture nurtured the deceased's soul and abetted its salvation. Among the services most sought by Mamluk sultans and amirs, Qurʾan reading was lavishly endowed in their tombs (**Fig. 4.2**). Muqri's were retained in sites of religious service that could afford them. They did double duty by instructing the young in basic scriptural reading. Institutions supported by massive endowments were often equipped with galleries where muqri's declaimed scripture day and night during festivals or momentous occasions. Their presence was ubiquitous during Holy Ramadan. The milieu of these rituals during

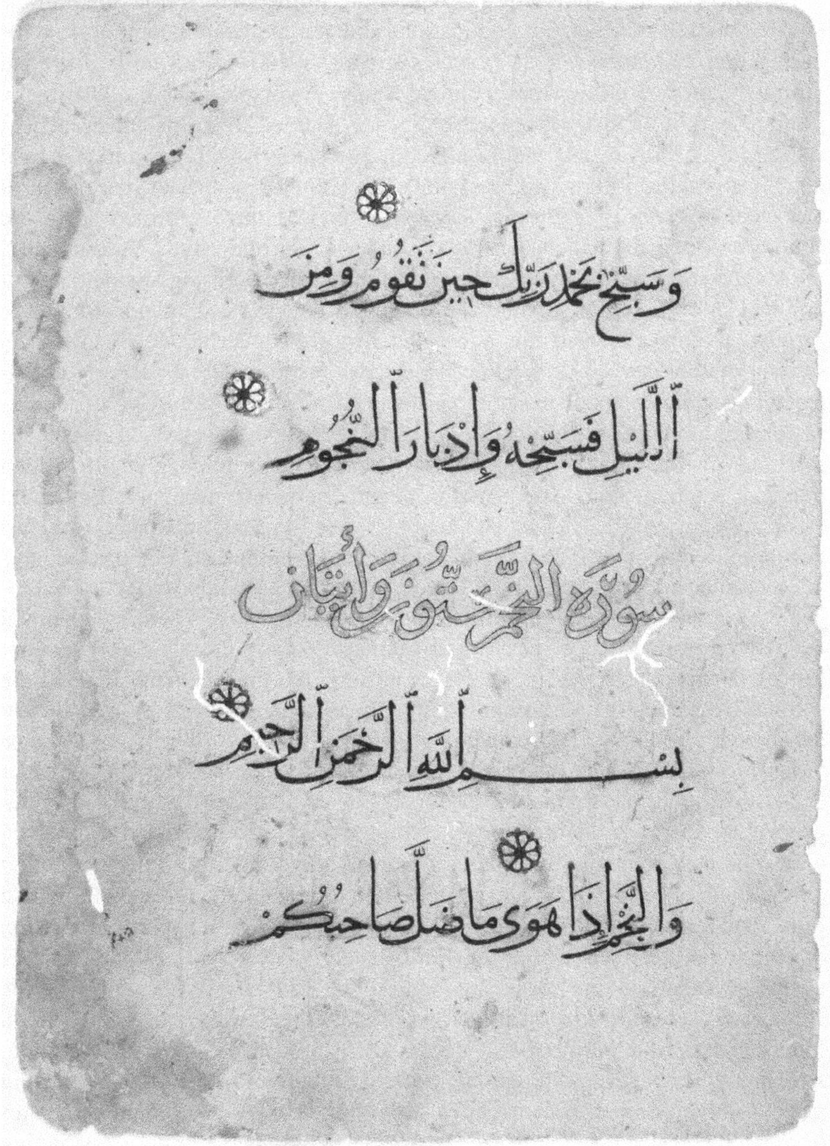


Fig. 4.2 Qur'an manuscript folio
Sura 53:1, al-Najm (the Star); seventh/thirteenth–eighth/fourteenth centuries; ink, gold, and colors on paper; sheet: 23.5 × 16.4 cm (9 1/4 × 6 7/16 in.); text area: 15.1 × 10.2 cm (5 15/16 × 4 in.).
(Photo by: Sepia Times/Universal Images Group via Getty Images)

a major feast day or impending crisis in settings like al-Azhar in Cairo must have stirred the passions of worshippers, inspiring them with a sense of Divine presence.

Muqri's were distinctive for their heterogeneity and familial legacies. While the origins of many were humble, others descended from generations of forebears who had recited the Qurʾan. Apprenticeship was a normative medium of instruction, but muqriʾs often taught the formal paradigms of recitation in institutional settings. When educations of muqriʾs are traceable, memorization of scripture and Hadith figured prominently, reflecting aptitudes for verbatim retention and a flair for rhyming. These skills were prerequisites to a successful career and to accruing the fame that garnered patrons. Muqriʾs often depended on affluent sponsors, since their maintenance signaled conspicuous piety, an act pleasing to God. An impediment pronounced among muqriʾs was blindness. Biographies of some of the most eminent highlighted this condition with terms emphasizing their eloquence and retentive powers. Muqriʾs seem to have engaged in quotidian activities of religious institutions more regularly than imams or khatibs, their vocation immersing them in the mundane rhythms of Muslim worship. Yet, muqriʾs were well represented among pedagogues holding endowed posts, due in part to their prominence as instructors of Qurʾan, Hadith, and public recitation.

Diversity among muqriʾs may be seen in profiles of individual readers. From the ranks of common people (*ʿawāmm*) was one Shams al-Din Muhammad ibn ʿAli al-Qahiri al-Sufi al-Shafiʿi, born at the Sufi khanqah of Saʿid al-Suʿadaʾ in Cairo, 809/1406–07.[40] Al-Shams Muhammad followed his father as gatekeeper (*bawwāb*) and initiated his studies within the hospice community. His skill at recitation brought him to the attention of the famed exegete Ibn Hajar al-ʿAsqalani and other scholars who certified his competence. Al-Shams Muhammad suffered from ophthalmia (*ramad*) from his youth and could only distinguish light from darkness. He was appointed muqriʾ in al-Azhar and Saʿid al-Suʿadaʾ and khatib in the mosque of Sharaf al-Din. Al-Shams Muhammad apparently prospered from his posts, since he owned a private house that was burglarized of valuable property. No such dwelling was mentioned for his gatekeeper father, for whom the hospice was home.

At the high end of the social scale was Zayn al-Din Jaʿfar ibn Ibrahim al-Qurashi al-Qahiri al-Azhari al-Shafiʿi.[41] Born in the Delta town of Sanhur in 810/1407–08, he memorized the Qurʾan and pursued his studies there. He then departed for Cairo to continue at several madrasas. More than sixty items appeared in his biography's curriculum list, many of which he was certified to teach. Al-Zayn Jaʿfar became famous for his capacity to absorb texts without error. He was appointed muqriʾ and mudarris of Qurʾanic recitation in the Muʾayyadiyya college and al-Azhar, where he took up residence. He was subsequently appointed supervisor (*nāẓir*) of the Suruja Mosque, presumably an opulent sinecure. Admired among a wide circle of colleagues and scholarly associates, he attracted the notice of several Mamluk officers. Al-Zayn Jaʿfar received a stipend of five dinars per month from Qayitbay's adjutant, Yashbak min Mahdi al-Dawadar, who was impressed by his flawless declamation of entire suras. He died in Cairo Dhu'l-Hijja 894/October–November 1489.

### Sufi Mystics

Individuals joined a mystic community to seek contemplation, self-perfection, and spiritual harmony – ideally. In practice, their search rarely meant withdrawal from society indefinitely (cf. Chapter 7). While such goals were often sought in consort with like-minded aspirants, isolation from temporal engagement was considered aberrant and misguided. Association with a Sufi community did not require removal from the world of affairs. Sufi orders themselves varied in styles of ritual observance and transcendence of temporal affairs. Persons who tied themselves to the term "Sufi" in some way were not uniformly committed to membership in an order (*tarīqa*: literally "road" or "path"). Biographical evidence from the Sultanate's urban populations mentions links to an order for only a minority of references to Sufis. Sufi identities for rural populations are sparsely traceable in biographical sources aimed at urban notables. Mention of a bond with Sufism without designation of a site occurred more often than reference to an order. Sufis in the Mamluk period were widely disbursed throughout both militarist and civilian domains of society. Yet, they do not appear to have been evenly distributed throughout the major vocational groups.[42] Fewer Sufis showed up in lists of diwan-related bureaucratic fields than among the ranks of jurist-scholars. And, for the latter, representation of Sufis seems to have diminished according to advancement through the judicial hierarchy. Still, Sufis were absent from no station of the judiciary, and their pronounced representation among scholastics in a wide range of subjects (in particular *Fiqh* and *Ḥadīth*) suggests their permeation of education and the learned classes generally. Biographical evidence for Sufis engaged in artisanal occupations or simply as laborers is pronounced. Their presence among religious functionaries indicates Sufis disbursed across the full range of mosques, shrines, and tombs rather than a proclivity for khanqahs or ribats. The ubiquity of Sufi mystics at all social stations throughout the Mamluk era symbolizes the multi-faceted character of the learned classes as a whole in Egyptian and Syrian society during the later medieval period. While assuming diverse roles in contrasting vocational settings, they attained renown simultaneously for expertise within distinct fields chosen for specialized erudition. These will be considered further in the contexts of broader social conditions.

A quality associated with mystic identity in the Mamluk Sultanate was conspicuous autonomy from the hegemony of the military class. Respect, even awe, for individuals manifesting *qurba*, or awareness of God, was embedded at all levels of the Mamluk elite. Those who compellingly expressed a commitment to piety and transcendence over worldly tribulation invoked deference inspired by a profound desire for association that lent the admirer some measure of a shared aura. That the masses revered this aura as well was not lost on the ruling authorities, who sought to incur the favor of Sufis resident in prominent convents and hospices. They expressed their esteem in lavish endowments of prominent sites. Whether formal endorsement of regime policies or implicit resignation to them, the stance of Sufi communities toward the ruling class was mutually appreciated.

An incident that reveals the influence of eminent Sufis over politics of the military elite, in particular during crises, occurred in Ramadan 922/October 1516, soon after the defeat and death of Qansawh al-Ghawri by the Ottomans at Marj Dabiq. It captures the tie between revered status and temporal power in Mamluk society. A caucus of senior amirs had pressured al-Ghawri's nephew and adjutant Tuman Bay to accept the sultanate. When he adamantly refused, the amirs sought resolution of the issue by a revered Shaykh. The historian Ibn Iyas reported the meeting:

> Upon the amirs' return to Cairo, they concurred that the Amir Tuman Bay the Dawadar should be designated Sultan, for which the grave circumstances qualified him. But he vehemently refused. The amirs then insisted: "We accept no one but you, willing or no." Then, the Amir al-Dawadar rode out, accompanied by several officers, . . . to the Shaykh Abu'l-Saʿud who resided at *Kūm al-Jāriḥ*. When they convened, he was informed of the Dawadar's refusal to accept the Sultanate. The Shaykh then brought out a copy of the Holy Qur'an, and compelled them to swear on it that, if they imposed the Sultanate on him, they would not betray, deceive, or conspire against him. They would consent to his speech and acts. The assembled officers agreed. The Shaykh then compelled them to pledge, from that day forward, not to resume their injustices against the populace, nor to restore the oppressive policies of al-Ghawri. They were to annul the monthly and weekly taxes on shops, and conduct affairs as they had been in al-Ashraf Qayitbay's time. They should return to market regulations as practiced by Yashbak al-Jamali when he was inspector. To this the amirs also consented. Then the Shaykh admonished them: "God the All-High defeated you, humbled you and granted authority over you to the Ottoman ruler because all humankind denounced you on land and sea." The amirs replied, "We repent our oppression before God the All-High as of this day." The meeting concluded, and the amirs departed from the Shaykh to confirm the Amir al-Dawadar as Sultan. The Shaykh had sworn them to abide by all they had pledged in his presence. The Dawadar's nomination was upheld, and he was installed as shall be related.[43]

# 5 The Political Economy
## Contexts of Innovation

The political economy of the Mamluk Sultanate evolved continuously throughout the two hundred and seventy years of its rule. Since the regime presided over an imperial union of territories that differed in their topography and ecology, the process of evolution in these disparate regions exhibited contrasting patterns of change. Agriculture as practiced in the Nile Valley manifested procedures unlike crop raising or animal husbandry along the Syrian coast, upland valleys, or semi-arid outback of the Syrian Sahel. Commodities imported from South or East Asia transited from ports in Yemen or Western Arabia through entrepôts on the Upper Nile to Alexandria, where they were transferred to European carriers that conveyed them to destinations on the Mediterranean north shore and beyond. Agents in each of these stages answered to differing sponsors, aligned their conduct of business with local politics, and extracted revenues at levels fluctuating within the mechanisms that governed interregional trade throughout this period. Domestic commerce in both urban and rural settings dealt in the exchange of myriad commodities produced locally in a workshop milieu. Control over (and profiteering from) marketing of lucrative staples that funneled revenues to the regime, such as spices, textiles, or sugar, became a principal objective of governmental authority, with results that enhanced the Sultanate's fisc in the short term but compromised its competitive position in the *longue durée*. The sole condition evident in all these aspects of the Sultanate's political economy was change itself.

The chapter will consider these issues from the perspective of agricultural practices or animal husbandry in Egypt and Syria, the varying extent of control exercised over them by the central bureaucracy, methods of fiscal extraction (formal or undercover), the conduct of interregional trade and its manipulation by the Sultanic regime over time, the domestic commercial economy, and finally the growing trend toward overt expropriation or clandestine extraction on which the regime progressively relied as licit sources of revenue diminished in the Sultanate's final century.

## Agriculture and Husbandry

Agriculture in the Nile Valley was based on irrigation methods implemented millennia earlier in the ancient Pharaonic period (ca. 3100–30 BCE).[1] The system depended on the annual flood from Aswan to the Delta that resulted from monsoonal rainfall over the Ethiopian highlands during late summer months, run-off from which flowed through the Atbara and Blue Nile tributaries into the main channel (White Nile). From Aswan north, the Nile rose on an average of 6.4 meters, cresting in September. Flood water was drained via canals into catch basins that were closed off by dykes after the crest to hold the silt-filled water until it saturated the soil and replenished the alluvium (thus negating the need for additional fertilizer). This network of water-retention basins extended the length of the Nile Valley from Aswan (**Fig. 5.1**). Dependent on the late summer/early fall flood, it produced winter crops primarily of grain (wheat, barley), broad beans, clover, sugar cane, and flax, staples that formed the foundation of the agrarian economy in Egypt. Alternate systems of irrigation occurred in regions removed from direct access to river flowage, in particular the oasis of the Fayyum. The Fayyum lay in a depression west of the main channel that had been transformed into a lush agrarian zone

Fig. 5.1 Catch basin irrigation farming in Edfu, Upper Egypt
(Credit: Andrew Holt/Getty Images)

during the Pharaonic Twelfth Dynasty (ca. 2100–1900 BCE).[2] The Twelfth Dynasty regime constructed a canal that extended 300 kilometers from far Upper Egypt to the depression and delivered water all year via a gravity-descent technique into the depression. From the time of the Arab conquest (19/640–41), the canal was known as the *Baḥr Yūsuf* or "River of Joseph," in reference to the Biblical Prophet sold by his brothers into slavery and renowned for convincing Pharaoh to settle the Israelites in Egypt. In the tradition of miraculous powers attributed to legendary figures in popular lore, Joseph was credited with the canal's construction. At the Bahr Yusuf's entry into the depression, its waters were diverted by a retainer dam into a lattice of canals that extended to the surrounding desert rim (**Fig. 5.2**). From Ptolemaic times (third–first centuries BCE) when detailed documentation is available, the Fayyum supported perhaps the most fecund agrarian zone in Egypt. Due to its perennial water supply, the district yielded summer crops of legumes, clover, flax, fruits (dates, melons), and sugar cane and was renowned for its poultry (chickens, ducks, geese, pigeons) and sheep raising. Rainfall agriculture was only marginally possible in the northern Nile Valley; sporadic cropping was confined to the Mediterranean coast and minimally documented.

Agriculture in Syria contrasted with the Nile Valley in its topographical diversity. Cultivation varied according to rainfall, altitude, and soil, with a

Fig. 5.2 Fayyum oasis at the western desert rim
(Credit: Emad Aljumah/Getty Images)

Fig. 5.3 Norias and aqueduct on the Orontes River, Hama
(Credit: PHAS/Contributor, Photo by: Prisma/Universal Images Group via Getty Images)

gradual demarcation between farming and husbandry extending from coastal regions east through mountain valleys into the semi-arid Sahel.[3] Although smaller-scale than in Egypt, irrigation in Syria was more locally differentiated and exhibited a wider range of techniques, from diversion to fields via sluice canals linked to stream channels, to water-raising wheels of massive proportions, such as the norias (Ar. *nawāʿīr*) in Hama (in modern Syria) (**Fig. 5.3**). Irrigation was confined to regional riverine systems such as the Jordan (*al-Ghūr*) between the Galilee and Dead Seas; its tributary, the Yarmuk; the Litani and Orontes in the Lebanon; the Ghuta oasis around Damascus; or the Euphrates in the Jazira district (northern Syria, northwestern Iraq). Tracts of land suited to rainfall agriculture (primarily in winter months) were located in the districts of *al-Sawād* (Ar. for black soil) in Damascus province (now modern Jordan), ʿAjlun, Hisban, Shawbak, and Salt (located in the Jabal ʿAwf and Balqaʿ regions, also in modern Jordan), the coastal plain of lower Syria (below the Jerusalem highlands in modern Israel/Palestine), the Biqaʿ Valley (between mountain ranges in modern Lebanon), and throughout the

Fig. 5.4 Hillside plowing in Lebanon
(Photo by Ivan Dmitri/Michael Ochs Archives/Getty Images)

Jazira in Iraq (**Fig. 5.4**). The coastal mountain slopes of the Lebanon were covered with orchards and forested in their higher elevations – stands of cedar trees provided one of the few sources of timber suited to construction in the Levant. Crops ranged from the predictable staples of wheat and barley to fruits and olives from orchards, legumes, and sugar cane (as in Egypt, the most lucrative cash crop and thus subject to the most regime control), particularly in the Ghur/Jordan Valley district. Husbandry based on herding sheep and goats by Bedouin tribes was basic to the economy of the Sahel and figured more prominently in regional politics than in Egypt.

### Administration and Taxation

Similar to contrasts in cultivation practices, regional administration of agrarian or pastoral land varied throughout the Sultanate's territories. In the Nile Valley, systems of control exhibited a genealogy also dating back millennia to the Pharaonic era. The theme apparent in their evolution is decentralization of authority with regard to tenancy of cultivators, jurisdiction of ownership, status of yield recipients, and methods of exploitation (via taxation). The critical stage of agrarian administration in the Nile Valley that culminated during the Mamluk period dated to the reign of Sultan Salah al-Din (564/1169–589/1193), founder of the Ayyubid Dynasty in Egypt. Salah al-Din introduced the system of land allotment and revenue extraction (*iqṭāʿ*), as practiced in Southwest Asia, that would prevail in the Nile Valley, with successive alterations, until the Ottoman Conquest of 923/1517.[4] The term *iqṭāʿ* derives from the Arabic root *qāf-ṭaʾ-ʿayin*, literally "to cut." In the context of agrarian administration, it may be defined as "apportionment," with reference to designating tracts of land, measuring their size, determining their purpose (cultivation, pasturage, arboriculture, wetland), ascertaining their produce (in cash or kind), and allocating yields to recipients. When European analysts initially encountered the term iqtaʿ in Arabic texts during the nineteenth century, they drew parallels with feudalism in medieval Europe. As feudalism evolved over several centuries in a variety of settings within the Latin West, they assumed that iqtaʿ developed in broadly similar ways throughout the medieval Islamic world. Such parallels are misleading.

From a fiduciary perspective, iqtaʿ referred to allotment of revenues from agrarian yields to members of the military institution, rather than to grants of title to ownership of land itself for indefinite periods. Nothing like the legal ordinances that sanctioned European feudal manorialism emerged in the context of iqtaʿ in the central Islamic lands. No landed estates with fixed boundaries bestowed by charter from a monarch or regional potentate, and presided over by a landlord who personally controlled peasant cultivators obliged to owe him service and yields under a regimen of formal statutes, emerged in the medieval Islamic setting. Nonetheless, a trend toward a sense of entitlement to long-term occupation of a distinct tract of land, effectively as private property, is discernible during the evolution of the iqtaʿ system in its various locales. European feudalism and Middle Eastern iqtaʿ also shared a second principle: usufruct (*istighlāl*), the granting of revenue or harvest from land in return for military service by a soldier in regime employ. The Middle Eastern recipient of such proceeds for the duration of his service was designated the allotment "holder" (*muqṭaʿ*). This principle of usufruct was noteworthy in the Middle Eastern context for its progressive devolution over time: from the ideal of temporary custody limited to fixed terms of service to the reality of privatization as personal property held indefinitely and transferable to heirs via techniques of appropriation, alienation, or purchase – at the regime's expense in progressive diminution of its state lands (*khāṣṣ*).

Antecedents of the iqtaʿ system predated Salah al-Din's reign and are discernible during the Fatimid period in Egypt (358/969–567/1171).[5] The variant of iqtaʿ Salah al-Din transferred to Egypt originated in the Saljuq Sultanate that ruled Iran and Iraq (431/1040–590/1194). Salah al-Din and his successors had to accommodate the Saljuq iqtaʿ system to Egyptian traditions of centralized state control over agrarian real estate. With the exception of grants to senior family members and favored officers, the muqtaᶜ under the Ayyubids in Egypt received his allotment primarily as a wage determined by the regime's fiscal bureaucracies (which had their origin under the Fatimids). He maintained few personal ties to the allotted real estate and rarely visited the site himself. Income from this allotment, the actual iqtaᶜ, was calculated according to a unit of account, the *dīnār jayshī,* literally "army (gold) coin," paid in cash (in actuality, dirhams at a ratio that varied between 10 and 13 dirhams/1 dinar jayshi; see Addendum) and kind, and doled out to the muqtaᶜ directly from the relevant bureau (*dīwān*). During the Fatimid and Ayyubid periods, the diwan primarily responsible for distributing iqtaᶜ revenues to holders experienced several phases of reorganization that aimed at tying the military apparatus more closely to the ruler and senior officers of his regime and separating its revenues from monies destined for civil services. Its shifting titles reflected this goal: from "bureau of the (imperial) council" (*dīwān al-majlis*), to "bureau of revenues" (*dīwān al-amwāl*), to "bureau of the armies and salaries" (*d. al-juyūsh wa'l-rawātib*), eventually shortened to "army bureau" (*d. al-jaysh*). Upon establishment of the Mamluk Sultanate and refinement of its fiscal administration under al-Ẓahir Baybars, the evolution of military fiscal administration would proceed in more complex ways, discussed below.

Revenues from agrarian land administered by the diwans were collected according to several classes of excises, the most significant of which was the "land tax" (*kharāj*).[6] Although traceable to Greek origins via Syriac transliterations, following the Muslim conquest the term was linked to the Arabic root *khā'-rā'-jīm*, designating in this context "extraction." Because the term kharaj appeared ubiquitously throughout the pre-modern Islamic world with regard to revenue collected from productive land in rural settings, its meanings varied widely according to location, purpose, and time. In Ayyubid and Mamluk Egypt, the kharaj applied to land under cultivation in rural areas for a broad range of crops. Agrarian land itself was classified according to its quality per unit (*faddān*, in Eg. 4200.8 $m^2$, 1.038 acres), as measured by: a) suitability for production of staple crops (themselves ranked in degrees of importance, as determined by price per unit of weight, the most common being the *irdabb*: in Eg. 198 liters, 69.6 kg.) – the highest rankings; b) cycles of cultivation alternating between irrigation, rotation of crops, or fallowing; and c) use confined to pasturage (lowest on the scale). The kharaj was charged against villages, each of which was assigned to one or more iqtaᶜs with a fixed number of faddans. Placing the burden of meeting quotas collectively on a village rather than on individual tenants assured the receipt of amounts stipulated per iqtaᶜ regardless of whether individual cultivators fell short of estimates for their own harvests.

Assessment of yields occurred annually in the flood's aftermath and, at least theoretically, involved on-site inspections of productivity based on past precedent, as recorded in detailed registers. The bureaucracy requisite to this process was substantial, not least because assessors and collectors sent from Cairo needed backup by enforcers from the military establishment itself. Assignment and distribution of iqtaᶜs were determined over time through surveys of land use throughout the Nile Valley and Syrian Provinces. These cadasters (*rawk/riwāk*) had likely been conducted in Egypt for millennia. Relevant to estimates calculated during the Ayyubid and Mamluk periods, the initial survey was ordered by Sultan Salah al-Din at the outset of his regime in 572/1185: the *Rawk al-Ṣalāḥī*.[7] Salah al-Din ordered this survey to prepare for the reorganization of iqtaᶜs he planned to support his army, composed of Turkish and Kurdish free cavalry for the most part. The cadaster's listing of yields according to land units served as the basis for calculating the value in proceeds (*ᶜibra*) from individual iqtaᶜs into the first century of the Mamluk period.

Changes in the status of military personnel under the Mamluk regime gradually rendered obsolete the categories and stipend levels supported by monies allotted via the Salahi Rawk. These categories were also perceived as inadequate for enhancing the Sultan's personal share of revenues derived from iqtaᶜ yields that he sought to bolster the loyalty of his favored troops: the Royal (*sulṭānī*) Mamluks. Prompted by worries that the several corps of free-born reservists (*ajnād al-ḥalqa*) were receiving excessive stipends out of proportion to their allegiance (regarded as ambivalent at best) at the expense of salaries for his Royal Mamluks, Sultan Husam al-Din Lajin al-Mansuri commissioned a second cadaster in 697/1297–98, *al-Rawk al-Ḥusāmī*. Although the muster of inspectors, clerks, accountants, and support troops required months to conduct their assessment of individual villages, revenues they generated, and verification of former boundary and tax registers, their work was nearly complete when Sultan Lajin and his adjutant Mankutamur were assassinated the following year. Lajin and Mankutamur had incurred the wrath of several rival officers and troops within the Ḥalqa ranks because of a steep reduction in stipends resulting from a shift in current shares of iqtaᶜ proceeds to the Royal Mamluks. Calculations of kharaj revenues collected from the Sultanate's iqtaᶜs overall were posited on twenty-four monetary portions (karats, *qīrāṭ*) per iqtaᶜ unit. According to the Salahi Rawk, twenty shares had been earmarked as iqtaᶜ: ten for non-Sultani officers, ten for Halqa personnel. The Husami Rawk halved this number to ten overall and allowed amirs among the Sultani Mamluks a gain of nine. The Sultan retained the four shares formerly designated for his office and entourage from the Salahi Rawk. The remaining share, officially set aside to supplement incomes for troops with iqtaᶜs deemed insufficient to support their combat readiness, in fact was alleged to have been usurped by Lajin and Mankutamur to enlarge their special funds. In addition, revenues collected from the poll tax charged against non-Muslims (*jawālī*) or property from persons who died without heirs (*mawārīth ḥashriyya*) that the muqtaᶜ had formerly claimed were also now appropriated by the regime. Although the assassination of Lajin and his adjutant temporarily destabilized the succession, adjustments imposed by the Husami Rawk survived their termination and continued in force until the implementation of the next, and more consequential, survey, commissioned by Sultan al-Nasir Muhammad ibn Qalawun.

As discussed in Chapter 1, al-Nasir Muhammad regarded his authority as dynastic, legitimated by right of succession as heir to a former ruler. He did not consider himself first among equals within a regiment of soldiers who shared his prerogatives, since he had not been imported from abroad with a cohort of foreign cadets and socialized within the regime's barracks culture. In fact, al-Nasir remained ambivalent, if not hostile, to this culture. He accordingly did not respect the principle of right to rule by acclamation even from senior officers because, by his standards, they were not his peers. Al-Nasir had personally experienced the insecurity of deposition twice before he gained his position the third time in 710/1310. Al-Nasir realized that retention of it required his consolidation of power, to which end he pursued measures to solidify support from within the Sultani Mamluks that had begun under Lajin and to enhance his control over fiduciary resources on a scale greater than his predecessors had envisaged.

To achieve these goals, al-Nasir launched a survey unprecedented in the Sultanate's history. It proceeded in four stages over more than a decade, the first focused on central and southern Syria (primarily Damascus Province) in 713/1313. While the survey increased the sultan's share of iqtaᶜ revenues, it abolished a series of taxes regarded as onerous to both officers who were assigned the iqtaᶜs and cultivators who worked them and was therefore regarded as equitable to the elite and masses alike. Two years later, al-Nasir initiated a survey of the Nile Valley. Contemporary sources uniformly concurred on the rigor of the officials who conducted it. Figures reported from the Husami Cadaster seventeen years earlier were minutely investigated, boundaries were resurveyed, and crop yields reassessed. As in Syria, unpopular miscellaneous taxes (twenty-nine in total) were abolished, in part to mollify the negative reaction by holders to the regime's claim of a larger share of iqtaᶜ revenue at their expense. Extraneous demands for submission of crops or animals from cultivators previously imposed by holders as ad-hoc "tribute" (*ḍiyāfa*) also came under scrutiny. The regime did not abolish these demands but added them to the iqtaᶜ yield (*ᶜibra*). It thereby formalized them, with the result of collection on a more regularized basis and subject to scales regarded by cultivators as less onerous and fickle than under individual muqtaᶜs. And since the "tribute" was now part of the ᶜibra, the regime gained access to resources heretofore the holder's sole prerogative. The final two phases of the cadaster surveyed territories surrounding Tripoli (*Ṭarābulus*) and Aleppo

(*Ḥalab*) Provinces, in 717/1317 and 725/1325 respectively. Details about specific procedures are obscure in comparison with policies during the initial two phases, due to the lack of comparable sources that summarized them.

But overall, the Nasiri Rawk implemented the following changes. First, the Sultanate increased its portion of revenue deducted from iqtaᶜ land from four to ten shares. This increment enabled the regime to create a separate fiscal domain from which the sultan could afford an increase in stipends paid to his Sultani mamluks over and beyond what they received from their officers and muqtaᶜ sponsors. By this device, al-Nasir's Muhammad's regime bound them more closely and bolstered their loyalty. Second, amirs at the several official ranks, Sultani and non-Royal, along with members of the Halqa corps, received fourteen shares total, a gain of four over the reduction imposed by the Husami Rawk but six less than the original portion of twenty set by the Salahi Rawk 140 years earlier. In consequence of this shift, members of the Halqa corps suffered the most severe reductions in stipends. Third, numerous miscellaneous taxes were abolished, a move appealing to both the military class and civilian/rural masses. The regime actually stood to benefit the most from a fiduciary perspective, since it managed to finesse its own enhancement of revenues under the cover of tax repeals. Fourth, Sultan al-Nasir's administration initiated a steady reduction in status and influence on the part of the Halqa corps, whom it regarded as excessively independent and thus a challenge to its own hegemony. Despite their massive losses, the Halqa's decline was gradual and would morph along unforeseen paths. But the diminution of its influence had been one of al-Nasir Muhammad's long-term objectives. Finally, the regime restored the usufruct principle (*istighlāl*) of service for revenue by blocking tendencies toward alienation and privatization of iqtaᶜs that were eroding its prerogative of their bestowal, removal, or transfer. As noted subsequently, this trend had already gained traction and might be stymied by fiat but not averted. Especially in remote districts throughout Syria, local militarists whose origins lay outside the system of Mamluk recruitment had often received appointments to iqtaᶜs in return for service. They frequently managed to retain their claims, sometimes under protest directly to the regime, and thus effectively gained possession of landed estates they could hold indefinitely. Overall, the cadaster overseen by Sultan al-Nasir Muhammad produced the results he intended: heightened control over the iqtaᶜ system, consequent enhancement of revenues at his disposal, and entrenchment of the Royal Mamluks as the foundation on which his military authority depended. The policies it implemented would remain in force until the end of the Qalawunid quasi-dynasty and the next phase of transformations initiated by Sultan al-Zahir Barquq.

The politics of land use in the Syrian provinces were less uniform than in the Nile Valley due to topographical variations and more diverse settlement patterns. They were also less precisely documented. The iqta$^{c}$ system officially applied to virtually all agrarian land watered by rainfall (*ba$^{c}$l*).[8] Irrigated land was more likely to be categorized as "private" (*milk*), in particular if sugar cane was cultivated on it due to the lucrative market for this crop. The sultan and senior amirs invested heavily in sugar production in both Egypt and Syria. The sultan exercised a monopoly over lucrative sugar cane cultivation in the Jordan Valley (*al-Ghūr*). Since its cultivation demanded intensive labor, the sultan ordered his governor in Damascus to conscript local peasants for the corvée (*sukhrī*) and to oversee the harvest personally. This duty required the governor's absence from Damascus for several months of the year, subjecting his own office to risks of insurrection. Iqta$^{c}$s in Syria were formally classified as "complete" (*darbastá*): subject to the muqta$^{c}$s' prerogative of seniority in the collection of relevant taxes. In this their privilege differed from policies in Egypt, where tax receipts were divided between the regime and holder in an elaborate, and formalized, system of shares due to the more pronounced intervention of fiscal bureaucracies in Cairo.

Overall, contrasts between official policies and local practices of cropping or harvesting were more apparent in Syria, a condition reflecting the lesser extent of administrative centralization generally. The range of cultivation procedures throughout the diverse Syrian topography also contributed to the tendency for more localized agrarian autonomy. Yet, paradoxically, the evidence in narrative sources, spotty as it is, suggests a more pronounced sense of personal identity by the muqta$^{c}$ in Syria with his holding as a distinct property over which he had fiduciary and heritable rights. While not paralleling the European manorial lord's sense of ownership as occupation sanctioned by Law, muqta$^{c}$s in Syria took up the process of alienation earlier and more consistently than their counterparts in Egypt. They often considered their entitlement as indefinite tenure from the time that their grant was assigned. Their sense of usufruct as obligatory seems to have been more pliable than was customary in Egypt. The extent to which muqta$^{c}$s in Syria relied on agents (*naqīb/nuqabā'; wakīl/wukalā'*) to interact with indigenous cultivators and collect taxes also may have differed from practices in Egypt. Syrian sources mention several officials responsible for local iqta$^{c}$ management: the *mushidd* or steward, the *mutakallim* or tax collector, and the *kāshif* or inspector. In Syria, these officials representing state interests tended to be mentioned in tandem with the muqta$^{c}$'s own agents: his wakil and accountants, who interacted with the regime's staff during harvests to divide tax revenues in money and kind. As noted, muqta$^{c}$s in Syria regarded their allotments as "grants in full," with the ultimate power to ascertain how revenues were collected from them. Their attitude was consistent with the widespread status of cultivators as tenants in Syria with no formal rights of ownership (in contrast with their permanent residency, which remained a right). Syrian sources sporadically mention the muqta$^{c}$'s authority to transfer peasant cultivators between iqtaᶜ holdings according to planting and harvesting schedules, although not to the extent of permanently uprooting them to distant regions.[9]

Security due to pillaging and destruction of environment posed risks for elites and commons alike in Syria that were more pressing than in Egypt. The Levantine "Corridor" linking Africa to Southwest Asia and beyond had exposed this region to foreign invasions since ancient times. Rural populations responded to episodic raiding or occupation by moving temporarily to less settled areas in the Sahel, an option more feasible to them than for their counterparts in the Nile Valley. They would return with the restoration of order. Inhabitants of marginal zones in the Sahel, where agriculture and pastoralism fluctuated according to seasons and short-term droughts, were accustomed to adapting their livelihoods to prevailing conditions. They interacted closely with pastoral tribes (more frequently referred to as *ᶜarab/ᶜurbān* than as *badw*), with whom they often shared kinship ties. Tribes were a significant economic and military presence throughout the Syrian provinces. Their influence ranged from symbiotic association with sedentary populations (for husbandry or crop transport that was mutually beneficial) to predation that inflicted long-term damage for all affected. The cumulative effects of sporadic foreign invasion and internal disruption from local tribes contributed to an abiding milieu of potential instability, to which the ruling authorities and indigenous population responded in ways that shifted markedly during the Sultanate's later years.[10]

## Fiscal Dilemmas, Counteractive Remedies

The measures legislated by Sultan al-Nasir Muhammad's cadaster to enlarge his financial base and bolster his political hegemony achieved their short-term goal. They also set in motion trends that led to fiscal shortfalls decades later. In the long term, these trends resulted in changes to landholding by the military class throughout the Empire that undercut sources of revenue established during the Sultanate's formative years and compelled the ruling administration to transform its bureaucratic apparatus in search of a remedy. The individual who presided over this transformation most prominently was Sultan al-Zahir Barquq (784/1382–801/1399 with interregnum), who demonstrated his acumen as a fiscal innovator along with ruthless political pragmatism.[11]

Policies implemented by the Nasiri Rawk initiated a process of diminution with regard to the iqtaᶜ system as the principal source of revenue to support the military establishment throughout the Sultanate's territories, although specific phases differed in Egypt and the Syrian provinces. Following Sultan al-Nasir Muhammad's death (741/1341), the four-decade span of largely figurehead rule by his descendants witnessed fiscal demands on this source that led to its insolvency when Barquq assumed the Sultanate in 784/1382. Several interest groups imposed these demands. As titular sovereigns, al-Nasir's descendants engaged in struggles for actual power with the most senior officers who held the largest iqtaʿs and monopolized the most lucrative fiscal offices. Factions among the several mamluk corps, primarily troops acquired by the current ruler's predecessors (*mustakhdamūn*) or senior amirs (*sayfiyya*), contested incessantly over preference for stipends and status. And the Royal Mamluks purchased (*mushtarawāt*) by the ruler inserted themselves into the political process as principal actors due to their pronounced military gain over other rivals in the capital. They demanded ever larger stipends and bonuses in return for stabilizing the sultanic ruling structure and upholding its administrative edifice. Their loyalty was bought, at inflating cost.

Sultan al-Nasir Muhammad's effort at hegemony by creation of an enhanced private domain through his rawk's increase of it from four to ten shares held by the Sultanic fisc was noted by competitors at subordinate levels of the military structure. They responded with acquisition of land to create mini-domains of their own. They exploited several tactics to achieve this goal: refusal to surrender iqtaʿs upon termination of service via bribery or other ploys, purchase of former iqtaʿs from personal resources to transform them into private property (*milk*), and alienation of iqtaʿs by making them over into charitable trusts (*waqf/awqāf*), which, under Shariʿa, were formally irrevocable and off-limits to taxation by the regime. The progressive diminution of the regime's landed inventory (*khāṣṣ*) that resulted was abetted by several phenomena, the most serious of which were pestilence and tribal resistance. In 749/1348–49, the Bubonic Plague (Black Death) broke out in Egypt for the first time. Successive epidemics over the next century and a half would reduce both urban and rural sectors of the population, with resultant declines in village occupation levels and local work forces to maintain the irrigation infrastructure (cf. Chapter 7). These declines were particularly noticeable in Upper Egypt, where some districts reverted in part to fallow or pastoralism. Plague was less of a demographic factor in the Syrian provinces, where the urban and rural economies continued largely unaffected. In the Nile Valley, maintenance of canals, dykes, and catch basins declined with downturns in productivity that had reduced kharaj proceeds substantially when Barquq assumed power.

The impact of these reductions was intensified by tribal rebellions. Tribes that identified as *ʿarab* (stereotyping them as Bedouin similar to nomads in the Arabian Peninsula is misleading; many tribes in both Egypt and Syria were semi-sedentarized) had obtained positions of regional prominence in both Upper Egypt and the Delta for centuries. In Upper Egypt, they had assumed de-facto political control over villages in several districts and asserted themselves as principal negotiators of kharaj rates for cash or crops collected by the central authorities. When the regime attempted to impose or renew miscellaneous excises that locals considered onerous, tribal leaders routinely declared rebellion, suppression of which proved difficult for the regime. Even the most vehement officers sent to crush tribal resistance, such as Sultan Qayitbay's adjutant Yashbak min Mahdi (cf. Chapter 2), achieved qualified results that were short-term at best. Tribal rebellion became a major source of resistance to control from the imperial center throughout the Circassian Mamluk period. It added significantly to the dilemmas that confronted al-Zahir Barquq upon his enthronement.[12]

When Barquq assumed sole rule, he reorganized the financial apparatus set up by al-Nasir Muhammad sixty years earlier. This apparatus consisted of several bureaus (*dīwān/dawāwīn*) that financed the military institution. While their lineage extended back to Fatimid origins, they had assumed the functions described by Mamluk-era observers in the decades following establishment of the Ayyubid regime. The principal funder of the military institution was the bureau of armies (*dīwān al-juyūsh*), responsible for paying salaries and bonuses to the several ranks of troops and officers. It worked in tandem with the collection bureau for land allotments (*dīwān al-iqṭāʿ*); both operated under the authority of the minister of revenue (*ṣāḥib dīwān al-māl, al-dawla*), often referred to in western sources as "chancellor of the exchequer." As the Ayyubid period evolved, authors of financial manuals claimed that these revenue departments were further refined, with a bureau of provinces (*dīwān bi'l-aʿmāl*) specifically responsible for collecting the kharaj and other excises from the provinces and border districts (*thaghr/thughūr*), in particular the port of Alexandria (discussed under interregional trade); and a bureau for the court (*dīwān bi'l-bāb*) responsible for collecting obligatory alms paid by Muslims (*zakāt*), excises on non-Muslims (*jawālī*), and inheritance duties (*mawārīth*) owed the state. Al-Nasir Muhammad effectively deactivated the vizierate, which previously had authority over the preceding bureaus, and replaced it with three officials: a supervisor of finances (*nāẓir al-māl*), superintendent of departments (*shādd al-dawāwīn*), and supervisor of his new personal domain (*nāẓir al-khāṣṣ*), noted above. It was these structures that Barquq contemplated when he initiated his financial reforms.

To supplement revenue from al-Nasir Muhammad's bureau of personal domain (*dīwān al-khāṣṣ*), Barquq formed a new "special" bureau (*al-dīwān al-mufrad*) by privatizing two large iqtaʿs: his own that dated from his days as *atābak al-ʿasākir* to Sultan al-Mansur ʿAli and that of his comrade-turned-rival, Baraka, whom he eliminated upon assumption of power. Barquq completed its creation by 797/1395.[13] The bureau's ostensible purpose was to augment the corps of mamluks Barquq had purchased himself through infusions of new recruits and raising their stipends. During the unsettled period following the deposition of Sultan Shaʿban II (778/1377), competing squadrons of Royal Mamluks had rioted for pay increases and threatened to unseat any sovereign who withheld them. Barquq thus resolved to exile his predecessors' mamluks upon his enthronement, replacing them with his own troops (*mushtarawāt*). Since proceeds from iqtaᶜs reserved for Royal Mamluks had diminished during the interval between al-Nasir Muhammad's death and Barquq's accession, due to alienation of state lands, Barquq intended to form a revenue source under his personal control to enhance the incomes of his own corps of purchased recruits, who numbered ca. 5000 men – the Ẓāhirī unit. Although a supervisor (*nāẓir*) directed the new bureau's distribution of revenues, one of the most senior officers of the realm presided over it: the *Ustādār al-Sulṭān* or superintendent of the Sultan's "House," that is, his estate, which Barquq intended to enlarge. In his heightened capacity, the Ustadar served as the sultan's chief minister of finance (cf. Chapter 2). His closest colleagues were appointed to it.

Barquq created complementary bureaus to oversee the collection of kharaj from districts not included in the two original iqtaᶜs subsumed in the Diwan al-Mufrad, or taxes levied at Alexandria and other ports on the Mediterranean (*D. al-Wizāra, D. al-Khāṣṣ*). Their portion of revenue-generating assets steadily diminished as the Diwan al-Mufrad enlarged from successive grafts of revenue sources over the next several decades. When Barquq established the bureau, it had jurisdiction over fourteen fiscal districts with an annual ᶜibra yield of ca. 200,000 jayshi dinars. By the middle years of Sultan Qayitbay's reign (872/1468–901/1496), the Diwan al-Mufrad controlled more than 150 districts located in seventeen of Egypt's twenty-one provinces. Its annual revenues exceeded 1.4 million jayshi dinars, or 17.3 percent (4 *qīrāṭ*s of 24) of total kharaj revenues from Egypt's rural districts.[14] Authority wielded by the Ustadar grew commensurately when Barquq's successors assigned him the viceroyship (*niyāba*) over Lower and Upper Egypt to assure his military power to enforce collection procedures throughout the Nile Valley.

Despite the Special Bureau's aggrandizement during the ninth/fifteenth century, its solvency was compromised by commensurate increases in its outlays, a development exacerbated by the inexorable alienation of remaining iqtaᶜ properties, their rural depopulation due to plague, reversion to pastoralism, and tribal resistance. Although sultans of the Circassian regime sought to privilege their corps of purchased mamluk troops, they were not positioned – or inclined – to disestablish fully the longstanding edifice of the military elite, which remained the foundation of the Sultanate's institutional identity. Units of troops who had served previous rulers retained their formal rank as Sultani mamluks despite their demotion. An incumbent ruler could not exile all of them and had to draw upon their service in times of local crisis or campaigns abroad. The various elements of the Halqa corps, among whom descendants of first-generation mamluks (*awlād al-nās*) remained their most prominent representatives by the Circassian period, were downgraded. They nonetheless endured as a class of notables (*aʿyān*) formally above the civilian commons. Since they were accustomed to subsidy, their stipends were reduced but not terminated. The Special Bureau thus found itself responsible for paying stipends to a host of groups that maintained ancillary ties to the military elite, many of whom no longer provided military service. It had become in practice a welfare agency for non-productive sectors of the ruling class, a function that compromised funding for the reigning sultan's purchased troops (*mushtarawāt*), the diwan's original mission. In consequence, by the reign of al-Zahir Jaqmaq (842/1438–857/1453) and his immediate successors, the Diwan al-Mufrad confronted the impending insolvency that had prompted Barquq to found it.

This irremediable context of endemic shortfalls motivated the fiscal policies of the Sultanate's final rulers: al-Ashraf Qayitbay and Qansawh al-Ghawri (906/1501–922/1516). These individuals adopted measures that counteracted demands by mamluk soldiers for inflating stipends or imposed tests of their qualifications for service.[15] Both addressed pressing issues with short-term solutions. Qayitbay convened his senior adjutants and fiscal advisors on several occasions to discuss salary and bonus rates. He then confronted troops of all ranks, on call for active duty or held in reserve, to defray their demands for pay hikes as a privilege of status. Qayitbay justified his refusal on grounds of international crisis. The meteoric rise of the Dhu'l-Qadrid rebel, Shah Suwar, in Southeastern Anatolia, and subsequent provocation of hostilities with the Ottomans presented the Sultanate with a formidable military challenge that required a vigorous – and expensive – reprisal (cf. Chapter 3). The several expeditions Qayitbay commissioned to quell the threat from Anatolia cost several million dinars, a sum that exceeded the Special Bureau's resources. The most favored units of the military hierarchy, the sultan's purchased soldiers among the Royal Sultani Mamluks, were poised to demand steep increases in stipends and bonuses for serving in these expeditions. Their tactics to leverage the demand were refusals to enlist or revolts that prompted rioting, which would paralyze the capital and shut down its markets. Qayitbay's achievement, lauded by contemporary observers such as the historians Ibn Taghri Birdi and Ibn Iyas, emerged from his adroit deferral of these demands. Qayitbay enjoyed sufficient stature among all levels of the military hierarchy to denounce ultimatums for increases from even his favored troops as manifestations of their greed and incompetence that compromised state security. He then summoned every unit requesting a stipend to trials for testing their readiness for service. The most rigorous involved drawing bows strung at increasing degrees of tension. Only those who could pull at the most strenuous level and accurately hit a target received a brevet to join an expedition at full pay and bonus. Those who failed received only token allotments that branded them as welfare recipients, unfit for service and a burden on the realm despite their residual place among the *aʿyān*.

The historian Ibn Taghri Birdi described one such incident in detail:

When the Sultan (Qayitbay) ascended to the Citadel (15 Rabīᶜ II 873/2 November 1468), he ordered a proclamation in Cairo's streets that whoever was due a stipend (*jāmakiyya*) ... should ascend the next day to claim it. He also summoned the senior judges to convene that day to discuss the multitude of stipends owed to the Sultani Mamluks and others. On Friday the 16th, the judges arrived along with learned persons (*ᶜulamāʾ*), and amirs. They assembled in the royal courtyard. The Sultan addressed them at length, noting that the *jāmakiyya* had, during al-Muʾayyad Shaykh's reign (815/1412–824/1421), amounted to 10,000 dinars per month. During al-Ashraf Barsbay's reign (825/1422–841/1438), it rose to 18,000/month. The Ustadar had been unable to cover that amount. In the days of al-Zahir Jaqmaq (842/1438–857/1453), it reached 28,000/month. The reason: al-Zahir had entrusted the Ustadar, Amir Zayn al-Din, with most of the (Mufrad) Diwan's operations, (enabling him) to spend as he wished, and defraying its grave consequences. Now the *jāmakiyya* stood at 46,000 plus five dinars. The Royal Diwan could not fulfill this amount from its proceeds. The Sultan then began to curse the situation, calling for (his own) death and threatening to abdicate. He then addressed the assembly: "Choose among you who should take over (my) authority." In subsequent discussions, the assertion was made that he (the Sultan) had failed to pay this money. He had given it to his own staff each month. Several judges claimed that the resultant oppression should not be imposed on a religious group (*milla*), since rumors were circulating that the Sultan intended to seize the people's assets and properties held in trusts (*awqāf*). The Sultan had authority over only assets to which he was entitled within the Diwan... *(from here follows a list of fiscal officials called upon the report their budgets.)*

The secretary of mamluks then summoned the host of stipend claimants, each according to his rank. The Sultan was positioned on the dais with three bows, each more resistant than the other. Those (formerly) receiving a *jāmakiyya* were tested, in particular the awlad al-nas who made up most of the claimants. The test was imposed on them because of their inclination to leisure and luxury, more than the Mamluks. ... A large group of awlad al-nas were deleted from the stipend lists, as were others. In consequence of this session, Sultani Mamluks (*troops, not officers*) were limited to 2000 dinars; any more was denied. If a mamluk had ordered more (equipment and victuals) at further cost, he was to return it to the supplier, or compensate him from his own iqtaᶜ. ... Every Sultani Mamluk was to receive three shares of fodder (*ᶜalīq*); each *Khāṣṣakī* received five, officeholders excluded. Each (Sultani Mamluk) was entitled to a bowl (*zabdiyya*) of meat weighing three ratls; more was denied. Previously, each one had (subsequently) received three bowls, then four, ten and fifteen (*increments not explained*). All of this was deleted. Likewise, fodder was limited to only three shares per man. The Sultan treated no one unjustly with these reductions because customarily, in ... Barsbay's days, portions had been set at these levels. We are not aware of any Sultani Mamluk who was due more than 2000 dinars, a (three-ratl) bowl of meat, and three (fodder) shares. Indeed, most had received less than one bowl each, and a purse containing only 250 dirhams, and only if he were a Sultani Mamluk. The session continued until a vast host had appeared before the Sultan. Yet the turbaned (officials, jurists and *ᶜulamāʾ*), *awlād al-nās*, merchants and commons (*al-ᶜāmma*), even Christians, could not all be counted or examined. ... The vizierate was unable to supply the meat rations; likewise the Ustadar's office could not convey the stipends and fodder. (Formerly), the rulers complemented (the deficit) with assets from the Treasury. Now, they could no longer (make it up). Thus, the (whole) burden of these problems fell on officials of the Diwan (al-Mufrad) ... on this day of abomination. Indeed, there was no feasible solution, nor reform. This situation dated from the Sultanate of al-Zahir Jaqmaq, may God grant him mercy, until the present.[16]

Both Qayitbay and Qansawh al-Ghawri were aware of the dilemmas depicted above that diminished the regime's finances and compromised its military effectiveness. Both contemplated long-term solutions, of which the fiscal devices previously noted represented the progressive abandonment of the *iqṭāʿ* system of revenue allotment. Over the course of the Circassian period, the system was replaced by privatization of assets in real estate formerly held by the state and their relocation to personal domains reserved for the ruler's agenda of political entrenchment and preparedness for campaigns against foreign rivals. Qayitbay and Qansawh al-Ghawri enlarged their domains on a scale unprecedented in the Sultanate's history. The range of assets they tapped became more diverse and included urban commercial establishments, mercantile networks, and a wide variety of craft shops (*ḥānūt/ḥawānīt*). In addition to this agenda, Qansawh al-Ghawri, the regime's penultimate ruler who observed radical shifts in the regional balance of power, contemplated the creation of new militia, such as a corps of fuseliers trained in the use of firepower, and experimented with novel technology such as artillery. Whether al-Ghawri was motivated to adopt these measures, which proved marginally effective, by innovations on the part of regional rivals (Europeans and Ottomans) remains a matter of debate. How they would have played out in practice was terminated by the Ottoman conquest of 923/1517.

Contemporary sources that addressed fiscal policies applied to the Syrian Provinces provide no depiction of bureau reorganization equivalent to changes documented in Egypt. They focus on a dramatic increase in miscellaneous taxes charged against asset holders in urban centers primarily and collected by agents sent from Cairo backed up by *khaṣṣakī* troops. They often exploited methods described by contemporary writers as extortionist. With regard to the rural sector, a significant portion of properties converted by Qayitbay and al-Ghawri into waqf were located in the Syrian Provinces. Their charters specify the return of ʿibra yields exceeding amounts reserved formally for local charitable purposes to their royal sponsors in Cairo. From Sultan Barquq's time, the pace of "waqfization" increased noticeably and embraced whole villages.[17] The network of territories converted to waqf by senior Mamluk officials extended out beyond sedentary zones to grazing lands in the Sahel, although degrees of extractive control likely varied according to the potential for resistance from pastoralists. Tribes in the Sahel were militarily capable and remained formidable adversaries if confronted with strong arm tactics. Yields remained a matter of mutual negotiation.

The preceding discussion summarizes a multi-faceted process of transformation in which the iqta[c] allotment system that funded the military institution when Sultan Baybars consolidated the Mamluk Sultanate had been eroded when the Ottomans defeated Qansawh al-Ghawri and annexed it. The privatization of former state lands into personal domains either by alienation or purchase of iqta[c]s had steadily whittled down the state's landed reserve so that it no longer yielded revenues sufficient to support the regime's troops, either to stabilize the regime or conduct its defensive operations abroad. The process itself reveals a series of innovations and devices concocted by sultans and their fiscal staff that were remarkable for their ingenuity. These innovations, despite charges of corruption lodged against their architects, kept the regime afloat when it faced the prospect of bankruptcy. Whether the Ottoman administration that inherited their legacy resolved these dilemmas more effectively remains an issue beyond the scope of this study.

## Interregional Commerce

Long-distance commerce between geographic zones in Africa, Asia, and the Mediterranean Basin (China, Indonesia, the Indian Subcontinent, Greater Iran, Zanzibar, East and West Africa, the Levant, Nile Valley, and Southern Europe) dates to periods that preceded the Arab Conquest by millennia. By the height of the unified ʿAbbasid Caliphate (ca. third/ninth–fifth/eleventh centuries), advances in maritime navigation and overland transport via pack animals in caravans had linked these zones in an elaborate system of trade networks. These networks transferred, on a reliable schedule, a variety of expensive commodities to their ultimate consumers who were willing to bear their high cost as indispensable items rather than as exotic luxuries. Two developments that followed the Caliphate's dissolution, the Crusader occupation of the Levant from Europe and the Mongol conquests across Central Asia, did not dismantle the structure of interregional trade in these zones but promoted its transformation into the system that prevailed during the Ayyubid and Mamluk periods. The Crusades brought the mercantile states of the Italian Peninsula and southern Europe into a sustained commercial relationship with the post-Mongol militarist regimes in Egypt and Syria that sought to profit from their control over the sea routes through which these commodities reached the consumers who were progressively conditioned to their access. Nautical shipment of these exotic wares via the Red Sea became the mode of transport most feasible for both parties due to disruption of overland routes through Asia (the Silk Road) temporarily imposed by the Mongol Imperium. Although successive Mongol regimes sought to restore overland trade from East Asia to the Mediterranean for their own advantage, several European commercial states – most prominently Venice – and the two Syro-Egyptian Sultanates regarded the

Mongols as competitors. Both sides aimed to build relations that benefited their mutual interests.[18]

Arabic sources that specified commodities transiting through Egypt and Syria date initially from the Fatimid period. Their lists of items include: textiles (cotton and linen produced domestically; silk, velvet, woolens, and other exotic cloths from Africa and Asia) either in raw bulk or finished (spun, woven, brocaded, or embroidered) in a wide range of processes; metalwork (brass, copper, iron) primarily of armor, implements, or weaponry; jewelry of gold, silver, and gems; crystal, glassware, and porcelains from Asia and Europe; paper and parchment finished as media for literary products; timber and naval stores from Anatolia and the Lebanon; and foodstuffs: primarily grains, olive oil, and dried fruits or vegetables produced locally or imported from Africa, Asia, and Europe (olive oil from Italy, North Africa, and Syria was regarded as superior to its counterpart in Egypt). Salt processed in blocks of varying weights represented a signal item of commerce transported by caravan from sub-Saharan Africa to the Maghrib and Mediterranean Europe. Aloe vera was similarly exported to the Maghrib and Europe from Africa for finishing of wool and cotton textiles. Traffic in persons, widespread throughout the Mediterranean and Southwest Asia from pre-Islamic times, figured prominently in interregional commerce in this period due to the demand for slave cadets imported from Central Asia or the Caucasus via the Black Sea and trained in military institutions of regimes that emerged in Syro-Egypt and elsewhere throughout the Islamic world during the Mongol era.[19] Trade in slaves from other regions destined for concubinage, domestic chattel, or emasculation as eunuchs for service in barracks, harems, or religious sanctuaries is also depicted in contemporary sources. They offer details that imply a lesser degree of significance with regard to expense if not quantity.[20]

But the category of commodities that assumed primacy of place in these sources, as measured by cost and demand, was spices cultivated in South or Southeast Asia and shipped to consumers throughout the Mediterranean and beyond for culinary or medicinal purposes. By the Ayyubid and Mamluk periods, pepper had become an item regarded as essential to preparation (and preservation) of meats and other perishables in cuisine cultures from the Middle East through northern Europe. During the eighth/fourteenth and ninth/fifteenth centuries, its price in Egyptian or Syrian markets and spice fairs in Italy would rise steadily, exhibiting meteoric spikes and declines in the final decades before the Portuguese entered the Indian Ocean and initiated a revolution in global commerce. While pepper consistently topped cost lists, it did not monopolize trade in spices overall. Cinnamon, ginger, cloves, nutmeg, and camphor appear on merchant ledgers in quantities and prices only marginally below figures reported for pepper.[21]

The cadre of merchants who oversaw this trade in the Ayyubid and Mamluk periods was labelled "*Kārimī*" in Arabic sources. The term's morphology remains indeterminate. It derives from no Arabic root, although medieval topographers in Egypt linked it to colloquial words for amber (*kārim* or *kahramān)* in the context of Cairene markets where amber was bought and sold. Whatever its origins, Arabic sources applied the term to spice merchants operating fleets throughout the Indian Ocean and Red Sea.[22] References to the word appear initially in chronicles that discussed blockage of European Crusaders from accessing the Red Sea during the Ayyubid period. In 577/1181, Sultan Salah al-Din demanded taxes from Karimi merchants (*tujjār al-kārim*) operating out of Aden in Yemen in return for allowing their fleets to dock at Egyptian coastal ports such as *Aydhāb*. The following year, the Ayyubid Sultan upheld the Egyptian monopoly over transit through the Red Sea when he defeated the Crusader commander Renaud de Châtillon, who had attempted to establish a European presence there. Although Karimi merchants continued to preside over the spice trade throughout the Ayyubid period, references to their activities occur sparsely in contemporary narrative sources. They became more visible after the coup that placed the Mamluks in power. Their ascendancy as effective arbiters of the interregional trade in spices via the Red Sea and Nile Valley dates roughly from the reign of Sultan al-Mansur Qalawun (678/1279–689/1290) to the enthronement of al-Ashraf Barsbay (825/1422). During these decades, the Karimis constituted an elite of two to three hundred merchants whose wealth in cash, ships, spices, and staff (free and slave) became proverbial. The sources mention several families from which eminent traders emerged that each managed assets in excess of ten million dinars. Religious minorities rarely appeared within their ranks. Karimis who received detailed attention in the biographical and narrative literature were consistently depicted as native-born Muslims, with only a few listed as converts from Christian or Jewish ancestors. In light of the Karimis' hegemony over a trade network that extended from China to North Africa and Europe, they were sophisticated with regard to regime politics, currency fluctuations, market conditions, and nautical seafaring throughout this wide expanse. Yet, while the sources often point to expertise and influence of individuals, they do not indicate their participation in formal organizations resembling merchant guilds of medieval Europe. The Karimis interacted with each other apparently on an ad-hoc basis. The extent to which they liaised as competitors or collaborators remains largely a matter of guesswork based on scattered inferences in period narratives. The narratives had more to say about their relationship with political authorities in the militarist Sultanate.

The Ayyubid and Mamluk regimes were governed by cadres of military officers who answered to the authority of a ruler who held his office by right of dynastic descent, acclamation by peers, or a combination of both. These cadres inherited a longstanding tradition of funding their caste and its military operations in part from extractions levied against civilian asset holders. When events presented fiscal demands exceeding returns from revenues generated from the official agrarian or commercial taxes previously outlined, the regime did not hesitate to call upon affluent asset holders in the civilian sector. The Karimis figured prominently in this relationship. Their fortunes prompted their service as bankers to individual sultans, underwriting loans that were negotiated in terms mutually favorable to both sides. Up to the rule of Barsbay, the Karimis oversaw their hegemonic control of the spice trade without overt intervention from the ruling authorities. The wealth that accrued to them during the eighth/fourteenth and early ninth/fifteenth centuries had enabled them to prosper while paying excises the regime charged against the spice traffic and defraying the often exorbitant sums "loaned" to rulers in need of cash due to exceptional circumstances. Proceeds from taxes on spices and other high-demand commodities were collected by bureaus distinct from the diwans managing the kharaj and supplementary agrarian revenues. From the reign of Barquq, these were centralized in the Sultan's private bureau, the diwan al-khass. For his part, Barquq and his advisors astutely appreciated the fiscal implications of the global forces that rendered the Sultanate's monopoly over the Red Sea/Nile trade so profitable to all involved parties. They allowed the Karimis to conduct their operations autonomously, within constraints imposed by the informal – albeit onerous – arrangement of demand and "loan" mutually understood on both sides. Barquq also placed sites of trade, emporia, and warehouses in the port of Alexandria under regime control so as to oversee collection of customs dues directly. The decades up to Barsbay's reign witnessed an unprecedented surge in profits accruing to the Karimi merchants. This sultan reflected on the growth of their wealth in the context of rising fiscal challenges confronting his regime that extant revenues no longer allayed. He therefore elected to depart from his predecessors' laissez-faire policies for the autonomous spice trade.

Sources contemporary to Sultan Barsbay's reign (to 845/1438) commented at length on decisions he reached to intervene directly in the spice trade and commerce in other high-demand commodities such as cotton and sugar.[23] They linked these decisions to Barsbay's introduction of a monopoly over buying and selling of pepper in 832/1429. Barsbay paired this action with an attempt to take over sugar production by appropriating refineries concentrated in Cairo's Nile port of Bulaq.[24] Barsbay issued edicts compelling both indigenous Karimi merchants and their European counterparts (by this time, largely Venetians) to purchase, at prices above market value, pepper stocks the regime had effectively confiscated from Asian shippers or their agents at rates artificially lower. The extent to which Barsbay and his successors were able to sustain the monopolies they officially imposed on pepper, sugar production, and other spices subsequently remains an issue of debate at present. Individuals bearing the nisba title "*kārimī*" continued to turn up in chroniclers' annals until the late ninth/fifteenth century. They described sugar refineries operated by the sultan's rivals or civilian entrepreneurs until the Ottoman occupation and beyond. But the era of the Karimis' commercial hegemony, proverbial wealth, and exalted social status in Egypt did come to an end with the implementation of Barsbay's policies. Those who successfully navigated these challenges by taking service under the regime's auspices were no longer positioned to retain their previous profit levels.

## The European Presence: Competition and Cooption

Agents of states situated in the Italian Peninsula or the Mediterranean north coast that engaged in commerce with regimes based in Egypt and Syria are sporadically noted in Arabic sources from the Fatimid period onward. Their activities are elaborated in more detail after the erosion of the Crusader era in the Levant that began with the reign of Salah al-Din and foundation of the Ayyubid Dynasty. After the coup that established the Mamluks in power, Sultans Baybars and Qalawun terminated the Crusaders as a political entity in Syria, a process that culminated with the fall of their last coastal port, Akko/Acre, in 690/1291. The Papacy responded to this seemingly catastrophic blow to European Christian interests in the region with a ban that year on traders who served European states against dealing with counterparts in the Mamluk Sultanate.[25] The states that faced a loss of access to the inflating market in commodities from South and East Asia transiting through the Sultanate's ports, of which spices were the most lucrative and vulnerable, pragmatically regarded the ban as a threat to their economies. Venice took the lead in pressuring the Vatican to lift its embargo, which it achieved in 746/1345. The Venetians and their commercial rivals mutually accepted the fact of a Muslim political order ensconced in the Levant, with which they would have to negotiate the terms of their commercial operations.

The Venetian Republic would eventually attain a position of preference in the lucrative trade with the Sultanate that ensued, a profitable status it exploited until the latter lost the monopoly over maritime routes with the Portuguese arrival in the Indian Ocean at the end of the ninth/fifteenth century. One hundred and fifty years earlier, the supremacy of Venice was not assured. Several states competed for access to the inflating market in commodities from the Orient. Catalonia, Florence, Pisa, and Padua emerge in the sources as prominent players in this arena. But it was Genoa that posed the gravest challenge to Venice's "special relationship" with the Cairo Sultanate.[26] In the decades after the Papacy lifted its ban on trade, Genoa aggressively contested Venice's efforts at commercial hegemony and territorial expansion throughout the eastern Mediterranean. In 1261, the Genoese had contributed to termination of the Latin "Dynasty" in Constantinople, imposed after the Fourth

Crusade (1204), and restoration of independent Byzantine rule under the Palaeologi emperors. The new Byzantine regime rewarded Genoa with preferred trade status and concessions over commerce in the Black Sea. Since most of the traffic in slaves that supplied the Mamluk Sultanate with its military personnel passed through the straits linking the Black Sea to the Aegean and beyond, the Genoese gained a position of primacy in regulating their transport to Egypt. The Genoese also maintained ties to the Lusignan Dynasty in Cyprus. They exploited their dockage privileges in Famagusta and elsewhere on the Island to assault Venetian vessels in acts of piracy. When King Peter I launched his "Crusade" against Alexandria in Safar 767/October 1365 (cf. Chapter 1), both Venetians and Genoese participated in the port's sack that followed. But the Venetians out-maneuvered the Genoese by formally submitting their Republic to the Mamluk Sultan as his adjunct subject. The Venetians also offered vessels that provided the Sultanate naval services, for troop transport and protection of its ports, that Cairo was prepared to outsource. Hostilities between Genoa and Venice came to a head in a series of conflicts known as the War of Chioggia (1378–81). Chioggia was a fishing town with a garrison that guarded the southern entrance of the Lagoon of Venice at the north end of the Adriatic. The Genoese had occupied the town with the aim of isolating Venice and blocking its further expansion into the Adriatic and Aegean Seas. Through audacious strategies implemented by the Doge Andrea Contarini, the Venetians broke the siege, defeated the Genoese decisively, and won recognition by their allies, Austria, Hungary, and Padua, of Venetian control over Adriatic and Aegean ports.

With regard to their preference in trade, the Venetians negotiated a relationship with the Sultanate that amounted *de facto* to a status of subordinate membership within its empire, rather than a bilateral partnership as a mutually sovereign state.[27] This relationship enabled the *Serenissima* to bypass prohibitions of its commercial activities that might accrue from its formal allegiance to Latin Christianity. The Doge of Venice officially rendered the Republic an extension of Mamluk imperial sovereignty by concluding treaties that allowed commercial privileges the Sultan personally authorized with him. No aspect of Venice's political autonomy or religious practice in its own territory was affected by this act of submission; it applied solely to commercial transactions within Egyptian or Syrian ports. The Doge's agreements with the Sultan were agnostic. He surrendered no commercial or fiduciary prerogatives his agents had gained in Egypt and Syria and in fact enhanced them by affirming their religious neutrality. Through this ploy, Venice proceeded to lobby the Sultanate to approve taxes and tolls below rates previously set according to extant laws governing commerce between religious minorities (*ahl al-dhimma*) and Muslims. In the Sultanate's ports, these often exceeded the customary tithe or *ʿushr* sanctioned by Shariʿa. They had in fact reached levels of 20 percent or higher per unit of a commodity's purchase price in the pre-1345 period and lifting of the Papal Ban, attainment of which the Venetians used to bargain these lower rates with the Sultanate. The Venetians aimed at brokering rates of 10 percent per unit, which they occasionally achieved at the cost of bribes and payment of "special gifts" to the Sultan's khass fund. In Qayitbay's time, when he confronted expenses of dinars in the millions to fund his campaigns in Anatolia, these gifts were onerous but deemed a necessary prerequisite for maintenance of Venice's special relationship. Until the Portuguese turned up in the Red Sea, they paid off. While the Portuguese were harbingers of the revolution in nautical routes of global commerce that would unfold over the next fifty years, their presence did not immediately terminate Cairo's centrality in the spice trade. Since the Ottomans would absorb the Mamluk Sultanate within two decades of the Portuguese arrival, losses as measured by short-term declines in volume and prices of the commodities noted above must be weighed against the larger scope of maritime and overland commerce as it evolved across the Ottoman Imperium's vast domains in these years.

## The Domestic Economy

In contrast with detailed treatises compiled in the Mamluk period that address regime management of agrarian land, interregional commerce and its commodities, or complexities of multiple currencies in circulation that resulted from successive alterations in ratios of precious metals to base imposed by the government, realities of economic life as experienced by the majority population received less attention in the abstract. This dearth of theoretical commentary is compensated by references in narrative chronicles, topographical surveys, and trust documents (*awqāf*) to prices of commodities locally produced and wages of salaried personnel. These ranged from elites of the learned classes who staffed the fiscal bureaucracy, civil judiciary, colleges of law (*madrasa/madāris*), and religious institutions (mosques, hospices, Sufi convents, churches, synagogues) through diverse grades of brokers, merchants, and artisans to the broad spectrum of laborers who performed mundane activities that maintained the urban infrastructure. Sustenance of population sectors in rural settings can only be roughly estimated from percentages of yields from crops or herds allotted to them in relevant tax registers or trust documents.

Compilers of the preceding sources routinely provided price variations at monthly or annual intervals for staples such as unprocessed grains (wheat, barley),[28] flour and baked bread, broad beans and other legumes, sugar and raw cane, honey, textiles (cotton, linen, wool), poultry (chickens, ducks, geese, pigeons), eggs, meats (beef and mutton), fish, dates and other orchard fruits (fresh and dried), vegetables, olive and sesame oil, and animal fodder (hay or *barsīm* clover). They also minutely recorded fluctuations in Nile levels during flood months (the reason behind Egypt's reliance on solar and lunar calendars). As the basis for irrigation agriculture in Egypt, the annual Nile flood attracted the government's critical concern that hearkened back millennia. The chroniclers' details reflected it (Syrian historians were less consistent at disclosing prices and dealt with no event paralleling the Nile flood). The historians also tracked variations in prices of imported items such as spices, apparel (in particular silk), glassware, ceramics, paper, implements, and weaponry. They frequently commented on shifts in rates of monetary exchange (the resultant array of terms for specific numismatic issues in gold, silver, and copper confronts analysts with formidable problems of valuation). Historians such as al-Maqrizi compiled extensive surveys of markets, shops, factories, textile mills, sugar presses, caravanserais for foreign merchants, and warehouses throughout Cairo. Their counterparts were traced in the empire's other cities (**Fig. 5.5**).

Fig. 5.5 Bab al-Badistan, entry gate to market district, former Fatimid quarter in Cairo
(Credit: Emad Aljumah/Getty Images)

The impression that emerges from these data depicts a continuation of economic stability that extended, despite short-term fluctuations, from the Ayyubid period through the Bahri segment of the Mamluk Sultanate that ended with the death of al-Nasir Muhammad (741/1341) and the plague epidemic that broke out in 747/1348. Thereafter, the domestic economy allegedly commenced a process of decline with sporadic spikes and dips that lasted to the Ottoman Conquest of 923/1517. How this decline is measured (changes in ratios of cultivated land to pastoralism, tax receipts, commercial activity, prices, and wages), whom it affected, and to what degree remain issues that provoke controversy in the field.[29]

With regard to comparative rates of prices for domestic produce, the consistent position of wheat and barley as most frequently reported throughout all districts within the Sultanate testifies to the ubiquity of these two grains among food staples available to the masses. In the Nile Valley, the third-place rank of broad beans in price lists confirmed its centrality as a basic sustenance crop in Egypt. Prices for all three were reported per *irdabb* of weight (**Fig. 5.6**). Price lists for wheat are the most replete and often appeared annually from 663/1264 to 918/1512. They also provide a record of variations in currency imposed by Egypt's rulers that revealed steady debasement: from dirhams containing two-thirds silver or higher (*darāhim nuqra*) in the Sultanate's formative years through Sultan al-Nasir Muhammad's third reign, to coins with diminishing ratios of silver to copper (*darāhim min al-fulūs*, see Addendum), to dirhams restored to a high percentage of silver (by Sultan al-Mu'ayyad Shaykh: *d. niṣf-fiḍḍa*, literally "half silver"), to coins entirely of copper or even iron passing for dirhams by the end of the century (largely replacing issues with silver after Sultan Jaqmaq's reign).[30] Prices listed in gold dinars occurred rarely, during crises of extreme scarcity. Correlation of values for these shifts in specie reveals a record of broadly stable wheat prices, interrupted by periodic spikes and dips, of 10–13 dirhams per irdabb, which continued to the famine years of 805–06/1402–03. Severe grain shortages in those years set off a gradual trend toward rising prices that becomes progressively difficult to evaluate due to the explosion in copper "dirhams" during the Sultanate's final decades. Contemporary sources routinely listed figures of several hundred dirhams per irdabb for wheat and only marginally less for barley and beans.[31] Prices for processed foods were predictably reported most frequently for flour and bread (listed in *raṭls,* according to varying degrees of "fineness," with sharp differences between milled wheat and barley). Despite short-term spikes or declines and a gradual price rise overall, all of these grain staples seem to have remained within the masses' reach throughout the Sultanate's duration. Short-term scarcities routinely stimulated hoarding by grain brokers, among whom senior officers with access to vast grain stocks figured prominently. They exploited panics to drive up prices. Such tactics often provoked rioting,

Fig. 5.6 Scales with pulley and counterweight, from ms. eighth/fourteenth c. (Photo by Werner Forman/Universal Images Group/Getty Images)

which in turn induced sultans, who held the largest reserves, to prohibit price gouging by their subordinates or to release their own stocks for sale on the open market at pre-scarcity rates. Their actions, motivated by the overarching need for order, served as a corrective to profit-seeking regarded by the ʿulamaʾ and masses alike as akin to usury condemned by Shariʿa.

Charitable foundations in major cities also offset scarcities from famines or hoarding due to their lavish endowments in arable land or urban real estate. Attached to these foundations were repositories and kitchens for preparing large quantities of staple foods distributed to the poor or hungry in times of scarcity. Commentaries provided by contemporary observers indicate that these institutions made a real difference between privation and starvation. Prices for meats, poultry, fish, fruits, and other vegetables were reported less regularly. They parallel the broad trends set for staple grains. Costs of remaining items exhibited variations that indicate contrasts in availability and consumption that mitigate discernment of common trends. Most occupied an intermediate status between staple and luxury, the latter sought as a marker of affluence rather than sustenance for survival.

Patterns for wages revealed contrasts that underscored differences in occupational status, social station, and access to assets in real estate, commodities, or currency. Reference has previously been made to the gulf between stipends (*jāmakiyyāt*) accruing to the Sultan, his entourage of senior officers, and their praetorian guard of Royal Mamluks, and wages paid to the lower ranks of recruits, auxiliaries such as free infantry (*ajnād al-ḥalqa)* or descendants of first-generation Mamluk soldiers (*awlād al-nās*, cf. Chapter 2). This disparity widened during the ninth/fifteenth century as sultans sought to augment their positions against the threat of insurrection from potential rivals among senior amirs. During the Sultanate's formative decades, the ḥalqa infantry corps recruited from non-mamluk cadres were compensated at levels roughly equaling those allotted to imported mamluk troops: 80–125 dinars/month. Following the stipend reforms implemented by Sultan Husam al-Din Lajin that accompanied his rawk, these were reduced roughly by half and diminished steadily thereafter. Descendants of mamluks, who in the Sultanate's latter years rarely saw military service, fared worse. By the regime's end, *a walad al-nās* received a monthly stipend that ranged from 1000 to 2000 copper "dirhams" per month. Since these were now valued at 250–300 per dinar, he took no more than the equivalent of three to five monthly. By contrast, those who belonged to the elite corps of Royal Mamluks saw their stipends rise markedly in the ninth/fifteenth century. Mature line troops who had received five and ten dinars/month during the Bahri period obtained twice that amount by Sultan Qayitbay's time. The vast sums accruing to the several ranks of officers, initially from iqtaʿs and later from the sultan's bureaus (*dawāwīn al-khāṣṣ, al-mufrad*) have been previously noted (cf. Chapter 2).[32] These were largely spent on staff and households or stipends for soldiers in an officer's employ. The figures do not take into account rations, weaponry, or fodder for mounts provided to each soldier. Nor do they include monies expected for a soldier's bonus (*nafaqa*), demanded as a prerequisite to his fighting in a campaign or joining an expedition.[33] By the late Circassian period, bonuses placed such a drain on regime finances that rulers routinely pleaded insolvency and threatened to abdicate. To some extent their act was a posture cynically dismissed by obdurate troops since sultans invariably complied and bonuses were handed out, although at lesser amounts negotiated after arduous bargaining.

Wages received by various sectors of the civilian majority paralleled these disparities. Wages for day laborers are limited to impressionistic estimates gleaned from sporadic statements in narrative literature of the period. These statements often appeared in the context of singular events, such as canal clearage or dyke repairs in advance of impending floods, construction projects commissioned by sultans, structural restorations in the aftermath of calamities such as fires or destruction from mob violence, or water portage due to shortfalls following low Niles. The motive of urgency mattered in this context. Amounts reported for these wages may have reflected incentives offered to attract workers after emergencies or to induce completion of projects by target dates. In any case, medial figures ranged between one to three dirhams a day from the mid-seventh/thirteenth through eighth/fourteenth centuries, or 1.5–4 dinars per month. During the ninth/fifteenth century, figures for commensurate work rose distinctly, an increase linked by both contemporary observers and modern analysts to labor shortages resulting from plague epidemics. Their frequency and high mortality combined to reduce the population across diverse segments of society in both urban and rural settings until the Ottoman Conquest and beyond. The ninth/fifteenth-century historian al-Maqrizi asserted that a stable groom (*ghulām khayl*) in Cairo who took a daily wage of 30 dirhams before the epidemic of 747/1348 could demand 80 in its aftermath.[34] Wages received by artisans and functionaries were more explicitly recorded in charitable trust documents (*awqāf*). They confirm a similar elevation of wages paid to skilled workers as a consequence of epidemics after the mid-seventh/thirteenth century.[35]

Income accruing to members of learned professions was rarely limited to a formal salary. A senior judge (*qāḍī*) who was salaried at 50 dinars per month for his service in court typically held one or more professorships of jurisprudence (*manāṣib tadrīs al-fiqh*) in a college of Law (*madrasa*) at stipends ranging from 10 to 20 dinars/month according to the institution's endowment. Subordinate staff that oversaw mundane pedagogical duties in these colleges, such as the repetitor (*muʿīd*) who drilled students in memorization of texts or reader (*muqri'*) who instilled canonical variants of oral recitation, were allotted stipends significantly lower than for the holder of a professorial chair in

Jurisprudence (*kursī al-fiqh*). Figures of five to seven dinars per month are typically listed. Stipends granted to staff at religious sites (mosques, shrines, Sufi hospices) broadly paralleled figures for scholars and pedagogues, on a sliding scale according to the wealth and prestige of particular institutions. In marked contrast with the stimulus to wage boosts prompted by plague mortality throughout the ninth/fifteenth century, which was driven by market forces of supply and demand, stipends associated with learned personnel remunerated from endowments saw declines in their incomes during this period.[36] Whether this decrease was due to diminished revenues from reduced waqf yields straitened by abandoned or fallowed properties, money laundering on the part of corrupt accountants, or appropriation by militarist donors reserving larger yield shares for their personal expenses or heirs, contemporary sources cite a decline in revenues accruing to the literary and scholastic vocations during the Circassian Mamluk period. This phenomenon occurred within a larger context of privatization and clandestine procedures for extracting revenue that marked the era, discussed below.

The environment in which commerce was conducted is well documented in its urban context. Commerce in rural settings may be deduced, marginally, from references to agrarian taxes as listed in iqṭāᶜ or dīwān registers. Trade in cities was referenced primarily in relation to locales where it was transacted. The historian who described them most fulsomely was al-Maqrizi in his topographical survey of Cairo: *al-Mawāʾiẓ wa'l-iᶜtibār bi-dhikr al-khiṭaṭ wa'l-āthār*.[37] The *Khiṭaṭ* lists more than one hundred markets (*sūq/aswāq*), arcades (*qaysāriyya/-āt*), hostels (*khān/-āt*), caravanserais (*wakāla/-āt*), and hospices for lodging merchants (*funduq/ fanādiq*).[38] Many were named for specific commodities, the range of which suggests the diversity of items bought and sold: traders (*murḥilīn*) with reference to camel saddlers, arrow/blade cutters (*rawwāsīn*), chandlers (*shammāᶜīn*), poulterers (*dajājīn*), weaponers/armorers (*silāḥ*), baskets/cages (*qafīṣāt*), spur makers (*mahāmiziyīn*), harness makers (*lujumiyīn*), broad clothiers (*jūkhiyīn*), sharbūsh hat makers (*sharābishiyīn*), belt/sash sellers (*ḥawāʾiṣiyīn*), confectioners (*ḥalāwiyīn*), meat grillers/roasters (*shawwāʾiyīn*), camel traders (*jamalūn*), shell carvers (*maḥāʾiriyīn*), book dealers (*kutubiyīn*), cabinet makers (*ṣanādiqiyīn*), silk dealers (*ḥarīriyīn*), amber dealers (*ᶜanbariyīn*), chart/map makers (*kharrāṭīn*), furriers (*farrāʾiyīn*), headgear/veil makers (*bakhāniqiyīn*), robe dealers (*khalaᶜiyīn*), shoe/slipper dealers (*akhfāfiyīn*), meat ball cookers (*kuftiyīn*), felt hat makers (*aqbāᶜiyīn*), rag dealers (*saqaṭiyīn*), banners (*bunūd*), and produce (cabbages/turnips: *kurunb/lift*). While terms for commodities often applied initially to a market's main function at its founding, few were confined to a single activity. Markets evolved over time; new proprietors introduced differing wares that related to or contrasted with former merchandise. Many markets offered prepared foods as a convenience to customers shopping for other items.

## Privatized Assets, Clandestine Revenues

Trends toward alienation of agrarian real estate from state ownership through conversion to trust (*waqf/awqāf*) or allodial (*milk/amlāk*) properties provided the backdrop to adoption by the Sultanic regime of clandestine means of acquiring revenue. These would become noticeable during the Circassian Period (784/1382–923/1517). They are to be considered along with factors such as demographic decline from plague epidemics and its impact on rural and urban work forces, diminished land under cultivation or reversion to pastoralism (especially in Upper Egypt), intensified tribal (*ʿurbān*) aggression in both Egypt and Syria, and changes in ratios of products imported to or exported from the Sultanate, Europe, and elsewhere. The Sultanate formally responded to consequent reductions of income from agrarian taxes by increasing its reliance on revenues generated by excises on the high-priced commodities shipped from South and Southeast Asia (mainly spices), over which it exercised a virtual monopoly from the mid-eighth/fourteenth century until the Portuguese arrival in the Indian Ocean and Red Sea. The measures it employed – attempts to impose monopolies over these high-cost, high-demand commodities, their forced purchase and sale, and direct intervention in their shipment through the Red Sea – attest to the gravity of the regime's fiscal dilemmas and the strategies it used to confront them. But these strategies do not tell the whole story.

Contemporary sources refer to procedures for acquiring revenue of dubious legality under Shariʿa but expedient in the face of straitened finances. Procedures that were openly implemented, such as confiscation (*maṣādara*), bribery (*barṭala*), gifting (*badhl*), or sale (*bayʿ*) of offices were openly discussed.[39] More covert tactics were hinted at frequently but obliquely. They proved no less significant as generators of revenue, since their clandestine application effectively exempted monies so derived from taxation. How much revenue such tactics actually yielded at specific points in time remains a matter of conjecture since specific amounts were rarely tallied in formal registers. The ruling authorities that extracted them were not disposed to leaving records that would expose illicit stratagems.[40] But contemporary sources provide evidence sufficient for plausible estimates. The sources also disclose stratagems that, considered conjointly, reveal coherent but *sub rosa* policies. These paralleled the procedures of privatization, bureaucratic reform, and intervention in trade or artisanal production that formally constituted the regime's response to fiscal shortfalls that compromised its durability long term. A review of conditions that contributed to the decline in agricultural production and commercial vitality establishes the context in which these covert stratagems were imposed.

Although trends that in hindsight were harbingers of future stasis, if not diminution, in the Sultanate's economy are discernible from the late Fatimid period (ca. 427/1036–567 /1171), the demographic downturn following the outbreak of plague after 747/1348 transformed a gradual phenomenon into enduring crisis. Contemporary sources described epidemics that erupted successively from the mid-eighth/fourteenth century to the Ottoman Conquest of the early tenth/sixteenth century and beyond. While first-generation Mamluk troops imported from abroad were particularly vulnerable, no sector of either the urban or rural populations was immune. Plague epidemics decimated whole districts throughout the Nile Valley. In cities and towns, contemporary sources report figures for the deceased that daily reached hundreds. Syrian sources present a less drastic scenario, partially due to less replete data. Rural districts and urban centers in Syria do not seem to have suffered such cataclysmic losses. But in Cairo, the regime's attempt to enhance the capacity of funerary oratories or corpse-washing stations to handle the onslaught of casualties at the height of outbreaks leaves a sobering impression of demographic catastrophe. The resultant reductions of population impacted disparate sectors of society differently, however. Work forces in both urban and rural settings stood to benefit from resultant labor shortages. As noted, their wages rose steadily from the mid-eighth/fourteenth century.[41] But their gain in remuneration prompted rising costs of work they performed or price increases of commodities they crafted. Agricultural production overall diminished, although to what extent in specific regions remains debated. While abandoned villages were reported throughout Egypt, an impression of districts being effectively emptied is qualified by gains in rural autonomy and retention of larger crop shares by cultivators and, particularly in Upper Egypt, of local control often overseen by shaykhs of *ʿurbān* tribes. Nonetheless, revenues generated from the kharaj land tax that reached the central government declined, from ca. eleven million dinars annually during the early Bahri period to less than two million by 922/1517.[42] This drop was due in part to reduced land in production and in part to the privatization procedures that withdrew a substantial portion of former state property from tax rolls. Estimates that more than 50 percent of land under cultivation in Egypt during the Bahri period had gone out of production by the turn of the tenth/sixteenth century are likely qualified by depletion due to privatization and local autonomy. But the regime's revenue losses overall were real.[43] If the Sultanate were to endure, it had to adopt alternative strategies that tapped into funds generated from privatization or autonomy that were hoarded secretly and thus remained unreachable through official channels.

Of measures applied by the regime's bureaucracy to access these sources, confiscation (*maṣādara*) was the most salient, according to period sources. Episodic appropriation of assets garnered by affluent persons or groups long antedated the Mamluk Sultanate. And spectacular confiscations occurred even during the alleged halcyon days of the Bahri period under Sultan al-Nasir

Muhammad. Techniques of extraction were overseen by individuals who had risen to the apex of fiscal bureaucracies because of their demonstrated acumen in accessing hidden resources. Among persons so skilled, al-Nasir's senior fiscal advisor stands out: one Shams al-Din ibn Faḍl-Allah, familiar to both critics and admirers by his sobriquet al-Nashw.[44] His career, marked by success at extricating assets from holders whose stubbornness matched their affluence, was terminated by the ruler who had enabled him for their mutual benefit. Sultan al-Nasir Muhammad appointed al-Nashw supervisor of the Private Bureau (*nāẓir al-Khāṣṣ*) in anticipation of the potentially massive sums his agent could produce – and did. He valued al-Nashw's capacity to ferret out concealed fortunes. Al-Nasir removed him, with reluctance, only when pressured by officers powerful enough to challenge the Sultan's supremacy if sufficiently aroused. When al-Nasir could no longer ignore their anger, the sultan made al-Nashw a scapegoat for clandestine methods he himself had endorsed. A significant aspect of the relationship that joined the ruler with a bureaucrat of al-Nashw's sort involved the latter's total dependence on the former for his advancement and personal security. From the ruler's perspective, the client would deflect public charges of corruption from his own person to the agent who perforce bore liability for them. Since the agent realized the risks he faced, he had to gamble on beating the odds. To the civilians who opted for this route, many of whom were identified as Copts, either practicing or converts, the odds seem to have been worth taking. Few alternative paths to equivalent power and wealth were open to them. Persons from such backgrounds who were adept in fiscal maneuvers emerged consistently throughout the annals of Mamluk histories (cf. Chapter 4).[45] Their stratagems provoked ire at all levels of society, from powerful officers whose own extractive devices these agents compromised, merchants and other wealthy asset holders bitter over plundered fortunes, down to the masses resentful over illicit taxes and price fixing. But the visions of fiscal reform that underlay the actions of these individuals may have been perceived as a graver threat to longstanding prerogatives of competing elites.

Al-Nashw impressed al-Nasir Muhammad with more than lucrative extractions. He devised an agenda for his patron that evolved to influence much of the fiscal transformation the Sultan sought to impose over his realm. Al-Nashw may have been an instigator behind al-Nasir's plan to enlarge his personal estate through raising the royal claim to state land from four to ten shares as a policy complementing his rawk. He also likely helped shape tactics aimed at diminishing the capacity of potential rivals among senior officers to enhance their own estates at the sovereign's expense. Al-Nashw was noted as one of the initial figures to exploit forced purchases as a means to profit from prices that exceeded levels set by market forces. The adverse consequences of these tactics for the interests of al-Nasir's rivals led to their concerted focus on al-Nashw's removal that compelled the sultan to terminate him. When al-Nasir realized that their opposition could engulf the ruler as a complicit patron, he acted to condemn the client who had served him so adroitly. Al-Nashw was formally tried for corruption (by the amirs who bore him the most rancor), tortured, stripped of his gains, and executed as a traitor who had undermined the realm. His demise was celebrated by the masses, whose resentment over price gouges the regime exploited as a restoration of the "moral" economy defended by Shariʿa. But the legacy of tactics designed by figures such as al-Nashw would outlast him.

Consequences of the straitened economy continued to prompt fiscal decisions of al-Nasir Muḥammad's successors. They were evident in policies implemented by al-Zahir Barquq, innovative founder of the Circassian line. When al-Ashraf Qayitbay was enthroned in 872/1468, he confronted conditions whose gravity warranted further elaboration of this clandestine agenda. It is during his reign and that of his successor, Qansawh al-Ghawri, that contemporary observers disclosed this agenda most pointedly. Qayitbay confronted a challenge to his regime's territorial integrity immediately upon his enthronement. The Dhu'l-Qadrid rebel Shah Suwar had defeated the first expedition sent against him at the end of his predecessor's reign (cf. Chapter 3). Stung by the humiliation of a provincial upstart's success, Qayitbay and his staff recognized the deeper threat Shah Suwar's victory posed to the Sultanate's claim as regional hegemon. Given their apprehension over how other contenders, such as the rising Ottoman power in western Anatolia, would interpret this failure to subdue an insurgent vassal, Qayitbay and colleagues such as Yashbak min Mahdi concluded that a decisive response was necessary. But how was it to be funded? Contemporary sources outlined a fiscal dilemma that superficially arose from an allegedly depleted treasury. The seemingly draconian measures Qayitbay's oligarchy pursued were driven by suspicions of substantial assets concealed by the agents appointed to procure them. The sums they proceeded to extract, initially to fund a response to Shah Suwar's revolt but subsequently to deal with financial exigencies throughout the next fifty years, provide substance to their intuition. The context of their reasoning may be seen in depictions by the historians Ibn Taghri Birdi and Ibn Iyas of the council in which Sultan Qayitbay convened his judicial and military advisors to address the funding crisis. To quote the former:

When the Sultan learned of this (Suwar) affair, he was distraught. . . . He complained about the scarcity of money in the treasury and lack of supplies in the royal magazines. Yet he realized that it was incumbent upon him to pay bonuses (*nafaqa/nifāq*) to the officers and soldiers designated to do battle with Shah Suwar. He immediately ordered the senior judges to present themselves along with the Caliph and personnel learned in the Law (*ʿulamāʾ* and *fuqahāʾ*) the next day (24 Dhu'l-Qaʿda 872/15 June 1468) to consult them about collecting the money from merchants and yields (*mutahaṣṣil*) from trusts (*awqāf*) set up by iqta$^c$ holders. The Sultan had resolved to inflict measures on the people that were unprecedented. The populace spent that night in alarm over potential calamities. Everyone harbored foreboding thoughts over the magnitude of the Sultan's avarice and his lack of concern for the welfare even of his realm's notables. The Sultan possessed a violent temper, prone to tantrums and inconstancy. He lacked solicitude for those who mediated for him or were respectful to him. He belittled individuals who voiced an (objective) opinion or who ameliorated a difficult affair. ... The Sultan's inclination from his youth to maturity was to act solely according to what seemed plain to him rather than by consulting the view of others with informed opinions. ... When the Sultan ordered the judges to advise him on collecting money, each one realized that his (own) assets might be seized, with none to intercede for him. There is no protection save that of God the All-High. ... The next day, the Caliph al-Mustanjid bi'llah Yusuf arrived with the four magistrates, amirs of 1000 and the $^c$ulama'. Then, Zayn al-Din Ibn Muzhir, Confidential Secretary (*kātib al-sirr*), stood to address them, stating that the Sultan was confronting a catastrophe but possessed no means from the Muslims' treasury to supply the Islamic army. He therefore requested an emolument from the people drawn from their salaries, rents and yields from iqta$^c$s and awqaf. This he would spend on preparing the army to do battle against this deviant (*kharajī*, i.e. Shah Suwar). The Caliph replied in agreement as did the four magistrates, for nothing remained but to acquiesce. But then the Shaykh al-Shuyukh Amin al-Din Yahya ibn al-Aqsara'i al-Hanafi, rector of the Ashrafiyya Barsbay Madrasa, stood up ... to disavow Ibn Muzhir's statement. He opposed the Sultan's demand for money under any circumstances, save by following legal procedure (*ṭarīq shar$^c$ī*). If the treasury had been depleted nothing should be extracted from anyone before assets held by the amirs and troops had been tapped first. These should include their supplies and uniforms not required for the war. Such was the gist of his words. A prolonged debate ensued between the Shaykh Amin al-Din and the Katib al-Sirr. The Secretary overtly supported the ruler but secretly sided with the Shaykh. Likewise for the Caliph and judges. The katib al-sirr had shown off his rhetorical skills. Yet the Sultan was stymied from achieving his goal.[46]

Ibn Iyas noted that even the officers in attendance congratulated al-Aqsara'i, whose popularity soared when word of his admonition spread among the masses. But the Sultan was furious over this rebuttal.[47] Nor was he dissuaded from pursuing his plan, despite his public stance as a defender of Shari$^c$a. Over the following weeks, Qayitbay and his colleague Yashbak, who held the office of Executive Counselor (*Dawādār*), proceeded with the shakedowns of significant asset holders they had devised. They did negotiate the bonuses of officers and troops delegated for the expedition down to levels well below their original demands. Upon his succession, Qayitbay had pressured Kha'ir Bak, dawadar to his predecessor al-Zahir Khushqadam, to provide 60,000 dinars for back payments of stipends and bonuses that had been delayed during the interregnum. He had incarcerated Khushqadam's officer of council (*amīr majlis*), Shihab al-Din Ahmad ibn al-$^c$Ayni, until he divulged assets gleaned from his former post that were rumored to exceed 200,000. These expropriations enabled the new regime to stave off revolts by disgruntled opponents of its consolidation. But they could not defray the costs of a major expedition abroad. Qayitbay therefore convened the first council. Qayitbay couched his demand in terms of defending Islam against a heretic and traitorous rebel. The Shaykh's rebuttal did not thwart the Sultan from proceeding with the expropriation of propertied classes he had laid out. Their worries were justified. The sums Qayitbay acquired to fund this expedition signaled a harbinger of future extractions from diverse asset holders.

Over the next twenty-seven years, the Sultan would expend upwards of seven million dinars on campaigns aimed at blocking the Ottoman advance through Anatolia, suppressing restive vassals, and warding off incursions from Iran. While chroniclers claimed that this figure was unprecedented, its significance is attributable to the regime's success in obtaining such a trove by uncovering assets closeted clandestinely for the most part. The sums did exist, as the ruling oligarchy suspected. Their disclosure thus qualifies the record of fiscal decline exhibited by official sources. Even in its later years, marked by incessant claims of reduced acreage, diminished cultivation, population decline, dependence on tariffs from foreign trade, and predation from groups who defied regime authority, the Sultanate in fact continued to harbor vast untapped resources. Their concealment induced the government to devise strategies to access them, which it managed to do. But the fact of their existence does mitigate the impression of wholesale economic deterioration that has been associated with the Sultanate since the writings of its own historians. The Sultanate was better off financially than they claimed. The Sultan's actions also qualify the impression of the ʿulamaʾ as stalwart upholders of Shariʿa against its corruption and defenders of property rights generally, from wealthy hoarders to the allegedly downtrodden masses.

The historians who shed light on procedures of fiscal procurement imparted no record that approaches statistical validity because its agents left none. For yields from overt policies, they could abridge sporadic proclamations issued after council deliberations or quote sums derived from trial transcripts of "mulctees" or procurers who were arrested. With regard to clandestine measures, they relied on informed hearsay. Several of the historians who commented on bribery, confiscation, or office-selling had established themselves as jurists, with access to court hearings in Cairo or provincial capitals. Others maintained connections to the ruling establishment either by family ties or appointment to high office. As descendants of Mamluk officers, Ibn Taghri Birdi and Ibn Iyas belonged to the latter group. The statements they and their colleagues made about fiscal procurement during Qayitbay's reign revealed more than ninety incidents occurring between 872/1468 and 901/1496. The majority involved compulsory payments from occupational groups or socio-religious communities to fund military campaigns or confiscation of individual fortunes garnered by fiscal bureaucrats themselves. The sums derived from these statements must be interpreted as rough estimates of actual amounts that remain unobtainable. Two-thirds of the confiscations reported for Qayitbay's reign quoted no specific monetary figure but simply referred to a "vast quantity." The reports did often distinguish between an initial sum demanded and an ultimate sum extracted. For Qayitbay's reign, the figures are ca. 1,080,000 and 900,000 dinars respectively, a disparity of 10 percent. But since two-thirds of the ninety incidents did not specify an amount, total amounts acquired may have exceeded these figures.

The procurement record for Qayitbay's eventual successor, Qansawh al-Ghawri, revealed contrasting methods and larger yields. Sultan al-Ghawri's reign was shorter: 901/1506–922/1516. Yet, the figures for confiscations demanded and extracted are roughly 3,200,000 and 1,200,000 dinars respectively. However, the ratio between quotes for specific amounts and generalized references was reversed: two-thirds for the former, one-third for the latter (of seventy incidents total). The contrast is due in part to proximity of the individual who remains the primary commentator on al-Ghawri's reign, Ibn Iyas. As an on-site witness to its major events, Ibn Iyas had access to sources familiar with the regime's finances. On the other hand, Ibn Iyas bore a personal grudge against Qansawh al-Ghawri, since the Sultan had confiscated the iqtaᶜ of the historian's ancestor. Ibn Iyas did not conceal his biased assessment of al-Ghawri's motives, which he condemned as driven by greed. But the historian's care in distinguishing between sums demanded and actual extractions complements his readiness to credit al-Ghawri's military innovations at a time of crisis. Both lend credibility to his factual reportage, if not his objectivity.[48] Qansawh al-Ghawri did not aim at duplicating the esteem his predecessor had received from the military or civil elites and even the commons. He nurtured few close ties to his militarist peers, the senior officers who made up the ruling oligarchy, and rarely sought acclamation based on mutual trust from the cadres of Royal Mamluks, the regime's Praetorian Guard. In fact, the Royal Mamluks suspected al-Ghawri of plotting to demean their status and diminish their combat readiness. Qansawh al-Ghawri attained notoriety for his stinginess with regard to stipends and bonuses for them while he experimented with alternative weaponry and a new brigade of soldiers. Al-Ghawri began testing cannons soon after his enthronement when he learned about their use by foreign rivals. These artillery pieces produced no positive results before his defeat in 922/1516, although the Ottomans' victory was not wholly attributable to a gain in artillery. Al-Ghawri began developing a brigade that was labeled the "Fifth Corps," due to its pay distribution set after the four days allotted to stipending the several ranks of Mamluk soldiers. This Fifth Corps (*al-Ṭabaqat al-Khāmisa*) was not recruited from cadets formally trained in the barracks culture of the Mamluk institution. Contemporary sources referred to freeborn foreigners from Iran or Turkistan in its ranks, or reservists (*awlād al-nās*) who had not passed fitness tests in archery or lance-casting. But they did drill with firearms, arquebuses manufactured in Europe and already used by Ottoman infantry. Al-Ghawri stationed his new brigade in Suez port, northern entry to the Red Sea. As with artillery, they played no role in the Sultan's confrontation of the Ottomans at Marj Dabiq. Yet, their presence provoked the ire of Royal Mamluks, who held them up to al-Ghawri as a personal affront to their privileged status as the essential element of the regime's military prowess. Their hostility is evident in a rendition by Ibn Iyas of a strained session between the Sultan and soldiers chosen by troops from the Royal Mamluks to represent their grievances and demands for bonuses and stipends that were in arrears:

On Sunday the 20th (of Safar 920/4 April 1514), the Sultan sat on the dais in the Citadel Courtyard where the wazir Yusuf al-Badri and the diwan officials convened. Also in attendance were the rations purveyors and cooks. They presented their accounts to the Sultan. The Sultan found shortfalls in moneys due to the government, and ordered the officials to repair to the Citadel Mosque (of al-Nasir Muhammad) and revise their ledgers. ... This was a day marked by tension. The Mamluk (recruits) had assumed a menacing stance. It was rumored among the populace that a revolt against the Sultan was pending. It was also speculated that the Sultan had summoned ... several prominent khassaki troopers and had rebuked them for their behavior. But one responded insolently, "It is you who has caused the arrears among the diwans. You have set up this Fifth Corps, and stopped the stipends (*jawāmik*) of orphans and women to fund it. It is composed of Turkmen, Persians (*i.e.,* aliens: *aʿjam*), meat vendors (*suwaykhāta*),[49] cobblers (*asākifa*), and awlad al-nas – a ragged mob of scum." The Sultan replied, "I created this new corps only to relieve you of foreign travel and expeditions." The Mamluk responded, "This was not the policy of al-Ashraf Qayitbay. You have beggared the diwans, so that five months of meat and fodder rations have been delayed. The granaries give us wheat so rotted that the horses won't eat it. The stipend you offer us is not enough to rent a house or a stable, nor to pay a groom or to buy uniforms or clothing. All of these are costly. Even unworked broad cloth (*khām*) is scarce. Medicinal syrup (*uqsimá*: oxymel) sells for two *niṣf-fiḍḍas* per jar. Throughout your reign we have never been adequately provisioned in meat or medicine. We are starving and naked." The Sultan sat silently for a moment, then replied, "You are right. I shall pay you the delayed meat and fodder rations which I shall distribute. I will make the uqsima available at one *niṣf-fiḍḍa* per jar." Voices were raised to the Sultan in praise. He distributed the rations to those attending him. They thanked him and the dispute gradually resided. The Mamluk recruits had threatened to pillage the houses of officers and officials. They plundered Cairo's markets and shops, burning homes of occupants. But thanks to God, peace was restored. Yet the threat of discord continued since no inquiry was made (into the arrears).[50]

Tensions arising from feelings of mutual suspicion between Qansawh al-Ghawri and the Mamluk soldiery persisted until his defeat at Marj Dabiq. How these tensions induced al-Ghawri's officers to contemplate treason was shown in the sudden departure of Khaʾir Bak min Yilbay, governor of Aleppo, from the battlefield. His betrayal at a critical moment of the conflict shifted the outcome decisively to the Ottomans. How the tensions would have evolved if the confrontation had turned in al-Ghawri's favor remains unanswerable. What did stand out in the battle's aftermath was the enormous fortune al-Ghawri hoarded under allegedly straitened circumstances that burdened his reign. When the Sultan departed Cairo for Aleppo in Syria in Rabiᶜ II 922/May 1516, he emptied the Citadel vaults of a trove that included gold and silver currency, bullion, weapons, saddles, and bridles encrusted with precious gems. His motives for doing so stemmed from (well founded) worries over their security in his absence, when a potential rival might use them to buy support from troops whose loyalty was already ambivalent. Al-Ghawri may also have considered them collateral essential to bargaining a possible deal with the Ottoman Sultan Selim Yavuz that might salvage his position. Whatever al-Ghawri's rationale, the size of this trove is another telling sign of the Sultanate's hoarded wealth despite the penury of its final years. After Selim defeated al-Ghawri, he sojourned briefly in Aleppo to inventory the treasure his adversary had deposited there. The details of its contents, as described by Ibn Iyas, attest to the historian's incredulity if not his hyperbole. From what source Ibn Iyas acquired the figures remains unclear, but records kept in the Citadel may have been available to him in the early years of the Ottoman occupation, which he witnessed. In any case, Ibn Iyas claimed that al-Ghawri effectively appropriated the fiscal legacy, as measured in specie and objects, of the Egyptian state that had accumulated from Salah al-Din's time:

It was rumored that the Ottoman ruler, after he took possession of Aleppo, only entered the city three times. On the first visit, he ascended the Citadel to review its contents. He marveled at the currency, weapons and precious objects. He confiscated money, some 100,000,000 dinars (*mi'at alf alf*), also saddle cloths (*kanābīsh*) embossed in gold, gold neck liners for horses (*arqāb*), the parasol and bird (*emblems carried over the sultan in processions*), gold saddles embossed with crystal, enameled drums, gem-encrusted bridles, chrome steel-embossed horse caparisons (*barkustuwānāt*), multi-colored nap fabrics, gold-embossed swords, coats of mail, countless caskets and caches of arms. He beheld a sight unseen by him or any of his ancestors or previous rulers of Anatolia (*al-Rūm*). This trove al-Ghawri had assembled from moneys seized unjustly, precious objects he had withdrawn from treasuries amassed by previous rulers from the Kurdish House of Ayyub and others, and from the Turkish and Circassian monarchs (of Egypt). Salim Shah confiscated all of this trove with no effort or ordeal on his part. Nor did the treasure include properties of commanders of one thousand, forty or ten, or of civil officials and all the troops stationed in Aleppo – their moneys, weapons, outfits and baggage. He was said to have occupied thirteen fortresses in the Sultan's territory, and seized caches of money, baggage and luxury items. Thus, the total value of the currency and weapons appropriated by Salim Shah this year was beyond calculation. He also confiscated horses, mules and camels beyond counting. He took tents and baggage conveyed by the Sultan, his amirs and troops. Such would seem to supply him for eternity.[51]

### Agents of Procurement

The status of bureaucrats who finessed the Sultanate's extractions was tenuous, even hazardous. Throughout the Sultanate's history, several of these individuals stood out for the exceptional skills that made them indispensable to the rulers or officers who condoned their access to the regime's clandestine assets. Yet, success at fulfilling their sponsors' agenda heightened their vulnerability. The career of Shams al-Din al-Nashw emerged as the prominent instance of such a relationship during al-Nasir Muhammad's reign. Similar figures were active in the Circassian period during the tenures of Barquq, Barsbay, and Jaqmaq, when the regime's finances verged on bankruptcy. As noted, some of the most prominent were Muslims descended from Christian ancestors. Their lineages marked them as a class distinct from the native-born Muslim majority even if they were not converts themselves. In depictions of contemporary chroniclers, they were regarded as innately adept at fiscal administration but prone to duplicity and hoarding. During Qayitbay's early reign, an exemplar of this class was allegedly of Armenian origin: Yahya ibn ᶜAbd al-Razzaq ibn Abi'l-Faraj al-Armani, known as Zayn al-Din al-Ustadar.[52] This Zayn al-Din rose to the top of the fiscal bureaucracy as head of the Diwan al-Mufrad and subsequently Ustadar under Sultan Jaqmaq. He was alleged to have amassed the largest fortune held by a civilian in the realm and purchased a body guard of 250 mamluks. Zayn al-Din ferreted out concealed assets so effectively that Jaqmaq's successors, Inal and Khushqadam, retained him. He combined fiscal expertise and shrewd bargaining with the mercantile elite to advance their mutual interests while funding military expenses. His distribution of grain and bread to the masses and endowment of corpse-washing facilities during plague epidemics won him popularity that redounded to his patrons. But Qayitbay and his adjutant Yashbak min Mahdi held grievances against Zayn al-Din that dated from interactions with him when they were line troopers. Qayitbay dismissed the former Ustadar's initial account of his fortune as deceptive, despite its magnitude, and accused him of hiding a trove that dwarfed his offer. Yashbak took over Zayn's interrogation and subjected him to floggings that "stripped the flesh from his bones." When Zayn died under torture (28 Rabiᶜ I 874/1 October 1469) without a disclosure that met Qayitbay's expectations, the sultan demanded to view his body before it was interred. He cursed the former ustadar and kicked his corpse before allowing it to be washed and shrouded.

Some of the most notorious figures did not rise from the ranks of Muslim Copts. An individual noteworthy for his humble origin, extractive ingenuity, and stubborn resolve served Qansawh al-Ghawri as his director of the reserve fund (*ustādār al-dhakhīra*): Shams al-Din ibn ᶜAwad. Born a peasant in the provincial town of Minyat Masir, Ibn ᶜAwad gained renown for his ability to raise money while on staffs of several senior amirs. Ibn ʿAwad drew his expertise entirely from personal experience since he was unlearned and had no training in bookkeeping. Ibn Iyas claimed that he never abandoned his rustic demeanor or crude dialect. His knowledge of markets and street life from the bottom was unmatched by any formally schooled rival. He was especially skilled at guiding petitioners through intricacies of the diwans and legal courts. Soon after al-Ghawri took him on, the Sultan made Ibn ʿAwad his senior civilian official and shared an "exceptional bond of mutual trust." But Ibn ʿAwad had made enemies, one of whom was a mamluk officer and prefect (*kāshif*) of Gharbiyya Province in the Delta named Kha'ir Bak. Ibn ʿAwad had taken the side of a local shaykh in a dispute over revenues claimed by the prefect. When the shaykh won his suit with Ibn ʿAwad's advice, Kha'ir Bak denounced the ustadar before al-Ghawri for concealment of assets from his employer worth 150,000 dinars. Al-Ghawri arrested Ibn ʿAwad and turned him over to his ablest interrogator, Zayni Barakat ibn Musa, who subjected Ibn ʿAwad to "the full gamut of tortures": lashing, head compression in a vice, and burning fingers. Yet the interrogator could not break Ibn ʿAwad's resistance. He died in confinement (18 Jumada II 920/10 August 1514) after disclosing only a fraction of his fortune. Subsequent torture of his son proved equally unproductive.[53]

The interrogator who had pledged to force Ibn ʿAwad's divulgence shared his lowly origin but advanced through a contrasting trajectory.[54] Zayn al-Din Barakat ibn Musa entered royal service as the son of a Bedouin falconer and groom in the Citadel stables. His name initially appears in a succession of petty offices such as curtain drawer and herald of the sultan's arrival at public audiences. Qansawh al-Ghawri appointed Zayni Barakat market inspector (*muḥtasib*) of Cairo in 910/1505, a position he would manipulate into a mechanism for cultivating popular support invaluable to the Sultan's own security and fiscal aggrandizement. Zayni Barakat became al-Ghawri's senior inquisitor. During his tenure as muhtasib, he forged bonds with sectors of society that ranged from street vendors to affluent spice merchants. He was personally connected to commercial agencies crucial to the economy at all levels such as the grain exchange. His influence at that institution was so pervasive that he could compel powerful hoarders of wheat or barley among the amirs to lower prices on popular demand. Upon any hint of his dismissal or arrest, Zayni Barakat could call on the masses to rally behind him. Al-Ghawri routinely turned over the richest asset procurers to him for interrogation. Ibn ʿAwad was among the few whom he failed to budge, even on the point of death. Al-Ghawri had reason to fear Zayni Barakat's formidable store of information and loyal constituents. His popularity rendered him invulnerable and secured his position even after the Sultan's termination. Zayni Barakat's career would outlast al-Ghawri's defeat and continue on to successful appointments under the sultan's betrayer at Marj Dabiq. The former governor of Aleppo, Kha'ir Bak min Yilbay (no relation to the prefect), was rewarded by Selim Yavuz with the viceroyship of Egypt. Zayni Barakat served this nemesis of his previous patron for several years.

## Privatization of Charitable Trusts

Privatization of assets donated to charitable trusts (*awqāf*) evolved as an investment strategy throughout the economy's mounting exigencies and shortfalls. In the reigns of Qayitbay and Qansawh al-Ghawri, their alienation of waqf properties assumed proportions indicative of the fiscal system's radical transformation in the Sultanate's latter years. These rulers exploited the security of the charitable trust under Law from diminution or appropriation to create personal fiscs sufficient to fund their goals of building a loyal military base and warding off challenges from foreign rivals. Their strategies can be traced through the documentation of properties each ruler acquired over several decades. A waqf could be legally sold (*bayᶜ*), substituted for another asset in real estate (*istibdāl*), reassigned (*intiqāl*), alienated, or transferred (*tamlīk*), provided that its value remained equivalent to the original principal and its yield for charitable purpose was not reduced. Donors could, within limits fixed by inheritance law, set aside properties for their descendants' support. They could designate a family member as supervisor (*nāẓir*), charged with allocation of waqf proceeds and the right to choose successor trustees. These prerogatives theoretically ensured control of waqf yields within a lineage over generations. They evolved as a consequence of the trust's ad-hoc status in Shariᶜa.

While interpreted by analogy as an instrument of charity linked to the third pillar of Islam (*zakāt*), the term waqf does not appear in the Qur'an. Commendations of charitable donation do occur in Hadith literature, acquiring their sanctity from Prophetic endorsement rather than from Divine injunction. The waqf's standing as a licit procedure confirmed by tradition rather than by revelation legitimated its malleability. By the later Middle Ages in the central Islamic lands, the charitable trust had become the prime instrument of public welfare and protector of estate integrity in settings that compromised each.

Waqf deeds issued by Qayitbay, al-Ghawri, and their accountants reveal similarities and contrasts in the two sultan's objectives. Qayitbay began placing properties in trust decades before his enthronement. The earliest surviving deed in his name dates from 29 Dhu'l-Qaᶜda 855/23 December 1452, seventeen years before his accession.[55] He purchased roughly one-third of an agrarian plot in Gharbiyya Province for 1100 dinars. This property is not listed in subsequent deeds and may have been reserved for his personal estate. From this time until the year before his death (900/1495), Qayitbay acquired a broad assortment of urban real estate and rural tracts, most of which he placed in subsequent waqfs. The documents date from 24 Jumada II 879/5 November 1474 to 15 Dhu'l-Hijja 895/30 October 1490. They supported fourteen charitable foundations, including the sultan's mausoleum/mosque (*jāmiʿ al-madfan*) located in the Desert Cemetery (*Ṣaḥrāʾ*) east of Cairo, public fountains, orphanages, other mosques in Cairo or the Delta, and a college (*madrasa*) in Jerusalem.[56] Qayitbay's primary deed, issued 24 Jumada II 879/5 November 1474, amended several times, listed properties that supported his mausoleum, three fountains, two Qur'an schools, a mosque, and an irrigation wheel in Gharbiyya and Minufiyya Provinces. Since the mausoleum was the deed's primary beneficiary, its staff listed religious functionaries, Sufi mystics who read the Qur'an over the deceased's tomb, and scholastics and custodians to maintain its devotional, pedagogical, and welfare activities. They were salaried in coins (at this time copper *darāhim min al-fulūs*), each worth a minute fraction of an Ashrafi dinar. Collectively, the deed allotted staff and their supplies a million-plus dirhams annually for this foundation alone. With regard to income, yields from properties that supported the eight foundations in Qayitbay's primary trust deed generated an estimated annual sum of 58,000+ dinars.[57] Annual disbursements to the designated foundations, calculated from rent estimates based on 10 percent of property values compared with staff salaries in copper "dirhams" (exchanged at 300 per dinar), came to 4000+ dinars, 7 percent of total income. Since these figures may underestimate actual revenues provided for staff salaries, student stipends, food allotments, or upkeep costs, a calculation allowing twice the preceding disbursement would still approach only 14 percent. More than 80 percent of revenues generated from Qayitbay's trust properties were not allotted to support of its designated functions. The implications of this disparity acquire a rationale when compared with similar calculations for Qansawh al-Ghawri's trusts.

In contrast with Qayitbay, al-Ghawri issued no waqfs before his enthronement. His earliest alleged purchases of property date from 907/1501, several months later. From that time, until his departure for Syria to confront Selim Yavuz, al-Ghawri assumed control of properties held in preexisting trusts at an unprecedented rate. Three hundred documents – consisting of sales, substitutions, reassignments, or transfers – bear his name. They amount to slightly less than a third of all trust documents from the Mamluk Sultanate preserved in modern archives. Despite this preponderance of documentation, al-Ghawri's charitable donations were more restricted than Qayitbay's. Al-Ghawri issued only one major trust deed. It supported four foundations, with the sultan's own mausoleum and mystic hospice in Cairo (*al-Qubba wa'l-Khānqāh al-Ghawriyya al-Sharīfa*) as the chief beneficiary. From 907 to the first transaction of his primary waqf deed, dated 26 Muharram 909/21 July 1503, a two-year period, al-Ghawri amassed a network of properties that generated an estimated annual yield of 52,000+ Ashrafi dinars. By late 914/April 1509, he had added holdings to the trust that provided 30,000+ more per year. By this year, the sultan thus acquired title to a network of properties that generated more than 80,000 dinars annually, sheltered in a blanket trust that officially endowed his mausoleum.[58] Al-Ghawri's other foundations (primarily a flood gauge, mosque, and belvedere known today as the Nilometer on the southern tip of Rawda Island) received revenues amounting to 700+ dinars annually. Disbursements listed in the primary document for the mausoleum complex itself came to ca. 6000 dinars per year – a percentage that paralleled the yield/expense ratio for Qayitbay's tomb. In both cases, between 90 and 80 percent of total yields from properties held in their waqfs remained undesignated. In what context did this procedure emerge?

In Dhu'l–Hijja 906/June–July 1501, following the initial rebellion by Mamluk recruits of his reign, al-Ghawri consulted with both his diwan accountants and jurist advisors as to how he could meet their demands with the treasury empty. After the assembled judges declared their opposition to any withdrawals from waqf funds, he met in private with his confidant who was most informed about legal procedure and receptive to his dilemma, Sari al-Din ibn al-Shihna al-Ḥanafī, to work out a plan. Ibn Iyas depicted the objective as follows:

> The Sultan intended to confiscate waqfs of mosques, colleges and other benevolent foundations, leaving them funds sufficient to cover daily operations only. As an incentive to the amirs responsible for the expropriations, he planned to grant them trust properties in their own names – thereby alienating them permanently.[59]

Although Ibn Iyas denounced this measure as draconian, if the surpluses generated by Qayitbay's and al-Ghawri's trusts provide a plausible indicator of yield/expense ratios that presumably applied to confiscated waqfs generally, the expropriations did not appreciably affect their designated charities. The residual amounts would not interrupt existing disbursements, even allowing for the most severe extractions.

In contrast with al-Ghawri's primary trust instrument, amended through several transactions to 922/1516, the 300 remaining documents exclusively depicted sale, substitution, transfer, and repossession procedures for specific properties. Original transactions in these documents, often dated decades before al-Ghawri's acquisition, frequently listed purchase or sale prices. These were absent from the final transaction certifying al-Ghawri's acquisition. Their dates often clustered on the same day, indicating a process of mass appropriation. Examples of these certificates read as follows:

> The entirety of the site described above was transferred to the possession (*milk*) of our Sovereign Sultan al-Ghawri from the possession of ______, as a lawful (*sharʿī*) transfer according to lawful sale at a price mutually accepted by the aforementioned seller, a legal contract in fullness and perfection (*bi'l-tamām wa'l-kamāl*) from assets of our

sovereign Majesty, in his Royal Name, as the above dated bill of sale on Damascene paper guarantees.[60]

A more detailed designation:

All of the ______, and what it encompasses within its boundaries described (above), was certified as a lawful waqf among the aggregate trusts of our Sovereign Majesty, Sultan al-Ghawri, may his Name be exalted, for maintenance of the Royal and Sultanic College (*madrasa*), its Mausoleum (*qubba*), its Hospice (*khanqāh*), its school (*maktab*), and its Fountain (*sabīl*), which our Sovereign Majesty, may his Name be exalted, founded, and for (support of) learned poets (*arbāb al-shaʿāʾīr*), esteemed shaykhs (*al-sādá al-mushāʾikh*), mystics (*al-ṣūfiyya*), orphans (*al-aytām*), custodial staff (*arbāb al-waẓāʾif*) and other specified emoluments (*al-jawāmik al-murattaba*) appertaining thereto by clear and explicit provision in His (al-Ghawri's) Royal trust deed inscribed on Ḥamá paper.[61]

None of the 300-odd certificates listed a price in figures. Phrases such as "at a mutually accepted price" (*bi-thamani ḥālin maqbūḍin*) approved by "legal proxy" (*tawakkul sharʿī*) appeared consistently. Since between 25 and 30 percent of persons listed in the documents as sellers to al-Ghawri were confirmed by the chronicles as victims of dismissal, arrest, and confiscation, the validity of these phrases is questionable. The probable scenario was their relinquishment of title in exchange for acquittal, avoidance of a monetary fine, and release. The impression of something akin to a rump court with regard to these proceedings emerges from dates affixed to these certificates. On 20 Safar 911/23 July 1505, sixty-eight received signatures endorsing their transferal to al-Ghawri's mausoleum trust. A decade later, on 18 Rabiʿ II 922/1 June 1515, fifty-two more were added. The latter date occurred six weeks after al-Ghawri annulled a monthly tax on grain sale futures, at a loss Ibn Iyas estimated of 76,000 dinars annually. While al-Ghawri's motive as an attempt to bolster his popular standing in light of rising tensions abroad was clear, Ibn Iyas puzzled over how the sultan made up the loss. The income gained from this mass acquisition of real estate may have provided partial compensation.

How did these proceedings mesh with the larger issues of endemic shortfalls, foreign challenges, and unrest among the military class? Research into these issues raises several possibilities. The iqtaʿ system of revenue extraction and allotment from agrarian properties to militarist recipients, subjected to alterations from al-Nasir Muhammad's time that intensified after Barquq's reign, may have approached a state of virtual abandonment under Qayitbay and Qansawh al-Ghawri. The Ottomans, after taking stock of the former regime's finances, did so outright. Was al-Ghawri considering the creation of a genuinely autonomous financial preserve under his legal authority and exclusive access to its proceeds? The regime seems to have been moving in this direction, again from al-Nasir Muhammad's time, and at an accelerated pace from al-Zahir Barquq's reign. Was al-Ghawri in particular considering a phase-out of the most intractable factions of the Mamluk corps once he had trained a viable alternative recruited from nontraditional cadres? These scenarios remain speculative since they join a range of hypothetical trajectories cut short by the Ottoman occupation.

Beyond dilemmas of the moment, these scenarios, and the innovations they imply, confirm the tenacity of the Mamluk oligarchy. Under trying circumstances, the military institution was capable of exploring creative ways of reconstituting its hegemony. The measures discussed in this chapter are indicative of the institution's continued vigor at the end of its independent sovereignty. Rather than consigning itself to an inevitable fate, the Mamluk oligarchy confronted its final dilemmas with the special combination of pugnacity and élan that had sustained its dominion over Egypt and Syria for so many preceding decades. While surrendering formal authority to the Ottomans after 922/1517, the Mamluk institution would continue to exhibit the resilience that had overcome the intimidating odds of its last episode of independence. Such resilience would enable the Mamluk institution to adapt itself to its new condition of subordination and eventually to assimilate its conquerors.

## Addendum: Currency

Tax rates, commodity prices, salaries, stipends, and wages were expressed in terms for currency and rates of exchange that reflected shifts in the Sultanate's economy over the two and a half centuries of its existence. Coins were issued in gold (*dīnār/danānīr*), silver (*dirham/darāhim*), and copper (*fals/fulūs*). Mints operated in Cairo, Alexandria, Damascus, Aleppo, Hama, and Tripoli. The Sultanate's monetary system originated during the Fatimid Caliphate, under which gold dinars weighing 4–4.25 grams (one *mithqāl*) were the basis for commercial transactions. During the first Fatimid century in Egypt (ca. 341/953–427/1036), the regime maintained a high standard of fineness (ratio of precious to base metal), exceeding 95 percent. The later Fatimid period (to 567/1171) witnessed production of dinars reduced in weight due to gold shortages, fiscal crises caused by extended droughts, and challenges from abroad – in particular the Crusader occupation at the end of the fifth/eleventh century. Their standard of fineness remained high at 90+ percent. Silver currency known as "black dirhams" (*darāhim waraq*) because of high copper content (two-thirds) was introduced as a partial remedy to dinar shortages. After Salah al-Din founded the Ayyubid Sultanate (564/1169), he issued dinars that were slightly debased in an attempt to restore circulation of gold coins. Under his successors, Fatimid-era ratios of gold/silver were attained. The Ayyubid regime increased production of dirhams to the extent that silver coinage became the primary basis for exchange. Debasement ensued as a consequence of this policy. Sultan al-Malik al-Kamil (615/1218–635/1238) claimed that dirhams minted at his orders would reverse the silver/copper ratio that had declined to 1/3:2/3, but this standard was only partially achieved after his reign.

During the early Bahri period, gold and silver currency paralleled Ayyubid coinage. Sultan Baybars confiscated troves of gold and silver coins minted by Ayyubid, Crusader, and Mongol rulers after his solidification of control over Syria. Dinars maintained previous high gold levels (90+ percent) while dirhams continued the two-thirds/one-third silver/copper standard. The Bahri period witnessed changes in foreign trade that caused flowage of currency and bullion from the Sultanate to external powers. The high cost of Mamluk slave-cadets contributed significantly to the drain, as did rising levels of trade with Europe. Import/export ratios increasingly favored the European side. Sultan al-Nasir Muhammad responded by issuing debased dinars at a gold/silver ratio of 1:9.3. A spike in trade with West Africa (*al-Takrūr*) contributed to a temporary rise of gold in circulation (cf. Chapter 3) and an improved exchange rate for silver. Throughout the remaining eighth/fourteenth century, dinars retained high gold standards (90+ percent), while dirhams gradually returned to a 1/3:2/3 silver/copper ratio.

The mid-eighth/fourteenth century saw an infusion of Italian gold coins (ducats, ar. *Ifrantī*) on a massive scale. The unsettled politics following Sultan Barquq's death (801/1399) induced his son Faraj to buy support from contending factions by issuing massive quantities of debased dinars to pay bonuses. Their presence undermined confidence in the Sultanate's currency and stimulated preference for ducats, in particular coins minted by Venice. When Sultan al-Ashraf Barsbay was enthroned (825/1422), the ducat was approaching the standard medium of gold coinage in the Sultanate. Barsbay attempted to alleviate this problem by issuing dinars that allegedly paralleled ducats in weight and ratios of gold to silver. These so-called *Ashrafī* dinars encountered resistance in competition with Ifranti/ducats until Barsbay received a ransom in ducats from the Cypriot King James I (ar. *Jānus*) in 832/1429. Barsbay reminted 50,000 of these and placed them in circulation. In consequence, ducats were largely driven out of the market in Egypt, while Ashrafi dinars dominated the spice trade – at least in the Nile Valley, Hijaz, Red Sea, and Aden. The Ashrafi dinar remained the Sultanate's standard of gold coinage until late in Qayitbay's reign when demands for increased stipends to troops necessitated gradual debasement.

After Barquq's death, silver currency exhibited complexities stemming from debasement and supply shortages. Ratios of silver to copper fluctuated so frequently that transactions were often recorded in "trade dirhams" (*darāhim min al-fulūs* or dirhams of copper *fals*). These may not have been actual coins but rather units of account calculated according to prevalent market conditions.

Faraj's ultimate successor, al-Mu'ayyad Shaykh, managed to stabilize silver currency somewhat when he defeated his Syrian rival Nawruz and confiscated his treasury (817/1414). Nawruz had issued dirhams in Syria that weighed 1.45 grams, half (*niṣf*) the weight of their counterparts in Egypt. Their silver content approached 100 percent. When Shaykh acquired Nawruz's stock of dirhams, he intended to issue dirhams at weight and fineness ratios that had prevailed in the early Bahri period. But his plan did not succeed. Dirhams labeled *niṣf-fiḍḍa*s, varying in weights between three and four-eighths of earlier issues, dated from Shaykh's reign and circulated throughout the ninth/fifteenth century. Their silver/copper ratio held generally at 1/3:2/3 until Sultan Jaqmaq's reign (842/1438–857/1453), when drastic debasement lowered the percentage of silver to miniscule levels. By Qayitbay's reign (872/1468–901/1496), the majority of "dirhams" in circulation may actually have been copper or iron coins, trading at rates of several hundred to one dinar (occasionally 1/900 in al-Ghawri's time).[62]

Currency figures listed in tax registers and yields from property in trust (*waqf*) deeds were reported in a medium known as the *dīnār jayshī*, literally "the army dinar." The term referred to a unit of account, composed of a fraction of one dinar and partial units of wheat and barley. Although a combination of 1/4 dinar plus 2/3 irdabb wheat and 1/3 irdabb barley has been assumed, variations appear ubiquitously in surviving registers or waqf documents due to the currency fluctuations noted above.[63]

# 6 Cultural Legacy

## Patronage, Audience, Genres, Historiography

The Sultanate's cultural legacy outlasted its political demise in 923/1517. The Mamluks' patronage of literary and scholastic arts inspired written products remarkable for their quantity and diversity. During the era of Mamluk rule in Egypt and Syria, bureaucrats, jurists, essayists, poets, scholars, and theologians generated a massive corpus of legal compendia, religious commentaries, political treatises, trust documents, literary anthologies, historical chronicles, manuals of diplomatic and statecraft, and handbooks of urban/rural topography. These works have enabled a generation of contemporary researchers to revise longstanding interpretations of traditional disciplines and to reconsider subjects previously regarded as inaccessible due to a presumed lack of sources. These include: literary theory, popular culture, historical method, rural life, gender relations, and religious diversity. Since the Sultanate presided over the central Islamic lands during their transition from the medieval to early modern periods (seventh/thirteenth–tenth/sixteenth centuries), the insights provided by these sources, and their revisionists, are reshaping the field of Islamic History overall.

This chapter will address the context of patronage of literary products by the Mamluk ruling class and other social groups with the means and inclination to do so. It will consider the audiences reflected in their contents, the evolution of languages in which they were written (primarily Arabic, but representation of Persian and Turkish as well), their principal genres (poetry/prose), and the development of historiography. A subsequent chapter will address the issues of rural life, gender studies, minority communities, and religious diversity, with a focus on Sufism.

### Patronage and Authorship

In light of their political hegemony, the Mamluks appropriated a share of the realm's fiduciary assets inversely proportional to their numeric minority – on a vast scale. The wealth garnered from this fiscal gain enabled the Mamluk ruling class to sponsor many aspects of literary production and to underwrite the milieus in which those who wrote them were trained. Although patronage by militarist ruling elites has a long history in this region (NE Africa, SW Asia), its context in the Sultanate exhibited paradoxes. These stemmed from changing attitudes toward literary accomplishment on the part of the Mamluks themselves and prejudices about its quality by self-styled custodians of literary refinement (*adab*) – primarily the ʿulamaʾ, who regarded themselves as trustees of a literary canon inherited from the idealized age of the ʿAbbasids. The Mamluks themselves commented minimally on their literary court culture, especially in the Sultanate's early decades.[1] The regime's founder, al-Zahir Baybars, was likely illiterate and evinced little interest in poetics. He did, however, enjoy listening to episodes of the panegyric lauding his military achievements, *al-Rawḍ al-ẓāhir fī sīrat al-malik al-ẓāhir* (The Splendid Garden of the Life of al-Malik al-Zahir), read aloud by its author, the katib al-sirr Muhyi al-Din Ibn ʿAbd al-Ẓahir.[2] The sultan's immediate successors were similarly insouciant. But they were not indifferent to their recruits' schooling in letters or religion.

From its start, barracks training of Mamluk cadets did not focus solely on proficiency in military arts. Inculcating tenets of Islam and literacy in Arabic and Qipjaq Turkish was central to their regimen. As noted in Chapter 2, cadets were drilled in Arabic grammar, calligraphy, and the basics of Sunni religious sciences. They transcribed works that focused on lives of the Prophet Muhammad, religious poetry and prayers, and principles of sound government as exemplified in the "Mirror for Princes" format widespread in the court culture of Muslim regimes throughout the region. The copies they transcribed were destined for libraries of their patrons: senior officers or the Sultan himself. These reveal errors and corrections indicative of their function as exercise books and syllabi for topics of instruction. Although numerous specimens survive, the majority date from the Circassian period.[3] The origins of this system of mentored "learn by doing" are less discernible in the Sultanate's formative years. Manuscript copying may have become a fixture of literary instruction relatively late in the evolution of cadet training in the barracks. Yet, the frequency of surviving copies in libraries of the cadets' patrons implies the exercise of manuscript copying as the end stage of a process of literacy training with a trajectory extending back to the origins of barracks culture at the Sultanate's founding. That the hierarchy of officers, with the sultan at its apex, sought to accumulate personal libraries by exploiting their cadets' efforts also suggests a learning curve of rising expectations for status as patrons of learning and personal accretion of erudition.

These expectations were also motivators for architectural sponsorship on an imposing scale. Most of the individuals who successfully warded off competitors to consolidate their hold on the Sultanate made the foundation of monumental legacies a signal objective of their reigns. The aforementioned Sultan Baybars established one of the regime's first large congregational mosques

Fig. 6.1 Sultan Qalawun mausoleum interior
Pillars of Aswan Granite support the Dome.
(Photo credit: KHALED DESOUKI/AFP via Getty Images)

north of the Fatimid city on his own polo grounds. He built on his personal property, a site vacant of existing structures, to avoid insinuations of confiscation or razing by rivals and nay-saying ʿulamaʾ. Baybars's eventual successor, Qalawun, endowed the hospital that bore his honorific title, al-Mansuriyya. His tomb, its dome supported by massive columns of Aswan red granite, is adjacent to it (**Fig. 6.1**). The interior leaves an impression similar to the Dome of the Rock in Jerusalem.[4] Sultan Baybars II al-Jashankir (r. 708–09/1309–10) endowed one of the most prominent hospices (*khānqāh*s) for Sufis in Cairo and amassed a library, much of which was recirculated in collections of his peers after his deposition (**Fig. 6.2**). The impulse of sponsorship endured through the Sultanate's final years, with the foundation of Cairo's last Sufi khanqah by the regime's penultimate ruler, Qansawh al-Ghawri: the *Ghūriyya* in local parlance (**Fig. 6.3**). Even rulers with unsavory reputations left their mark. Sultan al-Zahir Barquq's son, al-Nasir Faraj (801–15/1399–1412, with interregnum), who spent much of his two turbulent reigns battling his father's aggressive amirs for survival, and who ignominiously abandoned Damascus to the Central Asian conqueror, Timur Lenk, contributed to Cairo's architectural profile (cf. Chapter 1).

The Mamluk elite, inclusive of subordinate cadres such as the Habashi eunuchs who trained cadets (cf. Chapter 2), endowed monuments that

Fig. 6.2 Minbar in hospice (*khānqāh*) of Sultan Baybars II al-Jashankir
(Photo by Michel Setboun/Corbis via Getty Images)

Fig. 6.3 Sultan Qansawh al-Ghawri Complex (*al-Ghūriyya*)
(Photo by Frédéric Soltan/Corbis via Getty Images)

advertised their role in the defense of Sunni Islam, support of public worship, propagation of Shariᶜa Law, endorsement of Sufi observance, and commemoration of the founder's piety (**Fig. 6.4**). These goals were embodied in structures that communicated their "expressive" intentions: the mosque (*jāmiᶜ*, *masjid*) for congregational prayer, college (*madrasa*) for legal instruction, hospice (*khānqāh*, *ribāṭ*) for Sufi ritual, and donor's tomb (*qubba*, *turba*) for memorializing his legacy.[5] The manifestations of these objectives in monumental structures tied the triumphant hegemony of Sunni Islam in the central Arab lands to the military elite that took credit for imposing it. As the Mamluk era progressed, sultans and amirs tended to found complexes that combined these functions. Sultan al-Nasir Muhammad, at once praised for his building program and castigated for its cost, constructed several in the Citadel and city center along the Bayn al-Qaṣrayn (**Fig. 6.5**). Mamluk donors lavishly endowed the activities centered in these institutions: prayer leading, sermon preaching, juridical instruction, Sufi observance, and Qur'an reading over graves. They established charitable trusts (*waqf/awqāf*) that drew revenues from yields on properties (rural agrarian land and urban real estate) acquired by the ruling elite. While the pragmatic goals of rulers and officers who created these trusts transcended impulses of generosity and aimed at privatizing assets formerly held by the regime as personal estates (cf. Chapter 5), their munificence cannot

Fig. 6.4 Mosque lamp of Amir Qawsun al-Nasiri, ca. 730–35/1329–35
Blown glass showing Amir's Cup Blazon; colorless with brown tinge; blown applied foot, enameled and gilded, H. 14 1/8 in. (35.9 cm), attributed to Ali ibn Muhammad al-Barmaki(?).
(Photo by Sepia Times/Universal Images Group via Getty Images)

Fig. 6.5 Citadel Mosque of Sultan al-Nasir Muhammad ibn Qalawun Constructed 717–18/1318 as the center for Friday worship at the Royal Residence.
(Credit: Lola L. Falantes via Getty Images)

be denied. The topographer and historian al-Maqrizi listed numerous such institutions founded by Mamluk sponsors in his survey of Cairo's monuments, the *Khiṭaṭ*. Medieval Cairo's architectural legacy, which has lasted to the present day, is overwhelmingly the consequence of Mamluk-era sponsorship (**Fig. 6.6**).

Cultural enrichment stemming from Mamluk sponsorship extended beyond architecture. Despite persistent accusations of mediocre linguistic competence by the ʿulamaʾ, many members of the military class were literate in both Arabic and Turkish. Individuals imported from outside Arabic-speaking regions as adolescents without formal educations often sought tutelage to remedy this shortcoming following their manumission and promotion, if their training as cadets had left them deficient. Those who wielded power and amassed wealth frequently sought to acquire the trappings of learned accomplishment. The Dawadar who served as chief adjutant to Sultan Qayitbay, Yashbak min Mahdi, was notorious for his brutal suppression of Bedouin tribes in Upper Egypt and his defeat of the rebel, Shah Suwar, in Anatolia (cf. Chapter 2).

Fig. 6.6 Mausoleum of Sultan al-Ashraf Qayitbay in cemetery east of former Fatimid District
Lithography by David Roberts, ca. 1845.
(Photo by adoc-photos/Corbis via Getty Images)

He was also a patron of writers and scholars. The author of a genealogy of the Prophet and religious poems in Turkish, Yashbak collected manuscripts, founded a library, and commissioned the copying of works such as al-Busiri's ode in praise of the Prophet, *al-Kawākib al-durriyya* (see below). Al-Sakhawi, author of the ninth/fifteenth-century biographical compendium *al-Ḍaw' al-lāmiʿ*, wrote his supplement to al-Maqrizi's chronicle, *al-Tibr al-masbūk*, at Yashbak's request.[6] In it, he lauded Yashbak for his support of Sufis, pilgrims, and plague victims. Yashbak's example was duplicated by numerous peers who made it to the top of the ruling hierarchy and amassed personal fortunes. Aware of their vulnerability to rivals and the transience of worldly status, these individuals were motivated to leave a cultural legacy that would outlast their ascendance of the moment. The books and manuscripts they collected would pass after their deaths into libraries that served diverse constituencies broader than the formal literary circles of the ʿulamaʾ, as noted subsequently.

In the Sultanate's final decades, several rulers or their presumptive heirs presided over salons (*majālis*) convened to promote readings by authors whose works had been judged worthy of recitation before the regime's senior officers and scholars. The most replete documentation records sessions of the salon convened by Sultan Qansawh al-Ghawri (r. 906–22/1501–16), who regularly organized competitions among poets, chroniclers, and epic readers. Subjects listed in surviving registers of sessions, customarily held as soirees with banquets perfumed by rose water, included history, geography, mythology, politics, and satire. Religion figured prominently, but in a context of licitness with regard to aspects of court protocol or favored pastimes of the military class. Although poets who wrote in Arabic participated in the competitions, salon sessions gave preference to works in Persian and Turkish, languages of the ruling elite. They featured Turkish translations of such classics as Firdawsi's epic of pre-Islamic Iran, the Book of Kings (*Shahnahme*). The prevalence of Persian and Turkish at these *majālis* indicates the spread of a cosmopolitan court culture during the late ninth–early tenth/fifteenth–sixteenth centuries throughout the eastern Islamic lands, in which Arabic was not the principal literary medium.[7]

The impulse for sponsorship became pronounced among the Mamluks' progeny: the *awlād al-nās*. The awlad al-nas (literally: "sons of the people," with *nās* indicating elite ranks of society in contrast with the commons: *al-ʿāmma*) were not a homogenous group. They ranged from scions of rulers who regarded themselves as privileged by dynastic birthright, to offspring of line soldiers who could aspire to little more than sporadic service in the halqa militia, with an irregular pension.[8] But they all shared an identity split between their Mamluk forebears and the indigenous cultures of Egypt and Syria, which often entailed fluency in both Arabic and Turkish.[9] Those with elite (and affluent) parentage routinely received educations in the religious sciences (*ʿulūm al-dīn*) or literature (*adab*) by tutors hired from among eminent ʿulamaʾ. They were capable of studying intricate treatises in Arabic. The son and grandson of Sultan Qalawun, al-Nasir Muhammad and al-Nasir Hasan, both read compilations on Prophetic Traditions by the fourth/eleventh century Hadith scholar, Abu Bakr al-Bayhaqi (d. 458/1066) while confined after their depositions.[10] Another eminent walad al-nas had a *wāfidī* father (defector from the Mongol army). Muhammad ibn Jankali al-Baba (d. 741/1340) discharged his duties as an amir in Sultan al-Nasir Muhammad's court with reluctance, preferring the camaraderie of Hadith scholars, rhetoricians, and poets.[11] He kept company with the eminent (and controversial) author of licentious poems and shadow plays, Ibn Daniyal (see below), an association indicative of broad receptivity to the reach of discourses that pushed the boundaries of adab by flaunting pornography.

The historians Ibn al-Dawadari and Ibn Taghri Birdi were sons of Mamluk amirs. Sayf al-Din Abu Bakr ibn ʿAbdallah ibn Aybak ibn al-Dawadari (fl. mid-eighth/fourteenth c.) wrote a chronicle in nine volumes that extended from Creation to the events of Sultan al-Nasir Muhammad's time: *al-Kanz al-durar wa-jāmiʿ al-ghurar* (Trove of Pearls and Exemplary [Historical] Accounts). Significant for its insights to the military and political culture of the Mamluk elite during the mid-eighth/fourteenth century (vols. 8 and 9), the *Kanz* is regarded as a prime representative of the "medial" version of literary Arabic that was widely read by individuals outside the ʿulamaʾ, or ranks of formally learned scholastics. The *Kanz* also exemplified a trend toward "adabization" of historiography, with an emphasis on entertainment, anecdotes, marvels, and snippets of verse.[12]

Abu'l-Mahasin Yusuf ibn Taghri Birdi (d. 874/1470) was initially drawn to writing history by the example of the historian al-ʿAyni's recitations to Sultan Barsbay. His studies with al-ʿAyni's rival, al-Maqrizi, prompted respect for the eminent but acerbic chronicler's methods qualified by inferences about uncited borrowings, if not plagiarism. Ibn Taghri Birdi compiled a biographical dictionary to supplement al-Safadi's *Wāfī* (*al-Manhal al-ṣāfī wa'l-mustawfī baʿd al-wāfī*: The Pure Spring and Fulfillment after al-Wāfī); a voluminous chronicle of Egypt from the Arab conquest to 872/1467 (*al-Nujūm al-zāhira fī mulūk Miṣr wa'l-Qāhira*: Shining Stars among the Kings of Egypt and Cairo); and a detailed adjunct to al-Maqrizi's *Kitāb al-sulūk* (*Ḥawādith al-duhūr fī madá al-ayyām wa'l-shuhūr*: Episodes of the Epoch that Pass in Days and Months) that chronicled events between 845/1441 and 874/1469, immediately before his death.[13]

Lesser in rank but not erudition were such figures as Khalil ibn Aybak al-Safadi (d. 764/1363). Author of the biographical dictionary *al-Wāfī bi'l-wafayāt* (Perfection of the Necrologies), al-Safadi had emerged as a self-taught prodigy by the age of twenty, when he attached himself to the circle surrounding the revered but contentious Hanbali scholar Ibn Taymiyya in Damascus.[14] Al-Safadi's erudition facilitated his entry to a successful career in several diwans of government, particularly the chancery (*Dīwān al-Inshā'*). But he found distinction in the realm of letters. Al-Safadi's literary compass was exceptional and reflective of the diverse range of scholars, essayists, and poets he admired as colleagues and friends. Al-Safadi wrote across the full spectrum of *adab*, from treatises on ritual interpretations of numbers, to body parts associated with emotions, to stylistics, literary criticism, and alchemy. Al-Safadi's poems embraced themes of erotica, passion, unrequited love, and wine drinking. He copied the verse of numerous contemporaries, supplemented by commentaries on circumstances surrounding their composition and assessment of their quality.[15]

A pundit who followed a different path was ʿAli ibn Sudun al-Bashbughawi (d. 868/1464). Son of a Circassian Mamluk line trooper (not an officer), Ibn Sudun pursued formal studies in the madrasa founded by the grand amir Shaykhu, located on the Cross Street in the Citadel district of Cairo. Failing to secure his place as a scholar or cleric, Ibn Sudun turned to satire, odes mocking fraught love affairs, and depictions of miraculous events tinged with sardonic humor. In this genre, he scored. Ibn Sudun's anthology *Nuzhat al-nufūs wa-muḍḥik al-ʿabūs* (Diversion of Souls and Jester of Gloom) became something of a hit among literary circles in Cairo and Damascus that cherished high living and ribald humor. Self-styled fashionistas and vogue setters sought copies and attended public readings that provided Ibn Sudun with a living at the margins of elite (not "polite") society, although the ʿulamaʾ consistently scorned him.[16] Ibn Sudun's successful appeal to a receptive audience reveals the extent to which descendants of the ruling elite had assimilated into the broader civil society by the late Mamluk period.

## Change in Literary Culture and Growth of Audiences

The pursuits of these individuals suggest the range of social types among the Mamluk class that enriched the literary culture of the period through structures, endowments, and authorship. Their contribution should be considered within a larger context of reception by audiences that were changing during the eighth/fourteenth and ninth/fifteenth centuries. Reading communities evolved as they grew to embrace wider segments of society. Starting from the Ayyubid period (mid-fifth/eleventh–mid-sixth/twelfth centuries), an animated "writerly culture" flourished, notably in the urban environment of Syria.[17] Although paying tribute to literary models inherited from the ʿAbbasid period in Iraq that focused on tribal values of the Jahiliyya, idealization of the Prophet, transmission of traditions attributed to him, and themes of classical poetry, Syrian authors widened their range of subjects that appealed to an audience, broadening out from the ranks of diwan katibs, ʿulamaʾ scholastics, and religious clerics. The readership in this expanded constituency drew upon artisans, merchants, and tradespeople. They appreciated topics, in poetry and prose, that embraced heroism of figures in epics predating Arab tribes, themes of romantic love, humor (often bawdy), fantasy (often enlivened by alcohol and drugs), and spirituality refracted through Sufism. Subject matter increasingly dwelt on local issues with which this audience identified. Although literacy, as measured by the capacity to read and write, was increasing, dissemination of these topics was not limited to those so narrowly defined. Authors on the preceding topics joined compilers of historical chronicles, Hadith collections, and juridical treatises in reading their texts publicly to audiences who appreciated them despite their incapacity to peruse such works on their own. Individuals with pronounced retentive powers sporadically attained fame for erudition they acquired via aurality: "listening," despite their lack of literacy in the strict sense. Commentators would remark on their accuracy and breadth of knowledge.

These trends intensified in the era of centralized political authority under the Mamluks, when the Egyptian and Syrian writerly traditions combined to produce works diversified in scope and proliferating in quantity. During the Mamluk period, evidence for inculcation of literacy among children became more visible in the form of reading certificates certifying proficiency among pupils prepared either to continue in more advanced settings (madrasas, mosques, and khanqahs) or to enter commerce and the trades. These certificates did not bypass traditional media of instruction, such as memorization of Qurʾan or Hadith. But they stressed proficiency in active reduplication via writing along with passive oral recitation.[18] This development was enhanced by the phenomenon of patronage, largely on the part of the ruling elite, noted above. During the Mamluk period, a shift occurred away from manuscript copying and endowment of libraries primarily by the sultan's court to projects funded by amirs of several ranks that, because of their dispersion in the urban environment, were more locally accessible. The proliferation of kuttab schools and libraries endowed by amirs combined with the trends in literary instruction for children noted above to broaden out the ranks of persons with some degree of facility in the handling of written materials.[19] Not everyone involved possessed similar skill sets. These would vary between reading without writing, orality (transmission via recitation), and aurality (retention through hearing). Distinctions between levels of ability were not fixed. The evidence leaves a more realistic impression of sliding scales of competence intersecting with fluid skills in specific fields. But overall, as the Mamluk era unfolded, facility in some aspect of interaction with written materials became more widespread and reached more diverse components of society.[20]

Widening dispersion of readerships was reflected in lists of works catalogued in the local private libraries endowed by amirs and, to a lesser degree, by affluent civilians. These revealed a gradual shift in themes away from concentrations of texts on Qur'anic disciplines of commentary (*tafsīr*) and recitation (*qirā'a*), traditions (*Ḥadīth*), law (*fiqh/sharī'a*), theology (*kalām*), prayer (*ṣalāh*), pilgrimage (*ḥajj*), grammar (*nahw*), lexicography (*ṣinā'at al-mu'ajimiyya*), and history (*ta'rīkh*) that reflected professional needs of their primary users, 'ulama' who served as religious functionaries (Qur'an readers and imams). They were complemented, if not supplanted, by increasing frequency of works on secular (non-religious) literature (*adab*), the "rational" sciences of logic (*manṭiq*), medicine (*ṭibb*), alchemy (*kimiyā'*), mathematics (*rīyāḍiyāt*), and philosophy (*falsafa*), which addressed interests of groups more broadly engaged in practical fields and who were attracted to heroes of popular lore.[21] Among the most frequently cited in these catalogues were the *Maqāmāt* of al-Hariri (d. 516/1122); his anthology of rhymed prose and verse, richly illustrated, presented characters whose antics were of abiding appeal to the popular imagination. They were joined by renditions of epic stories (*sīrāt*) in which principal characters departed from their confirmed historical origins to perform deeds celebrated in fantasy across time and space. Prominent among these were the epics of: Antara ibn Shaddad, a warrior-poet of pre-Islamic fame; the Bani Hilal, tribal migrants across Egypt and the Maghrib during the fifth/eleventh century; Dalhamma/Dhat al-Himma, the princess (*amīra*) whose sons fought in wars between Umayyads and Byzantines; Baybars, the Sultanate's architect; and Sayf ibn Dhi Yazan, a semi-mythical king of Yemen (*Himyar*) in the sixth century CE, whose antagonist, the Axum monarch Sayfa Ar'ad, actually ruled Ethiopia in the eighth/fourteenth century.[22]

The popularity of these epics throughout the Mamluk and Ottoman periods often provoked the ire of 'ulama' scholars. They denounced their wide circulation as much for the implicit challenge they represented to authority by the official scholarly class over reading materials available to the expanding reading public as for the errors of chronology and historical fabrication they disclosed. Widespread reading or listening to these epics, so vividly depicting heroic events, did more than infect the masses with distortion of historical facts via fantasy. The epics compromised the status of the 'ulama' as self-styled custodians of sound belief, who claimed to determine what materials stood for "valid" reading. In earlier eras that preceded the expanded readership enabled by broadened literacy of the writerly culture emerging in Egypt and Syria under the Mamluks, such an agenda was more feasible. Denunciations of these works by the scholarly elite became more strident as their popularity, as signaled by their presence in library collections and references in chronicle narratives to public recitations, was on the rise.[23]

The trends toward audiences broadening to embrace receptive groups beyond the ranks of 'ulama' are traceable because of sources that were proliferating during the Mamluk period. Whether their abundance and diversity signal the emergence of genuinely new actors on the literary stage, or heightened visibility of extant groups moving in new directions, is an open question. But their impact on literary culture was transformative. That it occurred during the Sultanate's hegemony over Egypt and Syria was largely the consequence of patronage by the Mamluk elite. Their impetus for sponsorship derived in part from the elite's implicit linkage to promotion of Sunni Islam and the stature it brought them. But the Mamluks were also prompted by their own sense of engagement with this broadened audience, of which they were a constituent. How such engagement played out may be seen in the genres that shaped literary production in this era. Shifts in style and theme provoked debates over quality and substance that have persisted into contemporary discourses that enliven the field in the present day.

## Poetry: Formal Canons, Popular Modes

Of the genres poetry and prose, the former retained its preference as the medium most suited for expression of refined discourse and emotive feelings, a status that drew upon stylistic conventions fixed during the "Classical Age" of the ʿAbbasid Caliphate (third/ninth–fourth/tenth centuries). Such figures as Abu Nuwas (d. 198–200/813–15), composer of paeans to wine drinking and beautiful youths,[24] and al-Mutanabbi (d. 354/955), author of panegyrics (*mudīḥ*) at the courts of the Hamdanid amir Sayf al-Dawla in Syria and the Ikhshidid eunuch Abu'l-Misk Kafur in Egypt,[25] were among classical poets widely quoted by writers of the Mamluk period. But their prevalence as archetypes of refined style persisted within a milieu of shifting conventions that accompanied the literary transformations of the age. Among poetic forms, the ode (*qasīda*) continued as an esteemed model for eulogy (*rithāʾ*) and honorifics (*fakhr*) patterned after tribal precedents set before the advent of Islam (the *Jāhiliyya*).[26] Such themes as amorous love (*ghazal*), satire (*hijāʾ*), and wine drinking (*khamriyya*) were frequently expressed in forms adapted from external sources. Among the most common were the quatrain (*rubāʿī*) from Persia (*Fars*) and the strophic verse, typically of five stanzas (*muwashshaḥ*), from Iberia (*al-Andalus*).[27] From the late Ayyubid period, these forms placed emphasis on embellishment often derided by partisans of the classical tradition as ornamentation without force or passion. Their dismissal of poetic conventions that departed from hallowed classical styles castigated alleged replacement of vigorous content with trivial technique. This snubbing of poetic conventions by certain members of the ʿulama' from the Mamluk era has carried on into modern interpretations of the genre. Claims of "post-classical lassitude" have provoked revisionist rebuttals that depict poetics by authors from the Mamluk period as stylistically innovative, diverse in thematic content and inclusive of groups largely absent from social types idealized from a "classical" era already extinct by the later Middle Ages. The themes, conveyed in a myriad variety of stylistic modes, embraced a range of subjects that reflected tastes of the new literary classes.

Prominent among poets in the Mamluk Sultanate's formative years was Sharaf al-Din Muhammad ibn Saᶜid al-Sanhaji al-Busiri (d. 694–96/1294–97), author of a collection (*dīwān*) numbering some fifty works. Two of these have established al-Busiri among the luminaries who praised the Prophet in verse: the *Hamziyya* and the *Burda*. The *Hamziyya* recounts signal events in the Prophet's life: birth, receipt of Revelation, ascent to Heaven on the Buraq, and confrontations with Meccans over conversion. The *Burda* refers to the mantle that al-Busiri claimed the Prophet cast over him during a vision following a paralyzing stroke. Al-Busiri attributed his recovery to this miracle and composed an ode of 160 lines to commemorate it: *al-Kawākib al-durriyya fī madḥ khayr al-barriyya* (Luminous Stars in Praise of the Pious Best). The poem has been acclaimed as an exemplar tribute to the Prophet's healing powers, rendered in numerous stylistic forms and revered in more than ninety commentaries by later writers in Arabic, Persian, Turkish, and Berber. It set precedents for the profusion of elegies to the Prophet composed in the Mamluk and Ottoman periods.[28]

In the following century, a central figure was Safi al-Din ᶜAbd al-ᶜAziz ibn Saraya al-Hilli (d. ca. 749/1339). Born in the Iraqi town of his namesake (*Hilla*), al-Hilli sought sponsorship in the Ilkhanid principality of Mardin, whose ruler appointed him poet to the court. Al-Hilli later became famous in Egypt during his sojourn at the court of Sultan al-Nasir Muhammad ibn Qalawun in Cairo, following his Hajj (723–26/1322–26). At the sultan's request, al-Hilli composed the diwan subsequently regarded as his principal collection. Although his diwan was written in formal language (*fuṣḥá*), al-Hilli's output encompassed the full range of poetic forms in vogue during the period. It has influenced writers in a wide array of genres throughout the central Arab lands in subsequent centuries.[29] Although likely identifying with Shiᶜism because of his Iraqi heritage, al-Hilli addressed the Rashidun Caliphs, and the Prophet's Companions in general, with studied neutrality, if not positive terms, when they appeared in his works. He thereby avoided intimations of heresy. Al-Hilli is considered pivotal to the development of Arabic verse during the Mamluk period. Particularly affective was his poem: *al-ᶜĀṭil al-ḥālī wa'l-murakhkhaṣ al-ghālī* (The Decoratively Unadorned and the Valuably Underpriced), which laid out seven verse forms, starting with the classical qasida. Examples accompanied each form. The precedent set by this work was followed by subsequent generations as the "Seven Arts" of poetic style. Al- Hilli's career trajectory embodied the cosmopolitanism characteristic of the Sultanate's literary culture.[30]

Al-Hilli's diversity of styles, ranging from formal to colloquial, was embraced by his contemporaries and subsequent generations. Among these was an author whose verse was considered profound in style and content, Jamal al-Din Muhammad ibn Shams al-Din Muhammad ibn Nubata (d. 768/1366). Triviality was not attributed to his poems.[31] Born to a scholarly family in Cairo, Ibn Nubata sought sponsorship in Syria at the court of the penultimate Ayyubid ruler of Hama under Mamluk suzerainty, the Amir al-Mu'ayyad Ismaʿil (r. 710–32/1310–32), for whom he wrote a series of panegyrics: *al-Muʾayyadiyya*. Following the deposition and death of al-Mu'ayyad's son, al-Afḍal (742/1342), Ibn Nubata found employment in the chancery of Damascus under its Mamluk viceroy. His experience there, and subsequently in Cairo under the patronage of Sultan al-Nasir Hasan, led to the compilation of anthologies that included his poems in several modes (subsequently assembled as a formal *Dīwān* by Badr al-Din al-Bashtaki [d. 830/1427]), *inshāʾ* documents (*Taʿlīq al-dīwān*: Annotation of the Bureau), and private letters (*Zahr al-manthūr*: Flowering Prose).[32]

By the late eighth/fourteenth–early ninth/fifteenth centuries, poetry accessible to vernacular readers beyond the ʿulama' was departing from idealized topics of heroism or vendetta by long-dead tribes in the Jahiliyya and panegyrics to the Prophet to treat subjects that reflected current fashion and daily life. These are the stuff of popular culture. Former derision by the ʿulama' was becoming more muted as jurists and scholastics themselves contributed to the plethora of works touching on commonplace issues, where even the mundane was richly embellished. Wordplay and ornamentation became objectives independent of subject and may have been considered more readily suited to topics resonant with the expanded audience.

Poetry composed to typify a stance of hedonistic elegance was known as *adab al-ẓurufāʾ*, literally "expression by the refined." Terms derived from the root *ẓāʾ-rāʾ-fāʾ* (elegance, refinement) were discernible in literature from the ʿAbbasid era. By the Ayyubid and Mamluk periods, these had taken on insinuations of dandification visible in fancy dress, perfumed aromas, and delight in wine. Same-gender attractions were often hinted in verse by individuals labeled "*ẓarīf*." A vivid example may be seen in the brief but adulated career of Shams al-Din Muhammad ibn ʿAfif al-Din Sulayman al-Tilimsani, known as *al-Shābb al-Ẓarīf* (The Dandified Youth), who died in 688/1289 at the age of 27.[33] Son of a mystic from the Maghribi town of Tlemcen who had settled in the Cairo khanqah of Saʿid al-Suʿada', al-Shabb al-Zarif moved with his father to Damascus, where he pursued his education and wrote elegies for elite figures. But al-Shabb won renown, and infatuation, for his poems on love and wine addressed to men. These initially propelled him into elite male circles that flaunted sybaritic behavior. Why al-Shabb ultimately fell from favor and died young, isolated with a sense of suffering from conspiracy by rivals, remains unclear. Yet, his poems became paragons for later generations who emulated the "dissolute" self-indulgence they conveyed. These included Mamluk amirs and awlad al-nas who affected the *ẓurufāʾ* lifestyle.[34]

The "popular" genres ranged out from dandified elegance to embrace themes reflective of writers whose origins were in crafts and trades. Although many wrote poems celebrating time-honored topics such as love, panegyric, and wine, they set them in milieus congenial to their readerships. An early example was Jamal al-Din Abu'l-Husayn Yahya al-Jazzar, "the Butcher" (d. 679/1281), who wrote such pieces as *Taqṭīf al-jazzār* ("The Butcher's Deboning," or capturing the essence [meat] of a poem) under commission by the historian of Aleppo, Ibn al-ʿAdim. Al-Jazzar's treatment of begging and poverty, whether satirical or unfeigned, prompted a degree of invective from critics indicative of its positive appreciation by an audience familiar with realities of the working world. The stylistics of al-Jazzar's verse would inspire later writers such as Ibn Nubata.[35] In a similar vein was a comical poem titled *Al-Ḥarb al-maʿshūq bayn laḥm al-ḍa'n wa-ḥawāḍir al-sūq* (The Passionate War between Mutton and Refreshments of the Market), penned by one Ibn al-Hajjar (stonemason), who satirized a banquet where meat and vegetable dishes fought over which was more delectable.[36] Reflective of gastronomical tastes among craftspeople was a maqama composed by Muhammad al-Ansari al-Bilbaysi in 746/1345: *Kitāb al-mulāḥ wa'l-ṭuraf min munādabāt arbāb al-ḥiraf* (Witticisms and Novelties Shared by Convivial Masters of Trades). In this prosimetric text, representatives of forty-nine professions gather at a banquet to sardonically praise wine drinking, each with an epigram, before a qadi who has himself indulged. Only when the final narrator, a corpse washer (*ghāsil*), warns of their impending fall from salvation do the tradesmen and judge repent of their lapse.[37] Works like the above proliferated during the Mamluk period, although many survive only in fragments or unedited collections. They depict a context of tensions between legal conformity and lenient gratification genially celebrated as the good life by the commercial classes.

Tendencies verging on the countercultural may be seen in dramatic genres such as the Shadow Play. To what extent these genres represented mainstream attitudes about public morals or fetishes on the margins of propriety is an open question at present. Celebrated among their writers was Shams al-Din Muhammad al-Khuzaʿi al-Mawsili, known as *Ibn Dāniyāl al-Kaḥḥāl* ("the Oculist"; d. 710/1310).[38] An immigrant to Cairo from Mosul after the Mongol invasion, Ibn Daniyal sporadically treated eye diseases while he gained prominence for writing "serious" works such as a rhymed register (*urjūza*) of magistrates in Egypt from the Arab conquest to his own time. Commissioned by the Shafiʿi qadi Badr al-Din Ibn Jamaʿa, the register was widely cited by later chroniclers and legal scholars, including the eminent scholar Ibn Hajar al-ʿAsqalani, who modeled his own inventory of judges, *Rafʿ al-iṣr ʿan quḍāt Miṣr* (Removal of the Burden on the Judges of Egypt), on it. Ibn Daniyal composed numerous poems in a variety of styles that were subsequently collected in anthologies, sections of which were preserved by such polymaths as al-Safadi.

But Ibn Daniyal's fame – and notoriety – rest on his shadow plays and lewd verse. The shadow play (*khayāl al-ẓill*) evolved from antecedents in Iraq and elsewhere in Southwest Asia. In Mamluk Cairo, performances depicted protagonists cast as shadows on an illuminated screen from figures cut from leather, their dialogues accompanying the action. Full copies of only three plays by Ibn Daniyal survive, the sole examples of medieval Arabic theatrics in complete form. They present farcical scenarios of botched trysts, street entertainments, and infatuation with juvenile love interests expressed in colloquial language rich with vulgar terminology that audiences apparently found hilarious. Meanings of numerous words and phrases remain obscure, their usage likely the result of "on-the-spot" invention by copyists of the extant manuscripts.[39] The plays emerged within a context of tongue-in-cheek protest against censorship by sultans acting as self-styled guardians of morality. Ibn Daniyal belonged to a circle of authors who derided efforts of such rulers as al-Zahir Baybars (658–76/1260–77) and al-Mansur Lajin (696–98/1296–98) to crack down on alcohol or drug use, dancing, and music in public spaces. Since many members of the Mamluk ruling class, officers and soldiers alike, robustly indulged in these "vices," they shared the civilian masses' appreciation of the genre. Ibn Daniyal was a popular figure among the Mamluk corps despite his scoffing of prudism from the top.

Ibn Daniyal's "obscene" poetry (*mujūn*) raised more complex issues of covert intent masked by overt debauchery and pornography. Ibn Daniyal wrote several qasidas that parodied the customary sequence of the hero's prologue (*nasīb*), journey (*raḥīl*), and panegyric (*madīḥ*) by supplanting his traditional objectives, such as pursuit of heteronormative sex in defiance of tribal honor, with lustful exploitation of the youthful male body. But in some odes, the hero became Iblis, the arch-jinn cast out from Heaven by God for refusing to prostrate himself before Adam. In the odes, Iblis appears as a narrator who readily participates in lewd acts and laments their prohibition by the ruler. The odes are suggestive of a religious underground or counterculture that flourished in the Sultanate's urban centers despite its heterodox connotations and efforts by the regime to repress it.

## Prose: The Chancery Orbit, Popularization, and *Alf Layla wa-Layla*

Prose authors writing during the Mamluk period (mid-seventh/thirteenth–early tenth/sixteenth centuries) also inherited forms that had matured in the preceding centuries. The period itself is remarkable for proliferating genres and styles and for the quantity of textual products in prose. The environment in which these products were composed developed substantively as well. The institution responsible for much of the formal prose writing was the *Dīwān al-Inshāʾ*, literally "Bureau of Composition," in practice the Chancery. Officially organized for drafting documents related to diplomacy, statecraft, litigation, and finance, the Diwan al-Inshaʾ served as a principal training ground for prose authors who contributed to adab: literary genres regarded as cultivated or refined that were not formally within the purview of these professions.[40] Individuals writing within the Inshaʾ orbit composed treatises (*risālāt*) on a wide range of secular and religious subjects. Essays on stylistics, rhetorical embellishment, and canons of rhyme/meter shared company with treatises on theology, political theory, mathematics, the natural sciences, political economy, and topography, often penned by authors who considered themselves adept in multiple disciplines. Writing during the Mamluk era was marked by a sense of fluid boundaries between fields of knowledge. Modern distinctions between sacred and secular were not applicable to the literary mindset of this period; many thinkers regarded the supernatural as a genuine aspect of reality, worthy of exploration alongside the rational sciences. Divine intervention in the temporal world was ubiquitously assumed, although rarely in a reductive sense of fatalistic determinism.[41]

In the realm of more "popular" writing, the maqama or rhymed prose (*sajʿ*) that conveyed fables, folklore, and humoresque remained a prominent form among an array of literary media. Anthologies of anecdotes, tales, fantasies, and legends proliferated among the broadened audiences of the period's writerly culture. A survey that does justice to this diversification of literary output lies beyond the scope of the present chapter. But one work attracts such pervasive attention in modern literary circles that it merits comment: the collection of picaresque tales titled *Alf layla wa-layla* (1001 Nights), now known worldwide as the Arabian Nights. It is ironic that an anthology of stories with modest appeal to its contemporary premodern audience has attained iconic status in global popular culture of the present day.

Among the earliest known fragmentary references to an incident in the Nights' so-called frame tale recounted by the collection's protagonist, Shahrazad, to her husband the king was a marginal gloss. The textual scholar Nabia Abbott discovered it jotted on a manuscript sheet from Syria held by the Oriental Institute at the University of Chicago that dates from the third/ninth century.[42] But stories regarded as the narrative core of anecdotes with origins in ancient East and South Asia first emerge in versions familiar to current readers in collections copied during the Ayyubid and Mamluk periods. During the ʿAbbasid era, Ibn al-Nadim (d. 385–88/995–98), a Baghdadi manuscript dealer who compiled his index (*Fihrist*) as a catalogue of Arabic books comprehensive for the time, mentioned a collection known in Persian as A Thousand Stories (*Hazār afsān*), in which Shahrazad leaves the king

Shahriyar impatient for conclusions of tales deliberately left unfinished by each night's end.[43] Ibn al-Nadim's contemporary, al-Masᶜudi, in his collection, *Murūj al-dhahab*, noted the title A Thousand Nights (*Alf layla*) in a similar setting for the frame story. References to a final night added to the first thousand (*Alf layla wa-layla*) did not appear until the sixth/twelfth century, in a chronicle by al-Qurti, now lost, and the Geniza Documents (cf. Chapter 7).

As the tales cited by Ibn al-Nadim and al-Masᶜudi were translated into Arabic from Persian over subsequent periods, anecdotes relative to the politics and societies of the central Arab lands altered and enlarged the original group. Famous figures from the ᶜAbbasid era, such as the Caliph Harun al-Rashid (d. 193/809) and his vizier Jaᶜfar al-Barmaki (d. 187/803), became prominent characters in several story cycles. Their actions were inspired by fanciful imagination rather than historical fact. Of larger significance to the Nights' cultural tenor, many words depicting foodstuffs, apparel, and popular lore colloquial to Cairo between the seventh/thirteenth and ninth/fifteenth centuries infused the collection with this city's ambiance. The anthology that appeared in manuscripts encountered by European translators was composed in the dialect of Mamluk-era Cairo rather than in classical fusha and was loaded with terms reflecting local parlance. As a product of the writerly culture noted above, the Nights thus projected cultural norms of the nonelite groups who made up its audience. It also projected their fantasies about the elites whose lives they did not share but creatively imagined.[44]

Although Ibn al-Nadim and al-Masᶜudi mentioned a thousand nights, surviving manuscripts from the Mamluk period contain no more than 280-plus episodes narrated between dusk and dawn. Since individual stories often extend over several "nights," the number of distinct anecdotes is even less. At most, depending on how they are counted, some 200 anecdotes, several of which make up a longer story, often with convoluted plotlines (such as the multi-episodic Tale of the Hunchback),[45] comprise the collection recorded in manuscripts of the period. Their structure belongs to the milieu of storytelling and aurality that had become the primary medium through which this genre reached its audiences. Since references to popular stories in contemporary library catalogues sparsely mentioned the Nights, the collection itself in its own day seems to have enjoyed nothing like the enthusiasm it has stimulated outside the central Arab lands from the eighteenth century onwards. In fact, when the Nights attracted the attention of European translators, the paucity of surviving manuscripts and limited number of stories they contained prompted them to add tales separate from the collection. "The Seven Voyages of Sindbad the Sailor" is a prominent case in point. Some of the most popular stories for modern audiences, such as the Tale of Ala' al-Din (Aladdin), they heard from contemporary fabricators or made up themselves. The Arabian Nights known to modern readers has therefore experienced an extraordinary process of transformation and amplification at the hands of its translators, the first of whom was one Antoine Galland (1646–1715). Episodes from Galland's initial French translation drew such attention that he was prompted to embellish original stories and invent new ones. His example, and the consequent receptivity for the "oriental tale" among European readers generally, induced a series of subsequent writers to try their hand at producing versions of the Nights that would appeal to the exotic "Eastern" mode that was in such current fashion. These varied widely with regard to accuracy, contrivance, and distortion. For English readers, such names as Edward Lane (1801–76), John Payne (1842–1916), and Richard Francis Burton (1821–90) provoke debates over issues that extend far beyond matters of literary convention. Burton's translation in particular, although long the most complete (and heavily dependent on Payne's meticulous precedent), continues to spark altercations over alleged imperialism, colonialism, sexual fetishism, and racism. That it remains in print attests to the perennial fascination over Burton's ties to these subjects. Discussion of the Nights' remarkable trajectory in modern times also remains beyond the purview of this chapter. The marginality of the original anthology, one of many with broader appeal circulating during the Mamluk period, is the reality of the collection's place in the cultural imagination of its own day.

## The Growth of Historiography

Models for historical writing during the Mamluk period can be traced to composition of annals that flourished in the era of the centralized Caliphate under the ʿAbbasids, as is the case for other literary genres. Yet, these models were distant antecedents for characteristics of historical narratives distinctive to the seventh/thirteenth–ninth/fifteenth centuries in Egypt and Syria. Moreover, authors from these two regions themselves differed in both the style and content of their works. Narrating ta'rikh embraced a wide range of options for reporting the past. Diverse motives for doing so were especially noticeable during the "long" ninth/fifteenth century, which extended from the last decades of the eighth/fourteenth, when a figure such as Ibn Khaldun put finishing touches to his works, to a "journalist" such as Ibn Iyas, who lived through the Ottoman Conquest of 922–23/1516–17 and the occupation that followed. One generalization can be offered at the outset: unprecedented quantity. The output of historical writing under the late Ayyubids and throughout the Mamluk period is extraordinary. A scholar of political dynamics and coalition building during only one segment of this period (812–74/1410–70) has identified for relevant inclusion within a database, designed by his team, no less than seventy-four discrete compositions by twenty-seven authors who addressed matters of ta'rikh. These ranged from brief treatises of several folios to compendia in multiple volumes.[46] A comprehensive inventory of works that report historical events compiled throughout the Sultanate's duration (648/1250–922/1517) would number in the hundreds. Annalistic chronicles that listed incidents by year by no means encompassed the range of media that conveyed them. Dictionaries presenting biographies of individuals according to era, locale, occupation, legal affiliation, literary distinction, or social notoriety reached their culmination in Egypt and Syria during the Mamluk period. Among the longest, al-Safadi's *al-Wāfī bi'l-wafayāt* exceeds 30,000 biographies. Ongoing since 1931, its publication in thirty-two volumes was completed only by 2010. Manuals of diplomatic and statecraft became signature products of chancery bureaus (*dawāwīn al-inshā'*) in Cairo and provincial capitals. Beyond their significance as guides to transcription and principles of inter-regime relations, these manuals are valuable as repositories of original documents once housed in chancery archives that no longer exist. Since depiction of historical events was frequently enlivened by insertion of poetic verse, miraculous events, or sardonic gossip, much historical writing aimed at pleasing audiences beyond the ʿulamaʾ, as previously noted. Works composed for broad appeal shed light on styles and tastes that were foundations of popular culture. Individuals employed by bureaus of government, or scholars preoccupied with matters of political economy, compiled topographical surveys that remain primary sources for urban and rural history of the medieval environment. The range of sources for historical inquiry was diverse.

Yet, the legacy of historical writing from past eras is discernible in the educational resumés shared to varying degrees by most of these authors. While methods of historical reportage evolved from several disciplines in the classical Islamic curriculum, the science of prophetic traditions (*Ḥadīth*) assumed primacy of place as the template for presenting past events, in both technique and motive. The process for verifying authenticity of statements attributed to the Prophet that was devised during the Classical period, consisting of chains (*asnād*) of successive authorities across time and place, was largely responsible for procedures developed to report anecdotes and ascertain the reliability of their sources. The sense of ultimate purpose behind historical inquiry – linking reportage of past events to depiction of the Prophet's mission via his verified anecdotes – gave historians a profound motive that tied their work to God's divine plan. Even historians known for their alleged "secular" inclination or agnostic approach to interpreting the past have been shown to have nurtured deeply spiritual motives for writing it. When the curricula in which historians were trained are listed in their biographies, most began with studies in Qur'an and Hadith.

The influence of a figure in whose works historiography effectively culminated during its formative ʿAbbasid era may be discerned in their writings, despite the intervening centuries. Abu Jaʿfar Muhammad ibn Jarir al-Tabari (d. 310/923) was the primary author known to all of them and on whom they relied, to varying degrees, for their own summations of the Jahiliyya era and the subsequent Classical past from the Messenger's mission to the High Caliphate. Al-Tabari's focus on anecdotes related to the twin subjects of his history – prophets and kings – with its strict guidelines for verification via chains of authority, was acknowledged by historians of the Mamluk period as an impetus for their craft, if not its foundation. They also elaborated on how their own practices had broadened to include both wider swaths of society and incidents al-Tabari dismissed as irrelevant to his purpose. Al-Tabari apparently imagined his great work of history, lengthy as it is, as a summary to a compilation much longer (some reports claiming ten times) detailing events from Creation to the beginning of the fourth/tenth century (specifically, 22 Dhu'l–Hijja 302/12 July 915). A version of the full title found in one of al-Tabari's own manuscript colophons reads: *Mukhtaṣar ta'rīkh al-rusul wa'l-mulūk wa'l-khulafā'* (Abridged History of Messengers, Kings, and Successors [of the Prophet]).[47] Since the extant compendium, first edited by Dutch scholar M. J. de Goeje, numbers twelve massive volumes, excluding notes and indices, one can only speculate as to what the author initially envisioned.[48]

Al-Tabari's History was regarded as the indispensable source for coverage of Islam's first three centuries by medieval Islamic historians, and it remains so today in modern scholarship. Al-Tabari's presentation of events preceding Muhammad's mission – creation; patriarchs, prophets, and rulers of biblical Israel; pre-Islamic Iran; the mission of Jesus, the penultimate Prophet; and the Sassanid regime before the Arab invasion – reads as a succession of narrative summations. Following a discussion of Muhammad's lifetime, the History then proceeds with annalistic lists of discrete events (*akhbār*), usually with disparate accounts of "what happened" according to sources consulted by the author. These included king lists in Persian of pre-Islamic rulers of Iran and an array of akhbar compendia written in Arabic by authors regarded as authorities on the subjects al-Tabari considered relevant. "Relevance" is key to weighing al-Tabari's conception of ta'rikh and his influence on later generations of historians. The History addresses several broad subjects: the Arab conquests in Northeast Africa and Southwest Asia, rulers of the Umayyad and ʿAbbasid dynasties, and the activities of their governors in provinces of the resultant Caliphal Empire to the date noted above. Al-Tabari focused on activities of elite figures for the most part: conquerors, royalty, senior advisors, regional adjutants, religious leaders, and prominent converts. Individuals from social groups outside these elites figure in al-Tabari's annalistic reports marginally to the extent of their interaction with them. More significant than this restricted coverage was al-Tabari's commitment to veracity, as he interpreted the term. Al-Tabari was dedicated to reportage of events that he could verify, at the least, as transmitted by earlier authorities who themselves provided evidence of distinguishing fact from hearsay or deliberate falsification. It is this dedication to verification of source, rather than pronouncement of judgment about the rectitude, morality, or legacy of an event or individual, that remains the hallmark of al-Tabari's method – and its influence on historians who followed him. To what degree could a version of an episode be authenticated according to sources available in al-Tabari's time that he could scrutinize for their own accuracy and faithful transmission? Assessment as to "good" or "bad" al-Tabari considered peripheral to the mu'arrikh's essential duty; it amounted to insertion of personal opinion tangential to actual fact. This view of essential procedure stemmed directly from the science of Hadith transmission, with its obsession over authenticity that continued to evolve, replete with controversies over allegations of falsehood and intrusion of politics or heterodox theology, in al-Tabari's time. It is relevant to this discussion because most practitioners of ta'rikh writing in generations after al-Tabari, including those of the Ayyubid and Mamluk Sultanates, were also steeped in Hadith transmission. To what extent did they adhere to al-Tabari's example?

While historians of these regimes often modeled their summations of bygone eras – past long before their own times – on al-Tabari's archetype, they diverged from his precedent when they ventured into more contemporary events. Injection of personal opinion became progressively sharper as they proceeded. The author of Universal History during the Ayyubid period, ʿIzz al-Din ʿAli ibn al-Athir (d. 630/1233), relied heavily on al-Tabari for events preceding the rise and disintegration of the central Caliphate when he wrote his *Al-Kāmil fī'l-ta'rīkh* (The Perfection of History), which concludes in 628/1231.[49] Although recounting akhbar episodes in the fashion of Hadith chains (*asnād*), Ibn al-Athir identified his sources for events after the Crusader invasions sporadically. As he approached the ascension and campaigns of Salah al-Din Yusuf ibn Ayyub (Saladin) in his second history, *al-Bāhir fī ta'rīkh atābakāt al-Mawṣil* (The Dazzling History of the Overlords of Mosul), Ibn al-Athir derogated the founder of the Ayyubid confederacy in terms that appealed to his sponsors, the Atabaks of Mosul, Salah al-Din's rivals. Historians of the Mamluk era, such as al-Maqrizi and Ibn Khaldun, drew heavily upon his works. Several other Ayyubid authors contributed more objective assessments of Salah al-Din's achievements and those of his successors. The works of Baha' al-Din ibn Shaddad (d. 632/1235); Imad al-Din al-Katib al-Isfahani (d. 597/1201); ʿAbd al-Rahman ibn ʿAli, al-Qadi al-Fadil (d. 596/1200), Salah al-Din's secretary and biographer; and Jamal al-Din ibn Wasil (d. 697/1298) figure prominently.[50]

But it is the author of another universal history whose compilation influenced a multifarious group of successors in the Mamluk period in unique ways. This was Shams al-Din Abu'l-Muzaffar Yusuf ibn Qizoghlu (d. 654/1256), son of a Turkish freedman in the service of a vizier in Baghdad, and his wife, daughter of a famous preacher and author in that city, Ibn al-Jawzi. Since this scholar provided his education, the grandson took his name – as Sibt ibn al-Jawzi, by which he became known. Sibt ibn al-Jawzi produced the *Mir'at al-zamān fī ta'rīkh al-aʿyān* (Mirror of the Age for the History of Notables). Following sections that summarize remote events copied from al-Tabari, or developments of the sixth/twelfth century drawn from several authors noted above, Sibt ibn al-Jawzi contributed original details to the episode sequences of his own time. To these he appended obituaries of individuals deceased during the string of yearly events, a device he borrowed from his grandfather's practice and continued by his successors.[51] Sibt ibn al-Jawzi's rendition of the fourth–fifth/tenth–eleventh centuries, while also derivative, relied on histories of the period by al-Hilal al-Sabi' and his son that are now lost. His verbatim reproduction of several sections from these vanished works provides otherwise irretrievable information.

Nonetheless, Sibt ibn al-Jawzi's pivotal role in the evolution of historiography may be seen in its impact on a group of successor historians from Syria – and on analysts of their historical writing in the present day. With regard to the Syrians, four individuals stand out: Shihab al-Din Abu Shama ʿAbd al-Rahman al-Maqdisi (d.665/1268), Qutb al-Din Abu'l-Fath Musa al-Yunini (d. 726/1326), Shams al-Din Muhammad ibn al-Jazari (d. 739/1338), and ʿAlam al-Din Abu Muhammad al-Qasim ibn al-Birzali (d. 739/1339). These author-compilers did more than borrow substantively from the *Mir'a*. They adapted Sibt ibn al-Jawzi's annalistic method of episodes (which they termed *ḥawādith*, rather than *akhbār*) and obituaries (*wafāyāt*) to their own chronicles, each flush with rich detail. And al-Yunini went further. The uneven state of the numerous manuscript copies of the *Mir'a* left by Sibt ibn al-Jawzi points to a process of collation and editing incomplete by the author's death. One group of manuscripts appears to have been autographs filled with lacunae, a sign that the author left them as unfinished drafts. The other group results from al-Yunini's editing. Al-Yunini took up the task of organizing these manuscripts in a systematic fashion that rendered them coherent and located passages missing from lacunae in other copies. A monumental accomplishment, but al-Yunini did not stop there. He went on to write an abridgment (*mukhtaṣar*) of the *Mir'a* itself, followed by an addendum (*dhayl*) treating the years 654/1256–711/1311, which is a contribution in its own right.[52] Both were copied multiple times, an indication of their wide distribution and broad popularity. Recent scholarship on the subsequent transmission processes for the mukhtasar and dhayl has disclosed no less than nineteen manuscripts for the former and twenty-three for the latter, located in libraries throughout the Middle East, Europe, and Asia.[53]

The influence of Sibt ibn al-Jawzi's *Mir'a* on these historians raises the question of their working relationships. Al-Jazari, al-Birzali, and al-Yunini were contemporaries living in Damascus. Although degrees of their personal interaction are minimally known due to the lack of individual biographies (none wrote a memoir), parallels in their works and frequent mutual citations suggest close familiarity with each other's historical projects. This issue of interaction has been interpreted as evidence of a Syrian "school" of historiography discernible in the eighth/fourteenth century. Since none of these individuals, or other writers of ta'rikh in the same period, used terms indicative of a shared sense of localized professional identity, this hypothesis is problematic. But regional distinctions between career trajectories stand out. Syrian historians were, for the most part, members of the ʿulamaʾ. Virtually all had received madrasa educations that focused on the religious and judicial sciences, with Hadith transmission assuming primacy. They made their livings in pedagogy and litigation, colleges and the courts. By contrast, career paths of Egyptian historians were less uniform. Although the formal curricula of religious and judicial disciplines were visible, so was practical service in the regime's bureaucracy. As noted above, the Chancery, or *dīwān al-inshāʾ*, figured prominently in Egyptian literary scholarship generally. With regard to historiography, it served as both workplace and fount for sources. Several historians trained there. Experience in Cairo's fiscal diwans led to the profuse listing of financial data such as tax rates, Nile levels, staple prices, customs dues, and tariff fixing that were hallmarks of Egyptian chronicles. The presence of Mamluk officers and their progeny, the awlad al-nas, was conspicuous as well. Reports of troop drills, regional campaigns or local expeditions, factional rivalries, riots, and related unrest among competing cadres of troops occupy an outsized share of material in Egyptian chronicles. Their detail attests to the insights that participants directly involved could provide. The diversity of backgrounds among Egyptian historians also mitigates the presence of a "school" as expressed in ideological leanings or shared objectives. A sense of identity with a "court culture" by them because of the pervasive sultanic establishment in Cairo is more plausible, particularly as individual rulers courted their presence within the salon milieu they were promoting during the ninth/ fifteenth century.[54] And the aforementioned Ibn ʿAbd al-Zahir is a case in point with regard to the Sultanate's formative phase. He was Sultan Baybars's confidential secretary when he read the *Rawḍ al-Ẓahir* to him.

Among the historians who contributed to a distinctive intellectual environment in Syria during the eighth/fourteenth century, two further luminaries warrant comment. Although they participated in the interactive network characteristic of the individuals discussed above, they stand somewhat apart with regard to their works. The first was Shams al-Din Muhammad ibn Ahmad al-Turkumani al-Dimashqi (d. 748/1348), known as al-Dhahabi because of his father's craft as goldsmith. The father's commercial success and affluent marriage provided the son with a prosperous upbringing and cosmopolitan education. Al-Dhahabi studied with distinguished scholars in several cities, including eminent traditionist and jurist Ibn Daqiq al-ʿId in Cairo. Al-Dhahabi gained renown in Hadith transmission and was appointed shaykh in the Dar al-Hadith endowed by Amir Tankiz, governor of Damascus, and subsequently in al-Nafisiyya where he succeeded his colleague, al-Birzali.[55] Al-Dhahabi associated himself with the circle of savants surrounding the controversial jurist Ibn Taymiyya, whom he admired for his intellectual rigor but criticized for his polemics against the ʿulamaʾ. Al-Dhahabi wrote a long history, *Taʾrīkh duwal al-Islām* (History of the Nations of Islam), from the Prophet's life to 700/1301, followed by a supplement (*dhayl*) to 750/1349, its final year and obituaries added posthumously. The second, ʿImad al-Din Ismaʿil ibn ʿUmar ibn Kathir (d. 774/1373), belonged to a Qurayshi family from Busra, a village near Damascus. Ibn Kathir studied with numerous Damascene fuqahaʾ and muhaddithin, including al-Dhahabi. He was profoundly influenced by the traditionist Jamal al-Din Yusuf al-Mizzi, with whom he studied several canonical collections of Hadith and treatises in Maliki and Shafiʿi jurisprudence. He married his mentor's daughter, Zaynab, and joined the learned ranks in Damascus.[56] Ibn Kathir's most famous work on history was his universal survey, *al-Bidāya wa'l-nihāya* (The Beginning and the End). The section addressing the Mamluk period reveals Ibn Kathir's debt to his colleagues, al-Jazari and al-Birzali, for its content. Ibn Kathir shared his generation's mixture of awe and ambivalence toward the Damascene jurist and theologian Ibn Taymiyya[57] and included in the *Bidāya* many details on his life recounted nowhere else.

The preceding sketches on authors noted above do not embrace the full range of taʾrikh writing in Syria in the Mamluk era. But they suggest trends on which several modern analysts have elaborated. Among the most significant is the concept of "literarized" history argued by a German scholar, the late Ulrich Haarmann.[58] Haarmann asserted that, while Mamluk-era historians maintained the Tabari-style annalistic framework for presenting events, they departed from it with regard to their choice of subjects. Rather than confining themselves to al-Tabari's remote "prophet and kings" format, they marshaled an array of topics more relevant to the mundane world of the present. They animated these topics by inserting devices like poetry in the styles previously mentioned or marvels and miracles expressed with an aim to titillate the reader. Even elite political figures were depicted in terms that made them seem approachable and down to earth. Haarmann's thesis is in keeping with Hirschler's depiction of the writerly culture that was reaching new audiences. Haarmann's thesis did not go unchallenged. Another German scholar, Bernd Radtke, claimed that historical writing during the Mamluk period was not a radical departure from classical norms at all but in fact continued a long-standing tradition of explaining events according to either divine salvation based on Revelation (and thus "true": *ṭasdīq*) or celebration of the miraculous (thus "astounding": *taʿjīb*). Radtke utilized Ibn al-Dawadari's *Kanz al-durar* (the early material of which was largely copied from Sibt ibn al-Jawzi's *Mir'a*) to show that classical Islamic views of cosmography persisted unaltered in Mamluk historiography.[59] Radtke's assertion bears some merit, but he acknowledged himself that both rationales were affected by the trend toward popularization of history as entertainment from the eighth/thirteenth century onwards. Popularization of history is evident in the works of Egyptian historians as well. But its manifestation occurred in a milieu even more complex.

The diversity of occupational callings that set Egyptian historians apart from their Syrian counterparts augmented their visions of intended outcomes. These visions occasionally entangled goals that seem incongruous from a superficial perspective. Objectives of individuals high placed in the Chancery and close to their royal employers were clear. Ibn ʿAbd al-Zahir wrote panegyrics to Sultans Baybars, Qalawun, and Khalil. His nephew, Nasir al-Din Shafiʿ al-Misri (d. 730/1330), edited the uncle's *Rawḍ* and went on to compose a biography for Qalawun: *al-Faḍl al-ma'thūr min sīrat al-sulṭān al-malik al-manṣūr* (Virtue Transmitted from the Life of al-Malik al-Mansur).[60] Less laudatory were the goals of Shihab al-Din Ahmad ibn Yahya al-Qurashi al-ʿAdawi, known as Ibn Fadl Allah al-ʿUmari (d. 749/1349). Son of a distinguished chancery head in Damascus and Cairo, al-ʿUmari succeeded his father to the Cairo post but ran afoul of his patron, Sultan al-Nasir Muhammad ibn Qalawun. Inclined to acerbic confrontations with superiors, al-ʿUmari was on the losing end of a quarrel with the ruler. Sacked and imprisoned, al-ʿUmari returned to Damascus upon his release, where he took up the insha' directorship. He held the office three years before being fired for numerous complaints over his conduct. He remained out of service until his death, benefiting from the leisure time to write his monumental works.[61] Al-ʿUmari's fraught career inspired no panegyrics. But he produced a manual for drafting documents, *Al-Taʿrīf bi'l-muṣṭalaḥ al-sharīf* (Instruction of the Noble Procedure), and his magnum opus: *Masālik al-abṣār fī mamālik al-amṣār* (Paths of Discernment to Kingdoms of the Lands), an encyclopedia noteworthy for its excursuses on regions adjacent to the Mamluk Empire, such as the Arabian Peninsula, and farther afield, such as the Mongol Empire and India.[62]

An encyclopedist contemporary to al-ʿUmari wrote an even larger compendium that reflected the diversity of his multiple avocations. Shihab al-Din Ahmad ibn ʿAbd al-Wahhab al-Bakri al-Tamimi al-Qurashi, known as al-Nuwayri (d. 733/1333 in Cairo), experienced a multifaceted career as director of several fiscal bureaus, participant in Syrian campaigns against the Mongols, diplomat, provincial administrator, scholar in residence at the Nasiriyya Madrasa in Cairo, and confidant of sultans.[63] The range of al-Nuwayri's offices provided the manifold data for his master work: *Nihāyat al-arab fī funūn al-adab* (Epitome of the Desirable in the Literary Arts). Al-Nuwayri organized his encyclopedia into five "classes" (*funūn*): cosmography, natural history, humankind (peoples and tribes), flora and fauna, and history. The final section was a chronicle heavily dependent on his predecessors' histories but distinctive in its departure from their annalistic format.[64] Al-Nuwayri addressed issues unfolding over more than a year as topics that warranted elucidation separate from the stream of events occurring chronologically and simply mentioned rather than contextualized. With regard to the other *funūn*, al-Nuwayri interspersed his mass of factual details with anecdotes, fables, marvels, and poetry. Seventy-five poets were quoted in the *fann* on fauna. This tactic was a means to present bulky quantities of (potentially tedious) information in a manner that animated its reception to audiences of the period's writerly culture. In modern scholarship, al-Nuwayri's stratagem renders his *Nihāya* a source valuable for insights to popular views about culture and erudition. He provided a substantial edifice for doing so. Al-Nuwayri began compiling the *Nihāya* upon his retirement from government service in 716/1316. Over the next seventeen years, he produced a compendium of 9000 pages in thirty-one volumes (twenty-one for the historical section). Al-Nuwayri remarked that his aim throughout was *adab*, learning transmitted as a literary art.[65]

Eight decades after al-Nuwayri finished his *Nihāya*, a clerk in the Cairo Chancery compiled a manual of diplomatics that is considered the epitome of its genre and the ultimate product of the insha' institution in medieval Egypt. Shihab al-Din Abu'l-ʿAbbas Ahmad ibn ʿAli al-Fazari al-Qalqashandi al-Shafiʿi (d. 821/1418) grew up in a learned family from the Delta town of Qalqashanda that traced its ancestry to the Maghribi Arab tribe of Fazara.[66] Although he studied jurisprudence (*fiqh*) with the intention of pursuing a career in the Shafiʿi courts, he took up a position on the staff of the Chancery Head (*kātib al-sirr fī dīwān al-inshāʾ*). Al-Qalqashandi ultimately became a secretary of the Royal Bench (*kātib al-dast*), responsible for recording sessions presided over by the sultan in his capacity as ultimate appellate judge. The katib al-sirr attended the ruler as his senior legal adviser and informant (cf. Chapter 4). During his tenure at this post, al-Qalqashandi assembled the trove of documents that were integrated into the manual he was composing as a procedural guide for members of his profession. He completed it in 814/1412, with the title: *Subḥ al-aʿshá fī ṣināʿat al-inshāʾ* (Dawn for the Benighted Regarding the Chancery Craft). The *Subḥ* was organized in ten discourses (*maqālāt*), preceded by an introduction, that laid out in minute detail the evolution of documentary practice from the origins of Islam to the author's own day, protocols of form and style appropriate to specific types of correspondence, and practices to be followed by secretarial staff. In manuscript form, the *Ṣubḥ* occupied seven volumes (the printed Cairo edition takes up fourteen, of ca. 400 pages each). Beyond its intrinsic value as a reference that illustrates documentation in the medieval Islamic world, the *Ṣubḥ* included many transcriptions of original documents, copied as procedural examples for secretaries to follow, that are preserved nowhere else. As such, the *Ṣubḥ* stands as a unique repository of primary sources for the diplomatic history of the central Islamic lands in premodern times. Since it also included procedures of correspondence with non-Islamic states in Europe, Africa, and Asia, the *Ṣubḥ* is an important source for diplomacy beyond the Dar al-Islam.[67]

Prominent among members of the Mamluk military class who wrote works of ta'rīkh was Rukn al-Din Baybars al-Mansuri al-Khita'i (d. 725/1325). Imported for training as a cadet in 659/1261, Baybars was purchased by the amir Qalawun and adopted his patron's laqab as his nisba when the latter assumed the sultanate as al-Malik al-Mansur. Baybars was promoted an officer upon Qalawun's enthronement. Assigned the governorship of al-Karak in 685/1286, he was dismissed by Qalawun's successor, Khalil. Baybars successfully navigated the conspiracies surrounding Sultan al-Nasir Muhammad ibn Qalawun's two depositions. Steadfastly loyal, he was reinstated as Dawadar to reward his part in facilitating al-Nasir's final restoration in 709/1310.[68] A year later, he fell victim to al-Nasir's paranoia over potential insurrection and was imprisoned at al-Karak for five years. Upon his release in 716/1316, he was reinstated to his former rank as an officer of one hundred with stipend, a compensation that enabled retirement devoted to scholarship. Baybars's significant composition was his *Zubdat al-fikra fī ta'rīkh al-Hijra* (Essential Thoughts on History of the Hijra), a universal history from creation to the year 724/1324. Written in ornate style, the *Zubda* offers insights unique to Baybars's observations about reigns of the three sultans (Qalawun, Khalil, and al-Nasir Muhammad) whom he served. However, he depended on Ibn ʿAbd al-Zahir for much of his coverage of Qalawun and his predecessors.[69]

In addition to authors descended from first-generation Mamluks (*awlād al-nās*) previously discussed (Ibn al-Dawadari, Khalil al-Safadi, Ibn Sudun, and Ibn Taghri Birdi), two figures active at the end of the "long" ninth/ fifteenth century stand out. The first was the Sultanate's chronicler of its final decades and the Ottoman occupation, who exemplified prose writing in the medial Arabic that had been evolving over the preceding century and a half. He also contributed to the poetic milieu of the period. This was Shihab/Zayn al-Din Abu'l-Barakat Muhammad ibn Ahmad al-Nasiri al-Jarkasi al-Hanafi, known as Ibn Iyas (d. 930/1524). Ibn Iyas's chronicle remains a source unique for its detailed treatment, in annalistic fashion, of the late Sultanate. His *Badā'iʿ al-zuhūr fī waqā'iʿ al-duhūr* (Marvels Blossoming among Incidents of the Epochs) provides firsthand observations about politics, foreign affairs, fiduciary procedures, literary culture, and life among both elites and masses of society when it proceeds from the ascension of Sultan Qayitbay in 872/1468.[70] Despite the centrality of his chronicle to this *fin-de-siècle* era, Ibn Iyas remains something of an anomaly in Mamluk historiography. Beyond his position in an affluent lineage traced to an officer who served Sultans al-Nasir Hasan and al-Ashraf Shaʿban in the mid-eighth/fourteenth century, little is known about Ibn Iyas's personal life. He studied with two scholars, al-Suyuti and ʿAbd al-Basit ibn Khalil al-Hanafi, in the tutorial fashion preferred by elite families. How he acquired proficiency in both fusha and the semi-colloquial dialect of Cairene written Arabic cannot be ascertained since he wrote no memoir and received no biography by his ʿulamaʾ contemporaries. But of his proficiency there is no doubt. Ibn Iyas's fount of information is indispensable to understanding the late Mamluk period. Controversy persists over how his writings should be interpreted. Ulrich Haarmann asserted that the *Bada'iʿ* was not a work of history but rather an assemblage of disparate facts listed without context and interspersed with literary snippets.[71] Others, including this writer, have noted finite themes that include a largely negative assessment of regime policy, fiscal corruption, and the regime's diminishing capacity to rein in aggressive foreign rivals. Ibn Iyas's treatment of these themes reveals a nuanced understanding of practical politics. With regard to Ibn Iyas as a connoisseur of poetry, one scholar has discovered a hundred examples of his verse appended to a wide range of incidents colorfully recounted in the *Badāʾiʿ*. Ibn Iyas also quoted numerous other authors and commented on the salons of poets convened by Sultan al-Ghawri.[72] For these reasons, Ibn Iyas occupies a vital place among the Sultanate's historians.

The second was a Syrian who, similar to Ibn Iyas in Egypt, witnessed the final decades of Mamluk rule in the Levant and the subsequent Ottoman occupation: the Damascene Shams al-Din Muhammad ibn ʿAli ibn Ahmad al-Salihi al-Hanafi, known as Ibn Tulun (d. 953/1546). Born to a scholarly walad al-nas family descended from a Mamluk officer named Khumarwayh ibn Tulun, this individual paralleled al-Suyuti's status as a prodigy (noted below). He received an ijaza from him. Ibn Tulun had memorized the Qur'an by the age of seven; in his eleventh year he merited a stipend from a waqf that paid for his education in Jurisprudence (*fiqh*) at the Maridaniyya madrasa in Damascus.[73] Ibn Tulun's subsequent career was not distinguished. He held posts in the courts or madrasas, but few were prestigious. Only in his later years was he offered appointments as preacher (*khaṭīb*) in the Umayyad Mosque or Hanafi jurisconsult (*muftī*) of Damascus, both of which he turned down, pleading infirmity due to age. Yet, Ibn Tulun's writings offer an insightful commentary to the rising tensions over gang disputes and factional rivalries that plagued Syria's cities as the Sultanate's authority diminished in the region. Ibn Tulun compiled a chronicle that addresses events in Damascus occurring between 884/1479–80 and 926/1520: *Mufākahat al-khillān fī ḥawādith al-zamān* (Boon Banter over Anecdotes of the Age).[74] The author's choice of title may have expressed his sardonic reaction to the endemic violence that engulfed Damascus before the Ottoman invasion. The myriad incidents of theft, rioting, and pillage reported in the *Mufakaha* shed light on agendas of their perpetrators: factional leaders from the masses who took over wards of the city as the regime's police agencies abandoned their charge to uphold order. The *Mufakaha* depicts an environment of endemic turbulence that stymied the routine conduct of commerce and sapped the waning energies of the provincial authorities in their efforts to bring it under control. As such, Ibn Tulun's chronicle provides a telling commentary for the state of urban unrest in the Levant before the Ottoman Conquest.[75]

Historians who identified as jurist-scholars ranked among the most eminent intellectuals of their age. One need only mention a figure such as Ibn Khaldun, often labeled the first "secular" historian in Islamic historiography. Abu Zayd ʿAbd al-Rahman ibn Muhammad ibn Khaldun (d. 808/1406) was born in Tunis to a family that had migrated to North Africa from the Iberian Peninsula (*al-Andalus*). His lineage may be traced to tribal origins in the Hadramawt (southern Arabian Peninsula).[76] Following a career of distinguished service and political intrigue under several rulers in al-Andalus and the Maghrib, Ibn Khaldun departed Tunis, ostensibly on pilgrimage to Mecca. He settled in Cairo (784/1383), where he was honorably received by Sultan Barquq, who appointed him senior Maliki qadi, a post he would gain and lose several times. Ibn Khaldun is known in western scholarship primarily for his *al-Muqaddima fī'l-ta'rīkh* (Introduction to History), an appraisal of geography, political theory (*siyāsa*), economics, social structure, and learned disciplines as they related to the Islamic societies of his time. The methodology behind its argumentation and presentation of data is unique to medieval historical writing and is often interpreted as posited on principles that presage the modern social sciences. A comprehensive discussion of the *Muqaddima* exceeds the scope of this survey. Suffice to note that attribution of modern secularity to Ibn Khaldun's methods is misleading. This individual was a devout believer who regarded occult "sciences" of the miraculous and supernatural as worthy of serious scrutiny.[77] Ibn Khaldun's place among contemporary authors of ta'rikh may be more contextually assessed from his universal history: *Kitāb al-ʿibar wa-dīwān al-mubtada' wa'l-khabar* (The Book of Interpretation, a Treatise on the Beginnings and Topics). As the first volume of the *Kitab al-ʿibar*, the *Muqaddima* was composed to provide an analytical framework for digesting the voluminous information on populations and dynasties, primarily of the Maghrib and Egypt, which followed. The *Kitab al-ʿibar*'s structure paralleled works of the ta'rikh genre written by Ibn Khaldun's contemporaries. Ibn Khaldun drew substantively from his predecessors, al-Jazari, al-Yunini, and al-Nuwayri, for coverage of events in Egypt and Syria.[78]

An author who in his own time, and from the perspective of many modern scholars, has been considered the preeminent historian of Egypt from the Fatimids to the Mamluks is Taqi al-Din Abu'l-ʿAbbas Ahmad ibn ʿAli ibn ᶜAbd al-Qadir al-Maqrizi (d. 845/1442). His nisba refers to a quarter in the town of Baᶜlabakk in the Biqaᶜ Valley of the Lebanon, where he traced his paternal roots. Born and raised in Cairo to a prominent learned family, al-Maqrizi studied Hanafi jurisprudence with his grandfather but shared his father's affiliation with Shafiᶜism.[79] After appointments to several diwan offices, judgeships, and teaching posts in Cairo and Damascus, al-Maqrizi retired from active employment, apparently disillusioned over his failed prospects in the intrigue-ridden milieu of competition for patronage from sponsors in the ruling elite. Al-Maqrizi had successfully enhanced his status during the reigns of Sultans Barquq and Faraj but fell from favor when al-Mu'ayyad Shaykh assumed power (815/1412). His fortunes did not improve after al-Ashraf Barsbay consolidated his own position in 825/1422. The rival who won Barsbay's esteem as the sultan's spiritual advisor and confidant, al-ᶜAyni (noted below), supplanted al-Maqrizi and effectively served as historian to the royal court.[80] Following his recusal, al-Maqrizi addressed himself to writing works of urban topography, history, and political economy.

Foremost among these, as measured by citation across numerous disciplines, is al-Maqrizi's topographical survey of Cairo and its environs: *al-Mawāᶜiẓ wa'l-iᶜtibār bi-dhikr al-khiṭaṭ wa'l-āthār* (Admonitions and Reflections on Remembrance of Quarters and Monuments). The *Khitat* is an inventory of districts and structures, inclusive of edifices razed from former eras and known in al-Maqrizi's day only from textual references. It enumerates hundreds of palaces, mosques, madrasas, khanqahs, zawiyas, churches, synagogues, markets, streets, squares, bridges, and canals, each with contextual remarks about its construction, function, and longevity. Al-Maqrizi did not initiate the khitat genre; earlier surveys by Ibn ᶜAbd al-Zahir, al-Nuwayri, and al-ᶜUmari were sporadically cited. Nor did the *Khitat* avoid controversy over its originality. The biographer al-Sakhawi accused al-Maqrizi of plagiarizing parts of the *Khitat* from his colleague and neighbor, Ahmad ibn Hasan al-Awhadi (d. 811/1408), along with passages from the *Kitāb al-intiṣār li-wāsiṭat ᶜiqd al-amṣār* (Triumphal Book Highlighting Jewels of the Lands) by the walad al-nas chronicler, Ibn Duqmaq (d. 809/1407).[81] Al-Sakhawi's allegation has been verified by recent research, although only for limited sections of this immense compilation.[82] Al-Maqrizi may have regarded al-Awhadi's text as a legacy bestowed on him to appropriate. The *Khiṭaṭ* remains indispensable for research on medieval Cairo and urban topography in the Islamic world more generally.

Al-Maqrizi wrote chronicles about the Fatimid Caliphate: *Ittiᶜāẓ al-ḥunafā'* (Admonition of True Believers) and the Ayyubid and Mamluk regimes: *Kitāb al-Sulūk li-maᶜrifat duwal al-mulūk* (The Path to Knowledge of Royal Realms), the latter of which is among the most cited sources for the Mamluk Sultanate. Al-Maqrizi borrowed heavily from the authors noted above who addressed the Sultanate's pre-Circassian decades. From Sultan Barquq's reign, al-Maqrizi's reportage of events proceeds along their chronological order in the annalistic mode but is fleshed out by commentaries that provide contextual detail and inject personal opinion – copiously. Al-Maqrizi's negative regard for the Circassian rulers, and the ruling elite as a whole, pervades his narrative. The long-gone era of the Fatimids is held up as more than a nostalgic ideal from a glorious past. Al-Maqrizi was proud of his connection by lineage to the Fatimid Caliphate and extolled his sense of its principled governance and prosperity for all classes as a foil to the decline for which he held the Circassian rulers accountable.[83] Al-Maqrizi's obsessive focus on issues of corruption and malfeasance makes the *Sulūk* a rich source for crime and transgressive behavior in medieval Islamic societies. He frequently depicted criminal acts by common people as desperate reactions to oppression inflicted on them by the ruling class, formally pledged to uphold the law but in practice guilty of violating it for profit. Al-Maqrizi's views about corruption were also vividly expressed in treatises on political economy, such as his *Ighāthat al-umma bi-kashf al-ghumma* (Aiding the Community by Examining the Cause of Its Distress), which lamented the debasement of coinage that had become endemic during the Circassian period (cf. Chapter 5).[84]

Al-Maqrizi's rival contrived a more successful trajectory to prominence and favor by powerful patrons. Debate continues over the significance of his works in comparison with al-Maqrizi's. Badr al-Din Abu Muhammad Mahmud ibn Ahmad ibn Musa al-ʿAyni (d. 855/1451) was born in the north Syrian city of ʿAyntab (now Gaziantep in modern Turkey), where his father served as Hanafi qadi.[85] Al-ʿAyni belonged to a family of jurist-scholars from Aleppo and pursued his studies in Qurʾan and Hadith there. He also acquired fluency in spoken and written Turkish, a skill that would stand him well in the future. After his father's death, al-ʿAyni continued his education in Damascus and Jerusalem. He accompanied his teacher in Hanafi fiqh, ʿAlaʾ al-Din al-Sayrami, to Cairo, where his mentor held the post of Shaykh at the Sufi khanqah recently founded by Sultan al-Zahir Barquq. Al-Sayrami secured his student a place there. But, following al-Sayrami's death, al-ʿAyni fell out with a senior officer and departed Cairo for Damascus to take up the office of muhtasib. He soon returned to Cairo, where he supplanted al-Maqrizi as market inspector.[86] The enmity between the two began from this incident, as did al-ʿAyni's steady rise and al-Maqrizi's gradual fall to self-imposed isolation. Al-ʿAyni's cultivation of intimate rapport with Sultans al-Muʾayyad Shaykh, al-Zahir Tatar and al-Ashraf Barsbay as their confidant granted him the exceptional advantages that sponsors of supreme status in the realm could bestow. He also honed his skills at navigating succession crises and transferring allegiances. Al-ʿAyni went on to assume the lucrative post of supervisor of pious foundations (*nāẓir al-aḥbās*), which he occupied several times until shortly before his death.

He occupied the senior Hanafi judgeship concurrently. The wealth accrued from these positions enabled him to found his own madrasa.

Al-ᶜAyni prudently wrote panegyric eulogies to all three of his royal patrons, unlike al-Maqrizi, who castigated them in his *Sulūk* (also prudently after their deaths). Al-ᶜAyni acquired renown among Hadith scholars for his compilation of a commentary on the canonical collection of Traditions by the legist al-Bukhari (d. 258/870): *ᶜUmdat al-qārī fī sharḥ ṣaḥīḥ al-Bukhārī* (Prop of the Reciter on the Sound Commentary by al-Bukhari). His universal history, *ᶜIqd al-jumān fī ta'rīkh ahl al-zamān* (A Pearl Necklace on Peoples of the Times), differs from al-Maqrizi's *Kitāb al-sulūk* in its format for reportage of events, particularly from the Ayyubid through the Mamluk periods. Some modern historians have regarded al-ᶜAyni's departure from annalistic listing to discussions of discrete topics superior to al-Maqrizi's approach. Al-ᶜAyni also acknowledged his sources, especially for the Bahri decades, more consistently than al-Maqrizi.[87] Assessment of the *ᶜIqd* is complicated by its uneven sequences of publication. No edition of the full text from its origins in Creation has been completed. Sections of the Ayyubid and Mamluk periods have appeared.[88] This limited coverage by three different editors, despite consultation of the same manuscripts, obviates a comparative assessment of the *ᶜIqd* with the *Sulūk*. Nonetheless, contrasts in the two author's objectives are discernible. Al-Maqrizi's penchant for criticism lent his reportage a degree of credibility missing from al-ᶜAyni's predilection for panegyric. Al-Maqrizi also focused on conditions of "the street," in ways that provided a sense of what the masses were up to. Al-ᶜAyni concentrated his reportage on the elites, largely omitting perspectives of the social majority. Until the *ᶜIqd* is available in editions comparable to those for the *Sulūk*, further comparisons are not reliable.

A third individual dabbled in this milieu of competition over preference and sponsorship from the ruling elite, although his stature enabled him to remain somewhat aloof from open vituperation. Shihab al-Din Abu'l-Fadl Ahmad ibn Nur al-Din ᶜAli ibn Muhammad ibn Hajar al-ᶜAsqalani (d. 852/1449) was regarded as the preeminent scholar of Egypt in his own lifetime. His former student and admirer, al-Sakhawi, routinely referred to him as "Our Shaykh" (*shaykhunā*, on the assumption that any reader would know who this was. Ibn Hajar's forebears had moved to Alexandria from ᶜAsqalan in Palestine after the Ayyubid sultan, Salah al-Din, ordered the town razed during the Crusader wars. Ibn Hajar's immediate family resided in Cairo. His father had been trained in Shafiᶜi fiqh but had not secured a permanent position in the judiciary. Since he died when the son was only five, Ibn Hajar only dimly recalled him.[89] Ibn Hajar grew up in prosperity provided by his mother's family of affluent Karimi merchants and showed a precocious capacity for Hadith studies early on. Ibn Hajar held teaching posts in Cairo's most prestigious madrasas and occupied the senior Shafiᶜi judgeship intermittently for more than two decades.[90] Among his numerous writings on Hadith, the commentary on al-Bukhari's *Ṣaḥīḥ,* the *Fatḥ al-bāri'* (Victory of the Creator) became a standard of reference still consulted in the present day. The Timurid ruler, Shah Rukh, requested copies of the work-in-progress from Sultan Barsbay. Ibn Hajar wrote a chronicle on events in Egypt and Syria that occurred between 773/1372 (his birth) to 850/1446: *Inbā' al-ghumr bi-abnā' al-ᶜumr* (Enlightening the Ingenuous about Episodes of the Age). Although regime politics, foreign affairs, and intra-elite rivalries make their appearance, the author's proclivity to address judicial cases, doctrinal controversies, religious deviance or heresy, and tensions between Christians and Muslims shows abundantly in the *Inba'*'s topical coverage. Ibn Hajar also compiled a biographical dictionary: *al-Durar al-kāmina fī aᶜyān al-mi'a al-thāmina* (Hidden Pearls Regarding Notables of the Eighth Century) that contains more than 5000 biographies of individuals who attracted notoriety in Egypt and Syria during its period. Ibn Hajar relied heavily on al-Safadi for persons deceased before he was born.

Ibn Hajar's *Durar* was the model adopted by a figure whose work embodied the conceptual evolution of ta'rikh writing at the end of the "long" ninth/fifteenth century. Shams al-Din Abu'l-Khayr Muhammad ibn ᶜAbd al-Rahman al-Sakhawi al-Shafiᶜi (d. 902/1497) hailed from a prominent family of ᶜulama' who originally resided in the town of Sakhā in the Egyptian Delta. They had settled in the former Fatimid quarter of Cairo two generations before al-Sakhawi's birth.[91] Al-Sakhawi received his training in Hadith and related studies from numerous scholars, most notably his mentor, Ibn Hajar al-ᶜAsqalani, whom he revered. Al-Sakhawi's aptitudes inclined him toward production of works remarkable for their encyclopedic scope, as embodied in his monumental achievement: a biographical dictionary of prominent persons from both the military and civilian elites in the Sultanate during the ninth/fifteenth century: *Al-Ḍaw' al-lāmiᶜ fī aᶜyān al-qarn al-tāsiᶜ* (Light that Illumines Notables of the Ninth Century). While patterned after Ibn Hajar's *Durar*, the *Ḍaw'*'s plethora of detail reflected al-Sakhawi's obsession with evidence and perusal of diverse sources. Among its topics that illustrate the range and depth of scholarship during this period was al-Sakhawi's exhaustive listing of texts for which biographees were formally qualified to teach and transmit.[92] Al-Sakhawi obtained the relevant data from certificates (*ijāzāt*) he collected, signed by the instructors or attendant scholars who confirmed the biographee's accuracy of memorization and comprehension of arguments. For the military class, al-Sakhawi profusely sifted through his predecessors' chronicles to trace their careers. The *Ḍaw'* contains 11,000-plus biographies, of which more than a thousand address women (located in the final volume) who had attained prominence for their own erudition apart from status as spouses to husbands (cf. Chapter 7). Al-Sakhawi attained notoriety, deservedly, for his propensity to castigate what he regarded as erroneous transmission, shallow reasoning, or trivial reportage on the part of adversaries and colleagues alike. He was particularly dismissive of the polymath, al-Suyuti, noted below, who vehemently returned the favor. But al-Maqrizi and Ibn Taghri Birdi were also targeted for criticism. Al-Sakhawi's fulminations must be interpreted with caution, despite his stated goal of ascertaining his contemporaries' fitness, morally or scholastically, for transmitting religious texts or deciding legal cases. Nonetheless, the factual accuracy of al-Sakhawi's information is regarded as sound, if for no other reason than his keen awareness that opponents would expose errors or distortions of his own, in return for his denunciations of them and their works.

In addition to the *Ḍaw'*, al-Sakhawi compiled an inventory of ta'rikh writers and scholastics generally, from al-Tabari's time to his own, that he supplemented with a treatise on historiographical methodology and objectives. This was his *al-Iʿlān bi-tawbīkh li-man dhamma ahl al-ta'rīkh* (Open Denunciation of the Adverse Critics of the Historians). From a technical perspective, the *Iʿlan* was "an apologetic essay on historiography as a religious science derived from the science of ḥadīth."[93] More broadly, Franz Rosenthal considered the *Iʿlan* a summation of scholastic method as it was understood at the end of the "long" ninth/ fifteenth century, a work

> written in order to defend the study of history as an auxiliary subject in the extra-academic curriculum of religious studies. History, in this sense, preferably referred to the discussion of certain aspects of the biography of religious scholars. In fact, the work was written entirely from the point of view of the religious disciplines. However, at the same time, it was written by a man who was possessed by a passion for collecting details and who marked the end of a great era of research on the writing of history. The result was a work which constitutes a comprehensive and often brilliant exposition of Muslim historiography.[94]

Al-Sakhawi also wrote supplements to al-Dhahabi's history: *Dhayl duwal al-Islām*, noteworthy for its coverage of events in the Hijaz; and al-Maqrizi's chronicle: *al-Tibr al-masbūk fī dhayl al-sulūk* (Refined Gold as Sequel to the *Sulūk*), sponsored by the aforementioned Amir Yashbak, which continued the depiction of events to 857/1453.

The target of al-Sakhawi's derogation is regarded as the most productive author of the "long" ninth/ fifteenth century, or of any period in premodern Islamic history – if measured by quantity. Jalal al-Din Abu'l-Fadl ʿAbd al-Rahman ibn Abi Bakr ibn Muhammad al-Khudayri al-Suyuti (d. 911/1505) produced hundreds of texts on virtually every discipline in the traditional canon.[95] His multifarious works are read to this day from South Asia to West Africa. A prodigy who taught prophetic traditions at the age of eighteen, al-Suyuti eventually proclaimed himself an autonomous interpreter (*mujtahid*) of Imam al-Shafiʿi's corpus and even the renewer (*mujaddid*) of Islam for his era.

His audacity, clothed in pious affectation of humility before God, prompted al-Sakhawi's castigation. Al-Suyuti descended from Persian ancestors who had once lived in the Khudayriyya quarter of Baghdad. His more immediate forebears settled in Asyut in Upper Egypt and then transferred to Cairo. When al-Suyuti's father died in his sixth year, he was already immersed in Qur'anic and Hadith studies. He allegedly attended lectures by Ibn Hajar at the age of three. Among al-Suyuti's roster of traditionists were several female reciters of Hadith whom he held in high regard. His mentors included the eminent jurist ᶜAlam al-Din Salih al-Bulqini (d. 868/1463)[96] and the author of texts on grammar and logic, Muhyi al-Din al-Kafiyaji (d. 879/1474). The latter nominated al-Suyuti to the post of mudarris Hadith at the Shaykhuniyya Madrasa in Cairo in 877/1472. He eventually assumed the rectorship (*mashyakha*) of the wealthy Baybarsiyya khanqah (891/1486), into which sanctuary he progressively sought seclusion as antagonism mounted against his pronouncements. Al-Suyuti was not shy about his claim to mastery of the Islamic Sciences in their totality. He also issued fatwas refuting the opinions of eminent legists and refused to attend the customary consultations with the sultan each month on the grounds that the Mamluk ruler's charge as final arbiter of appellate cases was illegitimate and contradictory to the genuine authority of the ᶜAbbasid Caliph. He condemned the legacy of al-Zahir Baybars, who had established the policy of appointing senior judges in each of the four Sunni madhhabs. His relationships with Sultans Qayitbay and Qansawh al-Ghawri were strained. Al-Sakhawi could thus tap a reservoir of resentment shared by many in both learned and political circles when he denounced al-Suyuti's stance as mujaddid.[97] Al-Suyuti's works on ta'rikh were modest in comparison with his massive oeuvre on traditions, jurisprudence, philology, and Sufism. He wrote a short treatise on procedure, *al-Shamārīkh fī ᶜilm al-taᶜrīkh* (Date Panicles on the Science of History); a survey of the Caliphs, *Ta'rīkh al-khulafā'*; and a history of Egypt, *Ḥusn al-muḥādara fī akhbār Miṣr wa'l-Qāhira* (Excellent Lectures on Events in Egypt and Cairo). Al-Suyuti's impact on historiography was therefore minimal; al-Sakhawi's ire was directed at his grandiose claims to supremacy in the religious sciences.

## Concluding Thoughts

In his *Iᶜlān bi-tawbīkh*, al-Sakhawi mused over the evolution of historiography from its formation in the science of Hadith transmission during the Classical era to the multiplicity of genres in his own time. He acknowledged the template left by al-Tabari as a model for goals subsequent historians should aim to fulfill. Prominent among these was restraint from criticism of personalities. Al-Tabari eschewed character assessment of persons in preference for reportage of their actions via chains of transmission of variable soundness, usually without opining further. A statement that captures his intention appears in the foreword to his history:

The reader should know that with respect to all I have mentioned and made it a condition to set down in this book of ours, I rely upon traditions and reports (*akhbār*) which I have transmitted and which I attribute to their transmitters. I rely only very exceptionally upon what is learned through rational arguments and produced by internal thought processes. For no knowledge of the history of men of the past and of recent men and events is attainable by those who were not able to observe them and did not live in their time, except through information and transmission provided by informants and transmitters. This knowledge cannot be brought out by reason or produced by internal thought processes. This book of mine may (be found to) contain some information mentioned by us on the authority of certain men of the past, which the reader may disapprove of and the listener may find detestable, because he can find nothing sound and no real meaning in it. In such cases, he should know that it is not our fault that such information comes to him, but the fault of someone who transmitted it to us. We have merely reported it as it was reported to us.[98]

Al-Sakhawi admired al-Tabari for his foundational contribution but subtly qualified his concurrence with al-Tabari's refutation of personality criticism. With regard to his admiration, the following passage from the *Iʿlan* is illustrative:

Another representative (of this kind of straight [i.e. annalistic] history) is the great History of the religious leader Abu Jaʿfar aṭ-Ṭabari, which has remained the standard work of reference in the field for all later (scholars). Aṭ-Ṭabari, a religious leader of independent judgment, who had a greater knowledge (in the religious disciplines) than any of his famed contemporaries, collected the various chains of transmitters for the traditions and for the information about the world (contained in it), but restricted his work to its purpose, namely, history, wars, and conquests. He rarely bothered with personality criticism and the like, so that he had no complete information about any one religious leader. He was only concerned with the explicit and detailed, not summary story of wars and conquests and the history (*akhbār*) of the ancient prophets and kings of old, of past national entities and bygone generations, for which he also indicated the various ways (of transmission) and numerous different chains of transmitters. He had an inexhaustible knowledge of this and other subjects. (As to personalities), he was satisfied with his history of personalities (of the science of traditions).[99]

Al-Sakhawi revealed his own qualification about negative character assessment in a statement on the benefits offered by the study of history in his own time that prefaced his survey of individual authors:

Our reply to the critics is that the justification of (continued personality criticism) lies in the fact that it is advice, which is not limited to the transmission (of traditions). There are cases which permit one to state discreditable facts about a person, and it is not considered calumny but necessary advice. For instance, an office holder who does not discharge the duties of his office in the way that he should, either because he is not fit for the office, or because he is wicked, or negligent, or the like, should be exposed so

> that he may be removed and his place be taken by a person fit for it. A person who is observed frequenting an innovator of Sufi or other leanings, or some wicked man, for study and guidance, and who is in danger to suffer harm on account of that, should be told the truth about the condition (of his mentor). Further cases (which must be exposed) are men who are so accommodating as muftis, authors, judges, witnesses, transmitters or preachers that they publicly make false and untenable statements. There also are men who are so accommodating in making statements about (religious) scholars, or in giving and accepting bribes, in that they either practice bribery or permit its practice although they would be able to prevent it, as well as in appropriating other people's possessions through legal tricks and fraud. There are those who take scholarly books away from their owners, or they take them away from mosques, even inalienable waqfs, and make them (their) personal property. There are other cases of illegal activity. All of that should be exposed, in order to prevent any harm from arising. Such exposure is either permissible or necessary. It is thus obvious that (the practice of) negative personality criticism did not stop (at a certain moment) and that under the prevailing conditions it is necessary advice. Those who dispense it will be rewarded (in the other world).[100]

When al-Sakhawi wrote his *Iʿlān*, he had surveyed the profiles of several thousand individuals with standing in the Sultanate's capital and elsewhere during the "long" ninth/ fifteenth century in his *Ḍawʾ al-Lāmiʿ*. The nefarious antics of many led him to conclude that "prevailing conditions" did compel the historian to offer the reader advice. Al-Tabari's eschewal, defensible in an idealized halcyon age long past, was no longer warranted.

# 7 The Rural Environment, Gendered Issues, Minority Communities, Sufi Practice

In recent decades, research has proliferated on several topics that have invited new methodological approaches. These are: the rural setting, relations between men and women, communal status of minorities (Christians and Jews), and religious diversity among Muslims, in particular among those who identified as Sufi mystics. New sources and revisionist interpretations of them continue to transform the field of Mamluk Studies. Yet, in many instances, findings on these subjects are confined to discoveries of information on discrete conditions or isolated events that do not lend themselves to comprehensive analysis. They often depend on a single source or fragmentary data set and require imaginative speculation to formulate hypotheses that apply to questions about their broader contexts in society. This chapter will outline the state of research on these subjects and their potential to open new lines of inquiry by highlighting examples that have influenced revisionist interpretations.

## The Rural Environment

The issue of isolated sources mentioned above, often scattered in fragments, is particularly noticeable in study of the rural environment. Until recent decades, premodern Islamic cultural, economic, and social history has been primarily an urban enterprise. Most of the historical writers, topographical surveyors, or political commentators were city dwellers. They focused on the milieu in which they lived. City people wrote for urban audiences. The vast majority of documentary and narrative sources address urban issues. When these writers did refer to rural hinterlands, where the bulk of farming or pastoral populations lived, they remarked about them cursorily as generators of taxes in kind or revenue, or when they interacted with the urban environment. Some authors discussed in previous chapters did mention lineage ties to families in rural areas. Transgressive behavior was another marker for them. If rural types caused trouble, urban writers paid them more attention. Recovering the cultural patterns, economic pursuits, or political engagement of rural populations has thus required ingenuity on the part of intrepid investigators who have creatively sorted through the desultory information chroniclers, topographers, and tax assessors provided sporadically on rural districts and their residents. Their research often draws upon methodologies developed in the social sciences, in particular anthropology and archaeology, to uncover evidence not traceable in written sources or to place their narratives in contexts otherwise obscure.[1] The following studies are representative of this research.

A work that qualified the marginality of a town in the Sultanate's distant outback of Upper Egypt was also pathbreaking for its interpretation of madrasa learning there as integrative among scholars or traders whose backgrounds ranged from agrarian peasantry to commerce in spices. In 1976, Jean-Claude Garcin published *Un centre musulman de Haute-Égypte médiévale: Qūṣ*.[2] Qus was a port on the Nile that facilitated the transit of spices and other commodities from the Red Sea to Cairo and Alexandria. It was an entrepôt in the larger commercial network that connected South and East Asia to the Mediterranean and Europe. The town flourished in the eighth/fourteenth century at the height of the Bahri period, but saw its fortunes ebb during the ninth/fifteenth century due to depopulation from plague epidemics, strife between tribes, and shifts in nautical shipping routes (cf. Chapter 5). Despite its significance to international trade, Qus remained very much a provincial town whose inhabitants retained close ties to local villagers and *ʿurbān* tribes. Garcin's study therefore broke new ground because it revealed, via scrutiny of the town's residents and their connections to the surrounding hinterland, how a river port functioned within the administrative structure of the Mamluk Empire and yet remained distinctly "*Saʿīdī*" in its character.

For data on the town's notables, many of whom were only a generation or two away from ancestors who had been farmers or tribesmen, Garcin drew upon a biographical dictionary compiled by an author descended from Upper Egyptian immigrants to Cairo. Kamal al-din Jaʿfar al-Udfuwi (nisba for the town of Edfu) wrote *al-Ṭāliʿ al-saʿīd al-jāmiʿ li-asmāʾ al-fuḍalāʾ wa'l-ruwāt bi-aʿlá al-ṣaʿīd* (The Rising Star and Auspicious Compendium that Names Refined Notables and Narrators from Uppermost Egypt).[3] The *Ṭāliʿ*'s list of literati and ʿulama' from Upper Egypt numbered only some 600 individuals, in contrast with the thousands of notables who populated the urban-centric inventories by al-Safadi, Ibn Hajar, or al-Sakhawi. This figure is a telling indicator of the relative paucity of scholastics who traced their origins to Upper Egypt. But for Garcin's purposes, al-Udfuwi's contribution was essential. From its biographies, Garcin was able to link jurist-scholars active in Qus to their regional constituencies of villagers and tribesmen. Al-Udfuwi's personnel who served in tandem with the Sultanate's administrative apparatus and commercial network revealed how the regime's provincial governance actually functioned at a specific site. Their interactions with Mamluk officers who lived off iqtaʿ allotments in the region showed why the Sultanate created estates for the ruling cohort. These were designed to grant them autonomous powers of enforcement while assuring the regime ultimate suzerainty over a district vital to its commercial interests. Several of these officers had been exiled from Cairo for conspiring against the ruler. They could be of use to the regime while being neutralized from further intrigue far away from the capital. Garcin also discerned a special interaction between Mamluk officials and *ʿurbān* tribes that served their mutual interests. By granting iqtaʿs to senior shaykhs, the regime sought to coopt potential raiders into acting as guarantors of security for caravans and local villages. The reduction of iqtaʿ grants that resulted from the regime's privatization of assets during the "long" ninth/fifteenth century contributed to the decline of Qus's status in the Sultanate's hierarchy of priorities and a loss of leverage over the tribes. Garcin's pioneering thesis has influenced subsequent studies of tribal relationships with the Sultanate throughout Egypt and Syria.[4]

Stuart Borsch, a student of water usage in medieval Egypt, has considered irrigation practices and the impact of natural phenomena on them during the Mamluk epoch. Borsch interrogated possible causes for a dramatic decline in maintenance of Egypt's irrigation system that began in the mid- to late eighth/fourteenth century and persisted to the end of the ninth/fifteenth.[5] The effect of this decline on Egypt's agrarian output was catastrophic. Borsch's interest was initially piqued when the chroniclers al-Maqrizi and Ibn Iyas reported increases in levels of the annual flood during these decades, in contrast with lower levels in the preceding century. Borsch questioned the chroniclers' speculation that water volumes flowing from the South had likely increased (although their knowledge of monsoons over the Ethiopian highlands was sketchy at best), since sources for weather patterns over the Indian Ocean for the ninth/fifteenth century reported no events that would cause an unusual increase in monsoonal precipitation. Borsch instead linked the dramatic rise in flood levels to increases of alluvium deposited by the floodwaters that was not being dredged on a regular basis.

But why did Egypt's irrigation network suffer neglect, after a long era of steady maintenance? Borsch noted a correlation between a lapse in maintenance policies and declines in rural population due to successive epidemics of plague. The Black Death broke out in Egypt during the mid-eighth/fourteenth century, following migration of its bacterium into Syria and the Nile Valley from the Mongols' invasion routes in Central Asia or seafaring carriers docking at Red Sea and Mediterranean ports. Borsch estimated death rates for Egypt at ca. 50 percent in both urban and rural settings. He argued that the resultant decline of labor power could not be made up from resources in Cairo or other cities. As a consequence, dredging of irrigation canals and repairing of dykes or catch basins diminished to the extent that several regions of Upper Egypt effectively went out of cultivation. The vacuum was filled by a reversion to pastoralism exploited by local tribes (*ʿurbān*), who occupied districts that had been abandoned by settled farmers.

Borsch went on to compare the allegedly dismal fate of Egyptian agriculture with the agrarian situation in Plantagenet England, also devastatingly affected by plague mortality in the same period.[6] He argued a dramatically different response in that country. In England, the decline in peasant population effectively broke the grip of big landholders over access to large tracts by small owners. The resultant shortage of rural agrarian labor benefited the free peasant class by enhancing their power to demand higher wages and acquire tracts of land as personal property. In Egypt, the opposite occurred. The regime responded by tightening its grip over remaining agrarian land, in part by reducing iqtaᶜs to the Arab tribes, as noted above. Borsch's research has introduced a new set of arguments to the larger question of diminished economic production throughout the central Islamic lands in the late medieval period.

A study that qualifies Garcin's and Borsch's hypotheses has been evolving over more than a decade. In 2004, Yossef Rapoport published "Invisible Peasants, Marauding Nomads: Taxation, Tribalism, and Rebellion in Mamluk Egypt."[7] Several articles, a monograph, and translation of a text on this topic have subsequently appeared.[8] Rapoport's assertions are drawn from a treatise unique in the documentary record of medieval Egypt. In 642/1244–45, during the reign of the Ayyubid Sultan al-Malik al-Salih Ayyub (r. 637/1240–647/1249), the ruler passed through the Fayyum oasis on a provincial tour. Having been informed that the district was less prosperous than in earlier times, al-Salih commissioned a former official in the financial bureaus and fiscal advisor to his father, Sultan al-Malik al-Kamil, to survey the Fayyum and prepare an inventory of its productive lands for tax purposes. This was ᶜAla' al-Din Abu ᶜAmr ᶜUthman ibn Ibrahim al-Qurashi ibn al-Nabulusi (d. 660/1262), who, over a period of two months in 642, visited most of the villages in the Fayyum to observe agrarian practices and record tax yields. These were available to al-Nabulusi for the preceding year 641/1243–44. Al-Nabulusi submitted his inventory and detailed commentary with the simple title *Taʾrīkh al-Fayyūm*, usually listed as *Villages of the Fayyum* in edited editions.[9]

Rapoport's analysis of agrarian techniques, pastoral husbandry, ethno-demography, and irrigation maintenance, as they appear in the *Taʾrīkh al-Fayyūm*, has yielded the following conclusions. The district's resident population during the late Ayyubid and early Mamluk periods consisted of elements that cannot be neatly categorized as either agrarian "peasants" (*fallāḥīn*) or Bedouin "nomads" (*badw*), since these terms do not appear in Nabulusi's treatise. Rather, Nabulusi described most of the population as either "arabs" (*ᶜurbān*) in a sense of ethnic identity held by settled grain farmers who were largely Muslim (but not nomads) or "sedentary" (*ḥaḍar*), who raised cash crops (fruits, vegetables) and were primarily Christians. The latter were a distinct minority and inhabited fewer villages than the ᶜurban. Grain cultivation, especially in eastern districts of the Fayyum, relied largely on water from

Fig. 7.1 Water wheels near Fayyum oasis dam
(Credit: Emad Aljumah/Getty Images)

the adjacent Nile, while interior areas where cash crops were cultivated drew water from channels that fanned out from a dam located at the terminus of the Bahr Yusuf canal from Upper Egypt (cf. Chapter 5) (**Fig. 7.1**).

Al-Nabulusi did not mention roving nomads within these two groups. But he did discuss who controlled the land. Following the Ayyubid takeover after the Fatimids, productive land in the Fayyum had been allotted as iqtaᶜs to support the military establishment. According to al-Nabulusi, by regime policy tax revenues went directly to allotment holders. The central government in Cairo did not receive them. And, during Sultan al-Salih's reign, one officer held the entire district as an iqtaᶜ: Fakhr al-Din ᶜUthman, who served his sovereign as majordomo (*ustādār*). Fakhr al-Din initiated a program of dyke construction, dam repair, and canal dredging, the cost of which he paid from his own resources. That is, the central administration neither collected revenues nor supervised irrigation maintenance. Labor was conscripted from the local population. Since al-Nabulusi mentioned no state-imposed corvée, these laborers were presumably compensated by Fakhr al-Din or owed their work as part of their tax obligation to him, not the regime. Rapoport stressed the local initiative behind this procedure. He also held it up to qualify assessments of agrarian decline made by chroniclers and topographers in the later Mamluk period that Garcin and Borsch broadly accepted.[10] Rapoport hypothesized that the local reclamation for the Fayyum depicted by al-Nabulusi under the ustadar Fakhr al-Din could be applied in principle to similar projects in other districts throughout the Nile Valley. Since al-Nabulusi's *Taʾrīkh* is unique, Rapoport's claim remains speculative. His study nonetheless stands as the most incisive to date for any rural district of Ayyubid or Mamluk Egypt. But it depended on a single source.

What about conditions in Syria? As noted in Chapter 5, the rural scene was more diverse than in Egypt due to variations in local topography ranging from coastal plains to riverine systems, mountainous highlands, and the interior Sahel that melded into the Arabian Desert. The region's cities gave rise to numerous authors who did intermittently refer to contacts with families in the countryside or encroachments by Arab tribes. The latter appear to have acted more autonomously than their counterparts in Egypt. Yet, no bureaucrat or chronicler produced a survey similar to al-Nabulusi's *Taʾrīkh al-Fayyūm*. This dearth of topographical material comparable to sources available for Egypt has obliged analysts of the rural setting in Syria to seek evidence elsewhere. The most significant research in this vein has been conducted by Bethany Walker. In 2011, she published *Jordan in the Late Middle Ages: Transformations of the Mamluk Frontier.*[11] This study provides a comprehensive analysis that integrates regional commerce, rural settlement, agriculture and pastoralism, and policies of the Sultanic regime with regard to land tenure over vast terrains. These policies differed significantly from rural administration in Egypt since they often assigned mamluk officers usufruct – subsequently ownership – over territories unsuited to agriculture that were inhabited largely by sheep and goat herding nomads. Dues paid in wool were negotiated according to mutual interests of muqtaʿs and pastoralists. Similar to Egypt, they appeared in sources as *ʿurbān* rather than as Bedouin. They served prominently in provincial cadres of the mamluk military establishment as auxiliaries and frequently shared strategic leadership during campaigns.

Walker's findings draw on archaeological surveys she directed at several sites in modern Jordan. The results indicate broad changes in settlement patterns, land use, and concomitant systems of control by the regime. From the mid-eighth/fourteenth to the early tenth/sixteenth centuries (again, the "long" ninth/fifteenth century), permanent habitation of villages in many districts appears to have been replaced by their seasonal occupation or even abandonment. Few catastrophic events, such as destructive foreign invasions, devastating floods, or violent earthquakes, prompted this shift. The Timurid incursion was brief and inflicted little damage. Gradual desiccation due to periodic droughts may have played a role. State-sponsored control over the most important agrarian industry, sugar distilling, lapsed by the end of the ninth/fifteenth century. Usufruct tenure over land by iqta$^c$ allotments to regional officers was largely supplanted by privatized estates sheltered in trusts (*awqāf*). These enabled the ruler and his most powerful adjutants to assume possession over large swaths of territory. This policy, initiation of which is traced to the accession of Sultan Barquq (784/1382), aimed at heightening the regime's extractive capacity. Whether this goal was actually achieved is open to question since the internal migration resulting from seasonal occupation that occurred simultaneously led to more transitory use of land and small-scale agrarian practices at the local level. On the other hand, the significance of nomadic pastoralism by *ʿurbān* to the regional economy was on the rise, especially in the Sahel. Tribal leaders were positioned to set terms of their grazing rights and wool sales. They also became more aggressive – and destructive – as regime authority became more distant.[12] After 923/1517, the Ottomans would inherit these broad shifts in demography and land tenure. Walker's study is unique for the originality of its findings, based on archaeological evidence and revisionist interpretation of textual sources. The transition from Mamluk to Ottoman control is presented in a new context that ties into global changes that were altering the entire MENA region and territories further afield.

## Gendered Issues

Until recent decades, the field of gender studies in the premodern Muslim world was sparse. Eroticism among elites has attracted attention – and fantasy – since the popularization of the *Alf layla wa-layla.* Depicting life in royal harems, in particular the Ottoman, became a fashionable tradition that often drew upon impressions by European observers who indulged their salacious imaginations. More objective inquiry was largely confined to perusal of injunctions in the Qurʾan or Hadith that were relevant to relations between men and women. The extent to which these pronouncements addressed local practices in diverse social settings was considered beyond recovery. The cause was attributed to an alleged patriarchal bias of source materials. Works written by men for men would refer to women in contexts of their subordination to male interests – and then obliquely. This assumption has changed substantively. Scholars concerned about relations between men and women, and activities of women as autonomous persons, have discovered that sources generated during the Mamluk period offer pertinent data at many social levels. Their findings include the prominence of elite women who served as estate managers and fiscal advisors to their husbands, fathers, and brothers. Due to the high mortality rates men in military service faced because of casualties from battle or insurrections, they frequently charged these women with preserving their assets – on occasion, in preference over other men. Wives, daughters, and sisters often offered stability for the long term that their male relatives were less positioned to provide.[13]

Analysis of commodity production has shown that urban women predominated in textile spinning to produce thread or yarn ready for weaving as part of a putting-out system. Male factors supplied raw yarn, but women negotiated terms and wages. Women also embroidered finished cloth and sewed garments, which they could do in the privacy of their homes. They were compensated at levels at least comparable to what many men received for skilled craft work. When debasement began to replace silver coinage with copper during the late Mamluk period (cf. Chapter 5), the value placed on fine embroidery for high-priced garments was indicated by stipulations requiring payment in silver dirhams.[14] The income women earned as independent workers has been tied to rates of divorce effectively instigated by women, despite the male gain of repudiation sanctioned in the Qur'an. Instances of childrearing apart from the father's authority by divorcees has been discerned.[15] Examination of charitable institutions sponsored by female donors has disclosed hospices reserved for women coping with spousal abandonment, abuse, or post-divorce isolation.[16] Women active in criminal circles have been connected to ventures more nefarious – and "entrepreneurial" – than prostitution or harem intrigues.[17] Women seeking autonomous spiritual fulfillment in religious observance have shown up in Sufi mystic communities, some of their own founding.

A caveat is warranted before considering genres of sources pertinent to issues of gender. Men wrote the overwhelming majority of them. Despite the frequency of references and diversity of circumstances they yield, authenticable statements by women themselves are exceedingly rare. One of the few prominent examples appears below. The milieus in which women lived and interacted with male siblings, spouses, or children are transmitted through male lenses for the most part. This qualifier is significant and conditions the impressions left in literature contemporary to the Mamluk period. The woman's own voice or written word remains elusive.

The genre in which women might have been assumed to occupy a prominent place is in fact minimal. Biographical literature of the Mamluk period contributes little to the store of information about gender, with one exception. The final volume of al-Sakhawi's *Ḍawʾ al-lāmiʿ* contains a thousand-plus entries about women, predictably of high status, who resided in Cairo during the ninth/fifteenth century.[18] No other compiler provided an equivalent fount of gendered data. Al-Sakhawi did not elucidate his motives for doing so. But his commitment to a comprehensive portrayal of erudite or politically influential figures in Cairene society warranted the inclusion of high-status women. Although al-Sakhawi discussed most of them according to their ties to men, he emphasized the autonomous accomplishments of women in learned disciplines. Eminent Hadith transmitters featured notably, as did women adept at managing assets and accruing reputations for piety. Among the first scholars to comment on al-Sakhawi's roster of women's biographies was Huda Lutfi, who in 1981 published "al-Sakhawi's Kitāb al-Nisā' as a Source for the Social and Economic History of Muslim Women during the Fifteenth Century A.D."[19] While Lutfi acknowledged the limitations of al-Sakhawi's focus on elite women, her choice of individuals for discussion highlighted the capacity of several to overcome adversity resulting from divorce or fiscal mismanagement of property by their husbands. Individual initiative impressed al-Sakhawi, and he credited women for acting positively to salvage their status from a bad marriage. Initiative bolstered by piety merited praise, which al-Sakhawi cited consistently.[20] Al-Sakhawi acknowledged women who attained renown as Hadith transmitters and listed male scholars who attended their recitations to request ijazas. Individuals who wrote elegant script were commended, although whether they authored treatises of their own remains indeterminate since al-Sakhawi provided few titles.

The massive body of chronicle literature copiously references women in the predictable contexts of parentage, marriage, divorce, and inheritance. Obituaries of women listed in necrologies at the conclusion of yearly inventories of events routinely list familial details. Elaboration on activities that called attention to individual women often connotes behavior men regarded as aberrant or transgressive. With the exception of Shajar al-Durr at the Sultanate's beginning, the chronicles provide few examples of women openly influencing policy decisions by the ruling elite. Influence of women as asset managers or sustainers of lineages can be found in documentary waqf literature. But in chronicles, they are minimally involved in decision making. The chronicles did mention women alleged to have crossed normative boundaries or engaged in crime. This aspect of gendered behavior is noted subsequently.

Contrasted with the lack of commentary on personal interactions between men and women in historical texts are narratives left by male authors who wrote memoirs. Although these occurred less frequently than chronicles, they reveal insights ranging from the mundane to intimacy in daily life that that rarely appear elsewhere. Three cases are exemplary. Al-Sakhawi recounted the career and personal life of his esteemed teacher Ibn Hajar al-ᶜAsqalani (d. 852/1449) in a biography titled *Al-Jawāhir wa'l-durar fī tarjamat Shaykh al-Islam Ibn Ḥajar* (Jems and Pearls in the Profile of Shaykh al-Islam Ibn Hajar). Al-Sakhawi drew extensively on his bond with Ibn Hajar to comment on the savant's complicated relationships to women he cherished.[21] As al-Sakhawi tells it, Ibn Hajar was devoted to his wife, Uns (Joy), who inherited from her mother an estate that included cash assets and a house in which Ibn Hajar chose to live. After years of conjugal monogamy and the birth of several daughters, Ibn Hajar acted on his yearning for a female slave owned by his wife. He arranged for the slave's dismissal and subsequent sale to him in secrecy. After the waiting period, Ibn Hajar conceived a son with her. When Uns discovered her husband's act, she considered it a betrayal, confronted him with the concubine's male child, and prayed that the infant would not duplicate his father's status as a scholar. Ibn Hajar, who defended his behavior as a desire for sons, was "heart broken," but did not divorce his wife. He later wrote her a passionate love poem (*ghazal*) in which he extolled his unswerving devotion.[22] The details of this episode reveal how the intensity of sustained love could surmount a wife's grievance over violated monogamy. Yet, al-Sakhawi had nothing to say about the effect of all this on the concubine.

A second example may be discerned in the autobiographical writings of Burhan al-Din Ibrahim ibn ʿUmar al-Biqaʿi (d. 885/1480). Al-Biqaʿi is known primarily as a theologian and jurist who was on the losing side in controversies over lawfulness of the Bible for interpreting pre-Islamic figures in the Qurʾan. He also was embroiled over implications of incarnation and monism in the Sufi treatises of Ibn ʿArabi or poems of Ibn al-Farid.[23] Amid these disputes, al-Biqaʿi wrote a chronicle where he disclosed details of his personal life: *Iẓhār al-ʿaṣr li-asrār ahl al-ʿasr* (Lightening the Dusk Shrouding Secrets of People of the Age). Al-Biqaʿi's narrative revealed a web of nuptial relationships with the women whom he married, divorced, or liaised. The most fraught of these was his failed second marriage to one Suʿadat, daughter of Nur al-Din ʿAli al-Bushi, shaykh of the wealthy Sufi hospice (*khānqāh*) founded by Sultan al-Nasir Muhammad ibn Qalawun. It was located in the suburb of Siryaqus north of Cairo.[24] Two versions of this union offer contradictory reasons as to why it soured. Al-Biqaʿi's rendition depicted the ceremony and the couple's early months together as idyllic bliss shared by both sides. Suʿadat is alleged to have dreamed about a figure who appeared to her while she was intimate with her husband (who narrated the experience). Although not named, the figure's white robe and veil denoted the Prophet Muhammad, who beckoned the couple to enter a garden laden with fruits. After they ate, Suʿadat urged her husband to take more fruits as they departed. The figure then enjoined the two to remain, whereupon Suʿadat woke up.[25] Allusions to the Biblical garden and its fruits, plucking and absconding of which al-Biqaʿi imputed to his wife's instigation, cast their relationship as sanctioned by the Prophet and thus indirectly by God. When it waned after their son's birth, the wife was goaded into a nasty custody battle by her mother, whom Biqaʿi blamed for their eventual divorce.

Al-Sakhawi, already hostile over al-Biqaʿi's views about Sufism, told a different story.[26] He depicted Suʿadat as a naive ingénue linked to a greedy reprobate who had previously divorced a wife to improve his fiduciary lot. While al-Biqaʿi claimed custody of his son for a father's pure love, al-Sakhawi regarded his aim as solely financial, attested to by his demand against Suʿadat for 500 dinars in return for her visitation rights. Al-Sakhawi regarded Suʿadat as excessively smitten with her son, a bond that by implication was unhealthy and not shared by her ex-husband. For his part, al-Biqaʿi embellished his later amorous journey in the *Iẓhār* with a litany of ties to concubines. His narrative provides a rich store of impressions about how a contentious ʿalim closely linked to the ruling elite engaged with a diverse group of women. Biqaʿi often offered their views as verbatim quotes. To what extent these were genuine remains indeterminate since no versions independently attributable to these women are available to validate them. To quote Li Guo, who vividly recounted al-Biqaʿi's journey, "Al-Biqaʿi's women, in the final analysis, are like those in Dostoevsky's novel: they do not have their own personal history and voice – they enter the male heroes' lives, constitute part of their fate, and disappear."[27]

A third example is contained in the garrulous diary of a Damascene clerk, Ibn Tawq (d. 915/1509): *Al-Taʿlīq: Yawmīyāt Shihāb al-Dīn Ahmad ibn Ṭawq* (Commentary: The Diary of Shihab al-Din Ibn Tawq).[28] Ibn Tawq was a notary (*shāhid*) in the Shafiʿi courts of Damascus. His employer was the madhhab's chief judge, the Shaykh al-Islam Taqi al-Din Abu Bakr ibn ʿAbd Allah, known as Qadi ʿAjlun, about whose family's daily experiences Ibn Tawq had much to say. Ibn Tawq's diary proceeds according to daily events of the most mundane sort, described in minute detail. The work is extensive; it spans the years 885/1480–908/1502 and fills four printed volumes. Topics run the gamut from political activities of the Mamluk viceroys who ruled the city to the author's personal doings, such as changes of outfit, minor ailments, or decisions as to meals. Ibn Tawq's references to women focused primarily on his patron's family. Ibn Tawq mentioned disputes between the Shaykh's two wives and dwelled at length on the one he found belligerent, whom he called "that Egyptian woman."[29]

> We are told . . . that at the wedding of . . . Muhammad (the Shaykh's son), the mother-in-law, in her double capacity as the groom's step-mother and the bride's birth mother (she had been married to the Shaykh al-Islam's brother, whose daughter was to marry Muhammad), failed to show up. The woman, as Ibn Tawq tells it, was "possessed by Satan" and mentally unstable. Ibn Tawq then goes on to report that the party went on without a hitch: "the female guests" were fed with a feast of "eight grilled sheep," various kinds of rice dishes, bread, dairy products, and dessert, to be washed down with refreshments; that he (Ibn Tawq) personally accompanied the groom to the pre-nuptial bath; that the newlyweds consummated their union at "the early minutes of two o'clock." At the end of the day, the "Egyptian woman's wicked tricks" were defeated by divine intervention (p. 581). Inquiring minds, however, may still want to know: why an account of the food for "female attendees" only? Why such bitter animosity against this particular woman?"

One wonders indeed. For all his bavardage, Ibn Tawq offers no context as to why the Egyptian wife behaved as she did. His omission is typical of how women's deportment was depicted even in sources where they were featured. The woman's own voice remained unheard.

So, where *can* this voice be heard? Very few instances of writing by women appear in textual material from the Mamluk period. But one outstanding example was the poetry composed by a devout Sufi mystic active in Damascus and Cairo, again during the "long" ninth/fifteenth century. ʿA'isha ibnat Yusuf ibn Nasr al-Baʿuniyya was born midway through it to an eminent family of scholars from the village of Baʿun near the Syrian capital (she died in 923/1517). ʿA'isha studied the traditional curriculum of Qur'an and Hadith in Damascus with her father and other teachers.[30] But she was engrossed with the Sufi masters who had inducted her into the mystic universe she would embrace for the rest of her life:

> My education and development, my spiritual effacement and purification, occurred by the helping hand of the sultan of the saints of his time, the crown of the pure friends of his age, the beauty of truth and religion, the venerable master, father of the spiritual axes, the axis of existence, Ismaʿil al-Hawwari – may God sanctify his heart and be satisfied with him – and, then, by the helping hand of his successor in spiritual states and stations, and in spiritual proximity and union, Muhyi al-Din Yahya al-ʿUrmawi – may God continue to spread his ever-growing spiritual blessings throughout his life-time, and join us every moment to his blessings and succor.[31]

Although ʿA'isha married the Syndic of the Prophet's Descendants (*Naqīb al-Ashrāf*) in Damascus, she identified al-Hawwari as her guide to awareness of God. Following al-Hawwari's death in 900/1495, she built a tomb for him along with a house nearby where she lived. Every Friday, she placed a lamp on her mentor's grave.

ʿA'isha's devotion to al-Hawwari did not inhibit her relationship with her husband. Their marriage lasted until his death in 909/1503 and produced a daughter and son, whose career ʿA'isha advanced. ʿA'isha cherished her husband's lineage from the Prophet and praised it in her many writings.[32] Yet, ʿA'isha's poetry centers on her sense of nearness to, even union with, the Divine. If other individuals are cited, they are her spiritual guides or the Prophet, not her husband. But God is always her prime focus. To quote verses from ʿA'isha's collection, *Emanations of Grace*:[33]

From His inspiration upon her in a sudden intimation (*fī wārid*) (105/199)

1. When I sought union with the one I love,
   His majesty replied that there was no path to Him.
2. So, I closed my eyes that had tried so hard to see Him,
   while in my heart, desire burned with separation's fire.
3. I was about to meet my death, when He was kind,
   And sweetly spoke to my heart, saying:
4. If you want union from Us, be true to Us,
   Set aside all else, strive for Us, and be humble.
5. Leave yourself and come to Us with Our true love and grace.
   Make that your means to Me.

6. Draw near Us, be devoted to Us; don't fear rejection.
   Turn toward a sacred precinct filled with acceptance.
7. There, you will find providence draws you to Us,
   bringing sweet union,
8. And you will leave there all but Us
   and appear in a station where true men alight.
9. You will behold lights of power, and in their intensity,
   the shadow of difference will go and disappear.
10. You will pass away, nothing to preserve you save Our splendor,
    As you behold, truly, the climax of desire.
11. Then you will abide with Us, Our servant,
    pure, chosen by Us for Our secrets forever!

The passion of ʿA'isha's desire for immersion in God's emanation can be seen in one of her most famous poems, its verses followed by the strophic refrain: Oh He, Oh He, Oh God! (*Yā Hū, yā Hū, yā Allāh!*), repeated four times.[34] Its powerful message of union is hypnotic:

From His inspiration upon her (294–96/411–14):

You who annihilates mystically
Those absorbed in love of You,
Give to me! Give to me!
Grant me a good life and immortality
With clear vision in union.

*Yā Hū, yā Hū, yā Allāh; yā Hū, yā Hū, yā Allāh; yā Hū, yā Hū, yā Allāh; yā Hū, yā Hū, yā Allāh; yā Hū, yā Hū, yā Allāh!*

My love, my desire,
My goal, my being
Be mine! Be mine!
And mend my break and free me from poverty
with nearness and union.

(refrain)

Love of You bereaved one who loves You:
I was dazed when I lost my reason,
And love bewildered me and kept me up all night
as it led me on and wore me out.

(refrain)

Your beauty bound me tight,
and when the light appeared, gone was
My shadow, my shadow,
and it stripped me, and nothing remained with me,
as it annihilated me as was right.

(refrain)

I left myself and went away.
My veil was gone, and my nearness appeared
With my union, with my union!
For, He had astonished me, then revived me,
and He gave me new life in beauty.

(refrain)

In His epiphany, when He called out
from His brilliant fire,
He said to me, He said to me:
"Arise, drink, and enjoy
the goodness of grace!"

(refrain)

For He had set out for me a radiant cup
filled for me with the pure wine of truth.
He gave to me, He gave to me
This pure drink with relief,
And hope and peace.

(refrain)

These jars of wine are unveiled gifts
of gnosis to their tavern-mates,
My folk, my folk,
My masters, my loves,
My brothers in my mystical states.

(refrain)

I have an exalted axis among them
who appeared with his fidelity
To me, to me,
And he drew me and brought me near
and raised me up in nobility

(refrain)

My Master, the greatest to come among us
is the most exalted Prophet.
Bless him, bless him!
And all the apostles, his family
and closest friends, You Most High!

(refrain)

As long as Your cup comes to my heart
with Your wine in the tavern of nearness
As my drink, as my drink,
Given to me to drink, quenching me,
And reviving me in union!

(refrain)

ʿA'isha's poetry reaches across the span of centuries to evoke the rapturous longing for Divine emanation that she sought – emanation that some factions of modern Islamic belief might find uncomfortably close to intimacy. How ʿA'isha herself envisaged this sentiment remains elusive since mystic verse intentionally insinuates more than it spells out. Suffice to note here that ʿA'isha al-Baʿuniyya's poetry did not induce the controversy, or condemnation, that the verses of such a figure as ʿUmar ibn Farid (whom she admired) provoked. References in contemporary narrative sources do not dwell on prohibition of ʿA'isha's poems from public recitation or their interrogation in learned circles for implicit heresy. Nor did she spend time defending her poems in her treatises on Sufism. Terms for union (*waṣl, wiṣāl, jamʿ*) appear ubiquitously, but in the sense of "annihilation (*fanā'*) of the selfish soul in love of God, the One, the Real, Who, by an act of Grace, draws His worshipper near to abide in His loving presence."[35] On this potentially contentious issue, ʿA'isha's rapturous verse seems not to have crossed the line between enticement and provocation. Did ʿA'isha's gender grant her immunity denied to her male counterparts? Was she freer than they to expound her sentiments in rapturous verse? As so often in matters surrounding mystic belief, this question is veiled in mystery.

## Infractions Linked to Gender

Chroniclers of social behavior attributed enhanced impropriety to transgressions committed by women, in addition to the generalized concept of "social harm" applicable to acts by either gender. They focused on incidents that disclosed women crossing normative boundaries of "proper" decorum (such as adoption of immodest dress, overt self-assertion in the public sphere, or undisguised contradiction of decisions by males). Chroniclers signaled their sense of violated gendered space through word choices, selection of descriptive detail, or adoption of stylistic devices peculiar to these incidents. They resorted to these indirect, covert devices to signal aberrant behavior more often than explicitly denouncing it. Implication rather than condemnation appeared as a more subtle, and effective, means of highlighting departure from behavioral norms. The following two cases suggest the descriptive vocabulary chroniclers employed when they described actions that set women they regarded as transgressors apart from their law-abiding contemporaries.

An act of homicide against an officer by his slaves occurred in the tenth/sixteenth century and involved slave women and their free lovers. The historian Ibn Iyas tied their ethnicity and status to their actions.

On Saturday the ninth (of Jumādá II 921/21 July 1515), the sultan (Qānṣawh al-Ghawrī) ordered hanged four persons, a white female slave of Anatolian extraction, an Ethiopian female slave, a youthful son of a mamluk who was turbaned (indicating notable status), and a bowmaker. The reason: this mamluk's son and the bowmaker fornicated with the two slaves and urged them to assassinate their owner, who himself descended from a mamluk and held a military fief. They (presumably the slaves only) killed him, and thrust his corpse into the latrine (possibly midden). They stole everything in his house and then traveled toward Aṭfih (in Upper Egypt). Five months elapsed before their crime was discovered. They were denounced by a small slave girl. A (presumably Bedouin) shaykh in Atfih apprehended them and returned them to the sultan. Upon interrogation, they confessed to the murder and disposal of the body. The sultan ordered the wali police chief to investigate the case. He searched the latrine and found the cadaver there in a putrid state. It was removed and shown to the sultan, who ordered its burial. The victim's fief was reassigned to another mamluk. He (the sultan) ordered hanged those who were responsible. On their execution day, Cairo turned out to witness it. They were conducted to the murder scene and terminated.[36]

The notoriety and implicit threat behind this case influenced Ibn Iyas's choice for its inclusion. His emphasis on the perpetrators' lust, greed, and deception conveyed a more ominous message of latent menace beneath the facade of smoldering resentment over an owner's control and exploitation. That free members of society were ready to abet these sentiments – and share in the risk of execution if captured – heightened this threat to public order and the hierarchies of class and property that buttressed it. Ibn Iyas's depiction of the free men who incited the slave women to murder their owner hinted at their primary responsibility as instigators of homicide that violated status boundaries and compromised the hegemony of the military elite.

The Damascene historian al-Jazari commented on a case of seduction where the guilty party met execution by strangulation for her duplicity. The incident's notoriety was sufficient to sustain its detailed depiction in a chronicle compiled decades after the fact.

On Tuesday the third of Dhu'l-Qaʿda (737/3 June 1337), they (presumably police authorities) strangled, on the outskirts of Damascus, a procuress. She habitually frequented wedding festivals, to take note of the attending women. In this instance one was wearing gold and silver jewelry, trinkets, and attractive apparel. She (the procuress) spoke to the woman, awakening her desire. She (the procuress) said to her that she had with her a handsome young man (her husband) who, if he customarily offered a comely woman fifty dirhams (silver coins), he might raise the amount to one hundred (upon meeting this one). If she (the woman) responded to him (in the affirmative), she (the woman) would retain (the additional sum). She (the procuress) (then) walked with the woman to the outskirts of town, and induced her to stay at a certain place. She said to her, "You cannot meet up with someone in town because of neighbors or officials, but only in the orchard." She (the procuress) then left the woman with her husband. He (the husband) then put off the pledge to her. But she (the procuress) had plotted with a female hairdresser, who absconded with many trinkets as was her custom. Three days later, one of the hairdresser's female slaves went to the police chief (*wālī*), and informed on what her mistress had done (in collusion with the procuress). When they (police) summoned her (the hairdresser), she denied the affair. They tortured her repeatedly, but she refused to confess. The wali then stated that the female slave was lying. (Subsequently) investigators took three coins and sent them with (another) woman whose husband had given them to her to spend. He had enjoined her, "Do not indulge (in the act). I will give (these) so that you will not have need (to do so)." When this other woman met up with her (the procuress), she (the woman) asked, "Is he (the young man [husband]) well-disposed?" She (the procuress) replied, "yes, and his enticement is upon you. Until now, I have acknowledged nothing." They (investigators) informed the wali. He summoned her (the procuress) and bound one hand and foot. They inserted the other hand into poison aloe. She verged on death, and confessed that she had (so) acted with several other women. Her husband fled, and no further news was learned of him. Her (the procuress's) interrogation lasted throughout the month. The Viceroy ordered her strangulation, which was carried out on the aforementioned date. May God show her neither mercy nor favor, nor for her husband. May God curse her and diminish them both.[37]

Since al-Jazari redacted the details of this incident secondhand from earlier sources (the text is filled with lacunae), we cannot know whether he abridged or enhanced them. Yet, the specific date and vividness of his version attest to the abiding memory of a transgression regarded as sordid due to the perpetrator's duplicity. No mention was made of any crime worse than theft and fornication (the participants were lured from post-marital festivities). No victims were reported murdered to conceal the offenders' identities. It would seem that the duplicity of the procuress, who infringed upon the sanctity of marital rites to carry out her seductions for profit, endured to taint her memory as a woman damned by God and society. Note also that al-Jazari focused his most vehement condemnation on the procuress, not on her husband. Nor did he report any effort on the authorities' part to pursue him, despite his complicity in the crime.

He was to be diminished, but God's curse fell on her. Despite shared culpability, the procuress merited the ultimate penalty. The gendered distinction is significant.

## Communal Status of Minorities: Christians and Jews

Assessment of the status of Christian and Jewish communities during the Mamluk period is complicated by an impression of subjugation applicable to both groups. This impression has evolved from a sense of communal decline after an allegedly halcyon era of prosperity and tolerance that issued from policies of preceding regimes, in particular the Fatimid Caliphate (297/909–567/1171). The definitive shift from majority to minority status on the part of Christians in Egypt is widely assumed to have occurred during the two and a half centuries of Mamluk rule. While Jews were always a demographic minority, they too appear to have endured a qualitative deterioration in status under the Mamluks. Since the plausibility of impressions rests on surviving sources, the available evidence must be weighed in terms of context and genre. What types of sources address the two communities, and under what circumstances? This question should be considered within the larger issue of contrasts between the two communities. Christians and Jews have lived in Egypt and Syria under differing conditions since the Arab conquest and onset of Islam during the first/seventh century.

With regard to the Christian population, the majority in the Nile Valley identified with the Egyptian Orthodox Church, commonly referred to as "Copt/Coptic" (*Qibṭ/Qibṭī*). The term derives from ancient usage and connotes "Egypt/Egyptian."[38] The Coptic Church followed the Monophysite rite which laid stress on the single Divine nature of Christ, as opposed to the Orthodox Church of the Byzantine Empire, which emphasized the distinction between God the Father and Jesus the Son, divine and human.[39] This division stemmed from the Council of Chalcedon, convened in 451 CE, where the single nature doctrine was declared heretical. The ensuing schism ultimately split Orthodoxy into two branches. The Coptic Church was administered by a separate patriarchate in Alexandria with jurisdiction over liturgical procedures throughout the Nile Valley and Abyssinia. It was this institution that the invading Arabs encountered during the first/seventh-century Conquest. Other Christian communities existed in Egypt, notably the Melkite rite of the Greek Catholic Church and the Jacobite or Syriac Orthodox Church, which shared Monophysitism with the Copts. Although the Melkites and Jacobites maintained clerical hierarchies distinct from the Copts, they remained a small minority in Egypt. Christian practice in Syria did not follow the Coptic rite but was divided between the Syriac Church, the Orthodoxy of Constantinople, or the Maronite Catholic Church centered in the Lebanon.

For several centuries after the Arab Conquest, the majority of Egypt's population retained its Christian religion. The new regime did not promote mass conversion, since the resultant shift in demography would drastically reduce the poll tax (*jizya*) paid by non-Muslims. During the early years of Muslim rule, the minority ruling class lived off proceeds from the jizya collected from the majority. Under the Umayyads and ʿAbbasids, Coptic officials staffed the bureaucracy that administered Egypt. When in 87/706 the Umayyad governor ʿAbd Allah ibn ʿAbd al-Malik decreed that records be kept in Arabic rather than Greek or Coptic, accountants and clerks adopted the rulers' language and initiated the process of literary Arabization more broadly.[40] To what extent conversion paralleled the change of language is indeterminate, but the process gradually unfolded since individuals identifying as native-born Muslims or converts began to appear in the state diwans. Still, the Coptic Christian presence in administration was pronounced. Under the Tulunid, Ikhshidid, and Fatimid regimes, Copts were a prominent presence in the bureaucracy. Although census data applicable to the entire country are not available, most of the population overall is presumed to have remained Coptic Christian. As noted above, the Fatimid Caliphate is regarded as the era of maximal prosperity for the Copts of Egypt. Their positive status is considered to have continued under the subsequent Ayyubid sultans, although signs of discontent by the ʿulamaʾ are discernible.

Muslim chroniclers, functionaries, jurists, and clergy reacted to the presence of Coptic Christians and converts in several contexts throughout the Mamluk period. Their comments were focused on Copts in the diwan bureaus of Cairo and provincial centers where churches and mosques coexisted in close proximity, an environment conducive to intercommunal tensions. These tensions were pronounced in several towns of Upper Egypt.[41] Entries in chronicles tended to address actions by Copts that were depicted as corrupt with regard to fiscal administration or threatening to the Muslim community. They were frequently phrased to implicate members of the ruling elite as complicit in fiscal malfeasance that mutually profited Coptic officials and their employers in the regime.[42] Jurists and clergy aimed their tracts at alleged violations by Copts of strictures against church building or renovation, conduct of Christian rituals that affronted Muslim services, or preference in social status. Muslim diwan officials vehemently denounced their Coptic peers for covert embezzlement or open extortion. A sense of intolerable insult to Muslims, especially of the common people and rural peasantry who were humiliated by Coptic officials flaunting their illicit status, pervades many of their tracts. A more latent but ominous threat implied a desire for revenge among Copts for the occupation of their country by Muslim conquerors centuries earlier. A theme of perduring conspiracy is noticeable, although rarely expressed in a call for open revolution. Neither side regarded insurrection as feasible. Yet, statements describing measures taken by rulers to remedy alleged excesses by Copts were often couched in phrases such as “a second Muslim conquest of Egypt” or “the restoration of true Islam” to the realm.

Despite their periodic proliferation, these sources were sporadic and unevenly distributed. They often followed edicts issued by sultans condemning alleged Christian transgressions against Muslims or were responses to acts by foreign powers that challenged Muslim hegemony in the region. The Crusades from Europe and the Mongol invasions from Central Asia are prime examples, but subsequent aggression by Mediterranean states such as Aragon and Cyprus or Abyssinia south of the Sudan figured prominently during the Sultanate’s latter decades. Piracy and raiding of ports in the Levant and North Africa by ships in service to the European maritime states grew from a nuisance in the eighth/fourteenth century to a threat in the ninth/fifteenth (cf. Chapter 3).[43] Yet, foreign threats rarely seem to have motivated authors of tracts hostile to Coptic Christians or converts to Islam. Because of its uneven coverage, the largely ambivalent literature on Coptic–Muslim relations does not leave an impression that applies to the population of Egypt as a whole over time. Most of the commentaries address urban settings, in either the capital Cairo or regional centers. The state of relations between Christians and Muslims in rural areas outside these centers – where most people lived – remains largely uncharted. Second, despite the intensity of denunciations and calls for oppression or even persecution, these do not appear to have resulted in significant reductions of the Coptic presence in the bureaucracy or elimination of Christian practice throughout the Nile Valley. The generalized view that Egypt shifted definitively from a Christian to a Muslim majority during the Mamluk period cannot be documented by cadasters or censuses. Nor can it be linked to countrywide pogroms or deportations. Widespread conversion by Christians is assumed as a response to deteriorating status but is unconfirmed by statistical evidence. Nonetheless, a climate of rising animus between the two communities is palpable. This animus is vividly displayed in chronicles and tracts.

Among the most representative of these is a treatise by the same Nabulusi who produced the aforementioned survey of the Fayyum. Several years earlier, al-Nabulusi lost real estate and his position as a senior supervisor of provincial taxation, allegedly because of a conspiracy hatched by an amir who coveted the property. This amir, Nur al-Din, was the son of the previously mentioned Fakhr al-Din ʿUthman, who held the Fayyum as an iqtaʿ fief. In 634/1236–37, Nur al-Din accused al-Nabulusi of laxity at his post to the Ayyubid Sultan al-Kamil. As al-Nabulusi tells it, al-Kamil bought into Nur al-Din's claim, fired his trusted supervisor, appropriated his assets, and jailed him for more than a month. Nur al-Din and his accomplice, the Coptic convert al-Asʿad al-Faʾizi, arranged for the sale of al-Nabulusi's house on the Nile shore at a price below market value.[44] The proceeds were transferred to Sultan al-Kamil's charitable trust. After his release, al-Nabulusi remained unemployed and, from his perspective, impoverished until he recovered his status with the Fayyum survey under Sultan al-Salih. It was during these years that al-Nabulusi wrote his tract: *Tajrīd sayf al-himmah li-istikhrāj mā fī dhimmat al-dhimma* (The Sword of Ambition to Extract What the Dhimmis Hoard). Al-Nabulusi grounded his denunciation of Christians in government service by quoting Qur'anic verses and expounding on hostility toward them by early Caliphs. Al-Nabulusi attributed the menace posed by Copts in Egypt to a sinister plot they concocted soon after the Arab conquest. As he wrote in his treatise:[45]

The Second Section: Why the Copts Specialize as Secretaries and Neglect Other Professions.

It is important that I note here how it is passed down in the annals of history that when the rule of Egypt was wrested from the Copts and they entered into the pact with Islam, they devised a strategy to ensure that their voices would be heard by the Muslims and that their new overlords would be compelled to look after their interests. The wisest and greatest Copts said to their people, "You were once masters of this land. But the glory of the sword has been wrested from you. Strive, therefore, to attain the glory of the pen." "How shall we do this?" they asked. Their wise men said to them, "By teaching your children the secretarial art, that they may share with the Muslims in their property, their interests, and their decisions." They all agreed upon this plan, and the result is plain to see. They gained power in the Muslims' administration and did as they pleased in the government. How apposite are the lines a poet composed to describe the Jews and Christians, observing that the former train their children in medicine, the latter theirs in the secretarial art, as follows:

> God curse the Christians and Jews!
> They have attained what they wanted to gain from us;
> They have emerged as doctors and secretaries
> That they might seize both souls and property.
>
> (note 82)

Al-Nabulusi did not name Amir Nur al-Din's Coptic accomplice in his treatise, but his animus was aimed at individuals in the diwans like him. He could not risk mentioning Nur al-Din, the plot's instigator. As a member of the ruling elite, the amir stood above him in rank. The gist of the preceding passage provides a context to al-Nabulusi's antipathy that is tied to the alleged thirst for revenge by Copts for the loss of their country noted above. The final line of the verse is telling: seizure of both souls and property, religion and assets – twin props of identity. The sincere embrace of Islam by such appropriators could not be trusted.

Several other authors expressed this antipathy.[46] The aspersions they leveled against Copts implicated their employers among the military class as colluders in corruption and betrayal of the ʿulamaʾ as custodians of belief. The Mamluk officers who held the bulk of agrarian land as iqtaʿs and presided over its fiscal administration did rely on gains that were illicitly siphoned from yields and taxes, especially during the ninth/fifteenth century. The Coptic clerks they arrested were often suspected of concealing their extractions or minimalizing their patrons' share. Copts whose methods of extortion aroused public animus were also convenient scapegoats to deflect popular rancor over corruption from the Mamluk elite. The case of Sultan al-Nasir Muhammad's condemnation and execution of al-Nashw is a case in point (cf. Chapter 5).

The historian Ibn Taghri Birdi complained at length about humiliations allegedly inflicted by Christians on Muslims in the courts and countryside. And he did link resentment to foreign threats. Ibn Taghri Birdi appended his statement to the arrest by Sultan al-Muʾayyad Shaykh (r. 815/1412–824/1421) of the Coptic Patriarch in reprisal for oppression of Muslims by the king of Abyssinia in 822/1419. The sultan exploited widespread anger over this persecution by a Christian ruler to reduce the status of senior Copts on his staff. Ibn Taghri Birdi then condemned conditions at home:[47]

So I have said: Perhaps God forgave al-Mu'ayyad for all his transgressions because of these acts, for they figured large in the cause of Islam. Administration by Christians in the bureaus of Egypt was among the gravest of egregious conditions that promoted aggrandizement of the Christian religion. Because of it, most Muslim people were obliged to frequent the gates of realm officials to conduct their affairs. Most relevantly, their needs were tied to the diwan of that (specific) bureau head, and were thus forced to abase themselves before him who held in his hand control of the aforementioned diwan – were he a Christian, Jew or Samaritan. As the proverb goes, "The blind man in need seeks only a settlement." [The Muslim] who stood waiting on his feet for hours in the presence of that Christian [official] – who sat – in order to resolve his suit, was compelled to show [the Christian] civility that he did not offer learned shaykhs. The same for he who bowed his shoulder and proceeded on his mount to [the Christian's] house to resolve his case.

As for the village peasant, the Christian steward periodically beat him, demeaned him and bound him in chains. He justified his act by the need to redeem revenues owed his patron (*ustādh*). But the actuality differed, for [the steward] intended to impose judgement against the Muslim's [interest], nothing more. It was he who took the Muslim prisoner in European lands for his money, holding him in [debt] bondage and for no other cause. One of the trustworthy [persons] of Upper Egypt stated, "Most of the cultivators in our villages are esteemed Sharifs. Yet the local intendant (*ʿāmil*) is a Christian. When the intendant arrives in the village, the peasants go forth to greet him with the *salām* of reverence, exceeding the accepted bounds [of meeting a non-Muslim]. Those who walk with his riding animal to where he departs the village kiss his hand. He is either the impoverished supplicant or one who fears the village owner [presumably its muqtaᶜ, possibly its head man]. He [the supplicant] begs [the superintendent] to resolve his situation, since the latter was empowered to calculate [his share of] the land tax (*kharāj*), pleading his leniency in this matter."

When al-Malik al-Mu'ayyad forbade the Christians from [such] administration, he nullified all of the preceding. With this edict, al-Malik al-Mu'ayyad granted Egypt a second conquest. He exalted the word of Islam and diminished the word of unbelief. There is no matter more meritorious before God. When the Christians failed to regain their former status in the administration of the Egyptian realm, the sultan's edict weakened them, for he blocked them from their accustomed governance over Muslims. He said, "The custom is to charge [only] a fifth." This alarmed [the Christians], and several proceeded to manifest the religion of Islam. They pronounced the two attestations outwardly, [but] God is master of secrets [*i.e.* of their true inner beliefs].

Ibn Taghri Birdi's rant revealed resentments smoldering among the Muslim elite over their perception of undue Coptic influence within the regime's fiscal diwans. While Sultan al-Mu'ayyad's resentment was genuine, it coincided with a shrewd stratagem. Many of the Coptic officials in his service managed to regain their posts after a cooling-off period when tensions over the Ethiopian persecution died down. The sultan charged the Copts retention fees in return for restoring their posts. The deeper antipathy underlying Ibn Taghri Birdi's decrial was felt among the Muslim elite and commoners alike. His commendation of al-Mu'ayyad's edict as a "second conquest" of Egypt was deliberate. The historian applauded the sultan for enabling the majority religion to take back its hegemonic prerogatives, sullied by Christians and crypto-Christians whose false conversion, driven by avarice, parodied true allegiance to Islam. The incident discloses the latent ambivalence compromising Muslim–Coptic relations.

An act of church razing in Upper Egypt during the first decade of the eighth/fourteenth century disclosed conflicting attitudes by the ruling authorities that pitted rights of dhimmis to preserve places of worship against resentment of their restoration by Muslims. In 707/1307, a riot erupted in the Nile port of Qus in Upper Egypt that resulted in the destruction of thirteen churches in two hours.[48] While Muslim mobs inflicted most of the destruction, they were abetted by Sufi mendicants (*fuqarāʾ*) who militantly expressed their sense of "moral regulation" through violent means. Instigating them were several local jurists, among whom was a shaykh, ʿAbd al-Jaffar ibn Nuḥ al-Qusi. When aggrieved Christian residents informed the local governor, a Mamluk amir, of the church razing, he arrested the Sufis and jurists for vigilantism and flaunting the military authorities. Several of the former were flogged and paraded publicly on mules. For his part, Ibn Nuh al-Qusi was brought to Cairo, tried before Sultan al-Nasir Muhammad, interred in the Citadel, and forbidden to return to Qus over concerns that he might incite further conflict. Although he died the following year, Ibn Nuh found solitude in the Mosque of ʿAmr ibn al-ʿAs to write a treatise on Sufi practice: *al-Waḥīd fī sulūk ahl al-tawḥīd* (The Singular Conduct of the People of Unity). Ibn Nuh devoted a section of this treatise to the razing incident.[49] He vehemently defended the assault as justified by dating the construction of these churches in Qus after the first/seventh-century conquest of the country by Muslims. They therefore were "new" and thus unprotected by Shariʿa statutes. Ibn Nuh asserted that the razing was meritorious according to the principle of "ordering good and forbidding evil" (*al-amr bi'l-maʿrūf wa'l-nahy ʿan al-mankar*) incumbent on all pious believers. The church razing incident of 707/1307 was neither the first nor last act of its kind. Similar events occurred, especially in the Saʿid, until the Ottoman occupation. These progressively favored Muslim claims over Christian rights.[50] Remarks in narratives that relate the incidents suggest a rising tide of conversion to Islam by Copts. Given the lack of statistics, these narratives are among the few tangible indications of the assumed demographic shift from Christian to Muslim identity in Upper Egypt between the seventh/thirteenth and ninth/fifteenth centuries.

In contrast with the majority status of Christians for much of the Islamic period in Egypt, the Jews experienced nothing comparable in terms of demography. For the early centuries of Muslim rule, little is known about their communal governance or identity, although traditions that looked back to a rich pre-Islamic heritage survived.[51] Sources relative to Jewish cultural life or literary production are similarly rare. This paucity ended with transferal of the Fatimid Caliphate to Egypt in 358/969, noted above. Narrative sources from the Fatimid period depict a dramatic resurgence of Jewish cultural activity, particularly in the metropolis extending from the Nile port of Fustat to the new capital of Cairo (*al-Qāhira*). This was the age of Yaᶜqub ibn Killis (d. 380/991), the Jewish convert to Islam who served the first and second Fatimid caliphs in Egypt as their vizier and presided over Egypt's rise to regional hegemony. The Fatimid era witnessed the influence of a Jewish mercantile family, the Tustaris, over caliphal politics several decades later. Under the Fatimids' Ayyubid successors, the most renowned of Jewish thinkers in the medieval Muslim world, Abu ᶜImran Musa ibn ᶜUbayd Allah Maymun al-Qurtubi (the Cordovan), known as Moses Maimonides (d. 601/1204), was physician to Salah al-Din's adjutant al-Qadi al-Fadil and the Damascene prince al-Afdal ᶜAli.

It was during the Fatimid and Ayyubid periods (fourth/tenth–seventh/twelfth centuries) that members of a Jewish congregation in Fustat left behind an exceptional record of their daily activity and commercial enterprise in the form of the Geniza. The Geniza refers to a mass of documents numbering many thousands that touched on the full spectrum of Jewish communal existence. Their preservation stemmed from the practice of saving any paper with the name of God inscribed on it (which included virtually all correspondence, even the most mundane). The documents, ranging from brief notes to lengthy letters, were deposited in a storage room (*geniza*) of the Ben Ezra Synagogue, center of the Jewish community in Fustat.[52]

Brought to modern scholarship when the synagogue was renovated in the nineteenth century, the Geniza documents disclose events and people active before the Mamluk period for the most part. But documents written later have been discovered among contemporary collections in Europe. Of these, one is of particular relevance to conditions affecting the Jewish community of Cairo during the ninth/fifteenth century. The scholar of Jewish culture in the medieval Arabic environment, Mark Cohen, compared its depiction of a singular event with versions by the historians Ibn Hajar al-ᶜAsqalani and al-Sakhawi (cf. Chapter 6).[53] The event involved an inquisition by senior Muslim jurists over a charge of blasphemy brought against the leader of Cairo's Jewish community (*ra'īs al-yahūd*). The charge, as described by the historians, accused members of the congregation in a synagogue (*kanīsa*) located in the Coptic quarter of Fustat (*Qaṣr al-Shamᶜ*) of abducting a former Muslim prayer pulpit (*minbar*) for their services. When the jurists and market inspector, led by Ibn Hajar in his capacity as Shafiᶜi qadi, discovered the names "Muhammad" and "Ahmad" inscribed on the steps, they condemned the offenders of desecrating an Islamic implement of prayer. The Hanafi qadi demanded their immediate mutilation and execution, but Ibn Hajar insisted on investigating the circumstances behind the act. His subsequent inquiry found that the offenders who transferred the minbar had acted on their own initiative. They were executed, but the congregation was spared and the synagogue left standing. Nonetheless, the incident prompted further citations of Jewish and Christian structures for violating the Pact of ʿUmar, the second Caliph, which forbade building new places of worship for dhimmis or renovating extant ones. The inquisition occurred in Dhu'l–Hijja 845/April 1442. The historians claimed that the Karaite Jews and Melkite Christians suffered ongoing humiliation and abuse throughout the remaining year.

The geniza document confirmed the incident and laid blame on the ra'is, one ʿAbd al-Latif ibn Ibrahim ibn Shams.

The document, written in Judeo-Arabic, is a draft of a petition from the Jewish community to the senior Muslim jurists. It accused ʿAbd al-Latif of spending funds endowed for communal welfare on illicit activities. They labeled him an "extortionist" and "robber." They also claimed that the ra'is surrounded himself with a gang of "young Jewish auxiliaries (*i.e.*, ruffians), whose counsel he follows and who give him destructive and improper advice." The petition mentioned the minbar inscription and claimed that ʿAbd al-Latif should have been removed from office for knowingly violating Islamic law. It went on to mention "fiscal penalties of thousands of dinars during his regime through his wrongdoing, lack of knowledge and judgement." The petition listed further calamities inflicted on the Jewish community and concluded by stating that witnesses were prepared to name ʿAbd al-Latif as one among those who had ascended the minbar.

This incident allegedly sparked ongoing persecution of both Christians and Jews throughout 845/1442. It is telling of conditions that burdened their communities during the Sultanate's latter decades. The impression they leave is not positive. Yet, Cohen pointed out that the jurists' investigation of the minbar incident was conducted according to established legal protocol. The petition itself confirmed the congregants' right to file a protest to the Muslim judiciary and documented their power to remove a leader deemed malfeasant. According to the historians, execution was limited to the offenders found guilty of desecrating the minbar. The congregation was reprieved. Cohen contrasted this procedure, conducted under law, with the probable response of mass violence that would have followed alleged desecration by Jews of a Christian icon in a German town of the same period.[54] This is not to deny an atmosphere of oppression and malaise that seems to have characterized much of Jewish life in the Mamluk capital.

Complexities of this condition may be seen in acts depicted as transgressive by other historians. A case of counterfeiting that implicated both minorities occurred early in the Ottoman occupation of Cairo. The chronicler Ibn Iyas signaled the incident's gravity by dwelling on the penalties meted out to those convicted.[55] The viceroy who presided over their hearing, himself despised due to his betrayal of sultan Qansawh al-Ghawri to the Ottomans, sought to demonstrate his loyalty to his new masters by inflicting drastic sanctions. The arraigned were a diverse lot: a Christian and a Jew, each accused of counterfeiting in gold and silver, a local police captain, and the son of an eminent courtesan singer previously executed by drowning for prostitution. The Christian had plea-bargained for clemency by denouncing the Jew, in whose home evidence of counterfeiting was subsequently discovered. The police captain was charged with dereliction of duty when the courtesan's son murdered a Janissary soldier under the captain's jurisdiction. All four were condemned to a lingering death by impalement. Ibn Iyas noted that the viceroy sentenced them on the same day to equate forging false money with homicide against a member of the conquering elite and delinquency of an officer sworn to defend the Ottoman occupation – counterfeiting likened to treason. The case attracted notoriety when the Christian converted to Islam to parlay his execution. The viceroy dismissed his act as a ploy for survival, but the Christian's continued pronouncement of the attestation of Muslim belief (*shahāda*) while he was suspended from the stake convinced bystanders of his contrition. So was the Shafiʿi judge to whom the Christian's sentence was appealed posthumously. The magistrate ruled the Christian's act of conversion genuine and thus valid and permitted his burial in a Muslim cemetery. Mourners recited prayers before the bier prior to his interment and afterward in the Hakim Mosque. No mention was made of mourning for the Jew, who presumably did not convert.

Another case the same year highlighted the legal gain of religious affiliation over right of human property. Ibn Iyas discussed an appeal brought by a female Ethiopian slave who claimed manumission – and freedom – from her Jewish owner by conversion for herself and her daughter.[56] The slave belonged to one Ibrahim al-Yahudi, director of the mint (*muʿallim dār al-ḍarb*). Seven months after the slave bore Ibrahim a girl, she sought sanctuary with the senior Maliki qadi, Muhyi al-Din al-Damiri, on the ruse of departing for the bath. When she stood before al-Damiri with her daughter, the slave recited her attestations of faith twice. She rejected her master's claim to further ownership for herself and the daughter. Al-Damiri upheld both their conversions. He informed Ibrahim that the daughter's Muslim status was legal on the basis of her mother's wish, despite the effective separation of a father from his child. Ibrahim was rumored to have offered al-Damiri 500 dinars for a ruling in favor of his daughter adhering to her father's religion. When the qadi maintained his decision, Ibrahim appealed it before the viceroy. Ibn Iyas did not mention another attempt at bribery but concluded with the viceroy's denial of Ibrahim's suit. The viceroy stated that he was not one to abrogate a qadi's ruling and restore a convert "to the religion of the Jews."

This dispute over the Ethiopian slave who won freedom for herself and her daughter from her Jewish owner emerged in a broader setting in which Christians and Jews sporadically appealed adverse verdicts by junior magistrates to the senior qadis or the sultan himself. The judge who upheld the slave's conversion to Islam rejected the bribe offered by the Ethiopian's former master, who protested the loss of his progeny from his religious community. The case provides an indication of religion's ultimate gain over rights of ownership and patrimony, rendered more credible in a judicial environment that frequently witnessed positive outcomes for plaintiffs with deep pockets and lucrative bribes. The Ethiopian's gamble paid off, a tribute to the agency of a woman who overcame her seeming handicaps of gender and servility to maneuver herself from confinement in society's lowest rank to the status of a free person and member of the hegemonic religion (with standing higher than that of her former owner, an irony noted by Ibn Iyas).

## Religious Diversity and Sufi Practice

At the time of the Sultanate's founding in the mid-seventh/thirteenth century, Islam had evolved from a localized cult in western Arabia to a global religion. The range of Islam's devotional practices paralleled its territorial expanse. The term Sufism (ar. *taṣawwuf*) touches on many of these because of concepts intrinsic to it, such as "closeness" (*Qurb*) in awareness of God, "poverty" (*Faqr)* as liberation from material desire, or "purity" (*Ṣafā'*) as unadulterated love for God that underlie its appeal to believers.[57] Usually translated as Islamic mysticism, this definition may be considered restrictive because of its implicit focus on awareness of Divine presence to the exclusion of engagement with the temporal world. Sufi practices rarely advocated personal removal from interaction with society in its mundane aspects. In medieval Egypt and Syria, Sufism is best understood as a wide spectrum of practices for Muslims who shared a commitment to *Qurb, Faqr*, or *Ṣafā'* with active social engagement. This survey does not attempt to summarize the extraordinary range of concepts and rituals associated with *taṣawwuf* in the Mamluk Sultanate. It aims to outline the practice of Sufism in its diverse settings and the missions of individuals who charted its political actions and societal impact.

Sufi practice has been organized around principles of spiritual lineage (*ṭā'ifa/ṭawā'if)* from persons believed to have attained exceptional awareness of God's emanation, the essence of *Qurb*. Such persons are revered as the ultimate leader (*quṭb*, literally "pole"), whose example guides the lineage community. Sufi lineages are typically defined as "orders," although a sense of "path" or "trajectory" (*ṭarīqa/ṭuruq*) more closely approximates the conception of taṣawwuf among Muslims. A *ṭarīqa* traces the lineage that descends from a founding *quṭb* who experienced awareness down through generations of successors (*khalīfa/khulafāʾ*). Over time, successors have often branched out to form sub-lineages of their own. In Egypt and Syria during the Sultanate, several *ṭuruq* exercised broad influence over devotional practices in urban and rural settings. Of these, period sources consistently cited the Shadhili tariqa as among the most influential.[58]

This tariqa is known by an individual from the Ghumara district in what is now Morocco: Abu'l-Hasan ʿAli ibn ʿAbd Allah al-Shadhili (d. 656/1258).[59] After studying the religious disciplines in the city of Fez, he allegedly adopted the Sufi path and sought out eminent shaykhs in Iraq. After a sojourn there, he returned to the Maghrib and became a disciple (*murīd*) of a revered hermit, ʿAbd al-Salam ibn Mashish (d. 625/1228). It was this figure who urged Abu'l-Hasan to settle in the village of Shadhila near Qayrawan, by which he was subsequently known. This trajectory is likely apocryphal, and al-Shadhili may have traveled no further east than Alexandria in Egypt, where he is said to have met the Ayyubid ruler, al-Malik al-Kamil.[60] In any case, after a period of devotional isolation, al-Shadhili moved to Tunis, capital of Ifriyiyya. While in that city, he aroused the ire of officials in the court of its Hafsid rulers, possibly over accusations of claiming to be the Fatimid Mahdi. He returned to Alexandria, where he sought al-Kamil's patronage. Al-Shadhili spent the rest of his life there but took the Hajj numerous times. It was on the return from pilgrimage in 656/1258 that al-Shadhili died and was interred in Upper Egypt. His tomb there is revered to this day.

In Egypt, al-Shadhili received the cloak (*khirqa*) attesting his attainment of *Qurb* from two eminent Sufi guides (*murshidayn*). He became revered as a teacher and preacher of sermons that profoundly moved his listeners but left no writings of his own. It was his close disciple, an Andulusian named Abu'l-ʿAbbas al-Mursi, who continued to transmit al-Shadhili's teachings until his own death (686/1287). After al-Mursi's passing, tensions erupted as to appropriate successors who would assume al-Shadhili's growing legacy. Ultimately, acknowledgment was bestowed on a fellow Alexandrian, Ibn ʿAtaʾ Allah al-Iskandari (d. 709/1309), discussed below. Since al-Iskandari compiled the written trove that came to exemplify themes central to Shadhili beliefs, the tariqa over which he presided commenced its trajectory toward ascendancy throughout Egypt and North Africa.[61] The Shadhili tariqa would owe its appeal in large measure to its eschewal of a centralized doctrine based on the founder's teachings. Firmly rooted in Sunni practice, the Shadhili tariqa allowed for the proliferation of subbranches stemming from the diverse perspectives of successive generations of regional guides. The legacy of al-Shadhili's interment in Upper Egypt encouraged the growth of the guides' revered status into cults as local saints. Over time, these attracted legions of worshippers. By the eighth/fourteenth–ninth/fifteenth centuries, the Shadhili tariqa had become the preeminent Sufi network in the Sultanate according to written sources. Its adherents were dispersed in both urban and rural settings. While counting some of the most distinguished ʿulamaʾ among its ranks, the Shadhili tariqa retained its founder's ambivalence for cooption by the ruling elite. A tradition of pragmatic association with ruling circles to advocate for the needs of poor people came to embody the Shadhili stance. Nathan Hofer has depicted this stance as "wary political reciprocity," in which the Shadhili network elected to accept largesse from the regime on behalf of the indigent while standing aloof from factional politics.[62]

Other frequently referenced turuq in the Sultanate were the Qadiriyya, Rifaʿiyya, and Ahmadiyya Badawiyya. The Qadiri lineage descended from Muhyi al-Din Abu Muhammad ʿAbd al-Qadir ibn Abi Salih al-Jilani, a Hanbali theologian from Jilan Province in Iran (d. 561/1166).[63] Revered as one of the supreme Sufi saints by Muslims globally after his death, ʿAbd al-Qadir spent his adult life in Baghdad. He never departed Iraq. Introduced to tasawwuf by a lowly syrup seller *(dabbās)*, ʿAbd Qadir was 50 years old when he began preaching in the Sufi tradition. A renowned ʿalim and mufti, ʿAbd al-Qadir lectured on Hadith, fiqh, and tafsir. But his Sufi teachings affected a broad audience. Many Christians and Jews were moved to convert to Islam after hearing him. ʿAbd al-Qadir's message reached the rich and powerful as well. Their financial support enabled him to found hospices for poor relief, a precedent that would influence his successors in later generations. The Qadiri movement has spread throughout Iran, Anatolia, Syria, Egypt, and the Maghrib. In Egypt, the tariqa became one of the most respected of the so-called scholastic orders. It continued to maintain close ties with the founding community in Baghdad.[64]

By contrast with Qadiri sobriety, the Rifaʿi tariqa became notorious for provocative rituals.[65] Its founder grew up in a region famous for its idiosyncratic religious customs. Abu'l-ʿAbbas Ahmad ibn ʿAli al-Rifaʿi (d. 578/1182) was born in the Marsh country (*Baṭāʾiḥ*) of Lower Iraq.[66] His ancestors had ties to Mecca, Andalusia, and the Maghrib. The Marshlands were known for bizarre practices viewed as incongruous with Orthodox belief but appealing to fringe elements from all over the Muslim world. Upon his father's death, Ahmad's maternal uncle, Mansur, sent his nephew to Baghdad, where he received an ʿalim's traditional education. He may have interacted with al-Qadiri in these years. Ahmad returned to the Marshlands after adopting the Sufi path from his uncle, Mansur, who headed a community named after a distant Meccan ancestor, Rifaʿa. Mansur bestowed its leadership on Ahmad before he died. Ahmad himself was not known as the exemplar for bizarre rituals that would characterize the order that bore his ancestor's name. During the Ayyubid period, the Rafiʿi tariqa spread throughout Egypt and Syria. Its lodges (*ribāṭāt*) became renowned or notorious, according to perspectives of observers, for promoting such acts as fire-walking, riding wild animals, tongue-speaking, and feverish observance of reciting the Divine names (*dhikr*). They also were sought as places of healing and miracle working that enhanced the tariqa's aura of beneficence. The Rifaᶜiyya enjoyed enormous popularity that has lasted through the Mamluk and Ottoman eras into modern times.

The Ahmadi Badawi community was more localized to Egypt.[67] Founded by disciples of Egypt's most revered saint, al-Sayyid Abu'l-Fityan Ahmad al-Badawi (d. 674/1276), the Ahmadiyya Badawiyya have flourished as loosely connected brotherhoods (*akhāwiyyāt*) rather than as a cohesive lineage with distinct branches. Al-Badawi himself may have identified with the Rifaᶜi community.[68] Details of his life are recounted in sources that stress hagiography rather than verifiable evidence. Al-Badawi is said to have been born in Fez, made the Hajj with his family, mastered Qurʾanic recitation, and performed exceptional acts of horsemanship. After embracing tasawwuf and living in seclusion, he visited the tombs of al-Qadiri and al-Rifaᶜi in Iraq, rejected a proposal of marriage from a woman who had refused previous suitors, and received a vision summoning him to the Delta town of Tanta, where he spent the rest of his days. In Tanta, al-Badawi adopted a stance of extreme asceticism. He allegedly spent forty days meditating on a rooftop, staring at the sun and abstaining from food or drink. He attracted disciples who called themselves "roof-dwellers" (*Suṭūḥiyya*), one of whom was a boy named ᶜAbd al-Al who suffered from eye disease. He became al-Badawi's khalifa. When al-Badawi died, ᶜAbd al-Al founded the mosque-tomb that is today Egypt's most visited shrine (**Fig. 7.2**). By the ninth/fifteenth century, the Ahmadiyya Badawiyya had developed into numerous semiautonomous cults of saints, several of whom had been al-Badawi's disciples. After the last khalifa was killed at the Battle of Marj Dabiq between the Mamluks and Ottomans (922/1516), the head of one of these cults, Muhammad ibn ᶜAbd Allah al-Shinnawi, assumed control over the Tanta shrine. Although the Badawiyya network was confined to Egypt and Syria, it gained a vast following within these countries that persists to the present.

These turuq are only the more prominent of numerous Sufi communities that flourished in the Mamluk Sultanate.[69] What do their attributes imply about the quality of religious life among Sufis in that realm? When the Sultanate was founded in the mid-seventh/thirteenth century, Sufism was already dispersed in myriad forms throughout the Islamic world, from Morocco to Central Asia and the Indian subcontinent. But its practices and leadership experienced an upsurge from external stimuli, many of which originated in the Maghrib and Iraq during the preceding century. The career trajectories of the four founders noted above, all Maghribis or Iraqis, unfolded in the 50 years preceding the Sultanate's establishment. These founders did not act alone. Their missions should be seen in a broader context of Maghribi and Iraqi customs permeating

Fig. 7.2 Mosque of Ahmad al-Badawi in Tanta during his birthday (*mawlid*) celebrations, center of Ahmadiyya Badawiyya Sufi Order in Egypt. (Photo 20 October 2016 by Stringer /Anadolu Agency/Getty Images)

Egypt and Syria at this time. There is little evidence that conditions in Egypt and Syria were uniquely receptive to these influences because of alleged local "burn-out" due to "sterility" of ʿulamaʾ legalism. Nor did foreign events such as the European Crusades or Central Asian invasions by the Mongols traumatize Egyptian and Syrian societies in ways that are discernible in Sufi rituals.[70] The burgeoning of Sufi activism that established the Sultanate's prominent orders seems to have been self-generating under the influence of currents, many of which had their origin in the Maghrib or Iraq. That society was receptive to these currents was due in part to regime sponsorship. But the deeper reasons stem from their effect on qualities of spiritual renewal, cultural enrichment, and social equity intrinsic to them.

With regard to regime sponsorship, the Mamluk elite were generous to Sufi institutions. Their motives followed Ayyubid precedents. The most prestigious center of formal Sufi praxis in Egypt was the hospice (*khānqāh*) established in 569/1173–74 by Salah al-Din Yusuf, founder of the Ayyubid monarchy: Saʿid al-Suʿadaʾ (Happiest of the Happy), laqab of a eunuch who had served the last Fatimid Caliphs. After the eunuch's death, Salah al-Din confiscated his house and made it into the khanqah. Although Salah al-Din stipulated that the hospice "support the Sufi poor (*fuqarā'*) newly arrived from remote lands," the massive yields from its waqfs were a magnet for Egypt's civil luminaries. Throughout the Ayyubid and Mamluk periods, the roster of individuals who resided there, either full or short-term, included state officials, eminent jurists, renowned scholars, and religious functionaries. The historian al-Maqrizi claimed that, when al-Zahir Barquq assumed the sultanate, 300 Sufis lived in the hospice.[71] They were munificently supported and their rector was acknowledged as leader of the Sufi establishment (*shaykh al-shuyūkh*) in Egypt.

Yet, Saᶜid al-Suᶜada' did not become a preserve exclusively for luminaries. They rubbed shoulders with persons from across commerce and the trades to those who dedicated their lives to pious poverty. This most prestigious hospice in Cairo brought together representatives of the highest status and most humble callings in a forum of shared holy space. It created an environment that epitomized the equity that called upon the former to revere the latter for their innate wisdom that mitigated excesses of the powerful against society's weakest. Persons from all walks of life could seek guidance from those blessed with *Qurb*. This trait was perhaps the essence of Sufism's appeal across all strata of the populace. It flourished in the most eminent of Cairo's khanqahs.

The example set by Saᶜid al-Suᶜada' was replicated in multiple ways throughout the range of Sufi institutions, from other rich khanqahs endowed by the ruling elite to local hostels (*ribāṭāt/zawāyā*) in towns or the remote countryside. Particularly in Upper Egypt, Sufi communities conducted their observances primarily in ribats founded to commemorate veneration of local saints. They were rarely associated with the major turuq and vigorously upheld a posture of autonomy from Cairo, distant center of imperial power.[72] Their remoteness from regime-sponsored foundations enabled a kind of activism that cherished miracle working, disparaged ᶜulama' custodianship of "proper" belief, and sporadically challenged Christian services and ceremonials as effrontery. The aforementioned Ibn Nuh al-Qusi defended the razing of Christian churches led by Sufi rioters as a valid, indeed necessary, implementation of Islamic law. When Christian delegates petitioned the provincial governor for compensation and protection, his endorsement of their plea prompted Ibn Nuh to castigate the governor's demand for redress as complicity by the regime in abetting Christian status and denigrating Islam.[73] The visibility of Sufis in raucous – and violent – outbursts of local Muslim fervor like this incident became a pronounced feature of their engagement with society in Upper Egypt during the Mamluk period. It vividly conveyed one dimension of the distinctive stance adopted by Sufis that vitalized their presence in Upper Egypt and enhanced their popularity among local Muslims.

The diversity of social types who found a place in Sufi life within the Sultanate precludes identifying a single individual's mission as "typical." But two individuals stand out as authors of works that encompassed the ideological scope of tasawwuf as it evolved throughout this era. One, Ibn Ata' Allah al-Iskandari, was active at the Sultanate's start; the other, ʿAbd al-Wahhab al-Shaʿrani, at the Sultanate's end and transition to Ottoman rule. Taj al-Din Ahmad ibn Muhammad ibn ʿAbd al-Karim ibn Ata' Allah al-Iskandari (d. 709/1309) was born to a family of Maliki jurists in Alexandria. After excelling at his studies in Maliki fiqh, Ibn Ata' Allah was recognized as an accomplished scholar of jurisprudence, Qur'anic exegesis, and Prophetic tradition.[74] Although initially skeptical of Sufism, Ibn Ata' Allah ultimately embraced the Sufi path after he encountered al-Shadhili's successor, Abu'l-ʿAbbas al-Mursi, at the age of seventeen. When Ibn Ata' Allah was persuaded of al-Mursi's convictions and became his disciple, he queried the guide about his own apprehension over conflict between scholastic pursuits and spiritual devotion. Al-Mursi dismissed this tension and urged Ibn Ata' Allah to pursue both since he was uniquely equipped to harmonize them. After Ibn Ata' Allah followed al-Mursi as khalifa of the Shadhili tariqa (696/1287), he went on to lecture at the Mansuriyya madrasa and preach at the Azhar mosque in Cairo. His sermons had a profound effect on their listeners. Ibn Ata' Allah attained the status of a revered Sufi guide in the tradition of his predecessors and was esteemed as a mediator between the scholastic approach of the ʿulama' and the esoteric calling of the Sufis.

Ibn Ata' Allah's writings are among the most widely read tracts in Sufism. His *al-Ḥikam* is an anthology of several hundred aphorisms that contemporaries admired for capturing the theologian al-Ghazali's essential teachings while placing them in a format of maxims composed by such Sufi masters as the Andalusian Abu Madyan Shuʿayb (d. 594/1198). The *Ḥikam* continues to influence Sufi practice to the present day and is available in numerous translations. Among Ibn Ata' Allah's other works, his *Laṭā'if al-minan fī manāqib al-shaykh Abi'l-ʿAbbās al-Mursi wa-shaykhihi al-Shādhilī Abi'l-Ḥasan* (Subtle Blessings in the Saintly Lives of Abu'l-ʿAbbas al-Mursi and His Master Abu'l-Hasan al-Shadhili) is regarded as the principal explication of concepts essential to al-Shadhili's mission, sustained by his successor al-Mursi. The *Laṭā'if* articulated views about sainthood and succession that bridged a potential divide between al-Shadhili's role as inspirer and the nascent community for which his khalifa al-Mursi was responsible for nurturing.[75] By articulating this connection, Ibn Ata' Allah implicitly justified his own succession to al-Mursi. To subsequent generations, the *Laṭā'if* became a model for the progressive transfer of guidance within lineages that was central to Sufi doctrines of spiritual authority in the Mamluk Sultanate. It has inspired concepts of guidance and lineage in Sufism far beyond the Shadhili tariqa. The figure whose career summed up trends in Sufi thought and deportment during the transition from Mamluk to Ottoman rule was ʿAbd al-Wahhab ibn Ahmad al-Shaʿrani (d. 973/1565).[76] Brought up in a family steeped in Sufi tradition, al-Shaʿrani's forebears had migrated to the Delta from the Maghrib in the sixth/twelfth century. Al-Shaʿrani claimed that his distant ancestor was Musa Abu ʿImran, son of the Sultan of Tilimsan (Tlemcen) and disciple of the Maghribi saint Abu Madyan, who sent him to Egypt.[77] After childhood years in the Delta village of Saqiyat Abu Shaʿra (source of his nisba), al-Shaʿrani moved to Cairo when he was twelve. An official in the finance bureau with ties to the family had arranged to settle him at the prominent Ghamri mosque.[78] This official, one Shaykh Khidr, was impressed by the boy's memorization of the Qurʾan at the age of eight. The family's connections to affluent bureaucrats are significant, since al-Shaʿrani would later emphasize his admiration for those who labored for their living. He personally profited from both elevated social placement and fortuitous events that brought him a fortune. As related by his biographers, al-Shaʿrani became the beneficiary of a jurist's near-fatal artifice during the rebellion that followed the Ottoman Sultan Selim's death in 926/1520. The jurist, Qadi Muhyi al-Din al-Uzbaki, had amassed property from his appointment as a provincial inspector of agrarian land by a relative who headed the fiscal diwans under the Mamluks and Ottomans. The Qadi acquired a lucrative estate from tracts foreclosed on their legal owners. When new Ottoman officials detected the fraud, they threatened to arrest al-Uzbaki. To avoid confiscation by the Ottomans and a possible death sentence, al-Uzbaki placed the estate in waqf for a zawiya over which he made al-Shaʿrani the trustee. Some versions of the incident asserted that al-Shaʿrani, already a respected Sufi shaykh, had interceded for al-Uzbaki to the Ottomans.[79] Al-Shaʿrani and his family lived comfortably from the proceeds for the rest of their lives. When, decades later, the Ottoman Pasha governor discovered the circumstances surrounding al-Shaʿrani's trusteeship, al-Shaʿrani shrewdly offered to bestow the zawiya and estate on the Ottoman authorities in Istanbul, to aid their defense of Islam against heretics and infidels. The Ottomans reinstated al-Shaʿrani after enjoining him to pray for the Sultan's success.

Al-Shaʿrani himself avoided mentioning the incident in his own writings. He took pride in his position as trustee of a zawiya that had raised his family to an elite lifestyle. He acknowledged no contradiction between his affluence and reverence for guides who embodied an ethic of work and material abstinence. He pointed to his own modest station during his youth, in which he claimed to have tilled the land and performed menial chores reserved for novices in his early days at the Ghamri Mosque.[80] The murshid whom al-Shaʿrani esteemed as his supreme spiritual influence was ʿAli al-Burullusi, an illiterate palm-leaf plaiter (*khawwāṣ*) deceased in 939/1532–33. This ʿAli belittled the ʿulamaʾ's self-styled posture of custodianship over proper belief and formal learning. He stressed the innate wisdom of the unschooled who took pride in manual work that enhanced their awareness of God and the needs of common people.[81]

In his writings, Al-Shaʿrani continuously praised ʿAli's aphorisms about the godliness of pious poverty and Divine guidance shown to the illiterate. He also extolled admonitions of another shaykh who passionately equated wisdom of the unlettered with the illiterate Prophet Muhammad. This was an Egyptian, Ibrahim al-Matbuli (d. 880/1475). Al-Matbuli sojourned at Ahmad al-Badawi's tomb in Tanta in his youth. In Cairo, he was a chickpea seller when the Prophet urged him to found a zawiya for pilgrims.[82] Al-Matbuli drew a devoted following whom he urged to avoid begging for alms and earn a living through honest labor. Al-Matbuli rigorously disparaged the antics of tricksters who duped gullible visitors at saints' tombs for money despite his own fame as a miracle worker.[83] Respected by the devout Sultan Qayitbay, al-Matbuli did not hesitate to denounce the ruler's avarice. Al-Shaʿrani was profoundly affected by al-Matbuli's commitment to pious poverty and identity with the Prophet's example. He titled his treatise on ethics, *Al-Akhlāq al-Matbūliyya*, after him.

Al-Shaʿrani's equation of merit earned through labor with closeness to God is sustained throughout his writings. His sentiment was genuine, apparently with no sense of hypocrisy over his elite status in life. Al-Shaʿrani seems to have regarded his affluence as the consequence of personal accomplishment, the result of sincerity rather than luck. Al-Shaʿrani justified his social privilege by emphasizing the leverage it gave him over senior amirs. His depiction of a meeting with the departing governor, ʿAli Pasha, soon to become Grand Vizier, subtly hints at the spiritual gain eminent Sufis held over the most powerful officials:

> When I was about to enter the tent of Vizier ʿAli, Pasha of Egypt, as he was preparing for his journey in Muharram 961 (Dec. 1553), he rose toward me and met me outside the tent, supported me under my arm, made me sit on his cushions, and he himself sat at my feet. Then he told me: "Whatever need you will have, just send us a letter to Istanbul and we will arrange it for you there, since we shall be of more use to the people of Egypt there than here, because of our proximity to the Sultan." I replied: "Thank God, the Sufis (*fuqarāʾ*) do not need anything from the rulers. But if you need something, let us know, so that we may supplicate to God for you in this matter." He silently bowed his head for a while and then said: "I ask for God's pardon. You attached yourselves to Almighty God and we attached ourselves to one of his servants, and you were right, because God has power over everything."[84]

Al-Shaʿrani was reminding the Pasha that, despite his temporal supremacy in Egypt – and soon in Istanbul – the Sufis mediated between him and God. His need for them was greater than theirs for him, and his use to the people ultimately derived from God's sanction, implicitly via the Sufis. Shaʿrani could regard himself as among the fuqaraʾ since poverty in this context meant closeness to God rather than material abstinence. Shaʿrani's empathy for the rural peasants, for whom "faqir" did mean destitute, was real. When he quoted his idolized guide, ʿAli al-Khawwas, on the exploited peasant, he was conveying his own feelings:

> The fallah toils throughout the year in misery and hardship. He has to give the governors' agents and Arab chiefs all the milk, oil, chickens and sheep he possesses, until there is nothing left, and he is compelled to sell what his wife weaves. At year's end they make him cover the deficit of the village (*ʿuṭl al-balad*) in addition to the taxes (*kharāj*). Sometimes they foreclose his granary, and when he wishes to take from there to feed his children, he is not allowed to do so. I wish he was like the inspector's assistants; they at least have a regular income. It is known that the villages are the economic mainstay (*mādda*) of the cities and all that is in cities arrives there from the villages.[85]

Via his revered murshid, Shaʿrani expressed empathy for the peasants' lot. Yet, he lived off yields of their labor that maintained his own zawiya. Any implicit irony was likely mitigated by the contrast he drew between regime extraction that upheld oppression and support for spiritual observance that sought Divine succor. This kind of rationalization appeared in al-Shaʿrani's views about the ʿulama', whose role as interpreters of Shariʿa and custodians of proper belief he endorsed, if guided by the mercy and compassion personified in the Sufi masters he revered. Shaʿrani did not advocate eliminating distinctions between the four schools of law (*madhāhib*) as arbitrary impediments to the common person's understanding of Shariʿa. But he believed that there was potential for discord that could result from disputes among jurists over minutiae of fiqh. These could be alleviated by the guidance toward unity offered by the masters whose wisdom stemmed from spiritual intuition rather than formal learning. That these masters emerged from the common people assured their awareness of the people's needs and levels of comprehension. Al-Shaʿrani's views on these matters, as expressed in his writings, appealed to a broad audience. They stand as a summation of how Sufism had evolved during the era of Mamluk rule in Egypt and Syria and would continue into the Ottoman era that followed.

# Reflections

The preceding survey revealed ongoing change with regard to the traits Ibn Khaldun attributed to the Mamluk military elite. Their evolution over time reflected the elite's pragmatic adaptation to shifting circumstances of the political setting in which they pursued their careers, the economy they exploited to remunerate their hegemonic lifestyles, and the global environment they confronted that had altered profoundly in the course of 267 years. While contemporary observers sporadically disparaged the elite for lapsed martial skills, factional infighting, and fiscal corruption, their respect for its dedication to upholding the integrity of the Muslim Commonwealth was genuine, albeit tenuous in the Sultanate's latter years. When the Sufi shaykh Abu Saᶜud prodded the Mamluk officers, who accompanied Tuman Bay to his shrine in the face of impending invasion, to forswear betrayal in return for his reluctant acceptance of their acclamation, he also demanded they cease oppressing the masses – who were fellow believers (cf. Chapter 4). The shaykh's ultimatum stressed abjuration of fiscal malfeasance but also a return to moral values that had allegedly lapsed. He laid emphasis on the elite's fall from grace, their disrepute ubiquitous among Muslims regionally. To assuage it, they had to pledge themselves to a moral renewal and restoration of order according to Shariᶜa. The officers' acquiescence was predictable under the straitened circumstances. Whether they would have lived up to their oath cannot be known because of the Ottoman conquest the following year. This survey has aimed at tracing the circumstances behind the Mamluk cadre's evolution on a distinctive path that led them to accept the shaykh's admonition at this moment in time. It has underscored the cadre's capacity to persevere in the face of daunting challenges from abroad and within. The fact of the cadre's endurance has contributed to the Mamluks' legacy as seen by its successors and its analysts in modern times. This legacy indelibly shaped the impression left by the Mamluks for posterity.

The survey broadly upholds Ibn Khaldun's ascription to the Mamluks of a commitment to defend the religion of Islam. The Mamluks' dedication to bolstering Islam according to tenets of Sunni practice, as interpreted by the ᶜulama' and clerics, was motivated in part by a desire to mitigate the excesses of their authoritarian rule. But their commitment ran deeper, tapping into principles of sound belief and devotion to defense of religion that were sincerely felt despite temporal shortcomings innate to wielders of power. Ibn Khaldun's comments captured this sincerity. Other commentators, such as al-Maqrizi, were less generous. As an admirer of the Fatimid Caliphate as a golden age of progress and prosperity, the historian al-Maqrizi held the ruling elite of his own time accountable for a decline from this halcyon era. He was not alone. Yet, overall, the learned establishment that remarked so profusely on the Mamluk elite and its impact on society expressed appreciation for the fact of endurance itself. To many, endurance meant stability – a precious commodity. In a world of rising turbulence that threatened stability, this was no mean achievement and is one that modern observers have also come to appreciate. The study has examined this phenomenon of endurance from several angles, seeking to discern qualities intrinsic to the military elite that promoted its perseverance and conditions in the larger society that abided its domination. That the elite endured in an environment of rapid change bespeaks its remarkable capacity to adapt.

Ibn Khaldun did not dwell on support by the Mamluks for institutions that enriched the Sultanate's literary and scholastic culture. Yet, the outpouring of literary products during the Mamluk era, and their diversity, owed much to the patronage of the ruling class. The survey has shown the Mamluk elite as sponsors often actively engaged in the intellectual milieus they supported. Acting on a long tradition of literary patronage as a mark of prestige and ornamental display at the highest social levels, the Mamluks contributed distinctively to the expanding writerly culture that reached groups beyond the formally learned by competing among themselves to endow libraries and fund literary circles. The salon society that flourished in the Sultanate's final decades linked poetic genres in several languages spoken throughout the larger region to receptive groups in Cairo and provincial centers. And, with regard to literary genres that challenged established conventions of belief and morality, the Mamluk elite typically elected to adopt a stance of studied tolerance, if not open endorsement. That these genres found an enthusiastic audience among the Mamluk rank and file promoted a posture of this kind.

With regard to assessment of politics and the economy, opinions held by observers – contemporary and modern – have been unified only by contention over consequences. The survey has depicted a political process that prized competition and rivalry as positive and aspirational to its participants. Factional conspiracy appeared as a normative consequence of attitudes toward advancement and fulfillment of ambition engrained in the military class. The post-Mongol setting in which these attitudes evolved remains an object of fascination – and controversy – to current analysts, steeped in disciplines of the modern social sciences. Whether the ethos of the Mamluk military class, as they understood it according to their own values in their own time, can be objectively interpreted so long after their demise by scholars whose framework of analysis differs so greatly is a matter of debate in its own right. This is particularly relevant to contemporary attitudes toward the term "slavery" itself. In light of the dissension and emotion triggered by this term throughout the world today, the range of nuance and contexts surrounding slavery and indentured status in premodern societies generally, and the medieval Islamic world in particular, presents special problems for impartiality. Clearly the implications of slavery, and distinctions between ownership and chattel, carried meanings to observers who lived under the Sultanate that contrast radically with impressions held by analysts steeped in political conventions of the present time. Yet, this problem is not confined to debates over arcane topics relevant to societies long extinct. The Mamluk legacy today is often discussed in a wider backdrop of authoritarianism, militarism, and "strong man"-ism that allegedly emerged in the aftermath of the Mongol era and was indelibly imprinted on the central Islamic world over the following centuries. It is the militarist dimension of the Mamluk institution that allegedly carried on into the Ottoman era, which endured for 400 years in Egypt and Syria. More recently, the army-driven state that emerged under Gamal Abd al-Nasir in postcolonial Egypt is frequently discussed in terms of militarism and its abiding legacy dating back to the Mamluk period. Similar perspectives are frequently raised with regard to Egypt's political economy, which allegedly owes prioritization of military hegemonism as its primary goal to traditions that began with Saladin under the Ayyubids and attained their apogee under the Mamluks.

The preceding study acknowledges the controversies perpetuated by these issues. It has presented events in light of scholarship that has developed in their shadow but has not been diminished as a consequence. The Mamluk Sultanate is now recognized as one of the significant experiments in political systems that evolved in the premodern Islamic world. The survey has attempted to flesh out how the Sultanate affected the broader culture and institutions under its aegis during a period that marked the transition from medieval to early modern in Northeast Africa and Southwest Asia. While Ibn Khaldun praised the Mamluk cadets-to-be upon their arrival for being "undefiled by the ways of civilized living," he fulsomely expressed his admiration for the city whose marvels were owing to their largesse:

> I beheld in Cairo the Garden of the Universe, the orchard of the world, the assemblage of nations, the myriad flow of humanity, the portico of Islam, the seat of power. Palaces and arcades glimmer in her air. Monasteries and colleges blossom along her horizon. I beheld orbs and stars shining among her scholars. The shores of the Nile resembled the river of Paradise, the waters of Heaven. Its flow quenches the thirst of Egyptians without cease, collecting for them fruits and riches. I walked through the streets of the city crowded with the masses of passers-by, their markets filled with luxuries.

We continuously talked about this city, marveling at the extent of its buildings, the magnitude of its stature. Accounts of Cairo are frequent and varied from our savants and colleagues, returning from the Pilgrimage or commerce. I asked our colleague . . . Abu ʿAbd-Allah al-Muqriʾ . . . upon his return from the Pilgrimage . . . saying to him, "What is this city of Cairo like?" He replied, "Whoever has not seen it has not known the glory of Islam."[1]

# Notes

## Introduction

1 'Abd al-Rahman ibn Muhammad ibn Khaldun, *Kitāb al-'ibar wa-dīwān al-mubtada' wa'l-khabar* (Cairo: Bulaq, 1867–68), 5: 371, transl. B. Lewis, *Islam from the Prophet Muhammad to the Capture of Constantinople*, I: *Politics and War* (Oxford, 1987), 97–99; quoted by L. Northrup in the work cited in n. 3.
2 *The Middle East in the Middle Ages, The Early Mamluk Sultanate 1250–1382* (London: Croom Helm, 1986).
3 "The Bahri Mamluk Sultanate, 1250–1390," *The Cambridge History of Egypt*, v. I: *Islamic Egypt, 640–1517*, ed. by C. Petry (Cambridge, 1998), Ch. 10: 242–89.
4 "The Regime of the Circassian Mamluks," *The Cambridge History of Egypt*, v. 1: *Islamic Egypt, 640–1517*, ed. by C. Petry (Cambridge, 1998), Ch. 11: 290–317 (translation from French original).
5 "The Mamlūks in Egypt and Syria: The Turkish Mamlūk sultanate (648–784/1250–1382) and the Circassian Mamlūk sultanate (784–923/1382–1517)," *The New Cambridge History of Islam*, ed. by Maribel Fierro (Cambridge, 2010), II, Ch. 8: 237–84.

## Chapter 1

1 *EI2*: Ghulām: I.-The Caliphate; *EI2*: al-Muʿtaṣim bi'llāh; *EI3*: Caliph and Caliphate up to 1517.
2 *EI2*: Zangī.
3 *EI2/EI3*: Ayyūbids.
4 *EI2*: Shadjur al-Durr; D. F. Ruggles, *Tree of Pearls: The Extraordinary Architectural Patronage of the 13th-Century Egyptian Slave-Queen Shajar Al-Durr* (Oxford: Oxford University Press, 2020).
5 *EI2*: Ḳuṭuz.
6 *EI3*: Baybars I, al-Malik al-Ẓāhir Rukn al-Dīn.
7 *EI2*: E. Khalifa. The Institution of the Caliphate after 658/1258; M. Banister, *The Abbasid Caliphate of Cairo, 1261–1517: Out of the Shadows* (Edinburgh: Edinburgh University Press, 2021).
8 *EI2*: Ḳalāwūn.
9 *EI2*: Lādjīn.
10 *EI2*: al-Nāṣir (P. M. Holt).
11 *EI2*: Shaʿbān.

12 *EI2*: Ḳubrus, 2. The Frankish period (1192–1571).
13 *EI2:* Barḳūḳ; *EI3:* Barqūq, al-Malik al-Ẓāhir; al-Sakhawi, *al-Ḍaw' al-Lāmiᶜ* 3:10 #48.
14 *EI2*: Faradj; *EI3*: Faraj, al-Malik al-Nāṣir.
15 D. Behrens-Abouseif, *The Islamic Architecture of Cairo: An Introduction* (Leiden, 1989), 135–38; *idem, Cairo of the Mamluks: A History of the Architecture and Its Culture* (Cairo: American University in Cairo Press), 231–37.
16 *EI2:* al-Muʾayyad Shaykh; al-Sakhawi, *Ḍaw'* 3: 308 #1190.
17 *EI2/EI3*: Barsbāy, al-Malik al-Ashraf; al-Sakhawi, *Ḍaw'* 3: 8 #38.
18 *EI2*: Cakmaḳ; al-Sakhawi, *Ḍaw'* 3: 71 #287.
19 EI2*: Īnāl al-Adjrūd;* EI3*:* Īnāl al-Ajrūd; al-Sakhawi, *Ḍaw'* 2: 368 #1080.
20 *EI2*: Khushḳadam; al-Sakhawi, *Ḍaw'* 3: 175 #681; K. Yosef, "Mamluks of Jewish Origin in the Mamluk Sultanate," *Mamluk Studies Review* 22 (2019), 87–89, on possible Albanian background.
21 *EI2*: Ḳāʾit Bāy; al-Sakhawi, *Ḍaw'* 4: 201 #697.
22 A. Fuess (2020), "The Syro-Egyptian Sultanate in Transformation, 1496–1498, Sultan al-Nāṣir Muḥammad b. Qāytbāy and the Reformation of Mamlūk Institutions and Symbols of State Power," *Trajectories of State Formation across Fifteenth-Century Islamic West-Asia, Eurasian Parallels, Connections and Divergences*, ed. Jo Van Steenbergen; Leiden: Brill, Rulers and Elites, v. 18, 201–23.
23 *EI2*: Ḳānṣawh al-Ghawri.
24 Ibn Iyas, *Baḍāʾiᶜ* 5: 87.
25 Ibn Iyas, *Baḍāʾiᶜ* 5: 75.
26 *EI2*: Ṭūmān Bāy.

## Chapter 2

1 J. van Steenbergen, P. Wing, K. D'Hulster, "The Mamlukization of the Mamluk Sultanate? State Formation and the History of Fifteenth-Century Egypt and Syria: Part II – Comparative Solutions and a New Research Agenda," *History Compass* 14/11 (2016), 565.
2 With regard to the ethnic diversity of Mamluks in the Cairo Sultanate, the Turkic element diminished as the regime evolved. During the ninth/fifteenth century, individuals identifying as "Turk" had become a minority, while cadres traceable to Circassian (*Jarkasī*), Anatolian (*Rūmī*), or European (*Ifranjī*) origins predominated. Mamluks with backgrounds from farther afield were discernible.
3 *EI2*: Ghulām: I.-The Caliphate.
4 J. Loiseau, *Les Mamlouks*, XIII$^{e}$–XVI$^{e}$ siècle (Paris, 2014), 143–72.
5 *EI2*: Wāfidiyya; D. Ayalon, "The Wafidiya in the Mamluk Kingdom," *Islamic Culture* (Hyderabad, 1951), 81–104.
6 Loiseau, *Mamlouks*, 160–66.
7 Loiseau, *Mamlouks*, 79–85.
8 H. Barker, *That Most Precious Merchandise; The Mediterranean Trade in Black Sea Slaves, 1260–1500* (Philadelphia, 2019).
9 Shihab al-Sarraf, "Mamluk Furūsīyah Literature and Its Antecedents," *Mamluk Studies Review* 8/1 (2004), 141–200.

10 *EI2*: Khādim, Khāṣī; *EI3*: Eunuchs; D. Ayalon, "On the *Eunuchs* in Islam," *Jerusalem Studies in Arabic and Islam* 1 (1979), 67–124; D. Ayalon, *Eunuchs, Caliphs, and Sultans: A Study in Power Relationships* (Jerusalem, 1999).
11 D. Ayalon, "Studies on the Structure of the Mamluk Army," *Bulletin of the School of Oriental and African Studies* 15/2 (1953), 203–28.
12 W. Popper, *Egypt and Syria under the Circassian Sultans, 1382–1468* (Berkeley, 1955), 85–87.
13 A. Levanoni, *A Turning Point in Mamluk History: The Third Reign of al-Nāṣir Muḥammad ibn Qalāwūn (1310–1341)* (Leiden, 1995), 28–72.
14 *EI2*: Wabā'; *EI3*: Black Death; M. Dols, *The Black Death in the Middle East* (Princeton, 1977).
15 *EI3*: Awlād al-Nās.
16 *EI2*: Ḥalḳa.
17 Ibn Iyas, *Baḍā'iʿ al-Zuhūr* 5: 69–72.
18 Popper, *Circassians,* 90–96.
19 Sultan al-Zahir Barquq abolished the office of na'ib sultan in Cairo (*EI3*: Atabak). The na'ib of Damascus initially appointed holders of this office in several district capitals throughout Syria (Ba'labakk, Jerusalem, Nablus), but as sultans in Cairo sought to extend their authority, particularly in the Circassian period, they appropriated control over these positions.
20 J. van Steenbergen, "The Mamlūk Sultanate as a Military Patronage State: Household Politics and the Case of the Qalāwūnid Bayt (1279–1382)," *Journal of the Economic and Social History of the Orient* 56/2 (2013), 189–217.
21 J.-C. Garcin, "The Regime of the Circassian Mamlūks," *The Cambridge History of Egypt*, v. 1, ed. by C. Petry (Cambridge, 1998), 299–308.
22 For an example of a senior amir with these abilities, see J. van Steenbergen, "The Amir Qawṣūn, Statesman or Courtier," *Egypt and Syria in the Fatimid, Ayyubid and Mamluk Eras*, eds. U. Vermeulen, J. van Steenbergen (Leuven, 2001), 449–66.
23 J. van Steenbergen, *Order Out of Chaos: Patronage, Conflict and Mamluk Sociopolitical Culture, 1341–1382* (Leiden, 2006).
24 Ibn Iyas, *Baḍā'iʿ* 3: 166, 170–75.
25 Ibn Iyas, *Baḍā'iʿ* 4: 471.

## Chapter 3

1 C. Petry, *Protectors or Praetorians? The Last Mamlūk Sultans and Egypt's Waning as a Great Power* (Albany, 1994), 30.
2 P. Holt, "Some Observations on the Abbasid Caliphate of Cairo," *Bulletin of the School of Oriental and African Studies* 47 (1984), 501–07; M. Banister, "Naught Remains to the Caliph but His Title": Revisiting Abbasid Authority in Mamluk Cairo," *Mamluk Studies Review* 18 (2014–15), 219–45; M. Banister, *The Abbasid Caliphate of Cairo, 1261–1517: Out of the Shadows* (Edinburgh: Edinburgh University Press, 2021).
3 Michael Kohler, *Alliances and Treaties between Frankish and Muslim Rulers in the Middle East* (Leiden, 2013); *Mamluk Cairo, a Crossroad for Embassies; Studies on Diplomacy and Diplomatics*, ed. by F. Bauden, M. Dekkiche (Leiden, 2019), chs. 1 and 2.

4 Petry, *Protectors*, 35.
5 *EI2*: Filasṭīn.
6 *EI2*: Tankiz; E. Kenney, *Power and Patronage in Medieval Syria: The Architecture and Urban Works of Tankiz al-Nāṣirī* (Chicago, 2009).
7 Petry, *Protectors,* 36–37.
8 Petry, *Protectors*, 37.
9 Petry, *Protectors*, 38.
10 B. Walker, *Jordan in the Late Middle Ages: Transformation of the Mamluk Frontier* (Chicago, 2011), 111–33.
11 Petry, *Protectors,* 39.
12 *EI2*: Makka, 2: From the ʿAbbasid to the Modern Period; J. Meloy, *Imperial Power and Maritime Trade: Mecca and Cairo in the Later Middle Ages* (Chicago, 2010), 11–38.
13 R. Mortel, "Taxation in the Amirate of Mecca during the Medieval Period," *BSOAS* 58/1 (1995), 1–16.
14 *EI2*: Ḳatāda ibn Idrīs.
15 *EI2*: Barakāt.
16 Mortel, *Taxation*, 13.
17 *Taxation*, 14; for background on merchants, see R. Mortel, "The Mercantile Community of Mecca during the Late Mamlūk Period," *Journal of the Royal Asiatic Society* 3rd series 4/1 (1994), 15–35.
18 R. Mortel, "Grand 'Dawādār' and Governor of Jedda: The Career of the Fifteenth Century Mamlūk Magnate Gānibak al-Ẓāhirī," *Arabica* 43/3 (1996), 437–56.
19 *EI2*: Dhū'l-Ḳadr; *EI3*: Dulkadir.
20 S. Har-el, *Struggle for Dominion in the Middle East: The Ottoman–Mamluk War, 1485–91* (Leiden, 1995); C. Petry, *Twilight of Majesty: The Reigns of the Mamlūk Sultans al-Ashraf Qāytbāy and Qānṣūh al-Ghawri in Egypt* (Seattle, 1993), 57–72.
21 Petry, *Protectors*, 43; Ibn Taghri Birdi, *Ḥawādith al-duhūr* 4: 634.
22 Petry, *Protectors*, 44; *Ḥawādith* 4: 686; Ibn al-Sayrafi, *Inbāʾ al-Haṣr*, 47.
23 *EI3*: Īlkhānids; Hülegü b. Toluy b. Chinggis Khān.
24 R. Amitai, "Mongol Imperial Ideology and the Ilkhanid War against the Mamluks," *Empire and Its Legacy*, eds. R. Amitai-Price, D. O. Morgan (Leiden, 1999), 57–72.
25 *EI3*: Abāqā.
26 *EI3*: Ghāzān Khān Maḥmūd.
27 *EI3*: Abū Saʿīd Bahādur Khān.
28 R. Amitai, "The Resolution of the Mongol-Mamluk War," *Mongols, Turks, and Others: Eurasian Nomads and the Sedentary World*, ed. by R. Amitai, M. Biran (Leiden, 2005), 359–90.
29 D. Little, "Notes on Aitamish, a Mongol Mamlūk," *Die islamische Welt zwischen Mittelalter und Neuzeit: Festschrift für Hans Robert Roemer zum 65. Geburtstag*, ed. By U. Haarmann, P. Bachmann (Beirut/Wiesbaden, 1979), 387–401.
30 *EI2*: Tīmūr Lang.
31 *EI2*: Shāh Rukh.
32 *EI2*: Aḳ Ḳoyunlu; J. Woods, *The Aqquyunlu: Clan, Confederation, Empire* (Chicago, 1999).
33 *EI2*: Uzun Ḥasan.
34 Petry, *Protectors*, 45; Ibn Taghri Birdi, *Ḥawādith* 4: 652.

35 Petry, *Protectors*, 45; Ibn Taghri Birdi, *Ḥawādith* 4: 675; Ibn Iyas, *Baḍā'iʿ* 3: 19, 27.
36 Petry, *Protectors*, 48; Ibn Iyas, *Baḍā'iʿ* 3: 88, 90.
37 Petry, *Protectors*, 49; Ibn Iyas, *Baḍā'iʿ* 4: 39.
38 Petry, *Protectors*, 51; Ibn Iyas, *Baḍā'iʿ* 3: 181.
39 *EI2*: Ḳarāmān.
40 D. Ayalon, *Gunpowder and Firearms in the Mamluk Kingdom* (London, 1956); G. Agoston, *Guns for the Sultan: Military Power and the Weapons Industry in the Ottoman Empire* (Cambridge, 2005), 24.
41 A. Fuess, "Why Venice, Not Genoa: How Venice Emerged as the Mamluks' Favourite European Trading Partner after 1365," *Union in Separation: Diasporic Groups and Identities in the Eastern Mediterranean*, ed. by G. Christ (Roma, 2015), 251–66.
42 *EI2*: Ḳubrus; al-Iskandariyya; G. F. Hill, *A History of Cyprus* (Cambridge, 1940–52), v. 3.
43 G. Christ, *Trading Conflicts, Venetian Merchants and Mamluk Officials in Late Medieval Alexandra* (Leiden, 2012).
44 Petry, *Protectors*, 56–57, nn. 88–89.
45 Petry, *Protectors*, 57–58, nn. 90–92.
46 Petry, *Protectors*, 58; Ibn Iyas, *Baḍā'iʿ* 4: 259.
47 Petry, *Protectors*, 59; Ibn Iyas, *Baḍā'iʿ* 4: 109.
48 Petry, *Protectors*, 59–61, nn. 99–102.
49 *EI2*: Takrūr.
50 al-Maqrizi, *Sulūk* 2: 255; *EI2*: Mansa Mūsā; *EI3*: Mande (Mandingo).
51 Al-ʿUmari, *Masālik*, *Corpus of Early Arabic Sources for West African History*, ed. by N. Levtzion, J. F. P. Hopkins (Princeton, 2000), 266–74.
52 W. Schultz (2006), "Mansa Musa's Gold in Mamlūk Cairo: A Reappraisal of a World Civilizations Anecdote," *Post-Mongol Central Asia and the Middle East: Studies in History and Historiography in Honor of Professor John E. Woods*, eds. J. Pfeiffer, S. Quinn, E. Tucker (Wiesbaden: Harrassowitz Verlag), 428–47.
53 *EI3*: Askiyā Muḥammad.
54 *EI2*: Ḥabash, Ḥabasha; *EI3*: Ethiopia, Islam, and Muslims in; Hadiyya (Ethiopia).
55 Al-Maqrizi, *Khitat*, 2: 276–77.
56 J. Loiseau, "Abyssinia at al-Azhar: Muslim Students from the Horn of Africa in Late Medieval Cairo," *Northeast African Studies* 19/1 (2019), 64–69.
57 Al-Sakhawi, *Daw'*, 6: 53 #147.
58 *EI3*: Eunuchs.
59 D. Ayalon, "On the Term Khādim in the Sense of 'Eunuch' in the Early Muslim Sources," *Arabica* 32 (1985), 289–08.
60 C. Petry, "From Slaves to Benefactors: The Ḥabashīs of Mamlūk Cairo," *Sudanic Africa* 5 (1994), 57–66; M. Meineke, *Die Restaurierung der Madrasa des Amirs Sabiq al-Din Mitqal al-Anuki und die Sanierung des Darb Qirmiz in Kairo* (Cairo, 1980).
61 Distinct from Yalbugha al-Yahyawi, governor of Damascus and rebel against Sultan al-Kamil Shaʿban, cf. Ch. One.
62 C. Petry, "Crime and Scandal in Foreign Relations of the Mamluk Sultanate: Espionage and Succession Crises Linked to Cyprus," *La frontière*

*méditerranéenne du XV^e^ au XVII^e^ siècle*, ed. by A. Fuess, B. Heyberger, Centre d`études superieures de la Renaissance, Université de Tours (BREPOLS, 2013), 145–61; C. Petry, "'Travel Patterns of Medieval Notables in the Near East' Reconsidered," *Everything Is on the Move, the Mamluk Empire as a Node in (Trans-)Regional Networks*, ed. by S. Conermann (Bonn, 2014), 165–80.

63 J. Loiseau, "The Ḥāṭī and the Sultan: Letters and Embassies from Abyssinia to the Mamluk Court," *Mamluk Cairo, a Crossroads for Embassies: Studies on Diplomacy and Diplomatics*, ed. by F. Bauden, M. Dekkiche (Leiden, 2019), 638–57.

64 Ibn Iyas, *Badāʾiʿ* 3: 179; Loiseau, *Ḥāṭī*, 645.

65 Ibn Iyas, *Badāʾiʿ* 5: 10.

66 *EI2*: Ifriḳīya; *EI3*: Ifriqīya.

67 C. Petry, *The Civilian Elite of Cairo in the Later Middle Ages* (Princeton, 1981), 74–77.

68 *EI3*: Ibn Baṭṭūṭa.

## Chapter 4

1 *EI2*: Wazīr, 2: The Fāṭimid Caliphate, 3: The Ayyūbids; W. Popper, *Egypt and Syria under the Circassian Sultans, 1382–1468 A.D.* (Berkeley, 1955), 96.

2 *EI2*: Kātib, 1: in the Caliphate; C. Petry, *The Civilian Elite of Cairo in the Later Middle Ages* (Princeton, 1981), 203–05.

3 Petry, *Civilian*, 213–20; Popper, *Egypt and Syria*, 97–99.

4 Petry, *Civilian*, 205–09; Popper, *Egypt and Syria*, 97.

5 For the context of this relationship, see M. Chamberlain, *Knowledge and Social Practice in Medieval Damascus, 1190–1350* (Cambridge, 1994), 108–33.

6 Petry, *Civilian*, 207, n. 13; G. Wiet, "Les secrétaires de la chancellerie (*kuttāb el-sirr*) en Égypte sous les mamlouks circassiens," *Mélanges René Basset* v. 1 (Paris, 1925), 287 #11.

7 Petry, *Civilian*, 208, n. 14; Wiet, *Secrétaires*, 288 #12.

8 Wiet, *Secrétaires*, 294 #17.

9 Wiet, *Secrétaires*, 294 #18.

10 C. Petry, *Twilight of Majesty: The Reigns of the Mamlūk Sultans al-Ashraf Qāytbāy and Qānṣūh al-Ghawrī in Egypt* (Seattle, 1993), 55–56; Wiet, *Secrétaires*, 307 #32.

11 Petry, *Twilight*, 105; Ibn Iyas, *Badāʾiʿ al-Zuhūr* 3: 227–29.

12 Wiet, *Secrétaires*, 308–09 #33, 34, 35.

13 *EI2*: Ibn al-Shihna.

14 Wiet, *Secrétaires*, 304–05 #28, 30.

15 *EI2*: Shāhid; Petry, *Civilian*, 225, n. 45.

16 Petry, *Civilian*, 228–29.

17 K. Salibi, "Listes chronologiques des grands cadis de l'Égypte sous les Mamlouks," *Revue des Études Islamiques* 25 (1957), 102 #23.

18 Petry, *Civilian*, 232.

19 Petry, *Civilian*, 45–47, 232–40.

20 B. Martel-Thoumian, "The Sale of Office and Its Economic Consequences during the Rule of the Last Circassians (872–922/1468–1516)," *Mamluk Studies Review* 9/2 (2005), 49–83.

21 ʿA. Husayn, *Al-Sujūn wa'l-ʿUqūbāt fī Miṣr "ʿAṣr Salaṭīn al-Mamālīk"* (Jails and Punishments in Egypt in the Age of Mamluk Sultans) (Cairo, 2002).
22 Ibn Iyas, *Baḍā'iʿ* 4: 14–15.
23 Ibn Iyas, *Baḍā'iʿ* 4: 340–46; C. Petry, *Protectors or Praetorians? The Last Mamluk Sultans and Egypt's Waning as a Great Power* (Albany, 1994), 149.
24 *EI2*: Ḥisba, 1: General: Sources, Origins, Duties; *EI3*: Ḥisba; Petry, *Civilian*, 223; K. Stilt, *Islamic Law in Action: Authority, Discretion and Everyday Experiences in Mamluk Egypt* (New York, 2011).
25 Salibi, *Listes*, 102 #23.
26 Salibi, *Listes*, 104 #33.
27 Salibi, *Listes*, 105 #37.
28 Salibi, *Listes*, 111 #10.
29 *EI2*, *EI3*: Fatwā.
30 Salibi, *Listes*, 104 #35.
31 J. Berkey, *The Transmission of Knowledge in Medieval Cairo* (Princeton, 1992), Ch. 4; Petry, *Civilian*, 250.
32 K. Hirschler, *Medieval Arabic Historiography: Authors as Actors* (London, 2006).
33 Petry, *Civilian*, 145–48; C. Petry, "Educational Initiatives as Depicted in the Biographical Literature of Medieval Cairo, the Debate over Prestige and Venue," *Medieval Prosopography* 23 (2012), 101–23.
34 *Inbā' al-ḥaṣr bi-abnā' al-ʿaṣr* (Cairo, 1970); *Nuzhat al-nufūs wa'l-abdān fī tawārīkh al-zamān* (Cairo, 1970–73; 1994).
35 Petry, *Civilian*, 246–50.
36 Petry, *Civilian*, 258.
37 Berkey, *Transmission*, 142.
38 *EI2*, Khaṭīb; Petry, *Civilian*, 260.
39 *EI2*: Ḳirā'a; Petry, *Civilian*, 262.
40 Petry, *Civilian*, 264, n. 108.
41 Petry, *Civilian*, 265, nn. 110, 111.
42 Petry, *Civilian*, 386–87.
43 Ibn Iyas, *Baḍā'iʿ* 5: 85.

## Chapter 5

1 S. Borsch, "Nile Floods and the Irrigation System in Fifteenth-Century Egypt," *Mamluk Studies Review* 4 (2000), 131–45.
2 Y. Rapoport, "Irrigation in the Medieval Islamic Fayyum: Local Control in a Large-scale Hydraulic System," *Journal of the Economic and Social History of the Orient* 55 (2012), 1–31.
3 B. J. Walker, *Jordan in the Late Middle Ages; Transformation of the Mamluk Frontier* (Chicago, 2011), Ch. 2: Mamluk Administration of Jordan; Ch. 4: Jordan's Economy at the Turn of the Fifteenth Century.
4 *EI2*: Iḳṭāʿ; C. Cahen, "L'Évolution de l'iqtaʿ du IXᵉ au XIIIᵉ siècles," *Annales, Économies, Sociétés, Civilisations* 8/1 (1953), 25–52.
5 C. Wickham, "The Power of Property: Land Tenure in Fatimid Egypt," *Journal of the Economic and Social History of the Orient (JESHO)* 62/1 (2019), 67–107.

6 *EI2*: Kharādj; C. Cahen, "Un traité fiancier inédit d'époque Fatimide-Ayyubide," *JESHO* 5/2 (1962), 139–59; C. Cahen, "Contribution à l'étude des impots dans l'Égypte médiévale," *JESHO* 5/3 (1962), 244–78; R. S. Cooper, "The Assessment and Collection of Kharāj in Medieval Egypt," *Journal of the American Oriental Society* 96/3 (1976), 365–82; R. S. Cooper, "Land Classification Terminology and the Assessment of the Kharāj Tax in Medieval Egypt," *JESHO* 17/1 (1974), 91–102; R. S. Cooper, "A Note on the Dīnār Jayshī," *JESHO* 16/2 (1973), 317–18.
7 *EI2*: Rawk, ii: Egypt; T. Sato, "The Evolution of the *Iqṭāᶜ* System under the Mamlūks – an analysis of *al-Rawk al-Ḥusāmī* and *al-Rawk al-Nāṣirī*," *Memoirs of the Research Department of the Toyo Bunko (The Oriental Library)* 37 (1979), 99–131; T. Sato, *State and Rural Society in Medieval Islam: Sultans, Muqtaᶜs and Fallahun* (Leiden, 1997); G. Frantz-Murphy, *The Agrarian Administration of Egypt from the Arabs to the Ottomans* (Cairo: IFAO, 1986); I. Lapidus, "The Grain Economy of Mamluk Egypt," *JESHO* 12/1 (1969), 1–15.
8 Y. Frenkel, "Agriculture, Land-Tenure and Peasants in Palestine during the Mamluk Period," *Egypt and Syria in the Fatimid, Ayyubid and Mamluk Eras*, ed. by U. Vermeulen, J. van Steenbergen (Leuven: Peeters, 2001), 193.
9 Walker, *Jordan*, 197–201.
10 Walker, *Jordan*, 119–33.
11 D. Igarashi, *Land Tenure, Fiscal Policy and Imperial Power in Medieval Syro-Egypt* (Chicago: MEDOC, 2015), 23–46.
12 J.-C. Garcin, "La 'Méditerranéisation' de l'empire mamelouke sous les sultans bahrides," *Rivista degli studi orientali* 48 (1973–74), 109–16.
13 D. Igarashi, "The Establishment and Development of al-Dīwān al-Mufrad: Its Background and Implications," *Mamluk Studies Review* 10/1 (2006), 117–40.
14 This figure, based on 17.3 percent, does not align with the sum of 2 million dinars total reported in the chronicle literature for the end of Sultan al-Ghawri's reign several decades later; cf. n. 40. The latter amount was listed solely as "dinars" rather than "d. al-jayshi," but the disparity reveals inconsistencies in contrasting sources.
15 D. Igarashi, "The Financial Reforms of Sultan Qāytbāy," *Mamluk Studies Review* 13/1 (2009), 27–51.
16 Ibn Taghri Birdi, *Ḥawādith al-Duhūr* 8/4: 689–91.
17 Walker, *Jordan*, 239–68.
18 E. Ashtor, *Levant Trade in the Later Middle Ages* (Princeton, 1983), 3–17.
19 H. Barker, *That Most Precious Commodity: The Mediterranean Trade in Black Sea Slaves, 1260–1500* (Philadelphia, 2019).
20 Ashtor, *Levant*, 11, 28, 47, 82–83, 127, 293, 308; D. Ayalon, "L'esclavage du Mamelouk," *Oriental Notes and Studies* 1 (Jerusalem, 1951), 1–4; D. Ayalon, "Aspects of the Mamlūk Phenomenon I: The Importance of the Mamluk Institution," *Der Islam* 53/2 (1976–77), 203–04; A. Ehrenkreutz, "Strategic Implications of the Slave Trade between Genoa and Mamlūk Egypt in the Second Half of the Thirteenth Century," *The Islamic Middle East, 700–1900*, ed. by A. Udovitch (Princeton, 1981), 335–45. J. Loiseau, *Les Mamelouks, XIIIᵉ–XVIᵉ siècles* (Paris, 2014), 25–56.
21 W. Fischel, "The Spice Trade in Mamluk Egypt, A Contribution to the Economic History of Medieval Islam," *JESHO* 1/2 (1958), 157–74; E. Ashtor, "The Volume of Levantine Trade in the Later Middle Ages, 1370–1498," *Journal of European*

*Economic History* 4 (Rome: 1975), 573–612; E. Ashtor, "Profits from Trade with the Levant in the Fifteenth Century," *Bulletin of the School of Oriental and African Studies* 38 (1975), 250–75; E. Ashtor, "Spice Prices in the Near East in the 15th Century," *Journal of the Royal Asiatic Society* (1976), 26–41.

22 *EI2*: Kārimī; E. Ashtor, "The Kārimī Merchants," *JRAS* (1956), 45–56.

23 J. Meloy, "Imperial Strategy and Political Exigency: The Red Sea Spice Trade and the Mamluk Sultanate in the Fifteenth Century," *JAOS* 123/1 (2003), 1–19.

24 M. Sobernheim, "Das Zuckermonopol unter Sultan Barsbai," *Zeitschrift fur Assyriologie und Verwandte Gebiete* 27 (1912), 75–84.

25 Ashtor, *Levant*, 17–18.

26 A. Fuess, "Why Venice, not Genoa: How Venice emerged as the Mamluks' Favourite European Trading Partner after 1365," *Union in Separation: Diasporic Groups and Identities in the eastern Mediterranean*, ed. by G. Christ (Roma, 2015), 251–66.

27 G. Christ, "A King of Two Seas? Mamluk Maritime Trade Policy in the Wake of the Crisis of the 14th Century," *Ulrich Haarmann Memorial Lecture* 13, ed. by S. Conermann (Berlin, 2017), 20–31.

28 B. Shoshan, "Money Supply and Grain Prices in Fifteenth-Century Egypt," *The Economic History Review*, new series 36/1 (1983), 47–67.

29 E. Ashtor, *Histoire des prix et des salaires dans l'orient médiévale* (Paris, 1969), chs. 6, 7; M. Shatzmiller, "Economic Performance and Economic Growth in the Early Islamic World," *Journal of the Economic and Social History of the Orient* 54/2 (2011), 132–84; M. Shatzmiller, S. Pamuk, "Plagues, Wages, and Economic Change in the Islamic Middle East, 700–1500," *Journal of Economic History* 74/1 (2014), 196–229.

30 Valued according to the number or weight necessary to equal the value of one silver dirham; cf. W. Schultz, "The Monetary History of Egypt, 642–1517," *The Cambridge History of Egypt*, v. 1: *Islamic Egypt, 640–1517*, ed. by C. Petry (Cambridge, 1998), 337, n. 88.

31 C. Petry, *Protectors or Praetorians? The Last Mamlūk Sultans and Egypt's Waning as a Great Power* (Albany, 1994), Appendices 2 and 4.

32 Ashtor, *Prix*, 378–79.

33 Ashtor, *Prix*, 380–81.

34 Maqrizi, *Kitāb al-sulūk li-maʿrifa duwal al-mulūk* 2: 786.

35 Ashtor, *Prix*, 373–75.

36 Ashtor, *Prix*, 376–78.

37 Cairo, 1853–54.

38 Maqrizi, *Khiṭaṭ* 2: 86–107.

39 B. Martel-Thoumian, "The Sale of Office and Its Economic Consequences during the Rule of the Last Circassians, 872–922/1468–1516," *Mamluk Studies Review* 9/2 (2005), 57–82.

40 Petry, *Protectors*, 166–76.

41 Ashtor, *Prix*, 373.

42 But cf. n. 14.

43 S. Borsch, *The Black Death in Egypt and England: A Comparative Study* (Austin, 2005), 40–54.

44 A. Levanoni, "The al-Nashw Episode: A Case Study of Moral Economy," *Mamluk Studies Review* 9/1 (2005), 1–14; C. Petry, *The Criminal Underworld in a Medieval Islamic Society* (Chicago, 2012), 86–87, 120–21, 301–02.

45 D. Little, "Coptic Converts to Islam during the Baḥrī Mamluk Period," *Conversion and Continuity: Indigenous Christian Communities in Islamic Lands, Eighth to Eighteenth Centuries*, ed. by M. Gervers, R. Bikhazi (Toronto, 1990), 263–88; D. Richards, "The Coptic Bureaucracy under the Mamlūks," *Colloque international sur l'histoire du Caire* (Cairo, 1969), 373–81.
46 Ibn Taghri Birdi, *Ḥawādith* 8/4: 635.
47 Ibn Iyas, *Badā'iʿal-Zuhūr* 3: 13.
48 C. Petry, *Twilight of Majesty: The Reigns of the Mamlūk Sultans al-Ashraf Qāytbāy and Qānṣūh al-Ghawrī in Egypt* (Seattle, 1993), 120–21.
49 D. Ayalon, *Gunpowder and Firearms in the Mamluk Kingdom* (London, 1956), 75, n. 157.
50 Ibn Iyas, *Badā'iʿ* 4: 369.
51 Ibn Iyas, *Badā'iʿ* 5: 75.
52 Al-Sakhawi, *al-Ḍaw' al-lāmiʿ fī aʿyān al-qarn al-tāsiʿ* 10: #983; Ibn al-Sayrafī, *Inbā' al-haṣr bi-abnā' al-ʿaṣr*, 144; Ibn Iyas, *Badā'iʿ* 3: 39.
53 Ibn Iyas, *Badā'iʿ* 4: 376, 382, 387.
54 Petry, *Protectors*, 144–46, 222.
55 *Petry, Protectors*, 198, n. 26.
56 Petry, *Protectors*, 198, n. 28.
57 Petry, *Protectors*, 199, n. 34.
58 Petry, *Protectors*, 202; appendices 7 and 8.
59 Ibn Iyas, *Badā'iʿ* 4: 14.
60 Petry, *Protectors*, 206, n. 50.
61 Petry, *Protectors*, 207, n. 51.
62 For complexities surrounding this issue, see J. Meloy, "Copper Money in Late Mamluk Cairo: Chaos or Control?," *Journal of the Economic and Social History of the Orient* 44/3 (2001): 293–21.
63 Ashtor, *Prix*, 274–82; J. Bacharach, "The Dinar versus the Ducat," *International Journal of Middle East Studies* 4/1 (1973), 77–96; J. Bacharach, "Circassian Monetary Policy: Copper," *JESHO* 19/1 (1976), 32–47; W. Schultz, "The Monetary History of Egypt, 642–1517," *The Cambridge History of Egypt*, v. 1: *Islamic Egypt, 640–1517*, ed. by C. Petry (Cambridge, 1998), 327–38; B. Shoshan, "From Silver to Copper: Monetary Changes in Fifteenth-Century Egypt," *Studia Islamica* 56 (1982), 97–116.

## Chapter 6

1 U. Haarmann, "Arabic in Speech, Turkish in Lineage: Mamluks and Their Sons in the Intellectual Life of Fourteenth-Century Egypt and Syria," *Journal of Semitic Studies* 33/1 (1988), 82–83.
2 *EI3*: Ibn ʿAbd al-Ẓāhir; R. Irwin, "Mamlūk Literature," *Mamluk Studies Review* 7/1 (2003), 1.
3 Haarmann, *Arabic*, 86–87; K. Stowasser, "Manners and Customs at the Mamluk Court," *Muqarnas* 2 (1984), 14; B. Flemming, "Literary Activities in Mamlūk Halls and Barracks," *Studies in Memory of Gaston Wiet*, ed. by M. Rosen-Ayalon (Jerusalem, 1977), 249–60.

4 R. S. Humphreys, "The Expressive Intent of the Mamlūk Architecture of Cairo: A Preliminary Essay," *Studia Islamica* 35 (1972), 117.
5 Humphreys, *Intent*, 74.
6 Haarmann, *Arabic*, 91; Irwin, *Mamluk*, 5.
7 Irwin, *Mamluk*, 4, 27–28; M. Awad, "Sultan al-Ghawri: His Place in Literature and Learning (Three Books Written under His Patronage," *Actes du XX^e^ Congrès international des orientalistes* (Louvain, 1940), 321–22; D. Behrens-Abouseif, "Sultan al-Ghawrī and the Arts," *Mamluk Studies Review* 6 (2002), 71–94; Y. Frenkel, *The Turkic Peoples in Medieval Arabic Writings* (New York, 2015), 21–23.
8 Haarmann, *Arabic*, 103.
9 Haarmann, *Arabic,* 111.
10 Haarmann, *Arabic,* 88; Irwin, *Mamluk*, 2.
11 Haarmann, *Arabic*, 109.
12 *EI3*: Ibn al-Dawādārī; D. Little, "Historiography of the Ayyūbid and Mamlūk Epochs," *The Cambridge History of Egypt*, v. 1: *Islamic Egypt*, ed. by C. Petry (Cambridge, 1998), 424; Haarmann, *Arabic*, 110.
13 *EI2*: Abu'l-Maḥāsin Djamāl al-Dīn Yūsuf Ibn Taghri Birdi; D. Little, "Historiography," 442.
14 *EI2*: al-Ṣafadī, Khalīl ibn Aybak.
15 D. Little, "Historiography," 421; Irwin, *Mamluk*, 20.
16 Al-Sakhawi, *al-Ḍaw' al-lāmiᶜ fī aᶜyān al-qarn al-tāsiᶜ*, 5: 229, #769; *EI3*: Arabic Literature, section 6: Ibn Ṣūdūn; M. Larkin, "Popular Poetry in the Post-Classical Period, 1150–1850," *The Cambridge History of Arabic Literature* v. 6: *Arabic Literature in the Post-Classical Period*, ed. by R. Allen, D. Richards (Cambridge, 2006), 227; Irwin, *Mamluk*, 20; K. Hirschler, *The Written Word in the Medieval Arabic Lands* (Edinburgh, 2012), 190; A. Elbendary, *Crowds and Sultans: Urban Protest in Late Medieval Egypt and Syria* (Cairo, 2015), 81.
17 Hirschler, *Written Word*, Introduction.
18 Hirschler, *Written Word,* 84.
19 A. Sabra, *Poverty and Charity in Medieval Islam; Mamluk Egypt, 1250–1517* (Cambridge, 2000), 81–83.
20 Hirschler, *Written Word*, 19–25; Elbendary, *Crowds*, 87–96, 106; Irwin, *Mamluk*, 18.
21 Hirschler, *Written Word*, 145–46.
22 Hirschler, *Written Word,* 165–83.
23 Hirschler, *Written Word,* 170–72; Irwin, *Mamluk*, 20.
24 *EI2/3*: Abū Nuwās.
25 *EI2*: Al-Mutanabbī.
26 *EI2*: Ḳasīda.
27 T. E. Homerin, "Reflections on Arabic Poetry in the Mamluk Age," *Mamluk Studies Review* 1 (1997), 65; Larkin, *Popular Poetry*, 195.
28 *EI2*: Burda; *EI3*: al-Būsīrī.
29 EI2*: Ṣafī al-Dīn ᶜAbd al-ᶜAzīz b. Sarāyā al-Ḥillī.*
30 *EI3*: Arabic Literature, section 6: al-Ḥillī.
31 For example, Ibn Nubata's ode commemorating his son's death: T. Bauer, "Communication and Emotion: The Case of Ibn Nubātah's *Kindertotenlieder*," *Mamluk Studies Review* 7/1 (2003), 49–95.

32 *EI2:* Ibn Nubāta al-Miṣrī; *EI3*: Anthologies, Arabic Literature (post-Mongol period), section 1: Mamluk Anthologies: Ibn Nubāta; Irwin, *Mamluk*, 11.
33 *EI2*: Ibn al-ʿAfīf al-Tilimsānī; S. Jayyusi, "Arabic Poetry in the Post-Classical Age," *The Cambridge History of Arabic Literature*, v. 6, ed. by R. Allen, D. Richards (Cambridge, 2006), 50; Homerin, *Reflections*, 65.
34 Irwin, *Mamluk*, 9, n. 26; M. F. Ghazi, "Un groupe sociale: Les Raffinés (Ẓurafāʾ)," *Studia Islamica* 11 (1959), 69–70.
35 *EI3*: al-Jazzār.
36 *EI3*: Banquet; Larkin, *Popular Poetry*, 220; G. van Gelder, *God's Banquet* (New York), 97.
37 *EI3*: al-Bilbaysī.
38 *EI2, EI3*: Ibn Dāniyāl.
39 L. Guo, *The Performing Arts in Medieval Islam: Shadow Play and Popular Poetry in Ibn Dāniyāl's Mamluk Cairo* (Leiden, 2012).
40 L. Guo, "Mamlūk Historiographic Studies: The State of the Art," *Mamluk Studies Review* 1 (1997), 28.
41 R. Irwin, "Al-Maqrīzī and Ibn Khaldūn, Historians of the Unseen," *Mamluk Studies Review* 7/2 (2003), 217–30.
42 D. Reynolds, "A Thousand and One Nights: A History of the Text and Its Reception," *The Cambridge History of Arabic Literature*, v. 6: *Arabic Literature in the Post-Classical Period*, ed. by R. Allen, D. Richards (Cambridge, 2006), 170; N. Abbott, "A Ninth-Century Fragment of the *'Thousand Nights'*: New Light on the Early History of the Arabian Nights," *Journal of Near Eastern Studies* 8 (1949), 129–64.
43 Reynolds, *Nights*, 271.
44 R. Irwin, *The Arabian Nights: A Companion* (New York, 2004), Ch. 5: "Street Entertainments."
45 Reynolds, *Nights*, 274.
46 J. van Steenbergen et al., "The Mamlukization of the Mamluk Sultanate? State Formation and the History of Fifteenth-Century Egypt and Syria: Part II – Comparative Solutions and a New Research Agenda," *History Compass* 14/11 (November 2016), 560–69.
47 *EI2*: al-Ṭabarī; R. S. Humphreys, *Islamic History: A Framework for Inquiry* (Princeton, 1991), 73–74.
48 Leiden: Brill, 1901; English translation: *The History of al-Tabari*, 40 volumes, ed. by E. Yarshater (Albany: SUNY, 1985–99).
49 D. Little, "Historiography," 414.
50 D. Little, "Historiography," 416–18.
51 *EI2*: Ibn al-Djawzī.
52 *EI2*: al-Yūnīnī; Guo, *Studies*, 32; L. Guo, *Early Mamluk Syrian Historiography: al-Yūnīnī's Dhayl Mirʾat al-zamān* (Leiden, 1998), 1: 81–96.
53 Guo, *Historiography*, 22–28, 208–11.
54 Guo, *Studies*, 32, n. 92; Haarmann, *Arabic*, 82, 86.
55 *EI3*: al-Dhahabī.
56 *EI3*: Ibn Kathīr, ʿImād al-Dīn.
57 *EI2*: Ibn Taymiyya.
58 Guo, *Studies,* 34, n. 100.

59 Guo, *Studies*, 35, n. 101.
60 D. Little, "Historiography," 421–22.
61 *EI2*: Ibn Faḍl Allāh al-ʿUmarī.
62 D. Little, "Historiography," 430.
63 *EI2*: al-Nuwayrī.
64 D. Little, "Historiography," 430.
65 E. Muhanna, *The World in a Book: al-Nuwayri and the Islamic Encyclopedic Tradition* (Princeton, 2018), 23–27.
66 *EI2*: al-Ḳalḳashandī.
67 *EI3*: Archives and Chanceries; *EI3*: Chancery Manuals; D. Little, "Historiography," 444.
68 D. Little, "Historiography," 423.
69 *EI3*: Baybars al-Manṣūrī.
70 *EI2*: Ibn Iyās; D. Little, "Historiography," 440; C. Petry, *The Criminal Underworld in a Medieval Islamic Society: Narratives from Cairo and Damascus under the Mamluks* (Chicago, 2012), 19.
71 D. Little, "Historiography," 440, n. 78.
72 L. Guo, "Ibn Iyās, the Poet: The Literary Profile of a Mamluk Historian," *Mamluk Historiography Revisited*, ed. by S. Conermann (Bonn, 2018), 77–90.
73 *EI2*: Ibn Ṭūlūn.
74 2 vols. (Cairo: 1962, 1964).
75 Elbendary, *Crowds*, 111; M. Toru, "Urban Society in Damascus as the Mamluk Era Was Ending," *Mamluk Studies Review* 10/1 (2006), 157–93.
76 *EI2*, *EI3*: Ibn Khaldūn, ʿAbd al-Raḥmān.
77 D. Irwin, *Unseen*, 217–24; D. Irwin, *Ibn Khaldūn: An Intellectual Biography* (Princeton, 2018), 118–42.
78 D. Little, "Historiography," 435.
79 *EI2*: al-Maḳrīzī; N. Rabbat, "Who Was al-Maqrīzī? A Biographical Sketch," *Mamluk Studies Review* 7/2 (2003), 1–19.
80 A. Broadbridge, "Academic Rivalry and the Patronage System in Fifteenth-Century Egypt: al-ʿAynī, al-Maqrīzī, and Ibn Ḥajar al-ʿAsqalānī," *Mamluk Studies Review* 3 (1999), 85–107.
81 *EI3*: Khiṭaṭ; *EI3*: Ibn Duqmāq; D. Little, "Historiography," 437; N. Rabbat, "Was al-Maqrīzī's *Khiṭaṭ* a Khaldūnian History?" *Der Islam* 89/1 (2012), 118–40.
82 F. Bauden, "Maqriziana IX: Should al-Maqrizi Be Thrown Out with the Bath Water? The Question of His Plagiarism of al-Awhadi's Khitat and the Documentary Evidence," *Mamluk Studies Review* 14 (2010), 159–232.
83 P. Walker, "Al-Maqrīzī and the Fatimids," *Mamluk Studies Review* 7/2 (2003), 83–98.
84 Petry, *Criminal*, 13, n. 16.
85 *EI3*: alʿAynī, Badr al-Dīn.
86 Broadbridge, *Rivalry*, 88.
87 D. Little, "Historiography," 437; D. Little, "An Analysis of the Relationship between Four Mamlūk Chronicles for 734–45," *Journal of Semitic Studies* 19 (1974), 259–61; D. Little, "A Comparison of al-Maqrīzī and al-ʿAynī as Historians of Contemporary Events," *Mamluk Studies Review* 7/2 (2003), 205–15.
88 Mahmud Rizq Mahmud initiated publication of the years 565/1169 to 647/1250, but to date only one volume – to 578/1182 – has appeared (Cairo, Maṭbaʿa Dar

al-Kutub, 2003). ʿAbd al-Razzaq al-Tantawi al-Qarmut edited the years 815/1412–850/1447 (2 v., Cairo: al-Zahra li'l-Iʿlam al-ʿArabi, 1985–89). Muhammad M. Amin began publication from 648/1250 but left the project unfinished at volume 4, ending with the year 707/1307 (Cairo: al-Ḥay'at al-Miṣriyya al-ʿAmma li'l-Kitāb, 1992). See K. Hirschler, *Mamluk Studies Review* 8/2, 213–15).

89 *EI2*: Ibn Ḥadjar al-ʿAsḳalānī.

90 D. Little, "Historiography," 442.

91 *EI2*: al-Sakhāwī.

92 D. Little, "Historiography," 443; C. Petry, *The Civilian Elite of Cairo in the Later Middle Ages* (Princeton, 1981), 8–10.

93 D. Little, "Historiography," 443.

94 F. Rosenthal, *A History of Muslim Historiography* (Leiden, 1952), 195.

95 EI2: al-Suyūṭī; E. Sartain, *Jalāl al-Dīn al-Suyūṭī: Biography and Background* (Cambridge, 1975).

96 *EI3*: al-Bulqīnī Family; Petry, *Civilian*, 236.

97 Al-Sakhawi, *al-Ḍaw' al-Lāmiʿ* 4: 65–70, #203.

98 *The History of al-Ṭabarī*, v. 1, ed. by F. Rosenthal (Albany: SUNY, 1989), 170; Humphreys, *Framework*, 73–74.

99 Rosenthal, *History*, 410.

100 Rosenthal, *History*, 270.

## Chapter 7

1 EGYLandscape Project, www.egylandscape.org. Association based at Marburg University dedicated to analysis of the rural environment in premodern Egypt.

2 Cairo, Institut français d'archéologie orientale.

3 Edited by Sa'd Muhammad Hasan, Taha al-Hijri; Cairo: al-Dār al-Miṣriyya li'l-Ta'lif wa'l-Tarjama, 1966.

4 Garcin, *Qūṣ*, 359–410; J.-C. Garcin, "La 'Méditerranéisation' de l'empire mamelouk sous les Sultans Bahrides," *Revista degli studii orientali* 48 (1974), 109–16.

5 "Nile Floods and the Irrigation System in Fifteenth-Century Egypt," *Mamluk Studies Review* 4 (2000), 131–45; S. Borsch, "Environment and Population: The Collapse of Large Irrigation Systems Reconsidered," *Comparative Studies in Society and History* 46/3 (July 2004), 451–68.

6 *The Black Death in Egypt and England, A Comparative Study* (Austin, 2005).

7 *Mamluk Studies Review* 8/2 (2004), 1–22.

8 *Mamluk Studies Review* 8/2, 5, n. 16; J. Rapoport, *Rural Economy and Tribal Society in Islamic Egypt: A Study of al-Nabulusi's* Villages of the Fayyum, *The Medieval Countryside*, v. 19 (Brepols, 2018); *The Villages of the Fayyum, A Thirteenth-Century Register of Rural, Islamic Egypt*, ed./transl. by Y. Rapoport, I. Shahar, *The Medieval Countryside*, v. 18 (Brepols, 2018).

9 R. S. Humphreys, *Islamic History: A Framework for Inquiry* (Princeton, 1991), 174.

10 "Irrigation in the Medieval Islamic Fayyum: Local Control in a Large-Scale Hydraulic System," *Journal of the Economic and Social History of the Orient* 55 (2012), 1–31.

11 Chicago: Middle East Documentation Center.

12 Walker, *Jordan,* 231

13 C. Petry, "Class Solidarity vs. Gender Gain: Women as Custodians of Property in Later Medieval Egypt," *Women and Middle Eastern History: Shifting Boundaries in Sex and Gender*, ed. by N. Keddie, B. Baron (Yale University Press, 1991), 122–42; C. Petry, "Conjugal Rights vs. Class Prerogatives: A Divorce Case in Mamluk Cairo," in *Women in the Medieval Dar al-Islam: Power, Patronage and Piety*, ed. by G. Hambly (St. Martin's, Press, 1997), 227–40; C. Petry, "The Estate of al-Khawand Fatima al-Khassbakiyya: Royal Spouse, Autonomous Investor," *The Mamluks in Egyptian and Syrian Politics and Society*, ed. by M. Winter, A. Levanoni (Leiden: Brill, 2004), 277–94; Y. Rapoport, *Marriage, Money and Divorce in Medieval Islamic Society* (Cambridge, 2005); Y. Rapoport, "Women and Gender in Mamluk Society: An Overview," *Mamluk Studies Review* 11/2 (2007), 1–47; D. Igarashi, T. Ito (eds.), "Women and Family in Mamluk and Early-Ottoman Egypt, Syria and Hijaz," special issue: *Orient, Journal of the Society for Near Eastern Studies in Japan* 54 (2019).

14 Rapoport, *Marriage*, 32–38.

15 Rapoport, *Marriage,* 73.

16 Cf. n. 13.

17 C. Petry, *The Criminal Underworld in a Medieval Islamic Society: Narratives from Cairo and Damascus under the Mamluks* (Chicago, 2012), 365: index; B. Martel-Thoumian, *Délinquence et order social: l'état mamlouk syro-égyptien face au crime à la fin du IX^e-XV^e siècle* (Bordeaux, 2012), 389: index; G. Leiser, *Prostitution in the Eastern Mediterranean World* (London, 2017).

18 D. Little, "Historiography of the Ayyubid and Mamluk Epochs," *The Cambridge History of Egypt*, v. 1: *Islamic Egypt*, ed. by C. Petry (Cambridge, 1998), 443.

19 *The Muslim World* 71/2 (1981), 104–24.

20 C. Petry, "Gendered Nuances in Historiographical Discourses of the Mamluk Period; Muted Praise? Veiled Trivialization? Enigmatic Transgressions?" in *Mamluk Historiography Revisited: Narratological Perspectives*, ed. by S. Conermann (Göttingen, 2018), 153–74.

21 Y. Rapoport, "Ibn Ḥajar al-ᶜAsqalānī, His Wife, Her Slave-girl," *Annales Islamologiques* 47 (2013), 327–51.

22 Rapoport, "Ibn Hajar," 342.

23 *EI3*: al-Biqāᶜī.

24 L. Guo, "Tales of a Medieval Cairene Harem: Domestic Life in al-Biqāᶜī's Autobiographical Chronicle," *Mamluk Studies Review* 9/1 (2005), 101–21; Petry, *Gendered Nuances*, 157–58.

25 Guo, *Tales*, 104–05.

26 Al-Sakhawi, *Al-Ḍaw' al-lāmiᶜ fī aᶜyān al-qarn al-tāsiᶜ* 12: 62, #377.

27 Guo, *Tales,* 120, n. 70.

28 Damascus: al-Maᶜhad al-Faransi li'l-Dirasat al-ᶜArabiyya bi-Dimashq (2000), 4 v.; S. Conermann, "Some Remarks on Ibn Ṭawq's (d. 915/1509) Journal *Al-Taᶜlīq*, v. 1 (885/1480 to 890/1485)," *Mamluk Studies Review* 11/2 (2007), 121–35; T. Wollina (2012), "A View from Within: Ibn Ṭawq's Personal Topography of 15th Century Damascus," *Bulletin d'études orientales* 61: 271–95.

29 L. Guo, review of *al-Taᶜlīq*, *Mamluk Studies Review* 12/1 (2008), 214.

30 *EI3*: ᶜĀ'isha al-Bāᶜūniyya.

31 T. Homerin, *Emanations of Grace: Mystical Poems by ʿĀʾisha al-Bāʿūnīyah* (Louisville, 2011), 14, n. 10.
32 Homerin, *Emanations*, 16; glossary, 141; bibliography, 149.
33 Homerin, *Emanations*, 64; n. 8 on Qur'an 50:38.
34 Homerin, *Emanations*, 80–82.
35 Homerin, *Emanations*, 148.
36 Ibn Iyas, *Badāʾiʿ* 4, 461.
37 Al-Jazari, *Ḥawādith* 3, 393.
38 *EI2:* Ḳibt; T. Wilfong, "The Non-Muslim Communities: Christian Communities," *The Cambridge History of Egypt*, v. 1: *Islamic Egypt*, ed. by C. Petry (Cambridge, 1998), 175–81.
39 Since 1964, the Oriental (including the Coptic rite of Alexandria) and Greek (Byzantine) Orthodox Churches have initiated a dialogue to resolve the schism that emerged in the aftermath of the Council of Chalcedon. The Coptic Church now formally declares its doctrine with regard to the nature of Christ to be miaphysite: his single nature simultaneously divine and human. This modern distinction from the term monophysite is not relevant to the stance of the Coptic clerical hierarchy during the Mamluk period.
40 G. Anawati, "The Christian Communities in Egypt in the Middle Ages," *Conversion and Continuity: Indigenous Christian Communities in Islamic Lands, Eighth to Eighteenth Centuries*, ed. by M. Gervers, R. Bikhazi (Toronto, 1990), 241.
41 T. el-Leithy, "Sufis, Copts and the Politics of Piety: Moral Regulation in Fourteenth-Century Upper Egypt," *Le développement du soufisme en Égypte à l'époque mamelouk*, ed. by R. McGregor, A. Sabra (Cairo, 2006), 75–119.
42 C. Petry, "Copts in Late Medieval Egypt," *The Coptic Encyclopedia*, ed. by A. Atiya (New York, 1991) 2: 618–35; C. Petry, *The Civilian Elite of Cairo in the Later Middle Ages* (Princeton, 1981), 272–74; D. Little, "Coptic Converts to Islam during the Baḥrī Mamluk Period," *Conversion and Continuity*, 264–88.
43 C. Petry, *Criminal Underworld*, 259–60.
44 L. Yarbrough (ed./transl.), *The Sword of Ambition: Bureaucratic Rivalry in Medieval Egypt* (New York, 2016), xx; Rapoport, *Rural Economy*, 4–5.
45 Yarbrough, *Sword*, 55–60.
46 *EI2*, *EI3*: Dhimma; P. Lewicka, "Projecting the Enemy: Non-Muslims in the Mamluk State," *Conflict and Coexistence: Proceedings of the 29th Congress of the Union Européene des Arabisants et Islamisants*, ed. by T. Bauer, M. Springberg-Hinsen (Leuven: Peeters); M. Perlmann, "Notes on Anti-Christian Propaganda in the Mamlūk Empire," *Bulletin of the School of Oriental and African Studies* 10/4 (1942), 843–61; M. Perlmann, "Asnawi's Tract against Christian Officials," *Ignaz Goldziher Memorial*, vol. 2, ed. by S. Löwinger, J. Somogii (Jerusalem, 1958), 172–208; R. Gottheil, "An Answer to the Dhimmis," *Journal of the American Oriental Society* 41 (1921), 383–457; E. Strauss, "L'Inquisition dans l'état mamlouk," *Revista degli studi orientali* 25/1 (1950), 11–26; el-Leithy, *Sufis*, 76, n. 6.
47 *Al-Nujūm al-zāhira fī mulūk Miṣr wa'l-Qāhira* (Cairo, 1970) 14: 82.
48 el-Leithy, *Sufis*, 75; N. Hofer, *The Popularization of Sufism in Ayyubid and Mamluk Egypt* (Edinburgh, 2015), 215.

49 D. Gril, "Une Émeute anti-Chrétienne à Qūṣ au début du viii$^{e}$/xiv$^{e}$ siècle, *Annales Islamologiques* 16 (Cairo: IFAO, 1980), 241–74.
50 el-Leithy, *Sufis*, 80–82.
51 N. Stillman, "The Non-Muslim Communities: The Jewish Community," *The Cambridge History of Egypt*, 1: *Islamic Egypt*, ed. by C. Petry (Cambridge, 1998), 198–210; N. Golb, "The Topography of the Jews of Medieval Egypt," *Journal of Near Eastern Studies* 24/3 (1965), 251–70.
52 S. Goitein, *A Mediterranean Society: The Jewish Communities of the Arab World as Portrayed in the Documents of the Cairo Geniza*, 5 vols. (Berkeley, 1967–88); J. Lassner, *A Mediterranean Society: An Abridgment in One Volume* (Berkeley, 1999); P. Ackerman-Lieberman, *The Business of Identity: Jews, Muslims and Economic Life in Medieval Egypt* (Stanford, 2014).
53 M. Cohen, "Jews in the Mamlūk Environment: The Crisis of 1442 (a Geniza Study)," *Bulletin of the School of Oriental and African Studies* 47/3 (1984), 425–48; "Additional Series" Taylor-Schechter collection, vols. 145–53.
54 Cohen, Jews, 446.
55 *Baḍāʾiʿ* 5, 445: 8 Jumada I 928/4 April 1522.
56 *Baḍāʾiʿ* 5, 442; Rabiʿ II 928/February–March 1522.
57 C. Ernst, *Sufism: An Introduction to the Mystical Tradition of Islam* (Boulder, 2011): on meanings of term "*ṣūf*" (woolen garment), 18–31.
58 *EI2*: Shādhiliyya; on the influence of turuq generally: B. Shoshan, *Popular Culture in Medieval Cairo* (Cambridge, 1993), 9–12.
59 *EI2*: al-Shādhilī.
60 Hofer, *Popularization*, 114.
61 Hofer, *Popularization*, 117.
62 Hofer, *Popularization*, 141
63 *EI2*: ʿAbd al-Ḳādir al-Djīlānī.
64 *EI2*: Ḳādiriyya.
65 *EI2*: Rifāʿiyya.
66 *EI2*: al-Rifāʿī.
67 *EI3*: Aḥmadiyya (Badawiyya).
68 *EI2*: Aḥmad al-Badawī.
69 J.-C. Garcin, "Les soufis dans la ville mamelouke d'Égypte; histoire du soufisme et histoire globale," *La développement du Soufisme in Égypte à l'époque mamelouke*, ed. by R. McGregor, A. Sabra (Cairo; IFAO, 2006), 11–40; Hofer, *Popularization*, introduction; R. McGregor, *Sanctity and Mysticism in Medieval Egypt; the Wafāʾ Sufi Order and the Legacy of Ibn ʿArabi* (Albany, 2004), introduction.
70 Hofer, *Popularization*, 106–9.
71 Hofer, *Popularization*, 35–38; Petry, *Civilian Elite*, 327.
72 Hofer, *Popularization*, 184–89.
73 Hofer, *Popularization*, 214, 231; Gril, *Émeute*, 241–74.
74 *EI3*: Ibn ʿAṭāʾ allāh al-Iskandarī.
75 Hofer, *Popularization*, 112–14; Shoshan, *Popular*, 13–16.
76 *EI2*: al-Shaʿrānī.
77 M. Winter, *Society and Religion in Early Ottoman Egypt: Studies in the Writings of ʿAbd al-Wahhāb al-Shaʿrānī* (New Brunswick, 1982), 46.

78 D. Behrens-Abouseif, "Craftsmen, Upstarts and Sufis in the Late Mamluk Period," *Bulletin of the School of Oriental and African Studies* 74/3 (2011), 388, n. 62.
79 Winter, *Society*, 48.
80 A. Sabra, "Illiterate Sufis and Learned Artisans: The Circle of ʿAbd al-Wahhāb al-Shaʿrānī," *La développement du Soufisme in Égypte à l'époque mamelouke*, ed. by R. McGregor, A. Sabra (Cairo; IFAO, 2006), 160.
81 Winter, *Society*, 272; Sabra, *Illiterate*, 158.
82 Winter, *Society*, 95.
83 Sabra, *Illiterate*, 159.
84 Winter, *Society*, 65, n. 87.
85 Winter, *Society*, 274, n. 44.

## Reflections

1 *Al-Taʾrīf bi-Ibn Khaldūn, Riḥlatuhu Gharban wa-Sharqan*, ed. by M. Tanji (Cairo: Lajnat al-taʾlif wa-tarjama wa-nashr, 1951), 246-47; trans. by W. Fischel, *Ibn Khaldun in Egypt, His Public Functions and His Historical Research, 1382–1406: A Study in Islamic Historiography* (Berkeley, 1967), 18, n. 12.

# Bibliography

The list of secondary studies highlights foundational works and more recent research on specific topics.

A comprehensive bibliography, updated regularly, is compiled by the Middle East Documentation Center, University of Chicago: http://mamluk.lib.uchicago.edu/.

### Primary Sources


Ibn ʿAbd al-Zahir (1976). Muhyi al-Din ʿAbdallah ibn Nashwan. *al-Rawḍ al-ẓāhir fī sīrat al-Malik al-Ẓāhir*. Riyadh: A. A. Khuwaytir; 1956 partial edition and translation: Syedah Fatima Sadeque, *Baybars I of Egypt*, Dacca.

Ibn Ataʾ Allah (1972). Muhammad ibn ʿAbd al-Karim al-Iskandari. *Laṭāʾif al-minan fī manāqib al-Shaykh Abūʾl-ʿAbbās al-Mursī wa-shaykhihi al-Shādhilī Abūʾl-Ḥasan*. Cairo: Al-Maktaba al-Saʿidiyya, min turathina al-Sufi.

Ibn al-Athir (1963). ʿIzz al-Din ʿAli. *Al-Bāhir fī taʾrīkh atābakāt al-Mawṣil*. A. A. Tulaymat, ed. Cairo: Dar al-Katib al-ʿArabi.

(1867–76). *Al-Kāmil fīʾl-taʾrīkh*. C. J. Tornberg, ed. Leiden: Brill.; 1965–67 Beirut: Dar Sadir. 13 vols.

Al-ʿAyni (2003). Badr al-Din Mahmud ibn Ahmad. *ʿIqd al-jumān fī taʾrīkh ahl al-zamān*. Cairo: Matbaʿat Dar al-Kutub; 1985–89: al-Zahra liʾl-Iʿlam al-ʿArabi; 1992: al-Hayʾa al-Misriyya al-ʿAmma liʾl-Kitab.

(2005). *ʿUmdat al-qārī fī sharḥ Ṣaḥīḥ al-Bukhārī*. Beirut: Dar al-Fikr; numerous editions.

Baybars al-Mansuri (1998). Rukn al-Din. *Zubdat al-fikra fī taʾrīkh al-hijra*. Beirut: Dar al-Nashr, al-Kitab al-ʿArabi.

Al-Biqaʿi (1992). Ibrahim ibn ʿUmar. *Iẓhār al-ʿaṣr li-asrār ahl al-ʿaṣr*. M. Salim ibn Shadid al-ʿAwfi, ed. Cairo/Jiza: Hajar liʾl-Tibaʿa waʾl-Nashr waʾl-Tawziʿ waʾl-Iʿlan.

Al-Busiri (1973). Sharaf al-Din Muhammad ibn Saʿid. *Dīwān al-Būṣīrī: al-Qaṣīda al-hamziyya fīʾl-madāʾiḥ al-nabawiyya*. Cairo: Sharika wa-Maktaba wa-Matbaʿa Mustafa al-Babi al-Halabi.

(1987). *al-Burda: al-Kawākib al-Durriyya fī madḥ khayr al-barriyya*. Cairo: al-Hayʾa al-Misriyya al-ʿAmma liʾl-Kitab.

Ibn al-Dawadari (1960–94). Abu Bakr ibn ʿAbdallah ibn Aybak. *al-Kanz al-durar wa-jāmiʿ al-ghurar*. Cairo/Beirut: Matbaʿat ʿIsa al-Babi al-Halabi/Wiesbaden: F. Steiner. 9 vols.

Al-Dhahabi (1919, 1944–45). Shams al-Din Muhammad ibn Ahmad al-Turkumani. *Kitāb duwal al-Islām fī'l-ta'rīkh.* Haydarabad al-Dakan: Matbaʿa Darat al-Maʿarif al-Nizamiyya. 2 vols. in 1.

Ibn Duqmaq (1893). Ibrahim ibn Muhammad. *Kitāb al-intiṣār li-wāsiṭat al-amṣār.* Cairo: al-Matbaʿa al-Kubra al-Amiriyya.

Ibn Hajar al-ʿAsqalani (1966). Shihab al-Din Ahmad ibn ʿAli. *al-Durar al-kāmina fī aʿyān al-miʾa al-thāmina.* Cairo: Dar al-Kutub al-Haditha. 5 vols.; several subsequent editions.

(1967). *Inbāʾ al-ghumr bi-abnāʾ al-ʿumr.* Haydarabad: Matbaʿa Majlis Daʾirat al-Maʿarif al-ʿUthmaniyya; Cairo 1969–: Lajnat Ihyaʾ al-Turath al-Islami li'l-Kitab. 4 vols.

Al-Hariri (1883). Abu Muhammad al-Qasim ibn ʿAli al-Basri. *Maqāmāt.* Cairo: Matbaʿat Bulaq, 2nd printing; numerous editions.

Al-Hilli (1883). Safi al-Din ʿAbd al-ʿAziz ibn Saraya. *Dīwān*: incl.: *al-ʿĀṭil al-ḥālī wa'l-murakhkhaṣ al-ghālī.* Damascus: Matbaʿat Habib Afandi Khalid; 1982 Cairo: Husayn Nassar, ed.

Ibn Iyas (1960–63, 1970–75). Muḥammad ibn Aḥmad. *Badāʾiʿ al-zuhūr fī waqāʾiʿ al-duhūr.* Cairo: al-Hay'a al-Misriyya al-'Amma li'l-Kitab; Wiesbaden: F. Steiner: Bibliotheca Islamica. 5 vols.; French translation: G. Wiet. *Histoire des Mamlouks Circassiens.* Cairo: Institut français d'archéologie orientale, 1945; *Journal d'un bourgeois du Caire.* 2 vols. Paris: A. Colin, 1954, 1960.

Al-Jazari (1997). Shams al-Din Muhammad. *Ḥawādith al-zamān wa-anbāʾihi wa-wafāyāt al-akābir wa'l-aʿyān min abnāʾihi.* Beirut: al-Maktaba al-ʿAsriyya.

Al-Jazzar (2006). Jamal al-Din Yahya. *Shiʿr Abī'l-Ḥusayn al-Jazzār*, incl.: *Taqṭīf al-jazzār.* Cairo: Ahmad ʿAbd al-Majid Muhammad Khalifa, ed.

Ibn Kathir (1932–39). ʿImad al-Din Ismaʿil ibn ʿUmar. *al-Bidāya wa'l-Nihāya.* Cairo: Matbaʿat al-Saʿada. 14 vols.; several subsequent editions.

Ibn Khaldun (1867–68). Abu Zayd ʿAbd al-Rahman ibn Muhammad. *Kitāb al-ʿibar wa-dīwān al-mubtadaʾ wa'l-khabar fī ayyām al-ʿarab wa'l-barbar.* Cairo: Matbaʿat Bulaq. 7 vols.; 1956–59 Beirut: Dar al-Kitab al-Lubnani. 8 vols.

(1951). *Al-Taʿrīf bi-Ibn Khaldūn, Riḥlatuhu Gharban wa-Sharqan.* M. Tanji, ed. Cairo: Lajnat al-ta'lif wa-tarjama wa-nashr; English translation: W. Fischel, *Ibn Khaldun in Egypt, His Public Functions and His Historical Research, 1382–1406: A Study in Islamic Historiography.* Berkeley, University of California Press, 1967.

Al-Maqrizi (1853–54). Taqi al-Din Ahmad ibn ʿAli. *al-Mawāʿiẓ wa'l-iʿtibār bi-dhikr al-khiṭaṭ wa'l-āthār.* Cairo/Bulaq: Dar al-Tibaʿa al-Misriyya. 2 vols.; 2002–04 Ayman Fu'ad Sayyid, ed. London: al-Furqan Islamic Heritage Foundation. 7 vols.

(1956–58). *Kitāb al-sulūk li-maʿrifa duwal al-mulūk.* Cairo: Lajnat al-Taʾlif wa'l-Tarjama wa'l-Nashr; 1970–73 al-Hay'a al-Misriyya al-ʿAmma li'l-Kitab. 4 vols./3 parts each.

Al-Misri (1998). Nasir al-Din Shafiʿ ibn ʿAli ibn Asakir. *al-Faḍl al-maʾthūr min sīrat al-sulṭān al-malik al-manṣūr.* Beirut: al-Maktaba al-ʿAsriyya.

al-Nabulusi (2019). Abu ʿAmr ʿUthman ibn Ibrahim al-Safadi. *Tajrīd sayf al-himmah li-istikhrāj mā fī dhimmat al-dhimma.* L. Yarbrough, ed. New York: New York University Press.

(1898). *Taʾrīkh al-Fayyūm wa-bilādihi.* Matbu'at al-Kutubkhana al-Khidiwiyya; al-nashra 11. B. Moritz, ed. Cairo: Publications de la Bibliothèque Khédiviale; *idem*

(1899) *Description du Fayoum au VII$^{me}$ siècle de l'Hegire par Abou 'Osman il Naboulsi il Safadi*, Cairo.

Al-Nuwayri (1923–98). Shihab al-Din Ahmad ibn ʿAbd al-Wahhab al-Tamimi. *Nihāyat al-arab fī funūn al-adab.* Cairo: al-Mu'assasa al-Misriyya al-ʿAmma li'l-Ta'lif wa'l-Tarjama wa'l-Tibaʿa wa'l-Nashr, Maktaba al-ʿArabiya; Dar al-Kutub al-Misriyya. 33 vols.

Al-Qalqashandi (1913–19). Shihab al-Din Ahmad ibn ʿAli. *Ṣubḥ al-aʿshá fī ṣināʿat al-inshāʾ*. Cairo: al-Matbaʿa al-Amiriyya, Dar al-Kutub al-Khidiwiyya. 14 vols.

Al-Safadi (1931–2010). Salah al-Din Khalil ibn Aybak, *al-Wāfī bi'l-wafāyāt*; Leipzig: Deutche Morgenländische Gesellschaft; Wiesbaden: Bibliotheca Islamica; Beirut: al-Nashara al-Islamiyya. 32 vols.

Al-Sakhawi (1934–36). Muhammad ibn ʿAbd al-Rahman. *Al-Ḍawʾ al-lāmiʿ li-ahl al-qarn al-tāsiʿ*. Cairo: Maktabat al-Qudsi. 12 vols.; several subsequent editions.

(1992). *al-Dhayl al-tāmm ʿalá duwal al-Islām li'l-Dhahabī*. Kuwait: Maktabat Dar al-ʿUruba; Beirut: Dar Ibn al-ʿImad.

(1986). *al-Jawāhir wa'l-durar fī tarjamat Shaykh al-Islām Ibn Ḥajar*. Cairo: Wizarat al-Awqaf, al-Majlis al-Aʿla li'l-Shu'un al-Islamiyya, Lajnat Ihya' al-Turath al-Islami.

(1979). *al-Iʿlān bi-tawbīkh li-man dhamma ahl al-taʾrīkh*. Beirut: Salih Ahmad al-ʿAli; English translation: F. Rosenthal (1968). *A History of Muslim Historiography*. 2nd ed. Leiden: Brill, 263–529.

(2002–07). *Al-Tibr al-masbūk fī dhayl al-Sulūk*. Cairo: Matbaʿa Dar al-Kutub wa'l-Watha'iq al-Qawmiya, Markaz Tahqiq al-Turath.

Al-Sayrafi (1970). ʿAli ibn Da'ud al-Jawhari. *Inbāʾ al-ḥaṣr bi-abnāʾ al-ʿaṣr*. Cairo: Dar al-Fikr al-ʿArabi.

(1970–73, –94). *Nuzhat al-nufūs wa'l-abdān fī tawārīkh al-zamān*. Cairo: Wizarat al-Thaqafa, Markaz Tahqiq al-Turath. 4 vols.

Al-Shabb al-Zarif (1967). Shams al-Din Muhammad ibn ʿAfif al-Tilimsani. *Dīwān al-Shābb al-Ẓarīf*. al-Najaf: Matbaʿat al-Najaf.

Al-Shaʿrani (1977). ʿAbd al-Wahhab ibn Ahmad. *al-Akhlāq al-matbūliyya al-mazʿūma li'l-Shaʿrānī*. Muhammad ʿAbd Allah Samman, ed. Cairo: Dar Harra'.

Sibt ibn al-Jawzi (1907). Abu'l-Muzaffar Yusuf ibn Qizughlu. *Mirʾat al-zamān fī taʾrīkh al-aʿyān*. J. R. Jewett, ed. Chicago: University of Chicago Press; several subsequent editions.

Ibn Sudun (1998). ʿAli al-Bashbughawi. *Nuzhat al-nufūs wa-mudḥik al-ʿabūs*. Leiden: Brill.

Al-Suyuti (1967–68). Jalal al-Din ʿAbd al-Rahman ibn Abu Bakr. *Huṣn al-muḥādara fī akhbār Miṣr wa'l-Qāhira*. Cairo: Matbaʿat Idarat al-Watan. 2 vols.

(1894). *al-Shamārīkh fī ʿilm al-taʾrīkh*. Leiden: Brill.

(1976). *Taʾrīkh al-khulafāʾ*. Cairo: Dar Nahda Misr.

Al-Tabari (1901). Abu Jaʿfar Muhammad ibn Jarir. *Taʾrīkh al-rusul wa'l-mulūk*. M. J. de Goeje, ed. Leiden: Brill. 12 vols.; several subsequent editions; (1985–1999) English translation: *The History of al-Tabari*. E. Yarshater, ed. Albany: State University of New York Press. 40 vols.

Ibn Taghri Birdi (1929–52, 1970–72). Abu'l-Mahasin Yusuf. *Al-Nujūm al-zāhira fī mulūk Miṣr wa'l-Qāhira*. Cairo: Dar al-Kutub, al-Hay'a al-Misriyya al-ʿAmma li'l-Taʿrif wa'l-Nashr. 16 vols.; partial English translation: W. Popper. *History of*

*Egypt, 1382–1469 A.D, translated from the Arabic annals of Abu'l-Mahasin ibn Taghri Birdi.* Berkeley: University of California Press, 1954–63: University of California publications in Semitic Philology: vols. 13–14, 17–19, 22–24.

(1930–42). *Ḥawādith al-duhūr fī madá al-ayyām wa'l-shuhūr.* University of California Publications in Semitic Philology. Berkeley: University of California Press, vols. 8/1–4, W. Popper, ed.; (1990–) Beirut: Alam al-Kutub, Muhammad Kamal al-Din ʿIzz al-Din, ed.; (1990) Cairo: Jumhuriyat Misr al-ʿArabiyya, Muhammad Shaltut, ed.

(1932). *al-Manhal al-ṣāfī wa'l-mustawfī ba'd al-wāfī*; resumé edition by G. Wiet. *Les Biographies du Manhal Safi, Mémoires présentés à l'Institut d'Égypte.* Cairo, t. 19; (1984–) Arabic edition ongoing: Cairo: al-Hay'a al-Misriyya al-'Amma li'l-Kitab.

Ibn Tawq (2000). Shihab al-Din Ahmad. *Al-Ta'līq: Yawmīyāt shihāb al-dīn ahmad ibn ṭawq* (Commentary: The Diary of Shihab al-Din Ibn Tawq). Damascus: al-Maʿhad al-Faransi li'l-Dirasat al-ʿArabiyya bi-Dimashq. 4 vols.

Ibn Tulun (1962–64). Shams al-Din Muhammad ibn 'Ali. *Mufākahat al-khillān fī ḥawādith al-zamān.* Cairo: al-Mu'assasa al-Misriyya al-ʿAmma li'l-Ta'lif wa'l-Tarjama wa'l-Tibaʿa wa'l-Nashr. 2 vols.

Al-Udfuwi (1966). Kamal al-din Jaʿfar. *al-Ṭāliʿ al-sa'īd al-jāmiʿ li-asmā' al-fuḍalā' wa'l-ruwāt bi-a'lá al-ṣa'īd.* Cairo: al-Dar al-Misriyya li'l-Ta'lif wa'l-Tarjama. Sa'd Muhammad Hasan, Taha al-Hijri, eds.

Al-Umari (1988–89). Shihab al-Din Ahmad ibn Yahya al-Qurashi, Ibn Fadl Allah. *Masālik al-abṣār fī mamālik al-amṣār.* Frankfurt: Maʿhad Ta'rikh al-ʿUlum al-'Arabiyya wa'l-Islamiyya fi Itar Jamiʿat Frankfurt. 27 vols.; numerous editions.

(1894). Ibn Fadl Allah. *al-Ta'rīf bi'l-muṣṭalaḥ al-sharīf.* Cairo: Matbaʿat al-ʿAsima.

Al-Yunini (1954–61). Qutb al-Din Abu'l-Fath Musa. *Dhayl mir'at al-zamān fī ta'rīkh al-a'yān.* Hyderabad; (1998) Leiden: Brill. L. Guo, ed. 2 vols.

## Studies

Abbott, Nabia (1949). "A Ninth-Century Fragment of the '*Thousand Nights*': New Light on the Early History of the Arabian Nights." *Journal of Near Eastern Studies* 8: 129–64.

'Abd ar-Raziq, Ahmad (1970). "Un document concernant le marriage des esclaves au temps des Mamluks." *Journal of the Economic and Social History of the Orient* 13: 309–14.

(1973). *La femme au temps des mamlouks en Égypte.* Cairo: Institut français d'archéologie orientale.

(1977). "Le *ḥisba* et le *muḥtasib* en Égypte au temps des Mamluks." *Annales Islamologiques* 13: 115–78.

Abdelhamid, Tareq Gamal; El-Toudy, Heba, eds. (2017). *Selections from Subh al-A'shā by al-Qalqashandi, Clerk of the Mamluk Court: Egypt: "Seats of Government" and "Regulations of the Kingdom," From Early Islam to the Mamluks.* London: Routledge.

Abou El Fadl, Khaled (2001). *Rebellion and Violence in Islamic Law.* Cambridge: Cambridge University Press.

Abu-Ghazi, 'Imad Badr al-Din (2000). *Fī ta'rīkh Miṣr al-ijtimā'ī: Taṭawwur al-ḥiẓāya al-zirā'iyya fī Miṣr zamān al-Mamālīk al-Jarākisa*. Cairo: 'Ayn li'l-Dirasat wa'l-Buhuth al-Insaniyya wa'l-Ijtima'iyya.

Abu-Lughod, Janet (1971). *Cairo: 1001 Years of the City Victorious*. Princeton: Princeton University Press.

(1989). *Before European Hegemony: The World System A.D. 1250–1350*. Oxford: Oxford University Press.

Ackerman-Lieberman, Phillip (2014). *The Business of Identity: Jews, Muslims and Economic Life in Medieval Egypt*. Stanford: Stanford University Press.

Agoston, Gabor (2005). *Guns for the Sultan: Military Power and the Weapons Industry in the Ottoman Empire*. Cambridge: Cambridge University Press.

Aigle, Denise (2004). "Loi mongole vs. loi islamique: Entre mythe et réalité." *Annales: Histoire, Sciences Sociales* 59/5–6: 971–96.

(2006). "La légitimité islamique des invasions de la Syrie par Ghāzān Khān." *Eurasian Studies* 5/1–2: 5–29.

Alhamzah, Khaled (2009). *Late Mamluk Patronage: Qānṣūh al-Ghūrī's Waqfs and His Foundations in Cairo*. Boca Raton: Universal Publishers.

Allouch, Adel (1994). *Mamluk Economics: A Study and Translation of al-Maqrīzī's Ighāthah*. Salt Lake City: University of Utah Press.

Amin, M. Muhammad (1980). *Al-Awqāf wa'l-ḥayāt al-ijtimā'iyya fī Miṣr, 648–92/ 1250–1517*. Cairo: Dar al-nahdat al-'arabiyya.

(1981). *Catalogue des documents d'Archives du Caire de 239/853 à 922/1516 (depuis le IIIᵉ/IXᵉ siècle jusqu'à la fin de l'époque mamlouke)*. Cairo: Institut français d'archéologie orientale.

Amitai, Reuven (1987). "Mongol Raids into Palestine (A.D. 1260 and 1300)." *Journal of the Royal Asiatic Society of Great Britain & Ireland* 119/2: 236–55.

(1988). "Mamluk Espionage among Mongols and Franks." *Asian and African Studies* 22: 173–81.

(1990). "The Remaking of the Military Elite of Mamlūk Egypt by al-Nāṣir Muḥammad Ibn Qalāwūn." *Studia Islamica* 72: 145–63.

Amitai-Preis, Reuven (1992a). "'Ayn Jalut Revisited." *Ta'rih* 2: 119–50.

(1992b). "Mamluk Perceptions of the Mongol-Frankish Rapprochement." *Mediterranean Historical Review* 7: 50–65.

(1994). "An Exchange of Letters in Arabic between Abaγa Ilkhan and Sultan Baybars (A.H. 667 / A.D. 1268–9)." *Central Asiatic Journal* 38: 11–33.

(1995). *Mongols and Mamluks: The Mamlūk-Īlkhānid War, 1260–1281*. Cambridge: Cambridge University Press, 1995.

(1996). "Ghazan, Islam and Mongol Tradition: A View from the Mamluk Sultanate." *Bulletin of the School of Oriental and African Studies* 59: 1–10.

(1997). "The Mamluk Officer Class during the Reign of Sultan Baybars." *War and Society in the Eastern Mediterranean, 7th–15th Centuries*. Y. Lev, ed. Leiden: Brill: 267–300.

(1999). "Mongol Imperial Ideology and the Ilkhanid War against the Mamluks." *Empire and Its Legacy*. R. Amitai-Price, D. O. Morgan, eds. Leiden: Brill: 57–72.

(1999b). "Northern Syria between the Mongols and Mamluks: Political Boundary, Military Frontier and Ethnic Affinity." *Frontiers in Question: Eurasian*

*Borderlands c. 700–1700*. N. Standen, D. Power, eds. London: Macmillan Press: 128–52.

(2001a). "Al-Nuwayrī as a Historian of the Mongols." *The Historiography of Islamic Egypt (c. 950–1800)*. H. Kennedy, ed. Leiden: Brill: 23–36.

(2001b). "Turco-Mongolian Nomads and the iqṭāʿ System in the Islamic Middle East (1000–1400 AD)." *Nomads in the Sedentary World*. A. Wink, A. M. Khazanov, eds. London: Curzon Press: 152–71.

(2002). "Whither the Ilkhanid Army? Ghazan's First Campaign into Syria (1299–1300)." *Warfare in Inner Asian History*. N. Di Cosmo, ed. Leiden: Brill: 221–64.

(2003a). "Al-Maqrizi as a Historian of the Early Mamluk Sultanate (or: Is al-Maqrizi an Unrecognized Historiographical Villain?)." *Mamluk Studies Review* 7/2: 99–118.

(2003b). "Foot Soldiers, Militiamen and Volunteers in the Early Mamluk Army." *Texts, Documents and Artifacts: Islamic Studies in Honour of D.S. Richards*. C. F. Robinson, ed. Leiden: Brill: 232–49.

(2004). "The Mongol Occupation of Damascus in 1300: A Study of Mamluk Loyalties." *The Mamluks in Egyptian and Syrian Politics and Society*. A. Levanoni, M. Winter, eds. Leiden: Brill: 21–41.

(2005a). "The Conquest of Arsūf by Baybars: Political and Military Aspects." *Mamluk Studies Review* 9: 61–83.

(2005b). "The Resolution of the Mongol-Mamluk War." *Mongols, Turks, and Others: Eurasian Nomads and the Sedentary World*. R. Amitai, M. Biran, eds. Leiden: Brill: 359–90.

(2005c). "Some Remarks on the Inscription of Baybars at Maqam Nabi Musa." *Mamluks and Ottomans: Studies in Honour of Michael Winter*. D. J. Wasserstein, A. Ayalon, eds. London and New York: Routledge: 45–53.

(2006). "Some More Thoughts on the Logistics of the Mongol–Mamluk War (with Special Reference to the Battle of Wadi al-Khaznadar)." *Logistics of War in the Age of the Crusades*. J. Pryor, ed. Aldershot: Ashgate: 25–42.

(2007a). "An Arabic Biographical Notice of Kitbughā, the Mongol General Defeated at 'Ayn Jālūt." *Jerusalem Studies in Arabic and Islam* 33: 219–34.

(2007b). *The Mongols in the Islamic Lands: Studies in the History of the Ilkhanate*. Aldershot, UK, and Burlington, VT: Ashgate.

(2008a). "Mamlūks of Mongol Origin and Their Role in Early Mamlūk Political Life." *Mamluk Studies Review* 12/1: 119–38.

(2008b). "Diplomacy and the Slave Trade in the Eastern Mediterranean: A Re-examination of the Mamluk–Byzantine–Genoese Triangle in the Late Thirteenth Century in Light of the Existing Early Correspondence." *Oriente Moderno* 88/2: 348–68.

(2010). "Armies and Their Economic Basis in Iran and the Surrounding Lands, ca. 1000–1500 C.E." *The New Cambridge History of Islam*, vol. 3: *The Eastern Islamic World Eleventh to Eighteenth Centuries*. D. O. Morgan, A. Reid, eds. Cambridge: Cambridge University Press: 539–60.

(2011a). "Dealing with Reality: Early Mamluk Military Policy and the Allocation of Resources." *Crossroads between Latin Europe and the Near East: Frankish*

*Presence in the Eastern Mediterranean (12th to 14th Centuries)*. S. Leder, ed. Würzburg: Ergon Verlag: 127–44.

(2011b). "Im Westen nichts Neues? Re-examining Hülegü's Offensive into the Jazīra and Northern Syria in Light of Recent Research." *Historicizing the "Beyond": The Mongolian Invasion as a New Dimension of Violence?* F. Krämer, K.Schmidt, J. Sinder, eds. Heidelberg: Universität Verlag Winter Heidelberg: 83–96.

(2013a). *Holy War and Rapprochement: Studies in the Relations between the Mamluk Sultanate and the Mongol Ilkhanate (1260–1335)*. Turnhout: Brepols.

(2013b). "Mamluks, Franks and Mongols: A Necessary but Impossible Triangle." *Ferdowsi, the Mongols and the History of Iran: Art, Literature and Culture from Early Islam to Qajar Persia*. R. Hillenbrand, F. Abdullaeva, A. Peacock, eds. London: I.B. Tauris: 137–46.

(2013c). "Rashīd al-Dīn as an Historian of the Mamluks." *Rashid al-Din, Agent and Mediator of Cultural Exchanges in Ilkhanid Iran*." A. Akasoy, C. Burnett, R. Yoeli-Tlalim, eds. London and Turin: The Warburg Institute and Nino Aragno Editore: 71–88.

(2014). "Dangerous Liaisons: Armenian–Mongol–Mamluk Relations (1260–1292)." *La Méditerranée des Arméniens, XII^e–XV^e siècle*. G. Dédéyan, C. Mutafian, eds. Paris: Geuthner: 191–206.

(2015a). "Ibn Khaldūn on the Mongols and Their Military Might." *Nomad Military Power in Iran and Adjacent Areas in the Islamic Period*. F. Kurt, W. Holzwarth, eds. Wiesbaden: Reichert Verlag, 193–208.

(2015b). "The Impact of the Mongols on the History of Syria: Politics, Society and Culture." *Eurasian Nomads as Agents of Cultural Change*. Perspectives on the Global Past. R. Amitai, M. Biran, eds. Honolulu: University of Hawai'i Press: 228–51.

Anawati, Georges (1990). "The Christian Communities in Egypt in the Middle Ages." *Conversion and Continuity: Indigenous Christian Communities in Islamic Lands, Eighth to Eighteenth Centuries*. M. Gervers, R. Bikhazi, eds. Toronto: Pontifical Institute of Mediaeval Studies: 237–51.

Ankawi, Abdullah (1974). "The Pilgrimage to Mecca in Mamluk Times" *Arabian Studies* 1: 146–70.

Apellaniz Ruiz de Galaretta, Francisco (2009). *Pouvoir et finance en Méditerranée pré-moderne: Le deuxième État mamelouk et le commerce des épices (1382–1517)*. Barcelona: Consejo Superior de Investigiones Cientificas.

Arbel, Benjamin (1993). "Slave Trade and Slave Labor in Frankish Cyprus." *Studies in Medieval and Renaissance History* 14: 151–90.

(1995). *Trading Nations: Jews and Venetians in the Early Modern Eastern Mediterranean*, Leiden: Brill.

(2000). *Cyprus, the Franks and Venice (13th–16th Centuries)*. London: Ashgate (Variorum Collected Studies Series CS 688).

(2017). *Studies on Venetian Cyprus*. Nicosia: Cyprus Research Centre.

Ashtor, Eliyahu (1956). "The Kārimī Merchants." *Journal of the Royal Asiatic Society* 88: 45–56.

(1969). *Histoire des prix et des salaires dans l'orient médiévale*. Paris: S.E.V.P.E.N.

(1970). "Quelques observations d'un Orientaliste sur la thèse de Pirenne." *Journal of the Economic and Social History of the Orient* 13: 166–94.

(1971). *Les Métaux précieux et la balance de payements du Proche-Orient à la basse époque*. Paris: S.E.V.P.E.N.

(1975a). "Profits from Trade with the Levant in the Fifteenth Century." *Bulletin of the School of Oriental and African Studies* 38: 250–75.

(1975b). "The Volume of Levantine Trade in the Later Middle Ages, 1370–1498." *Journal of European Economic History* 4: 573–612.

(1976a). *A Social and Economic History of the Near East in the Middle Ages*. Berkeley: University of California Press.

(1976b). "Spice Prices in the Near East in the 15th Century." *Journal of the Royal Asiatic Society:* 26–41.

(1977). "The Levantine Sugar Industry in the Later Middle Ages – An Example of Technological Decline." *Israel Oriental Studies* 7: 226–80.

(1983). *Levant Trade in the Later Middle Ages*. Princeton: Princeton University Press.

(1984). "The Wheat Supply of the Mamluk Kingdom." *Asian and African Studies* 18: 283–95.

ʿAshur, ʿAbd al-Fattah (1962). *al-Mujtamaʿ al-miṣrī fī ʿaṣr salāṭīn al-mamālīk*. Cairo: Dar al-Nahda al-ʿArabiyya.

(1965). *ʿAṣr al-mamālīk fī miṣr wa'l-shām*. Cairo: Dar al-Nahda al-ʿArabiyya.

Assef, Qais (2012). "Le Soufisme et les soufis selon Ibn Taymiyya." *Bulletin d'études orientales* 60: 91–121.

Atil, Esin (1981). *Renaissance of Islam: Art of the Mamluks*. Washington, DC: Smithsonian Institution Press.

Atiya, Aziz S. (1938a). *The Crusade in the Later Middle Ages*. London, Methuen.

(1938b). *Egypt and Aragon: Embassies and Diplomatic Correspondence between 1300 and 1330 A.D.* Leipzig: F.A. Brockhaus.

(1955). *The Arabic Manuscripts of Mount Sinai: A Hand-List of the Arabic Manuscripts and Scrolls Microfilmed at the Library of the Monastery of St. Catherine, Mount Sinai*. Baltimore: Johns Hopkins University Press.

(1962a). *Crusade, Commerce, and Culture*. Bloomington: Indiana University Press.

(1962b). *The Crusade: Historiography and Bibliography*. Bloomington: Indiana University Press.

Atiyeh, George, ed. (1995). *The Book in the Islamic World: The Written Word and Communication in the Middle East*. Albany: State University of New York Press.

Awad, Muhammad (1940). "Sultan al-Ghawri: His Place in Literature and Learning (Three Books Written under His Patronage)." *Actes du XX^e Congrès international des orientalists, Bruxelles, 5–10 September 1938*. Louvain: 321–22.

Ayalon, David (1946). "The Plague and its Effects upon the Mamluk Army." *Journal of the Royal Asiatic Society*, 67–73.

(1949). "The Circassians in the Mamluk Kingdom." *Journal of the American Oriental Society* 69/3: 135–47.

(1951a). "L'esclavage du Mamelouk." *Oriental Notes and Studies (Jerusalem)* 1: 1–4.

(1951b). "The Wafidiya in the Mamluk Kingdom." *Islamic Culture* (Hyderabad): 81–104.

(1953–54). "Studies on the Structure of the Mamlūk Army." *Bulletin of the School of Oriental and African Studies* – I: "The Army Stationed in Egypt." 15/2: 203–28;

II: "The Ḥalqa." 15/3: 448–76; III: "Holders of Offices Connected with the Army." 16/1: 57–90.
(1956). *Gunpowder and Firearms in the Mamlūk Kingdom*. London: Frank Cass.
(1958). "The System of Payment in Mamluk Military Society." *Journal of the Economic and Social History of the Orient* 1/1: 37–65; 1/3: 257–96.
(1960). "Studies on the Transfer of the Abbasid Caliphate from Baghdad to Cairo." *Arabica* 7:41–59.
(1961). "Notes on the Furūsiyya Exercises and Games in the Mamlūk Sultanate." *Scripta Hierosolymitana* 9: 31–62.
(1967). "The Mamluks and Naval Power: A Phase of the Struggle between Islam and Christian Europe." *Proceedings of the Israel Academy of Sciences and the Humanities* 1/8: 1–12.
(1968). "The Muslim City and the Mamluk Military Aristocracy." *Proceedings of the Israel Academy of Sciences and Humanities* 2/14: 311–29.
(1971–73). "The Great Yasa of Chingiz Khān: A Reexamination." *Studia Islamica* 33: Part A: 97–140; 34: Part B: 151–80; 36: Part C1: 113–58; 38: Part C2: 107–56.
(1972). "Discharges from Service, Banishments and Imprisonments in Mamlūk Society." *Israel Oriental Studies* 2: 25–50.
(1975a). "Names, Titles and 'Nisbas' of the Mamlūks." *Israel Oriental Studies* 5: 189–232.
(1975b). "Preliminary Remarks on the Mamluk Military Institution in Islam." *War, Technology and Society in the Middle East*. V. J. Parry, M. E. Yapp, eds. London: 44–58.
(1976–77). "Aspects of the Mamlūk Phenomenon I: The Importance of the Mamlūk Institution." *Der Islam* 53/2: 196–225; "II: Ayyūbids, Kurds and Turks." *Der Islam* 54/1: 1–32.
(1979). "On the Eunuchs in Islam." *Jerusalem Studies in Arabic and Islam* 1: 67–124.
(1980). "Mamlūkiyyāt: (A) A First Attempt to Evaluate the Mamlūk Military System; (B) Ibn Khaldūn's View of the Mamlūk Phenomenon." *Jerusalem Studies in Arabic and Islam* 2: 321–49.
(1981). "From Ayyubids to Mamlūks." *Revue des études islamiques* 49/1: 43–57.
(1985). "On the Term Khādim in the Sense of 'Eunuch' in the Early Muslim Sources." *Arabica* 32: 289–308.
(1987). "Mamlūk Military Aristocracy: A Non-Hereditary Nobility." *Jerusalem Studies in Arabic and Islam* 10: 205–10.
(1988). "The Auxiliary Forces of the Mamlūk Sultanate." *Der Islam* 65: 13–37.
(1993). "Some Remarks on the Economic Decline of the Mamlūk Sultanate." *Scripta Hierosolymitana: Studies in Islamic History and Civilization* 9: 31–62.
(1999). *Eunuchs, Caliphs, and Sultans: A Study in Power Relationships*. Jerusalem: Magnes Press, Hebrew University.
Al-Azmeh, Aziz (1997). *Muslim Kingship, Power and the Sacred in Muslim, Christian and Pagan Politics*. London: I. B. Tauris.
Bacharach, Jere (1973). "The Dīnār versus the Ducat." *International Journal of Middle East Studies* 4/1: 77–96.
(1976). "Circassian Monetary Policy: Copper." *Journal of the Economic and Social History of the Orient* 19/1: 32–47.

Bacqué-Grammont, Jean-Louis; Kroell, Anne, eds. (1988). *Mamlouks, Ottomans et Portugais en Mer Rouge: l'affaire de Djedda en 1517*. Cairo: Institut français d'archéologie orientale.

Badawi, Mustafa (1992). "Medieval Arabic Drama: Ibn Dāniyāl." *Three Shadow Plays by Muḥammad ibn Dāniyāl*. P. Kahle, ed. Cambridge: Gibb Memorial Trust: 6–30.

Bakhit, Muhammad (1982). *The Ottoman Province of Damascus in the Sixteenth Century*. Beirut: Librairie du Liban.

Balog, Paul (1964). "The Coinage of the Mamluk Sultans of Egypt and Syria." *Numismatic Studies* 12, New York.

Banister, Mustafa (2014–15). "'Naught Remains to the Caliph but His Title': Revisiting Abbasid Authority in Mamlūk Cairo." *Mamluk Studies Review* 18: 219–45.

(2021). *The Abbasid Caliphate of Cairo, 1261–1517: Out of the Shadows*. Edinburgh: Edinburgh University Press.

Barker, Hannah (2015). "Reconnecting with the Homeland: Black Sea Slaves in Mamluk Biographical Dictionaries." *Medieval Prosopography* 30: 87–104.

(2016). "Purchasing a Slave in Fourteenth-Century Cairo: Ibn al-Akfānī's Book of Observation and Inspection in the Examination of Slaves." *Mamluk Studies Review* 19: 1–24.

(2019). *That Most Precious Merchandise: The Mediterranean Trade in Black Sea Slaves, 1260–1500*. Philadelphia: University of Pennsylvania Press.

Bauden, Frédéric (2003). "Maqriziana I: Discovery of an Autograph Manuscript of al-Maqrīzī: Towards a Better Understanding of his Working Method, Description, Section 1." *Mamluk Studies Review* 7/2: 21–68; (2008). "Maqriziana II: Analysis." *Mamluk Studies Review* 12/1: 51–118.

(2004). "The Recovery of Mamluk Chancery Documents in an Unexpected Place." *The Mamluks in Egyptian and Syrian Politics and Society*. M. Winter, A. Levanoni, eds. Leiden: Brill: 59–76.

(2009). "The Sons of al-Nāṣir Muḥammad and the Politics of Puppets: Where Did It All Start?" *Mamluk Studies Review* 13/1: 58–81.

(2010). "Maqriziana IX: Should al-Maqrīzī be Thrown Out with the Bath Water? The Question of His Plagiarism of al-Awhaḍī's Khiṭaṭ and the Documentary Evidence." *Mamluk Studies Review* 14: 159–232.

"The Qalāwūnids: A Genealogical Database." http://mamluk.uchicago,edu/qalawunids.

Bauden, Frédéric; Dekkiche, Malika, eds. (2019). *Mamluk Cairo: a Crossroads for Embassies: Studies on Diplomacy and Diplomatics*. Leiden: Brill.

Bauer, Thomas (2003a). "Communication and Emotion: The Case of Ibn Nubātah's Kindertotenlieder." *Mamluk Studies Review* 7/1: 49–95.

(2003b). "Literarische Anthologien der Mamlūkenzeit." *Die Mamlūken: Studien zu ihrer Geschichte und Kultur, Zum Gedenken an Ulrich Haarmann (1942–1999)*. S. Conermann, A. Pistor-Hatam, eds. Hamburg: EB-Verlag: 71–122.

Bauer, Thomas; Neuwirth, Angelika, eds. (2005). *Ghazal as World Literature I: Transformations of a Literary Genre*. Beiruter Texte und Studien 89. Beirut: Orient-Institut.

(2005). "Mamluk Literature: Misunderstandings and New Approaches." *Mamlūk Studies Review* 9/2: 105–32.

(2007). "In Search of 'Post-Classical Literature'. A Review Article." *Mamlūk Studies Review* 11/2: 137–67.
(2008). "Ibn Nubātah al-Miṣrī (686–768/1287–1366): Life and Works. Part 1: The Life of Ibn Nubātah." *Mamluk Studies Review* 12/1: 1–35; "Ibn Nubātah al-Miṣrī (686–768/1287–1366): Life and Works. Part 2: The Dīwān of Ibn Nubātah." *Mamlūk Studies Review* 12/2: 25–69.
(2009). "Jamāl al-Dīn Ibn Nubātah." *Essays in Arabic Literary Biography*. J. E. Lowry, D. J. Stewart, eds. Wiesbaden: Harrassowitz: 184–202.
(2011). *Die Kultur der Ambiguität. Eine andere Geschichte des Islams*. Berlin: Verlag der Religionen im Insel Verlag.
(2013a). "Ayna hādhā min al-Mutanabbī!" Toward an Aesthetics of Mamluk Literature." *Mamluk Studies Review* 17: 5–22.
(2013b). "Mamluk Literature as a Means of Communication." *Ubi sumus? Quo vademus? Mamluk Studies – State of the Art*. S. Conermann, ed. Göttingen: V&R unipress: 23–56.
(2014). "Dignity at Stake: Mujūn Epigrams by Ibn Nubāta and His Contemporaries." *The Rude, the Bad and the Bawdy: Essays in Honour of Professor Geert Jan van Gelder*. A. Talib, M. Hammond, A. Schippers, eds. Cambridge: The E. J. W. Gibb Memorial Trust: 160–85.
Beaumont, Daniel (2004). "Political Violence and Ideology in Mamlūk Society." *Mamluk Studies Review* 8/1: 201–25.
Behrens-Abouseif, Doris (1981). "The North-Eastern Extension of Cairo under the Mamluks." *Annales Islamologiques* 17: 157–89.
(1984). *Egypt's Adjustment to Ottoman Rule: Institutions, Waqf and Architecture in Cairo (16th and 17th Centuries)*. Leiden: Brill.
(1985a). *Azbakiyya and Its Environs from Azbak to Ismā'īl, 1476–1879*. Cairo: Institut français d'archéologie orientale.
(1985b). "Change in Function and Form of Mamluk Religious Institutions." *Annales Islamologiques* 21: 73–93.
(1989). *The Islamic Architecture of Cairo: An Introduction*. Leiden, 1989: 135–38.
(1995). "Al-Nāṣir Muḥammad and al-Ashraf Qāytbāy – Patrons of Urbanism." *Egypt and Syria in the Fatimid, Ayyubid and Mamluk Eras*. III, Proceedings of the 1st, 2nd, and 3rd International Colloquium organized at the Katholieke Universiteit Leuven in May 1992, 1993, and 1994. U. Vermeulen, D. De Smets, eds. OLA 73. Leuven: Peeters: 276–84.
(1998). "Qāytbāy's Investments in the City of Cairo: Waqf and Power." *Annales Islamologiques* 32: 29–40.
(2002). "Sultan al-Ghawrī and the Arts." *Mamluk Studies Review* 6: 71–94.
(2007). *Cairo of the Mamluks: A History of the Architecture and Its Culture*. Cairo: American University in Cairo Press.
(2011). "Craftsmen, Upstarts and Sufis in the Late Mamluk Period." *Bulletin of the School of Oriental and African Studies* 74/3: 375–95.
Berkel, Maaike van (1997). "The Attitude towards Knowledge in Mamluk Egypt: Organization and Structure of the Ṣubḥ al-aʿshá by al-Qalqashandī (1355–1418)." *Pre-Modern Encyclopaedic Texts*. P. Binkley, ed. Leiden: Brill: 159–68.

(2011). "Embezzlement and Reimbursement: Disciplining Officials in ʿAbbasid Baghdad, 8th–10th Centuries A.D." *International Journal of Public Administration* 34: 712–19.

Berkel, Maaike van; Duindam, Jeroen, eds. (2018). *Prince, Pen and Sword: Eurasian Perspectives*. Rulers and Elites 15. Leiden: Brill.

Berkey, Jonathan (1991). "'Silver Threads among the Coal': A Well-Educated Mamluk of the Ninth/Fifteenth Century." *Studia Islamica* 73: 109–25.

(1992). *The Transmission of Knowledge in Medieval Cairo*. Princeton: Princeton University Press.

(1995). "Tradition, Innovation and the Social Construction of Knowledge in the Medieval Islamic Near East." *Past and Present* 146: 38–65.

(1998). "Culture and Society during the Late Middle Ages." *The Cambridge History of Egypt,* vol. 1: *Islamic Egypt*. C. Petry, ed. Cambridge: Cambridge University Press: 375–411.

(2000). "Storytelling, Preaching and Power in Mamluk Cairo." *Mamluk Studies Review* 4: 53–73.

(2001). *Popular Preaching and Religious Authority in the Medieval Islamic Near East*. Seattle: University of Washington Press.

(2003). *The Formation of Islam: Religion and Society in the Near East, 600–1800*. Cambridge: Cambridge University Press.

(2004). "The Muḥtasibs of Cairo under the Mamluks, toward an Understanding of an Islamic Institution." *The Mamluks in Egyptian and Syrian Politics and Society*. M. Winter, A. Levanoni, eds. Leiden: Brill: 245–76.

(2005). "Popular Culture under the Mamluks: A Historiographical Survey." *Mamluk Studies Review* 9: 133–46.

(2009). "Mamlūk Religious Policy." *Mamluk Studies Review* 13/2: 7–22.

Borsch, Stuart (2000). "Nile Floods and the Irrigation System in Fifteenth-Century Egypt." *Mamluk Studies Review* 4: 131–45.

(2004a). "Environment and Population: The Collapse of Large Irrigation Systems Reconsidered." *Comparative Studies in Society and History* 46/3: 451–68.

(2004b). "Thirty Years after Lopez, Miskimin and Udovitch." *Mamluk Studies Review* 8/2: 191–201.

(2005). *The Black Death in Egypt and England: A Comparative Study*. Austin: University of Texas Press.

Borsch, Stuart; Wan Kamal, Mujani (2014). "Peasants during the Mamluk Period: How They Have Struggled. "*Athens Journal of Mediterranean Studies* 1/3: 261–72.

(2015). "Plague Depopulation and Irrigation Decay in Medieval Egypt." *The Medieval Globe* 1/1: 125–56.

Borsch, Stuart; Sabraa, T. (2016). "Plague Mortality in Late Medieval Cairo: Quantifying the Plague Outbreaks of 833/1430 and 864/1460." *Mamluk Studies Review* 19: 115.

(2017). "Qānūn al-Riyy: The Water Law of Egypt." *Sophia: Journal of Asian, African, and Middle Eastern Studies* 35: 87.

Bosworth, Clifford (1963). "Some Historical Gleanings from the Section on Symbolic Actions in Qalqashandī's Ṣubḥ al-Āʿsā." *Arabica* 10: 148–53.

(1972). "Christian and Jewish Dignitaries in Mamlūk Egypt and Syria: Qalqashandī's Information on Their Hierarchy, Titulature and Appointment." *International Journal of Middle East Studies* 3: 59–74, 199–216.

(1975). "Recruitment, Muster and Review in Medieval Islamic Armies." *War, Technology and Society in the Middle East.* V. J. Parry, M. E. Yapp, eds. London: 59–77.

Brinner, William (1963). "The Significance of the *Ḥarāfīsh* and Their 'Sultan'." *Journal of the Economic and Social History of the Orient* 6: 190–215.

(1977). "Dār al-Saʿāda and Dār al-ʿAdl in Mamlūk Damascus." *Studies in Memory of Gaston Wiet.* M. Rosen-Ayalon, ed. Jerusalem: Institute of Asian and African Studies: 235–47.

Broadbridge, Anne (1999). "Academic Rivalry and the Patronage System in Fifteenth-Century Egypt: al-ʿAynī, al-Maqrīzī, and Ibn Ḥajar al-ʿAsqalānī." *Mamluk Studies Review* 3: 85–107.

(2008). *Kingship and Ideology in the Islamic and Mongol Worlds.* Cambridge: Cambridge University Press.

(2011). "Sending Home for Mom and Dad: The Extended Family Impulse in Mamlūk Politics." *Mamluk Studies Review* 15: 1–18.

Bulliet, Richard (1979). *Conversion to Islam in the Medieval Period: An Essay in Quantitative History.* Cambridge: Harvard University Press.

Burgoyne, Michael; Richards, Donald (1987). *Mamluk Jerusalem: An Architectural Study.* The British School of Archaeology in Jerusalem.

Burke, Katherine Strange (2004). "A Note on Archaeological Evidence for Sugar Production in the Islamic Middle Periods in Bilād al-Shām." *Mamluk Studies Review* 8/2: 109–18.

Cahen, Claude (1953). "L'Évolution de l'iqṭāʿ du IXe au XIIIe siècles." *Annales Économies, Sociétés, Civilisations* 8/1: 25–52.

(1962a). "Contribution à l'étude des impôts dans l'Égypte médiévale." *Journal of the Economic and Social History of the Orient* 5/3: 244–78.

(1962b). "Un traité fiancier d'époque Fatimide-Ayyubide." *Journal of the Economic and Social History of the Orient* 5/3: 139–59.

(1968). *Pre-Ottoman Turkey.* London: Sidgwick & Jackson.

(1971). "Notes sur une histoire de l'agriculture dans les pays musulmans médiévaux, I: Coup d'oeil sur la literature agronomique musulmane hors de l'Espagne." *Journal of the Economic and Social History of the Orient* 14: 63–68.

(1977). *Makhzūmiyyāt: Études sur l'histoire économique et fiancière de l'Égypte médiévale.* Leiden: Brill.

Canard, Marius (1935). "Le traité de 1281 entre Michel Paléologue et le Sultan Qalā'ūn." *Byzantion* 10: 669–80.

(1935–45). "Un traité entre Byzance et l'Égypte au xiii$^{e}$ siècle et les relations diplomatiques de Michel VIII Paléologue avec les sultans mamluks Baibars et Qala'un." *Mélanges Gaudefroy-Demombynes.* Cairo: Institut français d'archéologie orientale: 197–224.

Chamberlain, Michael (1994). *Knowledge and Social Practice in Medieval Damascus, 1190–1350.* Cambridge: Cambridge University Press.

Chih, Rachida (1997). "Zāwiya, ṣaha et rawda: développement et role de quelques institutions soufies en Égypte." *Annales Islamologiques* 31: 49–60.

Christ, Georg (2012). *Trading Conflicts, Venetian Merchants and Mamluk Officials in late Medieval Alexandria*. Leiden: Brill.

(2017a). "Collapse and Continuity: Alexandria as a Declining City with a Thriving Port (13th–16th Centuries)." *The Routledge Handbook of Maritime Trade Around Europe, 1300–1600: Commercial Networks and Urban Autonomy*. W. P. Blockman, ed. London: Routledge: 121–40.

(2017b). "A King of Two Seas? Mamluk Maritime Trade Policy in the Wake of the Crisis of the 14th Century." *Ulrich Haarmann Memorial Lecture*. Vol. 13. S. Conermann, ed. Göttingen: Vandenhoeck and Ruprecht Unipress.

(2017c). "Sliding Legalities: Venetian Slave Trade in Alexandria and the Aegean." *Slavery and the Slave Trade in the Eastern Mediterranean (c.1000–1500 CE)*. G. Christoph, R. Amitai, eds. Turnhout: Brepols: 210–29.

(2019). "The Sultans and the Sea: Mamluk Coastal Defence, Dormant Navy and Delegation of Maritime Policing (14th and Early 15th Centuries)." *The Mamluk Sultanate and Its Neighbors: Economic, Social and Cultural Entanglements*. S. Conermann, R. Amitai, eds. Göttingen: V & R Unipress: 215–56.

Clerget, Marcel (1934). *Le Caire: étude de géographie urbaine et d'histoire économique*. 2 vols. Cairo: E. and R. Schindler.

Clifford, Winslow (1997). "Ubi Sumus? Mamlūk History and Social Theory." *Mamluk Studies Review* 1: 45–62.

(1993). "Some Observations on the Course of Mamlūk-Safavī Relations (1502–1516/908–922)." I and II. *Der Islam* 70/2: 245–65, 266–78.

(2013). *State Formation and the Structure of Politics in Mamluk Syro-Egypt, 648–741 AH/1250–1340 CE*. Göttingen: Vandenhoeck and Ruprecht Unipress.

Cohen, Hayyim (1970). "The Economic Background and the Secular Occupations of Muslim Jurisprudents and Traditionalists in the Classical Period of Islam." *Journal of the Economic and Social History of the Orient* 13: 16–61.

Cohen, Mark (1984). "Jews in the Mamlūk Environment: The Crisis of 1442 (a Geniza Study)." *Bulletin of the School of Oriental and African Studies* 47/3: 425–48; "Additional Series" Taylor-Schechter collection. Vols. 145–53.

Conermann, Stephan; Saghbini, Suad (2002). "Awlād al-Nās as Founders of Pious Endowments: The Waqfīyah of Yahyá ibn Ṭughān al-Ḥasanī of the Year 870/1465." *Mamluk Studies Review* 6: 21–50.

Conermann, Stephan; Pistor-Hatam, A., eds. (2003). *Die Mamlūken: Studien zu ihrer Geschichte und Kultur, Zum Gedenken an Ulrich Haarmann (1942–1999)*. Hamburg: EB-Verlag.

Conermann, Stephan (2007). "Some Remarks on Ibn Tawq's (d. 915/1509) Journal al-Taʿlīq, vol. 1 (885/1480 to 890/1485)." *Mamluk Studies Review* 11/2: 121–35.

Cooper, Richard S. (1973). "A Note on the Dinār Jayshī." *Journal of the Economic and Social History of the Orient* 16/2: 317–18.

(1974). "Land Classification Terminology and the Assessment of the Kharāj Tax in Medieval Egypt." *Journal of the Economic and Social History of the Orient* 17/1: 91–102.

(1976). "The Assessment and Collection of Kharāj in Medieval Egypt." *Journal of the American Oriental Society* 96/3: 365–82.

(1977). "Agriculture in Egypt, 640–1800." *Handbuch der Orientalistik, Abteilung I: Der Nahe und der Mittelere Osten, bd. 6: Geschichte der Islamischen Länder,*

*Abschnitt 6: Wirtschaftsgeschichte des Vorderen Orients in Islamischer Zeit, part 1*. Berthold Spuler, ed. Leiden: Brill: 188–204.

Cornell, Vincent (1996). *The Way of Abū Madyan: The Works of Abū Madyan Shu'ayb*. Cambridge: Islamic Texts Society.

Coulon, Damien (2013). "La documentation pontificale et le commerce avec les musulmans." *Les Territoires de la Méditerranée, xi$^{e}$–xvi$^{e}$ siècle*. Annliese Nef, ed. Rennes: Presses Universitaires de Rennes: 161–92.

Coureas, Nicholas (2008) "Mamluks in the Cypriot Chronicle of George Boustronios and Their Place within a Wider Context." *Continuity and Change in the Realms of Islam: Studies in Honour of Professor Urbain Vermeulen*. K. D'Hulster, J. van Steenbergen, eds. OLA 171. Leuven: Peeters: 135–49.

Creswell, K. A. C. (1916). "A Brief Chronology of the Muḥammadan Monuments of Cairo to A.D. 1517." *Bulletin d'Institut d'archéologie orientale du Caire* 16: 39–164.

(1952–59). *The Muslim Architecture of Egypt*. 2 vols. Oxford: Oxford University Press.

Crone, Patricia (1980). *Slaves on Horses: The Evolution of the Islamic Polity*. Cambridge: Cambridge University Press.

Dankoff, Robert (2004). Review of *The Dīvān of Qānṣūh al-Ghūrī*. Mehmed Yalçun, ed. Istanbul, Bay, Studies on Turkish Culture, 2002; and *Kansu Gavrî'nin Türkçe Dîvânı*. Orhan Yavuz, ed. Konya: Selçuk Üniversitesi, Türkiyat Arastırmaları Enstitüsü, 2002. *Mamluk Studies Review* 8/1: 303–7.

Darrag, Ahmad (1961). *L'Égypte sous le règne de Barsbay, 825–841/1422–1438*. Damascus: Institut français.

(1963). *L'Acte de waqf de Barsbay*. Cairo: Institut français d'archéologie.

(1972). "La vie d'Abū'l-Maḥāsin Ibn Tagrī Birdī et son œuvre." *Annales Islamologiques* 11: 163–81.

(1963). "Les relations commerciales entre l'état mamlouk et la France." *Majallat Kulliyyat al-Adab, Jāmi'at al-Iskandariyya* 25/2: 1–21.

Deguilhem, Randi, ed. (1995). *Le waqf dans l'éspace islamique: Outil de pouvoir socio-politique*. Damascus: Institut français.

Denoix, Sylvie (1992). *Décrire Le Caire: Fusṭaṭ-Miṣr d'après Ibn Duqmāq et Maqrīzī*. Cairo: Institut français d'archéologie orientale.

(2010). "Construction sociale et rapport à la norme d'un groupe minoritaire dominant: les Mamlouks (1250–1517)." *Minorités et regulations sociales en Méditerranée medieval*. D. Boisselier, F. Clement, J. Tolan, eds. Rennes: Presses Universitaires de Rennes: 125–44.

De Jong, Frederick; Radtke, Bernd, eds. (1999). *Islamic Mysticism Contested: Thirteen Centuries of Controversies and Polemics*. Leiden: Brill.

D'Hulster, Kristof; van Steenbergen, Jo (2013). "Family Matters: The 'Family-in-Law Impulse' in Mamluk Marriage Policy." *Annales Islamologiques* 47: 61–82.

Dölger, Franz (1952). "Der Vertrag des Sultans Qalā'ūn von Ägypten mit dem Kaiser Michael VIII. Palaiologos." *Serta Monacensia Franz Babinger*. Leiden: Brill: 60–79.

Dols, Michael (1977). *The Black Death in the Middle East*. Princeton: Princeton University Press.

(1979). "The Second Plague Pandemic and Its Recurrences in the Middle East, 1347–1894." *Journal of the Economic and Social History of the Orient* 22: 162–89.

(1981). "The General Mortality of the Black Death in the Mamluk Empire." *The Islamic Middle East, 700–1900: Studies in Economic and Social History*. A. Udovitch, ed. Princeton: Darwin Press: 397–428.

(1992). *Majnūn: The Madman in Medieval Islamic Society*. New York: Oxford University Press.

Doufikar-Aerts, Faustina (2003). "Sīrat al-Iskandar: An Arabic Popular Romance of Alexander." *Oriente Moderno* 22: 505–20.

Eddé, Anne-Marie (1999). *La Principauté ayyoubide d'Alep (579/1183–658/1260)*. Stuttgart: Franz Steiner Verlag.

(2011). *Saladin*. Cambridge: Belknap Press.

EGYLandscape Project. www.egylandscape.org.

Ehrenkreutz, Andrew (1972a). "Another Orientalist's Remarks concerning the Pirenne Thesis." *Journal of the Economic and Social History of the Orient* 15: 94–104.

(1972b). *Saladin*. Albany: State University of New York Press.

(1981). "Strategic Implications of the Slave Trade between Genoa and Mamlūk Egypt in the Second Half of the Thirteenth Century." *The Islamic Middle East, 700–1900: Studies in Economic and Social History*. A. Udovitch, ed. Princeton: Darwin Press: 335–45.

Elayyan, Ribhi M. (1990). "The History of the Arabic-Islamic Libraries: 7th to 14th Centuries." *International Library Review* 22: 119–35.

Elbendary, Amina (2001). "The Sultan, the Tyrant, and the Hero: Changing Medieval Perceptions of al-Ẓāhir Baybars." *Mamluk Studies Review* 5: 141–57.

(2012). "Between Riots and Negotiations. Urban Protest in Late Medieval Egypt and Syria." *Ulrich Haarmann Memorial Lecture*. Vol. 3. S. Conermann, ed. Berlin: EB Verlag.

(2015). *Crowds and Sultans: Urban Protest in Late Medieval Egypt and Syria*. Cairo: American University in Cairo Press.

Elisséeff, Nikita (1959). *La description de Damas d'Ibn 'Asākir*. Damascus: Institut français.

(1967). *Nūr al-Dīn: Un grand prince musulman de Syrie au temps des croisades*. Damascus: Institut français. 3 vols.

El-Leithy, Tamer (2005). "Coptic Culture and Conversion in Medieval Cairo, 1293–1524 A.D." PhD diss. Princeton University.

(2006). "Sufis, Copts and the Politics of Piety: Moral Regulation in Fourteenth-Century Upper Egypt." *Le développement du soufisme en Égypte à l'époque mamelouk*. R. McGregor, A. Sabra, eds. Cairo: Institut français d'archéologie orientale: 75–119.

El-Shamsy, Ahmad (2013). *The Canonization of Islamic Law*. Cambridge: Cambridge University Press.

England, Samuel (2017). *Medieval Empires and the Culture of Competition: Literary Duels at Islamic and Christian Courts*. Edinburgh: Edinburgh University Press.

Ernst, Carl (2011). *Sufism: An Introduction to the Mystical Tradition of Islam*. Boulder: Shambhala.

Escovits, Joseph (1976). "Vocational Patterns of the Scribes of the Mamlūk Chancery." *Arabica* 23: 42–62.

(1982). "The Establishment of Four Chief Judgeships in the Mamlūk Empire." *Journal of the American Oriental Society* 102/3: 529–31.

(1984). *The Office of Qāḍī al-Qudāt in Cairo under the Baḥrī Mamlūks*. Berlin: Klaus Schwarz.
Evrard, James (1974). *Zur Geschichte Aleppos und Nordsyriens im letzten halben Jahrhundert der Mamlukenherrschaf (872–921 AH) nach arabischen und italienischen Quellen*. Munich: Trofenik.
Eychenne, Mathieu (2013). *Liens personnels, clientélisme et réseaux de pouvoir dans le sultanat mamelouk (milieu xiii^e-fin xiv^e siècle)*. Damascus: Institut français.
Fancy, Hussein (2016). *The Mercenary Mediterranean: Sovereignty, Religion and Violence in the Medieval Crown of Aragon*. Chicago: University of Chicago Press.
Fernandes, Leonor (1981). "Three Ṣūfī Foundations in a 15th-Century Waqfiyya." *Annales Islamologiques* 17: 141–56.
(1983). "Some Aspects of the Zāwiya in Egypt at the Eve of the Ottoman Conquest." *Annales Islamologiques* 19: 9–17.
(1985). "Change in Function and Form of Mamlūk Religious Institutions." *Annales Islamologiques* 21: 73–93.
(1987a). "The Foundation of Baybars al-Jashankir: Its Waqf, History, and Architecture." *Muqarnas* 4: 21–42.
(1987b). "Mamlūk Politics and Education: The Evidence from Two Fourteenth-Century Waqfiyyas." *Annales Islamologiques* 23: 87–98.
(1988a). *The Evolution of a Sufi Institution in Mamluk Egypt: The Khanqah*. Berlin: Klaus Schwarz.
(1988b). "On Conducting the Affairs of the State: A Guideline of the Fourteenth Century." *Annales Islamologiques* 24: 81–91.
(1997). "Mamlūk Architecture and the Question of Patronage." *Mamluk Studies Review* 1: 107–20.
(2000). "Istibdāl: The Game of Exchange and Its Impact on the Urbanization of Mamluk Cairo." *The Cairo Heritage: Essays in Honor of Laila Ali Ibrahim*. D. Behrens-Abouseif, ed. Cairo: American University in Cairo Press: 203–22.
(2002). "Between Qāḍīs and Muftīs: To Whom Does the Mamlūk Sultan Listen?" *Mamluk Studies Review* 6: 95–108.
Fischel, Walter (1951). "Ibn Khaldūn's Activities in Mamlūk Egypt (1382–1406)." *Semitic and Oriental Studies Presented to William Popper*. W. J. Fischel, ed. Berkeley: University of California Press: 103–24.
(1952). *Ibn Khaldūn and Tamerlane: Their Historic Meeting in Damascus, 1401 AD (803 AH)*. Berkeley: University of California Press.
(1958). "The Spice Trade in Mamlūk Egypt: A Contribution to the Economic History of Medieval Islam." *Journal of the Economic and Social History of the Orient* 1/2: 157–74.
(1959). "*Ascensus Barcoch*: A Latin Biography of the Mamlūk Sultan Barquq of Egypt (d. 1399) Written by B. de Mignanelli in 1416." *Arabica* 6: 57–74, 152–72.
(1967). *Ibn Khaldun in Egypt, His Public Functions and His Historical Research, 1382–1406: A Study in Islamic Historiography*. Berkeley: University of California Press.
(1969). *Jews in the Economic and Political Life of Medieval Islam*. New York: Ktav Publishing.

Flemming, Barbara (1977). "Literary Activities in Mamlūk Halls and Barracks." *Studies in Memory of Gaston Wiet*. M. Rosen-Ayalon, ed. Jerusalem: Hebrew University Press: 249–60.

Frantz-Murphy, Gladys (1986). *The Agrarian Administration of Egypt from the Arabs to the Ottomans*. Cairo: Institut français d'archéologie orientale.

Franz, Kurt (2015). "Bedouin and States: Framing the Mongol–Mamlūk Wars in Long-Term History." *Nomad Military Power in Iran and Adjacent Areas in the Islamic Period*. K. Franz, W. Holzwarth, eds. Wiesbaden: Reichert Verlag: 29–106.

Franz, Kurt; Holzwarth, Wolfgang, eds. (2015). *Nomad Military Power in Iran and Adjacent Areas in the Islamic Period*. Wiesbaden: Reichert Verlag.

Frenkel, Yehoshua (1999). "Political and Social Aspects of Islamic Religious Endowments (awqāf): Saladin in Cairo (1169–73) and Jerusalem (1187–93)." *Bulletin of the School of Oriental and African Studies* 62: 1–20.

(2001). "Agriculture, Land-Tenure and Peasants in Palestine during the Mamluk Period." *Egypt and Syria in the Fatimid, Ayyubid and Mamluk Eras*. III, Proceedings of the 6th, 7th, and 8th International Colloquium organized at the Katholieke Universiteit Leuven in May 1997, 1998, and 1999. U. Vermeulen, J. Van Steenbergen, eds. Leuven: Peeters: 193–208.

(2005). "Women in Late Mamluk Damascus in Light of Audience Certificates (*sama'āt*) of Ibn Mibrad." *Egypt and Syria in the Fatimid, Ayyubid and Mamluk Eras*, IV. U. Vermeulen, J. Van Steenbergen, eds. Leuven: Peeters: 409–23.

(2009). "Awqāf in Mamlūk Bilād al-Shām." *Mamluk Studies Review* 13/1: 149–66.

(2015). *The Turkic Peoples in Medieval Arabic Writings*. New York: Routledge.

Fromherz, Allen (2010). *Ibn Khaldun, Life and Times*. Edinburgh: Edinburgh University Press.

Fuess, Albrecht (2001a). "Rotting Ships and Razed Harbours: The Naval Policy of the Mamlūks." *Mamluk Studies Review* 5: 45–71.

(2001b). *Verbranntes Ufer: Auswirkungen mamlukischer Seepolitik auf Beirut und die syro-palästinensische Küste (1250–1517)*. Vol. 3. Leiden: Brill, Islamic History and Civilization.

(2005). "Was Cyprus a Mamluk Protectorate? Mamluk Influence on Cyprus between 1426 and 1517." *Journal of Cyprus Studies* 11: 11–28.

Fuess, Albrecht; Hartung, Jan-Peter, eds. (2011). *Court Cultures in the Muslim World, Seventh to Nineteenth Centuries*. Vol. 13. London: Routledge Studies on the Middle East.

(2015). "Why Venice, not Genoa: How Venice Emerged as the Mamluks' Favorite European Trading Partner after 1365." *Union in Separation: Diasporic Groups and Identities in the Eastern Mediterranean*. G. Christ, ed. Roma: Viella: 251–66.

(2019). "Three's a Crowd: The Downfall of the Mamluks in the Near Eastern Power Struggle, 1500–1517." *The Mamluk Sultanate from the Perspective of Regional and World History*. R. Amitai, S. Conermann, eds. Göttingen: Vandenhoeck and Ruprecht Unipress.

A. Fuess (2020). "The Syro-Egyptian Sultanate in Transformation, 1496–1498, Sultan al-Nāṣir Muḥammad b. Qāytbāy and the Reformation of Mamlūk Institutions and Symbols of State Power." *Trajectories of State Formation across Fifteenth-Century Islamic West-Asia, Eurasian Parallels, Connections and Divergences*. Ruler and Elites 18. Jo Van Steenbergen, ed. Leiden: Brill: 201–23.

(2020). "Going Back to Mamlūk Glory: How al-Nāṣir Muḥammad II (r. 1496–1498) Tried to Revive the Dynastic Principle." *Trajectories of Late Medieval State Formation across Fifteenth-Century Muslim West Asia – Eurasian Parallels, Connections, Divergences.* J. van Steenbergen, ed. Leiden: Brill.

Garcin, Jean-Claude (1967). "Histoire, opposition politique et piétisme traditionaliste dans le *Ḥusn al-Muhadarat* de Suyūṭī." *Annales Islamologiques* 7: 33–89.

(1969). "Le Caire et la province: constructions au Caire et à Qus sous les mamlouks baḥrides." *Annales Islamologiques* 8: 47–62.

(1973–74). "La 'Méditerranéisation' de l'empire mamelouk sous les sultans baḥrides." *Rivista degli Studi orientali* 48: 109–16.

(1976). *Un Centre musulman de la Haute-Égypte médiévale: Qūṣ.* Cairo: Institut français d'archéologie orientale.

(1977). "Deux saints populaires du Caire au début du XVI^e^ siecle." *Bulletin d'études orientales* 29: 131–43.

Garcin, Jean-Claude, B. Maury, J. Revault, Z. Mona, eds. (1982a). *Palais et maisons du Caire,* vol. 1*: Époque mamelouke, xiii^e^–xvi^e^ siècle.* Paris: Centre national de recherche scientifique.

(1982b). "Évolution de l'habitat médiéval et histoire urbain." *Palais et maisons du Caire*, vol. 1: *Époque mamelouke, xiii^e^–xvi^e^ siècle.* J-C. Garcin, B. Maury, J. Revault, Z. Mona, eds. Paris: Centre national de recherche scientifique.

(1988). "Le system militaire mamluk et le blocage de la société musulmane médiévale." *Annales Islamologiques* 24: 93–110; "The Mamluk Military System and the Blocking of Medieval Muslim Society." *Europe and the Rise of Capitalism.* J. Baechler et al., eds. Oxford: Oxford University Press: 113–30.

(1991). "Le Caire et l'évolution urbaine des pays musulmans à l'époque médiévale." *Annales Islamologiques* 25: 289–304.

Garcin, Jean-Claude; Taher, M. A. (1995). "Enquête sur le financement d'un waqf égyptien du XV^e^ siècle: les comptes de Jawhar al-Lālā." *Journal of the Economic and Social History of the Orient* 38/3: 262–304.

(1998). "The Regime of the Circassian Mamlūks." *The Cambridge History of Egypt*, vol. 1: *Islamic Egypt.* C. Petry, ed. Cambridge: Cambridge University Press: 290–317.

Garcin, Jean-Claude, ed. (2003). *Lectures du Roman de Baybars*. Marseille: Parenthéses.

(2004). "Sīras et Histoire." *Arabica* 51: 33–54, 223–57.

(2006). "Les soufis dans la ville mamelouke d'Égypte: histoire du soufisme et histoire globale." *La développement du Soufisme en Égypte à l'époque mamelouke.* R. McGregor, A. Sabra, eds. Cairo: Institut français d'archéologie orientale: 11–40.

(2013). *Pour une lecture historique des Mille et Une Nuits: Essai sur l'édition de Būlāq (1835).* Arles: Sindbad/Actes Sud.

(2016). *Les mille et une nuits et l'histoire*. Paris: Non Lieu.

Gaube, Heinz; Eugen Wirth (1984). *Aleppo: Historische und geographische Beiträge zur baulichen Gestaltung zur sozialen Organisation und zur wirtschaftlichen Dynamik einer vorderasiatischen Fernhandelsmetropole*. Wiesbaden: Beihefte zum Tübinger Atlas des Vorderen Orients (Reihe B) 58.

Gaudefroy-Demombynes, Maurice (1923). *La Syrie à l'époque des mamelouks d'après les auteurs arabes*. Paris: Paul Geuthner.

Geoffroy, Éric (1995). *Le Soufisme en Égypte et en Syrie sous les derniers Mamelouks et les premiers Ottomans: Orientations spirituelles et enjeux culturels*. Damascus: Institut français.

ed. (2005). *Un voie soufie dans le monde: la Shādhiliyya*. Paris: Maisoneuve et Larose.

Ghazi, Mhammed (1959). "Un groupe sociale: Les Raffinés (Ẓurafā')." *Studia Islamica* 11: 39–71.

Gilbert, Joan (1980). "Institutionalization of Muslim Scholarship and Professionalization of the *'Ulamā'* in Medieval Damascus." *Studia Islamica* 52: 105–34.

Gil, Moshe (1992). *A History of Palestine, 634–1099*. Cambridge: Cambridge University Press.

Goitein, Solomon (1958). "The Oldest Documentary Evidence for the Title Alf Laila wa-Laila." *Journal of the American Oriental Society* 78/4: 301–02.

(1967–88). *A Mediterranean Society: The Jewish Communities of the Arab World as Portrayed in the Documents of the Cairo Geniza*. 5 vols. Berkeley: University of California Press.

Goitein, Solomon; Dov, Shlomo; Friedman, Mordechai (2007). *India Traders of the Middle Ages: Documents from the Cairo Geniza*. Leiden: Brill.

Golb, Norman (1965). "The Topography of the Jews of Medieval Egypt." *Journal of Near Eastern Studies*. 24/3: 251–70.

Gonnella, Julia (2006). "The Citadel of Aleppo: Recent Studies." *Muslim Military Architecture in Greater Syria, from the Coming of Islam to the Ottoman Period*. Hugh Kennedy, ed. Leiden: Brill: 165–75.

(2012). "The Mamluk Throne Hall in Damascus." *The Arts of the Mamluks in Egypt and Syria – Evolution and Impact*. D. Behrens-Abouseif, ed. Göttingen: Bonn University Press: 223–45.

Gottheil, Richard (1921). "An Answer to the Dhimmis." *Journal of the American Oriental Society* 41: 383–457.

Gril, Denis (1980). "Une Émeute anti-Chrétienne à Qūṣ au debut du viii^e/xiv^e siècle." *Annales Islamologiques*. 16: 241–74.

(2001–06). "Miracles." *The Encyclopaedia of the Qur'ān*. J. McAuliffe, ed. Leiden: Brill 3: 392–99.

(2006). "Le soufisme en Égypte au début de l'époque mamelouke d'après le Waḥīd fī sulūk ahl al-tawḥīd de 'Abd al-Ġaffār ibn Nūḥ al-Qūṣī (m. 708/1308)." *La développement du soufisme en Égypte à l'époque mamelouke*. R. McGregor, A. Sabra, eds. Cairo: Institut français d'archéologie orientale: 51–73.

Guo, Li (1997). "Mamlūk Historiographic Studies: The State of the Art." *Mamluk Studies Review* 1: 15–44.

(1998). *Early Mamluk Syrian Historiography: al-Yūnīnī's Dhayl Mir'at al-zamān*. 2 vols. Leiden: Brill.

(2001a). "Al-Biqā'ī's Chronicle: A Fifteenth Century Learned Man's Reflection on His Time and World." *The Historiography of Islamic Egypt (c. 950–1800)*. H. Kennedy, ed. Leiden: Brill: 121–48.

(2001b). "Paradise Lost: Ibn Dāniyāl's Response to Sultan Baibars' Campaign against Vice in Cairo." *Journal of the American Oriental Society* 121: 219–35.

(2003). "The Devil's Advocate: Ibn Daniyal's Art of Parody in His Qasidah No. 71" *Mamluk Studies Review* 7/1: 177–209.

(2004). *Commerce, Culture, and Community in a Red Sea Port in the Thirteenth Century*. Leiden: Brill.
(2005). "Tales of a Medieval Cairene Harem: Domestic Life in al-Biqāʿī's Autobiographical Chronicle." *Mamluk Studies Review* 9/1: 101–21.
(2008). "Al-Taʿlīq." (review). *Mamluk Studies Review* 12/1: 214.
(2012). *The Performing Arts in Medieval Islam: Shadow Play and Popular Poetry in Ibn Dāniyāl's Mamluk Cairo*. Leiden: Brill.
(2017a). "Cross-Gender 'Acting' and Gender-Bending Rhetoric at a Princely Party: Performing Shadow Plays in Mamluk Cairo." *The Presence of Power: Courts and Performance in the Pre-modern Middle East: 700–1600 CE*. M. A. Pomerantz, E. Birge Vitz, eds. New York: New York University Press: 164–75.
(2017b). "The Monk's Daughter and Her Suitor: An Egyptian Shadow Play of Interfaith Romance and Insanity." *Journal of the American Oriental Society* 137/4: 785–803.
(2018). "Ibn Iyās, the Poet: The Literary Profile of a Mamluk Historian." *Mamluk Historiography Revisited, Narratological Perspectives*. S. Conermann, ed. Göttingen: Vandenhoeck and Ruprecht Unipress: 77–90.
(2020). *Arabic Shadow Theatre 1300–1900: A Handbook*. Leiden: Brill.
Haarmann, Ulrich (1980). "Regional Sentiment in Medieval Islamic Egypt." *Bulletin of the School of Oriental and African Studies*" 43: 55–66.
(1984a) "The Library of a Fourteenth-Century Jerusalem Scholar." *Der Islam* 61: 327–33.
(1984b). "The Sons of Mamlūks as Fief-Holders in Late Medieval Egypt." *Land Tenure and Social Transformation in the Middle East*. T. Khalidi, ed. Beirut: 141–68.
(1988a). "Arabic in Speech, Turkish in Lineage: Mamlūks and Their Sons in the Intellectual Life of Fourteenth-Century Egypt and Syria." *Journal of Semitic Studies* 33/1: 81–114.
(1988b). "Rather the Injustice of the Turks than the Righteousness of the Arabs – Changing ʿUlama' Attitudes toward Mamlūk Rule in the Late Fifteenth Century." *Studia Islamica* 68: 61–77.
(1990). "Regicide and the 'Law of the Turks'." *Intellectual Studies on Islam: Essays Written in Honor of Martin B. Dickson*. M. M. Mazzaoui, V. B. Moreen, eds. Salt Lake City: University of Utah Press: 127–35.
(1998). "Joseph's Law: The Careers and Activities of Mamluk Descendants before the Ottoman Conquest of Egypt." *The Mamluks in Egyptian Politics and Society*. T. Phillipp, U. Haarmann, eds. Cambridge: Cambridge University Press: 55–84.
(2001). "The Mamlūk System of Rule in the Eyes of Western Travelers." *Mamluk Studies Review* 5: 1–24.
Al-Hajji, Hayat Nasir (1978). *The Internal Affairs in Egypt during the Third Reign of the Sultan al-Nāṣir Muḥammad b. Qalāwūn, 709–741/1310–1341*. Kuwait.
Halm, Heinz (1979–82). *Ägypten nach den mamlukischen Lehensregistern*. TAVO 38. 2 vols. Wiesbaden.
Halperin, Charles (2000). "The Kipchak Connection: The Ilkhans, The Mamluks and ʿAyn Jalut." *Bulletin of the School of Oriental and African Studies* 63/2: 229–45.

Hamza, Hani (2008). "Some Aspects of the Economic and Social Life of Ibn Taghrībirdī: Based on an Examination of His Waqfīyah." *Mamluk Studies Review* 12/1: 139–72.

Hanna, Nelly (1983). *An Urban History of Būlāq in the Mamlūk and Ottoman Periods.* Cairo: Institut français d'archéologie orientale.

(2003). *In Praise of Books: A Cultural History of Cairo's Middle Class, Sixteenth to the Eighteenth Centuries.* Syracuse: Syracuse University Press.

Har-el, Shai (1995). *Struggle for Dominion in the Middle East: The Ottoman-Mamluk War, 1485–91.* Leiden: Brill.

Haridi, Ahmad A. (1983–84). *Index des Hitat: Index analytique des ouvrages d'Ibn Duqmāq et de Maqrīzī sur le Caire.* 3 vols. Cairo: Institut français d'achéologie orientale. Textes arabes et études islamiques. XX/1–3.

Al-Harithy, Howayda (1996). "The Complex of Sultan Hasan in Cairo: Reading between the Lines." *Muqarnas* 13: 6.

Hasan, 'Ali Ibrahim (1967). *Ta'rīkh al-Mamālīk al-Baḥriyya.* Cairo.

Hathaway, Jane (1998). "'Mamluk Households' and 'Mamluk factions' in Ottoman Egypt: a Reconsideration." *The Mamluks in Egyptian Politics and Society.* T. Phillipp, U. Haarmann, eds. Cambridge: Cambridge University Press: 107–17.

(2003). *A Tale of Two Factions: Myth, Memory and Identity in Ottoman Egypt and Yemen.* New York: State University of New York Press.

Heath, Peter (1996). *The Thirsty Sword: Sīrat 'Antar and the Arabic Popular Epic.* Salt Lake City: University of Utah Press.

Hennequin, Gilles (1974). "Mamlouks et métaux précieux à propos de la balance de paiements de l'état Syro-Égyptienne à la fin du moyen age – question de méthode." *Annales Islamologiques* 12: 37–44.

Hennequin, Gilles; Krebs, Gérard (1988). *Monnaies de l'Islam et du Proche-Orient.* Paris: Administration des monnaies et médailles.

(1995). "Waqf et monnaie dans I'Egypte mamluke." *Journal of the Economic and Social History of the Orient* 38: 305–12.

Herzog, Thomas (2003). "The First Layer of the Sīrat Baybars – Popular Romance and Political Propaganda." *Mamluk Studies Review* 7: 137–48.

(2013). "Mamluk (Popular) Culture." *Ubi Sumus? Quo Vademus? Mamluk Studies – State of the Art.* S. Conermann, ed. Göttingen: Vandenhoeck and Ruprecht Unipress: 131–58.

Hess, Andrew (1973). "The Ottoman Conquest of Egypt (1517) and the Beginning of the Sixteenth-Century World War." *International Journal of Middle East Studies* 4: 55–76.

Heyberger, Bernard; Fuess, Albrecht, eds. (2013). *La frontière méditerranéenne du 15. au 17. siècle: échanges, circulations et affrontements: textes réunis et édités.* Turnhout: Brepols.

Heyd, Wilhelm (1885–86). *Histoire du commerce du Levant au Moyen-Age.* Leipzig, 2 vols.

Hill, George F. (1940–52). *A History of Cyprus.* Cambridge: Cambridge University Press, vol. 3.

Hillenbrand, Robert (2000). *Islamic Architecture: Form, Function and Meaning.* Edinburgh: Edinburgh University Press.

Hirschler, Konrad (2004). “Badr al-Dīn Maḥmūd al-ʿAynī, ʿIqd al-Jumān fi Ta'rīkh Ahl al-Zamān: al-ʿAṣr al-Ayyūbī (Part 1).” *Mamluk Studies Review* 8/2: 213–15.

(2006). *Medieval Arabic Historiography: Authors as Actors*. London: Routledge.

Hirschler, Konrad; U. Hübner (2009). “Zwei neue mamlukische Inshriften aus Abū Mahtūb nahe as-Saubak.” *Zeitschrift der Deutschen Palaestina-Vereins* 125/1: 76–83.

(2012a). “Islam: The Arabic and Persian Traditions, Eleventh-Fifteenth Centuries.” *The Oxford History of Historical Writing*, vol. 2: *400–1400*. S. Foot, C. F. Robinson, eds. Oxford: Oxford University Press: 267–86.

(2012b). *The Written Word in the Medieval Arabic Lands*. Edinburgh: Edinburgh University Press.

(2013). “Studying Mamluk Historiography: From Source-Criticism to the Cultural Turn.” *Ubi Sumus? Quo Vademus? Mamuk Studies – State of the Art*. S. Conermann, ed. Göttingen: Vandenhoeck and Ruprecht Unipress: 95–117.

(2016). *Medieval Damascus: Plurality and Diversity in an Arabic Library: The Ashrafīya Library Catalogue*. Edinburgh: Edinburgh University Press.

(2020). *A Monument to Medieval Syrian Book Culture: The Library of Ibn 'Abd al-Hādī*. Edinburgh: Edinburgh University Press.

Hiyari, M. A. (1975). “The Origins and Development of the Amīrate of the Arabs During the Seventh/Thirteenth and Eighth/Fourteenth Centuries.” *Bulletin of the School of Oriental and African Studies* 38: 509–25.

Hofer, Nathan (2014). “The Origins and Development of the Office of the ‘Chief Sufi’ in Egypt, 1173–1325.” *Journal of Sufi Studies* 3: 1–37.

(2015). *The Popularization of Sufism in Ayyubid and Mamluk Egypt*. Edinburgh: Edinburgh University Press.

(2018). “The Ideology of Decline and the Jews of Ayyubid and Mamluk Syria.” *Muslim–Jewish Relations in the Middle Islamic Period: Jews in the Ayyubid and Mamluk Sultanates (1171–1517)*. S. Conermann. ed. Göttingen: V&R Unipress, Bonn University Press: 95–120.

Holt, Peter (1973). “The Sultanate of al-Manṣūr Lāchīn (696–8/1296–9).” *Bulletin of the School of Oriental and African Studies* 36/3: 521–32.

(1975). “The Position and Power of the Mamlūk Sultan.” *Bulletin of the School of Oriental and African Studies* 38/2: 237–49.

(1977a). *The Eastern Mediterranean in the Period of the Crusades. Warminster.*

(1977b). “The Structure of Government in the Mamluk Sultanate.” *The Eastern Mediterranean Lands in the Period of the Crusades*. P. Holt, ed. Warminster: Aris and Phillips: 44–61.

(1980a). “Qalāwūn's Treaty with Genoa in 1290.” *Der Islam* 57: 101–08.

(1980b). “The Treaties of the Early Mamlūk Sultans with the Frankish States.” *Bulletin of the School of Oriental and African Studies* 43: 67–76.

(1984). “Some Observations on the ‘Abbasid Caliphate of Cairo.” *Bulletin of the School of Oriental and African Studies* 47/3: 501–07.

(1985). “Succession in the Early Mamlūk Sultanate.” *Deutscher Orientalistentag* 16: 6–20.

(1986). *The Age of the Crusades: The Near East from the Eleventh Century to 1517*. London: Longman.

(1995). *Early Mamlūk Diplomacy (1260–1290): Treaties of Baybars and Qalāwūn with Christian Rulers*. Leiden: Brill.

(1995). "An-Nāṣir Muḥammad b. Qalāwūn (684–741/1285–1341): His Ancestry, Kindred and Affinity." *Egypt and Syria in the Fatimid, Ayyubid and Mamluk Eras*. III, Proceedings of the 1st, 2nd, and 3rd International Colloquium organized at the Katholieke Universiteit Leuven in May 1992, 1993, and 1994, OLA 73, Leuven: Peeters: 313–24.

(1998). "Literary Offerings: A Genre of Courtly Literature." *The Mamluks in Egyptian Politics and Society*, T. Phillipp, U. Haarmann, eds. Cambridge: Cambridge University Press: 3–16.

(2001). "The Last Mamlūk Sultan: al-Malik al-Ashraf Ṭūmān Bāy." *Jerusalem Studies in Arabic and Islam* 25: 234–46.

Homerin, T. Emil (1997). "Reflections on Arabic Poetry in the Mamlūk Age." *Mamluk Studies Review* 1: 53–86.

(1999). "Saving Muslim Souls: The *Khānqāh* and the Ṣūfī Duty in Mamlūk Lands." *Mamluk Studies Review* 3: 65–73.

(2001). *From Arab Poet to Muslim Saint: Ibn al-Fāriḍ, His Verse, and His Shrine.* 2nd ed. Cairo: American University in Cairo Press.

(2011). *Emanations of Grace: Mystical Poems by ʿĀʾisha al-Bāʿūniyah*. Louisville: Fons Vitae.

(2019). *Aisha al-Baʿuniyya: A Life in Praise and Love (Makers of the Muslim World)*. London: One World Academic.

Horii, Yutaka (2003). "The Mamlūk Sultan Qānṣūh al-Ghawrī (1501–16) and the Venetians in Alexandria." *Orient* 38: 178–99.

Humphreys, R. Stephen (1972). "The Expressive Intent of the Mamlūk Architecture of Cairo: A Preliminary Essay." *Studia Islamica* 35: 69–119.

(1977a). "The Emergence of the Mamlūk Army." *Studia Islamica* 45: 67–99; Conclusion 46: 147–82.

(1977b). *From Saladin to the Mongols: The Ayyūbids of Damascus*. Albany: State University of New York Press.

(1991). *Islamic History: A Framework for Inquiry*. Princeton: Princeton University Press.

(1998). "Egypt in the World System of the Later Middle Ages." *The Cambridge History of Egypt,* vol. 1*: Islamic Egypt*. C. Petry, ed. Cambridge: Cambridge University Press, 445–61.

(2005). "The Politics of the Mamlūk Sultanate: A Review Essay." *Mamluk Studies Review* 9/1: 221–31.

Husayn, ʿAlaʾ Taha Rizq (2002). *Al-Sujūn waʾl-ʿuqūbāt fī Miṣr ʿaṣr salaṭīn al-Mamālīk*. Jails and Punishments in Egypt in the Age of Mamluk Sultans. Cairo: ʿAyn liʾl-dirasat waʾl-buhuth al-insaniyya waʾl-ijtimaʿiyya.

Igarashi, Daisuke (2006). "The Establishment and Development of al-Dīwān al-Mufrad: Its Background and Implications." *Mamluk Studies Review* 10/1: 117–40.

(2008). "The Private Property and *Awqāf* of the Circassian Mamlūk Sultans: The Case of Barqūq." *Orient* 43: 167–96.

(2009). "The Financial Reforms of Sultan Qāytbāy." *Mamluk Studies Review* 13/1: 27–51.

(2010). "The Evolution of the Sultanic Fisc and *al-Dhakhīrah* during the Circassian Mamluk Period." *Mamluk Studies Review* 14: 65–108.
(2015) *Land Tenure, Fiscal Policy and Imperial Power in Medieval Syro-Egypt*. Chicago: Middle East Documentation Center.
(2019a). "The Waqf-Endowment Strategy of a Mamlūk Military Man: The Contexts, Motives and Purposes of the Endowments of Qijmās al-Isḥāqī (d. 1487)." *Bulletin of the School of Oriental and African Studies* 82/1: 25–53.
Igarashi, D.; T. Ito, eds. (2019b). "Women and Family in Mamluk and Early-Ottoman Egypt, Syria, and Hijaz." *Orient, Journal of the Society for Near Eastern Studies in Japan* (special issue on women) 54 (Tokyo).
Irwin, Robert (1986a). "Factions in Medieval Egypt." *Journal of the Royal Asiatic Society*, 3rd series: 228–46.
(1986b). *The Middle East in the Middle Ages: The Early Mamlūk Sultanate, 1250–1382*. London: Croom Helm.
(1997). "Eating Horses and Drinking Mare's Milk." *Furūsiyya, Riyad, vol.* 1: 148–51.
(1999). "What the Partridge Told the Eagle: A Neglected Arabic Source on Chinggis Khan and the Early History of the Mongols." *The Mongol Empire and its Legacy*. R. Amitai-Preis, D. Morgan, eds. Leiden: Brill: 5–11.
(2002). "The Privatisation of 'Justice' under the Circassian Mamlūks." *Mamluk Studies Review* 6: 63–70.
(2003a). "Mamlūk Literature." *Mamluk Studies Review* 7/1: 1–29.
(2003b). "Al-Maqrīzī and Ibn Khaldūn, Historians of the Unseen." *Mamluk Studies Review* 7/2: 217–30.
(2003c). "Tribal Feuding and Mamluk Factions in Medieval Syria." *Texts, Documents and Artefacts: Islamic Studies in Honour of D. S. Richards*." C. Robinson, ed. Leiden: Brill: 251–64.
(2004a). *The Arabian Nights: A Companion*. New York: I. B. Tauris.
(2004b). "*Futuwwa*: Chivalry and Gangsterism in Medieval Cairo." *Muqarnas* 21: 161–70.
(2004c). "Gunpowder and Firearms in the Mamluk Sultanate Reconsidered." *The Mamluks in Egyptian and Syrian Politics and Society*. M. Winter, A. Levanoni, eds. Leiden: Brill: 117–39.
(2018). *Ibn Khaldūn: An Intellectual Biography*. Princeton: Princeton University Press.
Ito, Takao (2003). "Aufsicht und Verwaltung der Stiftungen im Mamlukischen Ägypten." *Der Islam* 80: 46–66.
Jackson, Sherman (1996). *Islamic Law and the State: The Constitutional Jurisprudence of Shihāb al-Dīn al-Qarāfī*. Studies in Islamic Law and Society 1. Leiden: Brill.
(2012). *Sufism for Non-Sufis? Ibn 'Aṭā' Allah al-Sakandari's Tāj al-'Arūs*. New York: Oxford University Press.
Jayyusi, Lena, trans. (1996). *The Adventures of Sayf Ben Dhī Yazan: An Arabian Folk Epic*. Bloomington: Indiana University Press.
Jayyusi, Salma (2006). "Arabic Poetry in the Post-Classical Age." *The Cambridge History of Arabic Literature*, vol. 6: *Arabic Literature in the Post-Classical Period.* Cambridge: Cambridge University Press: 25–69.

Johansen, Baber (1988). *The Islamic Law on Land Tax and Rent: The Peasants' Loss of Property Rights as Interpreted in the Hanafite Legal Literature of the Mamluk and Ottoman Periods*. London: Croom Helm.

Jomier, Jacques (1953). *Le maḥmal et la caravane égyptienne des pélerins de la Mecque (XIII^e–XX^e siècle)*. Cairo: Institut français d'archéologie orientale, RAPH 20.

Kahil, Abdullah (2008). *The Sultan Ḥasan Complex in Cairo 1357–1365: A Case Study in the Formation of Mamluk Style*. Beirut/Würzburg: Ergon.

Kahle, Paul (1935–40). "Die Katastrophe des Mittelalterlichen Alexandria." *Mélanges Maspero III: Orient islamique. Cairo: Mémoires de l'institut français d'archéologie* 68: 137–54.

Kedar, Benjamin (1993). *The Franks in the Levant, 11th to 14th Centuries*. Collected Studies Series XXI. Brookfield: Aldershot.

Keddie, Nikki (1992). "Material Culture, Technology and Geography: Toward a Historic Comparative Study of the Middle East." *Comparing Muslim Societies: Knowledge and the State in a World Civilization*. J. Cole, ed. Michigan: 31–62.

Kenney, Ellen (2009). *Power and Patronage in Medieval Syria: The Architecture and Urban Works of Tankiz al-Nāṣirī*. Chicago: Middle East Documentation Center.

Khowaiter, Abdul-Aziz (1978). *Baibars the First: His Endeavors and Achievements*. London: Green Mountain Press.

Knysh, Alexander (1999). *Ibn ʿArabī in the Later Islamic Tradition*. Albany: State University of New York Press.

Kohler, Michael (2013). *Alliances and Treaties between Frankish and Muslim Rulers in the Middle East*. Leiden: Brill.

Labib, Subhi (1957). "Ein Brief des Mamluken Sultans Qāʾitbāy an dem Dogen von Venedig aus dem Jahre 1473." *Der Islam* 32: 324–29.

(1959). "Geld und Kredit: Studien zur Wirtschafts-Geschichte Aegyptens im Mittelalter." *Journal of the Economic and Social History of the Orient* 2: 225–46.

(1965a). "Al-Asadī und sein Bericht über Verwaltungs-und Geldreform im 15. Jahrhundert." *Journal of the Economic and Social History of the Orient* 8: 312–16.

(1965b). *Handelsgeschichte Ägyptens im Spätmittelalter (1171–1517)*. Wiesbaden: Franz Steiner.

(1974). "Medieval Islamic Maritime Policy in the Indian Ocean Area." *Recueils de la société Jean Bodin* 32: 225–41.

Lancaster, William; Fidelity (1999). *People, Land and Water in the Arab Middle East: Environments and Landscapes in the Bilād ash-Shām*. Amsterdam: Harwood Academic Publishers.

Lange, Christian (2008). *Justice, Punishment and the Medieval Muslim Imagination*. Cambridge: Cambridge University Press.

Lapidus, Ira (1967). *Muslim Cities in the Later Middle Ages*. Cambridge: Harvard University Press.

(1969). "The Grain Economy of Mamlūk Egypt." *Journal of the Economic and Social History of the Orient* 12/1: 1–15.

(1972). "The Conversion of Egypt to Islam." *Israel Oriental Studies* 2: 248–62.

(2002). *A History of Islamic Societies*. 2nd ed. Cambridge: Cambridge University Press.

Larkin, Margaret (2006). "Popular Poetry in the Post-Classical Period, 1150–1850." *The Cambridge History of Arabic Literature*, vol. 6: *Arabic Literature in the Post-Classical Period.* R. Allen, D. Richards, eds. Cambridge: Cambridge University Press: 191–242.

Lassner, Jacob (1999). *A Mediterranean Society: An Abridgment in One Volume.* Berkeley: University of California Press.

Laoust, Henri (1960). "Le ḥanbalisme sous les mamlouks baḥrides (685–784/ 1260–1382)." *Revue des études islamiques* 28: 1–71.

Leder, Stefan (2002). *Spoken Word and Written Text: Meaning and Social Significance of the Institution of Riwāya.* Tokyo: Islamic Area Studies Project.

(2005). "Damaskus: Entwicklung einer islamischen Metropole (12–14. Jh) und ihre Grundlagen." *Alltagsleben und materielle Kultur in der arabischen Sprache und Litteratur.* T. Bauer, U. Stehli-Werbeck, eds. Wiesbaden: Otto Harrassowitz: 233–50.

(2007). "Religion, Gesellschaft, Identität – Ideologie und Subversion in der Mythenbildung des arabischen, Volkepos." *Heros – Gott, Weltenwürfe und Lebensmodelle im Mythos der Vormoderne.* C. Schmitz, ed. Stuttgart: Franz Steiner: 167–80.

Leiser, Gary (1985). "The Madrasa and Islamization of the Middle East: The Case of Egypt." *Journal of the American Research Center in Egypt* 22: 29–47.

(2017). *Prostitution in the Eastern Mediterranean World.* London: I. B. Tauris.

(2020). "The Life and Times of the Ayyūbid Vizier al-Ṣāḥib b. Shukr." *Der Islam* 97/ 1: 89–119.

Lellouch, Benjamin (2012). "La politique mamelouke de Selim I^er^." *Conquête ottoman de l'Égypte, Arrière-plan, impact, échos.* B. Lellouch, N. Michel, eds. Leiden: Brill: 165–210.

Le Strange, Guy (1965). *Palestine under the Moslems.* Beirut: Khayats.

Lev, Yaacov (2005). *Charity, Endowments, and Charitable Institutions in Medieval Islam.* Gainesville: University Press of Florida.

(2012). "Coptic Rebellions and the Islamization of Medieval Egypt (8th–10th century): Medieval and Modern Perceptions." *Jerusalem Studies in Arabic and Islam* 39: 303–44.

Levanoni, Amalia (1990). "The Mamlūks' Ascent to Power in Egypt." *Studia Islamica* 72: 121–44.

(1994a). "The Consolidation of Aybak's Rule: An Example of Factionalism in the Mamlūk State." *Der Islam* 71: 241–54.

(1994b). "The Mamluk Conception of the Sultanate." *International Journal of Middle East Studies* 26: 373–92.

(1995). *A Turning Point in Mamluk History: The Third Reign of al-Nāṣir Muḥammad ibn Qalāwūn (1310–1341).* Leiden: Brill.

(1998). "Rank-and-File Mamlūks versus Amirs: New Norms in the Mamlūk Military Institution." *The Mamluks in Egyptian Politics and Society.* T. Phillipp, U. Haarmann, eds. Cambridge: Cambridge University Press: 17–31.

(2001a). "Al-Maqrīzī's Account of the Transition from Turkish to Circassian Mamlūk Sultanate: History in the Service of Faith." *The Historiography of Islamic Egypt (c. 950–1800).* H. Kennedy, ed. Leiden: Brill: The Medieval Mediterranean 31: 93–105.

(2001b). "Sagar al-Durr: A Case of Female Sultanate in Medieval Islam." *Egypt and Syria in the Fatimid, Ayyubid and Mamluk Eras.* III, Proceedings of the 6th, 7th, and 8th International Colloquium organized at the Katholieke Universiteit Leuven in May 1997, 1998, and 1999. U. Vermeulen, J. Van Steenbergen, eds. Leuven: Peeters, OLA 102: 209–18.

(2004). "The Sultan's Laqab: A Sign of a New Order in Mamluk Factionalism?" *The Mamluks in Egyptian and Syrian Politics and Society.* M. Winter, A. Levanoni, eds. Leiden: Brill: 79–115.

(2005). "The al-Nashw Episode: A Case Study of 'Moral Economy.'" *Mamluk Studies Review* 9/1: 1–14.

(2006). "Awlād al-Nās in the Mamlūk Army during the Baḥrī Period." *Mamluks and Ottomans: Studies in Honor of Michael Winter.* D. Wasserstein, A. Ayalon, eds. London: Routledge: 96–105.

(2011). "The Ḥalqah in the Mamlūk Army: Why Was It Not Dissolved When It Reached Its Nadir?" *Mamluk Studies Review* 15: 37–65.

(2013). "A Supplementary Source for the Study of Mamlūk Social History: The Taqārīẓ." *Arabica* 60: 146–77.

Levtzion, N; J. F. P. Hopkins, eds. (2000). *Masālik, Corpus of Early Arabic Sources for West African History.* Princeton: Markus Wiener.

Lewicka, Paulina (2005). "Restaurants, Inns and Taverns that Never Were: Some Reflections on Public Consumption in Medieval Cairo." *Journal of the Economic and Social History of the Orient* 48: 40–91.

(2011). *Food and Foodways of Medieval Cairenes: Aspects of Life in an Islamic Metropolis of the Eastern Mediterranean.* Leiden: 2011.

(2012). "Medicine for Muslims? Islamic Theologians, Non-Muslim Physicians, and the Medical Culture of the Mamluk Near East." *Annemarie Schimmel Kolleg Working Papers* 3; www.mamluk.uni-bonn.de/publications/workingpaper/ask-working-paper-03-22.pdf.

(forthcoming). "Projecting the Enemy: Non-Muslims in the Mamluk State." *Conflict and Coexistence: Proceedings of the 29th Congress of the Union Europėene des Arabisants et Islamisants.* T. Bauer, M. Springberg-Hinsen, eds. Leuven: Peeters.

Lewis, Bernard (1982). *Race and Color in Islam.* New York: Harper and Row.

(1984). *The Jews of Islam.* Princeton: Princeton University Press.

(1992). *Race and Slavery in the Middle East: An Historical Enquiry.* Oxford: Oxford University Press.

Little, Donald (1970). *An Introduction to Mamlūk Historiography: An Analysis of Arabic Annalistic and Biographical Sources for the Reign of al-Malik an-Nāṣir Muḥammad ibn Qalā'ūn.* Montreal: McGill-Queen's University Press.

(1983). "Religion under the Mamlūks." *The Muslim World* 7: 165–81.

(1974). "An Analysis of the Relationship between Four Mamlūk Chronicles for 734–45." *Journal of Semitic Studies* 19: 252–68.

(1979a). "The History of Arabia during the Baḥrī Mamlūk Period According to Three Mamlūk Historians." *Studies in the history of Arabia*, vol. 1: *Sources for the History of Arabia*, part 2. A. M. Abdalla, S. al-Sakkar, R. Mortel, eds. Riyadh: 17–23.

(1979b). "Notes on Aitmish, a Mongol Mamlūk." *Die Islamische Welt zwischen Mittelalter und Neuzeit: Festschrift für Hans Robert Roemer um 65. Geburtstag.* U. Haarmann, P. Bachman, eds. Beirut/Wiesbaden: 387–401.

(1984a). *A Catologue of the Islamic Documents from al-Ḥaram al-Sarīf in Jerusalem*. Beirut: Orient-Institut der Deutschen Morgenländischen Gesellschaft.
(1984b). "Relations between Jerusalem and Egypt during the Mamluk Period According to Literary and Documentary Sources." *Egypt and Palestine: A Millennium of Association, 868–1948*. A. Cohen, G. Baer, eds. New York: St. Martin's Press: 73–93.
(1990). "Coptic Converts to Islam during the Baḥrī Mamlūk Period." *Conversion and Continuity: Indigenous Christian Communities in Islamic Lands, Eighth to Eighteenth Centuries*. M. Gervers, R. Bikhazi, eds. Toronto: Pontifical Institute of Mediaeval Studies: 265–88.
(1998a). "Documents Related to the Estate of a Merchant and His Wife in Late Fourteenth-Century Jerusalem." *Mamluk Studies Review* 2: 93–193.
(1998b). "Historiography of the Ayyūbid and Mamlūk Epochs." *The Cambridge History of Egypt*, vol. 1: *Islamic Egypt*. C. Petry, ed. Cambridge: Cambridge University Press: 412–44.
(2002). "Notes on Mamlūk Madrasas." *Mamluk Studies Review* 6: 9–20.
(2003). "A Comparison of al-Maqrīzī and al-ʿAynī as Historians of Contemporary Events." *Mamluk Studies Review* 7/2: 205–15.
(2006). "Diplomatic Missions and Gifts Exchanged by Mamlūks and Ilkhāns." *Beyond the Legacy of Gengis Khan*. L. Komaroff, ed. Leiden: Brill: 30–42.
Loiseau, Julien (2002). "L'Émir en sa maison: Parcours politiques et patrimoine urbain au Caire, d'après les biographies du Manhal Ṣāfī." *Annales Islamologiques* 36: 117–37.
(2010). *Reconstruire la Maison du sultan: Ruine et recomposition de l'ordre urbain au Caire (1350–1450)*. 2 vols. Cairo: Institut français d'archéologie orientale.
(2012). "The City of Two Hundred Mosques: Friday Worship and Its Spread in the Monuments of Mamluk Cairo." *The Arts of the Mamluks in Egypt and Syria – Evolution and Impact*. D. Abou-Seif, ed. Göttingen: Vandenhoeck and Ruprecht Unipress: 183–201.
(2013). "Choisir sa famille: *Waqf* et transmission patrimoniale en Égypte au XV^e^ siecle." *Annales Islamologiques* 47: Histoires de famille: 175–95.
(2014). *Les Mamlouks, XIIIe–XVIe siècle: Une expérience du pouvoir dans l'Islam médiéval*. Paris: Éditions du Seuil.
(2019a). "Abyssinia at al-Azhar: Muslim Students from the Horn of Africa in Late Medieval Cairo." *Northeast African Studies* 19/1: 61–84.
(2019b). "The Ḥāṭī and the Sultan: Letters and Embassies from Abyssinia to the Mamluk Court." *Mamluk Cairo, a Crossroads for Embassies: Studies on Diplomacy and Diplomatics*. F. Bauden, M. Dekkiche, eds. Leiden: Brill: 638–57.
Lopez, Robert; Leonard, Irving (1955). *Medieval Trade in the Mediterranean World: Illustrative Documents Translated with Introductions and Notes*. New York: Columbia University Press.
Lopez, R.; Miskimin, H.; Udovitch, A. (1970). "England to Egypt, 1350–1500: Long-Term Trends and Long-Distance Trade." *Studies in the Economic History of the Middle East*. M. A. Cook, ed. London: 93–128.
Lutfi, Hoda (1981). "al-Sakhāwī's Kitāb al-Nisā' as a Source for the Social and Economic History of Muslim Women during the Fifteenth Century A.D." *The Muslim World* 71/2: 104–24.

Lutfi, Huda (1985). *Al-Quds al-Mamlūkiyya: A History of Mamluk Jerusalem based on the Haram Documents*. Berlin: Klaus Schwarz.

Lyons, M. C. (1995). *The Arabian Epic: Heroic and Oral Story-Telling*. Cambridge: Cambridge University Press.

Lyons, M. C., Jackson, D. E. P. (1982). *Saladin: The Politics of the Holy War*. Cambridge: Cambridge University Press.

Mahamid, Ayman (2003). "Developments and Changes in the Establishment of Islamic Educational Institutions in Medieval Jerusalem." *Annales Islamologiques* 37: 329–54.

Mahdi, Muhsin, ed. (1984–94). *The Thousand and One Nights (Alf Layla wa-Layla) from the Earliest Known Sources*. 3 vols. Leiden: Brill.

Makdisi, George (1981). *The Rise of Colleges: Institutions of Learning in Islam and the West*. Edinburgh: Edinburgh University Press.

Mann, Jacob (1970). *The Jews in Egypt and Palestine under the Fāṭimid Caliphs*. New York: Ktav Publishing.

Manz, Beatrice (2007). *Power, Politics and Religion in Timurid Iran*. Cambridge: Cambridge University Press.

Marmon, Shaun (1999). "Domestic Slavery in the Mamluk Empire: A Preliminary Sketch." *Slavery in the Islamic Middle East*. S. Marmon, ed. Princeton: Markus Wiener: 1–23.

Marsham, Andrew (2009). *Rituals of Islamic Monarchy*. Edinburgh: Edinburgh University Press.

Martel-Thoumian, Bernadette (1992). *Les Civils et l'administration dans l'état militaire mamlūk (IX^e/XV^e siècle)*. Damascus: Institut français.

(2003). *Les manuscrits historiques de la bibliothéque nationale de Damas: Periode Mamelouke, 648–922 H. 1250–1517*. Damascus: Institut français du Proche-Orient.

(2005). "The Sale of Office and Its Economic Consequences during the Rule of the Last Circassians (872–922/1468–1516)." *Mamluk Studies Review* 9/2: 49–83.

(2012). *Délinquence et order social: l'état mamlouk syro-égyptien face au crime à la fin du IX^e–XV^e siècle*. Bordeaux: Ausonius, Scripta medievalia 21.

Mas Latrie, Louis de (1852). "Note sur le transport des armes et des esclaves en Égypte pendant le Moyen Age." *Histoire de l'île de Chypre sous le règne des princes de la maison de Lusignan*, vol. 2: *Documents et mémoires servant de preuves à l'histoire de Chypre sous les Lusignans*. Paris: 125–28.

Massoud, Sami (2007). *The Chronicles and Annalistic Sources of the Early Mamluk Circassian Period*. Leiden: Brill.

Mauder, Christian (2021). *In the Sultan's Salon: Learning, Religion and Rulership at the Mamlūk Court of Qāniṣawh al-Ghawrī (r. 1501–1516)*. Leiden: Brill.

Mayer, Leo (1933). *Saracenic Heraldry*. Oxford: Clarendon Press.

(1938). *The Buildings of Qāytbāy as Described in his Endowment Deed*. London: Arthur Probsthain.

(1952). *Mamluk Costume, A Survey*. Geneva: Albert Kundig.

Mayeur-Jaouen, Catherine (1994). *Al-Sayyid Aḥmad al-Badawī: Un grand saint de l'Islam égyptien*. Cairo: Institut français d'archéologie orientale.

(2006). "Maitres, cheikhs et ancêtres: saints du Delta a l'époque mamelouke." *Le Développement du soufisme en Égypte a l'époque mamelouke*. R. McGregor, A. Sabra, eds. Cairo: Institut français orientale: 41–50.

McGregor, Richard (2002). "New Sources for the Study of Sufism in Mamluk Egypt." *Bulletin of the School of Oriental and African Studies* 65/2: 300–22.
(2004). *Sanctity and Mysticism in Medieval Egypt: The Wafāʾ Sufi Order and the Legacy of ibn ʿArabī.* Albany: State University of New York Press.
(2009). "The Problem of Sufism." *Mamluk Studies Review* 13/2: 69–83.
McGregor, Richard, Sabra, Adam, eds. (2006). *Le Développement du soufisme en Égypte à l'époque mamelouke.* Cairo: Institut d'archeologie orientale.
(2013). "Sufis and Soldiers in Medieval Egypt: Parading the Aesthetics of Agency." *Annales Islamologiques* 46: 215–26.
(2020). *Islam and the Devotional Object: Seeing Religion in Egypt and Syria.* Cambridge: Cambridge University Press.
Meinecke, Michael (1980). *Die Restaurierung der Madrasa des Amirs Sābiq al-Dīn Mitqāl al-Anūkī und die Sanierung des Darb Qirmiz in Kairo.* Cairo: Deutches Archäologisches Institut.
(1992). *Die mamlukische Architektur in Ägypten und Syrien (648/1250 bis 923/1517).* Islamische Reihe 5. Cairo: Abhandlungen des Deutschen Archäologischen Instituts. Glückstadt: Verlag J. J. Augustin.
Meloy, John (2001). "Copper Money in Late Mamluk Cairo: Chaos or Control?" *Journal of the Economic and Social History of the Orient* 44/3: 293–321.
(2003). "Imperial Strategy and Political Exigency: The Red Sea Spice Trade and the Mamlūk Sultanate in the Fifteenth Century." *Journal of the American Oriental Society* 123/1: 1–19.
(2004). "The Privatization of Protection: Extortion and the State in the Circassian Mamlūk Period." *Journal of the Economic and Social History of the Orient* 47/2: 195–212.
(2005). "Economic Intervention and the Political Economy of the Mamlūk State under al-Ashraf Barsbāy." *Mamuk Studies Review* 9/2: 85–13.
(2006). "Celebrating the Mahmal: The Rajab Festival in Fifteenth-Century Cairo." *History and Historiography of Post-Mongol Central Asia and the Middle East, Studies in Honor of John E. Woods.* J. Pfeiffer, S. A. Quinn, eds. Wiesbaden: Harrassowitz: 404–27.
(2010). *Imperial Power and Maritime Trade: Mecca and Cairo in the Later Middle Ages.* Chicago: Middle East Documentation Center.
(2011). "Money and Sovereignty in Mecca: Issues of the Sharifs in the Fifteenth and Sixteenth Centuries." *Journal of the Economic and Social History of the Orient* 53/5: 712–38.
Meri, Josef (2002). *The Cult of Saints among Muslims and Jews in Medieval Syria.* Oxford: Oxford University Press.
Michel, Nicolas (1998). "Les rizaq iḥbāsiyya, terres agricoles en mainmorte dans l'Égypte mamelouke et ottomane: Étude des Dafātir al-Aḥbās ottomans." *Annales Islamologiques* 30: 105–98.
(2018). *L'Egypte des villages autour du seizieme siecle.* Collection Turcica 23. Louvain: Bristol, CT: Peeters.
Mohamed, Bashir (2007). *L'Art des chevaliers en pays d'Islam: Collection de la Furusiyya Art Foundation.* Paris: Institut du monde arabe, Skira.
Moreh, Shmuel (1992). *Live Theater and Dramatic Literature in the Medieval Arab World.* Edinburgh: Edinburgh University Press.

Mortel, Richard (1994). "The Mercantile Community of Mecca during the Late Mamlūk Period." *Journal of the Royal Asiatic Society*, 3rd series 4/1: 15–35.
(1995a). "The Decline of Mamlūk Civil Bureaucracy in the Fifteenth Century: The Career of Abū'l-Khayr al-Naḥḥās." *Journal of Islamic Studies* 6/2: 173–88.
(1995b). "Taxation in the Amirate of Mecca during the Medieval Period." *Bulletin of the School of Oriental and African Studies* 58/1: 1–16.
(1996). "Grand Dawādār" and Governor of Jedda: The Career of the Fifteenth Century Mamlūk Magnate Gānibak al-Ẓāhirī." *Arabica* 43/3: 437–56.
Mostafa, Salih (1972). *Moschee des Farag Ibn Barqūq in Kairo*, mit einem Beitrag von Ulrich Haarmann. Glückstadt: Augustin.
Muhanna, Elias (2010). "The Sultan's New Clothes: Ottoman-Mamluk Gift Exchange in the Fifteenth Century." *Muqarnas* 27: 189–207.
(2018). *The World in a Book: al-Nuwayri and the Islamic Encyclopedic Tradition*. Princeton: Princeton University Press.
Mundy, Martha (2004). "Ownership or Office? A Debate in Islamic Hanafite Jurisprudence over the Nature of the Military 'Fief', from the Mamluks to the Ottomans." *Law, Anthropology, and the Constitution of the Social: Making Persons and Things*. A. Pottage, M. Mundy, eds. Cambridge: Cambridge University Press: 142–65.
Mundy, Martha;, Smith, Richard S. (2007). *Governing Property, Making the Modern State: Law, Administration and Production in Ottoman Syria*. London: Tauris.
Naamoune, Nasr al-Din (2003). "La 'modernisation' de la vie de Baybars au XV$^{e}$ siècle." *Lectures du Roman de Baybars*. J-C. Garcin, ed. Marseille: Éditions Parenthéses, Mémoires de la Mission Archéologique française au Caire: 143–58.
Nakamachi, Nobutaka (2006). "The Rank and Status of Military Refugees in the Mamluk Army: A Reconsideration of the Wāfidīyah." *Mamluk Studies Review* 10/1: 55–81.
Nielsen, Jorgen (1972). *Secular Justice in an Islamic State: Maẓālim under the Baḥrī Mamlūks*. London.
Northrup, Linda (1998a). *From Slave to Sultan: The Career of al-Manṣūr Qalāwūn and the Consolidation of Mamlūk Rule in Egypt and Syria (678–689/1279–1290)*. Stuttgart: Franz Steiner Verlag.
(1998b). "The Baḥrī Mamlūk Sultanate, 1250–1390." *The Cambridge History of Egypt*, vol. 1: *Islamic Egypt*. C. Petry, ed. Cambridge: Cambridge University Press: 242–89.
(2001). "Qalawun's Patronage of the Medical Sciences in Thirteenth-Century Egypt." *Mamluk Studies Review* 5: 119–140
(2007). "Military Slavery in the Islamic and Mamluk Context." *Unfreie Arbeit: Ökonomische und kulturgeschichtliche Perspektiven*. M. Erdem Kabadayi, T. Reichardt, eds. Zurich, New York: Georg Olms: 115–32.
(2014). "Al-Bimaristan al-Mansuri–Explorations: The Interface between Medicine, Politics and Culture in Early Mamluk Egypt." *History and Society during the Mamluk Period (1250–1517)*. Studies of the Annemarie Schimmel Research College 1. S. Conermann, ed. Bonn: V&R unipress/Bonn University Press.
Nwiya, Paul (1986). *Ibn ʿAṭāʾ Allāh (m. 709/1309) et la naissance de la confrérie šādhilite*. Beirut: Dar el-Machreq.

O'Kane, Bernard (2000). "Domestic and Religious Architecture in Cairo: Mutual Influences." *The Cairo Heritage: Essays in Honor of Laila Ali Ibrahim*. D. Behrens-Abouseif, ed. Cairo: American University in Cairo Press: 148–82.

Olesen, Henrik (1991). *Culte de saints et pélerinages chez Ibn Taymiyya*. Paris: Geuthner, Bibliothéque d'études islamiques.

O'Sullivan, Shaun (2006). "Coptic Conversion and the Islamization of Egypt." *Mamluk Studies Review* 10/2: 65–79.

Oualdi, M'hamed (2008). "D'Europe et d'Orient, les approaches de l'esclavage des chrétiens en terres d'Islam." *Annales: Histoire, sciences sociales* 63 année 4: 49–64.

Ouerfelli, Mohamed (2008). *Le sucre: production, commercialization, et l'usage dans la Méditerranée médiévale*. Leiden: Brill.

Pahlitzsch, Johannes (2010). "The Mamluks and Cyprus: Transcultural Relations between Muslim and Christian Rulers in the Eastern Mediterranean in the Fifteenth Century." *Acteurs des transferts culturels en Méditerranée médiévale: Ateliers des Deutschen Historischen Instituts Paris*. R. Abdellatif, Y. Benhima, D. König, E. Ruchaud, eds. Paris: 111–20.

Pascual, Jean-Paul (2003). *Poverty and Wealth in the Muslim Mediterranean World*. Paris: Maisonneuve.

Peake, Frederick G. (1958). *A History of Jordan and Its Tribes*. Coral Gables, FL: University of Miami Press.

Perlmann, M. (1942). "Notes on Anti-Christian Propaganda in the Mamlūk Empire." *Bulletin of the School of Oriental and African Studies* 10/4: 843–61.

(1958). "Asnawi's Tract against Christian Officials." *Ignaz Goldziher Memorial*, vol. 2. S. Löwinger, J. Somogii, eds. Jerusalem: R. Mass: 172–208.

Peters, Rudolph (2005). *Crime and Punishment in Islamic Law: Theory and Practice from the Sixteenth to the Twenty-First Century*. Cambridge: Cambridge University Press.

Petersen, Andrew (2005). *The Towns of Palestine under Muslim Rule, AD 600–1600*. Oxford: Oxford University Press.

Petry, Carl (1981). *The Civilian Elite of Cairo in the Later Middle Ages*. Princeton: Princeton University Press.

(1983). "A Paradox of Patronage during the Later Mamluk Period." *The Muslim World* 73/3–4: 182–207.

(1986). "Travel Patterns of Medieval Notables in the Near East." *Studia Islamica* 62: 53–87.

(1991a). "Class Solidarity vs. Gender Gain: Women as Custodians of Property in Later Medieval Egypt." *Women and Middle Eastern History: Shifting Boundaries in Sex and Gender*. N. Keddie, B. Baron, eds. New Haven: Yale University Press: 122–42.

(1991b). "Copts in Late Medieval Egypt." *The Coptic Encyclopedia*. A. Atiya, ed. New York: Macmillan, 2: 618–35.

(1991a). "Holy War, Unholy Peace? Relations between the Mamluk Sultanate and European States Prior to the Ottoman Conquest." *The Jihad and Its Times*. H. Dajani-Shakeel, R. Messier, eds. Ann Arbor: University of Michigan Press: 106–9.

(1993). *Twilight of Majesty: The Reigns of the Mamluk Sultans al-Ashraf Qāytbāy and Qānṣūh al-Ghawrī in Egypt*. Seattle: University of Washington Press.

(1994a). "From Slaves to Benefactors: the Ḥabashīs of Mamlūk Cairo." *Sudanic Africa* 5: 57–66.
(1994b). *Protectors or Praetorians? The Last Mamlūk Sultans and Egypt's Waning as a Great Power*. Albany: State University of New York Press.
(1997). "Conjugal Rights vs. Class Prerogatives: A Divorce Case in Mamluk Cairo." *Women in the Medieval Dar al-Islam: Power Patronage and Piety*. G. Hambly, ed. New York: St. Martin's Press: 227–40.
(1998a). "Fractionalized Estates in a Centralized Regime: The Holdings of al-Ashraf Qāytbāy and Qānṣūh al-Ghawrī according to their Waqf Deeds." *Journal of the Economic and Social History of the Orient* 41/1: 96–117.
(1998b). "The Military Institution and Innovation in the Late Mamlūk Period." *The Cambridge History of Egypt*, vol. 1: *Islamic Egypt*. C. Petry, ed. Cambridge: Cambridge University Press: 462–89.
(2000). "Waqf as an Instrument of Investment in the Mamluk Sultanate: Security or Profit?" *Slave Elites in the Middle East and Africa: A Comparative Study*. M. Toru, J. E. Philips, eds. New York: Kegan Paul: 95–115.
(2001). "Robing Ceremonials in Late Mamluk Egypt: Hallowed Traditions, Shifting Protocols." *Robes and Honor: The Medieval World of Investiture*. S. Gordon, ed. New York: St. Martin's Press: 353–377.
(2004). "The Estate of al-Khawand Fāṭima al-Khassbakiyya: Royal Spouse, Autonomous Investor." *The Mamluks in Egyptian and Syrian Politics and Society*. M. Winter, A. Levanoni, eds. Leiden: Brill: 277–94.
(2012a). *The Criminal Underworld in a Medieval Islamic Society: Narratives from Cairo and Damascus under the Mamluks*. Chicago: Middle East Documentation Center.
(2012b). "Educational Initiatives as Depicted in the Biographical Literature of Medieval Cairo: The Debate over Prestige and Venue." *Medieval Prosopography* 23: 101–123.
(2013). "Crime and Scandal in Foreign Relations of the Mamluk Sultanate: Espionage and Succession Crises linked to Cyprus." *La frontière méditerranéenne du XV^e^ au XVII^e^ siècle*. B. Heyberger, A. Fuess, eds. Centre d`études superieures de la Renaissance. Tours: BREPOLS: 145–61.
(2014). "'Travel Patterns of Medieval Notables in the Near East Reconsidered." *Everything is on the Move: The Mamluk Empire as a Node in (Trans-) Regional Networks*. S. Conermann, ed. Göttingen: Vandenhoeck and Ruprecht Unipress: 165–180.
(2018). "Gendered Nuances in Historiographical Discourses of the Mamluk Period: Muted Praise? Veiled Trivialization? Enigmatic Transgressions?" *Mamluk Historiography Revisited: Narratological Perspectives*. S. Conermann, ed. Göttingen: Vandenhoeck and Ruprecht Unipress: 153–74.
Philipp, Thomas; Haarmann, Ulrich, eds. (1998). *The Mamluks in Egyptian Politics and Society*. Cambridge: Cambridge University Press.
Pipes, Daniel (1981). *Slave Soldiers and Islam: The Genesis of a Military System*. New Haven: Yale University Press.
Poliak, A. N. (1934). "Les révolts populaires en Égypte a l'époque des Mamelouks et leurs causes économiques." *Revue des études islamiques* 8: 251–71.

(1935). "Le caractère colonial de l'État mamelouk dans ses rapports avec la Horde d'Or." *Revue des études islamiques* 9: 231–48.

(1937). "Some Notes on the Feudal System of the Mamlūks." *Journal of the Royal Asiatic Society* 69/1: 97–107.

(1939). *Feudalism in Egypt, Syria, Palestine and the Lebanon*. London: Royal Asiatic Society.

(1942). "The Influence of Chingiz-Khan's Yasa on the General Organization of the Mamluk State." *Bulletin of the School of Oriental and African Studies* 4: 862–76.

Popper, William (1955–57). *Egypt and Syria under the Circassian Sultans, 1382–1468: Systematic Notes to Ibn Taghrī Birdī's Chronicles of Egypt*. Vols. 15–16. Berkeley: University of California Publications in Semitic Philology.

Pouzet, Louis (1991). *Damas au VIIe/XIIe siècle. Vie et structures religieuses dans une métropole islamique*. Beirut: Dar el-machreq.

Prawer, J. (1972). *A History of the Latin Kingdom of Jerusalem*. London.

Al-Qarmut, 'Abd al-Razzaq al-Tantawi (1995). *Al-'Alaqāt al-Miṣriyya al-'Uthmāniyya*. Cairo: al-Zahra' li'l-I'lam al-'Arabi.

Rabbat, Nasser (1995). *The Citadel of Cairo: A New Interpretation of Royal Mamluk Architecture*. Leiden: Brill.

(2003). "Who Was al-Maqrīzī? A Biographical Sketch." *Mamluk Studies Review* 7/2: 1–19.

(2006). "The Militarization of Taste in Medieval Bilād al-Shām." *Muslim Military Architecture in Greater Syria, from the Coming of Islam to the Ottoman Period*. H. Kennedy, ed. Leiden: Brill: 84–105.

(2010). *Mamluk History through Architecture: Monuments, Culture and Politics in Medieval Egypt and Syria*. London: New York: I. B. Tauris.

(2012a). "In Search of a Triumphant Image: The Experimental Quality of Early Mamluk Art." *The Arts of the Mamluks in Egypt and Syria – Evolution and Impact*. D. Behrens-Abouseif, ed. Göttingen: Vandenhoeck and Ruprecht Unipress: 21–35.

(2012b). "Was al-Maqrīzī's *Khiṭaṭ* a Khaldūnian History?" *Der Islam* 89/1: 118–40.

(2020). "Brotherhood of the Towers: On the Spatiality of the Mamluk Caste." *Thresholds* 48: 116–21.

Rabie, Hassanein (1972). *The Financial System of Egypt: A. H. 564–741/A.D. 1169–1341*. London: Oxford University Press.

(1975). "The Training of the Mamlūk Fāris." *War, Technology and Society in the Middle East*. V. J. Parry, M. E. Yapp, eds. London: 153–63.

(1978). "Political Relations between the Safavids of Persia and the Mamluks of Egypt and Syria in the Early Sixteenth Century." *Journal of the American Research Center in Egypt* 15: 75–81.

(1981). "Some Technical Aspects of Agriculture in Medieval Egypt." *The Islamic Middle East, 700–900: Studies in Economic and Social History*. A. Udovitch, ed. Princeton: Darwin Press: 59–90.

Rafeq, Abdul-Karim. "The Application of Islamic Law in the Ottoman Courts in Damascus: The Case of the Rental of Waqf Land." *Dispensing Justice in Islam: Qadis and Their Judgements*. M. K. Masud, R. Peters, D. S. Powers, eds. Leiden: Brill: 411–25.

Rapoport, Yossef (2004). "Invisible Peasants, Marauding Nomads: Taxation, Tribalism, and Rebellion in Mamluk Egypt." *Mamluk Studies Review* 8/2: 1–22.

(2005). *Marriage, Money and Divorce in Medieval Islamic Society*. Cambridge: Cambridge University Press.

(2007). "Women and Gender in Mamluk Society: An Overview." *Mamluk Studies Review* 11/2: 1–47.

(2012a). "Irrigation in the Medieval Islamic Fayyūm: Local Control in a Large-Scale Hydraulic System." *Journal of the Economic and Social History of the Orient* 55: 1–31.

(2012b). "Royal Justice and Religious Law: *Siyāsah* and *Sharīʿah* under the Mamlūks." *Mamluk Studies Review* 16: 71–102.

(2013). "Ibn Ḥajar al-ʿAsqalānī, His Wife, Her Slave-Girl." *Annales Islamologiques* 47: 327–51.

(2014). "New Directions in the Social History of the Mamluk Era." *History and Society during the Mamluk Period 1(1250–1517)*. S. Conermann, ed. Bonn: Bonn University Press: 143–55.

(2018a). *Rural Economy and Tribal Society in Islamic Egypt: A Study of al-Nābulusī's* Villages of the Fayyūm, *The Medieval Countryside.* Vol. 19 (BREPOLS).

(2018b). *The Villages of the Fayyum, a Thirteenth-Century Register of Rural Islamic Egypt; The Medieval Countryside*. Vol. 18. Y. Rapoport, I. Shahar, eds., trans. BREPOLS.

Raymond, André (1973). *Artisans et commercants du Caire au XVIII^e siècle*. Damascus: Institut français.

Raymond, André, Wiet, Gaston (1979). *Les marchés du Caire: traduction annotée du texte de Maqrīzī*. Cairo: Institut français d'archéologie orientale.

Reid, Megan (2013). *Law and Piety in Medieval Islam*. Cambridge: Cambridge University Press.

Reinaud, M. (1829). "Traités de commerce entre la république de Venise et les derniers sultans mameloucs d'Égypte, traduits de l'Italien, et accompagnés d'éclairissements." *Journal Asiatique* 4/19: 22–51.

Reinfandt, Lucian (2002). "Religious Endowments and Succession to Rule: The Career of a Sultan's Son in the Fifteenth Century." *Mamluk Studies Review* 6: 51–62.

(2003). *Mamlukische Sultansstiftungen des 9./15. Jahrhunderts: Nach den Urkunden der Stifter al-Asraf Īnāl und al-Muʾayyad Aḥmad Ibn Īnāl*. Berlin: Klaus Schwarz.

(2011). "The Administration of Welfare under the Mamluks." *Court Cultures in the Muslim World: Seventh to Nineteenth Centuries*. A. Fuess, J.-P. Hartung, eds. London: Routledge: 263–72.

Renard, John (1998). "Mamluk Sultan Barquq's Waqf." *Windows on the House of Islam: Muslim Sources on Spirituality and Religious Life*. J. Renard, ed. Berkeley: University of California Press: 226–31.

Revault, Jacques (1982). "L'architecture domestique du Caire a l'époque mamelouke (XIII^e–XVI^e siècle" *Palais et maisons du Caire*, vol. 1: *Époque mamelouke, xiii^e–xvi^e siècle*. J.-C. Garcin, B. Maury, J. Revault, Z. Mona, eds. Paris: Centre national de recherche scientifique: 19–142.

Reynolds, Dwight (1995). *Heroic Poets, Poetic Heroes: The Ethnography of Performance in an Arabic Oral Epic Tradition*. Ithaca: Cornell University Press.

(2001). *Interpreting the Self: Autobiography in the Arabic Literary Tradition.* Berkeley: University of California Press.

(2006a). "A Thousand and One Nights: A History of the Text and Its Reception." *The Cambridge History of Arabic Literature*, vol. 6: *Arabic Literature in the Post-Classical Period.* R. Allen, D. Richards, eds. Cambridge: Cambridge University Press: 270–91.

(2006b). "Sīrat Banī Hilāl." *The Cambridge History of Arabic Literature*, vol. 6: *Arabic Literature in the Post-Classical Period.* R. Allen, D. Richards, eds. Cambridge: Cambridge University Press: 307–18.

Richards, Donald (1969). "The Coptic Bureaucracy under the Mamlūks." *Colloque international sur l'histoire du Caire*. Cairo: Ministère de la Culture: 373–81.

(1998). "Mamlūk Amirs and Their Families and Households." *The Mamluks in Egyptian Politics and Society*. T. Phillipp, U. Haarmann, eds. Cambridge: Cambridge University Press: 32–54.

(2004). "Glimpses of Provincial Mamluk Society from the Documents of the Ḥaram al-Sharīf in Jerusalem." *The Mamluks in Egyptian and Syrian Politics and Society.* M. Winter, A. Levanoni, eds. Leiden: Brill: 45–57.

Rogers, J. Michael (1990). "To and Fro: Aspects of Mediterranean Trade and Communication in the Fifteenth and Sixteenth Centuries." *Revue du monde musulman et de la Méditerranée* 55/56: 57–74.

Rosenthal, Franz (1952, 1968). *A History of Muslim Historiography*. Leiden: Brill.

ed. (1989). *The History of al-Ṭabarī,* vol. 1*: General Introduction and from the Creation to the Flood.* Albany: State University of New York Press.

Rowson, Everett (1991). "The Categorization of Gender and Sexual Irregularity in Medieval Arabic Vice Lists." *Body Guards: The Cultural Politics of Gender Ambiguity*. J. Epstein, K. Straub, eds. New York, London: Routledge: 50–79.

(1997). "Two Homoerotic Narratives from Mamluk Literature: al-Safadi's Lawàt al-shaki and Ibn Daniyal's al-Mutayyam." *Homoeroticism in Classical Arabic Literature,* J. W. Wright, E. K. Rowson, eds. New York: Columbia University Press: 158–91.

(2003). "An Alexandrian Age in Fourteenth-Century Damascus: Twin Commentaries on Two Celebrated Arabic Epistles." *Mamluk Studies Review* 7/1: 97–110.

(2008). "Homoerotic Liaisons among the Mamluk Elite in Late Medieval Egypt and Syria." *Islamicate Sexualities: Translations across Temporal Geographies of Desire*. K. Babayan, A. Najmabadi, eds. Cambridge, MA: Harvard University Press: 204–38.

Ruggles, D. Fairchild (2020). *Tree of Pearls: The Extraordinary Architectural Patronage of the 13th-Century Egyptian Slave-Queen Shajar Al-Durr.* Oxford: Oxford University Press.

Sabra, Adam (2000). *Poverty and Charity in Medieval Islam: Mamluk Egypt, 1250–1517*. Cambridge: Cambridge University Press.

(2004). "The Rise of a New Class? Land Tenure in Fifteenth-Century Egypt: A Review Article." *Mamluk Studies Review* 8/2: 203–10.

(2005). "Public Policy or Private Charity? The Ambivalent Character of Islamic Charitable Endowments." *Stiftungen in Christentum, Judentum und Islam vor der Moderne, Auf der Suche nach ihren Gemeinsamkeiten und Unterschieden in religiösen Grunlagen, praktischen Zwecken und historischen Transformationen.* M. Borgolte, ed. Berlin: Akademie: 95–108.

(2006). "Illiterate Sufis and Learned Artisans: The Circle of ʿAbd al-Wahhāb al-Shaʿrānī." *Le développement du Soufisme en Égypte à l'époque mamelouke.* R. McGregor, A. Sabra, eds. Cairo: Institut français d'archéologie orientale: 153–68.

Sabra, Adam; Margariti, Roxani Eleni; Sijpesteijn, Petra M., eds. (2011). *Histories of the Middle East: Studies in Middle Eastern Society, Economy and Law in Honor of A.L. Udovitch.* Leiden: Brill.

Sadek, Mohamed-Moain (1991). *Die mamlukische Architektur der Stadt Gaza.* Berlin: Klaus Schwartz Verlag, Islamkundliche Untersuchungen 144.

Salam-Liebich, Hayat (1983). *The Architecture of the Mamluk City of Tripoli.* Cambridge, MA: Aga Khan Program for Islamic Architecture.

Salibi, K. S. (1957a). "Listes chronologiques des grands cadis de l'Égypte sous les Mamlouks." *Revue des Études Islamiques* 25: 81–126.

(1957b). "The Maronites of Lebanon under Frankish and Mamluk Rule (1099–1516)." *Arabica* 4: 288–303.

(1958). "The Banū Jamāʿa: A Dynasty of Shāfiʿite Jurists in the Mamlūk Period." *Studia Islamica* 9: 97–109.

Sanders, Paula (1994). *Ritual, Politics and the City in Fatimid Cairo.* Albany: State University of New York Press.

(2008). *Creating Medieval Cairo: Empire, Religion, and Architectural Preservation in Nineteenth-Century Egypt.* Cairo; New York: American University in Cairo Press.

Al-Sarraf, Shihab (2004). "Mamluk Furūsīyah Literature and Its Antecedents." *Mamluk Studies Review* 8/1: 141–200.

Sartain, E. M. (1975). *Jalāl al-Dīn al-Suyūṭī: Biography and Background.* Cambridge: Cambridge University Press.

Sato, Tgusitaka (1979). "The Evolution of the *Iqṭāʿ* System under the Mamluks – An Analysis of al-Rawk al-Ḥusāmī and al-Rawk al-Nāṣirī." *Memoirs of the Research Department of the Toyo Bunko (The Oriental Library)* 37: 99–131.

(1997). *State and Rural Society in Medieval Islam: Sultans, Muqtaʿs and Fallahun.* Leiden: Brill.

(1998). "The Proposers and Supervisors of al-Rawk al-Nāṣirī in Mamlūk Egypt." *Mamluk Studies Review* 2: 73–92.

(2006). "Slave Traders and Kārimi Merchants during the Mamlūk Period: A Comparative Study." *Mamluk Studies Review* 10/1: 141–55.

(2007). "Fiscal Administration in Syria during the Reign of Sultan al-Nāṣir Muḥammad." *Mamluk Studies Review* 11/1: 19–37.

Sauvaget, Jean (1941a). *Alep, essai sur le développement d'une grande ville syrienne, des origines au milieu du XIXe siècle.* Paris: P. Geuthner.

(1941b). *La poste aux chevaux dans l'empire des mamelouks.* Paris: Adrien-Maisonneuve.

(1950). "Noms et surnoms des Mamelouks." *Journal asiatique* 238: 31–58.

Scanlon, George; ed., tr. (1960). *A Muslim Manual of War Being Tafrij al-kurub fi tadbir al-hurub by ʿUmar ibn Ibrahim al-Awsi al-Ansari.* Cairo: American University in Cairo Press.

Schilcher, Lynda (1991). "The Grain Economy of Late Ottoman Syria and the Issue of Large-Scale Commercialization." *Landholding and Commercial Architecture in the Middle East*. C. Keydar, F. Tabak, eds. Albany: State University of New York Press: 173–95.

Schimmel, Annemarie (1942). "Kalif und Ḳāḍī im Spätmittelalterlichen Ägypten." *Die Welt des Islams* 24: 1–128.

(1968). "Sufismus und Heiligenverehrung im spätmittelalterichen Ägypten." *Festschrift Werner Caskel*. Erwin Gräf, ed. Leiden: Brill: 274–89.

(1975). *Mystical Dimensions of Islam*. Chapel Hill, NC: University of North Carolina Press.

Schregle, Götz (1961). *Die Sultanin von Ägypten: Sagarat ad-Durr in der arabischen Geschichtsschreibung und Literatur*. Wiesbaden: Harrassowitz.

Schultz, Warren (1998a). "Maḥmūd b. ʿAlī and the New Fulūs: Fourteenth-Century Egyptian Copper Coinage Reconsidered." *American Journal of Numismatics* 10: 123–44.

(1998b). "The Monetary History of Egypt, 642–1517." *The Cambridge History of Egypt*, vol. 1: *Islamic Egypt*. C. Petry, ed. Cambridge: Cambridge University Press: 327–38.

(1999). "Mamlūk Monetary History: A Review Essay." *Mamluk Studies Review* 3: 183–205.

(2001). "Mamlūk Egyptian Copper Coinage before 759/1357–1358: A Preliminary Inquiry." *Mamluk Studies Review* 5: 25–43.

(2003a). "The Circulation of Silver Coins in the Baḥrī Period." *The Mamlūks in Egyptian and Syrian Politics and Society*, A. Levanoni, M. Winter, eds. Leiden: Brill: 221–44.

(2003b). "'It Has No Root among Any Community that Believes in Revealed Religion, Nor Legal Foundation for Its Implementation': Placing al-Maqrizi's Comments on Money in a Wider Context." *Mamluk Studies Review* 7/2: 169–81.

(2003c). "Mamlūk Metrology and the Numismatic Evidence." *Al-Masāq: Journal of the Medieval Mediterranean* 15/1 (March 2003): 59–76.

(2004). "The Circulation of Dirhams in the Baḥrī Period." *The Mamluks in Egyptian and Syrian Politics and Society*. M. Winter, A. Levanoni, eds. Leiden: Brill: 221–44.

(2006). "Mansa Musa's Gold in Mamlūk Cairo: A Reappraisal of a World Civilizations Anecdote." *Post-Mongol Central Asia and the Middle East: Studies in History and Historiography in Honor of Professor John E. Woods*. J. Pfeiffer, S. Quinn, E. Tucker, eds. Wiesbaden: Harrassowitz Verlag: 428–47.

(2010). "The Mechanisms of Commerce." *The New Cambridge History of Islam*. Vol. 4. R. Irwin, ed. Cambridge: Cambridge University Press: 332–54.

(2011). "Recent Developments in Islamic Monetary History." *History Compass* 9/1: 71–83.

Sharon, Moshe (1975). "The Political Role of the Bedouins in Palestine in the Sixteenth and Seventeenth Centuries." *Studies on Palestine during the Ottoman Period*. M. Ma'oz, ed. Jerusalem: Magnes Press: 11–30.

Shatzmiller, Maya (1994). *Labour in the Medieval Islamic World*. Leiden: Brill.

(2000). *The Berbers and the Islamic State: The Marinid Experience in Pre-protectorate Morocco*. Princeton: Markus Wiener.

(2001). "Islamic Institutions and Property Rights: The Case of the 'Public Good' Waqf." *Journal of the Economic and Social History of the Orient* 44/1: 44–74.

(2007). "A Misconstrued Link: Europe and the Economic History of Islamic Trade." *Relazionie conomiche tra Europae mondo Islamico secc. XIII–XVIII, a cura di S. Cavaciocci*. Firenze: Le Monnier/Instituto Internazionale di Storia Economica "F. Datini." *Atti delle Settimane di Studi e altri convegni* 38: 387–415.

(2011). "Economic Performance and Economic Growth in the Early Islamic World." *Journal of the Economic and Social History of the Orient* 54/2: 132–84.

(2012). "The Economic History of the Medieval Middle East: Strengths, Weaknesses and the Challenges Ahead." *International Journal of Middle East Studies* 44/3: 529–31.

Shatzmiller, Maya; Pamuk, S. (2014). "Plagues, Wages, and Economic Change in the Islamic Middle East, 700–1500." *Journal of Economic History* 74/1: 196–229.

(2015). "Industries, Manufacturing and Labour." *A Cosmopolitan City: Muslims, Christians and Jews in Old Cairo*. T. Vorderstrasse, T. Treptow, eds. Chicago: Oriental Institute Museum Publications: University of Chicago Press: 49–52.

(2018a). "The Adoption of Paper in the Middle East, 700–1300 AD." *Journal of the Economic and Social History of the Orient* 61/3: 1–32.

(2018b). "Recent Trends in Middle East Economic History: Cultural Factors and Structural Change in the Medieval Period 650–1500." *History Compass* 16/12 (Parts One and Two).

(2019). *From Berber State to Moroccan Empire: The Glory of Fez Under the Marinids*. Princeton: Markus Wiener.

Shoshan, Boaz (1980). "Grain Riots and the 'Moral Economy': Cairo, 1350–1517." *Journal of Interdisciplinary History* 10: 459–78.

(1981). "Notes sur les épidémis de peste en Égypte." *Annales de démographie historique*: 387–404.

(1982). "From Silver to Copper: Monetary Changes in Fifteenth-Century Egypt." *Studia Islamica* 56: 97–116.

(1983). "Money Supply and Grain Prices in Fifteenth-Century Egypt." *The Economic History Review*, n.s. 36/1: 47–67.

(1984). "On the Relations between Egypt and Palestine." *Egypt and Palestine: A Millennium of Association, 868–1948*. A. Cohen, G. Baer, eds. New York: St. Martin's Press: 94–101.

(1986). "Exchange-Rate Policies in Fifteenth-Century Egypt." *Studia Islamica* 55: 97–116.

(1991). "High Culture and Popular Culture in Medieval Islam." *Studia Islamica* 73: 67–107.

(1993). *Popular Culture in Medieval Cairo*. Cambridge: Cambridge University Press.

Singer, Amy (1992). "Peasant Migration: Law and Practice in Early Ottoman Palestine." *New Perspectives on Turkey* 8: 49–65.

(1994). *Palestinian Peasants and Ottoman Officials: Rural Administration around Sixteenth-Century Jerusalem*. Cambridge: Cambridge University Press.

(2002). *Constructing Ottoman Beneficence: An Imperial Soup Kitchen in Jerusalem*. Albany: State University of New York Press.

Sivan, Emmanuel (1967). "Le caractère sacré de Jérusalem dans l'Islam aux XII$^{e}$–XIII$^{e}$ siècles." *Studia Islamica* 27: 149–82.
Silverstein, Adam (2007). *Postal Systems in the Pre-modern Islamic World.* Cambridge: Cambridge University Press.
Smith, John M. (1984). "ʿAyn Jalut: Mamluk Success or Mongol Failure." *Harvard Journal of Asiatic Studies* 44: 307–45.
Sobernheim, M. (1912). "Das Zuckermonopol unter Sultan Barsbai." *Zeitschrift fur Assyriologie und Verwandte Gebiete* 27: 75–84.
Sourdel-Thoumine, Janine; Sourdel, Dominique (2001). "Certificats de pélinerage par procuration à l'époque mamelouke." *Jerusalem Studies in Arabic and Islam* 25: 212–33.
Staffa, Susan (1977). *Conquest and Fusion: The Social Evolution of Cairo A.D. 642–1850.* Leiden: Brill.
Stello, Annika (2012). "La traité d'esclaves en mer noire (premiére moitie. Du XV$^{e}$ siècle)." *Les Esclavages en Méditerranée: Espaces de dynamiques économiques.* F. Guillén, S. Trabelsi, eds. Madrid: Collection de la Casa de Velasquez 133: 171–80.
Stewart, Angus (2001). *The Armenian Kingdom and the Mamluks: War and Diplomacy during the Reigns of Het'um II (1289–1307).* Leiden: Brill.
Stewart, Devin (1996). "Popular Shiʿism in Medieval Egypt: Vestiges of Islamic Sectarian Polemics in Egyptian Arabic." *Studia Islamica* 84: 35–66.
Stillman, Norman (1998). "The Non-Muslim Communities: The Jewish Community." *The Cambridge History of Egypt*, vol. 1: *Islamic Egypt.* C. Petry, ed. Cambridge: Cambridge University Press: 198–210.
Stilt, Kristen (2011). *Islamic Law in Action: Authority, Discretion and Everyday Experiences in Mamluk Egypt.* Oxford: Oxford University Press.
Stowasser, Karl (1984). "Manners and Customs at the Mamluk Court." *Muqarnas* 2: 13–20.
Strauss, Eli (1950a). "L'Inquisition dans l'état mamlouk." *Revista degli Studi Orientali* 25/1: 11–26.
(1950b). "The Social Isolation of the Ahl adh-Dhimma." *Études orientales à la mémoire de Paul Hirschler.* O. Komlos, ed. Budapest: 73–94.
Sublet, Jacqueline (1974). "La folie de princesse Bint al-Asraf (un scandale financier sous les mamelouks baḥrīs)." *Bulletin d'études orientales* 27: 45–50.
(1976). "Le séquestre sur les jardins de la Ghouta (Damas, 666/1267)." *Studia Islamica* 43: 81–86.
(1991). *Le voile du nom: Essai sur le nom propre arabe.* Paris: PUF.
Tabbaa, Yasser (1997). *Constructions of Power and Piety in Medieval Aleppo.* University Park: Pennsylvania State University Press.
(2001). *The Transformation of Islamic Art during the Sunni Revival.* Seattle: University of Washington Press.
Talib, Adam; Hammond, M.; Schippers, A., eds. (2014). *The Rude, the Bad and the Bawdy: Essays in Honour of Professor Geert Jan van Gelder.* Cambridge: Cambridge University Press.
Talib, Adam (2017). *How Do You Say "Epigram" in Arabic? Literary History at the Limits of Comparison.* Leiden: Brill.
Tarmontana, Felicita (2012). "*Khubz* as *Iqṭāʿ* in Four Authors from the Ayyubid and Early Mamluk Periods." *Mamluk Studies Review* 16: 103–22.

Taylor, Christopher (1999). *In the Vicinity of the Righteous: Ziyāra amd the Veneration of Muslim Saints in Late Medieval Egypt*. Leiden: Brill.

Thorau, Peter (1992). *The Lion of Egypt: Sultan Baybars I and the Near East in the Thirteenth Century*. New York: Longman; English translation of *Sultan Baibars I. von Ägypten: ein Beitrag zur Geschichte des Vorderen Orients im 13. Jahrhundert*. Wiesbaden: L. Reichert, 1987.

Toledano, Ehud (2007). *As If Silent and Absent: Bonds of Enslavement in the Islamic Middle East*. New Haven: Yale University Press.

Toru, Miura (1995). "The Ṣāliḥiyya Quarter in the Suburbs of Damascus: Its Formation, Structure, and Transformation in the Ayyūbid and Mamlūk Periods." *Bulletin d'études orientales* 47: 129–82.

(1997). "Administrative Networks in the Mamlūk Period: Taxation, Legal Execution, and Bribery." *Islamic Urbanism in Human History: Political Power and Social Networks*. T. Sato, ed. London: Kegan Paul: 39–75.

(2006). "Urban Society in Damascus as the Mamlūk Era Was Ending." *Mamluk Studies Review* 10/1: 157–93.

Al-Toudy, Heba; Abdelhamid, Tareq Galal, eds. (2017). *Selections from Ṣubḥ al-A'shá by al-Qalqashandi, Clerk of the Mamluk Court: Egypt: "Seats of Government" and "Regulations of the Kingdom," from Early Islam to the Mamluks*. Routledge Medieval Translations, London: Routledge.

Tritton, A. S. (1948). "The Tribes of Syria in the Fourteenth and Fifteenth Centuries." *Bulletin of the School of Oriental and African Studies* 12: 567–73.

Tucker, William F. (1981). "Natural Disaster and the Peasantry in Mamlūk Egypt." *Journal of the Economic and Social History of the Orient* 24: 215–24.

(1999). "The Environmental Hazards, Natural Disasters, Economic Loss, and Mortality in Mamlūk Syria." *Mamluk Studies Review* 3: 109–28.

Tyan, Émile (1959). "Le notariat et le régime de la preuve par écrit dans la pratique du droit musulman." *Annales de la Faculté de droit de Beyrouth* 2, Beirut.

Udovitch, A. L. (1970a). "England to Egypt, 1350–1500: Long-Term Trends and Long-Distance Trade" *Studies in the Economic History of the Middle East*. M. Cook, ed. London: Routledge: 93–128.

(1979b). *Partnership and Profit in Medieval Islam*. Princeton: Princeton University Press.

ed. (1981). *The Islamic Middle East, 700–1900: Studies in Economic and Social History*. Princeton: Darwin Press.

Vallet, Éric (2010). *L'Arabie marchande: État et commerce sous les sultans Rasūlides du Yémen (626–858/1229–1454)*. Paris: Publications de la Sorbonne, Bibliothéque historique des pays d'Islam I.

Van Gelder, Geert J. H. (1988). *The Bad and the Ugly: Attitudes towards Invective Poetry (Higā') in Classical Arabic Literature*. Leiden: Brill.

(2000). *God's Banquet*. New York: Columbia University Press.

Van Steenbergen, Jo (2001). "The Amir Qawṣūn, Statesman or Courtier? (720–41 AH/1320–41 AD)." *Egypt and Syria in the Fatimid, and Mamluk Eras*. III, Proceedings of the 6th, 7th, and 8th International *Ayyubid* Colloquium organized at the Katholieke Universiteit Leuven in May 1997, 1998, and 1999. U. Vermeulen, J. Van Steenbergen, eds. Leuven: Peeters, OLA 102: 449–66.

(2006a). "The Mamlūk Elite on the Eve of al-Nāṣir Muḥammad's Death (1341): A Look Behind the Scene of Mamlūk Politics." *Mamluk Studies Review* 9/2: 173–99.

(2006b). *Order Out of Chaos: Patronage, Conflict and Mamluk Socio-Political Culture, 1341–1382*. Leiden: Brill.

(2007). "Is Anyone My Guardian...? Mamluk Under-Age Rule and the Later Qalāwūnids." *Al-Masāq* 19/1: 55–65.

(2011). "On the Brink of a New Era? Yalbughā al-Khāṣṣakī (d. 1366) and the Yalbughāwiyya." *Mamluk Studies Review* 15: 117–52.

(2012). "Qalāwūnid Discourse, Elite Communication and the Mamlūk Cultural Matrix: Interpreting a 14th-Century Panegyric." *Journal of Arabic Literature* 43/1: 1–28.

(2013a). "Caught between Heredity and Merit: Qūṣūn (d. 1342 and the Legacy of al-Nāṣir Muḥammad b. Qalāwūn (d. 1341)." *Bulletin of the School for Oriental and African Studies* 78/3: 429–50.

(2013b). "The Mamlūk Sultanate as a Military Patronage State: Household Politics and the Case of the Qalāwūnid Bayt (1270–1382)." *Journal of the Economic and Social History of the Orient* 56/2: 189–217.

(2013c). "Ritual Politics and the City in Mamlūk Cairo: The Bayna l-Qaṣrayn as a Dynamic 'lieu de mémoire,' 1250–1382." *Court Ceremonies and Rituals of Power in Byzantium and the Medieval Mediterranean: Comparative Perspectives*. A. Beihammer et al., eds. Leiden: Brill: 227–76.

(2015). "Mamlukisation between Social Theory and Social Practice: An Essay on Reflexivity, State Formation, and the Late Medieval Sultanate of Cairo." *ASK Working Papers* 22. Göttingen: Vandenhoeck and Ruprecht Unipress: 1–44.

(2016a). "Appearances of Dawla and Political Order in Late Medieval Syro-Egypt: The State, Social Theory, and the Political History of the Cairo Sultanate (Thirteenth–Sixteenth Centuries), History and Society during the Mamluk Period (1250–1517)." *Studies of the Annemarie Schimmel Institute for Advanced Study* 2. S. Conermann, ed. Göttingen: Vandenhoeck and Ruprecht Unipress: 53–88.

Van Steenbergen, Jo; Wing, Patrick; D'Hulster, Kristof (2016b). "The Mamlukization of the Mamluk Sultanate? State Formation and the History of Fifteenth-Century Egypt and Syria: Part I – Old Problems and New Trends, Part II – Comparative Solutions and a new Research Agenda." *History Compass* 14/11: 549–69.

Venzke, Margaret (2000). "The Case of a Dulgadir-Mamlūk Iqṭāʿ: A Re-assessment of the Dulgadir Principality and Its Position within the Mamlūk–Ottoman Rivalry." *Journal of the Economic and Social History of the Orient* 43/3: 399–474.

Vermeulen, Urbain (1978). "The Rescript of al-Malik al-Ṣāliḥ Ṣāliḥ against the Dimmīs." *Orientalia Lovaniensa Periodica* 9: 175–84.

Veinstein, Gilles (2005). "Le rôle des tombes sacrées dans la conquète ottomane." *Revue de l'histoire des religions* 222/4: 509–28.

(2010). "Les lieux saints du Hijāz sous les Ottomanes." *Routes d'Arabie: Archéologie et histoire du royaume d'Arabie saoudite*. Musée du Louvre, 17 juillet–27 septembre 2010. Paris: Louvre-Éditions: 523–33.

Verlinden, Charles (1977). *L'Esclavage dans L'Europe médiévale*, vol. 2: Italie, colonies italiennes du Levant, Levant Latin, Empire byzantine. Gand: Rijksuniversiteit te Gent.

Vigouroux, Élodie (2011). "La mosquée des Omeyyades de Damas après Tamerlan: Chronique d'une renaissance (1401–1430)." *Bulletin d'études orientales* 61: *Damas médiévale et ottomane: Histoire urbaine, société et culture matérielle*. M. Eychenne, M. Boqvist, eds.: 123–59.

(2013). "Les Banū Mangak à Damas: Capital social, enracinement local et gestion patrimoniale d'une famille d'*awlād al-nās* a l'époque mamelouke." *Annales islamologiques* 47: 197–233.

Wade Hatton, Rosalind (2012). "Mongol Influences on Mamluk Ceramics in the Fourteenth Century." *The Arts of the Mamluks in Egypt and Syria – Evolution and Impact*. Mamluk Studies 1. D. Behrens-Abouseif, ed. Göttingen: Bonn University Press: 96–113.

Walker, Bethany (1999). "Militarization to Nomadization: The Middle and Late Islamic Periods." *Near Eastern Archaeology* 62/4: 202–32.

(2004). "Mamlūk Investment in the Transjordan: A 'Boom and Bust' Economy." *Mamluk Studies Review* 8/2: 119–47.

(2007). "Sowing the Seeds of Rural Decline? Agriculture as an Economic Barometer for Late Mamluk Jordan." *Mamluk Studies Review* 11/1: 173–99.

(2008). "The Role of Agriculture in Mamluk–Jordanian Power Relations." "Le pouvoir à l'age des sultanats dans le *Bilād al-Shām*." B. Walker, J.-F. Salles, eds. *Bulletin d'études orientales* 57, supplement: 19–30.

(2009a). "Popular Responses to Mamluk Fiscal Reforms in Syria." *Bulletin d'études orientales* 58: 51–68.

(2009b). "The Tribal Dimension in Mamluk-Jordanian Relations." *Mamluk Studies Review* 13/1: 82–105.

(2010). "From Ceramics to Social Theory: Reflections on Mamlūk Archeology Today." *Mamluk Studies Review* 14: 109–58.

(2011). *Jordan in the Late Middle Ages: Transformations of the Mamluk Frontier*. Chicago: Middle East Documentation Center.

Walker, Paul (2003). "Al-Maqrīzī and the Fāṭimids." *Mamluk Studies Review* 7/1: 83–98.

Walmsley, Alan (2001). "Fatimid, Ayyubid and Mamluk Jordan and the Crusader Interlude." *Archaeology of Jordan*. B. MacDonald, R. Adams, P. Bienkowski, eds. Sheffield: Sheffield Academic Press: 515–59.

Wansbrough, John (1961). "A Mamlūk Letter of 877/1473." *Bulletin of the School of Oriental and African Studies* 24: 200–13.

(1963). "A Mamlūk Ambassador to Venice in 913/1507." *Bulletin of the School of Oriental and African Studies* 26: 503–30.

(1965a). "A Mamlūk Commercial Treaty Concluded with the Republic of Florence." *Documents from Islamic Chanceries*. S. Stern, ed. Oxford: Faber: 39–79.

(1965b). "Venice and Florence in the Mamlūk Commercial Privileges." *Bulletin of the School of Oriental and African Studies* 28: 483–523.

(1971). "The Safe-Conduct in Muslim Chancery Practice." *Bulletin of the School of Oriental and African Studies* 34: 20–35.

Wasserstein, David; Ayalon, Ami (2006). *Mamluks and Ottomans: Studies in Honour of Michael Winter*. New York: Routledge.

Whelan, Estelle (1988). "Representations of the *Khāṣṣakiyah* and the Origins of Mamluk Emblems." *Content and Context of Visual Arts in the Islamic World:*

*Papers from a Colloquium in Memory of Richard Ettinghausen*. University Park: Pennsylvania State University Press: 219–53.
(2006). *The Public Figure: Political Iconography in Medieval Mesopotamia*. London: Melisende.
Whitcomb, Donald (1994). *Ayla: Art and History in the Islamic Port of Aqaba*. Chicago: Oriental Institute, University of Chicago.
Wickham, Chris (2019). "The Power of Property: Land Tenure in Fāṭimid Egypt." *Journal of the Economic and Social History of the Orient* 62/1: 67–107.
Wiet, Gaston (1925). "Les secrétaires de la chancellerie (*kuttāb el-sirr*) en Égypte sous les mamlouks circassiens." *Mélanges René Basset*. Vol. 1. Paris: E. Leroux: 287–311.
(1937). *L'Égypte arabe de la conquète arabe à la conquète ottoman, 642–1517 de l'ére chrétienne. Histoire de la nation égyptienne*. G. Hanotaux, ed. Paris: Société de l'histoire nationale.
(1955). "Les marchands d'épices sous les sultans mamlouks." *Cahiers d'histoire égyptienne* 7: 81–147.
(1962a). "La grande peste noire en Syrie et en Égypte." *Études d'orientalisme: Mémorial Lévi Provençale* 1. Paris: Maisonneuve et Larose: 367–84.
(1962b). "Le traité des famines de Maqrīzī, traduction française." *Journal of the Economic and Social History of the Orient* 5: 1–90.
(1963). "Un refugié mamlouk à la cour mongol de Perse." *Mélanges Henri Massé, Tehran: Imprimerie de l'Université*: 388–404.
Wilfong, Terry (1998). "The Non-Muslim Communities: Christian Communities." *The Cambridge History of Egypt*, vol. 1: *Islamic Egypt*. C. Petry, ed. Cambridge: Cambridge University Press: 175–97.
Williams, Caroline (1993). *Islamic Monuments in Cairo: A Practical Guide*. Cairo: The American University in Cairo Press.
Williams, John (1984). "The Khānqāh of Siryāqūs: A Mamluk Royal Religious Foundation." *Quest of an Islamic Humanism: Arabic and Islamic Studies in Memory of Mohamed al-Nowaihi*. A. H. Green, ed. Cairo: American University in Cairo Press: 109–22.
Wing, Patrick (2007). "The Decline of the Ilkhanate and the Mamluk Sultanate's Eastern Frontier." *Mamluk Studies Review* 11/2: 77–88.
(2014). "Indian Ocean Trade and Sultanic Authority: The nāẓir of Jedda and the Mamluk Political Economy." *Journal of the Economic and Social History of the Orient* 57/1: 55–75.
(2015). "Submission, Defiance, and the Rules of Politics on the Mamluk Sultanate's Anatolian Frontier." *Journal of the Royal Asiatic Society* 25: 1–12.
Winter, Michael (1982). *Society and Religion in Early Ottoman Egypt: Studies in the Writings of ʿAbd al-Wahhāb al-Shaʿrānī*. New Brunswick: Transaction.
(2004a). "Mamlūks and Their Households in Late Mamlūk Damascus: A Waqf Study." *The Mamluks in Egyptian Politics and Society*. A, Levanoni, M. Winter, eds. *The Medieval Mediterranean* 61: 297–316.
Winter, Michael; Levanoni, Amalia, eds. (2004b). *The Mamluks in Egyptian and Syrian Politics and Society*. Leiden: Brill.

Wollina, Torsten (2012). "A View from Within: Ibn Ṭawq's Personal Topography of 15th Century Damascus." *Bulletin d'études orientales* 61: 271–95.
(2013). "Ibn Ṭawq's Taʿlīq. An Ego-Document for Mamlūk Studies." *Ubi Sumus? Quo Vademus? Mamluk Studies–State of the Art*. S. Conermann, ed. Göttingen: Vandenhoeck and Ruprecht Unipress: 337–58.
Yarbrough, Luke (2016). *The Sword of Ambition: Bureaucratic Rivalry in Medieval Egypt*. New York: New York University Press.
(2019). *Friends of the Emir: Non-Muslim State Officials in Premodern Islamic Thought*. Cambridge: Cambridge University Press.
Yosef, Koby (2012a). "Dawlat al-Atrāk or Dawlat al-Mamālīk? Ethnic Origin or Slave Origin as the Defining Characteristic of the Ruling Elite in the Mamlūk Sultanate." *Jerusalem Studies in Arabic and Islam* 39: 387–410.
(2012b). "Mamlūks and Their Relatives in the Period of the Mamlūk Sultanate (1250–1517)." *Mamluk Studies Review* 16: 55–69.
(2013a). "Ikhwa, Muwākhūn and Khushdāshiyya in the Mamluk Sultanate." *Jerusalem Studies in Arabic and Islam* 40: 335–62.
(2013b). "The Term Mamlūk and Slave Status during the Mamluk Sultanate." *Al-Qantara* 34/1: 7–34.
(2016). "Masters and Slaves: Substitute Kinship in the Mamlūk Sultanate." *Egypt and Syria in the Fāṭimid, Ayyūbid and Mamlūk Eras,* VIII: Proceedings of the 19th, 20th, 21st, and 22nd International Colloquium, University of Ghent, May 2010, 2011, 2012, and 2013. U. Vermeulen, K. D'hulster, J. Van Steenbergen, eds. Leuven: Peeters: 557–79.
(2017). "Usages of Kinship Terminology during the Mamluk Sultanate and the Notion of the 'Mamlūk Family'." Y. Ben-Bassat, ed. *Developing Perspectives in Mamluk History: Essays in Honor of Amalia Levanoni*. Leiden: Brill: 16–75.
(2019a). "Cross-Boundary Hatred: (Changing) Attitudes towards Mongol and 'Christian' Mamlūks in the Mamluk Sultanate." *The Mamluk Sultanate from the Perspective of Regional and World History: Economic, Social and Cultural Development in an Era of Increasing International Interaction and Competition*. R. Amitai, S. Conermann, eds. Bonn: Bonn University Press: 149–214.
(2019b). "Mamluks of Jewish Origin in the Mamluk Sultanate" *Mamluk Studies Review* 22: 49–96.
Zaki, Abdel Rahman (1964). *A Bibliography of the Literature of the City of Cairo*. Cairo: Société de géographie d'Égypte.
Zayadine, Fawzi (1985). "Caravan Routes between Egypt and Nabataea and the Voyage of Sultan Baibars to Petra in 1276." *Studies in the History and Archaeology of Jordan* 2: 159–74.
Ze'evi, Dror (2000). "My Slave, My Son, My Lord: Slavery, Family and State in the Islamic Middle East." *Slave Elites in the Islamic Middle East and Africa*. M. Toru, J. Philipps, eds. London: Kegan Paul: 71–80.
Ziyadeh, Nicola (1970). *Urban Life in Syria under the Early Mamluks*. Beirut: American University of Beirut Publications.

# Index

Ilkhan Abaqa, 55, 101–2
Ilkhan Abu Saʿid, 96
Ilkhanids, 14, 16, 87
Inal. *See* al-Nasiri, Inal al-ʿAlaʾi al-Zahiri
infractions, gender-based, against women, 257–59
  for homicide, 257–58
  Ibn Iyas on, 257–58
  al-Jazari on, 258–59
  for seduction, 258–59
instructor. *See mudarris*
interregional commerce, with Mamluk Sultanate, 172–76
  after Crusades, 172–73
  through Egypt, 173
  by Karimi merchants, 173–75
  with Mongol regimes, 172–73
  through Syria, 173
*Introduction to History. See al-Muqaddima fi'l-ta'rīkh*
iqtaʿ system
  administration of, 159–61, 163, 172
  in agriculture, 164–65
  under Barquq, 165–69
  charitable trusts and, 199–200
  in Egypt, 244–45
  under al-Ghawri, 171
  taxation under, 159–61, 163–65
Iran region. *See* foreign policy
Irwin, Robert, 2–3
al-Isfahani, Imad al-Din al-Katib, 226
Islamic Law, Maliki school, 1
Islamic Sciences, 144
  foundational sources of, 144
    Jurisprudence as, 144
    Prophetic Tradition as, 144
    Revelation as, 144
Ismaʿil Safawi, 50

Janam al-Ashrafi, 43–44
Jan-Birdi al-Ghazali, 100
Janibak al-Zahiri, 95
Jaqmaq. *See* al-Zahir Jaqmaq al-Jarkasi al-ʿAlaʾi
al-Jazari, Shams al-Din Muhammad, 258–59
al-Jazzar, Jamal al-Din Abu'l-Husayn Yahya, 219
Jews, communal status of, 259–69
  during Fatimid Caliphate, 259–60, 266
  Geniza documents, 266–68
  Ibn Iyas on, 267–68
*Jordan in the Late Middle Ages* (Walker), 248–49
judges, 135–40
  adjutant, 136–37
  case assignment of, 136–37
  corruption among, 140–41
  from elite classes, 137–38
  familial dynasties, 138–40
  full, 137–38
  historical career trajectory of, 136, 138–39
  jurisconsult compared, 142–43
  *muhtasib* (market inspector), 141–42
    duties of, 141–42
  role in religious services, 138
judicial class, distinction from other classes, 129
jurisconsult, judges compared to, 142–43
Jurisprudence, in Islamic Sciences, 144

al-Kafiyaji, Muhyi al-Din al-Kafiyaji, 240
al-Kamil Muhammad, al-Malik, 8
al-Kamil Muhammad, ibn al-Malik, 8
Karimi merchants, 173–75
Khalil, al-Ashraf, 14–15
Khan, Husam al-Din Berke, 56
*khatib. See* sermon preachers
Kha'ir Bak, 50–52, 69
al-Khita'i, Rukn al-Din Baybars al-Mansuri, 232
Khushqadam al-Mu'ayyadi, 43–44, 96–97
*Kitāb al-ʿibar* (Ibn Khaldun), 1–2
Kitbugha, Zayn al-Din, 15–16

Lajin, Husam al-Din, 16, 182
Lane, Edward, 223
Levanoni, Amalia, 2–3
literary patronage. *See* patronage
Louis IX (King), 8–9
Lu'lu', Badr al-Din, 9

madrasa (college of law), 122–23, 143–44
  *mudarris* in, 143–44
Maghrib region
  Almohads in, 126
  Mamluk foreign policy in, 117–28
  Marinids in, 126
  migration history in, 126–27
  Wattasids in, 126
Mahmud, Nur al-Din, 7
Maliki school of Islamic Law, 1
Mamluk institution, 5–8
  Ayyubid Dynasty, 7–8
    as major influence on, 5
  Fatimid Caliphate as influence on, 5, 7
  Great Saljuk Empire and, 7
  origins of, 5–6
    ʿAbbasid Dynasty, 5
    Caliphal Empire, 5
    etymological foundations, 6

For EU product safety concerns, contact us at Calle de José Abascal, 56–1°,
28003 Madrid, Spain or eugpsr@cambridge.org.

www.ingramcontent.com/pod-product-compliance
Ingram Content Group UK Ltd.
Pitfield, Milton Keynes, MK11 3LW, UK
UKHW020402140625
459647UK00020B/2603
* 9 7 8 1 1 0 8 4 5 6 9 9 9 *